# Lecture Notes in Artificial Intelligence 1455

Subseries of Lecture Notes in Computer Science
Edited by J. G. Carbonell and J. Siekmann

## Lecture Notes in Computer Science

Edited by G. Goos, J. Hartmanis and J. van Leeuwen

**Springer**
*Berlin*
*Heidelberg*
*New York*
*Barcelona*
*Hong Kong*
*London*
*Milan*
*Paris*
*Singapore*
*Tokyo*

Anthony Hunter   Simon Parsons (Eds.)

# Applications of Uncertainty Formalisms

 Springer

Series Editors

Jaime G. Carbonell, Carnegie Mellon University, Pittsburgh, PA, USA
Jörg Siekmann, University of Saarland, Saarbrücken, Germany

Volume Editors

Anthony Hunter
University College London, Department of Computer Science
Gower Street, London WC1E 6BT, UK
E-mail: a.hunter@cs.ucl.ac.uk

Simon Parsons
Queen Mary and Westfield College, Department of Electronic Engineering
University of London, London E1 4NS, UK
E-mail: s.d.parsons@elec.qmw.ac.uk

Cataloging-in-Publication Data applied for

Die Deutsche Bibliothek - CIP-Einheitsaufnahme

**Applications of uncertainty formalisms** / Anthony Hunter ; Simon Parsons (ed.).
- Berlin ; Heidelberg ; New York ; Barcelona ; Hong Kong ; London ; Milan ;
Paris ; Singapore ; Tokyo : Springer, 1998
  (Lecture notes in computer science ; Vol. 1455 : Lecture notes in artificial intelligence)
  ISBN 3-540-65312-0

CR Subject Classification (1998): I.2.3, F.4.1

ISBN 3-540-65312-0 Springer-Verlag Berlin Heidelberg New York

© Springer-Verlag Berlin Heidelberg 1998
Printed in Germany

Typesetting: Camera ready by author
SPIN 10638237      06/3142 – 5 4 3 2 1 0      Printed on acid-free paper

# Preface

Managing uncertainty is one of the key questions in a diverse range of areas in computing. Many researchers in both universities and commercial organizations are seeking better information on applying uncertainty formalisms. There is a particular need for analyses comparing and contrasting different approaches to uncertainty formalisms and we hope that the papers in this book help to fill this need.

The papers are divided into three sections:

- Papers in the first section outline some of the general problems being considered by researchers and introduce some of the range of uncertainty formalisms being proposed as the basis of solutions.
- Papers in the second section are case studies in applying uncertainty formalisms. Each paper in this category has a well-delineated application problem and an analysed solution based on an uncertainty formalism.
- Papers in the third section report on developments of uncertainty formalisms and supporting technology—such as automated reasoning systems—that are vital for making uncertainty formalisms applicable.

We believe that there is considerable synergy between the papers in this book. Furthermore, we believe that the critical mass of case studies and associated material should make this book a particularly important resource.

We would like to thank the following people, in addition to the authors, who helped to review the papers: Rachel Bourne, Paolo Giorgini, Wiebe van der Hoek, Jerome Lang, Jerome Mengin, Murray Shanahan, Yao-Hua Tan, Nic Wilson, and Michael Wooldridge.

We would also like to acknowledge the support provided by ESPRIT via the Basic Research Actions (3085) DRUMS and (6136) DRUMS2, the joint ESPRIT-NSF funded UMIS project, and the ESPRIT LTR Working Group 20001 FUSION project, in assisting us in our research into applications of uncertainty formalisms. Our special thanks go to Philippe Smets who was the prime mover behind all these projects.

July 1988

Anthony Hunter
Simon Parsons

# Table of Contents

## Section C: Technology for applications

# Introduction to Uncertainty Formalisms

Anthony Hunter[1] and Simon Parsons[2]

[1] Department of Computer Science, University College London,
Gower Street, London, WC1E 6BT
[2] Department of Electronic Engineering, Queen Mary and Westfield College,
University of London, London, E1 4NS, United Kingdom.

**Abstract.** The heterogeneity of uncertainty in the real-world has driven the development of a wide variety of formal approaches to representing and reasoning with uncertainty in knowledge. There is now a shift to analysing the application of many of these formalisms. Here, we briefly consider some of the issues in the application of uncertainty formalisms.

## 1 Introduction

Most of the information we have about the real world is uncertain. We are often uncertain about the information we need to run our lives; what the weather will be like tomorrow, what time the train we need to catch home will actually depart from the station, and how many students will make it to the next tutorial we organise. The ubiquitous nature of uncertainty coupled with the increasing computerisation of all areas of life means that uncertainty in information is a significant problem in computing. Increasing numbers of applications—such as diagnostic systems, data mining systems, scientific databases, information retrieval systems, knowledge-based systems, and natural language interfaces—require an ability to represent, manage, and reason with uncertain information. In order to handle uncertain information, we first need sufficiently expressive means to represent it. Then we need to incorporate a reasoning component into our computing systems in order to derive answers from the uncertain information. In addition, we assume that given the diverse kinds of uncertainty in information, we need to develop a range of techniques.

Adopting *ad hoc* approaches to computer-based handling of uncertain information can easily become counter-productive. Using computers in an organization is in some respects like delegating. Tasks are delegated when the delegator has confidence in what the delegatee will do. So for example, there is confidence in delegating payroll activities to computers because of the well-understood principles of arithmetic and accountancy. When handling uncertain information, the behaviour of even small datasets can be difficult to predict. Therefore, if we are to delegate handling of uncertain information, we should only do so within the context of well-understood principles.

Numerous formalisms for dealing with uncertainty have been studied over the years. These include those essentially numerical methods based on probability theory, fuzzy set theory, and possibility theory through to those largely symbolic methods such as default logics, paraconsistent logics and argumentation. We provide a review of key formalisms in Chapter 2, and other reviews include [3, 4, 7]. Whilst many questions remain in developing these kinds of uncertainty formalism, there is now a significant shift to developing applications using these formalisms. This shift to applications is raising many new questions of viability. In the past, interest often used to be focussed on questions such as:

- Does this formalism have a clear semantics?
- What are the properties of this formalism?
- How does this formalism relate to others?

Nowadays questions which relate more to the use rather than the development of the various formalisms are becoming important such as:

- Are we now ready to use these uncertainty formalisms in "real-world" problems?
- What kinds of applications have been successful?
- What are the shortcomings in the current formalisms?
- What developments will be required for uncertainty management techniques to be more widely used?
- In what ways can uncertainty formalisms be applied?
- What are the issues that need to be addressed for wider uptake?
- What limitations can we identify that currently prevent their application?

In this chapter, we discuss some of the background to these questions.

## 2 Application areas

The nature of uncertainty in information is complex. Many factors affect the types of uncertainty [2, 8], sources of uncertainty [1, 5], and the degrees of uncertainty. Nevertheless, there are many strategies that users adopt for aggregating such factors in order to minimize the negative ramifications of operating under uncertainty. Indeed, via learning, humans, and similarly organizations, can be become highly adept at using uncertain information.

The ubiquitous usage of uncertain information by people contrasts sharply with the low level of computer-based handling of uncertain information. Whilst many theoretical models have been proposed for the management of uncertainty, present generation information systems have very limited capabilities in this respect.

The situation seems set to change as the expanding role of computing means that handling uncertain information will become increasingly significant. Indeed as uncertainty pervades any real-world scenario, uncertainty handling must be incorporated into any computing system that attempts to provide a substantive model of the real-world. Even now, diverse types of information system such as database systems, information retrieval systems, expert systems, and groupware systems are currently being developed to incorporate uncertainty formalisms.

| Application feature | Chapter | | | | | | | | | | | |
|---|---|---|---|---|---|---|---|---|---|---|---|---|
| | 3 | 4 | 5 | 6 | 7 | 8 | 9 | 10 | 11 | 12 | 13 | 14 |
| Embedded knowledgebase | | | x | | | | x | x | x | x | | |
| Intelligent interface | | x | | | | x | | | | | | |
| Decision-support | x | | | x | x | | | | | | x | x |
| Information retrieval | | | | | | x | | | | | | |
| Classification | | | | x | | | | | x | | | x |
| Sensor interpretation | | | | | | | | x | x | | | |
| Real-time control | | | x | | | | x | x | | | | |

**Table 1.** Application features addressed in each chapter

In this book, we look at a number of case studies in which uncertainty formalisms are used in applications. These case studies can be grouped in a number of ways according to application features. In the following we discuss some of the key application features that are considered in one or more case studies. In Table 1, we identify which application features are addressed in each chapter.

**Embedded KBS.** Knowledge-based systems are frequently used within a larger software system. Here, high-level knowledge, such as rules, can be used to execute management or control activites in the wider software system.

**Intelligent interface.** Accessing information in computers can be difficult, so there is a need for computer interfaces to interact with users in a way that can help the user locate the information required, communicating in ways that are more appropriate for users.

**Decision-support systems.** The term "decision-support system" covers a wide range of tools designed to help end-users make decisions. This assistance can include provision of relevant information, reasoning with information to make arguments for possible decisions, and identifying qualifications, ramifications, or risk associated with possible decisions.

**Information retrieval.** The aim of information retrieval is to provide a user with information that best meets the user's request. This function involves various forms of uncertainty including determining, in some sense, the contents, of each document or article in the system, and determining the user's actual needs from the request.

**Classification.** Determining the classification for an instance given a number of attributes or observations can be a difficult problem in many spheres. Classification schemes can be complicated and interpreting them can involve resolving ambiguity, and handling the information about attributes or observations can require dealing with features such as incompleteness, inconsistency and imprecision.

**Sensor interpretation.** Devices are being designed with increasing numbers of devices incorporated. This is creating increasing pressure for automated means for interpreting the potentially enormous volume of data. The range of

| Problem area | Chapter | | | | | | | | | | | |
|---|---|---|---|---|---|---|---|---|---|---|---|---|
| | 3 | 4 | 5 | 6 | 7 | 8 | 9 | 10 | 11 | 12 | 13 | 14 |
| Biomedicine | x | | | x | | | | | | | x | |
| Biology | | | x | | | | | | | | | x |
| Telecommunications | | x | | | | x | | | x | | | |
| Manufacturing | | | | | | | | x | | | | |
| Mobile robotics | | | | | | | x | | | | | |

**Table 2.** Problem areas addressed in each chapter

devices incorporating sensors is very diverse and ranges from engine management systems through production line quality control systems and security systems, to mobile robots.

**Real-time control.** Software is increasingly being used to provide real-time control of systems ranging from avionics to chemical plants, and robots to medical monitors. A key compromise here is between correct/optimal inference in each scenario the system is used and the cost of engineering the system—so for example the approach of fuzzy control systems is popular for an application when it is relatively cheap to develop, and acceptable to use, a system that provides slightly sub-optimal reasoning.

The cases studies in this book show how an application feature can be potentially addressed using an uncertainty formalism. In Table 2, we then categorize the case-studies according to problem area. These areas are manufacturing, mobile robotics, telecommunications, biomedicine, and biology.

## 3   Technology questions

In this book we focus on applications where there is a need for the representation of information in a readily accessible and transparent form for the engineer or end-user. This need is prevalent in a wide range of systems including relational databases, decision-support systems, information retrieval systems, information filtering systems, and requirements engineering tools. For example, decision-support tools can be used by human decision-makers to enhance their performance. However, if the decision-support tool is opaque—as when the tool does not explain or justify its reasoning—then the confidence that the user has in the tool's output is decreased. Moreover, if the tool is opaque, then the user cannot qualify or adapt the output in the context of the wider sphere of information and experience that the user has access to.

The wide range of potential applications leads us to believe that we need a range of formal systems for handling uncertainty, and that each of these will incorporate a high-level language for representing uncertain information. In Table 3, we list the chapters in this book that use each of the main classes of uncertainty formalism.

| Application feature | Chapter | | | | | | | | | | | | | | | | | | |
|---|---|---|---|---|---|---|---|---|---|---|---|---|---|---|---|---|---|---|---|
| | 3 | 4 | 5 | 6 | 7 | 8 | 9 | 10 | 11 | 12 | 13 | 14 | 15 | 16 | 17 | 18 | 19 | 20 | 21 |
| Dempster-Shafer theory | | x | | x | | | x | | | | | | | | | | | | x |
| Probability theory | x | | | | | | | | | x | x | | | x | | | | | |
| Fuzzy set theory | | x | x | | | x | x | | x | | | | | | x | | | | |
| Default systems | | | | | | | | | | | x | x | x | x | | | | | |
| Modal logics | | | | | | | | | | | | | | | | | x | x | |
| Graphical models | x | | | | | | | | x | | | | | | x | | | | x |
| Argument systems | | | | | x | | | | | x | | | | | | | | | x |

**Table 3.** Approaches used in each chapter

Whilst the case studies discussed in this book and elsewhere demonstrate the utility of a range of uncertainty formalisms, many application problems remain unaddressed. Current uncertainty formalisms provide foundations, but further technology questions exist in bridging the gap with applications. We do not aim to provide a comprehensive coverage of current technology questions, rather we have included some papers that are of particular relevance to applications, which are in the following technology areas.

**Knowledge representation.** Clearly very general formalisms such as classical logic can be used for representing any kind of knowledge. Unfortunately, for some applications this may involve much effort in determining the appropriate predicates, functions and constants, and in writing the appropriate formulae. Consider an application for reasoning with temporal information. What is the model of time? Does it use intervals or time points? Is the model linear or does it branch in the future? Therefore, to facilitate the development of knowledge-bases, there is a need for formalisms that contain the appropriate language and inference techniques for each application. This means more sophisticated and more specialized formalisms are being developed that are useful for particular classes of application. In the case of temporal information, there are specialized temporal formalisms that incorporate constructs for different kinds of temporal reasoning thereby simplifying the task of a knowledge-base developer.

**Automated reasoning.** Given a knowledge-base, automated reasoning is required to generate inferences or answer queries. In most uncertainty formalisms, this is expensive—often involving reasoning that is intractable or undecidable in the worst case. Therefore there is a need to develop efficient algorithms for sublanguages and for approximation techniques. Since there are many possible sublanguages and approximation techniques, these need to be developed with respect to classes of application.

**Machine learning** This is about inducing, or refining, knowledge in some formalism from other relevant information. Given the difficulty and expense of developing knowledge-bases—particularly with uncertainty formalisms—

machine learning offers algorithms and techniques to partially automate the process of knowledge engineering. Machine learning is a large topic in artificial intelligence and some key problems reside in the intersection with uncertainty formalisms.

These topics incorporate many open questions. In the following chapters, there is some discussion of all of them.

# 4 Conclusions

The roles of computing systems are clearly very diverse, and as a result addressing the problem of handling uncertainty in such systems is a broad subject. In addition, the problem of handling uncertainty in any kind of system is a complex and difficult task, requiring a range of formalisms, and there are many choices to be made in adopting an uncertainty formalism. As a result, the application of uncertainty handling techniques across the whole range of computing systems is a tremendously complex problem to deal with. In order to minimize problems arising from using uncertain information in an application, there is pressure to adopt a rich and powerful model, but the development and computational costs of such a solution may be too great. So there is always a balance to be struck. Through considering case studies such as those contained in this book, it is hoped that sufficient experience will be compiled to make it possible to strike this balance.

Since the aim of this book is to look at applications of uncertainty formalisms, it would seem appropriate to offer some form of matrix relating particular uncertainty formalisms to particular classes of application problem. However, uncertainty is difficult to formalize—witness the problems of just trying to categorize the different kinds of ignorance in [8][1]. Therefore we at least need to better grasp the notions within uncertainty formalisms before we have the conceptual apparatus to relate formalisms to applications, and it will be some time before it is possible to provide a definitive mapping between formalisms and applications. However, we believe that this book is a useful contribution towards identifying such a mapping by comparing and contrasting a range of formalisms in some diverse case studies.

# References

1. P. P. Bonissone. Reasoning, Plausible. In S. Shapiro, editor, *Encyclopaedia of Artificial Intelligence*, pages 854–863. John Wiley & Sons, London, UK, 1987.
2. P. P. Bonissone and R. M. Tong. Editorial: reasoning with uncertainty in expert systems. *International Journal of Man-Machine Studies*, 22:241–250, 1985.
3. A. Hunter. *Uncertainty in Information Systems*. McGraw-Hill, London, UK, 1996.
4. P. Krause and D. Clark. *Representing Uncertain Knowledge: An Artificial Intelligence Approach*. Intellect, Oxford, UK, 1993.

[1] For a more extensive discussion of this problem see Chapter 2 of [6].

5. S. Kwan, F. Olken, and D. Rotem. Uncertain, incomplete and inconsistent data in scientific and statistical databases. In A. Motro and Ph. Smets, editors, *Uncertainty in Information Systems*. Kluwer, 1996.
6. S. Parsons. *Qualitative approaches to reasoning under uncertainty*. MIT Press, Cambridge, MA, 1998.
7. Ph. Smets and A. Motro, editors. *Uncertainty Management in Information Systems*. Kluwer, Boston, MA, 1997.
8. M. Smithson. *Ignorance and Uncertainty: Emerging Paradigms*. Springer Verlag, New York, NY, 1989.

# A Review of Uncertainty Handling Formalisms

Simon Parsons[1] and Anthony Hunter[2]

[1] Department of Electronic Engineering, Queen Mary and Westfield College,
University of London, London, E1 4NS, United Kingdom.
[2] Department of Computer Science, University College London,
Gower Street, London, WC1E 6BT, United Kingdom.

**Abstract.** Many different formal techniques, both numerical and symbolic, have been developed over the past two decades for dealing with incomplete and uncertain information. In this paper we review some of the most important of these formalisms, describing how they work, and in what ways they differ from one another. We also consider heterogeneous approaches which incorporate two or more approximate reasoning mechanisms within a single reasoning system. These have been proposed to address limitations in the use of individual formalisms.

## 1 Introduction

Practical AI systems are constrained to deal with imperfect knowledge, and are thus said to reason approximately under conditions of ignorance. Attempts to deal with ignorance, [45,91] for example, often attempt to form general taxonomies relating different types and causes of ignorance such as uncertainty, incompleteness, dissonance, ambiguity, and confusion. A taxonomy, taken from Smithson [91], that is perhaps typical, is given in Figure 1. The importance of such taxonomies is not so much that they accurately characterise the nature of ignorance that those who build practical AI systems have to deal with—they are far too open to debate for that—but more that they allow distinctions to be drawn between different types of ignorance. This has motivated the development of a multitude of diverse formalisms each intended to capture a particular nuance of ignorance, each nuance being a particular leaf in Smithson's taxonomy tree. The most important distinction is that made between what Smithson calls uncertainty and absence, though this may be confused by a tendency in the literature to refer to "absence" as "incompleteness". Uncertainty is generally considered to be a subjective measure of the certainty of something and is thus modelled using a numerical value, typically between 0 and 1 with 0 denoting falsity and 1 denoting truth. Absence is the occurrence of missing facts, and is usually dealt with by essentially logical methods. The wide acceptance of the suggestion that uncertainty and absence are essentially different, and must therefore be handled by different techniques has lead to a schism in approximate reasoning between the "symbolic camp" who use logical methods to deal with absence and the "numerical camp" who use quantitative measures to deal with uncertainty.

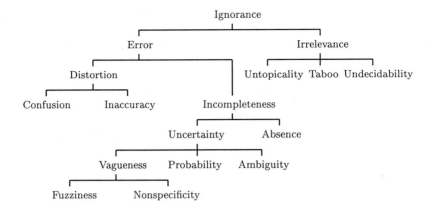

**Fig. 1.** Smithson's taxonomy of different types of ignorance.

This void between symbolic and numerical techniques, which remained unaddressed for many years as researchers concentrated on the finer technical details of their particular formalism, can be seen as symptomatic of the way in which research into approximate reasoning has been pursued. For many years researchers indulged in ideological slanging matches of almost religious fervour in which the formalism that they championed was compared with its "competitors" and found to exhibit superior performance. Examples of this behaviour abound, particularly notable are [10, 12, 42, 66, 88, 105]. It is only recently that a more moderate *eclectic* view has emerged, [13, 32, 48, 78] for example, which acknowledges that all formalisms are useful for the solution of different problems. A general realisation of the strength of this eclectic position has motivated research both into ways in which different formalisms may be used in combination to solve interesting practical problems, and into establishing the formal differences and similarities between different systems.

In this paper we discuss some of the best established and widely used formalisms from both the symbolic and numerical sides of the great divide. We suggest reasons for the introduction of the more novel techniques, and sketch in the technical differences between the approaches. With this background well established, we then consider work on bringing techniques together.

## 2 Numerical Approaches

Over the last two decades, numerous formal and informal systems have been introduced for reasoning under conditions of ignorance and uncertainty. The first uncertainty management technique to be introduced was probability theory. This was not only developed many years before the first computer, but was also used in computer decision aids before the advent of Artificial Intelligence as a discipline. Arthur Dempster generalised Bayes' theorem in 1967 [17, 18], though his work remained confined to the field of statistics until Glenn Shafer reformulated the theory and published it as "A Mathematical Theory of Evidence" in 1976 [82]. This body of work, often referred to as Dempster-Shafer theory, has several interpretations including the transferable belief model [87, 90]. Another much studied approach is possibility theory [26, 103] which grew out of work on fuzzy sets [102]. There are numerous other numerical techniques for dealing with uncertainty often developed from pragmatic considerations. These include certainty factors [86], probabilistic logic [63], and belief intervals [21] to name but a few.

## 2.1 Overview

The methods that we shall consider in the following sections are the main formal theories introduced to handle uncertainty—probability theory, possibility theory, and evidence theory. For theories that have traditionally been seen as rivals, one might expect that they would appear radically different, but this is not so. Indeed, they are remarkably similar, differing largely in subtleties of meaning or application, though this is not entirely surprising since they are intended to do much the same thing.

The basic problem is how to weigh up the degree to which several uncertain events are believed to occur so that the most believed may be unambiguously identified. The basis on which the "belief" is assigned is a contentious issue, though all the theories that we shall consider assume allocation by an assignment function that distributes belief to possible events under consideration. Belief may be distributed on the basis of statistical information [81, 92], physical possibility [103], or purely subjective assessment [12] by an expert or otherwise. The belief assigned is a number between 0 and 1, with 0 being the belief assigned to a fact that is known to be false, and 1 the belief assigned to a fact known to be definitely true. The infinite number of degrees of belief between the limits represent various shades of uncertainty. Now, some formalisms restrict the amount of belief that may be assigned. Both probability theory and evidence theory, which is after all derived from probability theory, limit the total belief that may be assigned by a particular distribution function by constraining the sum of all the beliefs to be 1. This may be interpreted as meaning that one particular observer cannot believe in a set of uncertain events more than she would have believed in a particular event of total certainty. There is no such restriction on a possibility distribution, since one may conceive of several alternative events that are perfectly possible, and so have a possibility of 1. Probability theory, unlike the other theories, also introduces a restriction on the belief that may be applied to a hypothesis based on the belief assigned to its negation. If we have an event A, then

$$\Pr(A) = 1 - \Pr(\neg A)$$

Given the result of a belief distribution, we are interested in how the assigned beliefs may be manipulated. Given our belief in two events, what is our belief in either of them occurring (our belief in their union), and what is our belief that both will occur (our belief in their intersection)? More importantly perhaps, especially for artificial intelligence applications where we often wish to assess the combined belief that results from several different pieces of information, we are interested in combining the effects of two or more belief distributions over the same set of hypotheses. Each distribution will, in general, assign different beliefs to a given hypothesis, and we require some means of assessing a final belief that takes account of all the different assignations. The way in which this is done is based upon the interpretation that the theory gives to the belief it assigns, and thus it is not surprising that each theory should "pool the evidence" in a different way.

## 2.2 Probability theory

Probability theory has existed in one form or another for several hundred years. During this time various alternative formulations have been introduced, and it is now difficult to say where the definitive account may be found. This is in contrast to the other methods described in this paper where the descriptions are drawn from the original paper on the subject. The introduction presented here is drawn from the discussion of probability theory in Lindley's excellent book "Making Decisions" [53]. Lindley asserts that probability theory is built on three axioms or laws that define the behaviour of a probability measure, which may be used as an estimate of the degree to which an uncertain event is likely to occur. The measure may be assessed by reference to a standard, such as the likelihood of drawing a black ball out of an urn containing five black balls and ten red balls. The first law of probability theory is the *convexity* law which states that the probability measure for an event $A$ given information $H$ is such that:

$$0 \leq \Pr(A|H) \leq 1$$

The second law is the *addition* law, which relates the probabilities of two events to the probability of their union. For two exclusive events $A$ and $B$, that is two events that cannot both occur, we have:

$$\Pr(A \cup B|H) = \Pr(A|H) + \Pr(B|H)$$

which is commonly written

$$\Pr(A \cup B) = \Pr(A) + \Pr(B)$$

without explicit reference to the information $H$, since the information is the same in all cases. If the events are not exclusive we have, instead:

$$\Pr(A \cup B) = \Pr(A) + \Pr(B) - \Pr(A \cap B)$$

Furthermore, the sum of the probabilities of a set of mutually exclusive and *exhaustive* events, the latter meaning that they are the only possible events that may occur, are constrained to sum to 1 so that:

$$\Pr(A) + \Pr(\neg A) = 1$$

or, more generally for a set of $n$ such events $A_i$:

$$\sum_{i=1,\ldots,n} \Pr(A_i) = 1$$

The final law is the multiplication law, which gives us the probability of two events occurring together; the probability of the intersection of $A$ and $B$:

$$\Pr(A \cap B | H) = \Pr(A|H).\Pr(B|A \cap H)$$

Again this may be written as

$$\Pr(A \cap B) = \Pr(A).\Pr(B|A)$$

without explicit reference to $H$. Note that $\Pr(A \cap B)$ is often written as $\Pr(A, B)$. The probability measure $\Pr(B|A)$ is the *conditional* probability of $B$ given $A$, the probability that $B$ will occur, given that $A$ is known to have occurred. From these laws we can derive two further results which are crucial from the point of view of artificial intelligence. The first of these is Jeffrey's rule:

$$\Pr(A) = \sum_{i=1,\ldots,n} \Pr(A|B_i)\Pr(B_i)$$

The second is Bayes' theorem, named after an eighteenth century non-conformist English clergyman. This states that:

$$\Pr(A|B) = \frac{\Pr(B|A).\Pr(A)}{\Pr(B)}$$

and thus gives a means of computing one conditional probability relating two events from another conditional probability.

Under the assumption that the events in which we are interested are mutually exclusive and exhaustive, and following some manipulation, we can obtain a version of Bayes' rule [14] that is suitable for assessing the probability of a hypothesis $h_i$ that is a member of the set $h_1, \ldots, h_n$ given a set of pieces of evidence $e_1, \ldots, e_m$, a set of probabilities of occurrence of the hypotheses $\Pr(h_1), \ldots, \Pr(h_n)$, and a set of conditional probabilities for each piece of evidence given each hypothesis $\Pr(e_1|h_1)$, $\Pr(e_1|h_2), \ldots, \Pr(e_m|h_n)$:

$$\Pr(h_i|e_1, e_2, \ldots, e_m) = \frac{\Pr(e_1|h_i)\Pr(e_2|h_i)\ldots\Pr(e_m|h_i)\Pr(h_i)}{\sum_{j=1,\ldots,n}\Pr(h_j)\Pr(e_1|h_j)\Pr(e_2|h_j)\ldots\Pr(e_m|h_j)}$$

This may be used, say, to reason about the likelihood of a particular disease ($h_i$), from a set of possible diseases $\{h_1, \ldots, h_n\}$, given a set of recorded symptoms $\{e_1, \ldots, e_m\}$.

There have been several adaptations of probability theory within the literature of artificial intelligence including the odds-likelihood formulation used by Prospector [28], and the cautious approach adopted by Inferno [74]. Another is

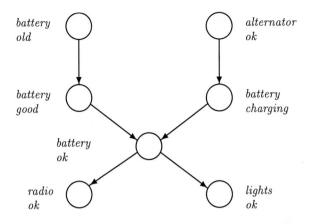

**Fig. 2.** Part of a probabilistic network for diagnosing faults in a car.

the use of probability theory by Tawfik and Neufeld [93] in their chapter in this volume where they consider the probability of failure of components over time and use this to guide diagnosis. Nilsson [63] provided an interesting variation with his probabilistic logic, an attempt to combine propositional calculus with a numerical uncertainty handling formalism by associating probability measures with logical sentences. Perhaps the most important feature of the formalism is it handles incompletely specified probabilistic models by computing the allowed bounds on the derived consequents.

An increasing important approach to using probability theory in computing is probabilistic networks, also called Bayesian networks or causal networks [39, 67, 68]. By augmenting the use of conditional probabilities with extra structural information, they can be used to represent and reason more efficiently with probabilistic information. In particular they incorporate assumptions about which propositions are independent of other propositions, thereby decreasing the dimensionality and number of conditional probability statements, and simplifying the computations. Essentially, probabilistic networks are a set of nodes with directed arcs (arrows) providing connections between nodes. Every node is connected to another node, but each node is not necessarily connected to every other node. Each node denotes a random variable, which is a variable that can be instantiated with an element from the sample space for the variable. They are used to model situations in which causality, or influence is prevalent, but in which we only have a partial understanding, hence the need to model probabilistically.

As an example, consider the network in Figure 2 which is part of a probabilistic network for diagnosing faults in a car (this example is drawn from [41]). This captures the fact that the age of the battery (the node *battery_old*) has an influence on whether or not the battery is good (*battery_good*), and that whether or not the alternator is good (*alternator_ok*) has an effect on whether or not the battery is charging (*battery_charging*), together the quality of the battery and whether or not the battery is charging affect whether the battery is working (*bat-

*tery_ok*), and this has an effect on the radio (*radio_ok*) and the lights (*lights_ok*). All the random variables in this example are either "true" or "false" so that the random variable *battery_old*, can be instantiated with the event *battery_old* meaning that the battery is old, or the event ¬*battery_old* meaning that the battery is not old.

Each of the links in the network is quantified by giving the relevant conditional probabilities, which in this case will include:

$$\text{Pr}(battery\_good | battery\_old) \qquad\qquad = 0.1$$
$$\text{Pr}(battery\_good | \neg battery\_old) \qquad\qquad = 0.8$$

$$\text{Pr}(battery\_ok | battery\_good, battery\ charging) \quad = 0.9$$
$$\text{Pr}(battery\_ok | battery\_good, \neg battery\ charging) \quad = 0.2$$
$$\text{Pr}(battery\_ok | \neg battery\_good, battery\ charging) \quad = 0.6$$
$$\text{Pr}(battery\_ok | \neg battery\ good, \neg battery\_charging) = 0.05$$

Note that the conditional probabilities reflect the direction of the arrows. Both, broadly speaking, capture a notion of causality (which is why probabilistic networks are also known as "causal networks")—if the battery is old it causes the battery to be less likely to be good, and it is therefore easier to assess Pr(*battery_good*|*battery_old*) than Pr(*battery_old*|*battery_good*) though the two probabilities may each be computed from the other using Bayes' theorem.

Now, given the network and the prior probabilities of the battery being old, Pr(*battery_old*), and the alternator being ok, Pr(*alternator_ok*), it is possible to compute the probability of each state of each random variable in the network (for instance Pr(*battery_good*) = 0.58 if Pr(*battery_old*) = 0.4) by simple application of Jeffrey's rule. It is also possible to take account of evidence that, for instance, the radio is not ok (which means that Pr(¬*radio_ok*) = 1) and to use Bayes' theorem to revise the probabilities.

Much attention has been given to the problem of propagating probabilities through probabilistic networks efficiently. Pearl [69] provides a comprehensive introduction to the use of probabilistic causal networks, along with an efficient scheme for the propagation of probabilities in singly-connected networks[1] between every that is based on autonomous message passing. Another network-based method that has received wide attention is that of Lauritzen and Spiegelhalter [52] which has been used as the basis of the expert system shell HUGIN [1], and the paper in this volume by Magni *et al.* [56] makes use of a graphical representation similar to that discussed above.

## 2.3 Evidence theory

Evidence theory is the term commonly used to refer to the body of work carried out by Arthur Dempster [17, 18] and Glenn Shafer [82] to remedy some of what

---

[1] Singly-connected networks are those in which for every pair of nodes there is at most one path along arcs which joins them. When assessing connectedness, arcs may be traversed both directions, but any arc may only be traversed once.

they saw as the limitations of probability theory, in particular [19] disposing with the "completeness" axiom of probability theory [42]. The theory deals with the so-called *frame of discernment*, the set of base elements $\Theta = \{\theta_1, ..., \theta_n\}$ in which we are interested, and its power set $2^\Theta$, which is the set of all subsets of the interesting elements. The basis of the measure of uncertainty is a *probability mass function* $m(\cdot)$ that assigns zero mass to the empty set, $m(\emptyset) = 0$, and a value in $[0, 1]$ to each element of $2^\Theta$, the total mass distributed being 1 so that:

$$\sum_{A \subseteq \Theta} m(A) = 1$$

Since we deal with all possible subsets of the set of all base propositions, rather than the propositions themselves as in probability theory, we can apportion the probability mass exactly as we wish, ignoring assignments to those levels of detail that we know nothing about. This allows us to model ignorance, $m(\Theta)$ being the probability mass we are unable, through lack of knowledge, to assign to any particular subset of $\Theta$. We can define our belief in a subset $A$ of the set of all propositions as the sum of all the probability masses that support its constituents:

$$\text{Bel}(A) = \sum_{B \subseteq A} m(B)$$

and the plausibility of A may be defined as the probability mass not supporting $\neg A$:

$$\text{Pl}(A) = \sum_{B \cap A \neq \emptyset} m(B)$$

which may also be written as:

$$\text{Pl}(A) = 1 - \text{Bel}(\neg A)$$

The interval $[\text{Bel}(A), \text{Pl}(A)]$ can be considered to be a measure of our ignorance about $A$, and can vary from zero when we have the same degree of belief in $A$ as would be generated by probability theory, to 1 when $A$ has belief 0 and plausibility 1. This means that no mass is assigned to $A$ or any of its subsets, but equally no mass is assigned to $\neg A$.

Evidence is combined by Dempster's rule of combination. This computes the probability mass assigned to $C \subset \Theta$ from the probability mass assigned to $A$ and $B$ where both $A$ and $B$ are also subsets of $\Theta$. If the distribution function assigning probability mass to $A$ is $m_1(\cdot)$ and the function distributing probability mass to $B$ is $m_2(\cdot)$, then the mass assigned to C is defined by:

$$m_{12}(C) = \frac{\displaystyle\sum_{A \cap B = C} m_1(A) m_2(B)}{1 - \displaystyle\sum_{A \cap B = \emptyset} m_1(A) m_2(B)}$$

where the division *normalises* the new distribution by re-assigning any probability mass which is assigned to the empty set, $\emptyset$, by the combination. To clarify

| | {Toyota, GM, Chrysler} 0.8 | Θ 0.2 |
|---|---|---|
| {Nissan, Toyota} 0.4 | {Toyota} 0.32 | {Nissan, Toyota} 0.08 |
| Θ 0.6 | {Toyota, GM, Chrysler} 0.48 | Θ 0.12 |

**Table 1.** Applying Dempster's rule.

what is going on here we will consider a simple example of the use of Dempster's rule in combining evidence.

Consider a world [14] with only four car manufacturers, Nissan, Toyota, GM and Chrysler, all trying to break into a new car market. We are interested in who will dominate the market. There are four singleton hypotheses corresponding to the assertions that each of the four manufacturers will dominate the market. Consider the case in which there are two mass functions $m_1$ and $m_2$ stemming from the opinions of two independent experts. Now, $m_1$ assigns 0.4 to {Nissan, Toyota}, the hypothesis that Japanese manufacturers dominate, and the remaining 0.6 to the set {Nissan, Toyota, GM, Chrysler} modelling ignorance about the behaviour of American manufacturers. Similarly, $m_2$ assigns 0.8 to the set {Toyota, GM, Chrysler} and 0.2 to Θ, and Dempster's rule of combination assigns the product of the two belief masses to the intersection of the sets to which they are assigned. Table 1 explains the calculation.

The masses after combination are as follows:

$$m_{12}(\{Toyota\}) = 0.32$$
$$m_{12}(\{Nissan, Toyota\}) = 0.08$$
$$m_{12}(\{Toyota, GM, Chrysler\}) = 0.48$$
$$m_{12}(\Theta) = 0.12$$

The belief that a Japanese manufacturer will dominate is computed from the sum of the belief masses of all the subsets of the hypothesis. Thus:

$$Bel_{12}(\{Nissan, Toyota\}) = m_{12}(\{Toyota\}) + m_{12}(\{Nissan, Toyota\})$$
$$+ m_{12}(\{Nissan\})$$
$$= 0.32 + 0.08 + 0$$
$$= 0.4$$

For this simple example, no normalisation is required.

The problems of the computational complexity of Dempster's rule have been discussed by several authors. Barnett [2] showed that the apparent exponential time requirement of the theory could be reduced to simple polynomial time if the theory was applied to single hypotheses, rather than sets of hypotheses, and the evidence combined in an orderly fashion. Gordon and Shortliffe [37] extended Barnett's approach to compute approximate beliefs in a space of hierarchically organised sets of hypotheses in linear time. This approach was then subsumed by that of Shafer and Logan [84], who provided an exact algorithm for hierarchically organised sets of hypotheses that is also linear in time whilst being slightly more general than that of Gordon and Shortliffe. More recently, Shenoy and Shafer[85] have introduced a method for the efficient propagation of belief functions in networks by means of local computations, and Nic Wilson [100] has proposed a method in which the explicit use of Dempster's rule of combination is avoided. This permits an exact calculation of belief to be performed in worse than polynomial but better than exponential time even when the hypotheses are not hierarchically structured. Wilson has also proposed an approximate calculation, based on a Monte-Carlo simulation, which gives results that are arbitrarily close to the exact solution, and which can be performed in linear time. More recent advances are explored in [61, 101].

The application of evidence theory is the subject of three papers in this volume. Lalmas [50] uses it as a means of deciding which document to retrieve, van Dam [96] uses it to control a radio communication system, and Duncan Wilson [98] considers how to apply it to the classification of faults in automated inspection.

## 2.4   Possibility theory

A formal theory of possibilities, based on the notion of a fuzzy set [102], was first introduced by Zadeh [103]. However, the concept of using the notion of possibilities as an alternative to probabilities was mooted much earlier. The economist G. L. S. Shackle [81], unhappy with the use of subjective probability for handling uncertainty, proposed an alternative formalism. This formalism was the calculus of *potential surprise* where uncertainty about an event is characterised by a subjective measure of the degree to which the observer in question would be surprised by its occurrence. Potential surprise is clearly linked to the intuitive notion of possibility. If an event is entirely possible, then there is no surprise attached to its occurrence. If an event is wholly impossible, or is believed to be so, then if it occurs it will be accompanied by the maximum degree of surprise. In this section we present a simple overview of Zadeh's theory, demonstrating its similarity to and differences from probability theory, and briefly discuss how possibility theory may be combined with logic.

Firstly we need the concept of a *fuzzy set* [102]. A fuzzy set is a set whose membership is not absolute, but a matter of degree, such as the set of tall people. A fuzzy set $F$ is characterised by a membership function $\mu_F$ which specifies the degree to which each object in the universe $U$ is a member of $F$. One way of considering $F$ is as a fuzzy restriction on $X$, a variable which takes values in $U$, in that it acts as an elastic constraint upon the values that may be assigned to $X$. The assignment of a value $u$ to $X$ has the form

$$X = u : \mu_F(u)$$

where $\mu_F(u)$ is the degree to which the constraint $F$ is satisfied when $u$ is assigned to $X$. To denote the fact that $F$ is a fuzzy restriction on $X$ we write:

$$R(X) = F$$

Now, the proposition "$X$ is $F$", which translates into "$R(X) = F$", associates a possibility distribution $\Pi_X$ with $X$ and this distribution is taken to be equal to $R(X)$:

$$\Pi_X = R(X)$$

Along with this we have a possibility distribution function $\pi_X$ which is defined to be equal to the membership function of $F$:

$$\pi_X = \mu_F$$

Thus $\pi_X(u)$, the possibility that $X = u$, is taken to be equal to $\mu_F(u)$. As an example, let $U$ be the set of positive integers, and $F$ be the fuzzy set of small integers. This set is described by the following set of pairs each of the form $(u, \mu_F(u))$:

$$F = \{(1,1), (2,1), (3,0.8), (4,0.6), (5,0.4), (6,0.2)\}$$

Given this, the proposition "$X$ is a small integer" associates the possibility distribution $\Pi_X$ with $X$ where $\Pi_X$ is written as a set of pairs $(u, \pi_X(u))$:

$$\Pi_X = \{(1,1), (2,1), (3,0.8), (4,0.6), (5,0.4), (6,0.2)\}$$

Thus, the possibility that $X$ takes the value 3, given that $X$ is a small integer, is 0.8. We can use possibility distributions to define possibility measures. If $A$ is fuzzy subset of $U$, then the possibility measure $\Pi(A)$ of $A$ is defined by

$$Poss(X \text{ is } A) = \Pi(A)$$
$$= \sup_{u \in U} \min(\mu_A(u), \pi_X(u))$$

When $A$ is a strict subset of $U$, this reduces to:

$$\Pi(A) = \sup_{u \in U} \pi_X(u)$$

Possibility measures clarify the comparison between possibility and probability theory. We can establish that:

$$\Pi(A \cup B) = \max(\Pi(A), \Pi(B)) \tag{1}$$
$$\Pi(A \cap B) = \min(\Pi(A), \Pi(B)) \tag{2}$$

which contrast with the corresponding results for probability theory[2]. Zadeh stresses the fact that possibility and probability are different concepts with the

---

[2] The use of maximum and minimum is not compulsory. For further discussion of this point, see [26].

example of Hans' breakfast. Consider the statement "Hans ate $X$ eggs for break-fast" with $X \in \{1, \ldots, 8\}$. We can associate both a possibility distribution (based on our view of the ease with which Hans can eat eggs) and a probability distribution (based on our observations of Hans at breakfast) with $X$, giving something of the form:

| u | 1 | 2 | 3 | 4 | 5 | 6 | 7 | 8 |
|---|---|---|---|---|---|---|---|---|
| $\Pi_X(u)$ | 1 | 1 | 1 | 1 | 0.8 | 0.6 | 0.4 | 0.2 |
| $\Pr_X(u)$ | 0.1 | 0.8 | 0.1 | 0 | 0 | 0 | 0 | 0 |

So that, while it is perfectly possible that Hans can eat three eggs for breakfast, he is unlikely to do so. There is a heuristic connection between possibility and probability, since if some thing is impossible, it is likely to be improbable, but (as the previous example shows) a high degree of possibility does not imply a high degree of probability, nor does a low degree of probability reflect a low degree of possibility. Dubois and Prade [25] point out that a weak theoretical connection exists since for all $A$,

$$N(A) \leq \Pr(A) \leq \Pi(A)$$

where $N(A)$ is the necessity of $A$, defined by:

$$N(A) = 1 - \Pi(\neg A)$$

It is possible to extend these ideas to possibility distributions that depend on more than one attribute, and marginal possibility distributions. Explanations of these concepts will be omitted in the interests of saving space (but see [103]), but it should be noted that the kind of graphical structures discussed above in relation to probability theory can be adapted for use with possibility theory as well [35].

Possibility has been applied to reasoning with vague statements [27, 104]. For example, suppose we have the following statement.

*If the clothes are dirty then wash them in hot water*

Both the concepts "dirty" and "hot" are vague or fuzzy in this context. For a given collection of clothes, we are interested in using this general statement to determine whether to wash them in hot water. In other words, we wish to determine whether for some fuzzy value for dirty, we should derive the instruction to wash the clothes in hot water.

Now, in classical logic we would perform this kind of reasoning using *modus ponens*, a rule for reasoning which formalises the argument that if $\alpha$ is *true* and $\alpha \supset \beta$ is *true*, then $\beta$ is *true*. For reasoning with fuzzy statements such as the one above about dirty clothes, we need to develop a notion of modus ponens which can handle fuzzy concepts. Generalized modus ponens is such a development [57]. For example, suppose the clothes are "not very dirty", then "not very dirty" does not directly match with "dirty". We need to adapt the statement to allow the data "not very dirty" to apply. This means changing the consequence in some way, perhaps to "warm water". Since "dirty clothes" and "hot water" can be modelled by fuzzy sets, the manipulations can be done on the fuzzy sets. For this, we represent propositions as:

$$X \text{ is } A$$

So for example, "clothes are dirty" is a a proposition, where $X$ is "clothes", and $A$ is "dirty". Generalized modus ponens is then of the following form.

$$\frac{\begin{array}{l} X \text{ is } A^* \\ \text{If } X \text{ is } A, \text{ then } Y \text{ is } B \end{array}}{Y \text{ is } B^*}$$

Here, $B^*$ is calculated from the possibility distribution of $A^*$, and of $A$ given $B$. The possibility distribution for $B$ provides an upper bound on the possibility distribution for $B^*$. This calculation decreases the possibility that $Y$ is $B^*$ is *true*, the further $A^*$ is from $A$. This combination of possibility theory and logic into *possibilistic logic* has been investigated at length by Dubois and Prade [23, 24]. Possibilistic logic is one of the techniques explored by Bigham in his paper in this volume [6], and both the contributions of Ramalho [75] and Saffiotti [79] make use of fuzzy inference of the kind discussed above, while Bosc *et al.* [7] consider the application of fuzzy techniques to databases.

## 2.5    Other approaches

There are a number of other numerical techniques which, although we do not have space to consider them in any detail, are worth mentioning for their particular historical or theoretical interest. Certainty factors [86], perhaps because of their simplicity and intuitive appeal, have been widely used to handle uncertainty. The certainty factor approach assigns a numerical weight, the certainty factor, to the consequent of every

If ⟨*evidence*⟩ then ⟨*hypothesis*⟩

rule in a rule-based system. The value of the certainty factor, which lies in the interval [-1, 1], is assessed by the domain expert from the degree, between 0 and 1, to which a given piece of evidence causes her belief and disbelief in the hypothesis to be increased. The certainty factor is then the difference of the degree of belief, $MB$ and the degree of disbelief, $MD$:

$$CF = MB - MD$$

The certainty factors of rules fired during inference are then combined to give an overall certainty for the support given to a particular hypothesis by the known evidence. Recently several people have challenged the validity of the certainty factor model. For instance, Heckerman [40] has shown that the original definition of the model is flawed since the belief in a hypothesis given two pieces of evidence will depend upon the order in which the effect of the pieces of evidence is computed.

Smets has adapted evidence theory as introduced by Dempster and Shafer in two important ways [87, 90]. The first was to relax the assumption that all hypotheses have been identified before the evidence is considered. Instead Smets makes an *open-world* assumption that the frame of discernment does not necessarily contain an exhaustive set of hypotheses. Under this assumption there is no normalisation in Dempster's rule of combination since the mass pertaining to the empty set is taken to indicate belief in a hypothesis outside the frame of discernment. The open world assumption requires a modification of the definitions given earlier for the calculation of belief and plausibility from probability mass distributions (which are just called "mass functions" by Smets). Belief is defined as:

$$\text{Bel}(A) = \sum_{B \subseteq A, B \neq \emptyset} m(B)$$

while plausibility is defined as:

$$\text{Pl}(A) = \sum_{B \cap A \neq \emptyset} m(B)$$
$$= 1 - (m(\emptyset) + \text{Bel}(\neg A))$$

Dempster's rule of combination becomes:

$$m_{12}(C) = \sum_{A \cap B = C} m_1(A) m_2(B)$$

Smets' other innovation was to introduce an alternative interpretation of the theory of evidence called the transferable belief model. The transferable belief model rejects any suggestion that the numbers manipulated by the theory are probabilities. Instead they are taken to be pure expressions of belief suitable for reasoning at an abstract *credal* level and are transformed into probabilities at the *pignistic* level when decisions are necessary. In the model, the basic belief mass $m(A)$ in any subset $A$ of a frame of discernment $\Theta$ is the amount of belief supporting $A$, that, due to ignorance, does not support any strict subset of A. If we have new evidence that excludes some of our original hypotheses, and so points to the truth being in $\Theta' \subset \Theta$, then the basic belief mass $m(A)$ now supports $A \subset \Theta'$. Thus the belief originally attributed to $A$ is transfered to that part of $A$ not eliminated by the new evidence, thus giving the system its name.

Another interesting proposal is due to Driankov [21]. In Driankov's system, we have degrees of belief and plausibility, related, as in the original theory of evidence, by:

$$\text{Bel}(A) = 1 - \text{Pl}(\neg A)$$

However the system also allows contradictory beliefs so that it is possible that:

$$\text{Bel}(A) + \text{Bel}(\neg A) > 1$$

These ideas lead to the definition of a calculus of belief intervals, where a belief interval for $A$ is $[\text{Bel}(A), \text{Pl}(A)]$, in which combination is carried out by a family of general functions called triangular norms and conorms [80], and explicit reasoning about the degree to which a proposition is believed and disbelieved is possible.

## 2.6 Limitations of numerical techniques

As one might expect, none of the systems mentioned in preceding sections is perfect, and there are a number of problems common to all numerical formalisms. The first is perhaps the simplest. When Cohen [14] criticises possibility theory saying:

> "relatively little has been made of the idea of fuzzy sets and possibility theory ... (this) may be because the idea does not improve on any of the difficult methodological problems that beset probability theory, such as the assessment of prior probabilities"

he is restating an argument that has been made time and again, perhaps most tersely by Cheeseman [11] who asked:

> "where are all the numbers coming from?"

Obtaining the "numbers", be they probabilities, possibilities, or mass distributions does seem to be a major problem. Clearly, without good numerical assessments sophisticated computational mechanisms are of little value. It is also true that there are domains in which it is not possible to obtain the kind of strong statistical data necessary to apply probability theory in its "frequentist" interpretation, where the probability of an event is the value to which the ratio of occurrences to non-occurrences converges after a large number of trials. This has been used by many (see for example [32]) to argue against the use of probability theory for dealing with uncertainty. However, the *personalist* and *necessarian* [83] schools of probabilists argue that probabilities may always be obtained, either from rational human reasoning, or because they exist as a measure of the degree to which sets of propositions confirm one another. It seems, then, as though there is no clear cut winner in this argument; the moral appears to be:

> "if you can obtain the numbers to your satisfaction, then use them."

As a final word, it is worth mentioning that it has also been convincingly argued in several places (see for example [9, 71]) that even if the numbers are available, they make little difference to the business of weighing up the evidence. This, however, is a different argument altogether, and we will say no more about it.

A second problem stems from the use of numbers; the interpretation of the results of applying a numerical formalism given the notorious irrationality that human beings exhibit when dealing with numbers [95]. All the techniques generate results as numerical values. These values, however, have been generated in different ways, and thus measure different things, although they are just numbers and may be compared and contrasted by the uninitiated as though they represented the same thing. Indeed, to interpret them correctly, it is perhaps necessary to label them with the type of belief that they measure to prevent a probability of 0.5 being compared unfavourably with a possibility of 0.8. In addition, there is the problem of ranking different solutions. A common argument for including numbers is in order to choose the best of several courses of action that must be differentiated between using uncertain knowledge, and of course numerical results can be used to do this. However, using the ordinal value of the results alone to do this can obscure important information concealed in the ratio of the results; namely how close the second largest value is to the largest. If they are close, but separated by a wide margin from the third, then, rather than choosing the first, it might be profitable to review the criteria upon which the assessment was made in the hope that some telling difference between the alternatives might be found.

Finally, there are the problems associated with computational expense. The massive amount of time needed to apply the full formal methods to realistically large problems was one of the main reasons that such *ad hoc* methods as certainty factors were introduced. Whilst, as outlined in earlier sections, there have been several recent attempts to find computationally efficient methods of calculating the results of applying probability and evidence theories in particular situations, the general problem of inefficiency remains.

## 3  Symbolic Approaches

Nonmonotonic logics were introduced in order to allow programs to deal with incompleteness by exhibiting "commonsense" reasoning, thus avoiding the need to state every possible exception to a general rule. Two key approaches are Reiter's default logic [76] and McCarthy's circumscription [60]. In this section we start with a discussion of the limitations of first order logic as a basis for practical reasoning systems, introducing the notions of retraction, monotonicity and defeasibility. Then we consider the family of default logic in more detail—as it is probably the most developed approach for non-monotonic reasoning. In the subsequent two sections, we consider the logic-based approaches of argumentation and truth maintenance systems.

### 3.1  Overview

The common motivation behind all of the systems of nonmonotonic logic that we will discuss below is the attempt to devise sound formal mechanisms for reasoning that overcome the limitations of first order logic. At first sight, first order logic seems to be a panacea for all the problems of knowledge representation and deduction for AI systems. This is unfortunately a naive impression, and there are many problems that beset the use of classical logic, especially when attempting to model the kind of "commonsense" reasoning which human beings excel at. Israel [44] credits Minsky with being the first to consider the matter, pointing out that there are two particular properties of first order logic that are at odds with commonsense human behaviour. The first results in the so called *qualification* problem. Say, to take the classic example, we are interested in building a system that reasons about animals and their athletic abilities. One of the facts that we want to encode is the fact that generally birds can fly. Unfortunately, there is no "generally" quantifier in first order logic, so we must approximate this by asserting that all birds fly:

$$\forall x, bird(x) \supset flies(x) \qquad (3)$$

This seems fine until we recall that penguins don't fly, and so we have to augment the rule. This may be done in several ways, we will choose to write:

$$\forall x, bird(x) \wedge \neg penguin(x) \supset flies(x) \qquad (4)$$

However, this formulation becomes problematic when we want to reason about ostriches, kiwis, and birds whose feet have been set in concrete. For any general rule of this kind, we can think up an arbitrarily large number of exceptions, and it is the provision of a compact means of handling all of these exceptions that is the qualification problem. The second troublesome property is that of monotonicity. In first order logic there is no mechanism for retracting inferences once they have been made, or facts once they have been added to the database. If a sentence $S$ is a logical consequence of a theory $A$ then it is still a consequence of any theory that includes $A$, such as the theory $A \cup \phi$. This is true even if we have $\phi = \neg S$, though in this latter case adding $\phi$ leads to inconsistency (since we can derive both $S$ and its negation). Monotonicity is particularly troublesome when, in attempting to solve the qualification problem, we allow systems to make "guesses" about the state of the world which are used in the absence of more detailed information. For instance consider making the assumption that a particular bird, Joe, flies when nothing is known to the contrary. In a monotonic system, when it is learnt that Joe has been nailed to his perch there is no means of retracting the inference that Joe can fly. To solve such problems researchers turned to nonmonotonic logical systems that allow for plausible inferences to be made to defeat the qualification problem, and then allow those inferences to be withdrawn if their falsity becomes apparent.

There are three main ways in which a solution to these problems have been attempted; closed world reasoning, prototypical reasoning, and reasoning about beliefs. These methods may be summarised as follows. Closed world reasoning makes the assumption that all relevant positive knowledge has been explicitly stated. Working on this assumption, systems are permitted to deduce any negative facts that they desire in order to reason about the state of the world. Thus a system reasoning about connecting flights which has no knowledge of a flight between London and Ankara is allowed to deduce that there is no such flight, and is only allowed to postulate the existence of a flight joining London and Paris if such a flight is explicitly recorded in its database. Prototypical, or default, reasoning proceeds from rules relating to typical individuals of some class to make plausible assumptions about particular individuals. If and when specific information about the individual that contravenes the plausible deduction comes to light, the assumptions are retracted. Our example about flying is of this kind. We know that birds fly in general, so that when we hear of a bird Opus we assume that he can fly. Later we learn that Opus is a penguin, and knowing that penguins don't fly allows us to retract our assumption that Opus is capable of flying. Finally, reasoning about beliefs allows a system to make sound deductions based on what it believes to be true. Assuming rationality, the system is allowed to logically deduce facts from what it knows and what it believes to be true, and what it believes to be false, which is everything that it does not believe to be true. Thus a system reasoning about its siblings can deduce that it is an only child because if it wasn't, it would know about a brother or sister.

In addition to the distinction between closed world reasoning, prototypical reasoning, and reasoning about beliefs, there is another distinction between systems of nonmonotonic logic which it is worth making. This is between *brave* systems and *cautious* systems (also known as *credulous* and *skeptical* systems, respectively). Brave systems are those which are prepared to accept any conclusion which they can hypothesise. As a result they typically suffer from being able to derive two contradictory conclusions, both of which they deem to be acceptable but are unable to choose between. Cautious systems on the other hand are only prepared to accept conclusions which cannot be contradicted. As a result if they can hypothesise both $\phi$ and $\neg\phi$, they conclude neither, even though one must be true.

## 3.2 Default logic

Default logic, introduced by Reiter in [76], models prototypical reasoning by allowing special inference rules, known as default rules, to be added to a standard first order logic. These rules differ from first order rules of the form:

$$\forall A(x) \supset B(x)$$

in that they include an explicit consistency check that prevents the rule being applied in inappropriate situations and allow the expression of rules such as:

$$\frac{Bird(x) : Flies(x)}{Flies(x)}$$

which is read as "if $x$ is a bird, and it is consistent to believe that $x$ flies, then conclude that $x$ flies". Default rules can be considered as meta-rules that tell us how to complete first order theories that are incompletely specified. Now, a default theory $(W, D)$, is a set of first order axioms $W$, and a set of default rules $D$ of the form:

$$\frac{\alpha(\tilde{x}) : \beta_1(\tilde{x}) \ldots \beta_m(\tilde{x})}{\gamma(\tilde{x})}$$

Where $\alpha(\tilde{x})$, $\beta_i(\tilde{x})$ and $\gamma(\tilde{x})$ are all formulae whose free variables are among those in $\tilde{x} = x_1, \ldots, x_n$. $\alpha(\tilde{x})$ is termed the precondition or prerequisite, the $\beta_i(\tilde{x})$ are known as the gating facts or justifications, and $\gamma(\tilde{x})$ is called the consequent. Given a set of default rules $D$ and a first order theory $W$, it is possible to define an extension of the default theory as the closure of $W$ plus a maximal consistent set of consequences of $D$. It is possible to distinguish several classes of such default rules, some of which have attractive properties such as always having extensions. Chief among these are those with a single justification $\beta(\tilde{x})$ which divide into normal defaults, the set of defaults such that $\beta(\tilde{x}) = \gamma(\tilde{x})$, and semi-normal defaults where $\beta(\tilde{x}) = \gamma(\tilde{x}) \wedge \omega(\tilde{x})$ for some $\omega(\tilde{x})$.

An extension $E$ of a default theory is a minimal set of beliefs that contain $W$ are deductively closed, and maximally consistent with the rules in $D$. Thus $E$ is an extension for $(W, D)$ if $\Gamma(E) = E$ where for any set of sentences $S$, $\Gamma(S)$ is a minimal set such that:

$$W \subseteq \Gamma(S)$$
$$Th(\Gamma(S)) = \Gamma(S)$$

where $Th(T)$ is the deductive closure of $T$, and if $D$ contains:

$$\frac{\alpha(\tilde{x}) : \beta_1(\tilde{x}) \ldots \beta_m(\tilde{x})}{\gamma(\tilde{x})}$$

and both $\alpha(\tilde{x}) \in \Gamma(S)$ and $\neg\beta_i(\tilde{x}) \notin \Gamma(S)$ for all $i$, then it is the case that $\gamma(x) \in \Gamma(S)$.

Reiter proved some interesting results for normal default theories that include no free variables. Firstly every closed normal default theory has an extension, so something can always be conjectured about such a theory. Secondly, if a closed normal default has two extensions, then the union of these are inconsistent, so that multiple extensions are only generated if the default rules have inconsistent consequents. Finally, Reiter showed that closed normal default theories are *semi-monotonic*. This means that if we have two default theories where the sets of default rules of one are a subset of the default rules of the other, then an extension of the theory with the smaller set of defaults will be a subset of an extension of the other. Thus adding default rules to a theory does not cause its extensions to need revision, instead new default inferences are simply added to the existing extensions (they may of course cause new extensions to arise). There are also some more general results, applicable to all closed default theories, the most important of which are that if such a theory $(D, W)$ has an inconsistent extension, then it is its only extension, and it is inconsistent because $W$ is inconsistent. Thus default rules alone do not generate inconsistent extensions.

Many authors have worked on default logic in the years since it was first introduced. One those whose work is worth considering is Łukaszewicz, who proposed two important extensions to the original formulation. The first of these [54] takes the form of translations between different types of default, in particular to replace the general default:

$$\frac{\alpha(\tilde{x}) : \beta(\tilde{x})}{\gamma(\tilde{x})}$$

by the semi-normal default:

$$\frac{\alpha(\tilde{x}) : \beta(\tilde{x}) \wedge \gamma(\tilde{x})}{\gamma(\tilde{x})}$$

and to replace the semi-normal default:

$$\frac{\alpha(\tilde{x}) : \beta(\tilde{x}) \wedge \gamma(\tilde{x})}{\gamma(\tilde{x})}$$

by the normal default:

$$\frac{\alpha(\tilde{x}) : \beta(\tilde{x}) \wedge \gamma(\tilde{x})}{\beta(\tilde{x}) \wedge \gamma(\tilde{x})}$$

The first is non-controversial, but the second, despite being applicable for a large range of practically occurring defaults, has some rather alarming exceptions [30]. By using both translations sequentially, we can replace the eminently sensible:

$$\frac{has\_motive(x) : guilty(x)}{suspect(x)}$$

by the rather unreasonable:

$$\frac{has\_motive(x) : suspect(x) \wedge guilty(x)}{suspect(x) \wedge guilty(x)}$$

In a further paper, Łukaszewicz [55] generalises default logic, providing an alternative formalisation of an extension, and proving that semi-normal default theories are guaranteed such extensions. He also shows that semi-normal default theories are semi-monotonic, that is monotonic with respect to default rules.

Despite the maturity of the theoretical work on default logic, there are as yet few applications, partly because there has been less attention paid to providing prospective application builders with useful tools for using default logic than has been paid to providing tools for using approaches such as probability. However this situation is beginning to change. This volume includes a paper by Nicolas and Schaub [62] which describes a system on which to build default logic applications, while Brazier *et al.* [8] have applied default logic to a problem from ecology.

## 3.3 Argumentation

Argumentation is the process by which arguments are constructed and compared. Following Toulmin [94], an argument can be structured so that from facts a qualified claim (a conclusion) can be argued (inferred) if and only if:

1. there is some warrant (some further assumptions) that can be used with the facts to logically derive the claim, and
2. there is no other argument that would act as a rebuttal of the claim (a counter-argument).

Argumentation can be further developed with the notion of an undercutting argument, which is an argument that acts as a rebuttal for one of the assumptions of an argument.

An argument can be modelled by a pair $(\Phi, \alpha)$, where $\Phi$ is a set of formulae, and $\alpha$ is a formula derived as a conclusion from the assumptions $\Phi$. These assumptions are also known as the grounds of the argument. For an argument $(\Phi, \alpha)$, a rebutting argument is an argument $(\Psi, \neg\alpha)$, and an undercutting argument is an argument $(\Pi, \neg\gamma)$, where $\gamma \in \Phi$. For a set of arguments $\{\Phi_1, ..., \Phi_n\}$, let $\Delta$ denote the union of the set of assumptions, ie. $\Delta = \Phi_1 \cup .. \cup \Phi_n$. Often in argumentation $\Delta$ will be inconsistent, and it may incorporate more than one minimally inconsistent subset[3]. Now, we can identify some arguments as safer than others according to the nature of the arguments and counter-arguments (both rebutting arguments and undercutting arguments). For example, an argument with no counter arguments is safer than an argument with counterarguments. As a result, we can rank conclusions on the basis of how safe the arguments for it are. As an example, suppose all maximally consistent subsets of $\Delta$ imply $\phi$, and so all arguments for $\phi$ are relatively safe, yet a more preferred conclusion is a formula that follows from the intersection of the maximally consistent subsets of $\Delta$. This approach to argumentation has been developed in [3, 29]. A number of other approaches to argumentation, including [70, 72, 97], focus on default reasoning by incorporating default connectives (which can be used to build up default statements similar to the default rules in default logic) into their languages together with associated machinery.

Argumentation can also be used to handle uncertain information by extending the pair $(\Phi, \alpha)$ to a triple $(\alpha, \phi, \delta)$ in which $\delta$ is a measure of the degree to which $\alpha$ is believed to be true on the basis of $\Phi$. In this way, argumentation can be used as a framework which can capture a number of different formalisms for handling uncertainty, with different formalisms entailing different meanings for $\delta$ (often called the "sign" of the argument) and different ways of handling the signs. This approach is described in more detail in this volume [33], and elsewhere [46], and its historical development is charted in [65]. It also forms the basis for one of the applications case studies in this book [47].

## 3.4   Truth maintenance systems

When reasoning with inconsistent information, questions of belief in assumptions and belief in conclusions arise. These questions include [58]:

**Inferences from beliefs.** How do new beliefs follow from existing beliefs?
**Default beliefs.** How do we record that a belief depends on the absence of other beliefs?
**Dependency recording.** How do we record that one belief depends on another belief?

---

[3] A minimally inconsistent set is a set of propositions which is inconsistent in the sense that $p \wedge \neg p$ can be derived from it for some $p$, and which is such that the removal of any one proposition from it will mean that the resulting set is not inconsistent.

**Disbelief propagation.** How do we withdraw belief in the consequences of a proposition that is disbelieved?

**Revision of beliefs.** How do we change beliefs in order to remove a contradiction?

These kinds of question led to approaches for truth maintenance[4]. A truth maintenance system (TMS) records information about each inference that is generated from a set of assumptions. The two main types of truth maintenance system are the justification-based truth maintenance system (JTMS) [20] and the assumption-based truth maintenance system (ATMS) [15]. A JTMS records a single set of consistent facts and all the inference which may be proved form them. When an inconsistency is detected some external system (which may be the user) is invoked to resolve the inconsistency and the JTMS then retracts the necessary inferences. In its simplest form, an ATMS maintains all the consistent subsets of the set of known facts and all the inferences which may be drawn from each. Inconsistency is handled by creating new consistent subsets and identifying which inferences may be made from them. Both types of system make it possible to identify consistent sets of beliefs and so make it possible to isolate inconsistency and avoid trivialization.

Truth maintenance can be considered to be concerned with lemma storage for non-monotonic reasoning. Thinking in terms of default logic, a JTMS can be considered to be a means of establishing a single extension and an ATMS as a means of establishing all the possible extensions. In a JTMS the discovery of a new fact which contradicts something in the existing extension will prompt the revisions necessary to establish a single new extension (if any exists). In an ATMS the introduction of a piece of contradicting information will generate a new set of extensions (if such extensions exist). The question of computational viability is then dependent upon the balance between on inferencing (consistency-checking and theorem proving) versus storage requirements (consistent subsets of data and inferential interdependencies). The aim of a TMS is to find the most parsimonious choice. A number of different implementations are given in [31], and a particular approach to assumption-based reasoning is described by Haenni [38]. In addition, more sophisticated truth maintenance systems will emerge from advanced theoretical frameworks such as that described by Benferhat and Garcia [4].

The notion of arguments discussed above provides useful concepts for formalising truth maintenance: For each explicit argument $(\Phi, \alpha)$ there is classical proof of $\alpha$ from $\Phi$ so addressing the question of inferences from beliefs, and for the belief $\alpha$, $\alpha$ is dependent on $\Phi$ so addressing the question of dependency recording. Let us assume that $(\Phi, \alpha)$ follows from some assumptions $\Delta$. To disbelieve some contradictory inferences from $\Delta$ requires a minimally inconsistent subset, $\Gamma$ of $\Delta$ to be removed. Furthermore, $\Gamma$ needs to be removed from the assumptions of all the argument, so all arguments $(\Psi, \beta)$ become $(\Psi - \Gamma, \beta)$. This of course may involve withdrawing some arguments since the revised assumptions

---

[4] Now often referred to as "reason maintenance".

no longer imply the conclusion. In this way it is possible to address the questions of disbelief propagation and the revision of beliefs.

Truth maintenance systems have proved to be of particular interest for incorporation in diagnostic systems. Given some set of observations, such as symptoms, diagnosis involves determining the cause of those observation by selecting an appropriate consistent set of hypotheses from which the observations can be logically derived. So diagnosis can be viewed as constructing an argument. Furthermore, since the diagnostic process can take place over time, new observations can be obtained that can be inconsistent with the current diagnosis, so forcing the need for revision of beliefs. Diagnosis can therefore benefit from appropriate truth maintenance.

## 4   Combining Approaches

Most of the research into uncertainty handling formalisms which has been mentioned so far has dealt with the use of single formalisms in isolation. However, if one accepts, as we do, that the eclectic position outlined in Section 1 is correct, then the following argument may be made. If different formalisms are good for representing different aspects of ignorance, then it follows that there are some problems which require the modelling of aspects of ignorance which are best covered by two or more different formalisms. Thus there is merit in investigating both the use of several formalisms in combination, and on determining the differences between different formalisms, and there is a growing body of work on this subject (though it should be noted that not all researchers working on such matters would explicitly acknowledge the validity of the eclectic position).

Possibly the most interesting strand of this kind of work is that which combines essentially logical techniques with numerical measures. This is commonly done by using a logical technique to establish a set of possible hypotheses from a larger initial set of exhaustive hypotheses, and then using a numerical techniques to rank the plausible set. Typical of such systems are those of Provan [73], Bigham [5] and Laskey and Lehner [51]. In all three of these systems, the semantic equivalence of the ATMS [15] and the Dempster-Shafer method, proved by Provan, is exploited ensuring that no information is lost in the initial round of inference. Bigham's system is particularly interesting in that it includes an extension of the clause based approach of McAllester's logic-based truth maintenance system (LTMS) [59] as a symbolic inference engine, and also permits beliefs based on possibility theory to be propagated. A similar system is de Kleer and Williams' [16] GDE for fault diagnosis. In GDE all inference directed at discovering the fault is carried out by symbolic methods, with probabilities invoked, not to determine the most likely of several solutions in a static analysis, but to suggest the next measurement to be taken by the user of the system. This measurement leads to new information which, when entered, leads to further symbolic computation. Thus the numerical computation sparks off another round of symbolic inference, and the cycle continues until the fault is found.

In contrast to these ATMS-based approaches, van Dam [96] uses a JTMS in combination with Dempster-Shafer theory.

It is also possible to use possibility measures with an assumption-based truth maintenance system instead of belief functions or probabilities. This is exactly the course followed by Dubois, Lang and Prade in their possibilistic ATMS [22]. A possibilistic ATMS is an ATMS in which both assumptions and justifications may be associated with a possibility weight, and, since the propagation of the weights is carried out for every clause in the ATMS, there is no separation of the management of uncertainty from the usual functionality of an ATMS. Bigham [6] has extended this work by adapting the possibilistic ATMS to take account of temporal information. Furthermore, the possibilistic ATMS allows inconsistent knowledge bases to be revised using the principles of epistemic entrenchment [34].

Another set of interesting developments which bridge the gap between symbolic and numerical techniques is the discovery of relationships between default logic and evidence theory. Wilson [99] considers the similarities between belief functions and default logic. He shows that, despite their initial dissimilarities they are, in fact, closely related. Indeed, in Łukaszewicz's [55] modification of default logic, the extensions of general closed default theories correspond to the sets of formulae whose beliefs, calculated by the theory of evidence, tend to 1 when the reliability of the sources of evidence tend to 1. The existence of a strong relationship between default logic and the theory of evidence is borne out by Smets and Hsia [89] who demonstrate how to represent normal defaults (both with and without prerequisites) using the transferable belief model. Both of these papers can be seen as an extension of the work of Rich [77] and Ginsberg [36], who considered ways of applying numerical certainty measures to logical inference rules.

It is also possible to use argumentation to combine symbolic and numerical reasoning. For instance, Fox and Krause [49] discuss a simple inference mechanism, based on argumentation, which is suitable for joint symbolic and numerical reasoning. Nonmonotonic reasoning about Tweety's ability to fly is handled in the following way. The result of applying the default rule that "typically birds fly" is marked as supported by a "possible" argument, thus explicitly recording the fact that the conclusion need not be true. A certain inference of the form that Tweety doesn't fly because she is an ostrich is supported by a true argument. When two facts are in conflict, reasoning that a default fact is a less powerful argument than a true one resolves the situation. Similarly, numerical techniques generate arguments quantified by numerical degrees of belief, which can be compared to order hypotheses. However, this method is more than just a fancy method for quantifying propositions. The quantifier also allows the reasoning mechanism to refer to the grounds of the argument, identifying why the argument was generated. This provides the vital connection between the degree of belief and the underlying uncertainty that is missing from most methods of approximate reasoning. From the grounds, we can establish the reasons for the uncertainty, and the nature of the uncertainty, and reasoning about this allows us to proceed when we would otherwise be held up by the incomparability of the degrees of belief with which the propositions we are dealing with are quantified.

## 5 Summary

In this introduction to uncertainty formalisms we have only been able to briefly cover some of the many uncertainty formalisms which have been proposed over the years[5]. However, despite this diversity, we strongly believe that no single approach is appropriate for all uncertainty handling problems. Furthermore, for some uncertainty handling problems, we believe that a mixture of approaches is required. While this statement is still controversial in some quarters, there seems to be a growing realisation that the position it represents has some merit, and so there are clear arguments for the development of a range of uncertainty formalisms. In particular, there is still more work to be done in developing the range of uncertainty formalisms and in learning more about how to use them effectively in a wider range of uncertainty problems.

## References

1. S. K. Andersen, F. V. Jensen, K. G. Olesen, and F. Jensen. HUGIN—a shell for building Bayesian belief universes for expert systems. In *Proceedings of the 11th International Joint Conference on Artificial Intelligence*, pages 783–791, San Mateo, CA, 1989. Morgan Kaufmann.
2. J. A. Barnett. Computational methods for a mathematical theory of evidence. In *Proceedings of the 7th International Joint Conference on Artificial Intelligence*, pages 868–875, Los Altos, CA, 1981. William Kaufmann.
3. S. Benferhat, D. Dubois, and H. Prade. Argumentative inference in uncertain and inconsistent knowledge bases. In *Proceedings of the 9th Uncertainty in Artificial Intelligence*, pages 411–419. Morgan Kaufmann, 1993.
4. S. Benferhat and L. Garcia. A local handling of inconsistent knowledge and default bases. In A. Hunter and S. Parsons, editors, *Applications of Uncertainty Formalisms (this volume)*. Springer Verlag, Berlin, 1998.
5. J. Bigham. Computing beliefs according to Dempster-Shafer and possibilistic logic. In *Proceedings of the 3rd International Conference on Information Processing and Management of Uncertainty, Paris*, pages 59–61, 1990.
6. J. Bigham. Exploiting uncertain and temporal information in correlation. In A. Hunter and S. Parsons, editors, *Applications of Uncertainty Formalisms (this volume)*. Springer Verlag, Berlin, 1998.
7. P. Bosc, L. Lietard, and H. Prade. An ordinal approach to the processing of fuzzy queries with flexible quantifiers. In A. Hunter and S. Parsons, editors, *Applications of Uncertainty Formalisms (this volume)*. Springer Verlag, Berlin, 1998.
8. F. Brazier, J. Engelfreit, and J. Truer. Analysis of multi-interpretable ecological monitoring information. In A. Hunter and S. Parsons, editors, *Applications of Uncertainty Formalisms (this volume)*. Springer Verlag, Berlin, 1998.

[5] For a more detailed survey, see [43, 48, 64].

9. T. Chard. Qualitative probability versus quantitative probability in clinical diagnosis: a study using a computer simulation. *Medical Decision Making*, 11:38–41, 1991.

10. P. Cheeseman. Probabilistic vs. fuzzy reasoning. In L. N. Kanal and J. F. Lemmer, editors, *Uncertainty in Artificial Intelligence*, pages 85–102. Elsevier Science Publishers, Amsterdam, The Netherlands, 1986.

11. P. Cheeseman. Discussion of the paper by Lauritzen and Spiegelhalter. *Journal of the Royal Statistical Society, B*, 50:203, 1988.

12. P. Cheeseman. An inquiry into computer understanding. *Computational Intelligence*, 4:58–142, 1988.

13. D. A. Clark. Numerical and symbolic approaches to uncertainty management in AI. *Artificial Intelligence Review*, 4:109–146, 1990.

14. P. R. Cohen. *Heuristic Reasoning about Uncertainty: An Artificial Intelligence Approach*. Pitman, London, UK, 1985.

15. J. de Kleer. An assumption-based TMS. *Artificial Intelligence*, 28:127–162, 1986.

16. J. de Kleer and B. C. Williams. Diagnosing multiple faults. *Artificial Intelligence*, 32:97–130, 1987.

17. A. P. Dempster. Upper and lower probabilities induced by a multi-valued mapping. *Annals of Mathematical Statistics*, 38:325–339, 1967.

18. A. P. Dempster. A generalisation of Bayesian inference (with discussion). *Journal of the Royal Statistical Society B*, 30:205–232, 1968.

19. A. P. Dempster. Comments on 'An inquiry into computer understanding' by Peter Cheeseman. *Computational Intelligence*, 4:72–73, 1988.

20. J. Doyle. A truth maintenance system. *Artificial Intelligence*, 12:231–272, 1979.

21. D. Driankov. A calculus for belief-intervals representation of uncertainty. In B. Bouchon-Meunier and R. R. Yager, editors, *Uncertainty in Knowledge-Based Systems*, pages 205–216. Springer-Verlag, Berlin, Germany, 1986.

22. D. Dubois, J. Lang, and H. Prade. A possibilistic assumption-based truth maintenance system with uncertain justifications, and its application to belief revision. In J. P. Martins and M. Reinfrank, editors, *Truth Maintenance Systems*, pages 87–106, Berlin, Germany, 1990. Springer Verlag.

23. D. Dubois, J. Lang, and H. Prade. Fuzzy sets in approximate reasoning, Part 2: Logical approaches. *Fuzzy Sets and Systems*, 40:203–244, 1991.

24. D. Dubois and H. Prade. Necessity measures and the resolution principle. *IEEE Transactions on Systems, Man and Cybernetics*, 17:474–478, 1987.

25. D. Dubois and H. Prade. Modelling uncertainty and inductive inference: a survey of recent non-additive probability systems. *Acta Psychologica*, 68:53–78, 1988.

26. D. Dubois and H. Prade. *Possibility Theory: An Approach to Computerized Processing of Uncertainty*. Plenum Press, New York, NY, 1988.

27. D. Dubois and H. Prade. Processing of imprecision and uncertainty in expert system reasoning models. In C. Ernst, editor, *Management Expert Systems*, pages 67–88. Addison Wesley, 1988.

28. R. O. Duda, P. E. Hart, and N. J. Nilsson. Subjective Bayesian methods for a rule-based inference system. In *Proceedings of the National Computer Conference*, pages 1075–1082, 1976.

29. M. Elvang-Gøransson and A. Hunter. Argumentative logics: Reasoning from classically inconsistent information. *Data and Knowledge Engineering Journal*, 16:125–145, 1995.

30. D. W. Etherington. *Reasoning with Incomplete Information*. Pitman, London, UK, 1988.

31. K. D. Forbus and J. de Kleer. *Building Problem Solvers*. MIT Press, Cambridge, MA, 1993.

32. J. Fox. Three arguments for extending the framework of probability. In L. N. Kanal and J. F. Lemmer, editors, *Uncertainty in Artificial Intelligence*, pages 447–458. Elsevier Science Publishers, Amsterdam, The Netherlands, 1986.

33. J. Fox and S. Parsons. Arguing about beliefs and actions. In A. Hunter and S. Parsons, editors, *Applications of Uncertainty Formalisms (this volume)*. Springer Verlag, Berlin, 1998.

34. P. Gärdenfors. *Knowledge in flux: Modelling the Dynamics of Epistemic States*. MIT Press, Cambridge, MA, 1988.

35. J. Gebhardt and R. Kruse. Background to and perspectives on possibilistic graphical models. In A. Hunter and S. Parsons, editors, *Applications of Uncertainty Formalisms (this volume)*. Springer Verlag, Berlin, 1998.

36. M. Ginsberg. Non-monotonic reasoning using Dempster's rule. In *Proceedings of the 4th National Conference on Artificial Intelligence*, pages 112–119, Los Altos, CA, 1984. William Kaufmann.

37. J. Gordon and E. H. Shortliffe. A method for managing evidential reasoning in a hierarchical hypothesis space. *Artificial Intelligence*, 26:323–357, 1985.

38. R. Haenni. Modelling uncertainty in propositional assumption-based systems. In A. Hunter and S. Parsons, editors, *Applications of Uncertainty Formalisms (this volume)*. Springer Verlag, Berlin, 1998.

39. D. Heckerman and M. Wellman. Bayesian networks. *Communications of the ACM*, 38:27–30, 1995.

40. D. E. Heckerman. Probability interpretation for MYCIN's certainty factors. In L. N. Kanal and J. F. Lemmer, editors, *Uncertainty in Artificial Intelligence*, pages 167–196. Elsevier Science Publishers, Amsterdam, The Netherlands, 1986.

41. M. Henrion, G. Provan, B. Del Favero, and G. Sanders. An experimental comparison of numerical and qualitative probabilistic reasoning. In *Proceedings of the 10th Conference on Uncertainty in Artificial Intelligence*, pages 319–326, San Francisco, CA, 1994. Morgan Kaufmann.

42. E. J. Horvitz, D. E. Heckerman, and C. P. Langlotz. A framework for comparing alternative formalisms for plausible reasoning. In *Proceedings of the 5th National Conference on Artificial Intelligence*, pages 210–214, Los Altos, CA, 1986. Morgan Kaufmann.

43. A. Hunter. *Uncertainty in Information Systems*. McGraw-Hill, London, UK, 1996.

44. D. J. Israel. Some remarks on the place of logic in knowledge representation. In N. Cercone and G. McCalla, editors, *The Knowledge Frontier: Essays in the Representation of Knowledge*, pages 80–91. Springer Verlag, New York, NY, 1987.

45. G. J. Klir. Where do we stand on measures of uncertainty, ambiguity, fuzziness, and the like? *Fuzzy Sets and Systems*, 24:141–160, 1987.

46. P. Krause, S. Ambler, M. Elvang-Gøransson, and J. Fox. A logic of argumentation for reasoning under uncertainty. *Computational Intelligence*, 11:113–131, 1995.

47. P. Krause, J. Fox, P. Judson, and M. Patel. Qualitative risk assessment fulfills a need. In A. Hunter and S. Parsons, editors, *Applications of Uncertainty Formalisms (this volume)*. Springer Verlag, Berlin, 1998.

48. P. J. Krause and D. A. Clark. *Representing Uncertain Knowledge: An Artificial Intelligence Approach*. Intellect, Oxford, UK, 1993.

49. P. J. Krause and J. Fox. Combining symbolic and numerical methods for reasoning under uncertainty. In D. J. Hand, editor, *AI and Computer Power; The Impact on Statistics*, pages 99–114. Chapman and Hall, London, UK, 1994.

50. M. Lalmas. Modelling information retrieval with Dempster-Shafer's theory of evidence. In A. Hunter and S. Parsons, editors, *Applications of Uncertainty Formalisms (this volume)*. Springer Verlag, Berlin, 1998.
51. K. B. Laskey and P. E. Lehner. Assumptions, beliefs and probabilities. *Artificial Intelligence*, 32:65–77, 1990.
52. S. L. Lauritzen and D. J. Spiegelhalter. Local computations on graphical structures, and their application to expert systems. *Journal of the Royal Statistical Society, B*, 50:157–224, 1988.
53. D. V. Lindley. *Making Decisions*. John Wiley & Sons, Chichester, UK, 1975.
54. W. Łukaszewicz. Two results on default logic. In *Proceedings of the 9th International Joint Conference on Artificial Intelligence*, pages 459–461, Los Altos, CA, 1985. Morgan Kaufmann.
55. W. Łukaszewicz. Considerations on default logic: an alternative approach. *Computational Intelligence*, 4:1–16, 1988.
56. P. Magni, R. Bellazi, and F. Locatelli. Using uncertainty management techniques in medical therapy planning: a decision theoretic approach. In A. Hunter and S. Parsons, editors, *Applications of Uncertainty Formalisms (this volume)*. Springer Verlag, Berlin, 1998.
57. P. Magrez and Ph. Smets. Fuzzy modus ponens: A new model suitable for applications in knowledge-based systems. *International Journal of Intelligent Systems*, 4:181–200, 1975.
58. J. Martins and S. Shapiro. A model of belief revision. *Artificial Intelligence*, 35:25–79, 1988.
59. D. A. McAllester. An outlook on truth maintenance. AI Memo 551, AI Laboratory, MIT, 1980.
60. J. McCarthy. Circumscription—a form of non-monotonic reasoning. *Artificial Intelligence*, 13:27–39, 1980.
61. S. Moral and N. Wilson. Importance sampling Monte-Carlo algorithms for the calculation of Dempster-Shafer belief. In *Proceedings of the 6th International Conference on Information Processing and the Management of Uncertainty*, pages 1337–1344, 1996.
62. P. Nicolas and T. Schaub. The XRay system: an implementation platform for local query-answering in default logics. In A. Hunter and S. Parsons, editors, *Applications of Uncertainty Formalisms (this volume)*. Springer Verlag, Berlin, 1998.
63. N. J. Nilsson. Probabilistic logic. *Artificial Intelligence*, 28:71–87, 1986.
64. S. Parsons. *Qualitative approaches to reasoning under uncertainty*. MIT Press, Cambridge, MA, 1998.
65. S. Parsons and J. Fox. Argumentation and decision making: a position paper. In *Formal and Applied Practical Reasoning*, pages 705–709, Berlin, Germany, 1996. Springer Verlag.
66. J. Pearl. How to do with probabilities what people say you can't. Technical Report CSD-850031, Cognitive Systems Laboratory, Computer Science Department UCLA, 1985.
67. J. Pearl. Fusion, propagation and structuring belief networks. *Artificial Intelligence*, 29:241–288, 1986.
68. J. Pearl. Bayesian decision methods. In *Encyclopedia of Artificial Intelligence*, pages 48–56. John Wiley, 1987.
69. J. Pearl. *Probabilistic Reasoning in Intelligent Systems: Networks of Plausible Inference*. Morgan Kaufmann, San Mateo, CA, 1988.

70. G. Pinkas and R. Loui. Reasoning from inconsistency: A taxonomy of principles for resolving conflict. In *Principles of Knowledge Representation and Reasoning: Proceedings of the Third International Conference*. Morgan Kaufmann, 1992.

71. M. Pradhan, M. Henrion, G. Provan, B. Del Favero, and K. Huang. The sensitivity of belief networks to imprecise probabilities: an experiemntal investigation. *Artificial Intelligence*, 85:363–397, 1996.

72. H. Prakken. An argumentation framework for default reasoning. *Annals of Mathematics and Artificial Intelligence*, 9, 1993.

73. G. M. Provan. Solving diagnostic problems using extended assumption-based truth maintenance systems: foundations. Technical Report 88-10, Department of Computer Science, University of British Columbia, 1988.

74. J. R. Quinlan. INFERNO: a cautious approach to uncertain inference. *Computer Journal*, 26:255–269, 1983.

75. M. Ramalho. Uncertainty measures associated with fuzzy rules for connection admission control in ATM networks. In A. Hunter and S. Parsons, editors, *Applications of Uncertainty Formalisms (this volume)*. Springer Verlag, Berlin, 1998.

76. R. Reiter. A logic for default reasoning. *Artificial Intelligence*, 13:81–132, 1980.

77. E. Rich. Default reasoning as likelihood reasoning. In *Proceedings of the 3rd National Conference on Artificial Intelligence*, pages 348–351, Los Altos, CA, 1983. William Kaufmann.

78. A. Saffiotti. An AI view of the treatment of uncertainty. *The Knowledge Engineering Review*, 2:75–97, 1987.

79. A. Saffiotti. Handling uncertainty in control of autonomous robots. In A. Hunter and S. Parsons, editors, *Applications of Uncertainty Formalisms (this volume)*. Springer Verlag, Berlin, 1998.

80. B. Schweitzer and A. Sklar. Associative functions and abstract semigroups. *Publicationes Mathematicae Debrecen*, 10:69–81, 1963.

81. G. L. S. Shackle. *Decision, order and time in human affairs*. Cambridge University Press, Cambridge, UK, 1961.

82. G. Shafer. *A Mathematical Theory of Evidence*. Princeton University Press, Princeton, NJ, 1976.

83. G. Shafer. Comments on 'An inquiry into computer understanding' by Peter Cheeseman. *Computational Intelligence*, 4:121–124, 1988.

84. G. Shafer and R. Logan. Implementing Dempster's rule for hierarchical evidence. *Artificial Intelligence*, 33:271–298, 1987.

85. P. P. Shenoy and G. Shafer. Axioms for probability and belief function propagation. In R. D. Shachter, T. S. Levitt, L. N. Kanal, and J. F. Lemmer, editors, *Uncertainty in Artificial Intelligence 4*, pages 169–198. North-Holland, Amsterdam, The Netherlands, 1990.

86. E. H. Shortliffe. *Computer-Based Medical Consultations: MYCIN*. Elsevier, New York, NY, 1976.

87. Ph. Smets. Belief functions. In Ph. Smets, E. H. Mamdani, D. Dubois, and H. Prade, editors, *Non-Standard Logics for Automated Reasoning*, pages 253–275. Academic Press, London, UK, 1988.

88. Ph. Smets. Belief functions versus probability functions. In B Bouchon-Meunier, L. Saitta, and R. R. Yager, editors, *Uncertainty and Intelligent Systems*, pages 17–24. Springer Verlag, Berlin, Germany, 1988.

89. Ph. Smets and Y-T. Hsia. Default reasoning and the transferable belief model. In P. P. Bonissone, M. Henrion, L. N. Kanal, and J. F. Lemmer, editors, *Uncertainty in Artificial Intelligence 6*, pages 495–504. Elsevier Science Publishers, Amsterdam, The Netherlands, 1991.

90. Ph. Smets and R. Kennes. The transferable belief model. *Artificial Intelligence*, 66:191–234, 1994.

91. M. Smithson. *Ignorance and Uncertainty: Emerging Paradigms*. Springer Verlag, New York, NY, 1989.

92. L. E. Sucar, D. F. Gillies, and D. A. Gillies. Objective probabilities in expert systems. *Artificial Intelligence*, 61:187–208, 1993.

93. A. Tawfik and E. Neufeld. Model-based diagnosis: a probabilistic extension. In A. Hunter and S. Parsons, editors, *Applications of Uncertainty Formalisms (this volume)*. Springer Verlag, Berlin, 1998.

94. S. Toulmin. *The uses of argument*. Cambridge University Press, Cambridge, UK., 1957.

95. A. Tversky and D. Kahneman. Judgement under uncertainty: Heuristics and biases. *Science*, 185:1124–1131, 1974.

96. K. van Dam. Using uncertainty techniques in radio communication systems. In A. Hunter and S. Parsons, editors, *Applications of Uncertainty Formalisms (this volume)*. Springer Verlag, Berlin, 1998.

97. G. Vreeswijk. Abstract argumentation systems. In M de Glas and D Gabbay, editors, *Proceedings of the First World Conference on Fundamentals of Artificial Intelligence*. Angkor, 1991.

98. D. Wilson, A. Greig, John Gilby, and Robert Smith. Some problems in trying to implement uncertainty techniques in automated inspection. In A. Hunter and S. Parsons, editors, *Applications of Uncertainty Formalisms (this volume)*. Springer Verlag, Berlin, 1998.

99. N. Wilson. Rules, belief functions, and default logic. In *Proceedings of the 6th Conference on Uncertainty in Artificial Intelligence*, pages 443–449, Mountain View, CA, 1990. Association for Uncertainty in AI.

100. N. Wilson. *Some theoretical aspects of the Dempster-Shafer theory*. PhD thesis, Oxford Polytechnic, 1992.

101. N. Wilson and S. Moral. Fast Markov chain algorithms for calculating Dempster-Shafer belief. In *Proceedings of the 12th European Conference on Artificial Intelligence*, pages 672–676, Chichester, UK, 1996. John Wiley & Sons.

102. L. A. Zadeh. Fuzzy sets. *Information and Control*, 8:338–353, 1965.

103. L. A. Zadeh. Fuzzy sets as a basis for a theory of possibility. *Fuzzy Sets and Systems*, 1:1–28, 1978.

104. L. A. Zadeh. A theory of approximate reasoning. In J. Hayes, D. Michie, and L. Mikulich, editors, *Machine Intelligence 9*, pages 149–194. Ellis Horwood, 1979.

105. L. A. Zadeh. Is probability theory sufficient for dealing with uncertainty in AI? a negative view. In L. N. Kanal and J. F. Lemmer, editors, *Uncertainty in Artificial Intelligence*, pages 103–116. Elsevier Science Publishers, Amsterdam, The Netherlands, 1986.

# Using Uncertainty Management Techniques in Medical Therapy Planning: A Decision-Theoretic Approach

Paolo Magni[1], Riccardo Bellazzi[1] and Franco Locatelli[2]

[1] Dipartimento di Informatica e Sistemistica, Università degli Studi di Pavia, Italy
[2] Clinica Pediatrica, IRCCS Policlinico S. Matteo, Pavia, Italy
E-mail: magni@aimed11.unipv.it, ric@aim.unipv.it, tmoped@ipv36.unipv.it

**Abstract.** Therapy planning is a very complex task, being the patient's therapeutic response affected by several sources of uncertainty. Furthermore, the modelling of a patient's evolution is frequently hampered by the incompleteness of the medical knowledge; it is hence often not possible to derive a mathematical model that is able to take into account the characteristics of the uncertain environment. An interesting way of coping with this class of problems is the Decision-Theoretic Planning approach, i.e. the formulations of policies on the basis of Decision Theory. This approach is able to provide plans in the presence of partial and qualitative information, while preserving a sound mathematical foundation. In this paper we will exploit a novel graphical formalism for representing Decision-Theoretic Planning problems, called Influence View. This method will be tested in an important therapy planning problem: the assessment of the Graft Versus Host Disease prophylaxis after Bone Marrow Transplantation in leukemic children.

## 1 Introduction

Therapy planning is a very complex task, since the patient's therapeutic response is affected by several sources of uncertainty, from inter- and intra-individual variability, to wrong implementations of the drug delivery protocol. Furthermore, the modelling of a patient's behaviour is frequently hampered by the incompleteness of the medical knowledge; it is hence often not possible to derive a mathematical model that is able to take into account the characteristics of the uncertain environment. In this case, the definition of an information system for supporting therapeutic decisions usually relies on heuristic rules, which exploit a representation of the patient's state based on discrete and qualitative variables.

An alternative way of coping with this class of problems is the Decision-Theoretic Planning approach, i.e. the formulation of policies on the basis of Decision Theory. This approach is able to provide plans in the presence of partial and qualitative information, while preserving a sound mathematical foundation.

In this context, finite-state Markov Decision Processes (MDPs) are often exploited for modelling time-dependent decision problems [19, 17]. In MDPs the stochastic process governing the dynamic system is a Markov Chain, i.e. a discrete-time/finite-state dynamic process in which the probability distribution of the state at time $t+1$ is independent of all past state realizations given the current one at time $t$. Control actions may be taken at each time instant (also called *decision stage*), and the plan is formulated according to a value function that takes into account the effectiveness and/or the costs of the action policy. A reasonable assumption is also that the value function will be *time separable*, i.e. it will be possible to calculate the overall value function as a combination of functions specified at each stage of the decision process. In order to calculate the best policy for MDP, tackling both finite and infinite-horizon decision problems, several algorithms have been defined: Dynamic Programming, Value Iteration and Policy Iteration [2] are examples of them.

The representational complexity of the system and the computational cost of the solution algorithms for MDPs is directly related to the dimensionality of the state space (i.e. the set of all possible values that the system state can assume), and hence with the capability to properly choose a suitable *state factorization*: the state factorization consists in the definition of a set of state variables, whose cartesian product defines the state space.

In practical applications, it is desirable to simplify the knowledge acquisition process and the system description through the explicit representation of the state variables and of the causal relationships among them.

Graphical models [16] are particularly appealing to cope with this task. In this paper we will exploit a novel graphical formalism for MDP knowledge acquisition called Influence View [11]. An Influence View is a directed acyclic graph that depicts the probabilistic relationships between the problem state variables in a generic time transition; additional variables, called event variables, may be added, in order to describe the conditional independence between state variables. By using the specified conditional independence structure, an Influence View may hence allow a parsimonious specification of a MDP.

This methodology has been applied by the authors to the Graft Versus Host Disease (GVHD) prophylaxis after Bone Marrow Transplantation.

The structure of this paper is hence the following one: after the introduction of the medical problem in section 2, we will define MDPs in section 3, and, in section 4, will address some problem definition issues and we will introduce the Influence View framework. Later, in section 5, we will model the medical problem as an MDP using the Influence View formalism, while, after the description in section 6 of the MDP solution algorithms, we will derive in section 7 the optimal policy for the GVHD prophylaxis problem. The last section is dedicated to a discussion on the above presented topics.

## 2 A Decision Support System for Assessing the GVHD Prophylaxis

Allogeneic Bone Marrow Transplantation (BMT) represents a curative treatment for patients affected by inborn errors of the immune system, as well as for patients who have acquired diseases such as severe aplastic anaemia and acute or chronic leukemias. The major complication of BMT is GVHD, a reaction of donor immunocompetent cells directed towards the recipient. GVHD is unfortunately frequent and life-threatening, and affects outcome and event-free survival as frequently as any other complication.

Nevertheless, in leukemic patients, GVHD is effective in preventing disease relapse, and hence a mild GVHD occurrence may affect the success of BMT. In fact, an immune-mediated anti-leukemia effect associated with GVHD, called Graft Versus Leukemia or GVL-effect, is widely reported in the literature [22].

Leukemic patients undergo a prophylactic treatment with immunosuppressive drugs in order to prevent or at least to control GVHD. The medical problem consists in assessing a plan that must specify both type and dosage of immunosuppressive drugs, in order to avoid or induce GVHD, according to the patient's specific condition and drugs toxicity.

In clinical practice, the physicians follow a therapeutic protocol that involves the delivery of two immunosuppressive drugs, Cyclosporine-A and Methotrexate. Cyclosporine-A dosage is given in two ranges of values, low or medium dosages $(1-2.9 \text{ mg/kg/day})$ and high dosages $(> 3 \text{ mg/kg/day})$; Methotrexate is instead delivered following a standard dose scheme, but it is not always given to patients, because of its high toxicity.

So, we may obtain four alternative different action schemes:

1. Cyclosporine-A low-medium dosage without Methotrexate;
2. Cyclosporine-A low-medium dosage with Methotrexate;
3. Cyclosporine-A high dosage without Methotrexate;
4. Cyclosporine-A high dosage with Methotrexate.

The initial prophylaxis (day 0 after BMT) is usually decided on the basis of the following main variables:

- the *age* of the patient: the younger the patient, the lower should be the probability of developing GVHD,
- the *donor histo-compatibility (HLA-compatibility)*: the more compatible the transplanted bone marrow cells, the lower the probability of developing GVHD,
- the *infection prophylaxis*: the more aggressive the infection prophylaxis before BMT, the lower the probability of *infections* after BMT and hence the lower the probability of developing GVHD;
- the *BMT conditioning regimen*: two different types of conditioning regimens are possible (Chemotherapy and Total Body Irradiation); Chemotherapy conditioning, producing a shorter period of neutropenia, reduces the risk of *infections* and hence of GVHD.

The prophylaxis is revised every two days depending on the patients conditions, measured in terms of *toxicity* (e.g. due to the immunosuppressive drugs) and of *drug concentration* in the blood. When a GVHD episode occurs the prophylaxis problem turns into a therapy problem.

The physicians must face a trade-off problem involving the following goals: 1) to avoid severe GVHD episodes that may lead to patient death; 2) to favour the development of mild GVHD episodes in leukemic patients in order to reduce the risk of relapse and hence mortality; 3) to avoid toxicity episodes caused by an excessive amount of immunosuppressive drugs.

To find the optimal control law (the optimal prophylaxis) it is necessary to model the evolution of the patient state during the follow-up period.

In our problem it is practically impossible to derive a mathematical model of the system dynamics, for at least the following reasons:

- the complexity of the system: the patient response dynamics depends on a great number of concurrent processes; the drugs absorption, the bone marrow cell production, the complex mechanisms of the immune system. At the present level of medical knowledge, a mathematical model of this system is not derivable (*uncertainty on the problem structure*).
- The therapeutic responses show considerable inter- and intra- individual variability (*uncertainty on the process evolution*);
- In clinical practice, the data coming from the monitoring of drug concentrations in the blood can be prone to high oscillations due to sampling time errors (*uncertainty on the measurements*).

In response to the above mentioned sources of uncertainty, we have hence decided to apply the Decision-Theoretic Planning techniques to this problem. In particular, we will model the decision making process using a MDP, whose transition probability matrix may be specified by conveniently exploiting graphical models.

## 3 Markov Decision Processes

In this section we will summarize the most important features of Markov Decision Processes, in order to introduce more easily our approach.

MDPs [21] are decision-theoretic extensions of discrete-time finite-state Markov Processes; in MDPs it is assumed that a decision maker is present and a time-separable utility (or cost) function is available.

A discrete-time finite-state Markov Process is a stochastic process $\{X_k\}$ with a finite set of states $\Omega_x$, where the state evolution $f(X)$ is described by the one-step transition probabilities $p_{ij} = P\{X_{k+1} = j \mid X_k = i\}$.

In MDPs the presence of the decision maker is modelled by transition probabilities depending on the action $A_k$ taken at time epoch $k$. The criterion to choose the proper decision is based on a time-additive utility function.

More formally, a discrete time MDP is a stochastic process that may be described in terms of:

- a discrete time domain $\Omega_t$;
- a finite state space $\Omega_x$;
- a set of possible actions $\Omega_u$, assumed to be finite;

- a reward function $v(i, a)$ that, for each temporal step $k$, specifies the contribution to a cumulative utility function. This reward function depends on the state $X_k = i$ and on the decision $A_k = a$ (with $a \in \Omega_u$) chosen by the decision maker, but is independent of the time epoch $k$;
- a set of one-step transition probabilities $p_{ij}^{(a)} = P\{X_{k+1} = j \mid X_k = i, A_k = a\}$, assumed to be time-independent.

We assume that the decision maker, at each time epoch $k$, takes his decision $A_k$ after the observation of the process state $X_k$. The decision maker's target is to get the maximum reward (i.e. to maximize the cumulative utility function) during the process evolution. The time period during which the decision maker is interested in observing the process is called the *time horizon* (in the following we will distinguish between finite or infinite time horizon). Since the decision maker does not know exactly the effects of his actions, the estimated state sequence over the time horizon is expressed by probabilistic relations and the decision optimality is evaluated on the expected value of the cumulative utility function.

Maximizing the expected utility function over the time horizon, it is possible to obtain an optimal dynamic policy $\{\mu_k\}$, that is a function which gives the optimal action $a = \mu_k(i)$ when the system is in state $i$ at decision epoch $k$.

When the policy is independent of the decision epoch $k$, it is said to be stationary.

# 4    Structuring Time Transitions: The Influence View Approach

The complexity of the solution algorithms for MDPs is directly related to the dimension of $\Omega_x$: the Dynamic Programming algorithm, used for the finite-horizon problem, performs a number of computations to solve $n$ stages $O(n \times |\Omega_x|^2 \times |\Omega_u|)$, while the Value Iteration algorithm, used for infinite-horizon problems, requires $O(|\Omega_x|^2 \times |\Omega_u|)$ computations for each iteration [12]. It is hence clear that a careful construction of the state space is crucial to obtain manageable problems. This building process may be viewed as a knowledge acquisition problem that can be subdivided into two fundamental steps: 1) a proper choice of the state variables, 2) a suitable structuring of the state space $\Omega_x$ and of the action space $\Omega_u$.

Here we will address the latter problem, while valuable approaches for the former are presented in [7]. We will hence assume that the state space has been already *factored*, by introducing a certain number of *state variables*; moreover we will assume that a proper *reduction* of the state space (considering only useful sub-domains of the state variables) and *abstraction* (e.g. a meaningful discretization of the state variables) has been performed.

A fundamental structuring operation consists in exploiting the *temporal conditional independencies* that can be identified in the state space transition.

For example, let us suppose that the state of a patient in the GVHD prophylaxis problem can be completely described by three variables: *Acute GVHD*

(G), the presence or the absence of *toxicity* (T), and *serum Cyclosporine-A concentration* (CS). The state of the system is hence the set $X = \{T, G, CS\}$.

$T$ can take two values *(Yes, No)*, while $G$ and $CS$ three values, ($\{No, Mild, Severe\}$ and $\{Low, Normal, High\}$, respectively).

The Acute GVHD at time $k$ may be considered as independent from the Toxicities at time $k-1$, so that $P(G_k \mid G_{k-1}, CS_{k-1}, T_{k-1}) = P(G_k \mid G_{k-1}, CS_{k-1})$.

More generally, if $\Omega_x$ is factored into $M$ state variables with at most $S$ values, and each state variable at a generic time is dependent on at most $N$ other state variables at previous one, the joint distribution $f(X)$ can be expressed by using $O(M(S^N))$ parameters instead of $O(S^M)$. It is hence clear that the more conditional independencies are found in the state space transition, the more efficient the knowledge elicitation and inference execution will be. For example, in the case of $M = 6, S = 4$ and $N = 2$ we will have a space of 96 elements instead of a space of 4096 elements: the advantage is clear.

Graphical models may be effectively used as instruments to exploit structure inside the state space and in the state space transition: in particular Bayesian Belief Networks and Influence Diagrams [16, 10] have been widely used in stochastic modelling and in decision problems. They are Directed Acyclic Graphs (DAGs) in which nodes represent variables, while arcs express direct dependencies between variables. These models are quantified by specifying the conditional probability tables of each node given its parents. They are able to represent the joint probability distribution of the variables by specifying only local conditional probability distributions. For further details see [16]. Influence Diagrams, DAGs in which decisions and value functions are also represented as nodes, have been proposed as an instrument for representing and solving dynamic decision problems [20] through the definition of Dynamic Influence Diagrams, and several applications have been developed in the medical field [17]. Although Dynamic Influence Diagrams represent a valuable solution to MDPs, their use is limited by a number of drawbacks.

In a Dynamic Influence Diagram it is necessary to describe the state space with a graphical model that is repeatedly drawn, at least conceptually, a number of times equal to the number of stages of the decision problem. This fact is of course a source of inefficiency for representational reasons. Moreover, Dynamic Influence Diagrams naturally represent only finite-horizon problems, and use a graph reduction algorithm that corresponds directly to the Dynamic Programming algorithm [20]. Finally, in order to impose a conditional independence structure on state variables and hence to simplify the knowledge acquisition process, it is often necessary to introduce, in the description of the system, additional variables, that we call *event variables* [11].

In order to clarify this crucial point let us refer to the "GVHD problem". The state space $X$ was $\{T, G, CS\}$. The CS state variable may be considered, at a generic instant, conditionally independent of each other variable, at the previous instant, if the Cyclosporine metabolism ($CS_M$) is known. In such a case we may say that, although the state of the patient may be exhaustively described by the variables $T$, $G$ and $CS$, the knowledge of an extra variable, like $CS_M$, may simplify the conditional dependence structure of the state space transition.

The problem in Dynamic Influence Diagrams is that event variables are treated as state variables, and this provokes an increase in the computational burden involved in the solution of dynamic decision problems. Generally speaking, the major drawback of Dynamic Influence Diagrams is related to the unnecessarily large number of state variables that they must manage. In our application example, this means that the state space must be increased, adding the variable $CS_M$.

In order to cope with this problem, in this work we have exploited a novel formalism for MDP knowledge acquisition, recently proposed by Tze-Yun Leong [11], called the *Influence View* approach.

Influence Views provide a graphical way to represent state transitions of a MDP using a synthetic and efficient formalism.

An Influence View is a DAG similar to Influence Diagrams. The probabilistic relationships among the problem variables (state and event variables) are graphically expressed by arcs between nodes and quantified by conditional probabilities [16].

An Influence View may contain the following kinds of nodes:

- **State nodes.** Each state node represents a state variable $x_k$ obtained by the factorization of the MDP space state. Since the Influence View specifies an MDP transition from a generic time epoch to the next one, each state node appears twice in this network, in order to express the same variable in two different time epochs. They are called *initial* and *final* state nodes. If in the Influence View there are $N$ state nodes representing the variables $x_1, x_2, \ldots, x_N$ with a sets of possible values $s_{x_1}, s_{x_2}, \ldots, s_{x_N}$, respectively, then the space state of the MDP described by this Influence View is $\Omega_x = s_{x_1} \times s_{x_2} \times \ldots \times s_{x_N}$.

- **Event nodes.** Each event node represents an event variable placed between initial and final state nodes. Event variables are introduced to help the user in the description of $f(X)$ by structuring the transition among the state variables. It is important to remark that event variables are not useful to describe the state of the system in order to take a decision, but they represent a way to simplify the building process of the system model.

  We can distinguish two types of event variables on the basis of their role: *context variables* and *transition variables*.

  - **Context variables.** In the Influence View network, a context variable is a root node or, more generally, a node that has no state nodes in its ancestral set (i.e. context nodes are not in any path between initial and final state nodes). The marginal distribution of these variables is hence independent from the values of the initial state nodes. The use of context variables is a way to parameterize $f(X)$ in dependence of problem features that are not supposed to change during the decision-making process. They allow a compact description of systems that have different behaviours according to some contextual information. In medical problems these kinds of variables can represent the specific characteristics of different patients or of different populations of patients.

- **Transition variables.** Transition variables are event nodes displaced in the path between initial and final state nodes. They are, by definition, not observable, and are used only for easier specification of the probability distribution that controls a generic time transition.

Event variables are never inferred in an Influence View, since they are not included in the set of the state variables, and hence are not directly useful for deriving the optimal policy.

Thanks to the distinction between event and state variables, it is possible to simplify the process of knowledge acquisition without increasing the computational complexity of MDP solution algorithms.

- **Utility node.** The utility node expresses the utility (cost) function of the MDP in a single transition. It is specified in dependence of the state and/or event variable values.

The role of the decision maker could be described using decision nodes that represent action variables. In order to allow a more general problem specification, we prefer to specify different networks corresponding to different actions instead of using decision nodes in the same network. In this way the Influence Views may differ both in the event nodes, and in the topological structure.

As stated before, Influence Views offer some advantages compared to MDP transition diagrams: they allow the user to specify probabilistic relationships among a small number of random variables instead of specifying the joint probability distribution. In other words, it is possible to describe the model specifying "local" knowledge about conditional dependencies among few related events, instead of giving "global" transition probabilities among all the possible states of the MDP.

## 5 The Influence View for the GVHD Prophylaxis

The GVHD prophylaxis problem introduced in Section 2 can be represented as a MDP:

- The actions to be compared at each decision point (every two days since BMT) are the following:
  1. Cyclosporine-A Low-Medium dosage without Methotrexate;
  2. Cyclosporine-A Low-Medium dosage with Methotrexate;
  3. Cyclosporine-A High dosage without Methotrexate;
  4. Cyclosporine-A High dosage with Methotrexate.
- The patient state, i.e. the collection of state variables that are exploited at each time instant for revising the prophylaxis, may be chosen depending on the medical knowledge [18] and in accordance with the medical practice described in Section 2. These variables are summarized in Tab. 1.

| State variable name | Set of values |
| --- | --- |
| Hepatic Toxicity | Yes, No |
| Renal Toxicity | Yes, No |
| Serum Cs-A Concentration | Low, Normal, High |
| Acute GVHD | No, Mild, Severe |
| Death | Yes, No |

**Table 1.** Patient state in the GVHD prophylaxis problem: the set of state variables and their values.

The probabilistic specification of the model was performed exploiting the Influence View formalism.

The main variables considered by physicians to assess the initial prophylaxis have been treated as *context event variables*. Moreover, a number of event variables have been specified in order to better express the mutual influences among state variables at time $k$ and at time $k + 1$. For example, the probability of *Toxicity* episodes at time $k + 1$ is related to the *serum Cs-A concentration* levels at time $k$; while the *serum Cs-A concentration* levels probability at time $k + 1$ is only indirectly dependent on *Toxicity* episodes at time $k$, through an alteration of *Cs-A metabolism*. This effect is modelled by the introduction of some event variables, namely *Cs-A renal clearance, Cs-A distribution volume, patient's age* and *Cs-A metabolism alterations*.

Tab. 2 summarizes the event variables used in the GVHD prophylaxis problem.

| Event variable name | Set of values |
| --- | --- |
| Age | $\geq 10$ years, $< 10$ years |
| BMT Conditioning | Chemotherapy, Total Body Irradiation |
| Infection prophylaxis | Yes, No |
| Donor histo-compatibility | Low, High |
| Distribution volume | Low, Normal, High |
| Renal clearance | Normal, Decreased |
| CS-A metabolism | Increased, Normal, Decreased |
| Infection | Yes, No |

**Table 2.** The event variables introduced in the GVHD prophylaxis problem for structuring the state space transition: the first four variables are context variables, the other ones are transition variables.

The resulting Influence View of GVHD problem is shown in Fig. 1.

It is important to notice that a different Influence View must be created for each of the four actions. In our case, we have specified four Influence Views with the same topology but with different conditional probability tables. For

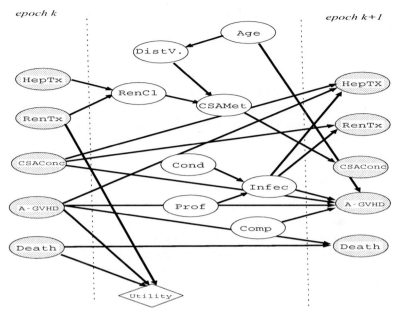

**Fig. 1.** The influence view describing the GVHD prophylaxis problem: filled ellipsis are state variables, empty ellipsis are event variables and the diamond is the utility function.

example, Methotrexate delivery decreases the probability of *GVHD* and increases the probability of toxicity episodes like *Hepatic Toxicity* and *Renal Toxicity*.

Some of the conditional probability tables of the Influence View have been derived through an elaboration of the data coming from the Italian National Registry of Acute Myeloid Leukemias. The utility model used is a survival model, modified to take into account the probability of toxicity episodes. So, we will take a policy that maximizes the survival time while minimizing the risk of drug toxicity.

It is worthwhile to notice that, in this particular problem, instead of specifying four probability transition matrixes of $72 \times 72 = 5184$ parameters, we need to specify only 4 sets of conditional probability tables with 325 parameters. This represents a considerable advantage in terms of knowledge acquisition.

## 6  The Influence View Solution

The solution of a decision problem described with an Influence View is an optimal policy that at each time specifies the best action on the basis of the values assumed by the state variables. An optimal policy may be dynamic or stationary.

In the Influence View framework the problem solution is derived in two steps:

1. Compute the transition probability matrix of the MDP described through Influence Views.
2. Solve the resulting MDP.

The above mentioned steps may be conveniently performed by using the following algorithms:

- The Elimination algorithm to *remove* event variables and to compute the equivalent MDP.
- The Dynamic Programming algorithm to solve optimization problems with a finite time horizon.
- The Value Iteration algorithm to find the optimal stationary policy for problems with an infinite time horizon.

**Elimination algorithm**

In order to compute the transition probability matrix of MDP described by the Influence Views framework we used an event variable elimination procedure, that we call *Elimination algorithm*. This algorithm, after setting the initial state nodes to fixed values, derives the joint probability distribution of the final state nodes, by applying the *elim-bel* algorithm proposed by Rina Dechter in [8]. In this way it is possible to derive the transition probability matrix using the conditional probability distributions specified in the Influence View.

The basic ideas of the Elimination algorithm are the following ones:

- Each row of the transition matrix represents the joint distribution of the final state nodes, given a fixed configuration of initial ones.
- Given an arbitrary order on $N$ stochastic variables it is always possible to express the joint distribution using the so-called chain rule:

$$P(Z_1, \ldots, Z_n) = \prod_{h=1}^{N} P(Z_h \mid Z_1, \ldots, Z_{h-1})$$

- The joint distribution of a subset $M$ of $N$ discrete variables can be computed starting from $P(Z_1, \ldots, Z_n)$ by eliminating all the variables $\notin M$ as follows:

$$\sum_{N_D} P(Z_1, \ldots, Z_n)$$

where $N_D$ is the set of all possible combinations of the variables that have to be eliminated.
- In general, the conditional probabilities that appear in the chain rule do not depend on every variables, so that, in the elimination step described above, some matrices can be migrated out of the summation.

In order to show how the algorithm works, we will refer to the Influence View in Fig. 2, that is a simplified version of the GVHD network. The state variables are $x_1 = T$ and $x_2 = CS$. The corresponding Markov process $\{X_k\} = \{x_{1k}, x_{2k}\}$ has space state $\Omega_x = \Omega_{x_1} \times \Omega_{x_2} = \{LowYes, LowNo, NormalYes, NormalNo,$

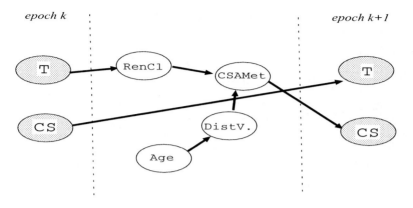

*epoch k*                          *epoch k+1*

**Fig. 2.** Influence view used in the forward propagation example.

$HighYes, HighNo\}$ since $\Omega_{x_1} = \{Yes, No\}$ and $\Omega_{x_2} = \{Low, Normal, High\}$. We can conveniently denote the state space as $\Omega_x = \{1, 2, 3, 4, 5, 6\}$. As a training example, in the following we will show how to compute the first row of the transition probabilities matrix $P_1 = P\{X_{k+1} | X_k = 1\}$.

So, after setting $X_k = 1$, that is $x_{1_k} = Yes$ (i.e. $T = Yes$) and $x_{2_k} = Low$ (i.e. $CS = Low$), we have to compute the distribution of $X_{k+1}$, that is the joint distribution of $x_{1_{k+1}}$ and $x_{2_{k+1}}$, using the *elim-bel* algorithm.

The first step is to find, in the Influence View, the subset of all nodes from which it is possible to reach the final state nodes (i.e. $T_k, CS_k, RenCl, CSAMet,$ $Age, DistV, T_{k+1}, CS_{k+1}$).

Then we have to fix an order into this subset. In particular we consider the following criterion based on the Influence View topology: the first elements are the final state nodes, the following ones are the event nodes (on the basis of the order of the backward visit in the graph starting from final state nodes) and the last elements are the initial state nodes (that are always instantiated). In our example the ordered[1] set is:

| $T_{k+1}$ | $CS_{k+1}$ | $CSAMet$ | $RenCl$ | $DistV$ | $Age$ | $T_k$ | $CS_k$ |
|-----------|------------|----------|---------|---------|-------|-------|--------|
| $Z_1$ | $Z_2$ | $Z_3$ | $Z_4$ | $Z_5$ | $Z_6$ | $Z_7$ | $Z_8$ |

where we denote with $Z_h$ the nodes in the ordered set.

Now we have to generate an ordered partition of the conditional probability matrices, called $\lambda$-partition, into *buckets*. Each $\lambda$ matrix depends only from a subset of the nodes: if the $h^{th}$ variable is the highest of them in the ordered set, $\lambda$ will be put in the $h^{th}$ bucket.

Our *buckets* are:

---

[1] The derived order is, in general, not unique.

| Bucket | $\lambda_1(\cdot)$ | $\lambda_2(\cdot)$ |
|---|---|---|
| $Bucket_8$ | $P(CS_k)$ | $P(T_{k+1} \mid CS_k)$ |
| $Bucket_7$ | $P(T_k)$ | $P(RenCl \mid T_k)$ |
| $Bucket_6$ | $P(Age)$ | $P(DistV \mid Age)$ |
| $Bucket_5$ | $P(CSAMet \mid RenCl, DistV)$ | |
| $Bucket_4$ | | |
| $Bucket_3$ | $P(CS_{k+1})$ | |
| $Bucket_2$ | | |
| $Bucket_1$ | | |

After the initialisation step we can start to eliminate initial nodes and event variables starting from the last nodes until only final state nodes are present in the reduced set.

The elimination step of the generic node $Z_h$ is obtained in this way:

1. Consider the $bucket_h$ and all $\lambda$ matrices in this $bucket$:
   - (a) if $Z_h$ is an instantiated variable (i.e an initial state nodes) then substitute, for each $\lambda$ matrix, the instantiated value;
   - (b) else compute $\lambda_{new}(\cdot) = \sum_{s=1}^{N_{Z_h}} \prod_{l=1}^{N_\lambda} \lambda_l(Z_h = s, \cdot)$ where $N_{Z_h}$ is the number of values of $Z_h$ and $N_\lambda$ is the number of $\lambda$ matrices in the $bucket$.
2. Put the obtained $\lambda_{new}$ matrix in the right $bucket$ (the one of the highest node which it depends from).
3. Eliminate the $Z_h$ from the ordered set.

In the example we have start considering the $bucket_8$. The node $Z_8$ (i. e. $CS_k$) is an instantiated node so we must apply step 1.(a) to eliminate it:

- $\lambda_2(Z_1, Z_8) = P(T_{k+1} \mid CS_k)$ turn into $\lambda_{2_{new}}(Z_1) = P(T_{k+1} \mid CS_k = Low)$
- we have to put $\lambda_{2_{new}}(Z_1)$ in the $bucket_1$.

| Bucket | $\lambda_1(\cdot)$ | $\lambda_2(\cdot)$ |
|---|---|---|
| $Bucket_1$ | $\lambda_{2_{new}}(Z_1)$ | |

- The reduced set of nodes is:

| $T_{k+1}$ | $CS_{k+1}$ | $CSAMet$ | $RenCl$ | $DistV$ | $Age$ | $T_k$ |
|---|---|---|---|---|---|---|
| $Z_1$ | $Z_2$ | $Z_3$ | $Z_4$ | $Z_5$ | $Z_6$ | $Z_7$ |

Now we have to consider the last node in the reduced set. $Z_7$ (i.e. $T_k$) is an instantiated node, so we must again apply step 1.(a):

- $\lambda_2(Z_4, Z_7) = P(RenCl \mid T_k)$ turn into $\lambda_{2_{new}}(Z_4) = P(RenCl \mid T_k = Yes)$.
- we have to put $\lambda_{2_{new}}(Z_4)$ in the $bucket_4$.

| Bucket | $\lambda_1(\cdot)$ | $\lambda_2(\cdot)$ |
|---|---|---|
| $Bucket_4$ | $\lambda_{2_{new}}(Z_4)$ | |

- The reduced set of nodes is:

| $T_{k+1}$ | $CS_{k+1}$ | $CSAMet$ | $RenCl$ | $DistV$ | $Age$ |
|---|---|---|---|---|---|
| $Z_1$ | $Z_2$ | $Z_3$ | $Z_4$ | $Z_5$ | $Z_6$ |

Again, we have to consider the last node in the reduced set. The node $Z_6$ (i.e. $Age$) is not an instantiated node, so we must apply step 1.(b):

- $\lambda_{new}(Z_5) = \sum_{s=1}^{N_{Z_6}} (\lambda_1(Z_6 = s) \times \lambda_2(Z_5, Z_6 = s))$ where $\lambda_1(Z_6)$ is $P(Age)$ and $\lambda_2(Z_5, Z_6)$ is $P(DistV \mid Age)$
- we have to put $\lambda_{new}(Z_5)$ in the $bucket_5$.

| Bucket | $\lambda_1(\cdot)$ | $\lambda_2(\cdot)$ |
|--------|--------------------|--------------------|
| $Bucket_5$ | $P(CSAMet \mid RenCl, DistV)$ | $\lambda_{new}(Z_5)$ |

- The reduced set of nodes turn into:

| $T_{k+1}$ | $CS_{k+1}$ | $CSAMet$ | $RenCl$ | $DistV$ |
|-----------|------------|----------|---------|---------|
| $Z_1$ | $Z_2$ | $Z_3$ | $Z_4$ | $Z_5$ |

Then we can process in a similar way the node $Z_5(DistV)$, $Z_4(RenCl)$, $Z_3(CSAMet)$.

When only the final state variables are in the simplified subset we have to compute to joint distribution probability on final state nodes by using the following expression:

$$P(Z_1, \ldots, Z_{N_f}) = \alpha \times \prod_{h=1}^{N_f} \times \prod_{l=1}^{N_{\lambda(h)}} \lambda_l^{(h)}(\cdot)$$

where $N_f$ is the number of final nodes, $\alpha$ is the normalization constant, $N_{\lambda(h)}$ is the number of the $\lambda$ matrices in to the $h^{th}$ $bucket$ and $\lambda_l^{(h)}$ is its $l^{th}$ element.

In order to derive the complete one-step transition matrix $P$, the overall propagation process must be repeated for all the possible values of $X_k$. The utility function may be obtained by applying the same procedure to the utility node. To obtain $(p_{ij}^{(a)})$, i.e. the transition probability form each state $i$ to each state $j$ under the action $a$, and $(v(i, a))$, i.e. the utility value associated with each state $i$ under $a$, we must run the Elimination algorithm over all the networks referring to the different actions. Once this step has been completed, it is possible to run the MDP solution algorithms.

## Dynamic Programming algorithm

The Dynamic Programming algorithm [3] is used to solve the MDP on a finite time horizon. It finds the optimal dynamic policy $\mu_k(i)$ that on each time epoch $k$ maximizes the expected value of the cumulative utility function. This policy is dynamic, so it may happen for a process which is in the same state on two different time epochs to be controlled by two different actions. The Dynamic Programming algorithm is able to manage discrete time dynamic systems with a time separable and additive over time utility function; in this sense it may manage more general problems than MDPs.

A convenient formulation for the MDP solution can be expressed as follows:

1. in correspondence of time $N$, we compute $J_N(i) = \max_a \{v(i,a)\}$;
2. for each time $k$, going backwards from $N-1$ to 0, we compute

$$J_k(i) = \max_a \left\{ v(i,a) + \sum_j p_{ij}(a) \cdot J_{k+1}(j) \right\} \quad k = N-1, N-2, \ldots, 0$$

$$\mu_k(i) = \arg\max_a \left\{ v(i,a) + \sum_j p_{ij}(a) \cdot J_{k+1}(j) \right\} \quad k = N-1, N-2, \ldots, 0$$

where $N$ is the time horizon, $J_k(i)$ is the expected value of the cumulative utility function evaluated from time $k$ to time $N$, $\mu_k(i)$ is the optimal policy on time epoch $k$ and $\arg\max_a\{V\}$ denotes the action that maximize the functional $V$.

In order to clarify the fundamental steps of dynamic programming algorithm we refer to a simple example.

Let us consider a problem with two states $(1,2)$ and two actions $(a_1, a_2)$ with the following transition probabilities and utilities:

Transition
probabilities

| | $a_1$ | | $a_2$ | |
|---|---|---|---|---|
| $k$ | $k+1$ | | $k+1$ | |
| | 1 | 2 | 1 | 2 |
| 1 | 0.3 | 0.7 | 0.8 | 0.2 |
| 2 | 0.4 | 0.6 | 0.5 | 0.5 |

Utilites

| | $a_1$ | $a_2$ |
|---|---|---|
| 1 | 10 | 5 |
| 2 | 1 | 15 |

We want to derive the optimal policy, using the dynamic programming algorithm, considering a two steps time horizon.

1. At the time 2 we compute $J_2$ as:
   - $J_2(1) = \max_a\{10, 5\} = 10$;
   - $J_2(2) = \max_a\{1, 15\} = 15$;
2. at time 1 we compute $J_1$ and $\mu_1$ as:
   - $J_1(1) = \max_a\{10 + 0.3 * 10 + 0.7 * 15, 5 + 0.8 * 10 + 0.2 * 15\} = 23.5$;
     $\mu_1(1) = a_1$;
   - $J_1(2) = \max_a\{1 + 0.4 * 10 + 0.6 * 15, 15 + 0.5 * 10 + 0.5 * 15\} = 27.5$;
     $\mu_1(2) = a_2$;
3. at time 0 we compute $J_0$ and $\mu_0$ as:
   - $J_0(1) = \max_a\{10 + 0.3 * 23.5 + 0.7 * 27.5, 5 + 0.8 * 23.5 + 0.2 * 27.5\} = 29.3$;
     $\mu_0(1) = a_1$;
   - $J_0(2) = \max_a\{1 + 0.4 * 23.5 + 0.6 * 27.5, 15 + 0.5 * 23.5 + 0.5 * 27.5\} = 40.5$;
     $\mu_0(2) = a_2$.

The optimal policy is hence:

| state | time 0 | time 1 |
|---|---|---|
| 1 | $a_1$ | $a_1$ |
| 2 | $a_2$ | $a_2$ |

## Value Iteration algorithm

The Value Iteration algorithm [21] is a recursive procedure that computes the optimal stationary policy for a MDP on an infinite time horizon. It is usually impossible to maximize the cumulative utility function over an infinite time horizon, because its expected value may be infinite. So, the Value Iteration algorithm maximizes the average utility per time unit referred to the long-run. It is important to note that an MDP controlled by a stationary policy with the rule $\mu : \Omega_x \to \Omega_u$ is equivalent to a Markov process with transition matrix $P_\mu$, where the $i$-th row is taken from $P^{(\mu(i))}$, that is the MDP transition matrix corresponding to action $\mu(i)$.

We can summarize this algorithm in the following way:

1. Let $k = 0$ and $V_0(i) = \max_a v(i, a)$ $\forall i$.
2. Let $k = k + 1$ and
$$V_k(i) = \max_a \left\{ v(i, a) + \sum_{j \in S} p_{ij}(a) \cdot V_{k-1}(j) \right\}$$
$$\mu_k(i) = \arg\max_a \left\{ v(i, a) + \sum_{j \in S} p_{ij}(a) \cdot V_{k-1}(j) \right\}$$
3. Compute:
$$m_k = \min_j \left\{ V_k(j) - V_{k-1}(j) \right\};$$
$$M_k = \max_j \left\{ V_k(j) - V_{k-1}(j) \right\}.$$
if $M_k - m_k \leq \epsilon \cdot m_k$ let $\mu^* = \mu_k$, otherwise go to step 2.

where $\epsilon$ is a pre-specified tolerance value, $V_k(i)$ is the optimal cumulative utility function earned on time $k$ when the current state is $i$, $m_k$ is the minimum utility value computed on time $k$, $M_k$ is the maximum utility value computed on time $k$, $\mu_k$ is the stationary policy used to compute the $k$-th step, $\mu^*$ is the optimal stationary policy.

The finite convergence of the algorithm is sure if a state $r$, which can be reached from any other state under policy $\mu$, exists for each stationary policy $\mu$ and the associated Markov process is aperiodic.

Referring to the simple example describe in the previous section, we can derive the optimal stationary policy by using Value Iteration through the following iteration scheme:

1. Choose the desired precision $\epsilon$.
2. k=0. Compute $V_0$:
   - $V_0(1) = \max_a\{10, 5\} = 10$;
   - $V_0(2) = \max_a\{1, 15\} = 15$;
3. k=1. Compute $V_1, \mu_1, m_1, M_1$:
   - $V_1(1) = \max_a\{10 + 0.3 * 10 + 0.7 * 15, 5 + 0.8 * 10 + 0.2 * 15\} = 23.5$;
   - $\mu_1(1) = a_1$;
   - $V_1(2) = \max_a\{1 + 0.4 * 10 + 0.6 * 15, 15 + 0.5 * 10 + 0.5 * 15\} = 27.5$;
   - $\mu_1(2) = a_2$;
   - $m_1 = \min\{23.5 - 10, 27.5 - 15\} = 12.5$;
   - $M_1 = \max\{23.5 - 10, 27.5 - 15\} = 13.5$;
   - $M_1 - m_1 = 1$;
   if $M_1 - m_1$ is less or equal to the chosen precision, take $\mu_1(1)$ and $\mu_1(2)$ as optimal stationary policy, otherwise continue the iteration.

# 7    Results on the GVHD Prophylaxis Problem

Exploiting the Influence View solution algorithms introduced in the previous section, it is possible to derive the optimal policy for the GVHD prophylaxis problem, calculated over 30 days after BMT.

In this case, it is not useful to find a stationary policy, as derived by the Value Iteration algorithm, because the interesting time horizon is limited to 30 days after BMT, and clearly in this period the patient's evolution cannot be modelled as a stationary random process. Moreover, the state variable death is a sink of the underlying Markov process; this means that the only stationary state (death) is not significant for the policy assessment. We have hence applied the Dynamic Programming algorithm for deriving a dynamic policy.

The Influence View formalism allows us to specialize the solution for different patient classes, by instantiating some event variables (context variables). In order to show a typical result of the proposed approach, let us consider the following specific patient class:

 - **age**: less than ten years old;
 - **Donor histo-compatibility**: high;
 - **BMT conditioning regimen**: chemotherapy;
 - **infection prophylaxis**: yes.

The results obtained may be expressed through a table (Tab. 3), in which depending on the patient state and the decision epoch, the optimal action is suggested. This table shows only the significant state variable values: for example, the *Death* state variable was set to *No*, and the *Acute-GVHD* state variable was equal to *No*.

The structure of the results table is the following one: in the first three columns the state variable values are reported, in order to identify the patient's state; in the remaining columns, the optimal therapies for the $1st, 2nd, \ldots, 15th$ decision stages are presented. Since in the GVHD problem the prophylaxis is revised every two days, the column labelled *"5"* reports the optimal policy for the ninth and tenth day, and so on.

It is worthwhile noticing that the optimal prophylaxis is dependent both on the patient's state and on time. For example, when the patient is in the state: *Hepatic Toxicity=Yes, Renal Toxicity=Yes, Serum Cs-A Concentration=Normal*, that corresponds to the second row of the table, the suggested prophylaxis is *CS-A=Low* and *Methotrexate=Yes* for the 5th and 6th decision stage, while it is *Cs-A=High* and *Methotrexate=No* for the 7th and 8th decision stages. Taking a look at the table, it is also possible to note that Methotrexate is suspended earlier when the levels of Cs-A concentration are high. This fact is clearly related to the need of preventing drugs toxicity: the system suggests a solution that copes with the trade-off of avoiding toxicity while preventing disease relapse. More generally, comparing the results coming from different classes of patients, the system suggest a more aggressive policy for the patients with a higher risk of developing GVHD.

| HepTx | RenTx | CSAConc | ... | 5 | 6 | 7 | 8 | ... |
|-------|-------|---------|-----|------|------|------|------|-----|
| Yes | Yes | Low | ... | L-Y | L-Y | L-Y | H-N | ... |
| Yes | Yes | Normal | ... | L-Y | L-Y | H-N | H-N | ... |
| Yes | Yes | High | ... | L-Y | H-N | H-N | H-N | ... |
| Yes | No | Low | ... | L-Y | L-Y | L-Y | H-N | ... |
| Yes | No | Normal | ... | L-Y | L-Y | H-N | H-N | ... |
| Yes | No | High | ... | L-Y | H-N | H-N | H-N | ... |
| No | Yes | Low | ... | L-Y | L-Y | L-Y | H-N | ... |
| No | Yes | Normal | ... | L-Y | L-Y | H-N | H-N | ... |
| No | Yes | High | ... | L-Y | H-N | H-N | H-N | ... |
| No | No | Low | ... | L-Y | L-Y | L-Y | H-N | ... |
| No | No | Normal | ... | L-Y | L-Y | H-N | H-N | ... |
| No | No | High | ... | L-Y | H-N | H-N | H-N | ... |

**Table 3.** The table containing the optimal policy for the GVHD prophylaxis. Four different actions are possible: H-Y: High Cs-A dose with Methotrexate, H-N: High Cs-A dose without Methotrexate, L-Y: Low Cs-A dose with Methotrexate, L-N: Low Cs-A dose without Methotrexate.

Other results are now still under study. Further efforts will involve a refinement of the conditional probability tables and of the utility model.

In order to derive the optimal prophylaxis, we used a software tool, called DT-Planner [2] [14], able to represent and solve the MDP described by IV framework.

# 8 Discussion and Related Works

MDPs have been recognized as a suitable framework for assessing optimal or sub-optimal policies in uncertain behaviour. Nevertheless, the complexity involved in the model assessment and solution often hampers their use in real applications. Recently, Decision Theoretic Planning efforts have been devoted to provide instruments for managing and solving more efficiently MDPs. The most influential work in this field has been carried on by Dean and collaborators [7, 6]; their approach proposes the utilization of graphical models for state structuring and hence for *partitioning* the state space. In this way it is possible to obtain convenient formulations and computationally efficient solutions for MDPs.

Other important contributions may be found in the works of Parr and Boutilier, that address the problem of managing Partially Observable Markov Decision Processes [15, 4]. In this setting , the state of the system is partially observable, and, hence, in a generic time instant it is described through the joint

---

[2] The tool has been developed at University of Pavia by Magni at al. in 1995. It is available for download free of charge via anonymous ftp from aimed11.unipv.it. Executable files are available both for Sun and HP workstation in /dist/DT-Planner/DT-Planner-sun.tar.gz and in /dist/DT-Planner/DT-Planner-hp.tar.gz respectively.

probability distribution of the state variables, also called *belief state*. The solution of the decision problem hence involves the maximization of a utility function that is dependent on the belief state.

A crucial problem of MDPs is related to the probabilistic specification of the model. To cope with this problem, several approaches have been presented to *learn* the probabilistic relationships between variables from the data [15, 9, 5, 1].

The necessity for a convenient and compact elicitation of the MDP underlying a dynamic decision problem is also addressed and discussed in [11, 4]. In particular, the work herein presented have been based on the Influence View formalism, whose first assessment and definition have been given in the PhD thesis of Tze-Yun Leong. In our work, we have investigated the capability of Influence View of representing a real medical problem, in which it is crucial to model the uncertainty of the patient's state evolution. In our problem, it was practically impossible to derive a deterministic model of the system dynamics, due to 1) the incompleteness of the knowledge available on the system, 2) the high inter- and intra- individual variability in the therapeutic response and 3) the measurement errors. Nevertheless, since the implications of the decision are of crucial importance for the patient's life, the need of an (in some sense) optimal solution, motivated us to look for a Decision-Theoretic Planning approach. The Influence View formalism gave us a suitable way for coping with this problem, allowing a manageable problem specification, and a computationally efficient solution.

The approach herein presented is now under evaluation. We are comparing the proposed methodology with other methods that relies on decision-theory based approaches, as Decision Trees or Influence Diagrams [18]; moreover we are testing the Influence View framework in different medical application areas, like the prophylaxis in patients affected by hereditary spherocytosis [13]. During this testing phase good results in increasing the clinicians acceptability of the Influence View method have been obtained. As a further step, we will design a clinical evaluation study of the GVHD Influence View.

## Acknowledgement

Mario Stefanelli and Silvana Quaglini are gratefully acknowledged for their methodological support and for revising an early draft of this paper. We are very grateful to Tze-Yun Leong, whose PhD thesis was the starting point of our work.

# References

1. R. Bellazzi and A. Riva. Learning conditional probabilities with longitudinal data. In *IJCAI'95 workshop working notes: Building probabilistic networks: Where do the numbers come from?*, pages 7–15, Montreal, Canada, 1995.
2. R. Bellman. *Dynamic Programming*. Princeton University Press, 1957.
3. D. Bertsekas. *Dynamic Programming*. Prentice Hall, Engelwood Cliffs, 1987.

4. C. Boutilier, R. Dearden, and M. Goldszmidt. Exploiting Structure in Policy Construction. In *Proceedings of IJCAI'95*, pages 1104–1112, Montreal, Canada, 1995.
5. W. L. Buntine. Operations for Learning with Graphical Models. *Journal of Artificial Intelligence Research*, 2:159–225, 1994.
6. T. Dean and S. H. Lin. Decomposition techniques for Planning in stochastic domains. In *Proceedings of IJCAI'95*, pages 1121–1128, Montreal, Canada, 1995.
7. T. Dean and M. Wellmann. *Planning and Control*. Morgan Kaufmann, San Mateo, CA, 1991.
8. R. Dechter. Bucket elimination: A unifying framework for probabilistic inference. In *Proceedings of UAI'96*, Portland, Oregon, USA, 1996.
9. D. Heckerman, D. Geiger, and D. M. Chickering. Learning Bayesian Networks: the combination of Knowledge and Statistical Data. Technical Report MSR-TR-94-09, Microsoft Research Advanced Technology Division Report, Microsoft Corporation, 1994.
10. R. Howard and J. Matheson. Influence Diagrams. In R. Howard and J. Matheson, editors, *The principles and applications of decision analysis*. Strategic decision group, Menlo Park, CA, 1984.
11. Tze-Yun Leong. *An integrated approach to Dynamic Decision Making under uncertainty*. PhD thesis, MIT, 1994.
12. M. Littman, T. Dean, and L. Kaebling. On the complexity of solving Markov Decision Processes. In *Proceedings of UAI'95*, pages 394–402, Montreal, Canada, 1995.
13. P. Magni. *Modelli decisionali Markoviani in medicina e pianificazione di terapie ottime: metodi e applicazioni*. PhD thesis, Università di Pavia, 1998. (in italian) to appear.
14. P. Magni and R. Bellazzi. DT-Planner: An environment for managing dynamic decision problems. *Computer Methods and Programs in Biomedicine*. (to appear).
15. R. Parr and Stuart Russel. Approximating optimal policies for Partially Observable Stochastic Domains. In *Proceedings of IJCAI'95*, pages 1088–1094, 1995.
16. J. Pearl. *Probabilistic Reasoning in Intelligent Systems*. Morgan Kauffman, Palo Alto, CA, 1988.
17. G. M. Provan. Tradeoffs in Knowledge-Based Construction of Probabilistic Models. *IEEE Trans. on System Man Cybernetics*, 24:1580–1592, 1994.
18. S. Quaglini, R. Bellazzi, F. Locatelli, M. Stefanelli, and C. Salveneschi. An influence diagram for assessing GVHD prophylaxis after bone marrow transplantation in children. *Medical Decision Making*, 14:223–235, 1994.
19. F. A. Sonnenberg and J. R. Beck. Markov Models in Medical Decision Making: A practical Guide. *Medical Decision Making*, 13:322–338, 1993.
20. J. Tatman and R. Shachter. Dynamic Programming and Influence Diagrams. *IEEE Trans. on System Man Cybernetic*, 20:365–379, 1990.
21. H. C. Tijms. *Stochastic Modelling and Analysis: A Computational Approach*. John Wiley & Sons, 1986.
22. R. L. Truitt, R. P. Gale, and M. M. Bortin. *Cellular Immunotherapy of Cancer*. Liss, New York, 1987.

# An Ordinal Approach to the Processing of Fuzzy Queries with Flexible Quantifiers

Patrick Bosc[1], Ludovic Liétard[1] and Henri Prade[2]

[1] IRISA/ENSSAT , Technopole Anticipa, BP 447,
22305 Lannion Cédex, France
e-mail: bosc||lietard@enssat.fr
[2] IRIT-CNRS, Université Paul Sabatier, 118 route de Narbonne,
31062 Toulouse Cédex, France
e-mail: prade@irit.fr

**Abstract.** This paper studies queries to a database, involving expressions of the form 'Q A-x's are B's' where A and B are properties which may be fuzzy and with respect to which objects x's are evaluated, and where Q is a quantifier which may stand for 'all', or may leave room for exceptions ('at least q%', '(at least) most', etc.). An example of such a query is 'Find the departments where *most young* employees are *well-paid*'. Such queries are discussed from a modeling and evaluation point of view, taking also into consideration what the user intends to ask when (s)he addresses this type of queries to a database system. Clarifying what has to be evaluated is specially important in the case where A is fuzzy, since then the boundaries of A are ill-defined and A may be somewhat empty.

## 1 Introduction

One reason for introducing fuzzy sets in query models [2][3] is the representation of the preferences of the user which thus can be expressed in a simple way. This is clearly the case in a query asking, for instance, for 'an apartment *not too expensive* and *not too far* from downtown'. A benefit of the fuzzy set modeling is then to provide a framework for rank-ordering the answers according to their compatibility with the fuzzy request. However, this is not always the motivation underlying the use of fuzzy terms in a query. If for instance, we ask for 'the average of the salaries of the *young* people' about whom information is stored in the database, the use of a fuzzy label such as 'young' is rather a matter of convenience, which avoids to refer to a precise and somewhat arbitrary age threshold. In order that the query makes sense, it is necessary that the result does not vary too much with the slightly different possible interpretations of the word 'young' (in the given context), and if there is some brittleness of the result with respect to the different interpretations, we expect that the system will inform us about this state of fact, or will take it into account in its evaluation. A range of possible values for the average salary, according to the different possible interpretations of 'young', should then be returned by the system; see [10] for the treatment of such queries.

Queries involving fuzzy quantifiers, such as 'Find the departments where most young employees are well-paid', or 'What are the days where almost all early trains are overcrowded?', seem also to be motivated by some robustness issue. Indeed 'most' (then understood as 'at least most') is often a way of expressing some implicit proviso for exceptions rather than a way of really specifying a proportion in a fuzzy way. It should be understood in a flexible way. Indeed, addressing queries involving the universal quantifier 'all' instead of 'most' to a database, such as asking for departments where *all* employees are well-paid, may very often lead to empty answers. As in the average salary example, the use of fuzzy categories like 'young' or 'well-paid' is also here a matter of convenience and implicitly presupposes that the result of the query does not vary too much with the possible interpretations of the words. In the following, a qualitative model is proposed for representing fuzzy expressions of the form 'Q A-x's are B's', and its use in the handling of queries is discussed.

Although this work could be related to different views of the cardinality of a fuzzy set and the modeling of fuzzily quantified statements [8, 12, 14, 16, 20], the evaluation of 'Q A-x's are B's' with respect to an ordinary database (data are supposed to be precise and certain) is not envisaged here as the result of the matching of a count of the A's which are B's against Q[1]. Thus, the evaluation we are interested in, is rather viewed here as the extent to which all A's are B's up to some exceptions. Indeed we are primarily interested in rank-ordering cases (in our above example, 'the departments') according to the extent to which they satisfy a requirement of the form 'Q A-x's are B's'. Moreover, the approach only assumes the use of a purely ordinal scale (e.g., a finite, totally ordered, chain of levels) for defining the fuzzy sets, even if numbers in [0,1] are used for convenience in the paper for encoding these levels.

Section 2 is devoted to a brief overview of basic notions related to fuzzy set theory involved in our evaluation problem. In Section 3, we assume that A is an ordinary subset of X, when evaluating expressions of the form 'Q A-x's are B's', before discussing the general case where A is a fuzzy set in Section 4. In each case, we first study the situation where Q is the universal quantifier ('for all'), before relaxing the evaluation with an exception-tolerant quantification.

In the following, $X = \{x_1, ..., x_n\}$ denotes a finite subset of objects, *a* and *b* are two attributes which apply to the elements of X, and A and B are two, fuzzy or not, subsets of the attribute domains of *a* and *b* respectively. For instance, X is a set of people, *a* stands for 'age' and *b* for 'salary', A for 'less than 30 years old', 'young', etc., and B for 'more than 10 k FF', 'well-paid', etc.

## 2 Background

This section recalls different concepts associated to fuzzy set theory which will be used later on. Some fuzzy set notions are restated in Subsection 2.1, whereas Subsection 2.2 is devoted to fuzzy implications and fuzzy inclusions. The modeling of fuzzy quantifiers such as 'most' is discussed in Subsection 2.3.

---

[1] Indeed we are not interested here in knowing to what extent it is true that, for instance, "there are approximately eighty per cent of the A's which are B's", but rather to find out under what acceptable weakening of "for all" into "most", it is completely true that "most A's are B's" (or at least, to know if such a weakening exists).

## 2.1 Fuzzy Sets

The concept of a fuzzy set, introduced by L.A. Zadeh [18], aims at extending the notion of a regular set in order to express classes with ill-defined boundaries (corresponding in particular to linguistic values, e.g., *tall, young, well-paid, important*, etc). This framework allows for a gradual transition between non-membership and full membership. A degree of membership is associated to every element, x and a fuzzy set F over the referential X (i.e., F is a fuzzy subset of X) is defined by means of a membership function: $\mu_F$ from X to [0,1]. For any x in X, $\mu_F(x)$ is the membership degree of x in F. It should be emphasized that the role of these degrees is first to rank-order the elements of the universe X, according to their compatibility with the fuzzy set F. Remember that we are using the interval [0,1] here as an ordinal scale only; thus the ordering of the degrees is more important than their exact values.

Let F be a fuzzy subset of X. The height of F is denoted by h(F) and is defined as the largest membership degree ($h(F) = \max_{x \in X} \mu_F(x)$). When h(F) = 1, F is said to be normalized. The $\alpha$-level cut of F is the ordinary subset defined by $\{x, \mu_F(x) \geq \alpha\}$ and is denoted by $F_\alpha$. The support of F is the ordinary subset defined by $\{x, \mu_F(x) > 0\}$. The core of F is the ordinary subset $\{x, \mu_F(x) = 1\}$ of elements which undisputedly belong to F.

**Example 1.** Let X be a set of individuals {Angela, John, Mick, Peter, Mary} and the fuzzy subset F of young people given by $\mu_F(Angela) = \mu_F(Peter) = 1$, $\mu_F(John) = 0.8$, $\mu_F(Mick) = 0.5$ and $\mu_F(Mary) = 0$. The intended meaning is that Peter and Angela are considered as young (completely) and form the core of the fuzzy set, while John is considered as rather young and Mick as somewhat young (whereas Mary is not at all young). F is normalized (h(F) = 1) and its support is the set {Angela, John, Mick, Peter}. The $\alpha$-level cut $F_{0.8}$ is the set {Angela, John, Peter} ◆

## 2.2 Fuzzy Implications and Inclusions

A fuzzy implication is an operator ($\rightarrow$) defined from [0,1] × [0,1] to [0,1] which must satisfy the characteristic properties [15]:

1) $(a \rightarrow 1) = 1$;

2) $(0 \rightarrow a) = 1$;

3) $(1 \rightarrow a) = a$;

4) if $b \geq c$, $(a \rightarrow b) \geq (a \rightarrow c)$ (increasing w.r.t. the second argument);

5) if $a \leq c$, $(a \rightarrow b) \geq (c \rightarrow b)$ (decreasing w.r.t. the first argument).

There are mainly two basic kinds of implication connectives: S-implications which are of the form 'not A or B' (or equivalently 'not (A and not B)'), and R-implications which are obtained by residuation, $a \rightarrow b = \sup\{t \in [0,1], a * t \leq b\}$

where $*$ is a conjunction operation. Since we restrict ourselves to ordinal scales in this paper, we should take $* = \min$, and then the S-implication is Dienes' implication $a \to b = \max(1 - a, b)$, while the R-implication is Gödel's implication $a \to b = 1$ if a $\leq b$ and $a \to b = b$ if $a > b$. Note that $1 - (.)$ denotes nothing more than the order-reversing function of the ordinal scale in case a non-numerical encoding would be used.

Given an implication connective $\to$, an inclusion index d between fuzzy sets [1] is naturally defined under the form:

$$d(A \subseteq B) = \min_x (\mu_A(x) \to \mu_B(x)).$$

For Dienes' implication the above index gives:

$$d(A \subseteq B) = \min_x \max(1 - \mu_A(x), \mu_B(x)),$$

and we have the characteristic property:

$$d(A \subseteq B) = 1 \Leftrightarrow \text{support}(A) \subseteq \text{core}(B).$$

While using Gödel's implication, the inclusion index is such that:

$$d(A \subseteq B) = 1 \Leftrightarrow \forall x, \mu_A(x) \leq \mu_B(x)$$

$$= \min_{x:\mu_A(x) > \mu_B(x)} \mu_B(x) \text{ otherwise.}$$

## 2.3 The Quantifier 'Most'

Fuzzy quantifiers have been proposed by Zadeh [20] for modeling linguistic expressions such as 'most', 'a few', 'almost all', etc. Such linguistic quantifiers express an intermediate attitude between the classical, universal and existential, quantifiers. A relative linguistic quantifier Q, referring to an ill-known proportion (e.g., 'most'), is represented by a membership function $\mu_Q$ from [0,1] to [0,1], such as $\mu_Q(i)$ is the level of satisfaction of the statement 'Q conditions are satisfied' when i is the proportion of satisfied conditions. Figure 1 gives an interpretation for 'most'. This interpretation is, however, clearly context-dependent.

**Example 2.** In the case of Figure 1, the fuzzy statement 'most conditions are satisfied' is completely false if the proportion of satisfied conditions is less than 75% ($\mu_{most}(i) = 0$ if $i \leq 0.75$). If the proportion equals 82.5%, the truth degree of the statement is 0.5 ($\mu_{most}(0.825) = 0.5$). When 90% (or more) of the conditions are satisfied, 'most conditions are satisfied' is completely true. In addition, if 'most' applies to a number m of conditions, it is possible to define 'most' directly on the number of satisfied conditions (i.e., on a subset $\{0, 1, 2,..., m\}$ of integers). In this last case, 'most' is represented by a function $\mu_Q$ defined by:

$$\forall\ i \in \{0, 1, 2, ..., m\},\ \mu_Q(i) = \mu_{most}\ (i/m).$$

For example, if m = 12, according to Figure 1, we get $\mu_Q(0) = \mu_Q(1) =... = \mu_Q(9) = 0$, $\mu_Q(10) = \mu_{most}(10/12) = 5/9$ and $\mu_Q(11) = \mu_Q(12) = 1$. The quantifier represented by $\mu_Q$ can be then interpreted as 'at least about 11' ♦

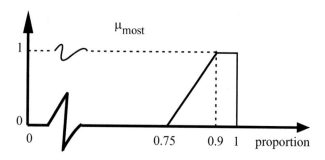

**Fig. 1.** A representation for the quantifier 'most'

In the following, we use a slightly different view for modeling 'most' in several examples. It is based on the idea of neglecting one or a few of the worst satisfied conditions (whereas the other conditions are fully taken into account). In that case, the quantifier is no longer genuinely gradual, and we are rather looking for the minimal relaxation of the requirement that 'all the conditions are satisfied' into 'all the conditions, except a few, are satisfied'.

## 3 Qualitative Modeling of 'Q A-x's are B's' with A Crisp

### 3.1 Case of the universal quantifier (Q = 'all')

Let us first assume that A and B are not fuzzy, and Q is the universal quantifier 'all'. The index E which estimates to what extent it is true that 'Q A-x's are B's' is given by:

$$E = \min_{x \in A} \mu_B(x) \text{ if } A \neq \emptyset \qquad (1)$$

$$= \begin{cases} 1 \text{ if } A \subseteq B \text{ and } A \neq \emptyset, \\ 0 \text{ otherwise.} \end{cases}$$

Note that (1) still makes sense when B becomes fuzzy, since E is then all the greater as all the objects in A have a high degree of membership in B. In particular, we have:

$$E = \max\{\beta \in (0,1] \text{ s.t. } A \neq \emptyset \text{ and } A \subseteq B_\beta\} \qquad (2)$$

$$= 0 \text{ if } A \not\subset \{x, \mu_B(x) > 0\} \text{ or } A = \emptyset,$$

where $B_\beta = \{x, \mu_B(x) \geq \beta\}$ denotes the β-level cut of the fuzzy set B.

**Example 3.** Let X be a set of employees described in Table 1, A (resp. B) be the predicate 'Age > 32' (resp. 'well-paid'). The evaluation of the query 'all employees over 32 are well-paid' yields:

$$E = \min_{e \in EMP \text{ s.t. } e.age > 32} \mu_{\text{well-paid}}(e)$$

$$= \min(1, 0.2) = 0.2 \blacklozenge$$

| EMP. | #emp | name | age | salary | $\mu_{\text{well-paid}}$ |
|------|------|------|-----|--------|--------------------------|
| | 189 | Smith | 56 | 60 | 1 |
| | 57 | Jones | 29 | 80 | 1 |
| | 876 | Kent | 43 | 38 | 0.2 |
| | 217 | Allen | 24 | 45 | 0.5 |

**Table 1**

E as a scalar evaluation may appear to be too crude. It is possible to refine the ordering introduced by E by using a leximin ordering [5]. Namely we can rank-order the elements of A according to non-decreasing values of $\mu_B$, i.e., $\mu_B(x_\tau(1)) \leq \ldots \leq \mu_B(x_\tau(m))$ where $\tau$ is a permutation and $|A| = m$. Then, if we have two evaluations E and E' such that E = E', corresponding in one of the above examples to two different departments for instance, the two departments can be ordered according to the leximin-ordering between the two corresponding vectors $(\mu_B(x_\tau(i)))_{i=1,m}$ and $(\mu_B(x'_\tau'(i)))_{i=1,m}$; i.e., E > E' if and only if $\exists k$, $\mu_B(x_\tau(t)) = \mu_B(x'_\tau'(t))$ for t = 1,k and $\mu_B(x_\tau(k+1)) > \mu_B(x'_\tau'(k+1))$ for k + 1 ≤ m. For instance, if E = min(0.2, 1, 1, 1), E' = min(0.2, 0.2, 0.2, 0.2), we will have E > E'. This type of refinement could be also extended to the evaluation of E in the more complex cases considered below. However, this would not be discussed further for the sake of brevity.

## 3.2 Relaxing 'all' into 'most' (Q = 'most')

The evaluation of 'all A-x's are B's', as expressed by (1) is the min-aggregation (which, indeed, considers the universal quantifier as a generalized conjunction) of the degrees of membership to B of all the x's in A. Going from 'all' to 'most', the idea is to relax the requirement into 'in most cases, the x's which are A's are B's', or equivalently 'there are only a few cases of A's which are not B's, or are 'bad' B's'. This can be done by weighting the min-aggregation and by giving little importance to these few cases.

The quantifier 'most' is then represented by a subset of the set of integers {0, 1, ..., m} where m is the cardinal of the set to which the quantifier refers (here A) rather than by a subset of proportions. More precisely, 'most' (understood as '(at least) most') has a non-decreasing membership function, i.e., $\mu_{\text{most}}(k) \leq \mu_{\text{most}}(k + 1)$ for k = 0, m − 1, and such that $\mu_{\text{most}}(m) = 1$. Q = 'all' is represented by $\mu_Q(k) = 0$, $\forall$ k ≤ m −

1 in this setting. In particular, 'at least k' will be represented by $\mu_Q(t) = 0$ if $t = 0, k - 1$ and $\mu_Q(t) = 1$ if $t = k, m$. Associated with 'most' is the (possibly fuzzy) subset I defined by $\mu_I(k) = 1 - \mu_{most}(k - 1)$ for $k = 1, m$ and $\mu_I(0) = 1$. Thus if most = {k, ..., m}, then $I = \{0, ..., k\}$. I represents the set of ranks of elements to be considered as important in the evaluation as we shall see in the following.

In this section, we consider the case where A is not fuzzy and $A \neq \varnothing$ (if $A = \varnothing$, E = 0). Let $A = \{x_1, ..., x_m\}$, $m \leq n = |X|$. Assume that the elements of A are reordered according to the decreasing values of $\mu_B$, i.e., $\mu_B(x_\sigma(1)) \geq \mu_B(x_\sigma(2)) \geq ... \geq \mu_B(x_\sigma(m))$ where $\sigma$ is a permutation of $\{1, ..., m\}$. Then the estimation E is expressed by:

$$E = \min_{i=1,m} \max(\mu_B(x_\sigma(i)), 1 - \mu_I(i)). \tag{3}$$

(3) can be rewritten in order to let A explicitly appear. Namely:

$$E = \min_{j=1,n} \max(\mu_B(x_{\sigma'}(j)), 1 - \mu_A(x_{\sigma'}(j)), 1 - \mu_I(j)) \tag{4}$$

where $\sigma'(j) = \sigma(j)$ for $1 \leq j \leq m$ and $\sigma' = $ identity for $\{m + 1, ..., n\}$, since $\mu_A(x_{\sigma'}(j)) = 0$, for $j = m + 1, n$ ($\mu_I(j) = 0$ for $j = m + 1, n$ for the sake of coherence). It can be easily checked that (1) is a particular case of (3)-(4), letting $I = \{0, 1, ..., m\}$, and E defined by (3) is always greater or equal to E given by (1). (4) expresses the extent to which the k objects of A which are the more important with respect to their membership in B are indeed elements of B with high membership. (3)-(4) is an example of an 'ordered weighted minimum' aggregation, and has been recently proposed in the context of the division of fuzzy relations [11].

As it can be seen, E has a high value as soon as the elements $x_\sigma(i) \in A$ which have low membership grades in B are neglected, i.e., are such that $\mu_I(i)$ is close to 0. In the particular case where $|A| = m = 1$, we get $E = 0$ if $\mu_B(x_\sigma(1)) = 0$ since in this case $\mu_I(1) = 1 - \mu_{most}(0) = 1$ with $\mu_{most}(0) = 0$ (if we want to keep at least one non-neglected element in A!). When $A = X$, (3)-(4) yields the degree of membership in B of the $k^{th}$ best element in X according to $\mu_B$. In practice, quantifiers of the form 'at least k' may be sufficient for our purpose, although (3)-(4) still make sense if 'most' and thus I becomes fuzzy (with monotonic, non-decreasing and non-increasing membership functions respectively, as already said).

**Example 4.** Let us consider 'most A-X's are B's' applying to the set $X = \{x_1, x_2, x_3, x_4, x_5\}$ and $A = \{x_1, x_2, x_3, x_4\}$. The degrees of membership to A and B are given in Table 2. The quantifier 'most' is defined on $\{0, 1, 2, 3, 4\}$, since $m = 4$, by:

$$\mu_{most}(0) = 0, \mu_{most}(1) = 0, \mu_{most}(2) = 0.1, \mu_{most}(3) = 0.8, \mu_{most}(4) = 1.$$

Then, $\mu_I(0) = 1, \mu_I(1) = 1, \mu_I(2) = 1, \mu_I(3) = 0.9, \mu_I(4) = 0.2$. According to formula (3):

$$E = \min(\max(\mu_B(x_1), 1 - \mu_I(1)), \max(\mu_B(x2), 1 - \mu_I(2)),$$
$$\max(\mu_B(x_3), 1 - \mu_I(3)), \max(\mu_B(x_4), 1 - \mu_I(4))).$$

We finally get:

$$E = \min(\max(1, 0), \max(0.8, 0), \max(0.6, 0.1), \max(0.2, 0.8)) = 0.6.$$

This result is not surprising since $x_4$, the worst B-element of A, (which would have given E = 0.2 for Q = 'all') is somewhat neglected since this last element is not completely important. Note that making $\mu_{most}(2) = 0$ and $\mu_{most}(3) = 1$, i.e., making Q = 'at least 3' would not change the result of the evaluation ♦

| X | A | B |
|---|---|---|
| $x_1$ | 1 | 1 |
| $x_2$ | 1 | 0.8 |
| $x_3$ | 1 | 0.6 |
| $x_4$ | 1 | 0.2 |
| $x_5$ | 0 | 0.7 |

**Table 2**

However, as already said, (3)-(4) evaluates the extent to which 'in most cases, the x's which are A's are also B's', and *not* to what extent 'most x's are A's and B's'. Indeed in Example 4, 'all x which are A's (except one) are B's' yields E = 0.6, while 'all x (except one) are A's and B's' would yield an evaluation equal to 0.2 (neglecting $x_5$).

# 4 Qualitative Modeling of 'Q A-x's are B's' with A Fuzzy

## 4.1 Case of the universal quantifier (Q = 'all')

### 4.1.1 A is a normalized fuzzy set

Let us now consider the general situation where A is also a fuzzy set. We again start with the case Q = 'all', before relaxing it. Then it seems natural to require that E is all the greater as, whatever the crisp interpretations of A and B in terms of level-cuts $A_\alpha$ and $B_\beta$, the condition $A_\alpha \subseteq B_\beta$ holds. We first consider the case where A is normalized, i.e., $\forall \alpha$, $A_\alpha \neq \emptyset$. This leads to state that:

$$E = \begin{cases} 0 \text{ if } \{x, \mu_A(x) = 1\} \not\subset \{x, \mu_B(x) > 0\} \\ \max\{\min(1 - \alpha, \beta), (\alpha, \beta) \in (0, 1)^2 \text{ s.t. } A_\alpha \subseteq B_\beta\} \\ 1 \text{ if } \{x, \mu_A(x) > 0\} \subseteq \{x, \mu_B(x) = 1\}. \end{cases} \qquad (5)$$

Indeed, since the $\lambda$-cut $F_\lambda$ of a fuzzy set F is all the larger as $\lambda$ is small, the statement 'all A-x's are B's' is all the more true as $A_\alpha \subseteq B_\beta$ holds for small $\alpha$ and large $\beta$, i.e., $A_\alpha$ is large and $B_\beta$ is small. Indeed when the support of A, $\{x, \mu_A(x) > 0\}$, is included in the core of B, $\{x, \mu_B(x) = 1\}$, we are completely certain that whatever the non fuzzy interpretations of A and B, we have $A_\alpha \subseteq$ support(A) $\subseteq$ core(B) $\subseteq B_\beta$, i.e., $A_\alpha \subseteq B_\beta$ holds for all $\alpha$ and $\beta$. In [13], it has been established that E is nothing but the necessity[2] of the fuzzy event B based on the possibility distribution $\mu_A$, i.e., we have the equality:

$$E = \min_{x \in X} \max(\mu_B(x), 1 - \mu_A(x)). \tag{6}$$

When A is non-fuzzy we recover (1). (6) can be also understood as a min-aggregation weighted in terms of levels of importance [9]. Namely, it is all the more important to take into account x in the evaluation as $\mu_A(x)$ is large, i.e., as x is indeed a typical element of A. In particular, if $\mu_A(x) = 0$, E does not depend on $\mu_B(x)$; if $\mu_A(x) = 1$, we should have $E \leq \mu_B(x)$, while if $0 < \mu_A(x) < 1$, E cannot be made equal to 0 just because we would have $\mu_B(x) = 0$ (in that case E will be just upper bounded by $1 - \mu_A(x)$ which reflects how much x is unimportant).

Note also that if $E = \theta > 0$, $\forall x \in \{x, \mu_A(x) > 1 - \theta\}$ then $\mu_B(x) \geq \theta$, i.e., $A_{\overline{1-\theta}} \subseteq B_\theta$, where $A_{\overline{\alpha}}$ denotes the strict $\alpha$-cut of the fuzzy set A ($A_{\overline{\alpha}} = \{x, \mu_A(x) > \alpha\}$). Moreover, if $E = \theta > 0$, $\exists x \in X$, ($\mu_B(x) = \theta$ and $\mu_A(x) > 1 - \theta$) or ($\mu_B(x) \leq \theta$ and $\mu_A(x) = 1 - \theta$). In particular, $E = 0$ if and only if $\exists x \in X$ such that $\mu_A(x) = 1$ and $\mu_B(x) = 0$, i.e., if and only if there is an unchallenged element of A which does not belong to B at all, which is satisfying.

Generally speaking, E can be viewed as an inclusion index [1] of the form:

$$E = \min_{x \in X} \mu_A(x) \rightarrow \mu_B(x) \tag{7}$$

where $a \rightarrow b = \max(1 - a, b)$ is known as Dienes implication in the fuzzy set literature, as recalled in Section 2.2. One may then wonder about the usefulness of other implications and their meaning in terms of conditions over $\alpha$-cuts. If Rescher-Gaines implication is chosen ($a \rightarrow b = 1$ if $a \leq b$, $a \rightarrow b = 0$ otherwise), $E = 1$ iff $\mu_B(x) \geq \mu_A(x)$ for all x, which means that for any $\alpha$, $A_\alpha \subseteq B_\alpha$. Thus, (7) with Rescher-Gaines implication estimates to what extent 'all x in X are at least as much B as they are A'; in particular if $\mu_A(x) = 0$, x has no influence on the evaluation.

Let us now consider Gödel implication: $a \rightarrow b = 1$ if $a \leq b$, $a \rightarrow b = b$ if $a > b$. In the context of (7), this implication leads to look for the smallest $\mu_B(x)$ such that $\mu_B(x) < \mu_A(x)$. Then it can be checked that

$$E = \min\{\alpha \in [0,1), A_{\overline{\alpha}} \not\subset B_{\overline{\alpha}} \text{ and } A_{\overline{\alpha}} \neq B_{\overline{\alpha}}\} \tag{8}$$

$$= 1 \text{ if } \forall \alpha, A_{\overline{\alpha}} \subseteq B_{\overline{\alpha}}.$$

---

[2] Given a possibility distribution $\pi$ from X to [0,1] such that $\pi$ is normalized ($\exists x, \pi(x) = 1$), the necessity of a fuzzy event B is defined by [6], $N(B) = \min_{x \in X} \max(\mu_B(x), 1 - \pi(x))$ which is dually associated with a possibility measure [19], $\Pi(B) = 1 - N(\overline{B}) = \max_{x \in X} \min(\mu_B(x), \pi(x))$. Note that $\Pi(B \cup C) = \max(\Pi(B), \Pi(C))$, while $N(B \cap C) = \min(N(B), N(C))$.

67

**Proof.** $\{\alpha \in [0,1),\ A_{\bar\alpha} \not\subset B_{\bar\alpha}$ and $A_{\bar\alpha} \neq B_{\bar\alpha}\} = \{\alpha \in [0,1),\ A_{\bar\alpha} \cap \overline{B_{\bar\alpha}} \neq \emptyset\} = \{\alpha \in [0,1),\ \exists x,\ \mu_A(x) > \alpha$ and $\mu_B(x) \leq \alpha\}$. Thus $E = \min_X \{\mu_B(x) \mid \mu_B(x) < \mu_A(x)\}$ and $E = 1$ if there is no x such that $\mu_B(x) < \mu_A(x)$ ♦

Thus E defined with Gödel implication refines the use of Rescher-Gaines implication, since in both cases $E = 1$ iff $\forall \alpha$, $A_\alpha \subseteq B_\alpha$, and E takes values intermediary between 0 and 1 if Gödel implication is used. These two implications express some simple conditions about the $\alpha$-cuts of A and B. This is particularly interesting, noticing that the inclusion of the $\alpha$-cuts of two fuzzy sets A and B is not monotonic with respect to $\alpha$. Indeed, we may have $A_{\alpha_1} \subseteq B_{\alpha_1}$, $A_{\alpha_2} \not\subset B_{\alpha_2}$ and $A_{\alpha_3} \subseteq B_{\alpha_3}$ with $\alpha_1 \geq \alpha_2 \geq \alpha_3$, as shown by the example $A = \{1/x_1, 0.9/x_2, 0.5/x_3\}$, $B = \{0.8/x_1, 0.6/x_2, 0.2/x_3\}$ where $A_1 \not\subset B_1$, $A_{0.6} \subseteq B_{0.6}$, $A_{0.5} \not\subset B_{0.5}$, but $A_{0.2} \subseteq B_{0.2}$. In this example $E = 0.2$ for Gödel implication since $A_{\overline{0.2}} \not\subset B_{\overline{0.2}}$ and $A_{\overline{0.2}} \neq B_{\overline{0.2}}$.

### 4.1.2 A is an unnormalized fuzzy set

Let us now consider the case where A is not normalized ($h(A) < 1$, where $h(A) = \max_{x \in X} \mu_A(x)$ denotes the height of the fuzzy set A). If we continue to use (6) in such a case, it can be easily checked that we would have $E \geq 1 - h(A)$. In particular if $A = \emptyset$, we get $E = 1$, which is not satisfying, since E should also reflect to what extent it makes sense to speak of the elements of A. Then E can be defined as:

$$E = \min(h(A), \min_{x \in X} \max(\mu_B(x), 1 - \mu_A*(x))) \qquad (9)$$

where $\mu_A*(x) = 1$ if $\mu_A(x) = h(A)$ and $\mu_A*(x) = \mu_A(x)$ otherwise. Note that we recover (6) when $h(A) = 1$. E is a graded version of the condition, $A \neq \emptyset$ and $A \subseteq B$, in the non-fuzzy case. A is renormalized in A* in (9) in order to have a meaningful degree of inclusion in (9). Indeed, if we keep A instead of A*, we would have $E \geq \min(h(A), 1 - h(A))$ which is a lower bound which does not depend on B, which is not satisfying. The method proposed for normalizing A is in agreement with the idea of a finite scale where the quotient $\mu_A(x) / h(A)$ does not make sense. Moreover, it leaves a maximum number of membership grades untouched. The renormalization involved in expression (9) is illustrated hereafter.

| X1 | A | B |
|----|-----|-----|
| $x_1$ | 0.7 | 0.6 |
| $x_2$ | 0.8 | 0.5 |
| $x_3$ | 0.6 | 0 |

**Table 3a**

| X2 | A | B |
|----|-----|-----|
| $x_1$ | 0.2 | 0.8 |
| $x_2$ | 0.5 | 0 |
| $x_3$ | 0.3 | 0.2 |

**Table 3b**

**Example 5**. Let us consider two sets X1 and X2 as described in Tables 3a and 3b. The evaluation of the query 'all A-x's are B's' yields:

$$E(X1) = \min(0.8, \max(0.6,0.3), \max(0.5,0), \max(0,0.4)) = 0.4$$

$$E(X2) = \min(0.5, \max(0.8,0.8), \max(0,0), \max(0.2,0.7)) = 0.$$

All the elements of X1 with the higher degrees of membership in A have a non-zero degree of membership in B and E is thus non-zero. On the contrary, the element $x_2$ of X2 with the highest degree $\mu_A(x_2) = h(A)$ is such that $\mu_B(x_2) = 0$, and E = 0, which is natural since $x_2$ is considered to be in A as soon as we sufficiently relax our idea of A (into $A_\alpha$ with $\alpha \leq 0.5$) in order to have A $\neq$ Ø (and $x_2$ is anyway the best representative of A in X2)♦

## 4.2 Relaxing 'all' into 'most' (Q = 'most')

More generally, we want to evaluate statements of the form Q A-x's are B's where 'all' is relaxed into a quantifier allowing for some exceptions. Three different types of evaluations can be distinguished (this is already the case when A is non-fuzzy). The first case corresponds to a relaxation of 'all A-x's are B's' into 'in most cases, if x is an A it is a B also'. Such an evaluation is clearly different of the statement 'in most cases, the x's are A's and B's', which correspond to a second type. Indeed, in the first case there is no restriction on the x's which are not A, while there are at most a few x's of this kind in the second case. In these two evaluations, the referential remains X. This was not the case in the evaluation (3), proposed in Section 3, where we were focusing on A only, ignoring what was happening in X – A. When A becomes fuzzy, this third type of evaluation becomes more tricky, since there are several crisp representatives of A depending on the $\alpha$-level cuts we consider thus leading to different evaluations in general. We now briefly discuss the three evaluations, starting with the two first ones, which were not developed for A crisp (although they apply as well to this case), in order to differentiate them from the third type of evaluation.

### 4.2.1 Interpretation 1: 'For most x's, those which are A's are B's'

The idea is then to give no importance to the worst counterexamples to the statement A's are B's, i.e., the x's which maximize $\min(\mu_A(x), 1 - \mu_B(x))$. Thus, we rank-order the x's in X according to the decreasing values of $1 - \min(\mu_A(x), 1 - \mu_B(x)) = \max(\mu_B(x), 1 - \mu_A(x))$ and we give no importance to the last $n - k$ x's (if Q = 'at least k' with $n - k$ much smaller than n in practice). The evaluation E is obtained by applying a formula close to (3) where $\mu_B(x_{\sigma(i)})$ is changed into $\mu_{\overline{A} \cup B}(x_{\sigma(i)})$, and m is changed into n which refers to the cardinality of X:

$$E = \min_{i=1,n} \max(\mu_B(x_{\sigma(i)}), 1 - \mu_A(x_{\sigma(i)}), 1 - \mu_I(i)) \tag{10}$$

where the values $\mu_{\overline{A}\cup B}(x_\sigma(i))$ are such that: $\mu_{\overline{A}\cup B}(x_\sigma(1)) \geq ... \geq \mu_{\overline{A}\cup B}(x_\sigma(n))$ and I is the set of ranks of elements somewhat important ($\mu_I(k) = 1 - \mu_Q(k-1)$ and $\mu_I(0) = 1$). Note that the x's outside the support of A have no direct influence in the evaluation (since they contribute a term equal to 1 in the min-aggregation). However, it is the whole cardinality of X which is taken into account in case I refers to a relative quantifier expressing a proportion.

**Example 6.** Let us consider the case described in Table 4. If the worst case $x_{10}$ is completely neglected (i.e., $\mu_I(10) = 0$ and $\mu_I(9) = ... = \mu_I(1) = 1$) we get E = 0.4. In the same spirit, if the worst two elements $x_9$ and $x_{10}$ are completely neglected (i.e., $\mu_I(10) = \mu_I(9) = 0$ and $\mu_I(8) = ... = \mu_I(1) = 1$) we get E = 0.5. Clearly, the greater the number of neglected elements, the greater the evaluation. Note that E may remain high although there are only a few x's which are A's◆

| X | A | B | $\max(\mu_B, 1-\mu_A)$ |
|---|---|---|---|
| $x_1$ | 0 | 1 | 1 |
| $x_2$ | 0 | 0.9 | 1 |
| $x_3$ | 0.9 | 1 | 1 |
| $x_4$ | 0.8 | 0.9 | 0.9 |
| $x_5$ | 0.9 | 0.8 | 0.8 |
| $x_6$ | 0.3 | 0.2 | 0.7 |
| $x_7$ | 1 | 0.5 | 0.5 |
| $x_8$ | 0.5 | 0.5 | 0.5 |
| $x_9$ | 1 | 0.4 | 0.4 |
| $x_{10}$ | 0.8 | 0.1 | 0.2 |

**Table 4**

### 4.2.2 Interpretation 2: 'Most x's are A's and B's'

In this case, we rank-order the x's according to the decreasing values of $\min(\mu_A(x), \mu_B(x))$. In other words, if Q means 'at least k', we are looking for a subset C of X such that:

$$|C| = k, C \subseteq A_\alpha, C \subseteq B_\beta \text{ with } \alpha \text{ and } \beta \text{ as large as possible,}$$

since:

$$C \subseteq A_\alpha \cap B_\beta \Leftrightarrow C \subseteq (A \cap B)_{\min(\alpha,\beta)}.$$

This leads to rank-order the k best elements of X according to their decreasing values of $\mu_{A\cap B}$ and to assign, via $\mu_I$, a degree of importance equal to 1 to the k best rated elements, the others having a level of importance equal to 0. Then E is given again by a formula close to (3) where $\mu_B(x_{\sigma(i)})$ becomes $\mu_{A \cap B}(x_{\sigma(i)})$ and n is the cardinality of X:

$$E = \min_{i=1,n} \max(\mu_{A \cap B}(x_{\sigma(i)}), 1 - \mu_I(i)) \qquad (11)$$

where the values $\mu_{A \cap B}(x_{\sigma(i)})$ are such that: $\mu_{A \cap B}(x_{\sigma(1)}) \geq ... \geq \mu_{A \cap B}(x_{\sigma(n)})$ and I is the set of ranks of elements somewhat important ($\mu_I(k) = 1 - \mu_Q(k-1)$ for $k > 0$ and $\mu_I(0) = 1$).

**Example** 7. Let us consider the condition 'At least about 4 x's are A's and B's' where the (fuzzy) quantifier is defined by $\mu_Q(0) = 0$, $\mu_Q(1) = 0$, $\mu_Q(2) = 0.2$, $\mu_Q(3) = .5$, $\mu_Q(4) = 1$, $\mu_Q(5) = 1$, $\mu_Q(6) = 1$ and the set X is given in Table 5.

Then $\mu_I(0) = 1$, $\mu_I(1) = 1$, $\mu_I(2) = 1$, $\mu_I(3) = 0.8$, $\mu_I(4) = 0.5$, $\mu_I(5) = 0 = \mu_I(6)$.

$E = \min(\max(\mu_{A \cap B}(x_4)), 1 - \mu_I(1)), \max(\mu_{A \cap B}(x_1)), 1 - \mu_I(2)),$
$\quad\quad \max(\mu_{A \cap B}(x_3)), 1 - \mu_I(3)), \max(\mu_{A \cap B}(x_2)), 1 - \mu_I(4)))$

$= \min(\max(0.9, 0), \max(0.8, 0), \max(0.5, 0.2), \max(0.2, 0.5))$

$= 0.5 \blacklozenge$

| X | A | B |
|---|---|---|
| $x_1$ | 1 | 0.8 |
| $x_2$ | 1 | 0.2 |
| $x_3$ | 0.5 | 0.5 |
| $x_4$ | 0.9 | 1 |
| $x_5$ | 0 | .9 |
| $x_6$ | 0.5 | 0 |

Table 5

Note that this view is in accordance with the usual result *when A is not fuzzy* stating that checking if 'at least k elements of A are B's' is equivalent to estimating if 'at least k elements of X are (A and B)'s'.

### 4.2.3 Interpretation 3: 'Most A's are B's' where A is fuzzy

As already said, in such an evaluation we restrict ourselves to the x's which are somewhat A. Clearly, depending on the $\alpha$-level cut $A_\alpha$ we consider, we would get different evaluations $E(A_\alpha)$ by applying (3). Note that $E(A_\alpha)$ does not vary in a monotonic way with $\alpha$ in general. This should not be surprising. Indeed, it is well-known that the proportion of A's which are B's varies in a nonmonotonic way when A is replaced either by a superclass, or a subclass of A. Then the information provided by the different $E(A_\alpha)$'s can be summarized in different ways.

A first approach is to propose the following evaluation:

$$E(A) = \max_\alpha \min(\alpha, E(A_\alpha)) \tag{12}$$

which corresponds to a weighted disjunction of the possible results. This is clearly an optimistic evaluation. Since we may have $E = 1$ because $E(A_1) = 1$ while for instance $E(A_{0.9}) = 0$!

**Example 8.** Let us consider the query 'most A-x's are B's' where the (fuzzy) quantifier 'most' means that *the* worst B element in A is neglected. The set X is given in Table 6. The different $\alpha$-level cuts are: $A_1 = \{x_1\}$ and $A_{0.9} = \{x_1, x_2, x_3\}$. We have for $A_1$: $\mu_I(1) = 1$ (because this set has only one element) and thus: $E(A_1) = \max (1 - \mu_I(1), \mu_B(x_1)) = 1$. Consequently the result given by (12) is $E = 1$ (because $E(A_\alpha) = 1$ for $\alpha = 1$). This result is obviously optimistic because, as it can be seen in Table 7, we would have to neglect the worst *two* elements in $A_{0.9}$ in order to keep this evaluation E ♦

| X | A | B |
|---|---|---|
| $x_1$ | 1 | 1 |
| $x_2$ | 0.9 | 0.1 |
| $x_3$ | 0.9 | 0.1 |

**Table 6**

Consequently, another natural evaluation which may be considered is:

$$E(A) = \min_\alpha E(A_\alpha) \tag{13}$$

which guarantees that, for any $\alpha$, $E(A_\alpha)$ is larger than or equal to E. This result corresponds to a conjunction of the possible results and is clearly a pessimistic evaluation (since we may have $E = 0$ because $E(A_{0.1}) = 0$ while for instance $E(A_\alpha) = 1$ for any $\alpha \neq 0.1$!

Expression (13) is a conjunction which can be weighted in order to modulate its pessimistic behavior:

$$E(A) = \min_\alpha \max (1 - \mu_I(\alpha), E(A_\alpha)) \tag{14}$$

where $\mu_I(\alpha)$ is the importance of the $\alpha$-level cut $A_\alpha$. The idea underlying (14) is that the $\alpha$-level cuts with large $\alpha$ are the most important ones, while $\alpha$-level cuts with low $\alpha$ can be neglected (since they involve elements which are not strongly in A). In the particular case where $\forall \alpha \geq \alpha'$, $\mu_I(\alpha) = 1$ and $\mu_I(\alpha) = 0$ otherwise, we obtain:

$$E(A) = \min_{\alpha \geq \alpha'} E(A_\alpha) \tag{15}$$

where α' can be viewed as a membership threshold for A-elements. It means that if $\mu_A(x) < \alpha'$ then x does not sufficiently belong to A and thus can be neglected.

In the special case where $\mu_1(\alpha) = \alpha$ in (14), which expresses that 'the higher α, the more important $A_\alpha$ and $E(A_\alpha)$', we get:

$$E(A) = \min_\alpha \max (1 - \alpha, E(A_\alpha)) \tag{16}$$

The expressions (12) and (16) can be viewed respectively as the possibility and the necessity (see note 2), of a fuzzy event corresponding to the $E(A_\alpha)$'s based on the possibility distribution $\pi(\alpha) = \alpha$ for $\alpha \in [0, 1]$ (α being the possibility that $A_\alpha$ represents the fuzzy set A; if $A_\alpha = \varnothing$ then $E(A_\alpha) = 0$). The estimates (12) and (16) can be viewed as scalar summaries of the fuzzy-valued estimate E* where $\mu_{E^*}(E_\alpha) = \alpha$; see Dubois and Prade [7]. In the particular case where Q is 'for all' (then $E(A_\alpha)$ is the minimum of $\mu_B(x)$ for x belonging to $A_\alpha$) it has been pointed out [4] that (6) and (16) lead to the same result. (It can be seen as a consequence of (5), by introducing the degree of inclusion of $A_\alpha$ into the fuzzy set B defined by (1)-(2), in the expression (5).)

**Example 9.** Let us consider the query 'most A-x's are B's' where the (fuzzy) quantifier 'most' means that *the* worst B element in A can be neglected. The set X is given in Table 7. The different α-level cuts are: $A_1 = \{x_1\}$, $A_{0.9} = \{x_1, x_2\}$, $A_{0.5} = \{x_1, x_2, x_3, x_4\}$, $A_{0.4} = \{x_1, x_2, x_3, x_4, x_5, x_6\}$. We have for $A_1$ $\mu_1(1) = 1$ (because this set has only one element) and thus (3) gives: $E(A_1) = \max (1-\mu_1(1), \mu_B(x_1)) = 1$. Considering $A_{0.9}$ we have $\mu_1(1) = 1$ and $\mu_1(2) = 0$ thus $E(A_{0.9}) = 1$ (the same result would be obtained even without neglecting $x_2$). Considering $A_{0.5}$ we have $\mu_1(1) = \mu_1(2) = \mu_1(3) = 1$ and $\mu_1(4) = 0$ and thus $E(A_{0.5}) = 0.8$ (neglecting $x_4$). Considering $A_{0.4}$ we have $\mu_1(1) = \mu_1(2) = \mu_1(3) = \mu_1(4) = \mu_1(5) = 1$ and $\mu_1(6) = 0$ thus $E(A_{0.4}) = 0$ (since we are neglecting at most one element). If definition (13) is chosen for E we have:

$$E(A) = \min_\alpha E(A_\alpha) = 0,$$

which is a pessimistic evaluation (since this result is induced by a poor member of A (0.4)). If definition (15) is taken for E, we face the problem of choosing α'. In this example, let α' be 0.5, we get:

$$E(A) = \min_{\alpha \geq 0.5} E(A_\alpha) = 0.8.$$

However, one may argue that α' is a precise boundary that cannot be always clearly justified. Furthermore, if we choose α' = 0.4 in this example we get E(A) = 0 which shows that two different but close thresholds (0.5 and 0.4) could lead to two extremely different results (0.8 and 0). Is 0.4 or 0.5 more appropriate to give a significant result? That is why the evaluation given by expression (16) may be preferred:

$$E(A) = \min_\alpha \max (1 - \alpha, E(A_\alpha)) = 0.6.$$

In this last case, each value $E(A_\alpha)$ is weighted by the importance $\alpha$ of the considered $\alpha$-level cut and the contribution of each $A_\alpha$ to the overall result is more significant when $A_\alpha$ only gathers elements which are strong members of A ♦

| X | A | B |
|---|---|---|
| $x_1$ | 1 | 1 |
| $x_2$ | 0.9 | 1 |
| $x_3$ | 0.5 | 0.8 |
| $x_4$ | 0.5 | 0.2 |
| $x_5$ | 0.4 | 0 |
| $x_6$ | 0.4 | 0 |

**Table 7**

## 5 Conclusion

This paper has mainly intended to provide a preliminary discussion of the qualitative handling of evaluations of the form 'Q A-x's are B's'. In practice, considering a query like 'Find the departments where most young people are well-paid', we would first rank-order the departments according to the extent to which *all* young people are well-paid'. If no (or too few) departments are retrieved with a positive evaluation, we would restart the evaluation process changing 'all' into 'all except one', and then relaxing the requirement still more, if necessary. It is also clear that when h(A) is less than 1, i.e., A is somewhat empty, this fact should be notified to the user.

Besides, we have insisted on the qualitative nature of the evaluation to provide, since it is not always clear in practice that the membership grades can receive a genuine interpretation in terms of a real number. It is then important to keep the evaluation and the ranking process as robust as possible. However, it would be interesting to clarify the differences between the approach proposed here and an OWA operation-based aggregation of the elementary evaluations for each item x [17], since OWA aggregation can be also nicely interpreted in terms of quantifiers. The expressions used in this paper are Ordered Weighted Minimums [11], rather than Ordered Weighted Averages (OWA's) which cannot be defined on purely ordinal scales as the Ordered Weighted Minimums. More generally, it would be useful to undertake some practical experiments in order to assess the approach and its situation with respect to those based on cardinalities (e.g., [17, 20]).

It could also be of interest to see the problem of the evaluation of expressions of the form 'Q-A's x are B's' as the detection of the (in)stability of the evaluations corresponding to various crisp approximations of A or B in terms of $\alpha$-cuts. For instance, we may look for what (high) values of $\alpha$ the evaluation of 'Q $A_\alpha$ elements are B's' remains constant (once the interpretation of Q is chosen). This can be related to data summarization issues since the $\alpha$-level cuts with high $\alpha$ may be viewed as different levels of approximation regarding the evaluation of the condition 'Q A-x's are B'. Going back to our example, once a department has been identified as satisfying the condition 'most young people are well-paid' to some extent (for some interpretation of 'most' of the type 'all except a few'), it might be interesting to find out if, for instance, the condition is more, or is less, satisfied if we neglect the people who are not really young. With such queries, it is also important to make clear that the evaluation may be quite different for apparently rather similar expressions, for example, if we look for 'the departments where all people are rather well-paid', or for 'the departments where almost all people are very-well-paid'.

# References

[1]     W. Bandler, L.J. Kohout, Fuzzy power sets and fuzzy implication operators. *Fuzzy Sets and Systems*, 4, 1980, 13-30.

[2]     P. Bosc, O. Pivert, SQLf: A relational database language for fuzzy querying. *IEEE Trans. on Fuzzy Systems*, 3, 1995, 1-17.

[3]     P. Bosc, H. Prade, An introduction to the fuzzy set and possibility theory-based treatment of soft queries and uncertain or imprecise databases. In: *Uncertainty Management in Information Systems: From Needs to Solutions* (Ph. Smets, A. Motro, eds.), Kluwer Academic Publ., 1997, Chapter 10, 285-324

[4]     P. Bosc, L. Liétard, Une interprétation pour 'Q B X sont A'. *BUSEFAL* (IRIT, Univ. P. Sabatier, Toulouse, France), 68, 1996, 9-19.

[5]     D. Dubois, H. Fargier, H. Prade, Refinements of the maximin approach to decision-making in fuzzy environment. *Fuzzy Sets and Systems*, 81, 1996, 103-122.

[6]     D. Dubois, H. Prade, Fuzzy Set and Systems: Theory and Applications. Academic Press, New York, 1980.

[7]     D. Dubois, H. Prade, Evidence measures based on fuzzy information. *Automatica*, 21, 1985, 547-562.

[8]     D. Dubois, H. Prade, Fuzzy cardinality and the modeling of imprecise quantification. *Fuzzy Sets and Systems*, 16, 1985, 199-230.

[9]     D. Dubois, H. Prade, Weighted minimum and maximum operations. *Information Sciences*, 39, 1986, 205-210.

[10]    D. Dubois, H. Prade, Measuring properties of fuzzy sets: A general technique and its use in fuzzy query evaluation. *Fuzzy Sets and Systems*, 38(2), 1990, 137-152.

[11]    D. Dubois, H. Prade, Semantics of quotient operators in fuzzy relational databases. *Fuzzy Sets and Systems*, 78, 1996, 89-93.

[12]    L. Liétard, Contribution à l'interrogation flexible de bases de données: Etude des propositions quantifiées floues. *Thesis*, Université de Rennes I, France, 1995.

[13]    H. Prade, Modal semantics and fuzzy set theory. In: *Fuzzy Set and Possibility Theory — Recent Developments* (R.R. Yager, ed.), Pergamon Press, New York, 1982, 232-246.

[14]    M. Wygralak, Vaguely Defined Objects. Kluwer Academic Publ., Dordrecht, 1996.

[15]    R.R. Yager, An approach to inference in approximate reasoning. *Int. J. of Man-Machine Studies*, 13, 1980, 323-328.

[16]    R.R. Yager, General multiple-objective decision functions and linguistically quantified statements. *Int. J. of Man-Machine Studies*, 21, 1984, 389-400.

[17]    R.R. Yager, On ordered weighted averaging aggregation operators in multicriteria decision making. *Trans. on Systems, Man and Cybernetics*, 18, 1988, 183-190.

[18]    L.A. Zadeh, Fuzzy sets, Information and Control, 8, 1965, 338-353.

[19]    L.A Zadeh, Fuzzy sets as a basis for a theory of possibility, *Fuzzy Sets and Systems*, 1, 1978, 3-28.

[20]    L.A. Zadeh, A computational approach to fuzzy quantifiers in natural languages. *Computer Mathematics with Applications*, 9, 1983, 149-183.

# Using Uncertainty Techniques in Radio Communication Systems

K. van Dam

Philips Research Laboratories, Redhill, UK

**Abstract.** This paper describes the application of uncertainty to a radio communication system. In this particular application, uncertainty information is used to optimise a Reason Maintenance System so that tight deadlines can be met. The advantages of using uncertainty techniques here are the capability of dealing with data which may have been corrupted, and the improved real-time performance. The experiences of using uncertainty techniques in a real application are summarised.

## 1 Introduction

In this paper the application of uncertainty to radio communication systems is investigated. The term 'radio' in this context refers to the transmission of information using a radio channel. Radio communication systems suffer from many problems that are virtually non-existent in their wired counterparts. Although removing the fixed wires can have many advantages such as mobility and ease of installation, many additional problems arise. These include transmission errors, power supplies, maintaining user subscriptions and so on. The main issue of concern for this paper relates to the error rate of the system. The probability of transmission errors occurring via a radio link is often significantly larger than via a fixed link. If uncorrected, transmission errors are immediately related to the perceived quality of the system and this is therefore an important issue in the competitive communications market.

## 2 Handover in Communication Systems

In order to counteract some of the effects of transmission errors, many radio communication systems have a facility called handover. This means that during transmission the routing of the connection is changed in such a way that the connection with the highest quality is maintained. Using DECT (Digital Enhanced Cordless Telecommunications) as an example, a system may contain several fixed terminals (base stations) and several portable terminals (portables), for example in the configuration shown in Fig.1. Here, the black squares represent base stations, situated within an area of 60mx60m . Connected portables are shown with a line to the base station they are connected to. When the signal received by a portable decreases in quality (perhaps due to movement or interference from other, nearby portables), the portable may choose to be connected to a different base station and thereby improve the quality of its connection. The decision to perform a handover is usually based on several available metrics. These would typically relate to the received signal strength and the estimated number of errors in the received data.

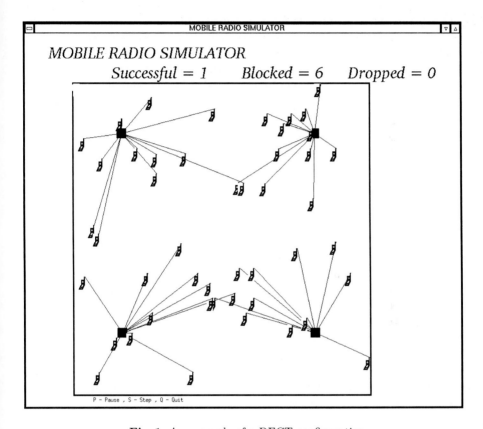

**Fig. 1.** An example of a DECT configuration

Most handover strategies assume that the metrics used for decision making are reliable and accurate. However, in practice this is not always the case. Due to the properties of radio propagation, errors may occur during transmission. The possibility of errors causes uncertainty in the correctness of both the metrics and the data. This leads to the requirement for a method to deal with uncertainty. We can distinguish several types of errors and uncertainty. Firstly, we consider errors during transmission. The transmitted data is normally protected at different levels by using error correction or error detection coding. This means that some redundant information is added to the transmitted data. When received, the redundancy provides information about the number of errors that occured during transmission. Signalling data (required to control the connection) has the highest protection level. Errors here would normally result in a request for retransmission. Errors in speech data are treated differently. Speech is protected to a much lower degree. That means that the amount of redundant information is lower than for signalling data. If the error rate of the transmission channel exceeds the error detection capabilities of the code, a proportion of the errors may remain undetected. Thus errors in the transmission system cause uncertainty in the estimated number of errors (CRC: Cyclic Redundancy Check). Uncertainty also occurs in the signal strength measurement (RSSI: Received Signal Strength Indicator). The signal strength is measured by the demodulator that transforms the modulated signal back into its original form. The RSSI is then quantised into one of several values. Uncertainty arises owing to the measurement accuracy in the demodulator and owing to the quantisation of the signal. The modulation method may also have an impact on the accuracy of the signal strength measurement. Errors may also occur due to equipment not operating correctly. This is particularly of concern for portable equipment and vulnerable parts such as antennas.

All these possible problems caused by the not so ideal world of radio communications give rise to the requirement to consider the incoming data with less than complete certainty.

An important condition on a handover control algorithm is that a response is required within certain time limits. A decision to perform a handover is not so useful any more after 5 minutes, when perhaps the call in question has already been completed. The metrics must be continuously monitored and handover decisions must be made within a few tenths of a second at most.

In order to deal with the complex issue of control in a real-time environment, a Reason Maintenance System (RMS or sometimes called TMS: Truth Maintenance System) will be used. Uncertainty propagation will take place in the RMS. The main reason for selecting an RMS approach here, instead of a rule based system, is that both the unreliability of the radio channel and the rapidly changing behaviour of a radio communication system are likely to cause inconsistencies in the received data.

## 3 Reason Maintenance Systems and Uncertainty

Reason Maintenance Systems (RMS) are often used in real-time Artificial Intelligence systems in order to maintain the consistency of beliefs and hypotheses based on changing data in a dynamic environment. A RMS is capable of resolving contradictions which might be caused, for example, by sensor faults. These systems are sometimes also called Truth Maintenance Systems (TMS). There are two main types of RMS: Justification- based TMS (JTMS) (Doyle, 1979) and Assumption-based TMS (ATMS) (De Kleer, 1986). A JTMS restores consistency using dependency-directed backtracking, where, if a contradiction is detected, the system will search through all possible causes for the contradiction until an assumption is found that would resolve the contradiction when retracted. The JTMS maintains a network of nodes where the nodes represent literals, and the connections between nodes represent the reasons (justification) for believing nodes. Each node can have one of two statuses: 'in' or 'out'. A node is labelled 'in' (in the current set of beliefs) if the JTMS has found reason to believe it. Otherwise the node is 'out'. This would be the case if there are no justification supporting the node. In addition, a node can be labelled as a contradiction. When a contradiction node becomes 'in', the dependency directed backtracking mechanism will be invoked. The aim of the system is to determine whether a set of initial assumptions is consistent with the available data, and if not, retract only those assumptions responsible for contradictions

An ATMS does not evaluate the status of each node (representing a literal) but instead defines a label for each node that specifies under which assumptions the node holds. The label consists of a set of minimal, consistent environments (assumption sets); a node holds in any environment that is a superset of one of the environments specified in the label. The ATMS avoids the need for context switching required in a JTMS as it describes the status of a node in all possible environments.

To find the approach most suitable for our application, it is necessary to compare the kind of problems each RMS approach solves best and how the systems would perform in a real-time environment.

According to de Kleer (1984), the ATMS approach is not suitable for every problem. It is most useful in situations when there are many solutions to a problem which are all required. If only one of these solutions is required, or only one solution exists, the advantages of an ATMS are not so clear. In the former case a JTMS approach is probably better, as in an ATMS all solutions will be explored, requiring much computational effort. In the latter case, the advantages of an ATMS depend on the amount of dependency-directed backtracking that is required. The more dependency- directed backtracking is required, the more efficient an ATMS will be.

In Provan (1990) it is shown that the algorithms used in an ATMS have exponential computational complexity for almost all problems. It is also argued that the case rarely occurs in which many solutions exist for a problem and all are required. Therefore Provan recommends the use of a JTMS, as it gives similar truth maintenance performance to the ATMS for only a fraction of the computational overhead.

In a radio communication system, only one solution to a problem will normally be required. The outputs of the system are in the form of controls, e.g. perform handover, switch antenna, and only one set of controls is required each time. Also, in a real-time environment, there may not be enough time available to generate and evaluate every solution. For our system, it will be more important that a reasonable solution is generated within a certain time, than that the perfect solution is generated after a deadline has passed. The problems in our application thus fall in the two categories mentioned before (only one solution exists, and only one solution is required) where according to De Kleer, it is not very clear which RMS approach gives the best performance. In view of this and Provan's complexity considerations above, the Justification-based TMS approach has been selected for our application.

Some modifications have been made to Doyle's initially proposed system in order to improve the efficiency of the system. One example is the decision to consider mainly fixed rule bases. This decreases the flexibility of the system, but allows for more efficient evaluation. For our application, the rule set is in most cases already known and it is not necessary to grant the flexibility of changing rules. A second important modification is the inclusion of an integrated uncertainty propagation system.

A discussed above, the properties of a radio communication system give rise to the requirement to deal with uncertainty. This can be done in several ways. In our case the RMS is already an important part of the reasoning system. Since the literals within the RMS are in some way derived from uncertain sensor data, it will be necessary to propagate uncertainty within the RMS.

Methods for dealing with uncertainty in a JTMS have been proposed elsewhere (Falkenhainer 1988), (Poznański, 1990). Neither of these methods propagate contradictions through the RMS network. They also do not acknowledge the existence of a measure of contradiction which we believe to be an important metric in deciding where and when to start backtracking in a resource limited system. Uncertainty techniques have also been used in an ATMS, for instance in (Laskey and Lehner, 1989) and (d'Ambrosio, 1988). The methods proposed in these two papers are very similar and use Dempster-Shafer propagation to calculate a belief value for each label in the ATMS. Again, the Dempster-Shafer technique is utilised only in order to calculate the certainty values of the results. Measures of contradiction are not used to assist in the process of reason maintenance.

In the literature many techniques are described for representing and propagating uncertain information. Selecting an uncertainty approach is not an easy task as many factors need to be considered. The interested reader is refered to (Van Dam, 1997) for a detailed account of how this selection was carried out for our application. It was decided to integrate a form of the Dempster-Shafer technique in the RMS. One of the deciding factors was the compatibility between Demster-Shafer belief values and the 'in' and 'out' status in an RMS.

In the Dempster-Shafer theory (see for example (Smets, 1988)) uncertainty is viewed as a degree of belief. These degrees of belief are values between 0 and 1, where 1 indicates total belief, 0 means lack of belief (which is not the same as disbelief), and an intermediate value means partial belief in a proposition.

Let $\theta$ be a set of hypotheses that are mutually exclusive and exhaustive, this is called the frame of discernment in Dempster-Shafer theory. Each of these basic hypotheses is called a singleton. The power set of $\theta$, is denoted by **2q and consists of all subsets of $\theta$, including the empty set and $\theta$ itself. Evidence can be combined using Dempster's rule of combination. Consider a proposition $C$ that is implied by two distinct pieces of evidence $A$ and $B$. The belief assigned to $C$ from evidence $A$ and $B$ is $m(A)$ and $m(B)$ respectively. The resulting belief

$m(C)$ is calculated as follows:

$$m(C) = \frac{\sum\limits_{A \cap B = C} m(A) * m(B)}{1 \quad \sum\limits_{A \cap B = \emptyset} m(A) * m(B)} \tag{1}$$

$$m(\emptyset) = 0$$

The factor in the denominator is a normalisation factor to ensure that the sum of the basic probability numbers equals 1, while the basic probability number assigned to the empty set ($\emptyset$) is equal to 0. In order to make the notation clearer, $m(A)$ is now called $t_A$, $m(\neg A)$ is called $f_A$ and $m(\Theta)$ is called $\theta_A$, denoting 'truth', 'false' and 'unknown' values respectively. The values $t_A$ and $f_A$ together now quantify the uncertainty of $A$. According to the Dempster-Shafer rule of combination, the sum of all m's assigned to members of $\Theta$ must add to one. Here, that means that the following equality must hold:

$$t_A + f_A + \theta_A = 1 \tag{2}$$

This in turn means that the support for $A$ and that for $\neg A$ can take any value between 0 and 1, provided that their sum is smaller or equal to one. The support for a literal $C$ supported with ($t_A$, $f_A$) from one source of evidence ($A$), and with ($t_B$, $f_B$) from another source ($B$) can now be determined using Dempster's rule.

As implied by equation 1, the support for C before normalisation (using only the numerator) is obtained by multiplying the support from A for C and the support from B for C. If this is carried out for each combination of support provided by A and B, the results are as follows:

$$t_C = t_A + t_B - t_A * t_B - t_A * f_B - t_B * f_A \tag{3}$$
$$f_C = f_A + f_B - f_A * f_B - t_A * f_B - t_B * f_A \tag{4}$$
$$\theta_C = (1 - t_A - f_A) * (1 - t_B - f_B) \tag{5}$$

In order to satisfy the condition $m_C(\emptyset) = 0$, the above values are normalised according to Dempster's rule. Here, the support for the empty set equals $t_A * f_B + f_A * t_B$ and all values are divided by the normalisation factor: $1 - (t_A * f_B + f_A * t_B)$. The resulting values for $t$, $f$ and $\theta$ satisfy equality (2). When normalising, the support for the empty set is redistributed proportionally over all non-empty sets without any formal justification. Some criticism has been expressed concerning the validity of the normalisation procedure (Clarke, 1988), (Zadeh, 1986). The next section describes an extension of Dempster-Shafer uncertainty propagation that does not require any normalisation.

## 4 Extended Dempster-Shafer Uncertainty Propagation

Using uncertainty propagation in a RMS can provide valuable information on measures of contradictions. This can be used to rank the contradictions, so that the one with the highest likelihood is resolved first. Particularly in real-time systems, where only limited time is available for contradiction resolution, it is advantageous to find some means of identifying which contradiction to resolve first.

In order to obtain this information, the Dempster-Shafer theory is extended such that any contradictions are not 'normalised away', but are considered as an additional parameter, c, for describing the status of a node. Below follows a brief description of the new technique. More detailed explanations can be found in (Van Dam, 1994) and (1997).

The above exercise of determining the support for and against a literal is now repeated, but including the possibility of contradictions. The support for the contradictory combinations $(A, \neg B)$ and $(\neg A, B)$ is now included in both $t_C$ and $f_C$. In addition, a new value $c_C$ is introduced that represents the support for a contradiction. Contrary to the previous example, the sum of $t$ and $f$ is now allowed to be larger than one.

$$t_C = t_A + t_B - t_A * t_B \tag{6}$$
$$f_C = f_A + f_B - f_A * f_B \tag{7}$$
$$c_C = t_A * f_B + f_A * t_B \tag{8}$$
$$\theta_C = (1 - t_A - f_A) * (1 - t_B - f_B) \tag{9}$$

The equality that now holds is:

$$t_C + f_C + \theta_C - c_C = 1 \tag{10}$$

Also, as in normal Dempster-Shafer propagation, the values of all $t$, $f$, $c$ and $\theta$ lie between 0 and 1. The above equations are for the special case when the antecedents themselves are free of contradictions. The support values for $C$ when both antecedents contain contradictions are shown in (11-14).

$$t_C = t_A + t_B - t_A * t_B \tag{11}$$
$$f_C = f_A + f_B - f_A * f_B \tag{12}$$
$$c_C = t_A * f_B + f_A * t_B + c_A * c_B + \tag{13}$$
$$c_B * (1 - t_A - f_A) + c_A * (1 - t_B - f_B)$$
$$\theta_C = (1 + c_A - t_A - f_A) * (1 + c_B - t_B - f_B) \tag{14}$$

When $c_A = c_B = 0$ (indicating that there were no contradictions in the antecedents), these equations reduce to those derived in (6-9). The difference between the support values for $C$ and $\neg C$ derived from Dempster-Shafer and our new method lies in the fact that the normal Dempster-Shafer method assigns only justified belief (ie belief that has not been contradicted). The extended approach represents a more tentative assignment of belief. The purpose of a Reason Maintenance System is to keep the consistency of different beliefs. Therefore the larger belief value, which includes the contradiction, is more appropriate in our case. The extended propagation technique differs from the conventional

Dempster-Shafer propagation in that it acknowledges that the 'rest' term represented by $\theta$ can represent contradictory knowledge as well as incomplete knowledge. The old $\theta$ from (2) now becomes $\theta$ - $c_A$ and is more flexible as it is allowed to be positive and negative. A positive 'rest' term can still include contradictory knowledge and negative one can include incomplete knowledge. While the proposed propagation technique allows easy reasoning with contradictory information, the Dempster-Shafer technique with normalisation becomes more unreliable (and even unstable) the more contradictory the evidence is. As an extreme, consider the result when $A$ is true and $B$ is false. The normalisation factor is $1 - (t_A * f_B + f_B * t_A)$ and here its value equals zero. The normalised support values would then be calculated by dividing by this normalisation factor!

## 5 Application of Extended Dempster-Shafer Theory to RMS

The above has shown how the existing Dempster-Shafer theory can be extended in order to obtain information on the severity of contractions. Now we will show how this information can be used in a Reason Maintenance System. The computational scheme outlined in the previous paragraph is used to calculate $t$, $f$ and $c$ for every node in the RMS.

In for instance Doyle's JTMS (Doyle, 1979), the detection of contradictions is straightforward, as there is either a contradiction or there is not a contradiction.

In our RMS, the case where the support for $C$ and $\neg C$ add to more than one, would seem to indicate a contradiction (Quinlan, 1983), (Poznański, 1990). However, this issue is rather more complicated since in an RMS that allows uncertain input values, it is only possible to evaluate a measure of contradiction. There is a definite contradiction when a node has values of $t$ and $f$ both equal to one. Without a computational scheme that calculates measures of contradiction as outlined above, all that can be concluded from the $t$ and $f$ values of a node are the lower and upper bounds of the measure of contradiction: the lower bound is equal to $(t_C + f_C - 1)$ and the upper bound is $\min(t_C, f_C)$, these quantities can be derived by examining the minimum and maximum overlap between $t_C$ and $f_C$ (Van Dam, 1997). The information on measures of contradictions is exploited in our system by ranking the contradictions depending on their $c$ value. Now, the most likely contradiction is resolved first. This arrangement ensures that if contradiction resolution can only be performed for a limited number of nodes due to time constraints, the worst contradictions will be resolved. With this scheme, most RMS nodes will have a non-zero value for $c$. As $c$ indicates a measure of contradiction, a non-zero value is not necessarily a problem. We have chosen to only resolve contradictions that have a c value of more that 0.5. This threshold corresponds to nodes that are more likely to contain a contradiction than not.

Once the decision to start backtracking on a contradiction has been made, the RMS algorithms will search through the contradictory node's justifications, and their justifications, and so on, for assumptions. If an assumption is found, it is provisionally retracted to see if it would resolve the contradiction. It is possible that more than one such assumption is found and a strategy needs to be defined that determines which assumption to retract. Possibilities for this include retraction of the least certain assumption and retraction of the assumption that only just resolves the contradiction, thus maintaining a maximum amount of knowledge in the RMS. When a culprit has been retracted, all its dependent nodes are marked, to indicate that their support is suspect (it may be based on the retracted node). The algorithms will now look for independent well founded support for the marked nodes.

A distinct advantage of propagating contradictions through the RMS is in guiding the search for assumptions. Each time a node is supported by more than one justification, the measure of contradiction in these justifications is used to find the most likely direction in which the assumption to be retracted lies. This can speed up the process of dependency directed backtracking when time constraints make it unfeasible to investigate the whole search space for assumptions.

When a literal is not supported by any assumptions, the measure of contradiction has no purpose. If the literal is selected for contradiction resolution, there are no assumptions that can be retracted. Therefore, when this is the case, the support values will be normalised, as in the normal Dempster-Shafer technique.

# 6 Simulations

The RMS with uncertainty has been tested using a simulation of a radio communication system (DECT). The simulator simulates the random setting up of calls and movements of the users. For each call, the received signal strength and the number of transmission errors are simulated taking into account interference from other portables.A snapshot during a simulation is shown in Fig.1. This also shows several metrics relating to call quality as follows: successful calls are is set up and terminated normally, dropped calls have lost their connection after set up and blocked calls never get connected.

If the performance of different methods is to be compared, it is necessary to define a quality metric. The quality metric used here is a combination of three separate quality indicators. An important measure for good performance of DECT is the grade of service. This is the weighted sum of the number of dropped calls and the number of blocked calls. Dropped calls are considered much more severe than blocked calls and are weighted ten times as much as blocked calls when calculating the grade of service. The DECT simulator keeps track of the number of successful, blocked and dropped calls. Another possible way to define the quality of a communication system, is to consider the speech quality. A frame is defined as a section of data (speech) that is transmitted in one identifiable packet. A bad frame ratio can then be defined as the total number of bad (or unintelligible) frames divided by the total number of frames. A third quality metric is the number of handovers per call. This is included in the overall quality metric since performing a handover represents an overhead on the system. The quality metric used in the simulation is a weighted combination of the three quality metrics. The weights were defined from the results of simulations (Van Dam, 1997).

One of the difficulties in assessing the performance of a communication system lies in the fact that, due to the statistical nature of the application, long simulations must be carried out before any significant conclusions can be drawn. The simulations have been run for 50000 frames. This takes approximately 10 hours on a SUN workstation.

A series of simulations have been carried out to test the performance of DECT with various control strategies. First the performance was determined without use of the RMS. This served as the base performance against which to compare the performance with the RMS.

In the next set of simulations faults were introduced in the DECT system. These faults represent faults in the DECT sensors. Three types of faults, each representing a fault in the DECT sensors, were evaluated. The first type of fault involves setting all CRC values to one. For the second type of fault all CRC values are set to zero. The third fault consists of the RSSI being set to a random value. The faults are intermittent with a random duration. Only one type of fault occurs per simulation. Results showed that for each of the faults, the performance was worse than that without faults. This was of course expected. The simulations so far did not involve the RMS. The following simulations use the RMS to demonstrate backtracking. The rule base was constructed in such a way that a contradiction was generated when the RSSI is very low (bad signal) and the number of CRCs is also very low (good signal) or vice versa. If a contradiction is detected, the dependency directed backtracking procedure is invoked which may result in the retraction of the 'no fault' literal. The performance with backtracking was significantly better than the performance without. The results show that the system can cope very well with intermittent faults. This is an important improvement over existing systems where faults usually have a detrimental effect on the performance of the radio system.

Further simulations use the uncertainty of the inputs in order to grade the contradictions. The most severe contradictions can then be resolved first. In the simulator, each portable is randomly assigned a probability of a fault occurring. During the intermittent fault periods, each portable radio will display a fault or not, depending on its fault probability. The probability of a fault is passed on to the reasoning system. The input values with faults are: received signal strength and the estimated number of transmission errors. In the rule base, these are always used in the form: IF (signal_strength > threshold) THEN ... The Dempster-Shafer support values for the proposition (signal_strength > threshold) are determined by looking at the probability of a fault ($p$, obtained from the simulation, see above). There is a probability of $1 - p$ that the value is uncorrupted. Nothing is known about the value if it is corrupted. If the value for the signal strength is higher than the threshold, the support values are thus as follows ($t = 1 - p$, $f = 0$). If the value of the signal strength is lower than the threshold, the support is ($t = 0$, $f = 1 - p$).

In order to illustrate the use of uncertainty here, simulations were carried out where only one contradiction per simulation time may be resolved. In the case of uncertainty, the contradiction with the highest measure of contradiction will be selected for resolution. Without uncertainty, the choice of contradiction is arbitrary.

The results show that when the fault involves setting all CRCs to zero, using uncertainty to select the contradiction to resolve results in better DECT performance (as defined by the quality metric described above) than when this is done randomly. For other types of faults the measured performance was better but may not be statistically significant.

The main value of using uncertainty in this way is that when contradictions arise, the backtracking is guided by the measures of contradiction, which in turn depend on the uncertainty values of the input values. This is important in the simulation since up to 60 connections are controlled at the same time. Any delay in dealing with the most severe contradictions may result in dropped calls.

# 7   Conclusions

This paper has described a novel method for controlling a radio communication system. Because data is transferred over the radio link, the received data is often unreliable. This gives rise to the requirement to use an uncertainty management technique. Here, this is integrated into an RMS in order to improve the real-time reasoining capabilities. Simulations have shown that using this arrangement can improve the performance of a radio communication system under fault conditions.

This research has provided the opportunity to gain experience in the question of the viability of using uncertainty techniques. Using uncertainty can be divided into three distinct stages: uncertainty acquisition, uncertainty propagation and uncertainty utilisation. These will now be considered in turn.

The experiences for this application have been that the most difficult exercise is assigning the uncertainty information. With numerical uncertainty in particular, it is very difficult to assess, for example, the implications of assigning a value of 0.7 or 0.8. As a result, uncertainty techniques should ideally be fairly robust to small changes in uncertainty values. This problem of course depends on the application, but it is our view that if this stage was easier, there would be a higher uptake of uncertainty techniques in the industrial world.

Once this is available, the uncertainty propagation itself is not difficult. The problem here is selecting an appropriate technique. Scientific literature is swamped by papers on uncertainty, most of which claim to report the one and only way! In order to apply uncertainty to a real application, one is first required to become an expert on uncertainty. This may well affect the uptake of these techniques.

Now the uncertainty values have been assigned and propagated, the next hurdle is to interpret the output values. Most real-world systems require their input as '1' or '0'. Therefore, if the output of the uncertainty propagation is used as an input to the next system, the uncertainty values need to be converted.

To summarise, using uncertainty techniques seems a natural way to deal with real data. However, there is a lot of work involved in applying an uncertainty technique to a real application. Although we believe that definite advantages can often be obtained from using such techniques, it may not always be clear during development whether it will be worthwhile.

# 8 Acknowledgements

The author would like to thank Dr T.J. Moulsley of Philips Research Laboratories for providing support and encouragement. This research was made possible by support from the DTI under grant number ITD 3/1/3098.

# References

M. Clarke, Discussion of Smets, P. 'Belief functions', Non-standard logics for automated reasoning, P. Smets et al (eds), Academic Press, (1988).

K. van Dam, Intelligent Control of Radio Communication Systems, PhD thesis, Queen Mary and Westfield College, (1997) (to appear).

K. van Dam and T.J. Moulsley, 'Extension of Dempster-Shafer Theory and Application to Fault Diagnosis in Communication Systems', 2nd Int Conf Intelligent Systems Engineering, (1994).

B. d'Ambrosio, 'A Hybrid Approach to Reasoning under Uncertainty', Int. Journal of Approximate Reasoning, **2**, 29–45, (1988).

J. Doyle, 'A Truth Maintenance System', Artificial Intelligence, **12**, 231–272, (1979).

B. Falkenhainer, Towards a General-Purpose Belief Maintenance System, 125–132, Uncertainty in Artificial Intelligence 2 (J.F. Lemmer, L.N. Kanal, eds.), North-Holland, (1988).

J. de Kleer, 'Choices without Backtracking', Proc. 4th AAAI, Austin, Texas, 79–85, (1984).

J. de Kleer, 'An Assumption-Based Tms', Artificial Intelligence, **28**, 127–162, (1986).

K.B. Laskey and P.E. Lehner, 'Assumptions, Beliefs and Probabilities', Artificial Intelligence, **41**, 65–77, (1989).

V. Poznański, 'Dempster-Shafer Ranges for an RMS', IEE Colloquium on 'Reasoning under Uncertainty, (1990).

G.M. Provan, 'The Computational Complexity of Multiple-Context Truth Maintenance Systems', Proc. ECAI '90, 522–527, (1990).

J.R. Quinlan, 'Consistency and Plausible Reasoning', Proc. IJCAI '83, 137–144, (1983).

P. Smets, Belief functions, Non-standard logics for automated reasoning, P. Smets et al (eds), Academic Press, (1988).

L.A. Zadeh, 'A Simple View of the Dempster-Shafer Theory of Evidence and its Implication for the Rule of Combination', AI Magazine, **7**, 85-90, (1986).

# Handling Imperfect Knowledge in *Milord II* for the Identification of Marine Sponges

Marta Domingo, Lluís Godo, Carles Sierra

Artificial Intelligence Research Institute, IIIA.
Spanish Scientific Research Council, CSIC.
Campus UAB, 08193 Bellaterra, Barcelona, Spain.
{domingo,godo,sierra}@iiia.csic.es

**Abstract.** In this chapter we present SPONGIA, a knowledge based system implemented using the **Milord II** programming environment. SPONGIA deals with the identification of sponges from the Atlanto-Mediterranean biogeographical province. It covers the identification of more than 100 taxa of the phylum Porifera from class to species. The effective handling of uncertainty has been critical to display an efficient performance in SPONGIA. This problem has been managed taking advantage of the multiple techniques provided by **Milord II**. The use of fuzzy logic makes it possible to accurately represent the imprecise knowledge which constitutes the classificatory theory of Porifera to a large extent. It also provides the user with some means of expressing his state of knowledge with accuracy. Easy design and incremental development of the knowledge base are possible thanks to modularity. Taxonomic knowledge is represented by means of plain modules hierarchically interconnected via submodule declarations and refinement operations. To emulate the reasoning strategies we use generic modules, which can take other modules as parameters. Thanks to the uncertainty handling and reflective deduction mechanisms it has been possible to emulate complex reasoning strategies displayed by experts in sponge systematics. Finally, the strict compartmentation of domain knowledge and knowledge concerning reasoning strategies into modules allows the reusability of pieces of knowledge.

## 1 Introduction

### 1.1 The identification problem

The study and description of living organisms has been practised by man for many centuries. The Swedish naturalist Linnaeus (1707-1778) devised the binomial nomenclature that has allowed scientists to discuss and improve the classification of organisms for generations, and to identify specimens on the basis of such a taxonomic representation.

Taxonomic identification is a complex task in which only experts in systematic biology have an authoritative voice. Very often these scientists have to spend their time identifying organisms for other researchers instead of concentrating on their own research. No ecological investigation can move forth without some taxonomic analysis of the organisms present. An error in identification at this stage could invalidate any subsequent work in a given area [26].

In the taxonomic context, the description of a species involves high information content. This complex description is reached thanks to the use of a natural language which can express imprecision, uncertainty and even incoherence. Experts in the field of systematic biology have to reason on the basis of this "imperfect" knowledge, that is, imprecise, uncertain or incoherent knowledge.

Automating the identification task has been a challenge in the field of systematic biology since computers began to be accessible. The first computerised identification tools appeared in the middle 70s when taxonomists began to build computer programs to identify species or to store descriptive information. These were classic programs that emulated any of the traditional identification procedures (dichotomous key, multiple-entry key or matching methods) by implementation of traditional search algorithms. They were called "on-line" identification programs because the interactive nature of these programs was then considered a critical advantage.

Nowadays, many on-line identification programs try to optimise their search by incorporating selection commands, such as the "best character" selection commands, that assess the goodness of characters[1] based on some kind of character weighting. However, on-line programs do not provide any mechanism to handle incomplete or imprecise knowledge in an effective way. Thus, if available data over a sample is incomplete or uncertain these programs can only continue the search by entering each of the branches where the unknown character is found. More details about the progress made on classic computerised identification tools are given by Pankhurst [30].

In the middle 80s, the weaknesses of classic identification programs led to the investigation of alternative techniques from the Artificial Intelligence (AI) field for taxonomic identification, see Edwards and Morse [16] review of the few knowledge-based systems that had been developed till the early 90s in the field of systematic biology. Other interesting uses of artificial intelligence techniques in systematic biology are discussed in [17].

This chapter focuses on a knowledge-based system, called SPONGIA, for taxonomic identification in the particular domain of marine sponges. The system SPONGIA, built over the **Milord II** knowledge base architecture, takes advantage of the approximate reasoning facilities provided by **Milord II** to deal in an efficient way with the identification of sponges from the Atlanto-Mediterranean biogeographical province, covering the identification of more than 100 taxa of the phylum Porifera from class to species.

## 1.2 The Porifera problem

Sponges are aquatic metazoans occurring both in marine and freshwater habitats. They are sedentary, thus belonging to the benthic community (*benthos*).

---

[1] **Character** 8. b. Now especially in Natural History. One of the distinguishing features of a species or genus. (The Compact Oxford English Dictionary, 1991).

The sponge body consists in a system of pores, ostia, canals and chambers with a single-layered epithelium of flagellated cells (*choanocytes*) that pumps a water current through its aquiferous system. The water current leaves the sponge throw one or several openings called *oscula*. By means of this low pressure pumping the sponge realises all essential exchanges, that is, food gathering, oxygenation and excretion.

Most sponges have a skeleton integrated by microscopic inorganic concretions (*spicules*) and/or organic tissue. The organic material is made of collagen which can be either disperse or in the form of fibrils and fibres (*spongin fibres*). Spicules may be made of silica or calcium carbonate. There is a special group of sponges whose skeleton is both calcareous and siliceous. Another group of sponges, which have a skeleton made of spongin in great quantity without inorganic spicules, are well-known because some species have been useful to man for centuries due to their capacity to absorb fluids.

In many sponges two kinds of spicules can be distinguished according to their morphology and disposition, namely megascleres and microscleres. Megascleres are the main bricks of the spicular skeleton whereas microscleres collaborate to support the structure making local reinforcement of the spicular skeleton. The so-called megascleres have bigger dimensions than microscleres. However, in many cases, the range of measures for the megascleres of some species overlaps with the range for the microscleres. Moreover, although some spicular morphologies are typical of megascleres or microscleres, other forms do exist in both spicular types. This may lead to uncertainty in the judgement of the observed data in a sponge sample. It is important to notice that relatively slight morphological differences in the spicular complement may characterise different species.

An elaborated terminology exists in reference to the shape, size and ornamentation of a given spicule. In Figure 1, the diversity and beauty of siliceous spicules can be appreciated in several scanning electron microscope (SEM) images.

A very characteristic aspect of the phylum Porifera is the variety of growth forms (see Figure 2). Many sponge species are very plastic and can adopt different growth forms in response to local and geographic environmental parameters. Generally speaking, we might distinguish among species with highly regular forms and species with irregularly massive bodies. We can list multiple growth forms which are present in the phylum. Encrusting forms that range from thin sheets (500 to 1000 $\mu$m in thickness) to thick encrustations or hemispherical forms. Massive forms with globular or subspherical bodies which may grow to a meter in height, or other forms like cup-shaped or ficiform. Erect forms which can take a branching, digitate, pinnate, or foliaceous pattern, among others, or pedunculate forms. Even endolithic forms, that is, sponges that have the capacity of excavating calcareous substrata or simply live in a hole previously made by other agents.

Porifera is a relatively small phylum. It contains some 5000 to 5500 described species and an unknown, but certainly extensive, quantity of undescribed species. As being the relative abundance of sponges in benthic assemblages high, the

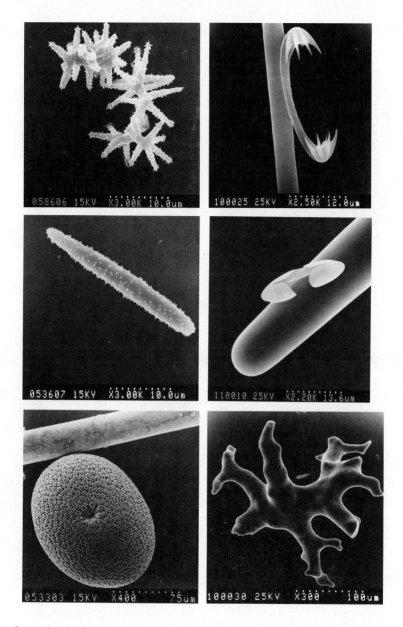

**Fig. 1.** Several spicule types in scanning electron microscope (SEM) views. Top-left) Microscleres: 'Streptasters' of *Poecilastra compressa.* Top-right) Microsclere: 'Isanchora' of a species from the order Poecilosclerida (on the right). Fragment of a megasclere (on the left). Mid-left) Microsclere: spiny 'microrhabd' of a species from the order Astrophorida. Mid-right) Microsclere: 'Isochelae' of a species from the order Poecilosclerida. Fragment of a 'style' (megasclere) behind. Bottom-left) Microsclere: 'Sterraster' of a species from the order Astrophorida (*Erylus pachydermata*). Fragment of a megasclere on top. Bottom-right) Megasclere: 'Desma' of *Desmanthus macphersoni,* a species of the Lithistida group.

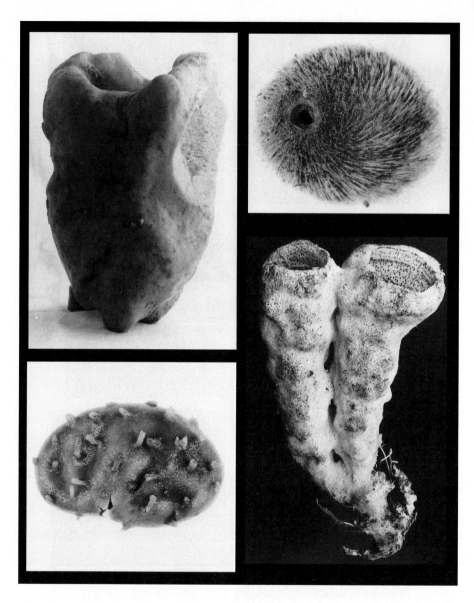

**Fig. 2.** Top-left) Specimen of *Stelleta hispida* (Order Astrophorida) with a massive growth form. Top-right) Specimen of *Tetilla capilosa* (Order Spirophorida) with a globular growth form with high hispidation in surface. A single oscule is distinguished. Bottom-left) Specimen of *Inflatella belli* (Order Poecilosclerida) with a massive subspherical body with several fistulas in surface. Bottom-right) Specimen of *Isodictya chichatouzai* (Order Haplosclerida) with an erect tubular body.

contributions to the understanding of the biology of sponges are fundamental in marine ecology studies. However, identification of specimens is the first step in such studies and identification of sponges is not a trivial task. Studies of biological diversity in marine habitats also needs accurate identifications.

On the other hand, sponges, among other benthic organisms, are active producers of chemical bioactive products (e.g. cytotoxic, antifungal, antimitotic, antiviral) [41]. This has drawn the attention of the pharmaceutical industry to such taxonomic groups and has laid bare the scarcity of experts in sponge taxonomy and the lack of good tools for sponge identification.

As identifying sponges is highly complex, it is confined to an expert's performance. Although this could be said of most marine invertebrate phyla, it is especially true for sponges. Years of experience are needed to become an expert on sponge systematics. Large specialised libraries and accurate laboratory observation are needed to identify species.

Expert research usually focus on one or several portions of the Porifera taxonomy. Thus, expertise is scarce and the knowledge of the phylum is usually scattered among several experts. In fact, taxonomic knowledge in any group depends on the past work of a systematic biologist in this group and the knowledge of the present experts, taking into account current scientific trends, may be lost when they retire.

For a novice the problems in identifying a specimen are not only associated with his skills but with his interpretation of scientific literature as well, because it reflects the conflicting classifications. Porifera is one of the most problematic marine invertebrate taxa with regard to its classification [5]. This is due to the morphological plasticity of its species, to the incomplete knowledge of many of their biological and cytological features, to the frequent description of new taxa (e.g. [8,6,27]), to the variety of specific terms [9] applied to homologous characters and, conversely, to the occurrence of single terms that name analogous characters [18]. Since taxa are closely alike, controversy around the species delimitation or even around higher taxonomic levels of the classification is common.

Different terms for the same concept are widespread in the literature; consensus among current experts is still hard to attain. Therefore, terminological incoherence is common. For example, the common expression "smooth acanthostyle" for a spicule is paradoxical as "acantho" means spiny. Or, the ambiguity of the concepts megasclere and microsclere, with a clear reference to size, that actually refer to two functions of spicules. Although these terms usually correspond to "big" and "small" spicules, the common size of some megascleres, e.g. some Haplosclerida, is similar to the general range for microscleres.

The problems listed so far, namely controversial classification, complex identification of specimens and scarce and scattered expertise, show the need for efficient taxonomic tools able to perform as experts in sponge systematics to be used by non-experts. To tackle the Porifera identification problem we have to capture the heuristics of experts and the (controverted) classification theory of sponges. That is, we need to a) represent imprecise predicates, b) represent uncertain statements, c) manage uncertain and imprecise propositions to propagate the certainty even in the absence of enough data, or with uncertain data, and d) simulate complex reasoning strategies.

## 1.3 Sources of uncertainty and imprecision in the Porifera

The lack of a well-established theory makes heuristic knowledge very important in the sponge systematics field. There are two elements that contribute to this situation. One is the high variability within the phylum Porifera, the other is the frequent new discoveries of species and new morphological and physiological characteristics in known species.

- *Variability.* The phylum Porifera seems to summarise all the growth strate-gies of sessile marine organisms. Thus, it is able to colonise even the most inhospitable habitats (e.g. deep inside dark caves, abyssal bottoms). An im-portant source of variability stems from the genetic content. Sponges have been proven to be genetically much more diverse than other marine inver-tebrates [38]. High variability is also present within species due to their capability of adaptation to environmental conditions.

  Variability of characters involves a great deal of uncertainty in taxa def-inition and description. In most cases, it is difficult to state the species boundaries clearly. Sometimes, what had been supposed to be a new species is discovered to be a morph of a previously known species. Further, some of the species reported in the literature are considered "bad species" by some experts because they do not seem distinctive to them.

  Description of species usually relies on measurable characters, for example on the spicules' size. However, the length and thickness of siliceous spicules may vary depending (at least) on water temperature. Then, when a taxonomic distinction is made on the basis of relative minor spicule variation there is some chance of introducing an artefact. Similarly, this may induce erroneous identifications when disregarding certain ecological constraints.

- *Incompleteness of the knowledge.* Sponges are a relatively little studied phy-lum and many existing species remain undescribed. On the other hand, many of the biological and cytological features of sponges are not fully known. His-torically, the skeleton has been the primary feature for description and, as a consequence, for identification. The main body of knowledge on sponges is still based on skeletal characters. Although biochemistry and genetics hold great promise, results in these disciplines are still preliminary and focus on few species.

## 1.4 Organisation of this chapter

As already pointed out, this chapter is devoted to describe the knowledge-based system SPONGIA, and in particular how it effectively deals with problems of imprecision and incompleteness in the domain theory and data.

After this introductory section, we survey in Section 2 the main features of the **Milord II** architecture, with special emphasis to those aspects related to the handling of imprecise or incomplete knowledge. In the description we address both the logical grounds of the deductive machinery and the computational constructs that implement them. Namely, after a brief introduction, in the second and third subsections the object-level component, based on finitely-valued fuzzy logics, is described and formalised. The fourth subsection is devoted to the meta-level component, while in the fifth subsection we describe the reflection mechanisms and their role in the dynamics of the execution of a module. Finally, in the sixth subsection we report on the modularisation techniques used in **Milord II**. In Section 3 we describe SPONGIA. After introducing the knowledge–based system, in the second subsection we explain the structure and functionality of the modular hierarchy. In the third subsection, we focus on the importance of a sensible management and representation of imprecise and unknown knowledge for the construction of automatic identification tools and particularly in the development of SPONGIA. In Subsection 3.3 we present the practical scenario of SPONGIA. Finally, we end up in Section 4 with some discussion on related work and conclusions.

## 2 Reasoning in Milord II

### 2.1 Introduction

Reasoning patterns that appear when modelling complex tasks, like sponge classification, cannot often be modelled only by means of a pure classical logic approach. This is due to several reasons, for instance, incompleteness of the available information, need to use and represent uncertain or imprecise knowledge, the combinatorial explosion of classical theorem proving when knowledge bases become large, or the lack of a methodology for building complex and large knowledge bases. In this section we provide a description of the main features of the system **Milord II**, a system that proposes a particular solution to these problems by a combination of approximate reasoning, reflection and modularisation techniques (more detailed descriptions of **Milord II** can be found elsewhere [33,34]):

In Artificial Intelligence there is very often a need for dealing with uncertain and/or imprecise information [11,31,24]. **Milord II** provides at the object-level a family of representation languages based on many-valued logics, where sets of truth-values stand for scales of linguistic terms representing different degrees of truth or belief. Moreover, fuzzy concepts can be represented in this base language. See [7,29] for similar approaches.

The use of reflection techniques is a common practice in several knowledge areas, natural language, philosophy, literature, etc. [4]. The application of reflection techniques to knowledge–based systems (KBS) has been widely used in the recent past as a clear separation between domain and control knowledge [28]; however, only a few systems such as OMEGA [2] and MC-Systems [20] have clear semantics. See [12] for a recent survey.

Modularisation is a standard technique to manage the complexity of highly interacting systems, such as KBSs [3,39]. A module can be understood as a functional abstraction, by fixing both the set of components it needs as input, and the type of results it can produce. This technique has been used in the context of functional programming, e.g. Standard ML [23], Logic Programming [37], and Artificial Intelligence architectures [40]. In the architecture of **Milord II**, reflection and modularisation are used together in order to define complex reasoning patterns in the large.

Figure 3 is a schematic picture of what a KB looks like in **Milord II**. It consists of a set of hierarchically interconnected modules, each one containing an Object-Level Theory (OLT) and a Meta-Level Theory (MLT) interacting through a reflective mechanism.

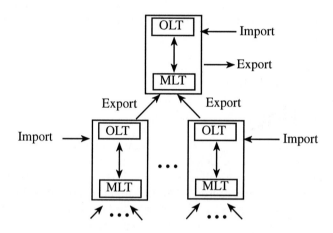

**Fig. 3.** Milord II KB structure.

Each module has also an import/export interface. The user of a KB provides information to modules via the import interface, and modules provide information to the user or to other modules via the export interface.

In this section we give an overview of the different components of the **Milord II** Architecture. In subsections 2-4 we detail the logical aspects of the object-level component. In subsection 5 we describe the meta-level component which plays a complementary role to the object level to define the dynamics of the reasoning as explained in subsection 6.. Finally, subsection 7 accounts for the modular structure of the language and the operations that can be applied on modules.

## 2.2   Object Level: Approximate Reasoning Model

**Milord II** provides the user with approximate reasoning capabilities at the object level in modules. The approximate reasoning mechanisms are generically based on the use of a finitely-valued fuzzy (or many-valued) logic. A particular logic can be specified inside each module by defining which is the algebra of truth-values, i.e. which is the ordered set of truth-values and which is the set of logical operators associated to them. The kind of algebras of truth-values used in **Milord II** are those defined as follows.

**Definition 1.** An **Algebra of truth-values** is a finite linearly ordered residuated lattice with a negation operation $A_{n,T} = \langle A_n, \leq N_n, T, I_T \rangle$, that is:

1. $(A_n, \leq)$ is a chain of $n$ elements: $\mathbf{0} = a_1 < a_2 < ... < a_n = \mathbf{1}$ where $\mathbf{0}$ and $\mathbf{1}$ are the booleans $False$ and $True$ respectively.
2. The negation operation $N_n$ is a unary operation defined as $N_n(a_i) = a_{n-i+1}$, which is the only operator that fulfils the following properties:
   - N1: if $a < b$ then $N_n(a) > N_n(b), \forall a, b \in A_n$
   - N2: $N_n(N_n(a)) = a, \forall a \in A_n$.
3. The conjunction operator $T$ is any binary operation such that the following properties hold $\forall a, b, c \in A_n$:
   - T1: $T(a, b) = T(b, a)$
   - T2: $T(a, T(b, c)) = T(T(a, b), c)$
   - T3: $T(0, a) = 0$
   - T4: $T(1, a) = a$
   - T5: if $a \leq b$ then $T(a, c) \leq T(b, c)$ for all $c$
4. The implication operator $I_T$ defined by residuation with respect to $T$ i.e.:

$$I_T(a, b) = Max\{c \in A_n | T(a, c) \leq b\}.$$

In many-valued logic there are several alternatives to define implication operators. One of the most usual choices is to define the implication by residuation with respect to the conjunction operator. In our case, the implication operator $I_T$ is defined by residuation with respect to $T$. Then the conjunction $T$ together with the residuated implication $I_T$ provides the set of truth-values $A_n$ with an structure of an *adjoint couple* [32]. The characteristic property of this kind of structures is the adjointness condition: $I_T(a, b) \geq c$ iff $T(a, c) \leq b$. As a consequence of this property, residuated implications in general, and $I_T$ in particular, enjoy a number of "good" properties like: ones:

- I1: $I_T(a, b) = 1$ if, and only if, $a \leq b$
- I2: $I_T(1, a) = a$
- I3: $I_T(a, I_T(b, c)) = I_T(b, I_T(a, c))$
- I4: if $a \leq b$ then $I_T(a, c) \geq I_T(b, c)$ and $I_T(c, a) \leq I_T(c, b)$
- I5: $I_T(T(a, b), c) = I_T(a, I_T(b, c))$

In particular, I1 is the generalisation of the property in two-valued logic stating that an implication $\varphi \to \psi$ is true iff the truth-value of $\varphi$ is less or equal to the truth-value of $\psi$. Moreover, the above adjointness condition guarantees a *sound* many-valued modus ponens in the following sense: from a lower bound $a$ of the truth degree $\rho(\varphi)$ of $\varphi$ and a lower bound $c$ of the truth degree $I_T(\rho(\varphi), \rho(\psi))$ of $\varphi \to \psi$ we get a lower bound $T(a, c)$ of the truth degree $\rho(\psi)$ of $\psi$.

As it is easy to notice from the above definition, any such truth-value algebras are completely determined as soon as the set of truth-values and the conjunction operator $T$ are determined. So, varying these two characteristics we obtain a parametric family of different many-valued logics. In this way, each module can have a local type of reasoning, potentially different from others. Additionally, in order to allow a flux of information between modules and submodules with different local logics, renaming mappings between sets of truth-values can also be specified inside a **Milord II** module [1].

In classical logic, we distinguish syntactically $A$ from $\neg A$ ($A$ being a formula) because the only two possible truth-value assignments to $A$ are *true* and *false*. Similarly, in our case, we need a syntactical representation for each truth-value assignment to a formula $A$. Moreover, to handle imprecision, intervals of truth-values are attached to formulas instead of single values: the more imprecision there is, the larger the intervals are. Then, the object level language of **Milord II** is such that sentences are pairs of type $(\varphi, V)$ where $\varphi$ is a classical-like sentence and $V$ is an interval of truth-values, possibly empty (represented as []). This representation leads to a classical satisfaction and entailment relations, as will be seen later, rather than having classical sentences but graded satisfaction and entailment relations, as for example in [39]. Another interesting characteristic of the object-level reasoning system is that deduction is based on what we call "Specialisation Inference Rule" (SIR), a more general inference rule than Modus Ponens, introduced in [35] to improve the input/output communication behaviour of the system.

In the sequel, the syntax, the semantics and the deduction system of the object-level logic are described given a particular algebra of truth-values $A_{n,T} = \langle A_n, N_n, T, I_T \rangle$.

**Syntax** [2]. The propositional language $OL_n = \langle A_n, \Sigma_O, C, OS_n \rangle$ of the object-level is defined by:

- A **Set of truth values** $A_n$.
- A **Signature** $\Sigma_O$, composed of a set of atomic symbols plus *true* and *false*.
- A set of **Connectives** $C = \{\neg, \wedge, \rightarrow\}$
- A set of **Sentences** $OS_n$ whose elements are pairs of classical-like propositional sentences and intervals of truth-values. The classical-like propositional sentences are restricted to literals and rules. That is, the sentences of the language (from now on called OL-formulas) are only of the following types:
  - OL-atoms: $(p, V)$ with $p \in \Sigma_O$
  - OL-literals: $(p, V), (\neg p, V)$
  - OL-rules: $(p_1 \wedge p_2 \wedge ... \wedge p_n \rightarrow q, V^*)$[3], being $p_i \neq p_j$, $p_i \neq \neg p_j$, $q \neq p_j$, $q \neq \neg p_j \; \forall i, j$

---

[2] The syntax used in this Object Level Language description is a simplification of the actual **Milord II**syntax.

[3] The corresponding rule in real **Milord II** syntax would be: If $\cdot p_1$ and $p_2$ and $\ldots$ and $p_n$ then conclude $q$ is $V^*$. In Annex A you can find the syntax BNF.

where $p_1, p_2, ..., p_n$ and $q$ are literals (atoms or negations of atoms), $V$ and $V^*$ are intervals of truth-values. Intervals $V^*$ for rules are constrained to be upper intervals, i.e. of the form $[a, 1]$, where $a > 0$. In the sequel, and for the sake of simplicity, we will identify intervals of type $[a, a]$ with the value $a$.

**Semantics.** The semantics of a particular logic is determined by the connective operators of the truth-value algebra $A_{n,T}$. Having truth-values explicit in the sentences enables us to define a classical satisfaction relation in spite of the models being multiple-valued assignments. *Models* are defined by valuations $\rho$ mapping the first components of sentences to the truth-values set $A_n$ fulfilling the following conditions:

$$\rho(true) = 1$$
$$\rho(\neg p) = N_n(\rho(p))$$
$$\rho(p_1 \wedge ... \wedge p_n \rightarrow q) = I_T(T(\rho(p_1), ..., \rho(p_n)), \rho(q))$$

The *Satisfaction Relation* between models and mv-formulas is defined as:

$$\rho \models_O (\varphi, V) \text{ iff } \rho(\varphi) \in V$$

We note $\models_O$ as the satisfaction relation at the 'Object level', to distinguish it from the satisfaction at the 'meta-level' ($\models_M$) that will be introduced later in the chapter.

**Deduction system.** The object-level deduction system is based on the following axioms:

(A-1) $(\varphi, [0, 1])$,
(A-2) $(true, 1)$,

and on the following inference rules:

- (RI-1) **weakening**: from $(\varphi, V_1)$ infer $(\varphi, V_2)$, where $V_1 \subseteq V_2$
- (RI-2) **not-introduction**: from $(p, V)$ infer $(\neg p, N_n^*(V))$
- (RI-3) **not-elimination**: from $(\neg p, V)$ infer $(p, N_n^*(V))$
- (RI-4) **composition**: from $(\varphi, V_1)$ and $(\varphi, V_2)\}$ infer $(\varphi, V_1 \cap V_2)$
- (RI-5) **SIR**: from $(p_i, V_i)$ and $(p_1 \wedge ... \wedge p_n \rightarrow q, V_r)$ infer $(p_1 \wedge ... \wedge p_{i-1} \wedge p_{i+1} \wedge ... \wedge p_n \rightarrow q, MP_T^*(V_i, V_r))$

$N_n^*$ is the point-wise extension of $N_n$ to intervals, $N_n^*([a, b]) = [N_n(b), N_n(a)]$, and $MP_T^*$ is a binary operation on intervals[4] of truth-values defined as follows:

$$MP_T^*([a, b], [c, 1]) = [T(a, c), 1]$$

The intuition behind the modus ponens function $MP_T^*$ is the following one. Given the OL-formulas

$$(p, V)$$
$$(p \rightarrow q, W)$$

---

[4] Notice that the second argument interval is always an upper interval.

a sound many-valued rule of Modus Ponens should derive the many-valued OL-literal:

$$(q, U)$$

where $U$ is the smallest interval such that $\rho(q) \in U$ whenever $\rho(p) \in V$ and $\rho(p \to q) = I_T(\rho(p), \rho(q)) \in W$, for any truth-evaluation $\rho$. In other words, $U$ must be the smallest interval containing $MP_T^*(V, W) = \{z \in A_n \mid \exists x \in V, \exists y \in W$ such that $I_T(x, z) = y\}$. However, since the syntax of **Milord II** requires $W$ to be an upper interval, it can be easily checked that, in this case, $MP_T^*(V, W)$ is an interval and, moreover, it holds that $MP_T^*([a, b], [c, 1]) = [T(a, c), 1]$.

The notion of *proof* is as usual. Let $\Gamma$ and $A$ be a set of sentences and a sentence respectively. We say that $A$ follows from $\Gamma$, written $\Gamma \vdash_O A$, if there is a finite sequence of sentences

$$B_1, ..., B_m = A$$

such that each $B_i$ is either an axiom, a sentence from $\Gamma$, or has been deduced from previous $B_j$ by application of some inference rule.

It is very easy to check that this deductive system is sound and complete with respect to OL-atoms. The proofs of these theorems can be found in [25].

**Theorem 2. (Soundness).** *Let $A \in OS_n$ be a sentence and $\Gamma \subseteq OS_n$ a set of sentences. Then, $\Gamma \vdash_O A$ implies $\Gamma \models_O A$.*

**Theorem 3. (Atom completeness).** *Let $A = (p, V)$ be an OL-atom and $\Gamma \subseteq OS_n$ a set of sentences. Then, $\Gamma \models_O A$ implies $\Gamma \vdash_O A$.*

## 2.3 Object level computational constructs: local logics and fuzzy sets declarations

The formal model presented in the previous subsection has a syntactical counterpart in the **Milord II** language as different object level language constructs. In this subsection we focus on two of such constructs which are of special interest: the declaration of many-valued local logics the management of vague knowledge by means of fuzzy sets.

**Local logics.** Any of the previously described algebras of truth-values is completely determined as soon as the set of truth-values and the conjunction operator are fixed. In **Milord II** these logics can be local to each module. To declare the local logic of a module the user has to write down[5] the set of linguistic terms and the conjunction operation best adapted to the solution of the problem the module represents. For instance,

---

[5] In fact, there is a default local logic in **Milord II** that is assumed by those modules that do not contain a local logic declaration. See Figure 9 and Annex B.

**Truth values** = (false, unlikely, may_be, likely, true)
**Conjunction** = **truth table**

        ((false false false false false)
        (false unlikely unlikely unlikely unlikely)
        (false unlikely may_be may_be may_be)
        (false unlikely may_be likely likely)
        (false unlikely may_be likely true))

The truth table is a matrix over pairs of truth values represented as a list of lists. That is, the value for $i \wedge j$ for $i, j \in Truth\ values$ is to be found at the intersection of the $i$th row and $j$th column. The order in the matrix respects the order established in the **Truth values** definition.

Different modules can have different local logics. We allow this because a very important part of any problem solving method is the way the programmer will deal with the uncertainty of the problem. And this may be particular to each subproblem: a richer set of linguistic terms can help in giving more precise answers to queries; different connectives represent different rule interpretations, and hence different deductive behaviours.

The main problem that has to be addressed in a system with local logics is how modules communicate and which are the properties that are to be preserved in that communication; that is, how a module has to interpret the answer to a query made to a submodule with a different logic. The practical aspect of it is that any language providing such local logic facilities has to permit a way of defining the relation between the values of different logics. In the case of **Milord II** we do so by the declaration, in the local logic of a module, of a renaming function that maps the linguistic terms of the local logics of submodules into intervals of the linguistic terms of the module. For instance, assume that a submodule $B$ of a module containing the previous pieces of code has the next set of linguistic terms: *impossible*, *may_be*, and *sure*. The translation of these terms into the previous ones could be done by means of the next sentence:

**Renaming**    B/impossible  ==> false
                 B/may_be     ==> [unlikely, likely]
                 B/sure        ==> true

**Milord II** checks whether the proposed translation between modules satisfies the requirements expressed in [1]. Notice that the translation can be made over intervals of linguistic terms as the previous example shows. If the local logics are the same, the identity renaming function is assumed by default and no renaming declaration is necessary. The interested reader on qualitative local uncertainty models can refer to [31].

**Fuzzy sets.** The simplest representation units are propositions and variables. There are three types of propositions, *boolean*, *many-valued* and *fuzzy*; and three types of variables, *numeric*, *set* and *linguistic*.

Numerical variables can get numerical values. Many-valued propositions roughly correspond to the atomic propositions presented in the previous subsection. Notice however that a comparison of a numerical variable with a particular value by using a comparison predicate is by no means different to an atomic proposition.

Fuzziness of concepts such as *big body size* is interpreted by the degree of membership of a numerical measure (in this case the *axis length* —the measure of the largest axis of the sponge[6]) to the fuzzy set associated to a fuzzy proposition like *big_body_size*. The syntax of the declaration of a fuzzy proposition (for instance, see *big_body_size* in Figure 4) contains the four points of a trapezoidal fuzzy set.

big_body_size =   **Type: fuzzy (10,15,25,30)**
                  **Relation: needs_quantitative body_measure**

The values of a fuzzy proposition is still an interval of truth values. The computation of the interval is done by the application of the fuzzy membership function to the value of the numerical variable which name must appear in the relation slot *needs_quantitative*. As long as the number of truth values is finite, the fuzzy membership of a numerical value is approximated by the minimum interval containing it, considering a uniform distribution of the truth values along the unit interval —that is, the range of the fuzzy set membership function.

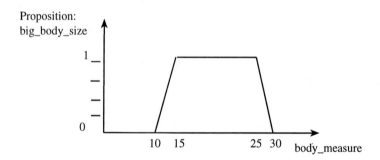

**Fig. 4.** *Big body size* concept representation.

Similarly, we can declare a linguistic variable (a variable receiving values from a finite user-defined set) giving for every element of its type a trapezoidal fuzzy set with respect to a numeric variable.

We can build fuzzy expressions in a similar way as numerical expressions[7]. We decided to use the same predicate names (v.g. "+", or "*") to build fuzzy

---

[6] Given the vast array of forms in which sponges have evolved we consider that the largest axis of the sponge body (horizontal or vertical) may be a suitable numerical reference of its body size.

[7] A numerical expression is composed by numbers, numerical variables and arithmetic operations (+,-,*,:). The evaluation of an expression of this type returns a number

expressions. So we have to consider them as overloaded predicate names (see Table 1).

| Relations | | Operations | |
|---|---|---|---|
| syntax | meaning | syntax | meaning |
| a < b | $A \subset B$ | a + b | $A \cup B$ |
| a > b | $A \supset B$ | $a * b$ | $A \cap B$ |
| a = b | $A = B$ | | |
| a /= b | $A \neq B$ | | |
| a int b | $A \cap B \neq \emptyset$ | | |

**Table 1.** Fuzzy relations and operations.

The operations "+" and "*" are interpreted as the fuzzy set union $\cup$ and the fuzzy set intersection $\cap$ respectively, defined as usual by: *Union:* $\forall \omega, \mu_{F \cup G}(\omega) = max(\mu_F(\omega), \mu_G(\omega))$
*Intersection:* $\forall \omega, \mu_{F \cap G}(\omega) = min(\mu_F(\omega), \mu_G(\omega))$

The allowed fuzzy relations are < (subset), > (superset), = (equal), /= (different) and **int** (intersection degree). The binary predicates apply over the evaluations of two expressions of the same type. The evaluation of these predicates is, as before, an interval of truth-values.

Now we define the inclusion, intersection and equality between two fuzzy sets and their meaning. *Inclusion degree:* $R_C(F, G) = min_\omega(\mu_{\bar{F} \cup G})$
*Intersection degree:* $R_\cap(F, G) = max_\omega(\mu_{F \cap G}(\omega))$
*Equality degree:* $R_=(F, G) = min(R_C(F, G), \cap R_C(F, G))$

These relations[8] return degrees of standard inclusion, intersection and equality respectively between two fuzzy sets.

**Linguistic Variables.** Linguistic Variables get values from a user-defined finite set of linguistic values (fuzzy sets).

Similarly to the case of fuzzy propositions we can declare a linguistic variable by giving, for every linguistic value, a trapezoidal fuzzy set with respect to a numerical variable.

For instance, in Figure 5 we can see the representation of the concept *body size* as a linguistic variable by means of four fuzzy sets *small, medium, big* and *very big*. A declaration of this new interpretation of the *body size* concept could be the following one:

body_size = **Type:**        (s "small" (0, 0, 1, 5),

---

over which we can apply predicates like < (less), > (greater), <= (less or equal), >= (greater or equal), = (equal), and / = (different).
[8] Notice that $R_C(F, G)$ and $R_\cap(F, G)$ definitions correspond respectively to the usual notions of necessity and possibility of $G$ with respect to $F$ [42].

m "medium" (1,5, 10, 15),
b "big" (10, 15, 25, 30),
vb "very big" (25, 30, 2000, 2000))
**Relation: needs_quantitative body_measure**

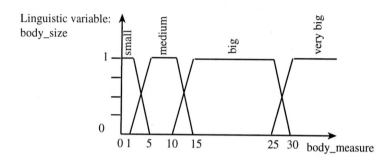

**Fig. 5.** Fuzzy values of the linguistic variable body size.

Notice that, as in the case of fuzzy propositions, it is necessary to declare the same relation *needs_quantitative* with a numeric variable, in this case again *body measure*. The optional string in the elements of the type (e.g. "small") is used only for informational purposes.

Linguistic variables, together with linguistic values, are used to build predicates of the form "*linguistic_variable* is *linguistic_value*". For instance:

R004 If body_size is big then conclude ...

Given a numerical value $s$ for the variable *body_measure*, the predicate "body_size is big" returns the value of

$$\mu_{big}^{body\_size}(s).$$

It is also possible to define more complex linguistic predicates of the form "*linguistic_variable* is ( *value_1* or *value_2* or ...)". For instance:

R004 If  body_size is (medium or big) then conclude ...

Now, given a value $s$, the predicate "body_size is (medium or big)" returns the value of:

$$max(\mu_{medium}^{body\_size}(s), \mu_{big}^{body\_size}(s)).$$

## 2.4  Belief modelling

In principle, many-valued logics are not suitable for belief or uncertainty modelling because of truth-functionality. It is well known that belief degrees cannot be fully truth-functional; for instance, there is no operation $\otimes$ in $[0, 1]$ such that

$probability(p \wedge q) = probability(p) \otimes probability(q)$, for any crisp propositions $p, q$ of a given propositional language. Nevertheless, nothing prevents graded truth from being functional with respect to connectives.

However, as proposed in [22], there is one way to properly deal with belief degrees as truth degrees: for each crisp proposition $\varphi$, consider a new proposition $Belief(\varphi)$ which is read as "$\varphi$ is believable". Then, $Belief(\varphi)$ is a typical fuzzy (many-valued) proposition and it clearly admits intermediary truth degrees: the higher is the belief on $\varphi$, the truer is the proposition "$\varphi$ is believable". For instance, we may postulate that

$$\text{truth degree of } "Belief(\varphi)" = \text{belief degree of } "\varphi".$$

But of course then, we have to be careful to distinguish, for instance, between "$Belief(\varphi \wedge \psi)$" and "$Belief(\varphi) \wedge Belief(\psi)$", which are clearly different things. The problem of the lack of truth-functionality is still there, but now we can use our many-valued logics as a kind of meta-logic to reason about beliefs if we let some of the propositional variables be of the form $Belief(\varphi)$, being $\varphi$ itself a possibly complex proposition. In such a case, the meaning of a (many-valued) rule like

$$(Belief(\varphi_1) \wedge Belief(\varphi_2) \rightarrow Belief(\psi), [a, 1])$$

has to be understood as saying nothing but

$$\text{belief-degree}("\psi") \geq T(a, T(\text{belief-degree}("\varphi_1"), \text{belief-degree}("\varphi_2"))).$$

In particular, when $\varphi_1$ and $\varphi_2$ are true, then the rule states that the belief degree in $\psi$ will be not smaller than $a$.

Finally let us comment some *implementation issues* of this belief handling in **Milord II**:

**Syntax.** In order to avoid the problems of the non truth-functionality of belief degrees, propositions of the form $Belief(\varphi)$, where $\varphi$ is a compound proposition, are not allowed, the only allowed "belief" propositions being of the form

$$Belief(p), Belief(\neg p)$$

where $p$ is an atom. Moreover, it is also assumed that truth evaluations of belief propositions only commute with the negation connective, that is,

$$\rho(Belief(\neg p)) = N_n(\rho(Belief(p))).$$

In a module specification, propositions whose belief can be a matter of degree are declared to be of *many-valued* type. In order to simplify notation on writing rules, many-valued propositions of type $Belief(p)$ or $Belief(\neg p)$ are written simply as $p$ and $\neg p$ since there is no possible ambiguity.

**Relationship between truth and belief scales.** In adopting the above relationship between truth degrees and belief degrees we are implicitly assuming that both scales are commensurate. This makes no problem when the common scale is the unit interval $[0, 1]$. However, in **Milord II**, truth scales are linearly ordered finite sets of linguistic terms. Even from a linguistic point of view, linguistic terms describing belief degrees cannot be the same than those describing truth degrees. This is an example of belief and truth scales with five terms:

| **truth** of "$Belief(\varphi)$" | **belief** of "$\varphi$" |
|---|---|
| *false* | *impossible* |
| *slightly true* | *quite possible* |
| *quite true* | *likely* |
| *fairly true* | *very possible* |
| *true* | *certain* |

For the sake of simplicity, in the local logic declaration, the user is only required to define a single scale in each module, either a qualitative truth or belief scale, and the corresponding one-to-one order preserving mapping between them is assumed.

## 2.5 Meta-level component

The **meta-level language** is a restricted classical first order language $ML = \langle \Sigma_M, C, MS \rangle$ defined by:

1. A **Signature** $\Sigma_M = \langle \Sigma_{rel}, \Sigma_{fun}, \Sigma_{con}, \Sigma_{var} \rangle$, where:
   - $\Sigma_{rel}$ = A set of predicate symbols plus $K$ and $WK$ (which play a special role in the reflection mechanism).
   - $\Sigma_{fun}$ = A set of classical arithmetic function symbols.
   - $\Sigma_{con}$ = A set of constants including the truth-values and object propositional symbols.
   - $\Sigma_{var}$ = A set of variable symbols; it can be empty.
2. The same set of **connectives** $C$ as in the object language.
3. A set of **sentences** $MS = MLL_G \cup MR$ where:
   - $MLL_G$ is the set of ground literals, in a classical sense, from $\Sigma_M$.
   - $MR$ is the set $\{P_1 \wedge P_2 \wedge \ldots \wedge P_n \to Q \mid P_i \text{ and } Q \text{ are literals from } \Sigma_M\}$ of meta-rules, where each variable occurring in $Q$ must occur also in some $P_i$. Variables in meta-rules, if any, are considered universally quantified. Quantifiers are all outermost.

The **semantics** of the language is a first order classical one. The meaning of the special predicates $K$ and $WK$ will be explained in the next subsection along with the definition of the reification correspondence. This correspondence gives sense to these predicates as a means to represent object-level sentences.

The **deduction** system is based on only one inference rule:

$$\text{from } \{P_1 \wedge P_2 \wedge \ldots \wedge P_n \to Q, P_1', P_2', \ldots, P_n'\} \text{ infer } Q'$$

where $P_1', \ldots, P_n'$ are ground instances of $P_1, \ldots, P_n$ respectively, such that there exists a unifier $\sigma$ for $\{P_1 \wedge P_2 \wedge \ldots \wedge P_n, P_1' \wedge P_2' \wedge \ldots \wedge P_n'\}$, and $Q' = Q\sigma$ is the ground instance of $Q$ resulting from $\sigma$. The deductive system of the meta-level of **Milord II** is then not complete with respect to the classical semantics we use for it. Nevertheless, the deduction mechanism based on this single inference rule is enough for our purposes of modelling the application of meta-rules. Meta-level Deduction will be denoted by the symbol $\vdash_M$.

## 2.6 Dynamics of the reasoning process

A complex KB in **Milord II** consists of a hierarchy of modules. Each module contains an Object-level Theory[9] (OLT) and a Meta-Level Theory (MLT). The goal of a module is to compute the most precise truth intervals for the propositions contained in its export interface. Then, a module execution consists of the reasoning process[10] necessary to compute the truth intervals for some of the propositions in the export interface: those the user is interested in.

The execution of a module can activate the execution of its submodules in the hierarchy. These executions only interact with the parent module through the export interface of the submodules, giving formulas back as result. So, submodule execution extends the OLTs of modules by adding the formulas returned by the submodules. The interaction is made only at the object-level.

**Reification.** The reification correspondence relates a subtheory of the OLT with the set of ground literals of the meta-language $MLL_G$. This is done by means of a set of bridge rules[11] and two meta-predicates $K$ and $WK$. To describe the meaning of these predicates and their corresponding bridge rules we first need to introduce the following notion.

**Definition 4.** Given an OLT, we define the *minimal literal theory $OLT^*$* as:
$OLT^* = \{(p, W) \mid p$ is literal, $W = \bigcap\{V_i \mid (p, V_i) \in OLT\}\}$[12].

So, intuitively, at any moment of the execution the minimal literal theory contains the more specific knowledge available for each literal at the object level. Given that the constant names used in the MLT are exactly the same as those used in the OLT as proposition names, the renaming operation is omitted in the following descriptions:

- **Meta-predicate K**: if $K(p, V)$ belongs to MLT it means that $V$ is the minimal interval such that the proposition $(p, V)$ belongs to the OLT. There is a closed world assumption on this predicate. The corresponding bridge rules are:

$$\frac{(p, V) \in OLT^*}{\vdash_M K(p, V)} \ , \ \frac{(p, V) \notin OLT^*}{\vdash_M \neg K(p, V)}$$

- **Meta-predicate WK**: if $WK(p, V)$ belongs to MLT means that $(p, V)$ is deducible in the $OLT$ by using the weakening inference rule. $\neg WK(p, V)$

---

[9] Theories are considered not closed under deduction. Hence, they are closer to the concept of *presentation* [36].

[10] Besides pure logical reasoning, execution of modules actually involve some control mechanisms (implicit and explicit) that are out of the scope of this chapter. The interested reader can consult [33,34].

[11] We use the term "bridge rule" according to [19].

[12] Recall that the object level does not contain variables, hence all $p$ are ground literals.

means that $OLT \vdash_O (p, V')$ with $V' \supset V$. The corresponding bridge rules are:

$$\frac{(p, V) \in OLT^* \text{ and } V \subseteq V^*}{\vdash_M WK(p, V^*)} \ , \ \frac{(p, V) \in OLT^* \text{ and } V \supset V^*}{\vdash_M \neg WK(p, V^*)}$$

**Reflection.** The reflection process maps meta-level $K$ predicate instances into object-level literals. The reflection rule that relates MLT with OLT is defined as:

$$\frac{\vdash_M K(p, V)}{\vdash_O (p, V)}$$

**Dynamics.** The reasoning process will be described in terms of extensions of the Object-level Theories and Meta-Level Theories. The initial OLT of a module consists of its set of rules, i. e. a partial KB. It is the same for the MLT, which initially consists of the set of meta-rules. **Milord II** provides the programmer with the possibility of specifying two types of evaluation for each module. The types of evaluation are *eager* and *lazy*. Their main difference being how they compute the import interface of the module, eager modules have a more greedy behaviour in getting values for the propositions and variables in the import interface than lazy ones (for a complete description refer to [33]). The reasoning dynamics follows the scheme outlined below:

**STEP 1:** The user selects a module $M$ to begin the system execution. The initial $M$'s OLT is the set of rules of the module, the current $M$'s MLT is the set of meta-rules plus the instances of meta-predicates $K$ and $WK$.

**STEP $2^{lazy}$:** The reasoning process starts at the object-level with the current OLT. If no *elementary extension* is produced then STOP, otherwise the reasoning process control is passed to the meta-level (STEP 3). By elementary extension we mean an extension of the OLT by adding a literal and closing by the weakening inference rule. This can be done either by inference on the OLT, or by importing a piece of data either from the user (as specified in the import interface), of the OLT from a submodule OLT or from the current MLT.

**STEP $2^{eager}$:** The reasoning process starts at the object level with the current OLT, and goes on until no more elementary extensions of the OLT can be obtained. If no elementary extension of the OLT has been produced then STOP, otherwise the reasoning process control is passed to the meta-level (STEP 3)

**STEP 3:** When the meta-level gets the control it builds the current MLT as the previous MLT plus the axioms coming from the reification of the current OLT. Then the meta-level reasoning process is activated. If no *extension*[13]

---

[13] By extension of the MLT we mean the extension of the current MLT by the set of ground literals resulting from the application of a single meta-rule over all the possible instantiations of its premise.

of the MLT can be obtained, the control is passed back to the object-level without extending the current OLT, i.e. the reflection does not modify the current OLT. On the other hand when an inference can be performed, and thus a meta-level extension is made, the control is passed to the object-level extending the current OLT by adding the reflection of the computed extension of the MLT[14]. In any case the control goes to STEP 2.

This dynamic process goes on till no possible extension of the OLT can be made.

## 2.7 Modularity

The most primitive structural construct of **Milord II** is the module. A program is composed by a set of module declarations that can recursively contain other module declarations, thus forming a hierarchy. Module declarations are surrounded by the keywords **begin** and **end**. Between these two keywords all the components of the module, including submodules, must be defined; nothing belonging to a module can be defined outside these two keywords. Module declarations can be given a name, that becomes its identifier, see **Homosclerophorida** in Figure 13. The scope of these identifiers is lexical. Then, to refer to a submodule component (proposition, variable, rule, ...) we must prefix the identifier of the component by the path of the identifiers of those modules placed syntactically between the point of reference and the point of definition. Components in a path are separated by "/". Top level modules are not prefixed.

Local names can be given to previously defined modules by allowing a reference to their name in the right part of a module name binding, see **structures** in Figure 13.

The contents of a module declaration can be clustered in the next sets of declarations: hierarchy, interface, deductive knowledge and control knowledge.

**Hierarchy:** It consists of a set of module declarations. We say that these modules are submodules of the module that contains them.

**Interface:** It has two components, the import and the export interface. They declare which variables and propositions could be asked to the user[15] (import) and those that can be results of the module (export). All variables and propositions inside a module not declared in the export interface are hidden from outside the module.

**Deductive and Control Knowledge:** These declarations allow modules to compute the components of its export interface (output) from the components of its import interface and those of the export interfaces of its submodules (input). Deductive knowledge includes the sentences of the object level

---

[14] In fact, the object-level will pass again the control to the meta-level as the reflected formulas represent an extension of the OLT as the condition of STEP 2 determines. This is an implicit iteration construct provided in **Milord II**

[15] In some cases the control of the module can give a value to an imported variable or proposition before asking it to the user (see [33]).

language. Control knowledge contains the sentences of the meta-language. A module with an empty deductive and control components is considered to be a pure interface (a signature).

A Knowledge Base consists then of a set of modules, each module containing submodules, and submodules containing subsubmodules and so on ..., and thus defining a hierarchy of modules. There are two types of modules: *plain* modules (as `Homosclerophorida`) and *generic* modules (as `Find_Skel_Chemistry (X)`). Generic modules are a type of high-order programming. They can be considered as functions between plain modules. That is, given one, or more, modules as arguments, a generic module computes a plain module as result. Some details of generic modules and of the operations between modules are given next.

**Generic Modules.** When a plain module contains a set of submodules, one way of looking at what the module performs is by seeing it as a combination of the results of the different submodules. The definition of generic modules opens to the user the possibility of defining specific, and reusable, operations of composition of modules. A generic module is indeed an abstraction of a combination by means of giving names to the submodules that will be obtained only at application time. Generic modules are then operations (or functions) on modules. The technique to define generic modules is the same as to define functions, that is, it consists of the isolation of a piece of program —or module— from its context by specifying:

1. Those modules upon which the abstracted module may depend (requirements or parameters of the generic module).
2. The contribution of the abstracted module to the rest of the program (results or export interface of the generic module).

A method for building large KB systems consists of applying generic modules to previously built plain modules. Keeping the common parts in a generic module we can save code and time, and make the code much more understandable. The application of a generic module over a set of arguments generates a plain module, and hence the application can appear in the code in the same places of a module declaration.

Consider the following example of chemical composition analysis of samples to determine the general type of skeleton in a sponge. With a simple test on a sample we can find, for instance, `silica` content. The chemistry of the skeleton can be analysed over different samples from different parts of the sponge body (surface, deep inside) to take into account all the possible locations of spicules.

We may deduce that the skeleton has an inorganic content (`siliceous` or `calcareous`) or exclusively an organic content (`collagenous`). We deduce that a sponge has siliceous spicules if in any of the studied samples a siliceous content appears. We deduce that a sponge has calcareous spicules if in any of the studied samples a calcareous content appears. We deduce that a sponge has only collagenous content if none of the studied samples presents a siliceous or calcareous content. There is a special case in which we can find both siliceous and calcareous content.

To encode this knowledge it is not necessary to define a different problem solution for each type of sample analysis; it would be enough to define a generic problem solution depending on the kind of sample.

**Module** Find_Skel_Chemistry (X) =
**Begin**
      **Export** siliceous, calcareous, collagenous
      **Deductive knowledge**
          **Dictionary**: ...
          **Rules:**   R001 **If** X/silica **then conclude** siliceous **is** sure
             ...
      **End deductive**
**End**

The parameters of a generic module are, as we said before, abstracted sub-modules. These parameter names are unbound until the instantiation of the generic module. If we want to refer to the exported variables or propositions of the submodules that will be bound at application time we must build a path using the names of the parameters (for instance, in the rule of module `Find_Skel_Chemistry` a reference to the proposition `silica` of a module eventually bounded is written `X/silica`). An example of the instantiation of the generic module seen above with data from a surface sample is the following:

**Module** Find_Skel_Chemistry_Surface = Find_Skel_Chemistry(Surface)

**Operations between Modules.** Incremental programming consists in writing a first (rough) prototype, testing it, then writing a second as a modification (refinement) of the first, and continuing until a final version is achieved. In classical programming languages the way of doing it is by changing the code of the program whenever a non-desired behaviour is observed or a more specific performance is required. However, to do this, the complete code has to be ready and at hand before performing any testing. A step forward in helping programmers in **Milord II** is by requiring: 1) that the partial specifications of modules, i.e. incompletely defined modules, must be executable to test them, and 2) a set of operations between modules for overseeing this process of incremental building of programs.

In **Milord II** modular syntax many components of modules are optional, although any module declaration is executable. For instance, if we execute a module which contains only an export interface, it will answer to all the questions about the value of exported variables or propositions with the constant *unknown*. Later on we can fill in the module with code details by *refining* it.

When we program a new version of a previous program we are interested in checking and declaring what the relation with the old version is. In **Milord II** this relation is defined between modules and can be either a refinement, a contraction or an expansion. Roughly speaking, we say that a module is a refinement of another one when the set of accessible[16] variables and propositions is the same as that of the previous one but the code is a particularisation. When we expand a module, the accessible variables and propositions in the next version will be extended, and reduced when we constrain it. The symbols ":", ">" and "<" stand respectively for the module refinement, expansion and contraction operations. They can be used in all module declarations including the parameter declaration of generic modules.

All these modular operations are based on three basic functions: enrichment verification, inheritance and information hiding.

**Enrichment Verification:** We say that the module M_1 is an *enrichment* of the module M_2, if and only if:
  1. The export interface of M_2 is a subset of the export interface of M_1.
  2. The submodule names of M_2 are a subset of the submodule names in M_1. If a submodule name is bound both in M_2 and M_1, the modules to which it is bound, let's say M_21 and M_11, must be such that either M_11 is an empty body, or otherwise M_11 must be an enrichment of M_21.
  3. Either the local logic declaration must be the same; or it is empty in M_2. That means that the module M_1 can extend the export interface and the submodules of M_2. When a submodule is declared in both modules M_1 and M_2, they must preserve the enrichment relation.

**Inheritance:** When we program a new version of a module we usually want to maintain several of its components. To avoid the programmer to write the components to be preserved twice, an inheritance mechanism is provided in **Milord II**. The components of a module that can be inherited are: submodules, variable and proposition definitions and local logics.

If M_1 inherits from M_2, then the module M_1 will inherit the bodies of the submodules of M_2 that are not present in the declaration of M_1. The inheritance operation makes a copy of the non redefined elements of the dictionaries as well. In the case of the local logic, M_1 inherits the logic of module M_2.

**Information Hiding:** If M_2 hides M_1 all the exported variables and propositions of M_1 not present in the export interface of M_2 are hidden[17]. Similarly, all the submodules of M_1 not visible in the hierarchy of M_2 are hidden.

Next, we explain the most important operation which makes use of these three basic functions in its definition: the refinement of modules. The other two operations are slight modifications of this refinement operation.

**Refinement.** Modules are the computational counterpart of the abstract units, usually called tasks, in which a programmer decompose a complex problem solving task [13]. These abstract units are characterised basically by the goal (query)

---

[16] Remember that the accessible variables and propositions of a module are those belonging to its export interface and those of the export interfaces of its submodules.

[17] Hiding a variable or a proposition means that no one, user or module, will be allowed to access its value.

they have to achieve. Hence, when designing a module the first decision is which is the goal, or the set of goals, that this module will solve. In **Milord II** these goals are represented by the set of accessible variables and propositions of that module. Then, when designing a particularisation of the module, that is, when filling the module with contents, we must keep the same set of goals, as far as the new module is still an implementation of the task that is being solved. The refinement operation has to guarantee that the new generated module fulfils this [21].

Consider the following example declaration that completes the example in the previous section:

**Module** Sample = **Begin Export** silica,calcium_carbonate, organic **End**

**Module** Surface : Sample =
**Begin**
    **Import** Surface_chem
    **Export** silica, calcium_carbonate, organic
    **Deductive knowledge**
        Dictionary: ...
        Rules:
            R001    **If**   Surface_chem = (SIL) **then conclude** silica **is** sure
          ...
    **End deductive**
**End**

The module `Sample` only contains an export interface. The second expression declares that the module `Surface` is a refinement of the module `Sample`.

This is the idea of incremental programming; all the modules that are refinements of the module `Sample` have the same export interface with, possibly, differences in other components that allows the module to obtain better, or different, results for the exported variables and propositions than the module `Sample`.

The refinement operation is specially useful when we declare generic modules. Remember that the instantiation of a generic module implies binding parameter names to submodules. The resultant module should use the exported variables and propositions of the bound submodules. It is obvious that not all the modules can be used to instantiate a generic module, because the code of the generic module will depend upon particular exported variables and propositions of those submodules.

For instance, we could modify the previous declaration of the generic module `Find_Skel_Chemistry` by changing the parameters' declaration:

**Module** Find_Skel_Chemistry (X : Sample) =
**Begin**
    **Export** siliceous, calcareous, collagenous
    **Deductive knowledge**
        Dictionary: ...
        Rules:   R001 **If** X/silica **then conclude** siliceous **is** sure

...
**End deductive**
**End**

This kind of declaration makes sure that the modules used to instantiate the generic module `Find_Skel_Chemistry` are only those which are refinements of the module `Sample`, that is, that have exactly its same export interface (in particular, we can assure that any argument module will export the proposition `silica`).

So, usually, any generic module will have parameters that are a refinement of a very simple module containing just an interface. More complex requirements on the arguments can be imposed by adding to the contents of the module of which they have to be a refinement.

A refinement operation is the result of the combined action of the functions presented above: enrichment, inheritance and hiding. The other two relations between modules are slight variations of refinement.

**Expansion and Contraction.** The expansion operation makes possible to build a module as an extension of a previous version of it either by extending the set propositions or variables in the import declaration of the module or by adding submodules. As it was the case in the refinement operation, when expanding a module we test that the new module is an enrichment of the previous one. Inheritance of components is performed as in the refinement operation, but information hiding is not applied.

In the following example, we force the argument (X) of the generic module `Generic` to have in its export interface *at least* the predicates in the export interface of module `Type`.

**Module** Generic (X > Type) = **Begin** ... **End**

So, the generic module will be applicable over a wider range of modules than if its argument was defined as a refinement of `Type`.

The contraction operation, e.g. `Module M = M_1 < M_2`, checks whether `M_2:M_1` holds. It is not necessary to apply information hiding because the module `M_1` exports at most the same variables and propositions as `M_2`. Inheritance of components is performed as in the refinement operation.

## 3    SPONGIA

### 3.1    Introduction

SPONGIA [14] is a KBS designed to emulate the identification skills exhibited by systematists in the Porifera field. It helps in the identification of marine sponges in the Atlanto-Mediterranean biogeographical province. It covers the identification of more than 100 taxa of different taxonomic ranks from class to species. In particular, SPONGIA is able to identify the orders and families of the class Demospongiae and the specimens of the family Geodiidae of the order Astrophorida to the species level. It was developed as a result of 3 years of periodic interaction with an expert in sponge systematics.

Validation of SPONGIA was performed by using data from 82 literature descriptions of sponge species, randomly selected. The data asked by SPONGIA to identify each case was obtained (if available) from the bibliographical description. The set of cases, in which each case was described by the data queried by SPONGIA, was presented to 5 independent experts internationally recognised in the field of sponge systematics. The identifications given by SPONGIA were compared with the identifications of these experts by means of a cluster analysis. The results of the cluster analyses show that SPONGIA is always close to anyone of the human experts. In particular, SPONGIA forms a cluster with two of the best considered experts in all of the dendrograms and it never remains isolate in any of the dendrograms. These results indicate that SPONGIA provides identifications of sponge samples with a reliability similar to the identifications given by the human experts in the field.

The knowledge base of SPONGIA constitutes a model of the *taxonomic* knowledge related to the phylum Porifera. Taxonomic knowledge concerns two separate knowledge models. The *structural model* focuses on knowledge related to the structure of the individual's body. The *classificatory model* focuses on knowledge related to classification of sponges. This involves both a domain model of the sponges classificatory tree and the classificatory problem solving methods. In the domain model we refer to characters which are introduced in the structural model to establish some kind of correspondence between features and ownership to a taxon.

The expert's reasoning strategies, namely their problem solving methods, seem to combine two general procedures: *elimination* and *matching*. Elimination consists in successively observe a new character in the unknown specimen and eliminate the taxa that does not present such character value. Matching is performed by comparison of the specimen with the standard descriptions of the taxa.

**Milord II** has provided the necessary requirements to tackle the Porifera's problem. That is, high expressivity to model the character variability, uncertainty handling mechanisms to represent imprecise and uncertain knowledge, reflective interaction between meta-level and object-level to implement the combination of the expert's problem solving methods, and, last but not least, modularity to allow an incremental development while preserving the integrity of each piece of knowledge. Moreover, the strict compartmentation of knowledge in modules allows for the implementation of modules containing reusable knowledge (i.e. problem solving methods).

## 3.2 Modular structure

SPONGIA consists of a hierarchy of modules. Each module is specialised to perform a given task, either the representation of a piece of classificatory theory or the definition of procedures to emulate the reasoning strategies of experts.

116

In the following, we detail the contents and structure of these modules in the structural model and classificatory model, respectively.

**Structural model.** Knowledge concerning the structural model, that is, the characteristics of the individuals to be identified, are represented using plain modules. The groups of characters are contained in different modules and sub-modules (e.g. external, ecology, anatomy, skeleton,...) hierarchically interconnected starting with Module **Structures** from top. That is,

**Module** Structures =
**Begin**
    **Inherit** Ext
    **Inherit** Eco
    **Inherit** Skel
    **Inherit** Ana
    **Inherit** Metrics
**End**

Each of a module's computational components is assigned a concept in the context of the taxonomic model. In Figure 6, we show a schema of a plain module, either from the structural or from the classificatory model, with the concepts assigned respectively. On the right, we show the concepts of the structural model assigned to the module's computational components. On the left, the concepts of the classificatory model assigned to the module's components are shown.

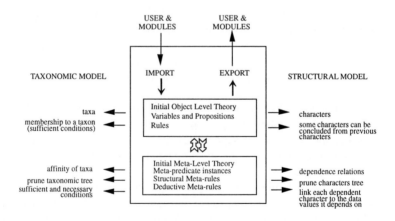

**Fig. 6.** Concepts assigned to the components of a module.

As shown in Figure 6, variables and propositions correspond to characters in a module of the structural model. Examples of different types of variables and propositions, taken from the structural model of SPONGIA, are shown in Figure 7.

| Name identifier | Type | Values | Question |
|---|---|---|---|
| grow:<br>Growth upon the substrate | Set | encrusting, massive, erect, repent | How is the sponge growing upon the substrate? |
| cribe:<br>Presence of cribes | Boolean | yes, no. | Is the surface of the sponge covered by cribes (circular perforated areas of some mm of diameter)? |
| numb:<br>Uni-, pauci- or multispicular tracts | Numeric | real number | How many spicules are there in the vertical tracts, alongside one another? |
| hierar:<br>Hierarchical reticulate spongin skeleton | Many_valued | sure, very possible, quite possible, possible, moderately possible, slightly possible, hardly possible, impossible | Do you observe a visible difference between two kinds of fibre? (primary=vertical and secondary = horizontal) |

**Fig. 7.** Examples of several variables and propositions of SPONGIA.

**Classificatory model.** Taking advantage of modularity we can decompose the Porifera classificatory model into its natural components, namely taxa. The modules of the classificatory model are interconnected via submodule declaration following the schema of the taxonomic tree. Figure 8 shows the modular structure of the SPONGIA's classificatory model. Each box stands for a module, and each module contains the taxonomic knowledge concerning a taxon, e.g. the knowledge concerning the class Demospongiae within the Module **Demos**, the knowledge concerning the order Astrophorida within the Module **Astro**, and so on. This constitutes a hierarchy of modules and submodules standing for taxa and subtaxa.

Representing a taxon within a module helps in designing the knowledge base in the beginning of the development. Afterwards, modules may be progressively filled with contents as soon as knowledge is available. In this way SPONGIA reaches different levels of the taxonomic tree depending on what has been developed yet. That is, SPONGIA identifies the sample until the level of species in a part of the taxonomic tree (e.g. *Geodia nodastrella* in Module **Geodia** or *Isops pachydermata* in Module **Isops**) but it remains at the level of family (e.g. family *Suberitidae* in Module **Hadro**) or genus in other branches that have not been filled with knowledge to the leaves yet.

On the other hand, the modular structure facilitates the cooperation of different experts in the same KBS. This is specially meaningful in domains, like sponges, where knowledge is scattered. Therefore, knowledge from different experts may expand the branches.

The modules of the classificatory model are interconnected through a refinement relation with a module named **Classification_task**. As shown in Figure 9, Module **Classification_task** defines the specific conditions that we impose

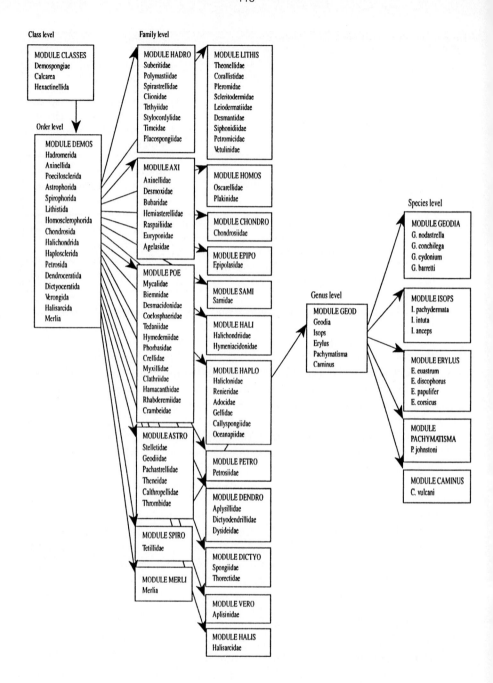

**Fig. 8.** Modular structure standing for the classificatory model in SPONGIA.

to the classification task. In this module we declare a submodule **Structures** which is the top module of the structural model, and a set variable **Taxon** to be given a value after the system consultation. We also define a local logic i.e. truth-values and connectives that will be applied to any refined version of this module.

```
Module Classification_task =
Begin
      Module Structures
      Export Taxon
      Deductive Knowledge
          Dictionary:
                Types:taxon_type
                Predicates: Taxon = Name: "Taxon" Type: taxon_type
          Inference System:
                Truth-values = (i, harp, slip, modp, p, qp, vp, s)
                Connectives: Conjunction: Truth table
                    ((i, i, i, i, i, i, i, i)
                    (i, harp, harp, harp, harp, harp, harp, harp )
                    (i, harp, harp, slip, slip, slip, slip, slip )
                    (i, harp, slip, modp, modp, modp, modp, modp)
                    (i, harp, slip, modp, modp, modp, p, p )
                    (i, harp, slip, modp, modp, p, qp, qp )
                    (i, harp, slip, modp, p, qp, vp, vp )
                    (i, harp, slip, modp, p, qp, vp, s ) )
      End Deductive
End
```

**Fig. 9.** Local logic definition.

Uncertainty (see Section 2.3) is expressed with linguistic labels (truth-values) ranging from true (or sure) to false (or impossible) (e.g. impossible (i), hardly possible (harp), slightly possible (slip), moderately possible (modp), possible (p), quite possible (qp), very possible (vp), sure (s)). They correspond to the verbal scale that a human expert may use to weight his statements.

To decide the granularity and the terms of this list we considered the opinion of several independent experts in the field. For practical reasons, we have chosen the default truth-values provided by **Milord II**. However, since most experts considered that the use of low certainties was very sporadic (e.g. hardly possible, slightly possible, moderately possible) we fixed the truth- threshold in all modules to the value **moderately possible**. In this way, the expert involved in the development of the rule base only used the truth-values over the truth-threshold because rules with lower certainty would not be fired. In consequence, the set of truth-values that SPONGIA used in the conclusions presented to the user was reduced (in practice) to six linguistic labels (i.e. impossible (i), moderately possible (modp), possible (p), quite possible (qp), very possible (vp), sure (s)).

A first refinement of Module `Classification_task` is done in Module `Sponges_Classification_task` that specifies the possible values for the set variable `Taxon` in the Porifera context (see Figure 10). Each module of the classificatory model inherits the interface and the inference system definition through a refinement of Module `Sponges_Classification_task`. For example, see the heading of Module `Homosclerophorida`, in Figure 13.

---

**Module** Sponges_Classification_task : Classification_task =
**Begin**
    **Export** Taxon
    **Deductive Knowledge**
        **Dictionary**:
            **Types**:
                TAXON_TYPE = (demos, calca, hexa, hadro, axi, poe, astro,
                    spiro, lithis, homos, chondro, sclero, hali, haplo, petro,
                    dendro, dictyo, vero,halis, sube, poly, spi, clio, tethy,
                    stylo,time, placo, latrun, axine, desmox, buba, hemi, raspa,
                    eury, agela, myca, clado, biem, desma, coelo, teda, hyme,
                    phorba, crelli, myxi, clath, hama, rhabde, crambe, stell,
                    geod, pacha, thene, calth, throm, teti, tetilla, theo, cora,
                    plero, scleri, leio, desman, sipho, petromi, vetu, plaki,
                    osca, oscarella, chondrilla, chondrosia, halichon, hymeni,
                    halicl, reni, ado, gelli, cally, oce, petrosia, aplysi,
                    hexadella, dysi, dictyoden, spongi, thorec, aplysina,
                    halisarca, epi, sami, geodia, pachymatisma, isops, caminus,
                    erylus, Gnodastrella, Gconchilega, Gcydonium, Gbarretti,
                    Ipachydermata, Iintuta, Ianceps, Eeuastrum, Ediscophorus,
                    Epapulifer, Ecorsicus, Pjohnstoni, Cvulcani)
            **Predicates**: Taxon = **Name**: "Taxon" **Type**: taxon_type
    **End Deductive**
**End**

**Fig. 10.** Refinement of Module Classification_task.

**Classificatory problem solving methods.** In SPONGIA, generic modules are used to model the complex identification skills of experts. A generic module implements a reasoning strategy, that is, a specific way of using the knowledge contained in the classificatory model to identify a specimen. Although the expert's identification skills are based on a matching-elimination strategy, several reasoning strategies (or problem solving methods) may be reported. Defining these methods into generic modules allows for the instantiation of each method over the same classificatory model. In this way, the KBS can be executed in different modes depending on the user needs.

Here we introduce the Refinement Method, a standard problem-solving method for classificatory tasks also known as *simple classification* [10]. This method consists of the iterative process of identifying the more promising taxa at a taxonomic level, and refining the taxonomic tree (i.e. pruning the branches that have been rejected). The generic module that implements this identification strategy is in Figure 11.

Complete details about **Milord II** syntax can be found elsewhere [33]. However, in order to grasp the meaning of Figure 11 we shall give a hint on some aspects of the syntax of generic modules. Variables may appear in metarules and are identifiers preceded by the sign '$'. Variables in metarules may be used to refer to variables and propositions at the object level, to submodules, to values, ... For instance '$z', in M0001 of the deductive control, refers to any submodule of the module generated when the generic module is applied to concrete arguments, '$z', in M0001 of the structural control, refers to the value of the set variable **Taxon** of parameter module DM. Reference to variables and propositions in a submodule down in the hierarchy is made by preceding the name by a sequence of module identifiers separated by '/'. The modules in the sequence are those in the path between the module where the reference is made and the module where the variable (or proposition) is defined. Hence '$z/taxon' refers to the set variable taxon defined in any submodule of the module generated by the application of this generic module. 'int(true, true)' is the representation at the meta-level of the interval of linguistic terms [true, true] at the object level, 'int(false,true)' corresponds to the whole interval of truth values, that is, it represents the complete ignorance, [false, true].

It should be noted that this generic module is declared to be an expansion of the task module (in the last line of the generic module's code, by > T ). Thus, according to Section 2.7, it is an enrichment of another module, in this case the task module (T), that the generic module itself takes as argument.

Another interesting feature is the recursive call of the Module **Refinement_method** itself, which is declared by **M0001** in the Structural Control. Hence, the instantiation of this generic module is made dynamically at each step of the iterative process. In this way, the Refinement method forces the user to bring in more and more details about the sample's characters, in order to identify each taxonomic level following the taxonomic tree.

The method in Figure 11is instantiated over the classificatory model of SPONGIA by means of the call:

**Module** Spong_IA = Refinement_method(Classes, Sponges_classification_task)

in which we specify the arguments to be taken by the generic module. That is, we write the name of the top module of the sponge classificatory model as first argument, i.e. **Classes** (corresponding to **DM** in the heading of the generic module); we write the name of a specific classification task, i.e. **Sponges_classification_task** as second argument (corresponding to **T**

```
Module Refinement_method (DM:T;T:Classification_task) =
Begin
    Control Knowledge
        Evaluation Type: eager
        Deductive Control:
            M0001    If    K(=($z/taxon ,$f),int(true,true)) and
                           K(=($z/taxon ,$ff), int($min, $max)) and
                           diff($f,$ff) and neq($min,true) and
                           K(=($f/taxon, $ff),int(false,true))
                           then conclude K(=(taxon, $ff), int(false,false))
            M0002    If    K(=($z/taxon ,$f), $c) and
                           K(=(taxon,$f), int(false,true))
                           then conclude K(=(taxon, $f), $c)
        Structural Control:
            M0001    If    K(=(DM/taxon ,$z),int($min,$max)) and
                           threshold(DM, $cut) and gt($min,$cut) and
                           submodule(DM, $z)
                           then conclude
                           Module(=($z,Refinement_method(DM/$z, T)))
    End Control
End > T
```

**Fig. 11.** Generic module modelling a refinement method.

in the heading of the generic module). Only those modules accomplishing the conditions specified in the generic module's heading can be taken as arguments. In this way, Module Classes is a refinement of the task module (T) and Module Sponges_classification_task is a refinement of Module Classification_task.

The Refinement method is a suitable method for users who are not especially acquainted with the domain problem, or for more experienced users facing up to a difficult case. It is a good method to detect inconsistency in the user's answers because it covers the taxonomic tree step by step, but experts may feel excessively guided. Even if the sample is a new species to science (i.e. a species never found until that moment) the refinement method could give a ranked list of hypotheses of higher taxonomic rank than species.

Figure 12 shows a schema of the complete modular structure of SPONGIA. Boxes stand for modules. When a box is drawn into another this indicates a module/submodule relation. Each generic module implementing an identification method (problem-solving method in Figure 12) may be instantiated over the modules standing for the classificatory model of the phylum Porifera. Questions are risen to the user according to the data needed by the classificatory model until the system can identify the sample case.

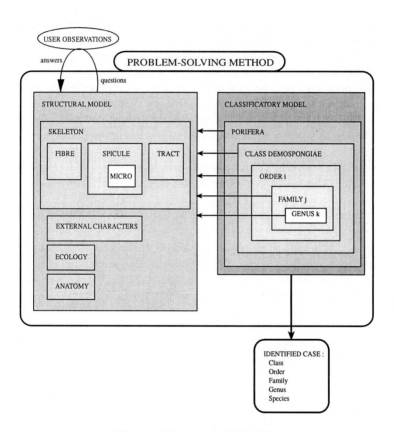

**Fig. 12.** Schema of SPONGIA.

## 3.3    Incompleteness and imprecision handling

**The rule-based paradigm and the representation of incompleteness
and variability.** As discussed below, in the phylum Porifera there is not enough
knowledge to build a definite theory. Many of the statements (or rules) expressed
by the experts are qualified with a term expressing uncertainty such as possibly,
often, sometimes, in general,... In other words, the practical taxonomic reasoning
involves complex uncertainty handling mechanisms [15]. Data supplied by specialised literature also reflects the uncertainty and incompleteness in the field.

The rule-based paradigm provides a natural means for expressing knowledge
about classification and identification. The deductive taxonomic knowledge may
be straightforward expressed by means of rules and meta-rules. In the classificatory model, rules may be seen as a mapping between combinations of characters
and taxa. Rules capture the matching strategy. For example, "if cheloid microscleres are present then order Poecilosclerida is sure". Meta-rules are mainly
intended to reject taxa, that is, to model the elimination strategy. For example, "if triaenas are present among the spicular complement then discard all the
orders except Astrophorida, Spirophorida and Lithistida".

In principle, the two previous examples could be perfectly represented using pure classical logic. But, very few taxonomic statements can be as precise
as these examples are. In general, rules have to cope with the representation
of the intra-taxon character's variability. For example, "if the external colour is
whitish, yellow or orange to red and the sponge is breakable then order Halichon-
drida is *possible*". Although the expert's heuristics concerning variability (i.e.
which range of variability is commonly found in a taxon) is not well-established
knowledge, they are essential in identification. Thus, the rule-based paradigm,
together with an approximate reasoning system, is critical in the representation
of the classificatory knowledge.

Module `Homosclerophorida` (see Figure 13) is an example to illustrate the
aspects of knowledge representation commented above.

The deductive knowledge within this module is concerned with the identification of the families of the order `Homosclerophorida`, namely family
`Oscarellidae` and family `Plakinidae`. Rules express combinations of characters
possibly matching the family `Oscarellidae` or the family `Plakinidae`. Meta-
rules emulate the elimination strategy. Each premise refers to a character that
has been conveniently defined in another module belonging to the structural
model. The conjunction operator **and** links a number of premises that have to
be satisfied to make the rule operative. The operator **int** has to be understood
as an intersection in the context of the fuzzy set theory, (see Section 2.3). It is
used to cope with a variety of possible combinations of states in a multi-state
character. Thus, a specimen displaying any possible subset of the set specified
in the rule will fit in this premise.

Incompleteness of knowledge about the classificatory model is expressed
by means of the use of a qualitative scale of linguistic labels (truth-values)
denoting uncertainty. The general conditions about the inference system
to be applied over the deduction have been previously defined in Module

```
Module Homosclerophorida : Sponges_Classification_task =
Begin
     Module Structures = Structural_model
     Open Structural_model
     Export taxon
     Deductive Knowledge
          Dictionary:
               Types: taxon_type
               Predicates:
                    taxon = Name: "Taxon" Type: taxon_type
               Rules:
                    R001 If no(skel/skel) and ext/colour int (blue,violet)
                         then conclude taxon = (oscarellidae) is sure
                    R002 If ext/form int (sheet,cushion) and
                         ext/hand int (rubbery) and ext/body_size int (small)
                         then conclude taxon = (oscarellidae) is quite_possible
                    R003 If skel/S/size int (polyaxon_medium_150) and
                         skel/S/actine int (two, more_than_two)
                         then conclude taxon = (plakinidae) is sure
                    R004 If eco/fix int (spots)
                         then conclude taxon = (plakinidae) is very_possible
                    ...
     End deductive
     Control knowledge
          Deductive control:
               M001     If K(not(skel/skel),int(s,s))
                        then conclude K(not(=(taxon, plakinidae)),int(s,s))
               ...
     End control
End
```

**Fig. 13.** Module Homosclerophorida definition.

Classification_task. Each taxonomic module is declared to be a refinement of Module Sponges_Classification_task, which is in turn a refinement of **Module** Classification_task. Therefore, every module of the classificatory model inherits these conditions.

In the structural model, the deductive knowledge is mainly involved in the definition of complex characters from simple observable data. For example, in Module **Tracts** of the structural model we find the rule "if the number of spicules alongside one another in the primary fibres is more than 1 and less than 6 then the sponge presents paucispicular tracts", where **numb1** is a numeric character. That is:

R004      **If** numb1>1 **and** numb1<6 **then conclude** paucil **is** sure

Other important aspects concerning the system's performance such as the order of the questions to the user, the dependence of characters or the possible exceptions are represented by meta-rules in the structural model. In Module **External** of the structural model we find for example "if the external form of the sponge is a sheet or thick encrusting then avoid any question about pedunculate habit". That is:

M002      **If**    K(=(form,$x),int(s,s)) **and** member($x,(sheet,thick_encrusting))
            **then conclude** K(not(ped),int(s,s))

**Uncertainty in the representation of characters.** Even for experts, the observation of some characters may involve some degree of uncertainty. In SPONGIA, we use many-valued propositions to represent characters that are usually expressed by experts with uncertainty. When the user is queried about the presence of such characters, he is allowed to qualify his answer with a linguistic certainty label. In this way, characters which are inherently difficult to observe with absolute certainty find a convenient representation.

For example, the observation of the hierarchical arrangement of the spongin in sponges with reticulate skeleton is not always straightforward. Then the character *skeleton* is represented by a many-valued proposition.

Even more, the user may qualify with a certainty label the values of a multi-state character if he is uncertain. And, the user answers "unknown" only if he does not know anything about the character.

**Fuzzy logic in the representation of characters.** In SPONGIA fuzzy propositions and linguistic variables are useful for representing multi-state characters with imprecise boundaries. This may happen in numeric characters that have some typified intervals of values. They are traditionally represented as simple numeric variables but they can be better represented as a fuzzy set.

For example, the body size of a sponge is usually referred as small, medium, big or very big. However, the representation of this character as a set variable would not be very sensible because the subjective user's answer could invalidate the data. On the other hand, defining a precise numeric interval for those qualitative values would be completely inadequate because experts are not able to define crisp boundaries for such character values. Thus, defining the character as a linguistic variable, where the qualitative values are represented as fuzzy sets, seems to be the right solution. Consider the example of **body-size** declaration in Section 2.3 and Figure 5). In this example, SPONGIA asks the user for the numeric value of variable **body measure**. The deductive knowledge does not use that numeric value but a qualitative abstraction of it. The qualitative value is the truth value associated to the fuzzy proposition **body-size**. This value is obtained by the piece of code in Figure 14. An example of how this fuzzy set is used in the premises of rules can be found in Figure 15.

```
Module Qualitative_Abstraction =
Begin
      Import Body_measure, ...
      Export Body_size, ...
      Deductive knowledge
          Dictionary:
          Predicates:
              Body_measure =
                  Name: "Measure of the largest axis of the sponge's body
                        (numeric value in cm)"
                  Question: "How much does it measure the largest axis of the
                        sponge's body (cm)?"
                  Type: numeric
              Body_size =
                  Name: "Body size of the sponge"
                  Type:    (small     (0, 0, 1, 5),
                           medium    (1, 5, 10, 15),
                           big        (10, 15, 25, 30),
                           very big  (25, 30, 2000, 2000))
                  Function:(lambda ()
                           (fuzzifier (type_all Body_size) (linguistic_terms)
                           (value Body_measure )))
              ...
      End deductive
End
```

**Fig. 14.** Schema of a qualitative Abstraction module.

Another example of a linguistic variable is the representation of the character *thickness of the cortex*. In sponges displaying a cortex, the thickness of the cortex ranges from a few $\mu$m to several mm in different species. There is also a certain degree of intra-specific variability. For instance, specimens of the genus Isops present a cortex that is thin or very thin in *Isops intuta*, thin or a little thick in

| | |
|---|---|
| R041 | If skel/pres and ext/body_size int (big) and<br>    ext/touc int (rough) and<br>    ext/colour int (whitish,cream_to_brown,black,grey,violet)<br>Then conclude taxon=(astro) is possible |
| R123 | If no(skel/skel) and ext/form int (sheet) and<br>    ext/surf int (conulose, even) and<br>    ext/body_size int (medium, big) and<br>    ext/colour int (violet, yellow)<br>Then conclude taxon=(dendro) is very possible<br>"Comment: possibly belonging to the genus Hexadella" |

**Fig. 15.** Rules for the identification of orders within the class Demospongia

*Isops anceps* and very thick in *Isops pachydermata*. As usually, to define these species in the knowledge-base we take into account both the experts heuristics and the literature descriptions but it is very difficult to state which interval corresponds to each of these qualitative terms.

Ideally, to make a fuzzy representation of a numerical character, its variability should be previously established experimentally. In practice, fuzzy sets are usually defined according to the heuristics of experts giving the difficulty in determining their precise shape and position. These heuristics may change because new discoveries are made, or because the actual range of character's variability could be statistically established. Given the flexibility obtained with a representation based on fuzzy sets, these difficulties are worth facing. As an example of flexibility we can see that a fuzzy representation of characters permits to change the membership degree of a specimen to a taxon, not by changing the classification rules but by changing the definition of the fuzzy sets defining the characters.

Another advantage of using fuzzy sets over numerical characters is the possibility of adapting the KBS to various ecological situations. For example, it has been demonstrated that the length and thickness of siliceous spicules vary depending on water temperature. The adaptation of the KBS may be done by modifying the membership functions of the characters according to the current values encountered in a given area. Again, this modification is external to the rule sets.

This feature increases the validity of the rule set as it may be actualised according to any new finding in the field or adapted to various specific situations. This is specially relevant in domains where there is continuous research and redefinition into the established theory, like Porifera.

**Example** The practical scenario of using SPONGIA is as follows. We have a computer in an actual laboratory which is perfectly equipped to observe a sample. SPONGIA, running on the computer, guides the user through the information gathering by means of a question-answer protocol. Questions made by

SPONGIA are answered by the user. In order to answer the questions the user will possibly need to use the equipment at the laboratory on the sample and some routinary examination may be done in advance to prepare some slides, for example. Once all the available information is gathered, SPONGIA presents a ranking of taxa to which the sample may belong.

SPONGIA provides the system developer with a detailed trace of the inference process which is too extensive to be presented here. In Figure 16 we present a summary of the system's trace for a sponge sample of *Geodia cydonium*. There we point out the main events in the inference process: the particular data asked to the user, the value answered by the user, the itinerary among the modules in the structural model, the conclusions reached, and the ultimate rules arriving at these conclusions in the classificatory model[18].

# 4 Discussion and final remarks

One of the main advantages of the knowledge-based approach is their ability to represent and manage imprecise and/or imperfect knowledge. However, this and other advantages are often eclipsed by the practical difficulties encountered by systematic biologists when developing knowledge-based systems. The main difficulty, in our opinion, is the lack of a methodology oriented to the development of knowledge-based systems for taxonomy. Conscious of this handicap, the actual development of SPONGIA as an application was preceded by the deployment of a knowledge-based system architecture for taxonomic domains [13] using the **Milord II** programming environment. This architecture was defined on the basis of a principled approach to the perception and organisation of taxonomic data by experts in systematic biology as elicited by a knowledge level analysis of taxonomic domains. In this architecture, the concepts, relations, data structures and problem-solving methods in biological taxonomy are mapped into computational elements that implement them.

However, the construction of computerised identification tools with powerful imprecision and uncertainty handling mechanisms would not be suitable nor necessary in all taxonomic groups. There are some taxa or local groups of species for which an agreed classification and monographs about fauna have existed for a long time. For these well-described groups it is probably not reasonable to make the effort of developing a knowledge-based system. In contrast, in low-structured taxonomic domains that involve a high degree of uncertainty and incompleteness, all that effort can be justified and necessary. The Porifera domain, with its large diversity and complex terminology is a paradigmatic case of the later group.

In this chapter, we have emphasised the essential role of uncertain and imprecise knowledge in the field of systematic biology, and particularly in the phylum Porifera. We have shown how this kind of knowledge may be represented and managed through the development of SPONGIA, a **Milord II** application

---

[18] Note that this is a small subset of the total number of rules and meta-rules that have been fired in the inference process from both the structural and the classificatory model to reach these conclusions.

| STEP | DATA REQUESTED TO THE USER | USER'S ANSWERS | VISITED MODULE | REACHED CONCLUSION | USED RULES |
|---|---|---|---|---|---|
| 1 | Geographical location | Atlantic | ECO | | |
| 2 | Presence of spicules | True | SKEL | | |
| 3 | Chemical composition | Silica | SKEL | | |
| 4 | Spicule categories | Megascleres_and_Microscleres | SPICULE | | |
| 5 | Number of axes of the megascleres | Four, One | SPICULE | Demos is **sure** | Classes/R003 |
| 6 | Spongin fibres present in the skeleton | False | SKEL | | |
| 7 | Number of actines of the megascleres | More_than_two, Two | SPICULE | | |
| 8 | Type of megascleres | Triaena, Oxea | SPICULE | | |
| 9 | Growth upon the substrate | Massive. | EXT | | |
| 10 | External form | Globular | EXT | | |
| 11 | Architecture of the spicular choanosomal skeleton | Perifery_radiate | SPICULE | | |
| 12 | Type of microscleres | Aster | MICROS | | |
| 13 | Type of aster | Oxyaster, Chiaster, Sterraster, Spheraster | MICROS | Astro is **sure** / Geod is **sure** | Demos/R047 / Astro/R005 |
| 14 | Type of sterraster | Globular | MICROS | | |
| 15 | Simple oscule/s clearly differentiated in the sponge surface | False | EXT | | |
| 16 | One or several superficial areas of some square cm, irregularly delimitated, where the cortex is microperforated and covers a cavity bearing oscula | True | EXT | Geodia is **sure** | Geod/R003 |
| 17 | Type of triaena | Orthotriaena, Anatriaena, Protriaena | SPICULE | | |
| 18 | Visual aspect of the surface | Unknown | EXT | | |
| 19 | Maximal length of the spicular complement (microns) | Unknown | METRICS | | |
| 20 | Form of globular sterrasters | Spherical | MICROS | Gconchilega is **possible** | Geodia/R006 |
| 21 | Maximal diameter of the sterrasters | 55 | METRICS | Gcydonium is **posible** | Geodia/R010 |
| 22 | Pronounced depression at the sponge's surface in which you can find the oscula located at the bottom when the cortex is removed | Unknown | EXT | | |
| 23 | Habitat | Unknown | ECO | | |
| 24 | Presence of cortex | Unknown | ANA | | |

**Fig. 16.** Example of *Geodia cydonium* case identification.

dealing with identification of marine sponges. From the user viewpoint, it is important to be able to give imprecise answers when he is not absolutely certain. As discussed in the previous section, the user may answer the query of SPONGIA with a certainty label (or interval) ranging from unknown to sure. Or, he can even express different possible answers, each one with a convenient certainty label. This flexibility in answering is not usually permitted when using classic computerised identification tools and is specially important for users who are not experts in sponge systematics.

In the course of the development of SPONGIA, through successive prototyping, we have experienced how the accuracy in the representation of uncertainty contributes to a more sensible performance of the system. Thus, we consider that the use of approximate reasoning mechanisms has been critical to construct a computerised tool for sponge identification. In particular, the use of fuzzy logic has made possible a suitable representation of the imprecise and/or incomplete knowledge which constitutes the classificatory theory of Porifera to a large extent.

Regarding the imprecision and uncertainty handling, as it has been described in Section 2, the approximate reasoning capabilities provided by **Milord II** at the object level languages are based on the use of many-valued logics, where the set of truth values is an ordinal scale of linguistic labels. In SPONGIA, this logical framework is actually used for two different purposes. First, as the underlying logical basis to handle imprecision by means of fuzzy sets; and second, for a qualitative uncertainty handling mechanism to deal with the incompleteness of the classificatory domain knowledge.

As already discussed in Section 2.4, from a formal and theoretical point of view, while truth-functional many-valued logics are considered to be a suitable model for fuzziness or vagueness, they are not suitable for dealing with uncertainty as belief, since belief is intrinsically not truth-functional. Indeed, having a full truth-functional uncertainty model may lead to completely erroneous conclusions. However, we think that the qualitative uncertainty handling mechanism has proved useful in the building of the knowledge base of SPONGIA. Moreover, we have avoided any potential source of conflicting uncertainty handling. The hierarchically modularity of the knowledge base, together with some built-in safeguard mechanisms[19] help in this task.

## Acknowledgements

The authors are indebted to M.J. Uriz for provision of scanning electron microscopy images and to José Manuel Fortuño for the fotographic reproduction. We thank the anonymous reviewers for their comments and suggestions that have helped in the improvement of the final version.

This project has received the support of the Spanish Research project SMASH (CICYT number TIC96-1038-C04001) and the European TMR *VIM*,

---

[19] For instance, the object level languages do not allow (see Section 2.2) $p$ and $\neg p$ in the premise of a rule or $p$ in the premise and $\neg p$ in the conclusion of the same rule

number PL93-0816. During the writing of this chapter, Carles Sierra was on sabbatical leave at Queen Mary & Westfield College, University of London, thanks to the Spanish Ministry of Education grant PR95-313.

# References

1. J. Agustí, F. Esteva, P. Garcia, L. Godo, R. Lopez de Mantaras, and C. Sierra. Local multi-valued logics in modular expert systems. *Journal of Experimental and Theoretical Artificial Intelligence*, 6:303–321, 1994.
2. G. Attardi and M. Simi. A formalisation of viewpoints. *Fundamenta Informaticae*, 23(2,3,4):149–174, 1995.
3. J. Balder, F. Van Harmelen, and M. Aben. A $KADS/(ML)^2$ model of a scheduling task. In Jan Treur and Thomas Wetter, editors, *Formal Specification of Complex Resoning Systems*. Ellis Horwood, 1993.
4. S. J. Barlett and P. Suber, editors. *Self-reference: Reflections on reflexivity*. Martinus Nijhoff, Dordrecht, 1987.
5. P.R. Bergquist. Poriferan relationships. In S. Conway-Morris, J.D. George, R. Gibson, and H.M. Platt, editors, *The origins and relationships of lower invertebrates*, volume 28 of *Systematics Association*, pages 15–27. 1985. Special Volume.
6. P.R. Bergquist and P.J. Fromont. The marine Fauna of New Zealand: Porifera demospongiae, part 4 (poecilosclerida). pages 1–21, 1988.
7. P. Bonissone. Summarizing and propagating uncertain information with triangular norms. *International Journal of Approximate Reasoning*, 1(1):71–101, 1987.
8. N. Boury-Esnault, M.T. Lopes, and M.J. Uriz. Spongiaires bathyaux de la mer d'alboran et du golfe ibero-marocain. *Memoires du Museum National d'Histoire Naturelle*, 160:174, 1994.
9. N. Boury-Esnault and K. Rützler, editors. *Thesaurus of Terms for Sponges*. Smithsonian Institution Press, Washington D.C., USA. In press.
10. W. J. Clancey. Heuristic classification. *Artificial Intelligence*, 27(3):289–350, 1985.
11. R. López de Mántaras. *Approximate Reasoning Models*. Ellis Horwood series on Artificial Intelligence, UK, 1990.
12. R. López de Mántaras (ed.). Special issue on Reflection and Meta-level AI Architectures. *Future Generation Computer Systems Journal*, 12, 1996.
13. M. Domingo and C. Sierra. A knowledge level analysis of taxonomic domains. *International Journal of Intelligent Systems*, 12(2):105–135, 1997.
14. Marta Domingo. *An Expert System Architecture for Identification in Biology*, volume 4 of *Monografies de l'IIIA*. IIIA – CSIC, Bellaterra (Barcelona), Spain, 1995.
15. Marta Domingo. Models of practical taxonomic reasoning in knowledge-based systems: an application to Porifera. *Bulletin de l'Institut Royal des Sciences Naturelles de Belgique – Biologie*, 66 suppl.:27–35, 1996.
16. M. Edwards and D.R.Morse. The potential for computer-aided identification in biodiversity research. *TREE*, 10(4):153–158, 1995.
17. R. Fortuner, editor. *Advances in Computer Methods for Systematic Biology: Artificial Intelligence, Databases, Computer Vision*. The Johns Hopkins University Press, Baltimore. London, 1993.
18. P.J. Fromont and P.R. Bergquist. Structural characters and their use in sponge taxonomy: When is a sigma not a sigma. In K. Rützler, editor, *New perspectives in sponge biology*, pages 273–278. Smithsonian Institution Press, Washington D.C., USA, 1990.

19. F. Giunchiglia and P. Traverso. Reflective reasoning with and between a declarative metatheory. In *IJCAI-91*, pages 111–117, 1991.
20. F. Giunchiglia, P. Traverso, and E. Giunchiglia. Multi-context systems as a specification framework for complex reasoning systems. In Jan Treur and Thomas Wetter, editors, *Formal Specification of Complex Resoning Systems*. Ellis Horwood, 1993.
21. L. Godo and C. Sierra. Knowledge base refinement in Milord. In *Proceedings of 14th IMACS World Congress*, Atlanta, USA, 1994.
22. P. Hajek, L. Godo, and F. Esteva. Fuzzy logic and probability. In P. Besnard and S. Hanks, editors, *Proceedings of the Uncertainty in Artificial Intelligence Conference, UAI-95*, pages 237–244, San Francisco, USA, 1995. Morgan Kaufmann.
23. R. Harper, D. MacQueen, and R. Millner. The Definition of Standard ML. Technical Report ECS-LFCS-86-2, Dept. Computer Science, Univ. of Edinburgh, 1986.
24. A. Hunter and S. Parsons, editors. *Uncertainty in Information Systems*, volume This volume. Springer.
25. J.Puyol, L.Godo, and C.Sierra. Specialisation calculus and communication. *International Journal of Approximate Reasoning*, 1998.
26. N. Knowtoln, E. Weil, L.A. Weigt, and H.M. Guzman. Sibling species in *montastraea annularis*, coral bleaching and the coral climate record. *Science*, 255:330–333, 1992.
27. C. Lévi. Nouveau spongiaires lithistides bathyaux affinites cretacees de la nouvelle-caledonie. *Bull. Mus. nat. Hist. nat. Paris*, 10(2):241–263, 1988.
28. P. Maes and N. Nardi, editors. *Meta-level Architectures and Reflection*. Academic Press, Amsterdam, 1988.
29. R. Martin-Clouaire and H. Prade. SPII-1, a simple inference engine capable of accommodating both imprecision and uncertainty in expert systems. In G. Mitra, editor, *Computer-Assisted Decision Making*, LNCS, pages 117–131. North Holland, 1986.
30. R. J. Pankhurst. *Practical Taxonomic Computing*. Cambridge University Press, Cambridge, 1991.
31. S. Parsons. *Qualitative approaches to reasoning under uncertainty*. MIT Press, Cambridge, USA, (in press), 1997.
32. J. Pavelka. On fuzzy logic I, II, III. *Zeitschr. f. Math. Logik und Grundl. der Math.*, 25:45–52, 119–134, 447–464, 1979.
33. J. Puyol and C. Sierra. Milord ii: Language description. *Mathware & Soft Computing*, 4:299–338, 1997.
34. Josep Puyol. *Modularization, Uncertainty, Reflective Control and Deduction by Specialization in Milord II, a Language for Knowledge-Based Systems*. PhD thesis, Universitat Autònoma de Barcelona, Barcelona, 1994.
35. Josep Puyol, Lluís Godo, and Carles Sierra. A specialization calculus to improve expert system communication. In *ECAI'92*, pages 144–148, Viena, 1992.
36. D. Sannella and A. Tarlecki. *Foundations of Algebraic Specification and Formal Program Development*. Cambridge University Press, Cambridge, (in press) edition, 1997.
37. D. T. Sannella and L. A. Wallen. A Calculus for the Construction of Modular Prolog Programs. *The Journal of Logic Programming*, pages 147–177, 1992.
38. A.M. Sole-Cava and J.P. Thorpe. High levels of genetic variation in marine sponges. In K. Rutzler, editor, *New perspectives in sponge biology*, pages 322–337. Smithsonian Institution Press, Washington D.C., USA, 1990.
39. Y. H. Tan and J. Treur. A bi-modular approach to non-monotonic reasoning. In *Proc. First World Congress on the Fundamentals of AI, WOCFAI-91*, pages 461–475, Paris, 1991.

40. J. Treur. On the use of reflection principles in modelling complex reasoning. *International Journal of Intelligent Systems*, 6:277–294, 1992.

41. M.J. Uriz, D. Martin, and D. Rosell. Relationships between taxonomical and biological characteristics and chemically mediated bioactivity in mediterranean sponges. *Marine Biology*, 113:287–297, 1992.

42. L. A. Zadeh. Fuzzy sets as a basis for a theory of possibility. *Fuzzy Sets and Systems*, 1:3–28, 1978.

# A  Syntax

| | |
|---|---|
| PROGRAM | ::= moddecl$^+$ |
| moddecl | ::= **Module** *amodid* [**(** [paramlist] **)**] [modoper modexpr] [$\equiv$ modexpr] |
| paramlist | ::= paramlist **;** paramlist \| *amodid* modoper modexpr |
| modoper | ::= **:** \| $\geq$ \| $\leq$ |
| modexpr | ::= bodyexpr modoper modexpr \| bodyexpr |
| bodyexpr | ::= **begin** decl **end** \| pathid [**(** [iparamlist] **)**] |
| iparamlist | ::= modexpr **;** iparamlist \| modexpr |
| pathid | ::= *amodid* \| *amodid*/pathid |
| decl | ::= [hierarchy] [interface] [deductive] [control] |
| hierarchy | ::= moddecl \| **Inherit** *modid* \| **Open** bodyexpr \| hierarchy hierarchy |
| interface | ::= [**Import** predicateidlist] [**Export** predicateidlist] |
| predicateidlist | ::= *predid* **,** predicateidlist \| *predid* |
| deductive | ::= **Deductive knowledge** |
| | [**Dictionary:** [**Types:** typebinding$^+$] **Predicates:** predicate$^+$] |
| | [**Rules:** rule$^+$] |
| | [**Inference system:** logcomp] |
| | **end deductive** |
| typebinding | ::= *typeid* [$\equiv$ typespec] |
| typespec | ::= **boolean** \| **many-valued** \| **numeric** \| **class** \| |
| | **fuzzy** char-funct \| **(** symbollist **)** \| **(** valuesspec **)** \| *typeid* |
| symbollist | ::= *symbol* [*string*] \| symbollist **,** symbollist |
| valuesspec | ::= *symbol* [*string*] char-funct \| valuesspec **,** valuesspec |
| char-funct | ::= **(** *number* **,** *number* **,** *number* **,** *number* **)** |
| predicate | ::= *predid* $\equiv$ attributes |
| attributes | ::= [name] [question] type [function] [relation$^+$] [explanation] [image] |
| name | ::= **Name:** *string* |
| question | ::= **Question:** *string* |
| type | ::= **Type:** typespec |
| function | ::= **Function: (** S-expression **)** |
| S-expression | ::= *atom* \| list \| predef-func \| S-expression S-expression |
| list | ::= **(** S-expression **)** \| **( )** |
| predef-func | ::= **( Type** *predid* **)** \| **( Linguistic_terms )** |
| relation | ::= **Relation:** relationid pathpredid |
| pathpredid | ::= pathid/*predid* \| *predid* |
| relationid | ::= **Needs** \| **Needs_true** \| **Needs_false** \| **Needs_value** \| |
| | **Belongs_to** \| **Needs_quantitative** \| **Needs_qualitative** \| *symbol* |
| explanation | ::= **Explanation:** *string* |
| image | ::= **Image:** *fileid* |
| rule | ::= *ruleid* **If** premisse-rule **Then** conclusion-rule [*documentation*] |
| premisse-rule | ::= condition-rule **and** premisse-rule \| condition-rule |
| condition-rule | ::= conditio \| **no (** conditio **)** |
| conditio | ::= operator **(** expression**,** ...**,** expression **)** \| |
| | expression operator expression \| |
| | pathpredid \| *ltermid* \| **true** \| **false** |
| expression | ::= operator-arit **(** expression**,** ...**,** expression **)** \| |
| | **(** expression operator-arit expression **)** \| |

```
                        number | pathpredid
operator          ::= < | > | <= | >= | = | /= | int |
operator-arit     ::= + | - | * | :
conclusion-rule   ::= conclude rconclusion is cert-value
rconclusion       ::= predid | predid = symbol | no ( predid ) | no ( predid = symbol )
logcomp           ::= [lingtermdef] [conjunction] [renaming]
lingtermdef       ::= Truth values = ( ltermidlist )
ltermidlist       ::= ltermid , ltermidlist | ltermid
conjunction       ::= Conjunction = truth-table
truth-table       ::= Truth table ( arrows )
arrows            ::= ( ltermid⁺ ) | arrows arrows
renaming          ::= Renaming lrenames⁺
lrenames          ::= pathid/ltermid ==> cert-value
cert-value        ::= ltermid | [ ltermid , ltermid ]
control           ::= Control knowledge
                      [Evaluation type: evaltype]
                      [Truth threshold: ltermid]
                      [deduccnt] [structcnt]
                      end control
evaltype          ::= lazy | eager | reified
deduccnt          ::= Deductive control: mrr⁺
mrr               ::= metaid If premisse-meta Then filter-mrr⁺
premisse-meta     ::= mexpr and premisse-meta | mexpr
filter-mrr        ::= inhibit rules [relation-id] pathpredid |
                      prune pathpredid | conclude gexpr | conclude known
structcnt         ::= Structural control: mre⁺
mre               ::= metaid If premisse-meta Then filter-mre
filter-mre        ::= filter amodid⁺ |
                      order amodid⁺ with certainty cert-value |
                      Open ( term ) | Module ( term ) | Inherit ( amodid )
mrx               ::= metaid If premisse-meta Then exception
exception         ::= definitive solution predid |
                      stop
mexpr             ::= known | mrel | msubmod | mthres | card | atom | member |
                      eqdif | moper | int | setof | pos | gexpr
symorvar          ::= symbol | $symbol
vpath             ::= symorvar | symorvar/vpath
known             ::= K ( fact, interval )
fact              ::= factex | not( factex ) | implies( list,list )
factex            ::= vpath | =( vpath, symorvar )
interval          ::= $symbol | int( symorvar, symorvar )
mrel              ::= relationid( symorvar, vpath )
msubmod           ::= submodule( symorvar, symorvar ) | submodule( symorvar )
mthres            ::= threshold( symorvar, symorvar ) | threshold( symorvar )
card              ::= cardinal( list, symorvar )
list              ::= $listid | ( listelem )
listelem          ::= elemid | elemid , listelem
atom              ::= atom( list )
```

| member | ::= __member__ ( symorvar, list ) |
|---|---|
| eqdif | ::= __equal__( listorsym,listorsym ) \| __diff__( listorsym,listorsym ) |
| listorsym | ::= symbol \| list |
| moper | ::= loper( symorvar,symorvar ) |
| loper | ::= __lt__ \| __le__ \| __eq__ \| __neq__ \| __ge__ \| __gt__ |
| int | ::= __intersection__( list,list ) |
| setof | ::= __set_of_instances__ ( $var,term,$var ) |
| pos | ::= __position__( symorvar,list,symorvar ) |
| gexpr | ::= predid ( term , ... , term ) |
| term | ::= $varid \| symbol \| termid(term, ..., term) |

# B  Default Logic

This is the default logic used in **Milord II** when there is no local logic declaration into a module.

**Truth-values**

$$A_8 = \{gp, mpop, llp, modp, p, fp, mp, s\}$$

where the meaning of each term is the following:

1. gp: Impossible
2. mpop: Very few possible
3. llp: Few possible
4. modp: Slightly possible
5. p: Possible
6. fp: Quite possible
7. mp: Very possible
8. s: Definite

**Conjunction** This operation is described in the Table 2.

| $T_8$ | gp | mpop | llp | modp | p | fp | mp | s |
|---|---|---|---|---|---|---|---|---|
| gp | gp | gp | gp | gp | gp | gp | gp | gp |
| mpop | gp | mpop | mpop | mpop | mpop | mpop | mpop | mpop |
| llp | gp | mpop | mpop | llp | llp | llp | llp | llp |
| modp | gp | mpop | llp | modp | modp | modp | modp | modp |
| p | gp | mpop | llp | modp | modp | modp | p | p |
| fp | gp | mpop | llp | modp | modp | p | fp | fp |
| mp | gp | mpop | llp | modp | p | fp | mp | mp |
| s | gp | mpop | llp | modp | p | fp | mp | s |

**Table 2.** Conjunction table for $A_8$.

# Qualitative Risk Assessment Fulfils a Need

Paul Krause[1], John Fox[1], Philip Judson[2] and Mukesh Patel[3]

[1]Imperial Cancer Research Fund, London WC2A 3PX

[2]Judson Consulting Service, Heather Lea, Norwood, Harrogate HG3 1TE

[3]LHASA UK Ltd., School of Chemistry, University of Leeds, LS2 9JT

**Abstract.** Classically, risk is characterised by a point value probability indicating the likelihood of occurrence of an adverse effect. However, there are domains where the attainability of objective numerical risk characterisations is increasingly being questioned. This paper reviews the arguments in favour of extending classical techniques of risk assessment to incorporate meaningful qualitative and weak quantitative risk characterisations. A technique in which linguistic uncertainty terms are defined in terms of patterns of argument is then proposed. The technique is demonstrated using a prototype computer-based system for predicting the carcinogenic risk due to novel chemical compounds.

## 1    Introduction

In the complex and dynamic world in which we live, risk assessment is taking an increasingly important role in both public and private decision and policy making. Decisions made on the basis of the possibility of global warming, for example, may have far reaching financial, environmental and sociological consequences. Equally, an inability to persuade a local authority to accept a subjective assessment of risk due to a "dangerous" road may have serious and tragic personal consequences. These two examples have been deliberately chosen as they can both be used to illustrate the extreme difficulty of providing a reliable point value measure of the likelihood of realisation of a perceived hazard. Nevertheless, the potential adverse consequences are so great that some meaningful risk characterisation is needed to enable a coherent decision to be made on the appropriate action.

This paper explores the problem of risk assessment in a domain, chemical carcinogenicity, for which quantitative risk assessment has been widely and publicly questioned [7]. Some of the arguments against quantitative risk assessment in certain domains will be rehearsed in the next section. It should be emphasised that the argument is not against the use of quantitative risk assessment *per se*. Rather, that there are situations where traditional methods of risk assessment need extending to enable weak quantitative, or even purely qualitative statements of risk to be made. A specific interest of the authors is the development of a computer-based assistant for the assessment of potential carcinogenic risk of novel chemical compounds. A prototype of this system will be used as a focus for discussing some approaches that have been taken to the qualitative and weak quantitative assessment of risk.

This paper does not claim to provide a full solution to the problem of qualitative risk assessment, although the results obtained to date are promising. The main reason for writing the paper at this stage is that it is a very important issue and needs to be raised as a matter of urgency. It is an unfortunate fact of life that information relating to many of the risks we face in our daily lives is often sparse and incomplete. If the uncertainty community could bend its collective mind to providing techniques for effective risk assessment and communication in such domains, this would be a major contribution to society as a whole.

## 2  The case for non-numerical risk assessment - not enough deaths

For certain technologies, such as electronic systems, civil-engineering structures and mechanical systems, established statistical models are available for making precise and reliable estimates of the likelihood of system failure. Significant quantities of historical data on the failure rates of standard components may be available, for example, or it may be possible to generate reliable simulations of system behaviour. Nevertheless, the contention that an objective, scientific assessment of risk is an achievable goal *is* being questioned. A 1992 report on *Risk Assessment* published by Britain's Royal Society included the comment that

the view that a separation can be maintained between "objective" risk and "subjective" or perceived risk has come under increasing attack, to the extent that it is no longer a mainstream position [22].

That is, there is no such thing as "objective" risk. Rather, risk is culturally constructed (see the next paragraph for an example of this). In fact, this quotation rather overstates the case in the context of the mainstream research and literature on safety and risk management. For example, Britain's Department of Transport draws a firm distinction between "actual" danger (objective risk) and perceived danger (subjective risk). Their position is that if a road does not have a fatality rate above a certain threshold which is considered normal, and therefore acceptable, it will not be eligible for funds for measures to improve safety ("normal" is about 1.2 fatalities per 100 million vehicle kilometres). Nevertheless, their position can lead to conflict. Consider the following scenario.

Increasing traffic over the years leads to a straight road through a residential area being considered "dangerous" by local residents. They plead with the local authority for something to be done to calm the traffic. In the meantime, children are warned to stay away from the road if possible, and to take extreme care if they do need to cross the road for any reason. As a result, the fatality rate on that road stays low - people are taking extra care not to expose themselves to a situation which they *perceive* as potentially risky. The local authority has no observable *measure* of increased risk, so nothing is done. Then a tragic accident does take place. Amidst public outcry, the local authority promises that traffic calming measures will be in place at the earliest opportunity. Which was the *real* risk: the perceived risk of the residents, or the objective risk (estimate) of the local authority?

Sadly, this is not an academic exercise. In 1991, Britain's Permanent Secretary for the Department of Transport announced that "funds for traffic calming will be judged on casualty savings, not environmental improvements or anxiety relief" [5]. This extreme position has led to many conflicts between local people and the Department of Transport, very tragically with consequences not dissimilar to the above hypothetical scenario. More recently the situation has changed slightly, but the whole issue of the distinction between one person's perceived risk and another's objective (estimate of) risk remains a major source of conflict in many fields [1]. Although it is not possible to quantify the subjective perceptions of risk, statistics are available on the risk management activities that are taken in response to these subjective judgements:

In 1971, for example, 80 per cent of seven and eight year old children in England travelled to school on their own, unaccompanied by an adult. By 1990 this figure had dropped to 9 per cent; the questionnaire survey disclosed that the parents' main reason for not allowing their children to travel independently was fear of traffic. ([1], p.13)

The above provides an example in which an authority has an objective estimate of risk which can be expressed as a single number (fatalities per so-many vehicle kilometres). This is questioned by a public which has a quite different perception of risk which they find much harder to express, other than through an extended debate with the authority. There are situations, however, where the authorities themselves cannot agree on an objective measure of risk. One such is the assessment of carcinogenicity due to chemicals. This will be the focus of attention for the remainder of this paper.

Of over five million known chemical substances, only thirty are definitely linked with cancer in humans, and only 7,000 have been tested for carcinogenicity: the rest is darkness [1].

There are several approaches which might be taken to assessing the carcinogenic risk due to a certain chemical. The surest way of obtaining a reliable, objective risk estimate is to establish a causal mechanism and/or obtain direct statistical data on a population of humans that have been exposed to the chemical. Clearly, it would be unacceptable to subject a population to a controlled release of the chemical, but epidemiological data are sometimes available on a population which is known to have been exposed in the past to a chemical (cigarette smoking is a case in point). However, as the quote from John Adams indicates, such information is available for very few chemicals. By far the most frequently used techniques for trying to establish the carcinogenic risk due to chemicals involve *in vivo* or *in vitro* tests. In the case of *in vivo* tests, regular doses of the substance under study are delivered to a population of test animals. The relative increase in tumour incidence with respect to a control population, as a function of dosage, is then used as the basis for an estimate of the increased risk to humans through exposure to the same substance. This estimate requires, however, a number of extrapolations to be made. In order for the experiment to be carried out within an acceptably short period of time, the test animals are subjected to a much higher dose rate than would be anticipated in the human population, so the first extrapolation is from a high dose rate to a low dose rate. Secondly, the results must be extrapolated across species from a population of test animals to humans.

The nature and validity of both forms of extrapolation are the subject of wide rang-

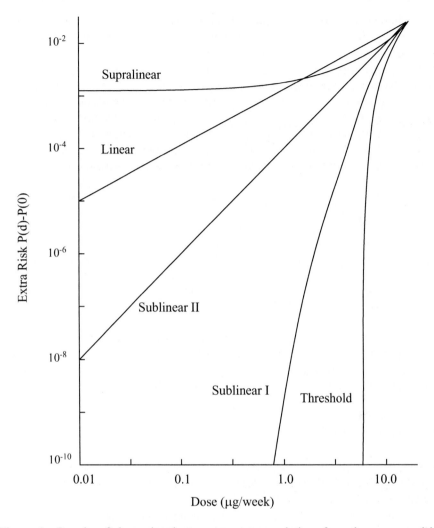

**Figure 1:** Results of alternative dose-response extrapolations from the same empirical data (after [18]). *Extra Risk* is the increase in probability of occurrence of an adverse effect, as a function of dose, above the probability of occurrence of that effect in the population as a whole.

ing disagreements between experts. Figure 1, for example, shows a number of alternative dose-response extrapolations from the same empirical data. It can be seen that the resulting risk predictions at low dose rates vary by many orders of magnitude. The extrapolation between animals and humans is subject to an equally high degree of disagreement. In an extreme case, suppose a chemical is seen to induce an increased incidence of tumours on a gland in rats that has no analogue in humans. What conclusions can be realistically made about that chemical's potential carcinogenicity in humans?

Even without considering the moral position associated with such experiments, serious questions can be asked about the ultimate value of these tests as predictors of human carcinogenic risk.

In the case of *in vitro* tests, such as the Ames Test [3], a "test tube" experiment is carried out to see if the chemical under study can induce mutations in DNA. However, although genetic mutation is a *necessary* prerequisite to the development of a cancer, mutagenicity is not a *sufficient* criterion for carcinogenisis. In addition, a "carcinogen" may not directly cause the genetic mutation that induces a cancer; it may play a role in facilitating rather than directly causing the genetic damage. Therefore, the results of *in vitro* tests as predictors of carcinogenic risk are also open to a wide range of interpretations (e.g. [2]).

In this domain questioning the value of "objective" point value measures of risk really *is* the mainstream position. The report of the UK Department of Health's Committee on Carcinogenicity of Chemicals in Food [7] concludes:

The committee does not support the routine use of quantitative risk assessment for chemical carcinogens. This is because the present models are not validated, are often based on incomplete or inappropriate data, are derived more from mathematical assumptions than from a knowledge of biological mechanisms and, at least at present, demonstrate a disturbingly wide variation in risk estimates depending on the model adopted.

Nevertheless, there are still situations when a meaningful risk characterisation is needed. The next section will introduce the StAR risk assessment project, and then the paper will continue with a discussion of the approaches to extending the scope of risk assessment which are being developed within that project.

## 3   Goals of StAR

The approach to risk assessment which will be reported in this paper is being developed in the project *StAR* (for *St*andardised *A*rgument *R*eport). The top level goals of this project are:

*   to develop a computer-based aid to risk assessment which can systematically accommodate diverse types of evidence, both qualitative and quantitative;
*   to develop techniques for risk communication which are both comprehensive and intelligible.

*StAR* draws on earlier work on the development of a model for reasoning under uncertainty based on a simple intuitive notion of constructing arguments "for" and "against" a hypothesis [13]. The net support for the hypothesis may then be evaluated using one of a number of techniques; the choice being dependent on the nature of the evidence available. Full details of the syntax and semantics of the formal model of argumentation may be found in [16]. The key points of the present paper can, however, be understood without further reference to the more technical material contained in the last reference.

This project is to a great extent problem driven. A concrete goal is to develop a risk adviser to support the prediction of carcinogenic risk due to novel chemical compounds. The problems of toxicological risk assessment in general have been introduced above, and are discussed in more detail in [15]. The following points summarise both these discussions:

- toxicological risk assessments for chemicals may at best cover a very wide range of possible values;
- point value estimates conceal the uncertainties inherent in risk estimates;
- judgements based on the comparison of point values may be quite different from those based on the comparison of ranges of possible values;
- in very many cases the spread of possible values for a given risk assessment may be so great that a numerical risk assessment is completely meaningless.

Our aim is to allow the incorporation of numerical data where available, and to allow a grading of risk characterisation from qualitative through semi- or weak-quantitative to quantitative, contingent on the reliability and accuracy of the data available. The purely qualitative risk characterisation is the most controversial of these, and is in most need of discussion. Hence, this will form the focus of the major part of the remainder of this paper, although some comments on numerical risk assessment will also be made.

## 4  Qualitative terms for risk assessment

The need for some form of qualitative risk characterisation has long been accepted by the U.S. International Agency for Research on Cancer (IARC) and Environmental Protection Agency (EPA). Their joint proposal for a qualitative classification scheme will be discussed in this section. This will be contrasted with a more general proposal for "symbolic uncertainty".

Both of the following approaches use terms whose semantics is defined in terms of logical states. This contrasts fundamentally with most of the existing work on the use of linguistic uncertainty terms, in which the underlying semantics is assumed to be probabilistic (e.g. [6]).

IARC Classification System.

This is based on the U.S. EPA classification scheme. It uses a small set of terms which are defined to represent the current state of evidence. They take as their basis a classification of the weight of evidence for carcinogenicity into five groups for each of human studies and animal studies. These classifications are summarised here, but are defined precisely in [24].

For human studies, the classifications are:

*Sufficient evidence* of carcinogenicity. There is an established causal relationship between the agent and human cancer.

*Limited evidence* of carcinogenicity. A causal relationship is credible but not established.

*Inadequate evidence.* Few available data, or data unable to support the hypothesis of a causal relationship.

*No data.* Self-explanatory.

*No evidence.* No association was found between exposure and increased incidence of cancer in well-conducted epidemiological studies.

For animal studies the classifications are:

*Sufficient evidence* of carcinogenicity. Essentially data are available from well conducted experiments which indicate an increased incidence of malignant tumours, or combined malignant and benign tumours, with a high degree of confidence.

*Limited evidence* of carcinogenicity. Data which are suggestive, but limited for one of a number of specified reasons.

*Inadequate evidence*. Data which cannot be interpreted as showing either the presence or absence of a carcinogenic effect.

*No data*. Self-explanatory.

*No evidence*. There is no increased incidence of neoplasms in at least two well-designed and well-conducted animal studies in different species.

Data obtained from these classifications are then used to provide an overall categorization of the weight of evidence for human carcinogenicity (again, full definitions can be found in [24]):

| | |
|---|---|
| *Known* Human Carcinogen | *Sufficient* evidence from human (epidemiological) studies. |
| *Probable* Human Carcinogen | *Sufficient* animal evidence and evidence of human carcinogenicity, or *at least limited* evidence from human (epidemiological) studies. |
| *Possible* Human Carcinogen | *Sufficient* animal evidence but *inadequate* human evidence, or *limited* evidence from human studies in the *absence of sufficient* animal evidence. |
| *Not Classifiable* | *Inadequate* animal evidence and *inadequate* human evidence, but *sufficient* evidence of carcinogenicity in experimental animals. |
| *Non carcinogenic* to Humans | Evidence for lack of carcinogenicity. |

Note that these uncertainty terms are defined specifically in the context of carcinogenicity risk assessment. Our criticism of them is primarily on this basis. It would be more useful to see a set of terms which were defined at a higher level of abstraction. This would enable their intention to be communicable to a person who was not necessarily familiar with the details of risk assessment in a specific domain. It would also enable their usage to be standardised across a wide range of domains.

## Elvang-Gøransson et al's "logical uncertainty" terms.

An alternative set of terms with a precise mathematical characterisation was defined in [9]. These terms take the notion of logical provability as primitive. They then express successively increasing degrees of "acceptability" of the arguments which support the propositions of interest; as one progresses down the list there is a decrease in the tension between arguments for and against, a hypothesis P. A precise characterisation of these terms is quite lengthy, and so is not reproduced here. Full details and a discussion of their properties can be found in [16]. The following is intended to give a reasonably intuitive informal description.

| | |
|---|---|
| P is *open* | if it is *any* well-formed formula in the language of the logic (one may be unable to construct any arguments concerning it, however). |
| P is *supported* | if an argument, possibly using inconsistent data, can be constructed for it. |
| P is *plausible* | if a consistent argument can be constructed for it (one may also be able to construct a consistent argument against it). |
| P is *probable* | if a consistent argument can be constructed for it, and no consistent argument can be constructed against it. |
| P is *confirmed* | if it satisfies the conditions of being probable and, in addition, no consistent arguments can be constructed against any of the premises used in its supporting argument. |
| P is *certain* | if it is a tautology of the logic. This means that its validity is not contingent on any data in the knowledge-base. |

No quantitative information is used in the definition of these terms; they use purely logical constructions. However, it should be clear that they allow a unidimensional scaling.

A problem still remains. Although these terms do have a precise definition, it is an open question whether they have "cognitive validity" (see the next section). If not, then they will be open to misinterpretation as a vehicle for communication.

# 5 The *StAR* demonstrator

An alternative strategy to either of the above is to see if it is possible to establish specific patterns of argument as qualitative landmarks. The aim is then to associate those patterns with linguistic terms in a way which has "cognitive validity"; that is, where the definitions reflect in some way people's intuitive usage of the associated terms. In order to explore these ideas further, a risk assessment demonstrator has been built which uses a small set of linguistic terms as part of the reporting facility. A brief run-through of the demonstrator will be used in this section to illustrate the general approach. Some more detailed definitions of argument structures will be given in the next section.

The demonstrator is a prototype for a computer based assistant for the prediction of the potential carcinogenic risk due to novel chemical compounds. A notion of hazard identification is taken as a preliminary stage in the assessment of risk. The hazard identification used here draws heavily on the approach taken in the expert system DEREK, which is used for the qualitative prediction of possible toxic action of chemical compounds [23]. DEREK is able to detect chemical sub-structures within molecules, known as structural alerts, and relate these to a rule-base linking them with likely types of toxicity. In the demonstration, the structural alerts have been taken from a U.S. FDA report identifying sub-structures associated with various forms of carcinogenic activity [25].

The user of the carcinogenicity risk adviser presents the system with the chemical structure of the compound to be assessed, together with any additional information

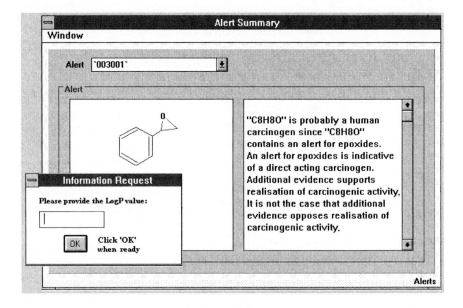

**Figure 2:** A capture of the summary screen following analysis by StAR of a simple chemical compound.

which may be thought relevant (such as possible exposure routes, or species of animal that will be exposed to the chemical). The chemical structure may be presented using a graphical interface.

The database of structural alerts is then searched for matches against the entered structure. If a match is found, a theorem prover tries to construct arguments for or against the hazard being manifest in the context under consideration. Having constructed all the relevant arguments, a report is generated on the basis of the available evidence.

For ease of presentation, the examples use a simplified database, and some of the following assessments may be chemically or biologically naive.

For the first screen (figure 2), the user has entered a relatively simple structure based on an aromatic ring. The system has identified that it contains an alert for epoxides (the triangular structure to the top right. Whilst constructing arguments, the system has recognised that the LogP value is relevant in this case, and so queries the user for this information (loosely, the value of LogP gives a measure of how easily the substance will be absorbed into tissue). The functional group for epoxides is indicative of a direct acting carcinogen, and the value of LogP supplied by the user is supportive of the substance being readily absorbed into tissue. Hazard recognition plus supportive evidence, with no arguments countering potential carcinogenic activity, yields the classification of a "probable human carcinogen" (the result might be different for different animals).

147

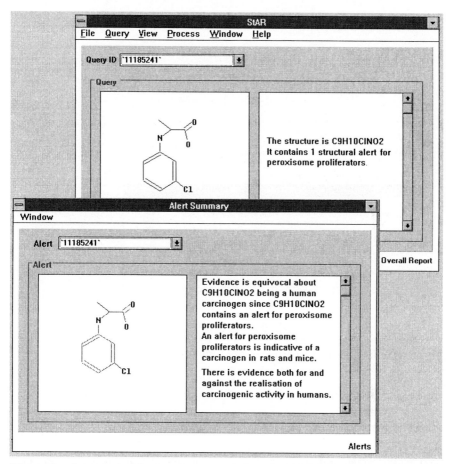

**Figure 3:** A capture of the summary screen following analysis by StAR of a chemical compound containing an alert for peroxisome proliferators.

Figure 2 shows the summary report. The query the user box is illustrated in this screen image, although it would normally have been closed by this stage.

In the second example (figure 3), a structure has been drawn which contains an alert for peroxisome proliferators. The top-most screen contains a simple non-judgemental statement to this effect. The lower screen contains the summary of the argumentation stage of analysis. Here, evidence is equivocal; there is evidence both for and against carcinogenic action in humans.

Further information on the evidence used for this assessment can be obtained. Figure 4 shows a more detailed report. It contains summaries of the arguments both for and against. Clicking on one of the argument summaries in turn yields more explanation still (on the reasons why the high doses used in experiments limits the applicability of the results to humans, in this case).

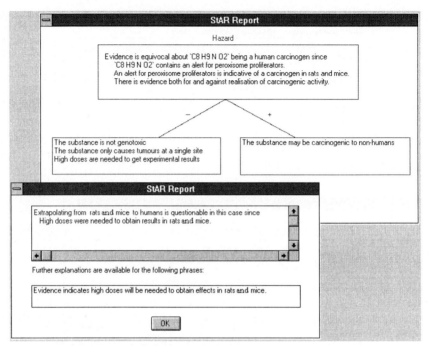

**Figure 4:** More detailed reporting is available from StAR at the user's request.

## 6   Arguments and cases

The previous section introduced the concept of matching linguistic uncertainty terms to structures of arguments. The thesis is that certain useful structures can be identified as "landmarks" in the space of all possible argument structures, and that natural language is capable of capturing the distinctions between these landmarks [11, 12].

Some example definitions of such landmarks will be given in this section. A more extensive set of definitions can be found in [14]. Experiments are currently under way to see if linguistic terms can be consistently associated in a meaningful way with such patterns of argument.

As a starting point four distinct "epistemic" states for a proposition $p$ can usefully be distinguished: p is confirmed; p is supported; p is opposed; p is excluded. It is useful to agree a notation to distinguish succinctly between these states. The following has been used in earlier work [13]:

p:+  $\equiv$  "p is supported"
p:−  $\equiv$  "p is opposed"

p:++ ≡ "p is confirmed"
p:—— ≡ "p is excluded"

We wish to raise arguments to the level of "first class objects" so that we may reason about *them*, as well as about the propositions of interest. *A* way of achieving this is to actually identify those facts and rules which are used to construct the argument. So a subset δ of the database Δ is identified which contains all and only that information which is needed to construct an argument for the proposition:

**Definition 6.1**

If $\delta \subseteq \Delta$ is minimal such that $\delta \vdash$ p:$q$ for some $q \in \{++, +, -, ——\}$, then (δ,p) is an argument for p from Δ. δ itself is referred to as the *grounds* of the argument.

If we now add in the above notation, we are able to distinguish four different basic classes of argument:

If $\delta \vdash$ p:+, then (δ,p) is a supporting argument;
If $\delta \vdash$ p:−, then (δ,p) is an opposing argument;
If $\delta \vdash$ p:++, then (δ,p) is a confirming argument;
If $\delta \vdash$ p:——, then (δ,p) is an excluding argument.

This discussion presupposes some proof mechanism for generating the labelled propositions p:$q$. Suitable examples can be found in [13, 16, 20], but others could be proposed. We do not wish to restrict this discussion to a specific entailment relation.

Cases

The set of all arguments which impact on a single proposition, constitutes the case concerning that proposition. This can now be stated in the above notation thus:

**Definition 6.2**

For a given proposition p

$\{(\delta,p) \mid \exists q \in \{++, +, -, ——\} \wedge \delta \vdash$ p:$q\}$     is the "*case concerning* p".

Two sub-cases of an overall case can be usefully distinguished. All those arguments which support or confirm the proposition p constitute the case for p. In contrast, all those propositions which oppose or exclude p constitute the case against p. To be precise:

**Definition 6.3**

For a given proposition p

$\{(\delta,p) \mid \exists q \in \{++, +\} \wedge \delta \vdash$ p:$q\}$          is the "*case for* p";
$\{(\delta,p) \mid \exists q \in \{-, ——\} \wedge \delta \vdash$ p:$q\}$          is the "*case against* p".

By altering the conditions on the kind of arguments, we may be able to define other useful sub-cases of an overall case.

Classes of cases

One further item of notation needs to be introduced now. Its usage will be slightly overloaded, but the precise meaning should be clear from the context.

**Definition 6.4**

$|(\delta,p)|$ is the "strength" of the argument (δ,p).

$|\{(\delta,p) \mid conditions\}|$ is the aggregate strength of those arguments $(\delta,p)$ satisfying *conditions*.

The latter may be just a "head count". This will usually be indicated by comparing the strength to some integer. For example $|\{(\delta,p) \mid \exists q \in \{++, +\} \wedge \delta \vdash p{:}q\}| \geq 1$ might be paraphrased as "there are one or more arguments for p". In contrast

$$|\{(\delta,p) \mid \exists q \in \{++, +\} \wedge \delta \vdash p{:}q\}| \quad > \quad |\{(\delta,p) \mid \exists q \in \{-, --\} \wedge \delta \vdash p{:}q\}|$$

means the aggregate strength of the *case for* is greater than the *case against* (be it a head count, probabilistic aggregation, or whatever).

Strength is a scalar quantity; it has magnitude but no direction. It is useful to think of the "force" of an argument as having both magnitude and direction. Although it is not used further in this document, the following definition is included for completeness:

**Definition 6.5**

The *polarity* of an argument indicates whether it is for or against its associated proposition.

The *force* of an argument is the product of its strength and its polarity.

Patterns identifying "classes of cases" can now be defined. Here are some examples. The first is a general pattern for all those cases where there are both arguments for and arguments against, the second where there are arguments for, but at least one excluding argument, and so on. For each pattern, an English language gloss precedes the formal definition.

For a given proposition p:

There is both a case for and a case against p. The term "equivocal" was used to describe this structure in the demonstrator.

$$|\{(\delta,p) \mid \exists q \in \{++, +\} \wedge \delta \vdash p{:}q\}| > 0 \wedge |\{(\delta,p) \mid \exists q \in \{-, --\} \wedge \delta \vdash p{:}q\}| > 0$$

There is a case for p, but at least one excluding argument

$$|\{(\delta,p) \mid \exists q \in \{++, +\} \wedge \delta \vdash p{:}q\}| > 0 \quad \wedge \quad |\{(\delta,p) \mid \delta \vdash p{:}{-}{-}\}| > 0$$

p has been confirmed, but there is still a case against p

$$|\{(\delta,p) \mid \delta \vdash p{:}{+}{+}\}| > 0 \quad \wedge \quad |\{(\delta,p) \mid \exists q \in \{-, --\} \wedge \delta \vdash p{:}q\}| > 0$$

p has been both confirmed and excluded

$$|\{(\delta,p) \mid \delta \vdash p{:}{+}{+}\}| > 0 \quad \wedge \quad |\{(\delta,p) \mid \delta \vdash p{:}{-}{-}\}| > 0$$

The last pattern means that it is possible to derive a contradiction in the classical sense. We can write the argument for the contradiction as $(\delta, \perp)$.

In the next group of patterns, either there is no case against, or there are at least no excluding arguments.

For a given proposition p:

There is a case for (although not a confirming case), but no case against p. This is the situation for which the term "probable" was used in section 5.

$$|\{(\delta,p)\,|\,\delta \vdash\ p{:}+\}| > 0 \qquad \wedge \qquad |\{(\delta,p)\,|\,\exists q \in \{-,--\} \wedge \delta \vdash\ p{:}q\}| = 0$$

There is a case for p and p cannot be excluded

$$|\{(\delta,p)\,|\,\delta \vdash\ p{:}+\}| > 0 \qquad \wedge \qquad |\{(\delta,p)\,|\,\delta \vdash\ p{:}--\}| = 0$$

p is confirmed and there is no case against p

$$|\{(\delta,p)\,|\,\delta \vdash\ p{:}++\}| > 0 \qquad \wedge \qquad |\{(\delta,p)\,|\,\exists q \in \{-,--\} \wedge \delta \vdash\ p{:}q\}| = 0$$

p is confirmed and there are no excluding arguments

$$|\{(\delta,p)\,|\,\delta \vdash\ p{:}++\}| > 0 \qquad \wedge \qquad |\{(\delta,p)\,|\,\delta \vdash\ p{:}--\}| = 0$$

Further cases can be defined in which there is either no case for, or at least there are no confirming arguments, and where purely negative statements are made about the state of evidence [14]. It is not clear whether all of these will be useful, however.

Apart from distinguishing between support and confirmation (or opposition and exclusion), the above patterns do not make any distinctions with respect to the strength of evidence. The following basic distinctions can be made.

For single arguments $(\delta,p)$ and $(\gamma,p)$, where $\delta \vdash\ p{:}+$ and $\gamma \vdash\ p{:}-$

A supporting and an opposing argument are of equal strength
$$|\,(\delta,p)\,| = |\,(\gamma,p)\,| \tag{1}$$

The supporting argument is stronger than the opposing argument
$$|\,(\delta,p)\,| > |\,(\gamma,p)\,| \tag{2}$$

The supporting argument is weaker than the opposing argument
$$|(\delta,p)\,| < |\,(\gamma,p)\,| \tag{3}$$

A supporting and an opposing argument are not of equal strength
$$\text{not}(|\,(\delta,p)\,| = |\,(\gamma,p)\,|) \tag{4}$$

Analogous patterns can be defined for sets of arguments.

Finally, there is the possibility that arguments themselves may be attacked. There is scope here for quite complex interactions between arguments; attacking arguments, attacking arguments that attack arguments, and so on. However, attention is restricted to some basic notions at this stage.

<u>"Undercutting defeat" of arguments.</u>

The reason for raising arguments to the level of first class objects is that we wish to be able to reason about the arguments themselves. We may annotate arguments as follows:

**Definition 6.6**
$(\delta, p){:}- \equiv$ "the argument $(\delta, p)$ is undermined".

**Definition 6.7**
$(\delta, p){:}-- \equiv$ "the argument $(\delta, p)$ is defeated".

In the work of Elvang-Gøransson et al. [9], the "arguments against the arguments" were all generated from same underlying database. Here we allow the possibility that the databases from which the arguments are constructed and from which the "meta-arguments" are constructed might be distinct [13].

For a knowledge base $\Delta$ and a (meta-)knowledge base $\Gamma$, the following cases can be defined (read "$A \bullet B$" as "$A$ such that $B$"):

A supporting argument is undermined

$$\exists \delta \subseteq \Delta, \gamma \subseteq \Gamma \bullet \delta \vdash p:+ \wedge \gamma \vdash (\delta, p):- \qquad (5)$$

A supporting argument is defeated

$$\exists \delta \subseteq \Delta, \gamma \subseteq \Gamma \bullet \delta \vdash p:+ \wedge \gamma \vdash (\delta, p):-- \qquad (6)$$

A confirming argument is undermined

$$\exists \delta \subseteq \Delta, \gamma \subseteq \Gamma \bullet \delta \vdash p:++ \wedge \gamma \vdash (\delta, p):- \qquad (7)$$

A confirming argument is defeated

$$\exists \delta \subseteq \Delta, \gamma \subseteq \Gamma \bullet \delta \vdash p:++ \wedge \gamma \vdash (\delta, p):-- \qquad (8)$$

Similar definitions can be provided for undermining and defeating opposing and excluding arguments.

The above just gives a selection of argument structures that *may* be useful as qualitative landmarks. To continue to develop the thesis outlined at the beginning of this section, we need to answer two questions. Which of these landmarks are recognised as important? Of those that are important in evaluating states of evidence, what is the language people use to recognise them?

A restricted set of linguistic terms linked to patterns of argument was used in the demonstrator discussed in Section 5. Preliminary user trials with this set have been very positive, and work now progresses to developing the demonstrator into a marketable product. This will provide a larger scale validation of this approach.

# 7 Discussion

There is an important difference between the system of argumentation that has just been presented, and the non-monotonic models that incorporate mechanisms of defeat and rebuttal such as Poole [21], Nute [19], Loui [17] and the various default logics. In the non-monotonic argumentation models, defeat and rebuttal may result in conclusions being retracted from the current belief state. This is not the case here. The argument structure is presented to the user, and the evidence state summarised by qualifying the conclusion with a linguistic term. This term indicates the general class of argument structures to which the specific case belongs. It is then up to the users of the system to be more, or less, cautious about which conclusions they accept, rather than the designer of the argument system.

This has important implications for risk communication. Even if the risk of some adverse effect has been strongly discounted, the risk is still presented together with the justification(s) for discounting that risk. The intent is that the risk characterisation should be transparent to the recipient, and he or she acts as final arbiter. The major benefit of this is that there is an explicit representation of the state of evidence concerning a proposition. However, the provision of a decision rule to aid the user in acting on the basis of the qualitative risk characterisation still needs to be addressed.

This paper focuses on qualitative risk assessment because it is the aspect of the StAR project that is most in need of discussion. However, the aim is to incorporate weak-quantitative and quantitative risk characterisations where possible. Some questions arise from this.

Although not illustrated here, numerical coefficients can be associated with the axioms in the demonstrator's database. However, an important question is raised if we do this. In this context, what precisely should the numbers mean? Remember that the system is intended to give some form of risk *prediction*, drawing on some prior general knowledge about indicators for potential carcinogenic activity. Should a numerical value, or interval of possible values indicate:

1. the lifetime likelihood of someone being exposed to the chemical developing cancer;

   or

2. a subjective estimate of belief in the statement "this chemical is carcinogenic"?

Given the difficulty of assessing risk due to chemicals that have been subject to some experimental study, discussed in section 2, it does not seem realistic to suppose that meaningful probabilities could be assigned to the general indicators of risk that are used in the *StAR* database. However, it *may* be possible to elicit subjective indications of the relative plausibility of the conclusions drawn from the generic knowledge that is elicited for the *StAR* database. So, whilst 1) above is unlikely to be achievable, an ability to include a value or range of values that conform to 2) *may* be realistic, at least in certain circumstances.

The *StAR* database can be viewed as consisting of facts (about the structure of the chemical of interest, its physical properties and the context in which it will be used) together with generic knowledge about possible mechanisms of carcinogenicity (chemical sub-structures with believed associations with carcinogenic activity, possible metabolic pathways, exposure routes, and so on). From this knowledge, *StAR* draws *plausible* conclusions. It may well be that it would be more appropriate to model the generic knowledge as conditional assertions [8] rather than by the more naive approach of rules with certainty coefficients as used here. In fact, the definition of an argument used in this paper is consistent with that of Benferhat, Dubois and Prade [4]. Hence a possibilistic encoding of rational inference may be an appropriate unifying framework for the qualitative and quantitative aspects of the risk characterisation, in the context where the numerical coefficient indicates a measure of plausibility of the conclusion.

A crucial issue is still outstanding, however. Although this paper offers some ideas for qualitative and (semi-)quantitative risk characterisations in the absence of reliable statistical data, there still remains the question of how to act on the basis of such a risk assessment. The implicit claim is that there is scope for fairer decisions to be made if a risk assessment is carried out in an argumentation framework, because:

1. The reasoning behind the risk assessment is readily open to inspection;

2. A party is able to counter a numerical risk assessment with a subjective, but clearly structured, risk characterisation.

In the case of the carcinogenic risk application being developed in StAR, we do not see the decisions that are made after consultation with the system as being along the lines of "we shall, or shall not allow this chemical into the public arena". Rather, it is intended to assist in the prioritisation of further investigations into the chemical of interest. That is, the decisions in question are of a different type from the rational choice of alternatives that is classically the domain of decision theory.

Apart from the specific application, it is hoped that the work described on providing a framework for the structuring of cases will contribute to a more orderly debate between two parties with differing conceptions of the risk associated with a specific situation.

# 8   Conclusion

This paper reports work on the development of qualitative techniques for risk assessment. The main aim of the paper is to bring the motivation for the work into the public arena. The main points are:

- there are situations in which a numerical assessment of uncertainty is unrealistic, yet;
- some structured presentation of the case that supports a particular assessment may still be required, and is achievable.

The concept of characterising risk by linguistic terms defined by relating them to patterns of argument has been demonstrated. This was then followed up with more detailed definitions of categories of cases (collections of arguments) which are being used as the basis for further studies.

As mentioned at the end of Section 6, some of the ideas from that section were trailed in the carcinogenicity risk advisor described in Section 5. This is now being developed as a product which is expected to be on the market in the near future.

# 9   Acknowledgements

The StAR consortium consists of: Judson Consulting; Imperial Cancer Research Fund, London; LHASA UK, School of Chemistry, Leeds University; Logic Programming Associates (LPA), London; Psychology Department, City University, London. The demonstrator was constructed in LPA Prolog for Windows, with the chemical structure window provided by Hampden Data Services, Nottingham. The assistance of Nicola Pappas and Alan Westwood is gratefully acknowledged.

This work was supported under the DTI/EPSRC Intelligent Systems Integration Programme, project IED/4/1/8029.

# 10 References

1.  J. Adams. *Risk*. UCL Press, London, 1995.
2.  J. Ashby. Benzyl acetate: from mutagenic carcinogen to non-mutagenic non-carcinogen in 7 years?. *Mutation Res.*, 306:107-109, 1994.
3.  J. Ashby and R.W. Tennant. Definitive relationships among chemical structure, carcinogenicity and mutagenicity for 301 chemicals tested by the U.S. NTP. *Mutation Res.*, 257:229-306, 1991.
4.  S. Benferhat, C. Cayrol, D. Dubois, J. Lang and H. Prade. Inconsistency management and prioritized syntax-based entailment. *Proc. International Joint Conference on Artificial Intelligence '93*, Chambery, France, 1993.
5.  P. Brown. Quoted in *Local Transport Today* (30 October), 1991.
6.  D.V. Budescu and T.S. Wallsten. A Review of Human Linguistic Probability Processing. *Knowledge Engineering Review*, 10:43-62, 1995.
7.  R.L. Carter. *Guidelines for the Evaluation of Chemicals for Carcinogenicity*. London: HMSO, 1991.
8.  D. Dubois and H. Prade. Non-standard theories of uncertainty in knowledge representation and reasoning. *Knowledge Engineering Review*, 9:399-416, 1994.
9.  M. Elvang-Gøransson, P.J. Krause and J. Fox. Dialectic reasoning with inconsistent information. In: Heckerman, D. and Mamdani, A. (eds.), *Uncertainty in Artificial Intelligence. Proceedings of the Ninth Conference*, San Mateo Ca: Morgan Kaufmann, 1993.
10. J. Fox. *Language, Logic and Uncertainty*. Technical Report, Imperial Cancer Research Fund, London, 1984.
11. J. Fox. Three arguments for extending the framework of probability. In: Kanal L.H. and Lemmer J.F. (eds), *Uncertainty in Artificial Intelligence*, Elsevier Science Publishers B.V. (North-Holland), 1986.
12. J. Fox and P.J. Krause. Symbolic decision theory and autonomous agents. In: D'Ambrosio B.D., Smets P. and Bonissone P.P., *Uncertainty in Artificial Intelligence, Proceedings of the Seventh Conference*, San Mateo Ca: Morgan Kaufmann, 1991.
13. J. Fox, P.J. Krause and S.J. Ambler. Arguments, contradictions and practical reasoning. *Proceedings of ECAI '92*, John Wiley and Sons, 623-627, 1992.
14. J. Fox and P.J. Krause. *Formal Definitions of Arguments and Cases*. ICRF Technical Report, 1994.
15. P.J. Krause, J. Fox and P. Judson. An Argumentation Based Approach to Risk Assessment, *IMA Journal of Mathematics Applied in Business and Industry*, 5: 249-263, 1994.
16. P.J. Krause, S.J. Ambler, M. Elvang-Gøransson and J. Fox. A Logic of Argumentation for Reasoning under Uncertainty. *Computational Intelligence*, 11:113-131, 1995.
17. R.P. Loui. Defeat among arguments: a system of defeasible inference. *Computational Intelligence*, 3:100-106, 1987.

18. National Research Council. *Risk Assessment in the Federal Government: Managing the Process*. Washington DC: National Academy Press, 1992.

19. D. Nute. Defeasible Reasoning and Decision Support Systems. *Decision Support Systems*, 4:97-110, 1988.

20. S. Parsons. Normative argumentation and qualitative probability. *Proceedings of the International Joint Conference on Practical Reasoning,* Bonn, 1997.

21. D.L. Poole. On the comparison of theories: preferring the most specific explanation. *Proc. IJCAI '85*, Los Angeles, USA, 144-147, 1985.

22. Roy. Soc. *Risk: Analysis, Perception & Management*. London: The Royal Society, 1992.

23. D.M. Sanderson and C.G. Earnshaw. Computer Prediction of Possible Toxic Action from Chemical Structure; The DEREK System. *Human & Experimental Toxicology*, 10:261-273, 1991.

24. U.S. EPA. Guidelines for Carcinogen Risk Assessment. *Federal Register*, 51, 33991-34003, 1986.

25. U.S. FDA. *General principles for evaluating the safety of compounds used in food-producing animals. Appendix 1. Carcinogen structure guide*. Washington: U.S. Food and Drug Administration, 1986.

# Information Retrieval and Dempster-Shafer's Theory of Evidence

## Mounia Lalmas

Department of Computing Science, University of Glasgow
Glasgow G12 8QQ, Scotland
mounia@dcs.gla.ac.uk

**Abstract.** This paper describes the use of the Dempster-Shafer theory of evidence to construct an information retrieval model that aims to capture four essential features of information: structure, significance, uncertainty and partiality. We show that Dempster-Shafer's initial framework allows the representation of the structure and the significance of information, and that the notion of refinement later introduced by Shafer allows the representation of the uncertainty and the partiality of information. An implementation of the model is briefly discussed.

## 1 Background

In [3, 6], some of the essential features of information in the context of an *Information Retrieval* (IR) system were discussed:

(i) *Structure:* A document often contains semantically related information items. An example of semantically related information is equivalent items of information. A document should not be more relevant to a query that uses many terms to express an information need than to a query using fewer terms to express the same information need. This equivalence of information can be taken into account by grouping equivalent terms into structures and treating the groups of equivalent terms as entities.

(ii) *Significance:* Not all the information contained in a document has the same significance. An item of information that occurs frequently in a document can imply that this item is a significant part of the document.

(iii) *Partiality:* Many items of information are not identified as part of a document's information content, though they are implicit in the document information content. The representation of a document is only partial; it can grow when the implicit information becomes available; for example, via the use of a thesaurus. That is, a document can have several representations, some being more exhaustive than others.

(iv) *Uncertainty:* The exact information content of a document cannot always be identified appropriately because of the difficulty in capturing the richness and the intensional nature of information. The relevance of a document with respect to a query depends on the existence of information explicit or implicit in the document, so the more uncertain this information, the less relevant the document.

To capture the partiality and uncertainty of information, the *Transformation Principle*[1] [3, 6] upon which to base a model of IR was proposed:

> Given a document representation $d$, a query representation $q$, and a knowledge set $K$; the measure of relevance, denoted $r(d, q)$, relative to $K$, is determined by the minimal transformation applied to $d$ to obtain some $d'$ such that $d'$ contains $q$.

The symbol $d$ refers to the original document, and represents the information explicit in the document.

The symbol $q$ is the query representation.

The symbol $K$, the knowledge set, contains the semantic relationships upon which the transformation is based. Examples of relationships in IR include synonyms, generic terms, broader terms, etc.

The original document, representing the information explicit in the document, can be transformed into a document, which can itself be transformed into another document until the document $d'$ is obtained. These documents and $d'$ are referred to as transformed documents. They contain the information explicit and implicit in the document. The transformed documents are not actual documents, but consist of more exhaustive representations of the original document. The different representations of the document capture the partiality of information.

The transformation may be uncertain. Suppose that the transformation of $d$ into $d'$ is based on a relationship linking, for example, the information item "database" to the information item "relational database". If it is not known which type of "database" is referred to in $d$, and since not all databases are relational ones, the use of the relationship is uncertain with respect to $d$: the information contained in $d'$ (i.e., "relational database") is uncertain with respect to $d$. The transformation of $d$ into $d'$ is uncertain.

The transformation of documents depends on how documents and queries are indexed. If documents and queries are indexed as sets of terms, which is common to many IR systems, the transformation of a document can be defined in terms of semantic relationships extracted, for example, from a thesaurus. A transformed document will then contain the terms that are contained in the original document and the terms that are semantically related to those used in the original document. The uncertainty of the transformation can be defined from the uncertainty introduced with the use of semantic relationships in transforming the document.

The uncertainty of the transformation process is used to compute the measure of relevance $r(d, q)$, also referred to as the degree of relevance, such that the more uncertainty is involved in the process, the lower the relevance.

Minimality ensures that the transformation process ceases as soon as the information being sought is reached. This indicates the obvious fact that a document that

---

[1] This principle is based on Van Rijsbergen's *Logical Uncertainty Principle* [12].

requires less transformations than another one is usually more relevant to the query than the other document.

The structure and significance of information are not explicitly expressed in the Transformation Principle, but they can be captured if the representation of the original document is defined a set of structures with their associated significance, and the transformation of a document is defined in terms of the transformations of these structures. This is illustrated in Fig. 1.

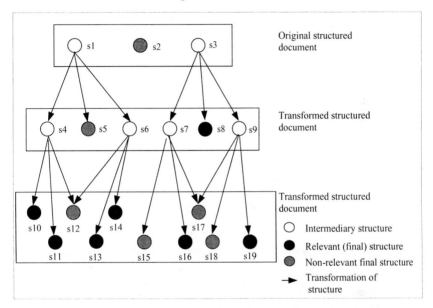

**Fig. 1.    Example of the transformation of a document in the structured representation**

Our task was to construct an IR model based on the Transformation Principle to capture partiality and uncertainty, and that takes into account structure and signif-icance. We use the Dempster-Shafer theory of evidence [2, 11] to express the IR model. The components of the IR model are described in section 2. The use of the Dempster-Shafer theory to express the model is presented in two steps. First, the initial theory as developed in [2] is described in section 3, and is shown to represent structure and significance. Second, the refinement function, later defined by Shafer [11], is described in section 4, and is given as a possible method for representing par-tiality and uncertainty. An implementation of the model was performed. We briefly discuss its outcomes in section 5. We conclude in section 6.

## 2    The Components of the Model

In this section, we define the components of an IR model that allows the capturing of structure, significance, uncertainty and partiality of information.

The structures considered in this work are those that contain semantically related information items and can be viewed as denoting a topic. Consider the following terms appearing in a document:

$$rose, Sun, giraffe, tulip, table, dog, Macintosh, elephant \qquad (1)$$

Four structures can be identified in this document denoting the topics "flower", "animal", "computer", and "furniture". An illustration of a structured representation of this document is given in Fig. 2.

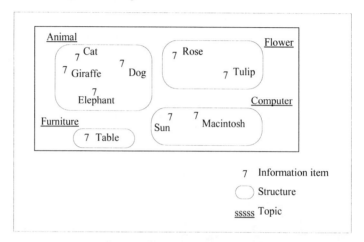

**Fig. 2. Example of a structured representation of a document**

We denote $I$ the set of information items (terms, phrases, whatever is used to index documents) and $S$ the set of structures. A document is represented as an element of $2^S$; thus capturing the structure of information.

Some structures may be more significant in a document than others because they constitute a more prominent part of the document information content than other structures. For example, the structure denoted by the topic "animal" can be considered more significant than the structure denoted by the topic "furniture" because the former structure contains more information than the latter. To represent this, a weight (a numerical value) is assigned to each structure to represent its significance. The higher the weight, the more prominent the structure.

To represent the significance of structures, we use a numerical function $w : S \rightarrow [0, 1]$: given a structure $s$ that belongs to a document, $w(s)$ represents the significance of the information contained in the structure $s$ (the weight of the structure) with respect to the document's information content.

The computation of $w(s)$ depends on whether $s$ belongs to an original document or a transformed document.

If $s$ belongs to an original document, then $s$ contains information explicit in the document. In this case, the value $w(s)$ increases with the prominence of the topic denoting that structure $s$, and this with respect to the document's explicit information content. Many standard IR methods can be used to compute $w(s)$ such as those based on term frequency information and inverse document frequency [9]. They come directly from the indexing process applied to the document.

If $s'$ belongs to a transformed document, $w(s')$ represents the weight of the structure $s'$ in that transformed document. However, its value is not determined from the indexing process; it depends on the weight of the structures of the original document that are transformed into $s'$ (eventually through intermediary transformations), and the uncertainty of these transformations.

A structure that is transformed into another structure can itself be the result of a transformation. If the two transformations are uncertain, then the information becomes increasingly more uncertain with each transformation. The uncertainty is said to be propagated along the sequence of transformations. This propagation of uncertainty must be taken into account in the formulation of $w(s')$.

Let $s$ be transformed into $s'$. In this case, $w(s')$ depends on $w(s)$ (i.e., the weight of $s$, which represents the uncertainty thus far propagated from the sequence of transformations that lead to $s$, or its significance if $s$ belongs to the original document) and the uncertainty in transforming $s$ into $s'$. Since information becomes more uncertain with each additional transformation, the values of $w(s)$ and $w(s')$ should be such that $w(s') \leq w(s)$.

Uncertainty, in addition to be propagated along transformations, can be aggregated. For example, in Fig. 1, two transformations lead to the structure $s_{12}$. This can be viewed as an accumulation of evidence towards the information contained in $s_{12}$; the information contained in $s_{12}$ should be less uncertain than if it was obtained by one transformation alone. Therefore, if $w^1(s_{12})$ and $w^2(s_{12})$ are the uncertainty[2] values attached to $s_{12}$ with, respectively, the first transformation (from $s_4$) and the second transformation (from $s_6$), then the overall uncertainty attached to obtaining $s_{12}$ from the original document, which is $w(s_{12})$, should be a combination of the values of $w^1(s_{12})$ and $w^2(s_{12})$ such that its value is at least as high as $w^1(s_{12})$ and $w^2(s_{12})$; that is, we have $w^1(s_{12}) \leq w(s_{12})$ and $w^2(s_{12}) \leq w(s_{12})$. This combination corresponds to an aggregation of uncertainty.

The relevance of a document to a query is expressed by the function $r : 2^S \times I \rightarrow [0, 1]$. For a document $d \in 2^S$, and a query $q \in I$, the value of $r(d, q)$ should increase with the number of transformations that lead to structures that contain[3] information pertinent to the query. This fact can be captured by defining the value of $r(d, q)$ as the aggregation of the uncertainty of those transformed structures that contain the query $q$: the value of $r(d, q)$ is defined as the aggregation of the values of $w(s')$ such that $s'$ is a structure in the transformed document and it contains $q$. If there is only one such structure $s'$, then $r(d, q) = w(s')$. Otherwise, $r(d, q)$ is such that $r(d, q) \geq w(s')$ for each $s'$.

In Fig. 1, the structures representing the original document are $s_1, s_2, s_3$. The structures that contain the information being sought by the query are $s_8, s_{10}, s_{11}, s_{13}$,

---

[2] The superscripts are used to differentiate the two transformations. If $a$ is the uncertainty associated with the first transformation and $b$ is the uncertainty associated with the second transformation, then $w^1(s_{12}) = a$ and $w^2(s_{12}) = b$.

[3] The notion of containment depends on how structures and information items are implemented. For example, if they are implemented, respectively, as sets of terms, and terms, containment corresponds to inclusion.

$s_{14}$, $s_{17}$ and $s_{18}$. The relevance of the document to the query will be the aggregation of $w(s_8)$, $w(s_{10})$, $w(s_{11})$, $w(s_{13})$, $w(s_{14})$, $w(s_{17})$ and $w(s_{18})$.

An aspect which has not been discussed so far is the minimality of the transformation. In this paper, a minimal transformation is a sequence of transformations in which all the transformations are necessary; the transformations are based on relationships that are essential to obtain the information being sought by the query.

## 2.1 Summary

In this section, we have describe the components of an IR model based on the Transformation Principle, and that captures the four features of information described in section 1. These components are:

(i)   a set of information items $I$.

(ii)  a set of structures $S$.

(iii) $w : S \rightarrow [0,1]$ expressing the significance of information. When related to original documents, its values are supposed determined. When related to transformed documents, its values must capture that uncertainty increases when propagated and decreases when aggregated.

(iv)  $r : 2^S \times I \rightarrow [0,1]$ expressing the measure of relevance. Its value must decrease with the number of transformed structures that contain information pertinent to the query.

The components and their properties are summarized in the following table:

| Given | To compute |
| --- | --- |
| $s$ is in the original document | $w(s)$ is assumed given. |
| $w(s) = a$ and $s$ is transformed into $s'$ | $w(s')$ in terms of $a$ such that $w(s') \leq a$ |
| Two transformations leading to $s'$, $w^1(s') = a$ and $w^2(s') = b$ | $w(s')$ in terms of $a$ and $b$ such that $w(s') \geq a, b$ |
| Two structures containing $q$, $w(s_1) = a$ and $w(s_2) = b$ | $r(d,q)$ in terms of $a$ and $b$ such that $r(d,q) \geq a, b$ |

Now that the components of the model and their properties have been defined, the next step is to express these components within a formal framework. This work advances the use of the Dempster-Shafer theory of evidence as the formal framework. First, we shown how the theory of evidence as originally introduced by Dempster [2] can be used to represent structure and significance. In section 4, we show how some concepts later defined by Shafer [11] can be used to express partiality and uncertainty.

# 3 The Initial Dempster-Shafer Theory of Evidence: Representing Structure and Significance

We describe first the initial theory as developed by Dempster. Then, we present an IR model based on the initial theory, and show how a similar approach can capture structure and significance as studied in this work. Finally, we show that the initial Dempster-Shafer theory cannot capture partiality and uncertainty.

## 3.1 The Initial Theory

The purpose of the theory of evidence is to represent beliefs in a set of elements referred to as *a frame of discernment*. A *belief function* $Bel : 2^U \rightarrow [0,1]$ is defined on a frame of discernment $U$. The beliefs are usually computed based on a density function $m$ called a *basic probability assignment* (BPA) which has the following properties:

$$m(\emptyset) = 0 \quad \text{and} \quad \sum_{A \subseteq U} m(A) = 1 \tag{2}$$

$m(A)$ represents the degree of belief that is exactly committed to the set $A$. If $m(A) > 0$ then $A$ is called a *focal element*. The set of focal elements and its associated BPA define a *body of evidence* on $U$. The belief associated with a set $A \subseteq U$, denoted as $Bel(A)$, is defined on $m$ as follows:

$$Bel(A) = \sum_{B \subseteq A} m(B) \tag{3}$$

$Bel(A)$ is the total belief committed to $A$, that is, the belief that the truth is in $A$.

A commonly used rule is *Dempster's combination rule*. This rule aggregates two bodies of evidence defined within the same frame of discernment into one body of evidence. Let $m_1$ and $m_2$ be two bodies of evidence defined in the frame of discernment $U$. The new body of evidence is defined by a BPA $m$ as follows:

$$m(A) = \frac{\sum\limits_{B \cap C = A} m_1(B) \times m_2(C)}{\sum\limits_{B \cap C \neq \emptyset} m_1(B) \times m_2(C)} \tag{4}$$

The notions thus far introduced constitute the Dempster-Shafer initial theory of evidence.

## 3.2 An IR Model Based on the Initial Theory

A number of IR models based on the Dempster-Shafer initial framework has been developed, for example [1, 10]. The basic characteristics of the models are similar, so we only discuss the model proposed in [1] by de Silva and Milidiu.

The model starts with the definition of a set of terms and their associated semantics (e.g., synonyms, related terms, etc.). Given a term $t$, $S(t)$ and $N(t)$ are the sets of synonyms and narrower terms of $t$ (e.g., part-of or instance-of relationships), respectively. $N(t) \subseteq S(t)$, where $\subseteq$ is viewed as semantically included. Examples of the narrower terms and the synonyms of the term "flower" are, respectively[4]:

$$N(flower) = \{rose, tulip\} \tag{5}$$

$$S(flower) = \{blossom, bud, flower, rose, tulip\} \tag{6}$$

For each set of synonyms $S(t)$, one term in this set is used as a descriptor. For example, the term "flower" is the descriptor of the above set of synonyms. A descriptor $\alpha$ is atomic if it does not have a narrower term, that is, $N(\alpha) = \emptyset$.

The set of atomic descriptors constitutes a frame of discernment $U$. Both the document and the query are defined as a body of evidence in this frame of discernment. $\alpha$ is a descriptor of the document if at least one term in $S(\alpha)$ appears in the document. Each descriptor of the document defines a focal element. The focal element associated to a non-atomic descriptor $\alpha$ of the document is defined as the union of the atomic descriptors in $N(\alpha)$. For example, suppose that "flower" is a descriptor of the document. If "rose" and "tulip" are atomic descriptors (i.e., $N(rose) = \emptyset$ and $N(tulip) = \emptyset$), then the focal element associated to the descriptor "flower" is:

$$\{rose, tulip\} \tag{7}$$

The BPA of a focal element representing the descriptor $\alpha$ is defined as follows:

$$m_d(\alpha) = \frac{\sum\limits_{t \in S(\alpha)} f(t, d)}{\sum\limits_{t \in T(d)} f(t, d)} \tag{8}$$

where $T(d)$ is the set of terms in the document and $f(t, d)$ is the frequency of the term $t$ in the document.

In de Silvia and Milidiu's model, the query is also represented as a body of evidence associated with the frame of discernment $U$. Let $T(q)$ be the set of terms used in the query $q$, which all correspond to descriptors. Let $w(\alpha)$ be the weight that represents a user's belief in $\alpha$ being a descriptor that represents the semantic content of the document to be retrieved. The BPA associated to this frame is defined in terms of this weight as follows:

$$m_q(\alpha) = \frac{w(\alpha)}{\sum\limits_{\alpha \in T(q)} w(\alpha)} \tag{9}$$

The relevance of the document to the query is computed as the agreement, denoted $A(d, q)$, between the document and the query. Several formulations of $A(d, q)$ are possible, depending on the properties attached to the terms. In one of them, the

---

[4] A term is a synonym of itself.

descriptors in the document and the query are independently determined, which leads to the following formulation of $A(d, q)$ (refer to [1] for the proof):

$$A(d, q) = \sum_{A \cap B \neq \emptyset} m_d(A) * m_q(B) \tag{10}$$

We can use a similar approach to represent the structures forming the original document and their significance. The document is represented by a frame of discernment, and the elements in this frame represent information items. Structures are represented by focal elements. The use of the relationships between information items to define the focal elements can be analogous to that above described (it depends on how semantically related information items are defined). The weights associated with these structures are represented by the BPA, which can be computed similarly to that above described (taking into account frequency information). If $m_d$ is the BPA associated to the original document, and $s$ is a structure in that document, then $w(s) = m_d(s)$.

## 3.3 Limitation of the Initial Theory

The initial theory of evidence can provide for the representation of structure and significance, but not for partiality and uncertainty.

The intuition behind the expression of the relevance degree in de Silvia and Milidiu's model is different from that in a model based on the Transformation Principle. In the former, the relevance consists of a comparison between the information contained in the document and the information need as phrased in the query. In the model discussed in this paper, the relevance is based on obtaining of a transformed document that contains the information need. Therefore, de Silvia and Milidiu's model cannot account for the representation of transformed documents, and hence partiality and uncertainty as studied in this work.

None of the other concepts of the initial theory of evidence can capture the transformation of a document. The belief function associated to the frame of discernment is computed based on the BPA of the focal elements of that frame. If that frame represents the original document, the belief function expresses relevance in terms of that document. This is not in accord with the Transformation Principle upon which our model is based.

As well, Dempster's combination rule cannot embody the transformed documents. Indeed, Dempster's combination rule aggregates two independent bodies of evidence into one body of evidence. Only the bodies of evidence change, not the elements of the frame of discernment. To embody the transformation of a document, both the original document and the transformed document must be represented by the same frame of discernment. Moreover, the first body of evidence would represent the original document, and the second body of evidence would model the transformed document. However, with Dempster's combination rule, the second body of evidence is not computed from the first body of evidence. In fact, Dempster's rule defines a third body of evidence in terms of the two previous ones. Therefore, it is not possible to represent that the transformed document is constructed in terms of the original document.

## 3.4 Conclusion

The initial theory of evidence can model the structure (by focal elements) and the significance (by a BPA) of information in a similar way to that done by de Silvia and Milidiu's model, but the other features of information cannot be expressed. The reason is that a single frame of discernment is used, so transformed documents cannot be represented. Shafer's refinement function [11] overcomes this problem.

# 4 Shafer's Refinement Function: Representing Partiality and Uncertainty

There are two aspects to the refinement function, a qualitative and a quantitative one. These are discussed in turn, and at the same time, we show how they can express, respectively, partiality and uncertainty. There is however a limitation with the use of Shafer's refinement function. This is discussed last.

## 4.1 The Qualitative Aspect of the Refinement Function: Representing Partiality

The refinement of a frame of discernment $U$ into a frame of discernment $V$ is defined by *splitting* the elements of $U$ into the elements of $V$. Splitting an element into a set of elements can be viewed as the latter representing more precise items of information that the former. For example, "animal" can be split into "dog", "cat" and "horse", since "dog", "cat" and "horse", are, each of them, more precise than "animal". The refinement is formally defined by a function $\omega : 2^U \to 2^V$ as follows:

(i)  $\omega(\{p\}) \neq \emptyset$ for all $p \in U$

(ii)  $\omega(\{p\}) \cap \omega(\{p'\}) = \emptyset$ if $p \neq p'$ for all $p, p' \in U$

(iii)  $\bigcup_{p \in U} \omega(\{p\}) = V$

(i) means that every element of $U$ is split into elements of $V$. (ii) means that two elements cannot be split into the same element. Finally, (iii) means that the result of a refinement is a frame of discernment. $U$ and $V$ are called the *coarse* and the *refined* frame, respectively.

In the above example, suppose that "animal" is in the coarse frame of discernment $U$, then:

$$w(\{animal\}) = \{dog, cat, horse\} \tag{11}$$

and "dog", "cat" and horse" are in the refined frame of discernment $V$. The refinement function is extended to set $A \subseteq U$ of elements as follows:

$$w(A) = \bigcup_{p \in A} w(\{p\}) \tag{12}$$

$\omega(A)$ consists of all the elements in $V$ that are obtained by splitting all the elements in $A$. For example, if "flower" is split into "rose" and "tulip", then:

$$w(\{animal, flower\}) = \{dog, cat, horse, rose, tulip\} \qquad (13)$$

The refinement function links two frames of discernment, such that one is defined in terms of the other. If the original document is modelled by the coarse frame, then the refinement function can represent the transformation of that document; the refined frame models the transformed document, and hence partiality can be represented.

The splitting process must then be defined in terms of relationships of the knowledge set $K$. The fact that an element $p$ is split into an element $p'$ (the information items these elements represent) can be viewed as a relationship of the knowledge set. For example, the splitting of the term "animal" into "dog", "cat" and "horse" means that animal is related to "dog", to "cat" and to "horse". Note that the relationships can be uncertain, since when mentioning "animal", it is not sure whether one means "dog", "cat" or "horse".

Shafer [11] demonstrates that the composition of two refinement functions is also a refinement function. That is, given the two refinement functions:

$$w_1 : 2^U \rightarrow 2^V \qquad (14)$$

$$w_2 : 2^V \rightarrow 2^W \qquad (15)$$

where $W$ is a frame of discernment, into which $V$ is refined, this means that ($\circ$ is the composition operator):

$$w_2 \circ w_1 : 2^U \rightarrow 2^W \qquad (16)$$

is also a refinement function. If a refinement function is used to model the transformation of a document, the composition of refinement functions can model a sequence of transformations.

In the model discussed in this paper, the structures of the transformed document are defined in terms of the structures of the original document. If the refined frame is to model the transformed document, the focal elements of the refined frame must be defined in terms of the focal elements of the coarse frame of discernment, since the focal elements model structures. However, in Dempster-Shafer's framework the focal elements of the refined frame are not explicitly defined in terms of the focal elements of the original frame, because the refinement function is defined at the element levels and then generalized to set levels. There are, however, properties relating the two sets of focal elements. These properties concern the BPA associated to the focal elements of the two frames. These are discussed next since they constitute a quantitative aspect of the refinement function.

## 4.2 The Quantitative Aspect of the Refinement Function: Representing Uncertainty

Let $Bel_U$ and $Bel_V$ be the belief functions defined on the coarse frame $U$ and the refined frame $V$, respectively. Let $m_U$ and $m_V$ be their respective BPAs. In Shafer's definition, $m_V$ is not explicitly defined in terms of $m_U$. However, the belief functions $Bel_U$ and $Bel_V$ must satisfy the criteria that the coarse and the refinement frames are *compatible*. This means that the two frames must agree on the information defined in them. Shafer explains [11] that for a given set $A$ of the frame of discernment $U$, and for a given refinement function $w : 2^U \to 2^V$, the sets $A$ and $w(A)$ represent the same information. That is, although refining a set means that more precise items of information are obtained, the union of these items carries the same information as the original set. For example, if the set:

$$A = \{animal\} \tag{17}$$

is refined into the set:

$$w(A) = \{dog, cat, horse, elephant, \ldots\} \tag{18}$$

where ... refers to any living animal. The same information is carried by the two sets. Shafer explains in detail this notion of compatible frames and formulates it. The details and the formalism are not given here since they involve notions that are not necessary to the understanding of the concepts used in this paper. What should be known is that the belief functions $Bel_U$ and $Bel_V$ are compatible if, for a given set $A$ of the frame $U$, the following property holds:

$$Bel_U(A) = Bel_V(\omega(A)) \tag{19}$$

It can be proven that this is satisfied if (see [11] for proof):

$$m_U(A) = \sum_{B \subseteq V, A = \bar{\theta}(B)} m_V(B) \tag{20}$$

where:

$$\bar{\theta}(B) = \{x \in U \,|\, w(\{x\}) \cap B \neq \emptyset\} \tag{21}$$

The set $\bar{\theta}(B)$ is called the *outer reduction* of the refinement of the set $B$. It is the set of elements $x \in U$ such that the refinement of $x$, that is $w(\{x\})$, intersects with $B$. This link between the BPAs $m_U$ and $m_V$ is illustrated in Fig. 3.

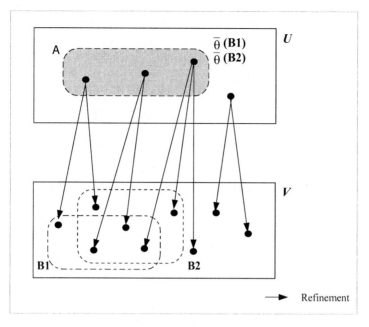

**Fig. 3. Outer reduction of a refinement**

Let $A$ be a focal element of $U$, and $B_1$ and $B_2$ be the focal elements of $V$. Both $\overline{\theta}(B_1) = A$ and $\overline{\theta}(B_2) = A$; that is $B_1$ and $B_2$ have the same outer reduction, $A$. Due to equation 20 above, the following equality must hold:

$$m_U(A) = m_V(B_1) + m_V(B_2) \tag{22}$$

The link between the focal element $A$ and the focal elements $B_1$ and $B_2$ and their respective BPAs can be used to model the transformation of structures, and the propagation of the uncertainty associated with the transformation. This is illustrated in Fig. 4, where $A_1$ and $A_2$ are focal elements of $U$, and $B_1$, $B_2$, $B_3$ and $B_4$ are focal elements of $V$.

Both $\overline{\theta}(B_1) = \overline{\theta}(B_2) = A_1$ and $\overline{\theta}(B_3) = \overline{\theta}(B_4) = A_2$. For the two frames $U$ and $V$ to be compatible, the following equalities must hold:

$$\begin{aligned} m_U(A_1) &= m_V(B_1) + m_V(B_2) \\ m_U(A_2) &= m_V(B_3) + m_V(B_4) \end{aligned} \tag{23}$$

which implies the following inequalities:

$$\begin{array}{ll} m_U(A_1) \geq m_V(B_1) & m_U(A_2) \geq m_V(B_3) \\ m_U(A_1) \geq m_V(B_2) & m_U(A_2) \geq m_V(B_4) \end{array} \tag{24}$$

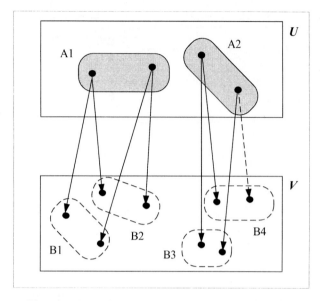

**Fig. 4.    Example of a refinement that leads to the representation of the transformation of structures**

The BPA associated to a focal element in the refined frame is lower than that of the focal element of the original frame which corresponds to its outer reduction. Consequently, if the focal elements represent structures, and if the BPAs $m_U$ and $m_V$ represent the significance attached to the structures in the original document and the transformed document, respectively, then the BPA associated to $V$ can be used to embed the propagation of the uncertainty since it captures the fact that uncertainty increases when propagated. Indeed, for a structure $s$ represented by a focal element of the original frame $U$ that is transformed into a structure $s'$, such that the outer reduction of the focal element representing that transformed structure in the refined frame $V$ is that exact focal element representing the structure $s$, the following equality holds:

$$m_U(s) \geq m_V(s') \tag{25}$$

What is left is to explicitly define the BPA $m_V$ in terms of the BPA $m_U$ so that $m_V(B_1)$ and $m_U(A_1)$ represent the focal elements associated to the structures $s$ and $s'$, where $m_V(B_1)$ is defined in terms of $m_U(A_1)$. Shafer's refinement function does not compute the BPA $m_V$ in terms of the BPA $m_U$. However, the explicit definition of $m_V$ in terms of $m_U$ does not contradict the ontology of Shafer's refinement function; it only expresses a specific use of the refinement function, for a BPA is defined in each frame.

Documents can be modelled by frames of discernment, and the transformation process can be modelled by a refinement function, and hence capturing partiality of information. The relationships between the BPAs can express the uncertainty of information.

The composition of refinement functions can model sequential transformations. The last refined frame can be viewed as a more refined (or detailed) representation of the document's information content. In [3], we show how this final frame can be define to constitute all the information items, either explicitly or implicitly, contained in the document[5]. The belief function associated with that frame can act as a measure of relevance. If $m_f$ is the BPA associated to that final frame, then the belief function is defined as the summation of the BPA of those focal elements that contain information relevant to the query represented by $q$. That is, if the two structures $s_1$ and $s_2$ contain information relevant to the query, then the relevance of the document to the query can be defined as:

$$r(d, q) = Bel(q) = m_f(s_1) + m_f(s_2) \tag{26}$$

The above formulation then captures the fact that the more such transformed structures are obtained, the higher the belief, and the higher the relevance. The formulation also captures the uncertainty generated by the transformations leading to these structures.

### 4.3 Limitation of the Refinement Function

There is however one problem with the use of a refinement function to model the transformation of a document; the fact that several structures are transformed into the same structures cannot be captured. An example of a refinement that would capture this case is given in Fig. 5.

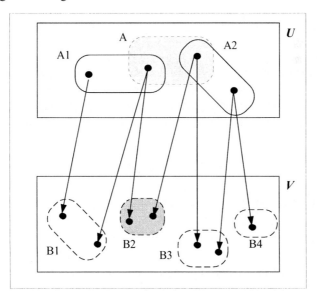

**Fig. 5.** Example of a refinement function that would lead to the case where structures are transformed into the same structures

---

[5] This is different to how refinement works in the Dempster-Shafer framework, but is not incompatible with it.

Suppose that $A_1$ and $A_2$ are the only two focal elements of the coarse frame, and $B_1$, $B_2$, $B_3$ and $B_4$ are those of the refined frame. To symbolize that the structures represented by the focal elements $A_1$ and $A_2$ can be both transformed into the structure represented by the focal element $B_2$, first, the outer reduction of $B_2$ must be defined as the union of $A_1$ and $A_2$, and, second, $m_V(B_2)$, $m_U(A_1)$ and $m_U(A_2)$ must be somewhat related. However, the outer reductions of the sets $B_1$, $B_2$, $B_3$ and $B_4$ are:

$$\bar{\theta}(B_1) = A_1 \quad \bar{\theta}(B_2) = A$$
$$\bar{\theta}(B_3) = A_2 \quad \bar{\theta}(B_4) = A_2 \tag{27}$$

For the two frames of discernment to be compatible, the following equalities must hold:

$$m_U(A_1) = m_V(B_1)$$
$$m_U(A_2) = m_V(B_3) + m_V(B_4) \tag{28}$$
$$m_U(A) = m_V(B_2)$$

That is, $A$ must be a focal element of the original frame, if $B_2$ is to be a focal element. Moreover, $m_V(B_2)$ does not relate to $m_U(A_1)$, nor $m_U(A_2)$. Therefore, it is not possible to capture that a structure is the result of several transformations based on the notion of outer reduction.

To make this possible, the property of the BPAs associated to the coarse frame and the refined frame must be weakened as follows:

$$m_U(A) \leq \sum_{B \subseteq V, A = \bar{\theta}(B)} m_V(B) \tag{29}$$

With a weaker property, the case where two elements (information items) are semantically related to the same element (information item) can be represented. This is not allowed in the Dempster-Shafer formalism because the refinements of two elements constitute two disjoint sets. With respect to natural language, this means that we cannot have:

$$horse \in w(\{animal\}) \cap w(\{transport\_method\}) \tag{30}$$

which is obviously too strong an assumption.

## 4.4 Conclusion

We have shown that the theory of evidence is an appropriate framework to represent an IR model that captures structure, significance, partiality and uncertainty of information. Expect for the problem occurring with the representation of the aggregation of uncertainty, all the other aspects of the model can be adequately represented by such a framework. A slightly modified definition of the refinement function that encompasses the problem related to the representation of the aggregation of uncertainty is however necessary.

# 5   Implementation Issues

We have implemented a system based upon our model to test its effectiveness. In this section, we briefly describe the main aspects and outcomes of the implementation. The reader should refer to [3] for a detailed description of the implementation, the experiments carried out, and their analysis.

We used a text document collection, and we implemented information items as terms extracted from the text documents.

An on-line thesaurus that stores manually-built terms associations was used to derive the semantic relationships which constitute the knowledge set. The thesaurus known as WordNet™ (Version 1.5) [7] is a general thesaurus that covers conventional English and a wide range of technical terms. WordNet takes into account the polysemic nature of terms, which we used to implement the uncertainty associated with the transformation process. Uncertain transformations arose when it was not known which sense of a term was used in a document. When performing our experiments, we did not have any information on the relative probability of the various senses of terms used in our document collection[6]. Therefore, we adopted a rather crude approach. Let the term $t$ be related to the term $t'$ (as extracted from WordNet). Let $\sharp t$ be the number of senses of the term $t$ in a structure $s$. If $\sharp t > 1$, then the use of the relationship in transforming $s$ was uncertain. If $s$ was transformed into a structure $s'$ based on this relationship only, the significance of $s'$ was set to that of $s$ multiplied by $1/\sharp t$; thus satisfying the property attached to the propagation of uncertainty. The aggregation of uncertainty was implemented as a summation.

Terms extracted from the text document were used to build the structures. The terms that were semantically related via WordNet were grouped together to form structures (the focal elements). The BPA $m$ capturing the significance of the structure was computed similarly to that done by [1].

This implementation of our model led to poor experimental results[7]. Although more relevant documents were retrieved with our model, the number of irrelevant retrieved documents increased dramatically. After looking more closely at the documents, the queries, and more importantly, the WordNet thesaurus, obtaining positive results would have been difficult for the following reasons:

(i)   The WordNet relationships were not specific to the document collection used in our implementation. They were ineffective in structuring documents, and transforming documents.

---

[6] In WordNet (Version 1.5), the synsets of a term are displayed in increasing order of the frequency of their senses. However, there is no information telling how often one sense of a term is used instead of another. The quantification of this ordering is not an obvious task. Also, the ordering may not be appropriate for all document collections. For this reason, this implementation ignores this feature of WordNet.

[7] In IR, there are standard metrics used to evaluate the effectiveness of an implemented model. These are not given here, although the discussion in this section is derived from the analysis coming from the use of those metrics.

(ii) More problematic, no disambiguation was done on both queries and documents terms, and many terms were erroneously obtained in the extended representations of documents.

Relationships extracted from a thesaurus or a knowledge base specific to the documents would have certainly led to more accurate structured representations of the documents and their transformations. Unfortunately, such a thesaurus or knowledge base was not available. This is a main drawback which, unfortunately, cannot be solved, unless other data are used, or a better use of the data is performed.

A more careful use of WordNet to derive the relationships might have let to more positive results. Some disambiguation could be performed, for example, based on methods studied in [13]. This would lead to a more controlled and hence more appropriate transformation process. Also, a more adequate measuring of the uncertainty associated to the use of relationships could be used. Some initial work towards this direction can be found in [8].

(iii) The expression of the relevance of a document to a query was a measure of specificity (i.e., the extent to which the information in the document concerned the query). The exhaustivity of the document to the query (i.e., the extent to which the document satisfied all the information required by the query) was not captured.

This problem could be attributed to the fact that only the document's information content had a structured representation in the model. A more appropriate measure of the relevance may be obtained if the information need of a query was also structured. This has the additional advantage that a richer semantic expression of the information need will be available. The Dempster-Shafer theory of evidence can be used for this purpose because it provides formalisms that allow the comparison, through the notion of common refinement [11], of the structured representations of a document's information content and a query's information need. This will be the purpose of future research.

## 6  Conclusion

The aim of this work was to develop a model where four essential features of information were captured: significance, uncertainty, partiality, and structure. To capture these features, the model was based on the Transformation Principle proposed in [6, 3]. The potential of the Dempster-Shafer theory of evidence in formulating the model was examined. The analogy between the theory and the components of the model was highlighted, and our conclusion is that the Dempster-Shafer formalism can be adopted to express the model.

The model was implemented, but its performance was not satisfactory. The effectiveness of the model depended strongly on the availability of a knowledge base or a thesaurus implementing the relationships and appropriate to the documents. This, we did not have. So no real conclusion can be drawn yet about the effectiveness of our model, other than the fact that an appropriate capturing of semantic relationships is primordial.

There is much work in order to obtain an effective implementation of our model, or any IR model based on the Dempster-Shafer theory of evidence. We are currently doing major experimental work in the use of Dempster-Shafer theory of evidence in modelling IR where we do not require the use of a thesaurus or a knowledge base [4]. We are considering another type of structures: the logical structure of documents (chapters, section, etc). Initial experimental results are looking promising [5].

# 7 References

[1] de Silva, W. T., and Milidiu, R. L. Belief function model for information retrieval. *Journal of the American Society of Information Science 4*, 1 (1993), 10–18.

[2] Dempster, A. P. A generalization of the Bayesian inference. *Journal of Royal Statistical Society 30* (1968), 205–447.

[3] Lalmas, M. *Theories of Information and Uncertainty for the modelling of Information Retrieval: an application of Situation Theory and Dempster-Shafer's Theory of Evidence*. PhD thesis, University of Glasgow, 1996.

[4] Lalmas, M. Dempster-Shafer's theory of evidence applied to structured documents: capturing uncertainty. In *Proceedings of ACM SIGIR Conference on Research and Development in Information Retrieval* (Philadelphia, PA, USA, 1997).

[5] Lalmas, M., Ruthven, I., and Theophylactou, M. Structured document retrieval using Dempster-Shafer's Theory of Evidence: Implementation and evaluation. In *Electronic Publishing'98 conference* (Saint Malo, 1997). Submitted.

[6] Lalmas, M., and van Rijsbergen, C. J. Situation Theory and Dempster-Shafer's Theory of Evidence for Information Retrieval. In *Proceedings of Workshop on Incompleteness and Uncertainty in Information Systems* (Concordia University, Montreal, Canada, 1993), V. Alagar, S. Bergler, and F. Dongs, Eds., pp. 62–67.

[7] Miller, G. A. WordNet: An On-Line Lexical Database. *International Journal of Lexicography 3*, 4 (1990), 235–312.

[8] Richardson, R., Smeaton, A. F., and Murphy, J. Using WordNet for conceptual distance measurement. In *Information Retrieval: new System and Current Research* (1994), R. Leon, Ed., vol. 2, Taylor Graham.

[9] Salton, G., and McGill, M. J. *Introduction to modern information retrieval*. McGraw-Hill Book Company, 1980.

[10] Schoken, S. S., and Hummel, R. A. On the use of the Dempster-Shafer model in information indexing and retrieval applications. *Int. J. Man-Machine Studies 39* (1993), 1–37.

[11] Shafer, G. *A Mathematical Theory of Evidence.* Princeton University Press, 1976.

[12] van Rijsbergen, C. J. A new theoretical framework for information retrieval. In *Proceedings of ACM SIGIR Conference on Research and Development in Information Retrieval* (Pisa, Italy, 1986), F. Rabitti, Ed., pp. 194–200.

[13] Voorhees, E. M. Using WordNet to disambiguate word sense for text retrieval. In *Proceedings of ACM SIGIR Conference on Research and Development in Information Retrieval* (Pittsburgh, PA USA, 1993), R. Korfhage, E. Rasmussen, and P. Willet, Eds., pp. 171–180.

# Uncertainty Measures Associated with Fuzzy Rules for Connection Admission Control in ATM Networks

Maria Fernanda N. Ramalho

Østfold Research Foundation (STØ),
P.O. Box 573 Busterud, N-1754 Halden, Norway

**Abstract.** This paper describes the application of Fuzzy Logic to Connection Admission Control (CAC) in Asynchronous Transfer Mode (ATM) broadband communications networks. CAC is a traffic control function that decides whether or not to admit a new connection on to the network, subject to ensuring the required quality of service of all the connections. Observations of the traffic in the ATM link (examples) are used to acquire knowledge on the behaviour of the ATM traffic. From this knowledge, the Fuzzy Logic based CAC (FCAC) can, then, infer the maximum expected ratio of cells lost per cells sent for a given connection in the presence of a particular traffic scenario. Uncertainty measures associated with each of the fuzzy rules enable to measure the uncertainty generated by the number of positive and negative examples for a rule. This way, not only the matching rule(s) for a certain input but also the uncertainty measure for this rule(s) will influence the fuzzily inferred output. A study is made to evaluate the cell loss ratio for an ATM link carrying variable bit rate traffic; the results obtained with the FCAC are compared with results obtained using analytical CAC algorithms.

**Keywords.** Fuzzy Logic, Uncertainty Measures, Learning from Examples, Connection Admission Control, ATM Networks.

## 1 Introduction

Any system can be described through the relation between its input and output variables. To identify such relation, a functional input-output description can be obtained via analytical methods. In the case of many complex non-linear processes, found in real life problems, such function is too complex to be implemented and, thus, alternative methods need to be considered. The use of fuzzy (logic) rules to describe systems that reason with fuzzy (vague) knowledge has been shown to be successful [1], [2].

A basic challenge associated with fuzzy systems is that of knowledge acquisition - that is, the transfer of knowledge from some source into a fuzzy rule base. Another challenge, related to knowledge acquisition, is the automatic design of the fuzzy rule base, that is, the definition of the fuzzy sets and the fuzzy rules. Among others, Pedrycz [3] used fuzzy discretisation and clustering techniques to identify fuzzy knowledge based systems and Takagi and Sugeno [4] investigated the identification of a fuzzy system where the consequent of the fuzzy rule is a linear input-output relation. Pedrycz's technique assumes that the number of fuzzy sets per variable is fixed and, therefore, so is the maximum number of fuzzy rules. The method of Takagi and Sugeno is only applicable to a particular rule format. Delgado and Gonzalez [5] proposed a method for designing fuzzy rule bases that does not exhibit such constraints. Basically, a method of 'learning from examples' is used, where the examples are input/output data pairs obtained from measurements of the system being studied. The fuzzy rules generated describe the system with a certain degree of uncertainty, given that for each rule there are not only a certain number of positive but also negative examples. In order to measure the uncertainty associated with the rule, Gonzalez [6] proposed a method to calculate the uncertainty distribution of each fuzzy rule, using the concept of frequency in fuzzy domains. Delgado and Gonzalez proved [7] that the notion of frequency in fuzzy domains is a plausibility function in the sense of Dempster-Shafer [8], [9]. The frequency measure (plausibility) and its dual (belief) constitute the upper and lower bounds, respectively, of the interval of uncertainty associated with each fuzzy rule.

In this paper, uncertainty measures are applied, in conjunction with a fuzzy logic based system, to a traffic control function: the Connection Admission Control (CAC), in ATM broadband communications networks. Section 2 describes the application area in a resumed fashion (for more details see Pitts and Schormans [10]). Section 3 shows how to calculate the interval of uncertainty for each fuzzy rule and section 4 presents the inference algorithm that allows to reason from fuzzy rules with an associated interval of uncertainty. Section 5 presents the predicted cell loss ratio results obtained when using the proposed Fuzzy Logic based CAC (FCAC) [11] for an experimental homogeneous (same type of traffic sources) ATM traffic scenario consisting of Variable Bit Rate (VBR) sources served into a single ATM link. A comparison of the cell loss ratio predicted by FCAC is made with cell loss ratios predicted by two other analytical approaches (the convolution algorithm and an approach based on Markov chains) and with cell loss ratios obtained from simulations. Finally, in section 6, the main conclusions and further work are presented.

## 2 Description of the problem

The Asynchronous Transfer Mode (ATM) has been widely recognised as a promising technique for implementing future high-speed communications networks carrying both variable and constant bit-rate traffic [12]. ATM allows for statistical multiplexing where the sum of the peak bit rates of all users on a link can exceed the capacity of the link although the sum of the mean bit rates will not. All connections share the network resources, namely the link bandwidth capacity (time resource) and the size of the link access buffer (space resource). The bandwidth required by a variable bit rate (VBR) connection varies between a mean and a peak value. Hence, if several VBR connections share a link, a more efficient usage of that link is achieved by assigning to each connection a bit rate which lies between its mean and peak bit rate values. This implies that there is a non-zero probability that cell losses will occur if the sum of the instantaneous rates of the multiplexed connections exceeds the link capacity and the size of the buffer is not sufficient to store the excess portion of the traffic. Hence, traffic control functions are required to achieve a high network utilisation whilst (1) avoiding congestion conditions (caused by an excessive network load) and (2) maintaining the network performance objectives (cell loss and delay statistics).

The Connection Admission Control (CAC) is a traffic control function which decides whether or not to admit a new connection into an ATM network (see figure 1), while preserving the Quality of Service (QoS) requirements of the existing connections and the new connection. QoS requirements are often formulated in terms of the constraints placed on the following network performance parameters: queueing delay,

delay variation and cell loss ratio (ratio of cells lost per cells sent). These are constraints which the end-user expects the network to maintain. In this study, the cell loss ratio will be the QoS parameter considered. It is assumed that cell delay requirements can be satisfied by appropriate buffer dimensioning [13]. In accordance with previous studies [14], this study focuses on the cell loss ratio experienced by each connection in a single ATM link and not on the cell loss ratio aggregated over all connections.

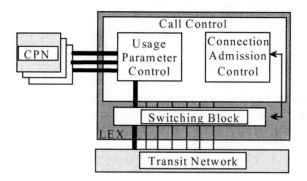

**Figure 1.** CAC as a Traffic Control function.
*Legend*: CPN, Customer Premises Network; LEX, Local Exchange.

Stochastic theory [15] can only provide an accurate description of traffic mixes which are far simpler than those which can be expected on a real ATM link. In addition, stochastic techniques (such as convolution) for predicting cell loss, incur computational time penalties, and, being based on a bufferless assumption, are too conservative [16]. This led to the idea of using techniques that exploit the tolerance for imprecision in the characterisation of the multiplexed traffic scenario in order to achieve a numerically tractable solution that predicts the effects on the cell loss ratio when several connections are multiplexed on an ATM link[17]. A Fuzzy Logic based technique was chosen because of (1) the easiness to design a fuzzy rule base system (using on-line data measurements for a variety of traffic scenarios) that empirically models the non-linearity between the load in an ATM link and the maximum cell loss ratio per connection and (2) its ability to provide a cell loss ratio prediction in real time.

The fuzzy logic based CAC (FCAC) is invoked every time the available bandwidth is insufficient to admit a new connection request on a peak rate allocation basis. The FCAC estimates the maximum cell loss ratio to be expected for each connection if the candidate connection is added to the traffic already present in the link (background traffic). If the estimated cell loss ratio value does not violate the cell loss ratio requirements of existing connections and the candidate connection, the new connection is admitted; otherwise it is rejected.

The FCAC algorithm takes as input the parameters with which the user characterises the traffic behaviour of the connection. The algorithm assumes that the declared parameters are being monitored by the Usage Parameter Control (UPC) function (see Figure 1); this is a "policing" function which protects the network against "dishonest" users. The parameters chosen to describe a VBR traffic source are the peak and mean bit rates (as recommended by the ITU [18]) as well as the mean burst length. The peak and mean bit rates characterise the traffic source in terms of its bandwidth (time resource) and the mean burst length characterises the buffer occupancy (space resource).

## 3 Uncertainty measure associated with fuzzy rules

This section is going to present the formalism used to calculate the upper and lower bounds of uncertainty associated with a fuzzy rule. Firstly, the notion of frequency in fuzzy domains is introduced. This notion is, then, extended to an M-dimensional domain allowing us to measure the uncertainty of a fuzzy rule given a set of examples. The notions of the set of positive and negative examples for a rule are also presented.

In the following it is assumed that the fuzzy logic based system has been identified previously, say using the "learning from examples" method proposed by Herrrera et al [19]. The later method enables us to automatically design (a) the fuzzy sets for the fuzzy variables in the antecedent and consequent of each fuzzy rule and (b) a finite set of fuzzy rules, given a set of examples consisting of input-output pairs obtained from on-line measurements.

Resuming, the problem solved in this section can be stated as follows. Given a set of fuzzy rules of the following form:

$$R_j: \text{If } X_1 \text{ is } A_{1j} \text{ and } ... \text{ and } X_n \text{ is } A_{nj} \text{ then } Y \text{ is } B_j \qquad [\alpha_i, \beta_i]$$

where
- $R_j$ denotes the $j$-th rule of implication,
- $A_{ij}$ and $B_j$ are fuzzy sets,
- $X_j$, for $i=1,...,n$, are input fuzzy variables on universe of discourse $[0, Umax_i]$ and
- $Y$ is the output fuzzy variable, defined on universe of discourse $[0, V_{max}]$.

An example of the rule above as used in FCAC is:
"*If* Mean-Load-of-the-link *is* High *and* degree-similarity-Bit-Rate-of-connections[1]-and-Constant-Bit-Rate *is* Low *and* Peak-Bit-Rate-of-connections *is* Medium *and* Mean-Burst-Length-of-connections *is* Long,
*Then* Maximum-Cell-Loss-Ratio-per-connection *is* High."

Consider also:
- the set of fuzzy sets (fuzzy domain) $D_i$ ($i=1,...,n$) and $V$. These fuzzy sets represent soft restrictions on the variables $X_j$ ($i=1,...,n$) and V, respectively;
- the set of examples $E$, whose elements are pairs $(x, y)$, $x$ is a vector of instances of the fuzzy variables $X_j$ ($i=1,...,n$) and $y$ is the instance of the fuzzy variable $Y$. The instances (also referred in the following simply as examples) are non-fuzzy (crisp) values.

In the following, a formalism is presented that calculates the upper and lower bounds ($\beta_i$, $\alpha_i$, respectively) of the interval of uncertainty $[\alpha_i, \beta_i]$, associated with each fuzzy rule.

---

[1] The connections are the already multiplexed connections and the new connection.

## 3.1 Definitions and assumptions

Let $U$ be a universe of discourse and $D$ a referential fuzzy domain containing a finite set of fuzzy sets defined in universe $U$ and denoted by $A_i, 1 \le i \le r$. Let $X$ be a fuzzy variable in $U$ taking values in the referential fuzzy domain $D$. Each of the fuzzy sets in domain $D$ has its meaning given by its membership function $A_i(U):U \to [0,1], 1 \le i \le r$. It is further assumed that each of the fuzzy sets in $D$ are normal ($\exists u \in U, A_i(u) = 1, 1 \le i \le r$) and satisfy the following completeness condition

$$\forall u \in U\ \exists i, 1 \le i \le r,\ \text{such that } A_i(u) \ge \delta$$

with $\delta \in [0,1]$ a threshold value representing the *completeness degree* of the referential fuzzy domain $D$.

If $E = \{e_1, e_2, ..., e_h\}$ is a set of examples, the frequency of any subset $A$ of $D$ through the set $E$ is

$$f_h(A) = \begin{cases} 0 & ,if\ A = \varnothing \\ \sum_k \dfrac{\Pi_A(e_k)}{h}, & otherwise \end{cases}$$

where:

- $\Pi_A(e_k) = \sup_{a \in A} \Pi_a(e_k), 1 \le k \le h$;
- $\Pi_a(e_k)$ is the normalised non-negative compatibility degree between fuzzy set $a$ and the example $e_k$.

The compatibility degree $\Pi_a(\cdot)$ is defined as:

$$\Pi_a(e_j) = \frac{\mu_a(e_j)}{\sup_{a \in D} \mu_a(e_j)},$$

when $e_j$ is a crisp example. It is also assumed that

$$\sup_{a \in D} \mu_a(e_j) > 0, j = 1, ..., h,$$

i.e., all examples are covered by domain $D$.

The compatibility degree as defined above, can be interpreted as the *possibility* measure of $A$ given the evidence $e_j$ (Dubois and Prade [20]).

Herrera et al ([19]) proved that the frequency $f_h(\cdot)$, defined above is a *plausibility* function. Its dual measure, $g_h(\cdot)$, defined as

$$g_h(A) = 1 - f_h(\overline{A}) = 1 - \sum_{j=1}^{h} \frac{\sup_{a \notin A} \Pi_a(e_j)}{h}$$

is a *belief*[2] function and $g_h(A) \le f_h(A), A \subseteq D$.

---

[2] Given a function $Bel: D \to [0,1]$ which assigns to each subset A of D a number in the unit interval [0, 1], the function $Bel$ is said to be a *belief measure* if it satisfies:
Axiom 1 (boundary conditions): $Bel(A) \ge 0, \forall A \subseteq D$ and $Bel(D) = 1$.
Axiom 2 (montonicity): If $A \subseteq B$, then $Bel(A) \le Bel(B)$.

From the above definitions, it can also be shown that the pair of dual measures $(f_h, g_h)$ is a *belief-plausibility* pair in the sense of Dempster-Shafer. Thus, for any subset $A$ of domain $D$, the interval $[\alpha, \beta] = [g_h(A), f_h(A)]$ measures the uncertainty about evidence $A$ that lies in the raw data set.

In the next section, the notion of interval of uncertainty is going to be extended to an M-dimensional domain. After that, the notions of positive and negative examples of a fuzzy rule are given. Finally, the interpretation of the interval of uncertainty by Herrera et al [19] will be presented.

## 3.2 Uncertainty interval of a fuzzy rule

Let us assume, to simplify the description, that the rules, $R$, have an M-dimensional antecedent and a one-dimensional consequent

$$R \equiv if \ X \ is \ A \ then \ Y \ is \ B \quad [\alpha, \beta]$$

with $X = (X_1, X_2, ..., X_M)$, $A = (A_1, A_2, ..., A_M)$.

Suppose that $E = \{e_1, e_2, ..., e_h\}$ is a set of examples for which:

- $e_k = (ex_k, \ ey_k)$, $k=1,...,h$;

- $ex_k = (ex_{1k}, ex_{2k}, ..., ex_{Mk})$, is an example of the variables $X$,

- $ey_k$ is an example of the variable $Y$,
- $ex_k$ and $ey_k$ belong to universe $U$ and $V$, respectively.

The extension of the definition of frequency to an M-dimensional domain uses the compatibility degree between the M-dimensional fuzzy vector, $A$, and the example $ex_k$ defined as:

$$\Pi_A(ex_k) = \underset{m=1...M}{*} \Pi_{A_m}(ex_{mk})$$

with * a t-norm.

The *frequency* of any fuzzy rule $R$ through the set of examples $E$ is, thus, defined as

Axiom 3 (continuity): For every monotonic sequence $A_i$, $i \in N$ of subsets of $D$, then

$$\lim_{i \to \infty} Bel(A_i) = Bel(\lim_{i \to \infty} A_i)$$

Axiom 4 (superadditivity to every positive integer order $n$): To the second order, this property is expressed as:

$$Bel(A_1 \cup A_2) \geq Bel(A_1) + Bel(A_2) - Bel(A_1 \cap A_2).$$

A *plausibility measure*, $Pl$, is a function that satisfies axioms 1 to 3 as well as:
Axiom 4' (subadditivity to every positive integer order $n$): To the second order, this property is expressed as:

$$Pl(A_1 \cap A_2) \leq Pl(A_1) + Pl(A_2) - Pl(A_1 \cup A_2).$$

It then follows the inequalities:

$$Bel(A) + Bel(\overline{A}) \leq 1, \ Pl(A) + Pl(\overline{A}) \geq 1, \text{ and } Bel(A) \leq Pl(\overline{A}), \ \forall A \in \Im(X).)$$

$$\Psi_E(R) = \frac{\sum_{k=1}^{h} R(e_k)}{h}$$

with $R(e_k) = \Pi_A(ex_k) * \Pi_B(ey_k)$ (* is a t-norm) being the compatibility degree between rule $R$ and example $e_k$, and $h$ the total number of examples in $E$. $\Pi_A(ex_k)$ is the compatibility degree between the rule's antecedent and example $e_k$, (defined above) and $\Pi_B(ey_k)$ is the compatibility degree between the rule's consequent and example $e_k$.

Bearing in mind the previous definitions, a method for calculating the interval of uncertainty $[\alpha, \beta]$, for each rule $R$, using the notion of positive and negative example for a rule R is presented in the following.

The set of examples that have an *effect* on rule $R$, $E(R)$, is defined as the fuzzy subset of $E$ characterised by

$$E(R) = \left\{ \left( e_k, \Pi_A(e_k) \right) \mid e_k \in E \right\}.$$

The set of *positive* examples for rule $R$ is the following fuzzy subset set of $E$:

$$E^+(R) = \left\{ \left( e_k, \Pi_A(e_k) * \Pi_B(e_k) \right) \mid e_k \in E \right\}.$$

Similarly, the set of *negative* examples for rule $R$ is:

$$E^-(R) = \left\{ \left( e_k, \Pi_A(e_k) * \Pi_{\overline{B}}(e_k) \right) \mid e_k \in E \right\},$$

where the symbol * stands for the Lukasiewicz t-norm defined by: $a * b = \max(a + b - 1, 0), \forall a, b$. The Lukasiewicz t-norm was chosen because it allows to concentrate the evidence provided by the examples in the most representative rules.

An example $e_k$ such as

$$\Pi_A(e_k) = 1 \text{ and } \Pi_B(e_k) = 1$$

has a membership of 1 to $E^+(R_i)$, and an example $e_k$ such as

$$\Pi_A(e_k) = 0.2 \text{ and } \Pi_B(e_k) = 0.001$$

has a membership of 0 to $E^+(R_i)$. It is easy to show that an example $e_k$ such that

$$\Pi_A(e_k) = 1 \text{ and } \Pi_B(e_k) = 0$$

belongs to $E^-(R_i)$ with a membership degree of 1, that is, $e_k$ ought to match with some other rule having the same antecedent but different consequent.

In case of a single variable consequent, the relation between $\Pi_B(e_k)$ and $\Pi_{\overline{B}}(e_k)$ is such that

$$\max\{\Pi_B(e_k), \Pi_{\overline{B}}(e_k)\} = 1,$$

and hence the following result:

$$\max\{\Pi_A(e_k) * \Pi_B(e_k), \Pi_A(e_k) * \Pi_{\overline{B}}(e_k)\} = \Pi_A(e_k).$$

Therefore, if the max t-conorm is used for defining the union of fuzzy sets, the following equality holds:

$$E(R) = E^+(R) \cup E^-(R).$$

The uncertainty interval $[\alpha, \beta]$ can be calculated for each rule from the above subsets of $E_h$. If the cardinality of a fuzzy subset is denoted by

$$|A| = \sum_{u \in U} \mu_A(u).$$

The quotient

$$\frac{\left|E^+(R_i)\right|}{\left|E(R_i)\right|}$$

represents the proportion of positive examples (among those having some effect on the rule) and coincides with $\beta$. Therefore, the upper measure of the rule's uncertainty quantifies the proportion of positive examples.

Similarly, the quotient

$$\frac{\left|E^-(R_i)\right|}{\left|E(R_i)\right|}$$

represents the proportion of negative examples and coincides with $(1 - \alpha)$. It measures to what extent $R$ is rejected (negatively supported) by the examples.

Therefore, the interval $[\alpha, \beta]$ has the following interpretation: each rule is affected by the fuzzy proportions of the positive examples $\beta$ (that is, examples matching the rule to a certain degree) and the fuzzy percentage of non-negative examples $\alpha$ (that is, one minus the percentage of examples matching the complement of the rule).

A rule with an uncertainty interval [0,1] has 100% positive examples and 100% negative examples, that is, 100% examples that do not affect the rule (we have no information about the rule). Such an interval represents the ignorance about the sentence "this rule represents the data set". In turn, if the rule's interval is [1, 1] the positive examples are 100% and the negative examples are 0%. In this case, the rule describes the data set accurately. The interval [0, 0] represents 0% positive examples and 100% negative examples, in which case all the information relative to the rule is concentrated in other rules with the same antecedent but different consequent.

## 4 The Inference model

This section presents an algorithm to infer from fuzzy rules with an associated interval of uncertainty, that is, rules of the form:

$$\text{If } X \text{ is } A \text{ then } Y \text{ is } B \ [\alpha, \beta]$$

where the interval $[\alpha, \beta]$ is a measure of the uncertainty that lies in the rule related to how well the rule describes a set of examples.

The two uncertainty measures, $\alpha$ and $\beta$, provide a means of weighting the influence of each of the fuzzy rules on the inferred output value. The inference model presented in the following is inspired on the work by Campos and Gonzalez [21] and adapted to fuzzy rules with a single output variable whose domain is a set of crisp (non-fuzzy) sets [11].

## 4.1 Inference without uncertainty

In order to simplify, for ease of understanding, the description of the fuzzy inference model, rules with no associated uncertainty degree are firstly considered, that is, rules with the format:

$$\text{If } X \text{ is } A \text{ then } Y \text{ is } B$$

where $X$ and $Y$ are variables on the reference sets $U_1$, $U_2$, respectively, and $A$ and $B$ are fuzzy sets of the domain of $X$ and $Y$, respectively.

Let $U_A = \{A, \neg A\}$ and $U_B = \{B, \neg B\}$ be two fuzzy partitions of $U_1$ and $U_2$. The fuzzy rule above defines a relation among the elements of $U_A$ and $U_B$. This relation is interpreted as a conditioning, that in turn, is represented by an uncertainty measure. Thus, the basic idea behind the inference model described hereafter is to replace $U_1$ and $U_2$ by the fuzzy partitions $U_A$ and $U_B$, respectively, and then to consider uncertainty measures on each fuzzy partition. The uncertainty measures on $U_A$ will be propagated to uncertainty measures on $U_B$ via the conditional information expressed in the rule (propagation model [21]).

The conditional information comes from a semantic interpretation of the rule in the following sense: the rule generates two conditional measures on $U_B$,

$$\left(l(/A), u(/A)\right), \quad \left(l(/\neg A), u(/\neg A)\right)$$

defined by:

| | |
|---|---|
| $l(B\mid A) = 1 \quad u(B\mid A) = 1$ | (1) |
| $l(\neg B\mid A) = 0 \quad u(\neg B\mid A) = 0$ | |
| $l(B\mid\neg A) = 0 \quad u(B\mid\neg A) = 1$ | (2) |
| $l(\neg B\mid\neg A) = 0 \quad u(\neg B\mid\neg A) = 1$ | |

Thus, the rule "If $X$ is $A$ then $Y$ is $B$" is interpreted as a conditioning (instead of a material implication); in other words:

- if $A$ *is true* is known, then we can assert that $B$ *is true* (modelled as the total certainty (1));
- if $A$ *is false* then nothing can be inferred about the truthfulness of $B$ (modelled as the total ignorance (2)).

Moreover, an upper probability measure on $U_A$ needs to be defined. This measure will be propagated to $Y$ through the conditional information expressed in the rule. The upper probability measure will be obtained by matching the input $A^*$ with each of the values in $U_A$, that is, by matching $A^*$ with $A$ and $A^*$ with $\neg A$. A matching mechanism based on the compatibility degree between two fuzzy sets, $F$ and $G$, is used to obtain the measure on $U_A$:

$$c(F,G) = \sup_{r \in U}\{\mu_F(r) * \mu_G(r)\} \tag{3}$$

where $*$ is a t-norm. Although any t-norm could be used in (3), the Lukasiewicz t-norm $a*b = \max(a+b-1,0)$ is chosen because it satisfies the non-contraction law ($a*(1-a) = 0$, $\forall a$) and, thus, the compatibility degree between two complementary fuzzy sets is zero:

$$c(F, \neg F) = \sup_{r \in U} \left\{ \max\left( \mu_F(r) + \mu_{\neg F}(r) - 1, 0 \right) \right\} = 0$$

with $\mu_{\neg F}(r) = 1 - \mu_F(r)$.

The upper measure on $U_A$ induced by the input $A^*$ is defined as

$$u_x(A/A^*) = c(A, A^*) = \sup_r \left\{ \max(\mu_A(r) + \mu_{A^*}(r) - 1, 0) \right\}$$

$$u_x(\neg A/A^*) = c(\neg A, A^*) = \sup_r \left\{ \max(\mu_{A^*}(r) - \mu_A(r), 0) \right\} \tag{4}$$

(the lower probability measure is given by $l_x(H) = 1 - u_x(\neg H)$ ).

Considering that the input $A^*$ is required to be a normalised fuzzy set, i.e.,

$$\exists r \in U_1 : \mu_{A^*}(r) = 1,$$

it can be easily proved that $c(A, A^*) + c(\neg A, A^*) \geq 1$. \hfill (5)

From (5), $u_x$ and $l_x$ can be interpreted as the upper and lower probability measure on $U_A$, respectively.

Using the propagation model (1), (2) and the upper measure on $U_A$, (4), an upper (lower) measure on $U_B$ is obtained. This measure is defined as:

$$u_Y(B) = 1, \quad u_Y(\neg B) = c(\neg A, A^*) \tag{6}$$

Considering the upper measure on $U_B$ as the fuzzy inference output, comes:

(rule)                   If $X$ is $A$ then $Y$ is $B$

(input)                  $X$ is $A^*$

(output)                 $Y$ is $B$ is $[1-\lambda, 1]$, $Y$ is $\neg B$ is $[0, \lambda]$, \hfill (7)

where $\lambda = c(\neg A, A^*)$ and "$Y$ is $C$ is $\theta$" means a proposition at *degree* $\theta$ [25]. In this study, the uncertainty degree $\theta$ is represented by the uncertainty interval $[\alpha, \beta]$ representing the lower and upper probability, respectively.

The fuzzy inference output generates certainty values for results $B$ and $\neg B$. Note that if the compatibility between $A^*$ and $\neg A$ is zero, that is, the input $A^*$ is included in $A$ and $\mu_{A^*}(r) \leq \mu_A(r)$, $\forall r$, the inference result is unambiguously $B$. If the compatibility between $A^*$ and $\neg A$ is maximum, that is,

$$\exists r \in U_1 : \mu_{A^*}(r) = 1 \text{ and } \mu_A(r) = 0,$$

(for example $A^* = \neg A$), then an uncertainty measure $U_B$ is obtained representing "total ignorance" about the truthfulness of $B$. This conforms with the conditional interpretation of the fuzzy rule previously made.

If the fuzzy inference output must be given in terms of a fuzzy set $B^*$, then the upper measure on $U_B$ and the membership functions of $B$ and $\neg B$ have to be combined in order to obtain a result $B^*$ as an expected value of $B$ and $\neg B$ weighted by the upper measures' value through a fuzzy integral (see [2] and [6] for more details). In order to be coherent at the membership level with the previously stated, the total ignorance about the universe $U_2$ (i.e. the fuzzy variable Y has no restrictions) must be expressed as a fuzzy set $B^*$ such that

$$\mu_{B^*}(r) = 1, \forall r.$$

This is achieved by defining an integral based on an operator which makes the fuzzy sets $B$ and $\neg B$ exhaustive (i.e. $B * \neg B = U_2$); more precisely the bounded sum t-conorm operator, defined as: $a \oplus b = a + b - ab$.

The fuzzy inference using the modified integral, produces the following result:

$$\mu_{B^*}(r) = \mu_B(r) + \lambda - \mu_B(r)\lambda$$

or, equivalently:

$$\mu_{B^*}(r) = \mu_B(r) \oplus \lambda \qquad (8)$$

where $\lambda = c(\neg A, A^*)$ and $\oplus$ is the bounded sum t-conorm.

The inference model verifies the following properties:

1. If $A^*=A$ then $B^*=B$. In effect, when $A^*=A$, the compatibility between $A^*$ and $\neg A$ is zero, and

$$\mu_{B^*}(.) = \mu_B(.) \oplus 0 = \mu_B(.),$$

that is, the inference model extends the classical *modus ponens*.

2. If $A^* \subseteq A$ then $B^*=B$:, that is, when the input $A^*$ is a subset of $A$, the compatibility between $A^*$ and $\neg A$ is zero, and we obtain a similar result to the previous case. When the input is more precise than the antecedent, the rule can only infer the consequent, without adding information not contained in the rule (the rule only says "if $X$ is $A$ then $Y$ is $B$", but it does not say, for instance, "*the more $X$ is $A$, then the more $Y$ is $B$*").

3. If $A^* \subseteq \neg A$ then $B^*=U_2$. In this case, the compatibility between $A^*$ and $\neg A$ is equal to one, and then

$$\mu_{B^*}(.) = \mu_B(.) \oplus 1 = 1.$$

Thus, for inputs completely different from $A$, the inference process gives no information about the universe $U_2$, that is, all the elements of the universe of the consequent variable are equally possible.

## 4.2    Inference with uncertainty

In the following, the inference model presented in the previous section is going to be extended (see also [21]) to include fuzzy rules of the form:

$$\text{If } X \text{ is } A \text{ then } Y \text{ is } B \text{ is } [\alpha, \beta]. \qquad (9)$$

where the interval $[\alpha, \beta]$ is a formalism used to represent the uncertain information expressed by the rule.

Similarly to (1), (2), the rule (9) generates two conditional measures on $U_B$ (pair of lower and upper uncertainty measures) given by:

| | | |
|---|---|---|
| $l(B\|A) = \alpha$ | $u(B\|A) = \beta$ | (10) |
| $l(\neg B\|A) = 1-\beta$ | $u(\neg B\|A) = 1-\alpha$ | |
| $l(B\|\neg A) = 0$ | $u(B\|\neg A) = 1$ | (11) |
| $l(\neg B\|\neg A) = 0$ | $u(\neg B\|\neg A) = 1$ | |

Propagating the measure (4) through these conditional measures, a measure on $U_B$ is obtained as follows:

$$u_Y(B) = \beta\,(1\text{-}c(\neg A, A^*)\,) + c(\neg A, A^*) = \beta \oplus c(\neg A, A^*) = \beta + \lambda \qquad (12)$$

$$u_Y(\neg B) = (1\text{-}\alpha)\,(1\text{-}c(\neg A, A^*)\,) + c(\neg A, A^*) = (1\text{-}\alpha) \oplus c(\neg A, A^*) = (1\text{-}\alpha) + \lambda \quad (13)$$

where $\lambda = c(\neg A, A^*)$.

The output $B^*$ produced by combining (12) and the membership function of $B$ and $\neg B$ is:

$$\mu_{B^*}(s) = \big(\mu_B(s) \oplus \lambda \oplus (1-\alpha)\big) - \big(\mu_B(s)(1-\beta)(1-\lambda)\big) \qquad (14)$$

The previous equation defines a non-normalised fuzzy set for $\beta \neq 1$. Imposing the condition $\beta = 1$, a normalised fuzzy set, $B^*$, is obtained; this way the kind of uncertainty in the rules is restricted to the possibilistic interpretation. Rule (9) is divided in two rules:

1. "If $X$ is $A$ then $Y$ is $B$ is $\alpha$ " and the conditional measure is now defined as:

$$\begin{aligned} l(B|A) = \alpha \quad & u(B|A) = 1 \\ l(\neg B|A) = 0 \quad & u(\neg B|A) = 1-\alpha \end{aligned} \qquad (15)$$

with (11) unchanged. The output fuzzy set generated is

$$\mu^1_{B^*}(s) = \mu_B(s) \oplus \big(\lambda \oplus (1-\alpha)\big) \qquad (16)$$

2. "If $X$ is $A$ then $Y$ is $B$ is $(1 - \beta)$" and the conditional measure is now defined as:

$$\begin{aligned} l(B|A) = 1-\beta \quad & u(B|A) = 1 \\ l(\neg B|A) = 0 \quad & u(\neg B|A) = \beta \end{aligned} \qquad (17)$$

with (11) unchanged. The output fuzzy set generated is

$$\mu^2_{B^*}(s) = \big(1 - \mu_B(s)\big) \oplus \big(\lambda \oplus \beta\big) \qquad (18)$$

Finally, the output $B^*$ is obtained by combining outputs (16) and (18) with the Lukasiewicz t-norm

$$\mu_{B^*}(s) = \mu^1_{B^*} * \mu^2_{B^*} \qquad (19)$$

## 4.3 FCAC inference algorithm

In the following, FCAC's inference algorithm is presented for a rule-base with $n$ fuzzy rules and for fuzzy rules with fuzzy sets in the antecedent of the rule and singletons in the consequent. The antecedent of the rules is composed of 4 fuzzy variables: Mean-Load-of-the-link, degree-similarity-Bit-Rate-of-connections-and-Constant-Bit-Rate, Peak-Bit-Rate-of-connections and Mean-Burst-Length-of-connections. The consequent fuzzy variable is the Maximum-Cell-Loss-Ratio-per-connection.

The fuzzy rules have the following format:

$$R_i \equiv \textit{if } X \textit{ is } A_i \textit{ then } Y \textit{ is } B_i \quad [\alpha_i, \beta_i]$$

where $x = (x_1, x_2, ..., x_4)$, $A_i = (A_{i1}, A_{i2}, ..., A_{i4})$, $1 \le i \le n$, $B_i \in \{\{y_1\}, \{y_2\}, ..., \{y_m\}\}$ and $y_r$, $1 \le r \le m$ is a crisp integer value that represents the integer negative power of ten of the cell loss ratio that the consequent variable, $Y$, can assume.

The inference algorithm shown in table 1 is inspired on the inference model presented in sections 4.1 and 4.2 but extended to a rule base of $n$ rules and adapted to the fuzzy rule format adopted in the FCAC tool and shown above (see for more details [11]).

## 5 Results from traffic experiments

An investigation was made on the accuracy of the cell loss ratio (CLR) predicted by FCAC for mixes of variable bit rate (VBR) sources representing data and image traffic multiplexed on a single ATM link. The cell loss ratio reference value, for each of the traffic mixes, was obtained via simulation using the LINKSIM cell rate simulator developed by Pitts[22]. Results from simulations were used due to the unavailability of an ATM test-bed to perform on-line CLR measurements for the high number of multiplexed traffic sources used in the experiments.

The cell loss ratio prediction given by FCAC was also compared with CLR predictions given by:
- the "enhanced" convolution approach (ECA), a convolution algorithm developed by Marzo et al [23],
- the ($M$+1)-MMDP approximation, an approach to estimate the cell loss probability in an ATM multiplexer for traffic scenarios with the same type of traffic sources (homogeneous traffic) described by Yang and Tsang [24], that uses the Markov Modulated Deterministic Process (MMDP) to approximate the actual arrival process and models the ATM multiplexer as an MMDP/D/1/$k$ queueing system.

The FCAC fuzzy rule base has 56 rules and the number of examples considered is 37 (each describing a different traffic scenario). The traffic sources used in the experiments are On-Off sources defined by parameters: peak and mean bit rate and mean burst length (see also table 2) and are in conformance with the traffic characteristics for the On-Off sources presented by Yang and Tsang (see table II, pp. 122 in [24]). The On-Off sources considered in each of the traffic mixes are assumed to be independent of each other.

**Table 2.** Description of the traffic sources

| Traffic Class | Peak Rate (Mbit/s) | Mean Rate (Mbit/s) | Mean Burst Length (cells) |
|---|---|---|---|
| Data | 10 | 1 | 339 |
| Image | 2 | 0.087 | 2604 |

The experiments consist of multiplexing traffic of the same type on a single ATM link for various traffic mixes and evaluating the cell loss ratio (CLR) predicted by each of the CAC approaches: ($M$+1)-MMDP, ECA and FCAC (see figures 2 to 6). The traffic mixes are obtained varying the number of traffic sources. The number of sources and the values of the link capacity and buffer size for each experiments were selected in order to get a wide range of CLRs (between $10^{-2}$ and $10^{-8}$).

**Table 1.** FCAC inference algorithm

1. *Initialisation*: $\lambda_{\min}[r] = 1$, $\quad \lambda_{\max}[i,r] = 0$, $\quad B^*[r] = 1$,
   where $i$ is the index for the rule, $1 \le i \le n$, and $r$ is the value assumed by the variable, $Y$, $r \in \{x \in N: 1 \le x \le m\}$.

2. *Normalisation and scaling*
   Calculate the crisp values $x_i$ for the crisp input vector $A^* = (x_1, x_2, x_3, x_4)$.

3. *Propagation through the fuzzy rule base (parallel inference)*
   For each of the $n$ rules do ($i$ is the index of the rule):

   3.1. Calculate $\lambda_{\max}[i, r] = \max\limits_{j=1..4}\left(1 - A_{ij}(x_j)\right)$ (see footnote [3])

   where $A_{ij}$ are the fuzzy sets assumed by variables $X_j$ ($j$=1...4) in rule $i$.

   3.2. If ($\lambda_{\max}[i, r] < \lambda_{\min}[r]$) then:

   3.2.1. Update $\lambda_{\min}[r]$ as $\lambda_{\min}[r] = \lambda_{\max}[i,r]$;

   3.2.2. Calculate the output fuzzy sets $B^1[r]$ as $B^1[r] = \lambda_{\max}[i,r] \oplus (1 - \alpha[i])$;

   3.2.3. Calculate the output fuzzy sets $B^2[r]$ as $B^2[r] = \lambda_{\max}[i,r] \oplus \beta[i]$.

   ($\alpha[i]$ and $\beta[i]$ are respectively, the lower and upper bounds of the uncertainty interval associated with rule $i$)

   3.3. For each of the possible $r$ values, $r \in \{x \in N: 1 \le x \le m\}$, of variable $Y$ do:

   3.3.1. If ($\lambda_{\min}[r] > 0.5$) then $B^*[r] = 0$;

   3.3.2. Else, for each of the possible $s$ values, $s \in \{x \in N: 1 \le x \le m\}$, that variable $Y$ can assume do (see footnote [4]):

   $$B^*[r] = \begin{cases} \min\left(B^*[r], B^2[s]\right) & s = r \\ \min\left(B^*[r], B^1[s]\right) & s \ne r \end{cases}$$

4. *Defuzzification*

   4.1. Calculate $M = \max\limits_{1 \le r \le m}\left(B^*[r]\right)$

   4.2. Calculate the output crisp value, $y^*$, using the *Mean of Maximum* defuzzification method, that is, by averaging the $n_r$ values of the support of the inferred fuzzy set $B^*$, whose membership function value, $B^*[r]$, reaches the maximum value, $M$:

   $$y^* = \frac{\sum\limits_{1 \le r \le m: B^*[r] = M} r}{n_r}$$

---

[3] Conjunction in the antecedents: $\lambda_{max}[i, r]$ is given by:

$$\lambda_{max}[i, r] = c(\neg A, A^*) = \max\limits_{j=1..4}\left(c(\neg A_{ij}, x_j)\right) = \max\limits_{j=1..4}\left(\sup\limits_{x \in U_{x_j}} \left\{\max\left(x_j(x) + \neg A_{ij}(x) - 1, 0\right)\right\}\right)$$

$$= \max\limits_{j=1..4}\left(1 - A_{ij}(x_j)\right), \text{ given } \neg A_{ij}(x) = 1 - A_{ij}(x) \text{ and } x_j(x) = \begin{cases} 1, & x = x_j \\ 0, & x \ne x_j \end{cases}.$$

[4] Disjunction in the antecedents: a set of $n$ rules of the form "If $X$ is $A(i)$ then $Y$ is $B$", $i$=1, ...., $n$, can be seen as a rule "If $X$ is $A(1)$ and ... and $X$ is $A(i)$ ... and $X$ is $A(n)$ then $Y$ is $B$", where $A(i)$ is the fuzzy vector in the antecedent of rule $i$.

All calculations were performed on Sun SPARC stations running SOLARIS and both the fuzzy-based CAC (FCAC) and the convolution-based approach (ECA) were developed in ANSI C.

**Table 3.** Specification of the network scenario and traffic types for the experiments.

| Experiment | Traffic type | Buffer size (cells) | Link Capacity (Mbit/s) |
|---|---|---|---|
| A.1 | data | 50 | 350 |
| A.2 | data | 50 | 52 |
| A.3 | image | 50 | 30 |
| A.4 | image | 50 | 7 |
| A.5 | image | 2000 | 7 |

The results of experiments A.1 to A.4 are plotted in figures 2 to 6 and show:
- the average CLR, $CLR_{avg}$, predicted by the $(M+1)$-MMDP approximation and ECA approach (against the average CLR obtained via simulations),
- the maximum CLR per connection, $CLR_{max}$, predicted by FCAC (against the maximum CLR obtained also via simulations).

Given that the traffic scenarios studied in the experiments are composed of traffic mixes with the same type of traffic in the mix, the maximum CLR per connection and the average CLR for all connections obtained by simulation are not significantly different (their difference is less than $10^{-1}$, as shown in figures 2 to 6). Therefore, comparative comments can be made from the CLR predicted by FCAC and the CLR predicted by ECA and $(M+1)$-MMDP approximation.

Note that the FCAC prediction is given in terms of an integer representing the negative power of ten for the maximum CLR per connection, whereas the predictions given by the $(M+1)$-MMDP approximation and ECA are given in terms of a floating point value for the average CLR. Hence, differences in the predicted CLR which are less than $10^{-1}$ are not considered for comparison purposes.

The value of the CLR considered in the examples used to train FCAC, is obtained by rounding the floating point CLR obtained by simulations to the nearest power of ten, that is, a CLR with a value of $4.13 \times 10^{-3}$ is actually "seen" by FCAC as $10^{-3}$ and a CLR value of $5 \times 10^{-3}$ as $10^{-2}$. This can be easily changed if, in a real implementation, the CLR predicted becomes too optimistic and, therefore, a more conservative prediction is required. For example, a CLR measured as $4.13 \times 10^{-3}$ might be truncated to $10^{-2}$, instead of $10^{-3}$.

## 5.1    Experiments with Data Traffic

The traffic studied in figures 2 and 3 is composed of data traffic, for which the mean bit rate of the traffic sources is 10% of the peak bit rate and the mean burst length is 339 ATM cells.

The CLR predicted by ECA provides an upper bound for the average cell loss probability for the traffic scenarios plotted in figures 2 and 3. The prediction given by the (M+1)-MMDP approach is also accurate and the accuracy increases with the number of data sources. FCAC predicts a CLR in the range of the value obtained by simulation, that is within a maximum error of $10^{-1}$. In figure 3, the values obtained via simulations for the maximum and average CLR differ significantly for a traffic mix of

12 sources (more than 0.05). This explains why FCAC predicts a more conservative value than ECA and ($M$+1)-MMDP for a traffic mix of 12 data sources.

The traffic sources that form the traffic mix for the experiments depicted in figure 3, have a high peak to link ratio (19%) compared to the same ratio for the traffic sources of figure 2 (0.03%) and this explains why the number of data sources that can be admitted to the link using FCAC, for a CLR requirement of $10^{-4}$, is much less in figure 3 (10 sources) then in figure 2 (220 data sources).

Yang and Tsang describe experiment A.1 (figure 2) as a traffic scenario where "burst-level congestion" is predominant and that accounts for the accuracy of the ($M$+1)-MMDP prediction for this traffic scenario. The mean burst length of the traffic sources is quite long (339 cells) and therefore, the influence on the CLR caused by queueing part of the burst is very significant in this experiment. Experiment A.2 (figure 3) is described by Yang and Tsang as the traffic scenario obtained when transferring large files across the link; the output buffer only copes with cell level fluctuations and all the loss is caused by lack of bandwidth resources. This constitutes an ideal scenario for the application of the ECA approach.

## 5.2    Experiments with image traffic

The traffic studied in figures 4 and 5 is composed of image traffic for which the mean bit rate is 4% of the peak bit rate and the mean burst length is very high: 2604 ATM cells. The peak to link ratio of the sources is small in the case of figure 4 (0.066), but quite high in figure 5 (0.28).

The CLR predicted by ECA is below the curve corresponding to the average CLR obtained via simulations, for both figures 4 and 5, although the difference between the two values is always less than $10^{-1}$. A similar comment is given for the CLR predicted by the ($M$+1)-MMDP. The CLR predicted by FCAC is as expected when reading the value obtained via simulations for the maximum CLR per connection.

Yang and Tsang describe experiment A.3 (figure 4) as a traffic scenario where "burst-level congestion" is, as in experiment A.1 (figure 2), the predominant cause of cell losses. The long term influence on cell loss ratio caused by the successive arrival of bursts is not taken into account by the traffic model used in the ($M$+1)-MMDP approximation and, thus, the predicted CLR is slightly optimistic. In both experiments A.3 and A.4, the mean burst length of the sources is very long (2604 cells) and the output buffer size chosen (50 cells) cannot cope with fluctuations at cell level. This explains why the ECA approach does not provide an upper bound for the average CLR both in figures 4 and 5.

Figure 6 shows an example of a traffic scenario for which ECA gives a very pessimistic prediction and ($M$+1)-MMDP cannot provide a prediction at all, given the complexity of the calculations involved. For this scenario, the characteristics of the traffic sources and the value of the link capacity are exactly the same as in figure 5. The output buffer size is increased to 2000 cells. ECA is based on a bufferless model and thus, the reduction on the number of lost cells obtained by queueing part of the burst is not taken into account when predicting the cell loss ratio value. This explains why the CLR prediction given by ECA is so pessimist. FCAC takes into account the actual size of the output buffer of the switch and, thus, predicts a CLR which conforms with the results obtained by simulation.

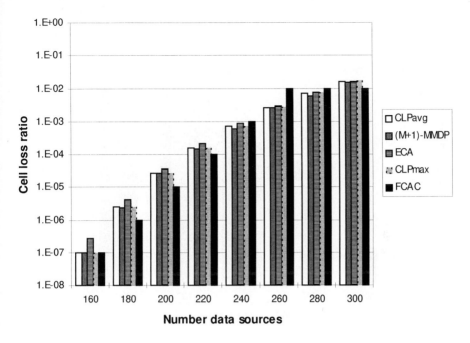

***Figure 2*** Traffic scenarios of *data* sources (C = 350 Mbit/s and K=50).

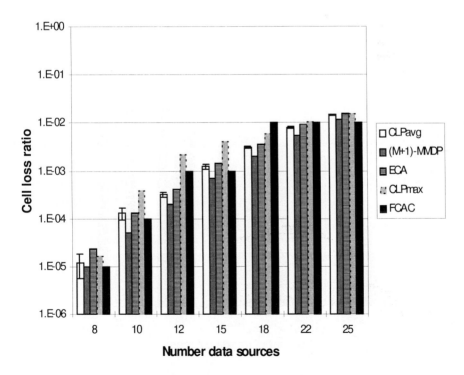

***Figure 3*** Traffic scenarios of *data* sources (C = 52 Mbit/s and K=50).

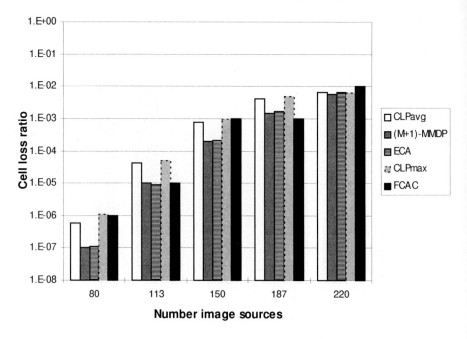

*Figure 4* Traffic scenarios of *image* sources (C = 30 Mbit/s and K=50).

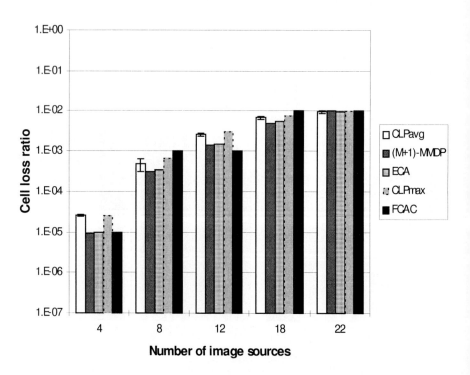

*Figure 5.* Traffic scenarios of *image* sources (C = 7 Mbit/s and K=50).

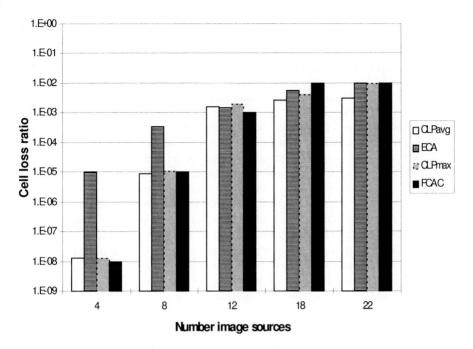

**Figure 6.** Traffic scenarios of *image* sources (C = 7 Mbit/s and K=2000)

## 6 Conclusions and Future Work

The application of fuzzy techniques to the CAC traffic control function has been described in this study. The FCAC uses a fuzzy inference method to estimate the maximum cell loss ratio obtained when a new connection is added to an existing multiplexed traffic scenario. If the estimated cell loss ratio does not violate the cell loss requirements of the already accepted connections nor the new connection, the new connection is admitted; otherwise it is rejected.

The use of uncertainty measures associated with each fuzzy rule allows to measure the uncertainty of a fuzzy rule in describing the process under study. The uncertainty interval is calculated using a method of "learning from examples" applied to fuzzy domains. The uncertainty of a rule exists because a fuzzy rule describes not only positive but also negative examples of the process under study. The uncertainty interval associated with a fuzzy rule allows to weight the contribution of each rule (the fuzzy inference is a parallel inference) in the inferred output value.

The cell loss ratio predicted by FCAC was compared with cell loss ratio predictions given by two theoretical CAC approaches: a CAC approach based on Markovian processes proposed by Yang and Tsang (the (M+1)-MMDP approximation) and a convolution based CAC approach developed by Marzo et al. (the ECA approach). The theoretical CAC approaches are generally accurate when compared with the average CLR obtained via simulation. The FCAC predictions are also in the range of the expected maximum CLR values obtained via simulation (within a maximum error of $10^{-1}$) for the totality of the experiments.

The network scenario shown in figure 6 is an example of a scenario where the application of FCAC can provide an advantage over ECA and (M+1)-MMDP. In this

196

figure, an ATM network scenario for which the switch has a long output buffer size has been studied (2000 cells). For this network scenario the ECA approach, being based on a bufferless model cannot take into account the decrease in lost cells obtained by buffering part or the whole traffic burst. The (M+1)-MMDP approximation does take into account the size of the output buffer, but for such long buffers will not be able to provide a prediction in real time. Long output buffers can provide low CLR for services which are not sensitive to delays but for which low data loss is the primer requirement, such as is the case for data file transfer and non-interactive image traffic.

The results obtained with the FCAC tool give us confidence in proposing it as a valid alternative to analytical approaches as long as the user requirements in terms of cell loss ratio can be expressed by a negative power of ten. It is important to note that the FCAC can deal with a system with buffers whereas the popular CAC methods such as the convolution approach assume a bufferless traffic model. The $(M+1)$-MMDP approximation can be used in a system with buffers but its complexity increases with the size of the buffer. Hence, it is not adequate for real time applications.

In order to fully test the accuracy of the cell loss ratio prediction given by FCAC, a wider set of examples would have been required. The assessment of different CAC methods is constrained by further knowledge of the development of ATM based technology and the behaviour of "real" ATM traffic.

Acknowledgements: The author acknowledges Mr. Marzo and Mr. Yang for having allowed to publish the results obtained with the "enhanced" convolution approach (ECA) and the $(M+1)$-MMDP approximation, respectively. Acknowledgements are also due to Mr. Herrera, Mr. Delgado and Mr. Gonzalez for the useful suggestions on the fuzzy inference method from fuzzy rules with an associated uncertainty interval.

# References

1   E.H. Mamdani and S. Assilian, An experiment in Linguistic Synthesis with a Fuzzy Logic Controller, in: D. Dubois, H. Prade, R. Yager, Ed., Readings in Fuzzy Sets for Intelligent Systems (Morgan Kaufmann, 1993) 283-289.
2   L.A. Zadeh, Fuzzy sets as a basis for a theory of possibility, Fuzzy Sets and Systems 1 (1978) 3-28.
3   W. Pedrycz, An identification algorithm in fuzzy relational systems, Fuzzy Sets and Systems 13 (1984), 153-167.
4   T. Takagi and M. Sugeno, Fuzzy identification of systems and its applications to modelling and control, IEEE Trans. Systems, Man Cybernetics 15 (1985), 116-132.
5   M. Delgado, Gonzalez, An inductive learning procedure to identify fuzzy systems, Fuzzy Sets and Systems 55 (1993), 121-132.
6   A. González, A learning methodology in uncertain and imprecise environments, International Journal of Intelligent Systems, 10 (1995), 357-372.
7   M. Delgado, A. González, A frequency model in a fuzzy environment, International Journal of Approximate Reasoning, 11 (1994), 159-174.
8   A. P. Dempster, Upper and lower probabilities induced by a multivalued mapping, Annual Mathematics Statistics 38 (1967), 325-339.
9   G. Shafer, A mathematical theory of evidence, Princeton University Press, Princeton, NJ, 1976.
10  J. Pitts, J. A. Schormans, Introduction to ATM Design and Performance (with Applications Analysis Software), John Wiley & Sons, 1996.
11  M. Ramalho, Application of an Automatically Designed Fuzzy Logic Decision Support System to Connection Admission Control in ATM Networks, PhD Thesis, Department of Electronic Engineering, Queen Mary and Westfield College, 1997.
12  L.G. Cuthbert, J.C. Sapanel, ATM The Broadband Telecommunications Solution, IEE Telecommunications Series 29, 1993.

13    H. Saito H., Call admission control in an ATM network using upper bound of cell loss probability, IEEE Transactions on Communications vol. 40 n. 9 (1992).

14    II. Kroner, G. Heburterne, P. Boyer and A. Gravey, Priority management in ATM switching nodes, IEEE J. Select. Areas Communications. vol. 9, n.3 (1991), 418-427.

15    R. Guerin, II. Ahmadi and Naghshineh, Equivalent Capacity and its Applications to Bandwidth Allocation in High-Speed Networks, IEEE J. Select. Areas in Commun. vol. 9 n. 7 (1991).

16    V.B. Iversen and Liu Y., "The performance of convolution algorithms for evaluating the total load in an ISDN system", 9th Nordic Teletraffic Seminar, Norway, pp. 14, Aug. 1990.

17    M.F. Ramalho and E.M. Scharf, Developing a Fuzzy Logic Tool using Genetic Algorithms for Connection Admission Control in ATM Networks", Proceedings. of the 6th IFSA World Congress 1 (1995), 281-284.

18    ITU, Traffic Control and Congestion Control in B-ISDN, in: Recommendation I.371 (Study Group 13, Geneva, 1995).

19    F. Herrera, M. Lozano, J. Verdegay, A Learning Process for Fuzzy Control Rules using Genetic Algorithms, Technical Report DECSAI-95108 (1995) (see WWW address http://decsai.ugr.es/difuso/pube.html).

20    D. Dubois, and H. Prade, Possibility Theory: An approach to computerized processing of uncertainty (Plenum Press, New York, 1988).

21    L.M. Campos and A. Gonzalez, A fuzzy inference model based on an uncertainty forward propagation approach, Int. Journal Approximate Reasoning 9 (1993), 139-164.

22    J.M. Pitts, Cell-rate simulation modelling of Asynchronous Tranfer Mode Telecommunications Networks, Ph.D. Thesis, Queen Mary and Westfield College, July 1993.

23    J.L.Marzo, R. Fabregat, J. Domingo, J. Sole. "Fast Calculation of the CAC Convolution Algorithm, using the Multinomial Distribution Function". Tenth UK Teletraffic Symposium, pp.23/1-23/6, 1993.

24    T. Yang, D.H.K. Tsang, A novel approach to estimating the Cell Loss Probability in an ATM Multiplexer loaded with Homogeneous On-Off sources, IEEE Trans. on Communications, vol. 43, no.1, 117-126, January 1995.

# Handling Uncertainty in Control
# of Autonomous Robots

Alessandro Saffiotti

IRIDIA, Université Libre de Bruxelles
50 av. Roosevelt, CP 194/6, Brussels, B 1050 Belgium
URL: http://iridia.ulb.ac.be/saffiotti
Email: asaffio@ulb.ac.be

**Abstract.** Autonomous robots need the ability to move purposefully and without human intervention in real-world environments that have not been specifically engineered for them. These environments are characterized by the pervasive presence of uncertainty: the need to cope with this uncertainty constitutes a major challenge for autonomous robots. In this note, we discuss this challenge, and present some specific solutions based on our experience on the use of fuzzy logic in mobile robots. We focus on three issues: how to realize robust motion control; how to flexibly execute navigation plans; and how to approximately estimate the robot's location.

## 1   I had a dream

It is Monday morning, and it is raining. I enter my office. Edi, my purple personal robot, promptly realizes my presence, and happily rolls out to get me some coffee. Down the corridor, it slips over the water left by somebody's shoes, and has to correct its trajectory by sensing the walls. The cafeteria's main door is closed, so Edi crosses the library and enters the cafeteria by its side door. Having obtained a cup of coffee from Gianni, the barman, it comes back by the same way, moving smoothly in order not to spill the coffee. Three people are smoking in the corridor, and Edi has to maneuver around them, and around a cart hiding behind them. I have just finished reading my mail when Edi comes in with my coffee on its head. It is still hot.

What makes this story a dream? After all, the task performed by Edi may not seem very complex to an outsider; and we know that industrial robots can perform seemingly elaborate tasks with high reliability. Yet, this story is probably close to the best that today's most advanced research robots can do. Having a commercially produced, inexpensive robot to reliably perform tasks of this type in our offices and houses is still a dream. Why?

A crucial observation to understand the difficulties involved is that control programs are typically based on a *model* of the controlled system. Control engineers use a mathematical description of the plant to design their regulators; and AI planning programs incorporate a symbolic description of the target system, of its dynamics, and of the effects of our actions on it. Now, in the case of robot operation the controlled system is composed of the robot *and* its workspace, and we need to account for both these elements in our models — see Figure 1.

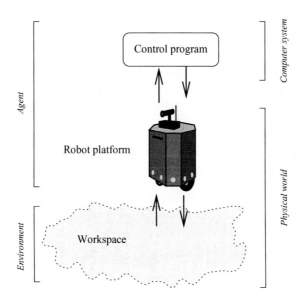

**Fig. 1.** The two facets of the robotic problem. The external observer sees a physical agent (the robot's body and its software) operating in an environment. The designer sees a control program controlling a physical system (the robot's body and its workspace).

A reasonably accurate model of the robot on its own can usually be obtained. For industrial robots, a complete model of the workspace is also usually available. The workspace is highly engineered and completely determined at design time: we know where the workpiece will be, and we know that there will not be a child standing in front of it (if these assumptions are wrong, the robot fails to perform its task). Unfortunately, the same amount of knowledge cannot be obtained in general for the type of real-world environments where we would like our autonomous robots to operate.

There are two sources of problems in getting a reliable model of the "robot + environment" system. The first one is the environment. Our prior knowledge of unstructured environments is necessarily incomplete, uncertain, and approximate: maps typically omit some details and temporary features, spatial relations between objects may have changed since the map was built, and the metric information may be imprecise and inaccurate. Moreover, the environment dynamics is typically complex and unpredictable: objects can move, other agents can modify the environment, and relatively stable features may change slowly with time (e.g., seasonal variations).

The second problem is that the interaction between the robot and the environment may be extraordinarily difficult to model. The results of the robot's actions are influenced by a number of environmental conditions which are hard to be accounted for: wheels may slip, and a gripper may lose its grasp on an object. And the relation between the perceptual information and the reality is elusive: noise in sensor measurements introduces uncertainty; the limited sensor range, combined with the effect of environmental features (e.g., occlusion) and of adverse observation conditions (e.g., lighting), leads to imprecise data; and errors in the measurement interpretation process may lead to incorrect beliefs.

Several of these sources of difficulties appear in the above dream. Edi must use a map to plan its route to the cafeteria, but this map turns out to be inaccurate (the door is closed) and incomplete (the people who are smoking are not in it). The effect of Edi turning its wheels is modified as a result of the wet floor. And the cart only comes into the sensor's view at the last moment. In general, builders of autonomous robots must face a great challenge: to design robust control programs that reliably perform complex tasks in spite of the large amount of uncertainty[1] inherent to real-world environments. As Lumelsky and Brooks already remarked in 1989 ([24], p. 714.)

> The next big leap of industrial and household automation depends on our ability to overcome the very expensive and often unrealistic requirement of structure and order characteristic of today's "hard" (industrial) automation.

In this note, we present some ways in which we can make it possible to take this leap. In the next section, we analyze the sources of uncertainty in the autonomous navigation task, and discuss how the robotics community has tried to deal with them. In the following sections, we present some possible solutions to the problem of uncertainty in robot navigation, based on the analysis of a test case: the use of fuzzy logic in the SRI International mobile robot Flakey (see [40] for more comprehensive reports on this work). We concentrate on three specific important problems: how to define robust behavior-producing modules; how to flexibly execute complex tasks; and how to reliably establish the robot's position with respect to a map of the environment. We conclude this note by a few remarks on the choice of a "best" way to deal with uncertainty in robotics.

## 2   The challenge of uncertainty

Consider again Figure 1, and recall our claim that many of the difficulties in modeling the "robot + environment" system come from the inherent uncertainty

---

[1] Throughout this note, we use the term "uncertainty" in its most general flavor; we shall use more specific terms like "imprecision," "vagueness" and "unreliability" when we want to focus on a specific facet of uncertainty.

of real-world environments. We now inspect this claim in deeper detail, and sketch the most common solutions adopted to circumvent this problem.

Suppose for concreteness that we are modeling our system by using the tools from the theory of dynamical systems (similar considerations could be made assuming a logic-based representation in the mainstream of AI). For example, we may model the system by the following pair of equations:

$$x_{t+1} = f(x_t, u_t)$$
$$y_t = g(x_t),$$

(1)

where $x_t$ denotes the state of the system "robot + environment" at time $t$; $u_t$ the control signals sent to the robot at $t$; and $y_t$ the signals returned by the robot's sensors at $t$. The $f$ function, usually called the state transition function, accounts for the dynamics of the controlled system; the $g$ function, usually called the output function, accounts for the observability of the system.

Equations (1) do not take any uncertainty into account: we know for sure that whenever we are in state $x_t$, we will observe the output $g(x_t)$; and that if we apply control $u_t$ in this state, we will end up in state $f(x_t, u_t)$. A possible way to bring uncertainty into the picture is by introducing two random variables $v$ and $w$ that represent the effects of the unknown factors, or *disturbances*. For instance, we might write

$$x_{t+1} = f(x_t, u_t) + v_t$$
$$y_t = g(x_t) + w_t.$$

To use this technique, we must be able to somehow specify the values taken by the $v_t$ and $w_t$ variables, for instance by defining two probability distributions for these variables. In other words, we must provide a *model of the uncertainty* that affects our model. This model can be provided for many physical systems; e.g., errors in the action of many effectors may be effectively modeled by assuming a Gaussian distribution over $v_t$. Unfortunately, in the case of most of the uncertainty that affects real-world unstructured environments, we are not able to precisely characterize and quantify the disturbances.

As an example of this, consider the uncertainty induced in the environment by the presence of people. People walk around, and they may change the position of objects and furniture. The actions of most persons cannot be described by a deterministic or a stochastic process — we just cannot write a meaningful probability distribution of when I will go to the printer room. As a consequence, we cannot write a meaningful model of the disturbances induced in the state transition function $f$ by the presence of people. A similar observation can be made for the disturbances introduced in the output function $g$. The reliability of visual recognition, for instance, is influenced by the lighting conditions, which may depend on the cloudiness. And the reliability of the distances measured by a sonar sensor is influenced by the geometry and the reflectance property of the objects in the environment. In each case, a probabilistic (or otherwise) model of uncertainty is either meaningless, or overly complex to obtain.

One possible way to approach this problem is to attack the uncertainty at its very source, by carefully engineering the robot and its workspace so that the uncertainty is minimized and the residual uncertainty can be fully characterized in some way. As we have noticed, this is typically done in industrial robots, where the dynamics of the work-cell is completely determined, and sensing is limited to internal precise sensors that monitor the position of the robot's parts. Some amount of environment engineering has often been applied to autonomous robotics too: from the early days of Shakey [28], where the observation conditions were carefully controlled, and the set of possible "unforeseen" events was known a priori; to the current service robots that patrol hospital floors by following a white or magnetic strip.

Careful engineering can result in good performance, but it has obvious draw-backs. First, adding sophisticated sensors to a robot may enormously increase its cost and fragility; domestic or service robots are expected to use cheap and "easy" sensors (typically, sonar sensors). Second, having to modify the environment is usually undesirable, as it increases the costs and reduces the autonomy of the robot: we do not want an autonomous wheelchair to be restricted to move in selected streets and buildings. Third, sometimes engineering the environment is just impossible: think of a rescue robot going to a disaster area. Fourth, relying on such engineering may reduce the robustness of the robot; for instance, robots that follow a white strip tend to get hopelessly lost if a long portion of the strip is obscured. Finally, and perhaps most importantly, not all sources of uncertainty can be eliminated in this way, and some uncertainty is inherent to the nature of the environment: the actions of humans and the variability of the lighting conditions are typical examples of this.

If we want to build easily available robots that inhabit our homes, offices, or factory floors, we should accept the idea that the platform cannot be overly so-phisticated, and that the environment should not be modified. Hence, we should strive to build robust control programs that reliably perform complex tasks in spite of the environmental uncertainties.

A strategy that has been widely employed in the robotics literature has been to abandon the idea to completely model the environment at the design phase, and endow the robot with the capability of building or updating the model on-line. This strategy led to the so-called *hierarchical* architectures, sketched in Figure 2. The robot uses exteroceptive sensors to acquire a model of the environment as it is at the moment when the task must be performed.[2] From this model, a planning program builds a plan that will perform the given task in the given environment. This plan is then passed to a lower-level control program for execution. Typically, execution proceeds "blindly" — the controller may use a model of the robot and monitor the state of the robot's effectors (proprioception), but it does not try to sense or model the environment anymore. In a sense, the hierarchical approach factors the environment out of the controlled system, thus

---

[2] Exteroceptive sensors, like a camera or a sonar sensor, observe the state of the environment; proprioceptive sensors, like a compass or shaft encoders on the wheels, observe the state of the robot's body. Although exteroceptive sensors are usually mounted on the robot, we prefer to draw them as a separate entity to emphasize the difference between exteroceptive and proprioceptive information.

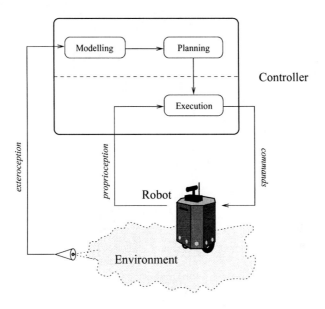

**Fig. 2.** Hierarchical architecture. The high-level layer builds a model of the environment and generates a plan for action. The low-level blindly executes this plan.

making the control problem tractable. This approach has been extensively used in the robotics literature; in most cases, the plan consists of a path leading to a goal position, and execution consists in tracking this path.

It is not difficult to see the limitations of the hierarchical approach when dealing with real-world environments. The model acquired by the robot is necessarily incomplete and inexact, due to the uncertainty in perception. Moreover, this model is likely to rapidly become out of date in a dynamic environment, and the plan built from this model will then turn out to be inadequate to the situation actually encountered during execution. The fact that the modeling and planning processes are usually complex and time consuming exacerbates this problem. Intuitively, the feedback loop with the environment must pass through all these processes — for this reason, this approach is also known as the "Sense-Model-Plan-Act", or SMPA approach. The complexity of the processes in the SMPA loop makes the response time of the robotic system far too long for dynamic environments (of the order of seconds).

By the mid-eighties technological improvements had caused the cost of mobile platforms and sensors to drop, and mobile robots began to appear in several AI research labs. Research on autonomous navigation was strongly pushed, and a number of new architectures were developed that tried to integrate perception and action more tightly. The general feeling was that planning should make as few assumptions as possible about the environment actually encountered during execution; and that execution should be sensitive to the environment, and adapt

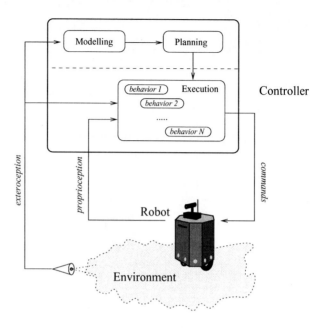

**Fig. 3.** Hybrid architecture. The lower layer uses perception to dynamically adapt plan execution to the environmental contingencies. Complexity in this layer is managed by a *divide et impera* strategy.

to the contingencies encountered. To achieve this, perceptual data has to be included into the executive layer, as shown in Figure 3 (we'll see the meaning of the "behavior" modules in a moment). Architectures of this type are often called *hybrid* because they combine ideas from hierarchical architectures and from behavior-based architectures [5].

Although a seemingly simple extension, the inclusion of perceptual data in the execution layer has two important consequences. First, it makes robot's interaction with the environment much tighter, as the environment is now included in a closed-loop with the (usually fast) execution layer. Second, the complexity of the execution layer has to be greatly increased, as it now needs to consider multiple objectives: pursuing the tactical goals coming from the planner; and reacting to the environmental events detected by perception.

Following the seminal works by Brooks [5], Payton [31] and Arkin [1], most researchers have chosen to cope with this complexity by a *divide et impera* strategy: the execution layer is decomposed into small independent decision-making processes, or *behaviors*, as shown in Figure 3. Other decompositions of the execution layer are possible: for example, in Khatib's proposal [32], an "elastic" path given by the planner is first modified to avoid collisions with sensed obstacles, and then it is given to a path tracking process. In all cases, the execution layer uses local sensor information to decide immediate reactions to the environmental contingencies, while trying to promote the overall goals.

Hybrid architectures do not solve the autonomous navigation problem, but they provide a convenient framework in which the different sub-problems can be dealt with and integrated. We still need to decide how the uncertainty in each sub-problem should be addressed. The rest of this paper is devoted to illustrating some ways to do so using the specific tools of fuzzy logic. As we shall show, fuzzy logic has features that are particularly attractive in light of the problems posed by autonomous robot navigation. Fuzzy logic allows us to model different types of uncertainty and imprecision; to build robust controllers starting from heuristic and qualitative models; and integrate symbolic reasoning and numeric computation in a natural framework. In the next pages, we shall illustrated these points by using our work on the robot Flakey as a test case. (See [36] for an overview of the uses of fuzzy logic in autonomous robotics.)

## 3 Robust behavior

The first issue that we consider is the design of the individual behavior-producing modules that appear in Figure 3. Each one of these modules fully implements a control policy for one specific sub-task, or behavior, like following a path, avoiding sensed obstacles, or crossing a door.

Fuzzy control is credited with being an adequate methodology for designing robust controllers that are able to deliver a satisfactory performance in face of large amounts of noise in the input and of variability in the parameters. The key to this robustness is to be found in the interpolation mechanism implemented by fuzzy controllers, which embodies the idea that similar inputs should produce similar actions. In addition to this, the rule format and the use of linguistic variables make fuzzy control an adequate design tool for non-linear systems for which a precise mathematical model cannot be easily obtained, but for which heuristic control knowledge is available. Finally, fuzzy controllers lend themselves to efficient implementations, including hardware solutions. (See, for instance, [18, 22] for a reminder of the basic principles of fuzzy control.)

These characteristics fit well the needs of autonomous robotics, where: (i) a mathematical model of the environment is usually not available; (ii) sensor data is uncertain and imprecise; and (iii) real-time operation is of essence. It is no surprise, then, if fuzzy control has since long attracted the attention of robot developers, and it represents today the most common application of fuzzy logic in the robotics domain. Notable examples include the early fuzzy controller developed in 1985 by Sugeno and Nishida to drive a model car along a track [43]; and the more recent behavior-based fuzzy controllers included in the award-winning robots Flakey [6], Marge [30], and Moria [44]. In the rest of this section, we detail our use of fuzzy control to implement basic behaviors in Flakey. (See [38, 40] for a more complete treatment.)

In our approach, we express desirable behavioral traits as quantitative *preferences*, defined over the set of possible control actions, from the perspective of the goal associated with that behavior. Following the formal semantic characterization of Ruspini [33, 34], we describe each behavior $B$ in terms of a desirability function

$$Des_B : State \times Control \rightarrow [0, 1],$$

where *State* is the internal state of the robot, including variables that represent relevant quantities in the environment or internal reference points, and *Control* is the set of possible robot's actions. For each state $x$ and control $c$, the value of $Des_B(x, c)$ measures the desirability of applying the control $c$ when the state is $x$ *from the point of view of attaining the goal associated with B*. For example, if the value of the state suggest that there is an obstacle on the left of the robot, then right turning control actions will have higher desirability than left turning ones from the point of view of an obstacle avoidance behavior.

A desirability function is given in the form of a set $R$ of fuzzy rules

$$\text{IF } A_i \text{ THEN } C_i, \quad i = 1, \ldots, n,$$

where $A_i$ is a propositional formula in fuzzy logic whose truth value depends on the state, and $C_i$ is a fuzzy set of control values. For each possible control value $c$, $C_i(c)$ quantifies the extent by which $c$ is a good instance of $C_i$. From these fuzzy rules, a desirability function $Des_R$ is computed by

$$Des_R(x, c) = [A_1(x) \wedge C_1(c)] \vee \cdots \vee [A_n(x) \wedge C_n(c)], \qquad (2)$$

where $\wedge$ and $\vee$ denote fuzzy conjunction and disjunction, respectively (these are min and max in our current implementation, but can be any t-norm / t-conorm pair in the general case). Intuitively, this equation characterizes a control $c$ as being desirable in the state $x$, if there is some rule in $R$ that supports $c$ and whose antecedent is true in $x$. This interpretation of a fuzzy rule set is that of a classical (Mamdani type) fuzzy controller [22], generalized so as to allow each antecedent $A_i$ to be an arbitrary fuzzy-logic formula.

---

IF (lane-too-right $\wedge$ ¬lane-angled-left) THEN turn-medium-right
IF (lane-too-left $\wedge$ ¬lane-angled-right) THEN turn-medium-left
IF (lane-angled-right $\wedge$ ¬centerline-on-left) THEN turn-smooth-right
IF (lane-angled-left $\wedge$ ¬centerline-on-right) THEN turn-smooth-left

---

**Fig. 4.** Fuzzy control rules for the FOLLOW behavior.

Figure 4 shows a set of rules that implement the FOLLOW behavior. This behavior is intended to make the robot proceed along the mid-line of a given lane; it can be used to go down a corridor, of drive on a road. The fuzzy predicates used in the rule antecedents depend on the the current position of the lane with respect to the robot. The consequents of the rules are triangular fuzzy subsets of the space of possible steering (and, in general, velocity) commands.

A desirability function specifies, for each input variable value, a ranking over possible controls rather than a unique control value to apply in that situation. The robot eventually employs this ranking to *choose* one specific control $\hat{c}$ that is sent to the controlled system. A possible mechanism to accomplish that selection is centroid defuzzification:

$$\hat{c} = \frac{\int c \, Des_R(x, c) \, dc}{\int Des_R(x, c) \, dc} , \qquad (3)$$

which computes the mean of possible control values, weighted by their degree of desirability. Centroid defuzzification has been found satisfactory in our experiments whenever the rules in a rule set do not suggest dramatically opposite actions. In these cases, centroid defuzzification obviously does not work as averaging of such multi-modal desirability measures might result in selection of a very undesirable choice (e.g., the best trade-off between avoiding an oncoming train by jumping to the left or to the right is hardly to stay on the track!). Our empirical strategy has been to design the rule sets so as to avoid production of multi-modal desirability functions — roughly, we insist that rules that propose opposite controls have mutually exclusive antecedents, so that only unimodal fuzzy sets are produced for every input. Other authors [47] have relied, however, on alternative defuzzification functions.

Up to this point, we have been a little vague on the content of the robot's internal state. In general, the state will contain variables holding the reference values for the controller, related to the behavior's goal. For example, in the FOLLOW behavior above, the state contains the current position of the lane to follow. For a path-tracking behavior, it may contain a representation of the path, or a set of way-points to achieve.

As we have discussed in the previous section, behaviors that rely on pre-computed paths can be ineffective in real-world dynamic environments, as the environment actually encountered during execution may differ significantly from the model used in the planning phase. For this reason, most behaviors in current autonomous robots are sensor-based: the controller takes as input data from the (exteroceptive) sensors, rather than an internal reference, thus moving the robot with respect to the perceived features in the environment. Typical examples include moving along a wall or a contour, reaching a light source or a beacon, and avoiding obstacles. Sensor-based behaviors can be more tolerant to uncertainty, in that they consider the environment as it is during actual execution.

One way to implement sensor-based behaviors is to include data from the sensors in the internal state, and to use these data as input to the controller. For example, to go down a corridor, we could use the sonar sensors to keep sensor contact with the corridor's walls. In our approach, we take a slightly more involved route: we use sensor data to update variables in the state that are related to the goal of the behavior, and then use these variables in the antecedents of the fuzzy rules.

More precisely, each goal-directed behavior in Flakey maintains in the state a *descriptor* of the object relevant to that behavior. For example, the FOLLOW behavior maintains a descriptor of the lane to follow, and uses the rules in Figure 4 with respect to it. An explicit procedure, called *anchoring* [35], is employed to maintain the correspondence between descriptors and environmental features detected by the sensors. Which features should be used for anchoring depends on the specific instance of the behavior. For example, to go down a given corridor, we use the FOLLOW behavior and anchor the lane to the walls of that corridor.

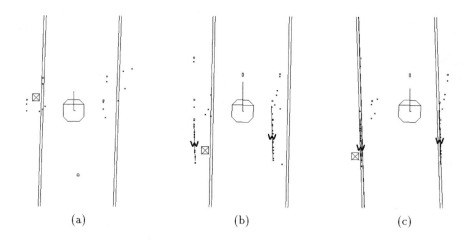

(a)                                      (b)                                      (c)

**Fig. 5.** Anchoring a corridor descriptor to sensor readings during corridor following; (a) the descriptor is used as a starting assumption; (b) the walls are detected; (c) the descriptor is updated.

Figure 5 shows an example of this. Initially (a), the robot is given a descriptor, produced from prior map information, of a corridor to follow (double lines), and FOLLOW operates with respect to this descriptor. After a while (b), enough sonar readings, marked by the small dots in the figure, are gathered to allow the perceptual routines to recognize the existence of two parallel walls, marked by "W." In this example, the descriptor does not match precisely the position of the real corridor: this may be due to errors in the robot's estimate of its own location, or to inaccuracies in the map. Finally (c), the perceived position of the walls is used to update the descriptor — i.e., the descriptor is *anchored* to the sensor data. As the rules of FOLLOW are based on the properties of the descriptor, anchoring implies that the robot will now follow the actual corridor. The corridor descriptor is normally re-anchored at each control cycle whenever the walls are visible. Note that the ability to recover from vague or imprecise assumptions originating from inexact prior knowledge is particularly important in practice, since our maps typically contain only approximate metric information (see Section 5 below).

Descriptors serve several functions. First, they allow us to give a behavior an explicit *goal* by initializing its descriptor using the relevant data (e.g., the position of a specific corridor to follow). Second, descriptors act as sources of credible *assumptions* when perceptual data is not available, as is the case when first engaging a new corridor, or when the walls are momentarily occluded by obstacles. Third, they allow us to *decouple* the problem of control from the problem of interpreting noisy data; the latter problem is confined to the anchoring process. Finally, the use of descriptors results in more *abstract* behaviors than those obtained by a purely reactive approach. For example, the FOLLOW behavior above follows the general direction of the corridor, and not the precise contour of the walls; following the contour may produce wrong decisions when the walls are interrupted by obstacles and open doors.

Not all behaviors are goal-directed, and not all behaviors need a descriptor to represent their goal object. For example, the obstacle avoidance behavior KEEP-OFF is implemented in Flakey by purely reactive rules, that is, rules whose antecedents only depend on the current readings from the sonars.[3] Figure 6 shows a run of this behavior in a completely unknown environment. The robot wanders around at random while trying to stay away from static and moving obstacles as they were perceived. The smoothness of motion, both in turning and acceleration, can be seen in the wake of small dots that indicate the robot's trajectory (one dot per second).

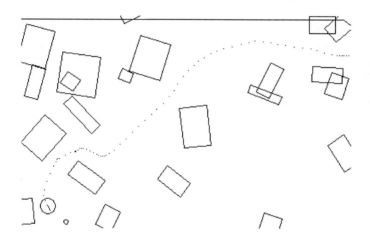

**Fig. 6.** A run of the obstacle avoidance behavior in an unknown environment.

In our experience, fuzzy behaviors are generally easy to write and to debug, and they perform well in face of uncertainty. We have written a dozen behaviors for Flakey, including behaviors for avoiding obstacles, for facing a given object,

---

[3] This is not entirely true, as KEEP-OFF also uses the last 50 readings in order to improve sonar coverage; this however does not change the essentially reactive nature of the behavior.

for crossing a door, and reaching a near location, and so on. Each behavior typically consists of four to eight rules involving up to a dozen fuzzy predicates. The main difficulty that we have encountered is that the debugging and tuning of the behaviors must be done by trials and errors — this is the price to pay for not using a mathematical model of the controlled system. Although writing most behaviors was very easy, some comparatively complex behavior, like KEEP-OFF, required extensive fine-tuning. In future, we may consider the use of learning techniques (e.g., [4, 14, 25]).

# 4  Flexible task execution

A behavior is a small unit of control aimed at achieving one simple goal in a restricted set of situations. Autonomous robots need to perform complex tasks, usually requiring the activation and cooperation of a number of behaviors. In this section, we focus on the problem of how to organize and coordinate the execution of basic behaviors in order to perform a given complex task. With respect to Figure 3 above, this means that we focus on the link between the behavior-based execution at the lower level, and the goal-oriented planning activity at the higher level. The simplest example is the coordination of an obstacle avoidance behavior and a target reaching behavior to achieve the goal of safely reaching a given position in the presence of unexpected or moving obstacles.

Since the first appearance of behavior-based approaches in the mid-eighties, authors have noticed the importance of the problem of behavior coordination. Many proposals are based on a simple on-off *switching* scheme: in each situation, one behavior is selected for execution and is given complete control of (some of the) effectors [5, 8, 10, 29, 31]. Unfortunately, this simple scheme may be inadequate in situations where several criteria should be simultaneously taken into account. To see why, consider a robot that encounters an unexpected obstacle while following a path, and suppose that it has the option to go around the obstacle from the left or from the right. This choice may be indifferent to the obstacle avoidance behavior. However, from the point of view of the path-following behavior, one choice might be dramatically better than the other. In most implementations, the obstacle avoidance behavior could not know about this, and would take an arbitrary decision.

To overcome this limitation, several researchers have proposed coordination schemes that allow the parallel execution of different behaviors, and perform a weighted combination of the commands they issue. These schemes bring about the important issue of how to resolve conflicts between the outputs of different concurrent behaviors. Consider the case where several behaviors are simultaneously active. Ideally, we would like the robot to select the controls that best satisfy all the active behaviors. This may not be possible, though, if some behaviors suggest different actions. In the rest of this section, we show how behavior coordination can be obtained by *context-dependent blending* (CDB), the behavior coordination technique that we have implemented in Flakey.

The key observation to CDB is that behaviors are not equally applicable to all situations: for instance, corridor following is most applicable when we are in a corridor and the path is clear, while obstacle avoidance is more applicable when there is an obstacle on the way. Correspondingly, we associate to each behavior a *context* of applicability, expressed by a formula in fuzzy logic. Given a set $\mathcal{B} = \{B_1, \ldots, B_k\}$ of behaviors, we denote by $Cxt_i$ the formula representing the context of $B_i$. We then define the *context-dependent blending* of the behaviors in $\mathcal{B}$ to be the composite behavior described by the following desirability function:

$$Des_{\mathcal{B}}(s, c) = (Cxt_1(s, c) \wedge Des_1(s)) \vee \cdots \vee (Cxt_k(s, c) \wedge Des_k(s)). \quad (4)$$

Intuitively, the composite desirability function is obtained by merging the individual recommendations from all the behaviors, each one discounted by the truth value of the corresponding context in the current state.

Equation (4) extends (2) to the meta-level, by merging the outputs of a set of behaviors rather than those of a set of control rules. Correspondingly, context-dependent blending may be expressed by a set of fuzzy meta-rules (or "context-rules") of the form

$$\text{IF } Cxt_j \text{ THEN } B_j, \qquad j = 1, \ldots, m, \quad (5)$$

where $Cxt_j$ is a formula in fuzzy-logic describing a context, and $B_j$ is a behavior.[4] A set of context-rules of this type can be evaluated to produce a combined desirability function using (4). This desirability function can then be defuzzified by (3) to produce a crisp control. This way to realize context-dependent blending corresponds to using a hierarchical fuzzy controller, as schematized in Figure 7. This is how CDB has been implemented in Flakey.

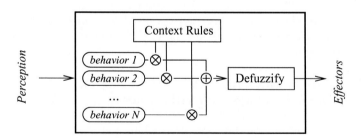

**Fig. 7.** A hierarchical fuzzy controller that implements Context-Dependent Blending.

A few observations should be made on Figure 7. First, it is essential that the defuzzification step be performed *after* the combination: the decision taken

---

[4] The hierarchical structure is reminiscent of the one previously proposed by Berenji et al. [2]. Context-dependent blending generalizes and extends that proposal by allowing dynamic modification of the degrees of importance of each goal.

from the collective preference can be different from the result of combining the decisions taken from the individual preferences [37]. Second, although in Figure 7 all the context-rules are grouped in one module, the same effect can be obtained by including each context-rule inside the corresponding behavior; this solution would be more amenable to a distributed implementation. Third, CDB can be iterated: we can use the structure in Figure 7 to implement each individual behavior, and combine several such (complex) behaviors using a second layer of context-rules; and so on. (Defuzzification should still be the last step.)

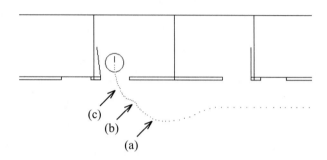

**Fig. 8.** Context-Dependent Blending of behaviors can compensate for inexact prior knowledge: (a) the CROSS behavior uses a wrong estimate of the door position; (b) KEEP-OFF intervenes to avoid a collision; (c) by blending both behaviors, the robot safely passes through the opening.

The CDB mechanism can be used to combine reactive and goal-directed behaviors. For example, the following context rules determine the blending between the obstacle avoidance behavior KEEP-OFF, and a behavior CROSS for passing through a doorway.

IF obstacle-close THEN KEEP-OFF
IF near-door $\wedge$ $\neg$(obstacle-close) THEN CROSS

An interesting outcome of this type of combination is an increased tolerance to imprecision in the prior knowledge. Figure 8 illustrates this point. In (a), the CROSS behavior is relying on the estimated position of the door to cross based on map information. This estimate turns out to be off by some 40 centimeters, and the robot is grossly misheaded. In (b), the edge of the door has been detected as a close obstacle, and the preferences of KEEP-OFF begin to dominate, thus causing the robot to slow down and re-orient toward the free space corresponding to the door opening. Later (c), both behaviors cooperate to lead the robot though the office door — i.e., through the sensed opening that is more or less at the assumed position. During these maneuvers, the preferences of both behaviors are considered, through (4), and contribute to the control choices.

| Context | Behavior |
|---|---|
| obstacle | KEEP-OFF(OG) |
| ¬obstacle ∧ at(Corr-2) ∧ ¬at(Corr-1) | FOLLOW(Corr-2) |
| ¬obstacle ∧ at(Corr-1) ∧ ¬near(Door-5) | FOLLOW(Corr-1) |
| ¬obstacle ∧ near(Door-5) ∧ anchored(Door-5) | CROSS(Door-5) |
| ¬anchored(Corr-2) | SENSE(Corr-2) |
| ¬anchored(Corr-1) | SENSE(Corr-1) |
| ¬anchored(Door-5) | FIND(Door-5) |

**Fig. 9.** A set of context rules forming a plan for reaching Room-5 in the environment of Figure 10 (see the text for explanations).

Context-dependent blending can also be used to execute full plans. In [37] we have proposed to represent plans as sets of *situation→action* rules of the form (5). These rules can be directly executed by the hierarchical controller above; interestingly, and differently from many languages for representing reactive plans, these rules can also be easily generated by classical AI planning techniques. For example, the set of rules shown (in a simplified form) in Figure 9 constitutes a plan to navigate to Room-5 in the environment shown in Figure 10 (top). The arguments passed to the behaviors are the object descriptors to be used to control motion ("OG" denotes the occupancy grid built from the sensor readings and used for obstacle avoidance). This plan has been generated by a simple goal regression planner from a topological map of the environment, and from a description (provided by the behavior designer) of the preconditions and effects of the basic behaviors available to the robot.[5] In this experiment, the map does not contain the position of Door-5, but states that it is the only doorway in Corr-1. Hence, the plan includes the behavior FIND, aimed at detecting the door; it also includes two more perception-oriented behaviors, called SENSE, whose aim is to help perception of the corridor walls when these are not anchored.

The lower part of Figure 10 shows the time evolution of the context values for the behaviors in this plan during the reported run. At (a), Flakey is in Corr-2, and FOLLOW(Corr-2) is active. As the robot approaches Corr-1 (c), the truth value of the context of FOLLOW(Corr-1) increases, and the robot smoothly turns into Corr-1 and follows it. At (g), the side sonars detect the door and Door-5 is anchored, and thus Flakey engages in the door crossing maneuvers. Notice that the perceptual behaviors become inactive once the corresponding feature has been detected and anchored (b, d, f, g), but they may come back to activity if anchoring is lost, like in (e), where a number of boxes occluded the left wall for some length. Also notice that at several occasions in the run the KEEP-OFF behavior blends in to go around unforeseen obstacles.

The above example shows that sets of fuzzy context rules can represent plans

---

[5] The planner uses the preconditions to build the contexts of activation. This is similar to building the triangular tables used in the robot Shakey [28].

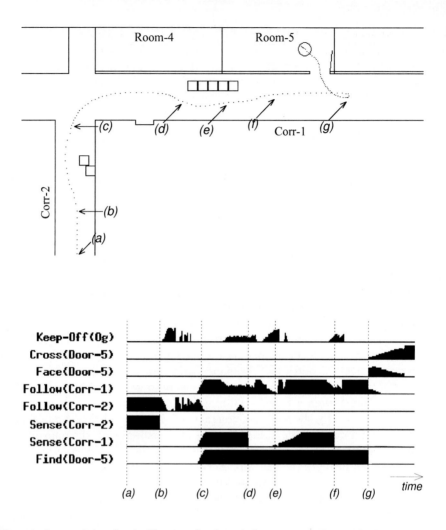

**Fig. 10.** A run of the plan in Figure 9 (top), and the corresponding evolution over time of the activation of the behaviors (bottom).

that are tolerant to uncertainty. Our plan could accommodate the extremely weak information available at planning time about the position of Door-5. The highly conditional nature of this plan also allows the robot to cope with the uncertainty in the effect of actions. For example, the effect of SENSE is to have the corridor anchored; however, this effect may be undone by later actions — like following the corridor in the area where a wall is occluded. This problem could not be detected at planning time, as the planner does not know about the obstacles in the corridor. However, the context rules just re-activate the SENSE behavior when the need to do so arises. (In this sense, our plans are similar to Schopper's universal plans [41].)

Following its implementation on Flakey [38], CDB has been used by several researchers in autonomous robotics [13, 26, 44, 45, 46]. CDB provides a flexible means to implement complex behavior coordination strategies in a modular way using a logical rule format. This modularity simplifies writing and debugging of complex behaviors: the individual behaviors and the coordination rules can be debugged and tuned separately; a few unforeseen interferences may remain, but identifying and correcting these have proved in our experience to be a much easier task than writing and debugging a complex monolitic behavior.

CDB is strictly more general than other coordination schemes commonly used in robotics. It can simulate both on-off behavior switching, and the vector summation scheme used in the popular potential field techniques [16, 20], but it differs from them in the general case. The fact that the same format is used for the control rules and the context rules has several advantages: it allows us to write increasingly complex behaviors in a hierarchical fashion; it facilitates the use of standard AI planning techniques to generate coordination strategies that achieve a given goal; and it allows us to formally analyze the resulting combined behavior. A more detailed analysis of CDB can be found in [37].

# 5  Approximate self-localization

The approaches that we have discussed up to here cope with uncertainty by *tolerating* it, that is, by building robust control programs that try to achieve their goals despite the presence of errors and inaccuracies in sensing and in prior knowledge. Another way to approach the uncertainty problem is by explicitly *representing* it, and by reasoning about its effects. To see the difference, consider the problem of building a robot navigation plan. A tolerant approach would generate a highly conditional plan, where a good amount of decision is postponed until the execution phase, and which includes provisions for real-time sensing in order to reactively adapt to the execution contingencies. The approach presented in the last section is an example of this. By contrast, an explicit representation approach would try to model the different sources of uncertainty, by estimating the (say) probability that an action will fail, that the position of an object will be different from what is expected, and so on; and would generate a plan that maximizes some measure of certainty of success.

One issue in robotics where an explicit representation of uncertainty is often preferred is reasoning with spatial knowledge. Spatial information about the environment can be obtained from several sources, including different types of sensors, motion history, and prior knowledge. If we have a measure of uncertainty for all items of information, then we can combine them to reduce uncertainty, for instance by synchronously fusing the data from different sensors, and/or by diachronically accumulating these data over time. The result of this process is usually to build a *map* of the environment.

Using a map brings about the important problem of *self-localization*: how to estimate of the robot's position with respect to this map. Knowing one's position

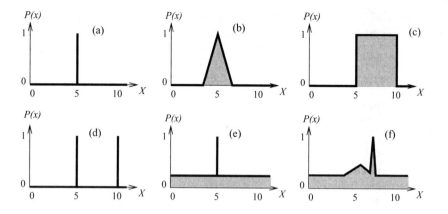

**Fig. 11.** Representing different types of uncertainty by fuzzy sets: (a) crisp; (b) vague; (c) imprecise; (d) ambiguous; (e) unreliable; (f) combined.

is necessary to relate the perceived world to the map, and to decide which actions to perform. Self-localization can use information from the odometric sensors (e.g., wheel encoders) to update the robot's position. Unfortunately, odometry has cumulative errors, and the robot's odometric estimate of its position can diverge from reality without bounds. Landmark-based techniques are commonly used to correct this problem [19]. A landmark can be any perceptually recognizable feature of the environment that is represented in the robot's map, like doors or walls. The robot uses the difference between the perceived and the expected locations of perceived landmark to correct the estimate of its own position.

Most existing approaches to landmark-based self-localization are based on a probabilistic representation of spatial uncertainty, and use some form of Kalman filter [15, 23, 27, 42] to update the robot's position estimate. These approaches can be very effective, provided that: (1) the underlying uncertainty can be given a probabilistic interpretation; (2) the initial estimate is good enough; and (3) the required data is available. In particular, the latter requirement means that (3a) we have an accurate dynamic model of the robot; (3b) we have an accurate stochastic model of the sensors; (3c) these systems do not change in unpredictable ways with time.

These conditions are pretty demanding, and they may easily be violated in the case of autonomous robots. In these cases, fuzzy logic may offer valuable alternatives which require less demanding assumptions: for example, fuzzy-based localization methods typically need only qualitative models of the system and of the sensors. In what follows, we illustrate this point by discussing the way we have used fuzzy logic for approximate map representation and for self-localization in Flakey (see [39] for more on this).

We represent the approximate location of an object by a fuzzy subset of a given space, read under a possibilistic interpretation [48, 49]: if $P_o$ is a fuzzy set representing the approximate location of object $o$, then we read the value of $P_o(\mathbf{x}) \in [0,1]$ as the *degree of possibility* that $o$ be actually located at $\mathbf{x}$. This representation allows us to model different aspects of locational uncertainty. Figure 11 shows six approximate locations in one dimension: (a) is a crisp (certain) location; in (b), we know that the object is located at approximately 5 (this is commonly referred to as "vagueness"); in (c), it can possibly be located anywhere between 5 and 10 ("imprecision"); in (d), it can be either at 5 or at 10 ("ambiguity"); (e) shows a case of "unreliability": we are told that the object is at 5, but the source may be wrong, and there is a small "bias" of possibility that it be located just anywhere. As an extreme case, we represent total ignorance by the "vacuous" location $P(x) = 1$ for all $x$: any location is perfectly possible. Finally, (f) combines vagueness, ambiguity and unreliability. Clearly, the information provided by a measurement device can present any of the above aspects, alone or in combination. It is important to emphasize that a degree of possibility is *not* a probability value: e.g., there is no necessary relation between the observed frequency of a location and its possibility; and degrees of possibility of disjoint locations need not add up to one.

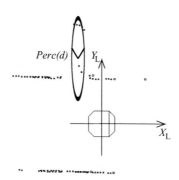

**Fig. 12.** The approximate location of a perceived door. The radiuses of the ellipsoid are proportional to the width of fuzzy location along the corresponding component. The "V" in the middle indicates the width of the fuzzy set of possible orientations.

We use fuzzy sets to represent the approximate position of objects in the map of the environment. More precisely, our approximate maps contain the approximate positions of the major environmental features (doors, walls, corridors, ...), represented by a fuzzy point in $R^3$ — that is, a fuzzy subset of the set of $(x, y, \theta)$ coordinates in a global Cartesian frame, where $\theta$ is the orientation of the object measured with respect to the $X$ axis. We also use fuzzy sets to represent the approximate position of features locally perceived by the sensors. For example, Figure 12 shows the fuzzy position *Perc(d)* of a door $d$ detected by the sonar sensors.[6] The shape of this fuzzy set is due to the fact that the sonar signature of a door on a side can only give a reliable indication about the position of the door along the longitudinal axis, while the distance and orientation of the door remains extremely vague. This set might also include a "bias" to reflect the unreliability of perceptual recognition, as in Figure 11 (e-f).

The above representation can be used by an algorithm for approximate self-localization. In [39] we have proposed a recursive algorithm of this type. Its outline is very simple. At each time-step $t$, the robot has an approximate hypothesis of its own location in the map, represented by a fuzzy subset $H_t$ of the map frame. During navigation, the robot's perceptual apparatus recognizes relevant features, and searches the map for matching objects using a fuzzy measure of similarity. Each matching pair is used to build a *fuzzy localizer*: a fuzzy set representing the approximate location in the map where the robot *should be* in order to see the object where the feature has been observed. So, each localizer provides one imprecise source of information about the actual position of the robot. All these localizers, plus odometric information, are combined by fuzzy intersection to produce the new hypothesis $H_{t+1}$, and the cycle repeats.

Figure 13 illustrates the operation of our algorithm. Each screen-dump shows: on the left, the robot's internal view of its local workspace (details of this view are not important for the discussion here); on the right, the internal map of the environment used by the robot; this includes the robot self-location estimate $H_t$, represented by the ellipsoid around the robot's shape (the narrow cone in front of the robot indicates the uncertainty in orientation). In (a) the robot has some uncertainty as to its position along the $X$ axis; however, there is little uncertainty along the $Y$ axis and in the orientation, due to a previous matching of the corridor's walls. After a while, the sonar sensors detect a door $D$ on the robot's right. By matching this percept to the approximate map, the robot builds the localizer $loc_D$ shown in (b): this indicates that the robot should be located somewhere in the fuzzy set $loc_D$. The robot also builds the dead reckoning localizer $loc_{dr}$ from the previous $H_t$ using odometric information from the wheel encoders. The $loc_D$ and the $loc_{dr}$ localizers are then intersected to produce the new, narrower estimate $H_{t+1}$ of the robot's position, as shown in (c).

The fuzzy self-localization algorithm above was able to keep Flakey well registered during several navigation experiments in an unstructured office environment. The algorithm was also able to produce a correct location hypothesis starting from a situation of total ignorance — a difficult task for probability-based methods. Finally, fuzzy locations can be smoothly integrated inside fuzzy-logic based controllers as the ones reported above. This is an important issue, as locational information eventually has to be used to take decisions.

---

[6] In our current implementation, a fuzzy location is encoded by three triangular fuzzy sets representing its projections on the three axes $X$, $Y$ and $\Theta$. Future implementations will use less restrictive representations.

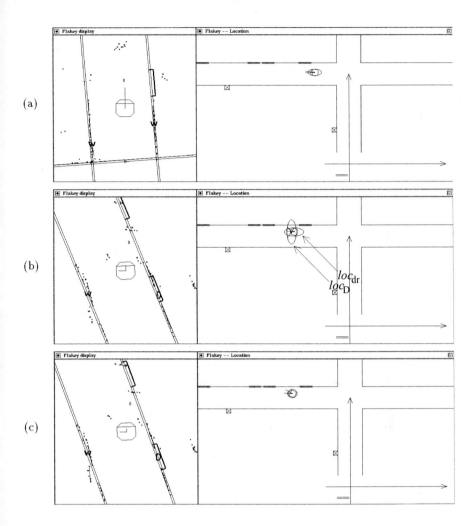

**Fig. 13.** Fuzzy self-localization. Left: the robot's internal view of its surroundings. Right: the robot's map of the environment, with (a) initial location hypothesis $H_t$; (b) dead reckoning and door localizers; (c) updated hypothesis $H_{t+1}$.

## 6  Concluding remarks

Several factors contribute to make truly autonomous robots still a dream — although a not entirely unrealistic one. For one thing, we do not fully understand the principles that underlie intelligent agency, and the intricate relation between agents and their environments. This is a fundamental problem that has been attracting attention from philosophers and scientists for centuries. On a more practical key, autonomous robotics needs the contributions of a number of different technologies developed in different fields, including artificial intelligence, control theory, vision, signal processing, mechatronics, and so on. Integrating these technologies in one system is a hard engineering problem. Finally, autonomous robots must operate in face of the large uncertainty which is inherent to the nature of real-world, unstructured environments, and to the robot-environment interaction. It is this last aspect that we have discussed in this note.

As with most problems involving uncertainty, we can take three different attitudes toward the presence of uncertainty in the robotics domain:

1. Get rid of it, by carefully engineering the robot and/or the environment;
2. Tolerate it, by writing robust programs able to operate under a wide range of situations, and to recover from errors; or
3. Reason about it, by using techniques for the representation and the manipulation of uncertain information.

Industrial robots show us that we can achieve remarkable performance taking the first attitude. If we want to build easily available robots that inhabit our homes, offices, or factory floors, though, we must live with the idea that the platform cannot be overly sophisticated, and that the environment should be only minimally modified. Then, we must consider the second or third attitudes to some extent.

By taking the tolerant attitude, we try to build control programs that provide a reasonable performance in face of large variability in the parameters of the model (due to poor prior knowledge), and large uncertainty in the state of the system (due to poor sensor data and errors in actions). We may express this by saying that these programs should rely on a weak model of the "robot + environment" system. By contrast, taking the third attitude we make the model richer, by explicitly including information about the uncertainty and variability of the parameters. The aim here is to build control programs that reason about this uncertainty in order to choose the actions that are more likely to produce the intended results.

Numerous examples of all these attitudes exist in the robotic domain, showing that often the same problem can be attacked with any one of them. It is difficult to say which uncertainty should be better eliminated by engineering the robot or the environment, and which one should be tolerated or explicitly represented. In general, there is a fundamental tradeoff between using better engineering or better programs (see [6] for an illustration of this tradeoff in the context of a robotic competition).

In this note, we have presented embodiments of the second and the third attitudes to address a few important issues in autonomous robot navigation. For the tolerant attitude, we have shown how we can implement robust behaviors that can tolerate uncertainty in sensing and action; and how we can use these behaviors to flexibly execute plans built from uncertain prior knowledge while adapting to the actual contingencies encountered. As for the representation attitude, we have shown how we can represent approximate spatial information, and reason about it in order to infer a good estimate of the robot's location. The solutions that we have presented were originally developed for the mobile robot Flakey, leading to good experimental results. These solutions have since been ported to a second robot, Edi; they have also been included in the general robot architecture Saphira [17], used on several robotic platforms. Two of these solutions are particularly novel: context-dependent blending, and fuzzy self-localization. The former is being increasingly applied in the autonomous robotics field; for the latter, some related work has been independently developed [12].

Needless to say, there are many other issues in autonomous robotics for which we need to take uncertainty into account, and which we have not touched here. Three omitted issues are particularly worth mentioning. First, perceptual interpretation and modeling. This is a huge field in itself, including a number of subproblems like signal processing, sensor fusion, image interpretation, 3D modeling, and active perception, just to mention a few. Each subproblem is the object of a vast literature, where dealing with uncertainty often plays an important role (see, e.g., [3] for a starting point). Second, planning. Several planning techniques that explicitly take uncertainty into account have been proposed both in the robotics and the AI literature (see, e.g., [7, 21]). Third, learning. Learning techniques can cope with the uncertainty in the model of the system by giving the agent the ability to discover and adaptively modify the model by itself (whether this model is explicitly or implicitly represented is not an issue here). Machine learning techniques have been widely used in autonomous robotics: an interesting sample can be found in two recent special issues [9, 11].

Whatever the issue, the problem of uncertainty needs to be addressed by choosing one of the three attitudes above and, if we opt for an explicit approach, by choosing a specific uncertainty formalism. Although most of the literature on dealing with uncertainty in robotics is based on probabilistic techniques, solutions based on fuzzy logic are being increasingly reported (see [36] for an overview). We have hinted at a few advantages of this choice in the pages above. Still, we emphasize that the choice of the formalism to use depends on the robot-environment-task configuration: there is no "best" way to deal with uncertainty in robotics, but there are as many best ways as there are different robots, environments and tasks.

## Acknowledgments

This research was partly supported by the BELON project, founded by the *Communauté Française de Belgique*. The work on Flakey was performed while the author was with the AI Center of SRI International, in strict collaboration with Enrique Ruspini, Kurt Konolige and Leonard Wesley.

# References

1. R. C. Arkin. Motor schema based navigation for a mobile robot. In *Procs. of the IEEE Int. Conf. on Robotics and Automation*, pages 264–271, 1987.

2. H. Berenji, Y-Y. Chen, C-C. Lee, J-S. Jang, and S. Murugesan. A hierarchical approach to designing approximate reasoning-based controllers for dynamic physical systems. In *Procs. of the 6th Conf. on Uncertainty in Artificial Intelligence*, pages 362–369, Cambridge, MA, 1990.

3. I. Bloch. Information combination operators for data fusion: A comparative review with classification. *IEEE Trans. on Systems, Man, and Cybernetics*, A-26(1):52–67, 1996.

4. A. Bonarini and F. Basso. Learning to to coordinate fuzzy behaviors for autonomous agents. *Int. J. of Approximate Reasoning*, 17(4), 1997. Forthcoming.

5. R. A. Brooks. A robust layered control system for a mobile robot. *IEEE Journal of Robotics and Automation*, RA-2(1):14–23, 1986.

6. C. Congdon, M. Huber, D. Kortenkamp, K. Konolige, K. Myers, E. H. Ruspini, and A. Saffiotti. CARMEL vs. Flakey: A comparison of two winners. *AI Magazine*, 14(1):49–57, Spring 1993.

7. C. Da Costa Pereira, F. Garcia, J. Lang, and R. Martin-Clouaire. Planning with graded nondeterministic actions: a possibilistic approach. *Int. J. of Intelligent Systems*, 1997. Forthcoming.

8. M. Dorigo and M. Colombetti. *Robot shaping: an experiment in behavior engineering*. MIT Press / Bradford Books, 1997.

9. M. Dorigo (Editor). Special issue on: Learning autonomous robots. *IEEE Trans. on Systems, Man, and Cybernetics*, B-26(3), 1996.

10. J. R. Firby. An investigation into reactive planning in complex domains. In *Procs. of the AAAI Conf.*, pages 202–206, 1987.

11. J. A. Franklin, T. M. Mitchell, and S. Thrun (Editors). Special issue on: Robot learning. *Machine Learning*, 23(2-3), 1996.

12. J. Gasós and A. Martín. Mobile robot localization using fuzzy maps. In T. Martin and A. Ralescu, editors, *Fuzzy Logic in AI — Procs. of the IJCAI '95 Workshop*, number 1188 in Lecture Notes in AI, pages 207–224. Springer-Verlag, 1997.

13. S. G. Goodridge, M. G. Kay, and R. C. Luo. Multi-layered fuzzy behavior fusion for reactive control of an autonomous mobile robot. In *Procs. of the IEEE Int. Conf. on Fuzzy Systems*, pages 579–584, Barcelona, SP, 1997.

14. F. Hoffmann and G. Pfister. Evolutionary learning of a fuzzy control rule base for an autonomous vehicle. In *Procs. of the Conf. on Information Processing and Management of Uncertainty (IPMU)*, pages 1235–1238, Granada, SP, 1996.

15. A. H. Jazwinski. *Stochastic processes and filtering theory*. Academic Press, 1970.

16. O. Khatib. Real-time obstacle avoidance for manipulators and mobile robots. *The International Journal of Robotics Research*, 5(1):90–98, 1986.

17. K. Konolige, K.L. Myers, E.H. Ruspini, and A. Saffiotti. The Saphira architecture: A design for autonomy. *Journal of Experimental and Theoretical Artificial Intelligence*, 9(1):215–235, 1997.

18. R. Kruse, J. Gebhardt, and F. Klawonn. *Foundations of Fuzzy Systems*. Wiley and Sons, 1994.

19. B. J. Kuipers. Modeling spatial knowledge. *Cognitive Science*, 2:129–153, 1978.

20. J. C. Latombe. *Robot Motion Planning*. Kluver Academic Publishers, Boston, MA, 1991.

21. A. Lazanas and J. C. Latombe. Motion planning with uncertainty: a landmark approach. *Artificial Intelligence*, 76(1-2):285–317, 1995.

22. C. C. Lee. Fuzzy logic in control systems: fuzzy logic controller (Parts I and II). *IEEE Trans. on Systems, Man, and Cybernetics*, 20(2):404–435, 1990.

23. J. J. Leonard, H. F. Durrant-Whyte, and I. J. Cox. Dynamic map building for an autonomous mobile robot. *Int. J. of Robotics Research*, 11(4):286–298, 1992.

24. V. J. Lumelsky and R. A. Brooks. Special issue on sensor-based planning and control in robotics: Editorial. *IEEE Conference on Robotics and Automation*, 5(6):713–715, 1989.

25. M. Maeda, M. Shimakawa, and S. Murakami. Predictive fuzzy control of an autonomous mobile robot with forecast learning function. *Fuzzy Sets and Systems*, 72:51–60, 1995.

26. F. Michaud. Selecting behaviors using fuzzy logic. In *Procs. of the IEEE Int. Conf. on Fuzzy Systems*, pages 585–592, Barcelona, SP, 1997.

27. P. Moutarlier and R. Chatila. Stochastic multisensory data fusion for mobile robot location and environment modeling. In *5th Int. Symp. on Robotics Research*, pages 207–216, Tokyo, JP, 1989.

28. N. J. Nilsson. SHAKEY the robot. Technical Note 323, SRI Artificial Intelligence Center, Menlo Park, California, 1984.

29. N. J. Nilsson. Teleo-reactive programs for agent control. *Journal of Artificial Intelligence Research*, 1:139–158, 1994.

30. I. Nourbakhsh, S. Morse, C. Becker, M. Balabanovic, E. Gat, R. Simmons, S. Goodridge, H. Potlapalli, D. Hinkle, K. Jung, and D. Van Vactor. The winning robots from the 1993 robot competition. *AI Magazine*, 14(4):51–62, Winter 1993.

31. D. W. Payton. An architecture for reflexive autonomous vehicle control. In *Procs. of the IEEE Int. Conf. on Robotics and Automation*, pages 1838–1845, San Francisco, CA, 1986.

32. S. Quinlan and O. Khatib. Elastic bands: connecting path planning and robot control. In *Procs. of the IEEE Int. Conf. on Robotics and Automation*, volume 2, pages 802–807, Atlanta, Georgia, 1993. IEEE Press.

33. E. H. Ruspini. On the semantics of fuzzy logic. *Int. J. of Approximate Reasoning*, 5:45–88, 1991.

34. E. H. Ruspini. Truth as utility: A conceptual synthesis. In *Procs. of the 7th Conf. on Uncertainty in Artificial Intelligence*, pages 316–322, Los Angeles, CA, 1991.

35. A. Saffiotti. Pick-up what? In C. Bäckström and E. Sandewall, editors, *Current Trends in AI Planning — Procs. of EWSP '93*, pages 166–177. IOS Press, Amsterdam, Nederlands, 1994.

36. A. Saffiotti. The uses of fuzzy logic for autonomous robot navigation: a catalogue raisonné. Technical report, IRIDIA, Université Libre de Bruxelles, Brussels, Belgium, 1997. Available on-line: http://iridia.ulb.ac.be/saffiotti/flarbib.html.

37. A. Saffiotti, K. Konolige, and E. H. Ruspini. A multivalued-logic approach to integrating planning and control. *Artificial Intelligence*, 76(1-2):481–526, 1995.

38. A. Saffiotti, E. H. Ruspini, and K. Konolige. Blending reactivity and goal-directedness in a fuzzy controller. In *Procs. of the 2nd IEEE Int. Conf. on Fuzzy Systems*, pages 134–139, San Francisco, California, 1993. IEEE Press.

39. A. Saffiotti and L. P. Wesley. Perception-based self-localization using fuzzy locations. In M. van Lambalgen L. Dorst and F. Voorbraak, editors, *Reasoning with Uncertainty in Robotics — Procs. of the 1st Int. Workshop*, number 1093 in LNAI, pages 368–385. Springer-Verlag, Berlin, DE, 1996.

40. A. Saffiotti (Maintainer). Fuzzy logic in the autonomous mobile robot Flakey: on-line bibliography. URL: http://iridia.ulb.ac.be/saffiotti/flakeybib.html. By ftp: ftp://iridia.ulb.ac.be/pub/saffiotti/robot/.

41. M. J. Schoppers. Universal plans for reactive robots in unpredictable environments. In *Procs. of the Int. Joint Conf. on Artificial Intelligence*, pages 1039–1046, 1987.

42. R. C. Smith and P. Cheeseman. On the representation and estimation of spatial uncertainty. *Int. J. of Robotics Research*, 5(4):56–68, 1986.

43. M. Sugeno and M. Nishida. Fuzzy control of model car. *Fuzzy Sets and Systems*, 16:103–113, 1985.

44. H. Surmann, J. Huser, and L. Peters. A fuzzy system for indoor mobile robot navigation. In *Procs. of the IEEE Int. Conf. on Fuzzy Systems*, pages 83–86, Yokohama, JP, 1995. IEEE Press.

45. E. Tunstel, H. Danny, T. Lippincott, and M. Jamshidi. Autonomous navigation using an adaptive hierarchy of multiple fuzzy behaviors. In *Procs. of the IEEE Int. Sym. on Computational Intelligence in Robotics and Automation*, Monterey, CA, 1997.

46. C. Voudouris, P. Chernett, C. J. Wang, and V. L. Callaghan. Hierarchical behavioural control for autonomous vehicles. In A. Halme and K. Koskinen, editors, *Procs. of the 2nd IFAC Conf. on Intelligent Autonomous Vehicles*, pages 267–272, Helsinki, FI, 1995.

47. J. Yen and N. Pfluger. A fuzzy logic based robot navigation system. In *Procs. of the AAAI Fall Symposium on Mobile Robot Navigation*, pages 195–199, Boston, MA, 1992.

48. L. A. Zadeh. Fuzzy sets. *Information and Control*, 8:338–353, 1965.

49. L. A. Zadeh. Fuzzy sets as a basis for a theory of possibility. *Fuzzy Sets and Systems*, 1:3–28, 1978.

# Some Problems in Trying to Implement Uncertainty Techniques in Automated Inspection

Duncan Wilson[1&2], Alistair Greig[1], John Gilby[2] & Robert Smith[2]


[1]Department of Mechanical Engineering, University College London,
Torrington Place, London, WC1E 7JE, UK
Email: ucaidjw@ucl.ac.uk

[2]Sira Technology Centre, Sira Ltd., South Hill,
Chislehurst, Kent, BR7 5EH, UK

**Abstract.** This paper discusses the difficulties in applying uncertainty management techniques to real world problems. Automated Inspection is a process where the data used to model the environment is uncertain. There is an existing body of knowledge within the research community which enables such uncertain information to be expressed. Although there have been successful applications in fields such as medical diagnosis, there are also problems in industry which currently cannot be solved. The process of industrial inspection is an environment where the method for applying uncertainty management techniques is not intuitive. The nature of the uncertainty and the difficulty in applying the theoretical techniques to real world problems shall be the focus of the following discussion.

## 1    Introduction

In many industrial process control situations the need to identify and classify defects is key to enabling process improvements. The task involves examining and then reporting. In the environment of visual inspection this can be translated as defect detection and defect classification. One of the major obstacles in this process is the management of uncertainty, which is inherent in the decision process of classification.

The purpose of classification is to assess the quality of the product. The measure of quality, and hence the category to which the product is classified, is dependent upon the customer requirements. The customer in this case may be the end user or the next stage in the manufacturing process. The important point to note is that inspection is required to meet customer requirements and that it must be undertaken regularly since the production environment is continuously open to change. This variation in environment may come through changes in the process, changes in raw materials or from increasing demands for product improvements and higher quality. A fundamental requirement is therefore a system which allows the reporting of information which is dependent on users end requirements and the production process, both of which are subject to change.

In the real world there is a need to manage uncertainty which is inherent in the system. This paper will review why it is necessary for the particular application of defect classification and will discuss the problems associated with implementing uncertainty management techniques. The following section describes a real world problem, automated inspection, and shows how it is different to other successful applications. Section three reviews how the uncertainty formalisms relate to the inspection environment. The fourth section illustrates the difficulties in applying the formalisms to the real world. Finally some concluding points are made assessing the requirements for further work.

## 2    A Real World Application - Automated Inspection

### 2.1    Detection and classification

Whilst there are many defect detection systems on the market [3, 11, 12, 17], there are few commercial products which also provide satisfactory classification. Research is focusing on the task of classification [4, 8, 9, 10, 13]. So why is this process of classification more difficult than detection?

Whilst detection is a fairly objective process (normally you are reporting if something is there or not) the classification stage is rather subjective. It is subjective because a decision must be made which assigns a classification to a defect which has been based on someone's perception of what a defect is. A fundamental point to be noted is that descriptions of defects do not normally exist. A common assumption people make when working with inspection systems is,

"There is some known measure of goodness which someone can describe."

Unfortunately this is not the case. It is the difficulty in representing what people perceive to be defects which will form much of the discussion in this paper.

Industry traditionally has difficulty in expressing what it thinks are defects [5, 14]. It is suggested this is because the functional end-use of the product is the actual criteria for inspection. That criteria may be 'Can I sell this stack of glass at a good price?' Such criteria are very difficult to quantify and therefore people look for an alternative that is quantifiable. The problem then is that this search can often lead further and further from the original criteria. Furthermore, which criteria look quantifiable depends on what can be expressed. Industry therefore has two methods by which it normally specifies what it wants. The first is to define defects in terms of some accessible parameter which is believed to correlate with defect severity. For example a measurement such as length. The second is to give the supplier samples of products with defects. In this case the defects used as examples are "what the customers want to be able to identify".

The former method is very subjective; defects are seldom high contrast objects with clearly defined parameters. Figures One A and B show the resultant images when a point light source is shone through a defect in glass and projected onto a screen. The defects in this case are a bubble and a ream knot. A bubble as the name suggests is a local area of trapped air. Ream is a waviness in the glass which sometimes occurs during production and a knot describes a local area of material with different physical properties within the glass. The images typify what might be 'seen' by a machine vision system. It is possible to construct signatures for different types of defects by analysing how they distort light. The difficulty lies in extracting the correct information to develop the signatures. It should also be noted that the amount of information available to describe the defect is often limited. (In the authors research the image size is usually less than 8*8 pixels). The limitation is usually due to small defect size compared to large areas of product and the speed at which the production lines operate.

There is a trade-off between detection and classification. Ideally, detection would result in a rich set of well defined parameters that map easily to the way people would naturally make the classification. However, at typical production speeds, it is usually not possible to obtain such information. Furthermore, obtaining the information requires extra hardware complexity in the inspection system (for example, extra optical channels). It should be apparent that in some applications the process of classification becomes much more difficult than that of detection due to the constraints on the inspection system.

Experience shows that in most cases of manual inspection different inspectors will classify the same defect differently. Whilst setting up an inspection system it is usual for the engineers to ask inspectors to give their verdict on samples of product with defects. Given these classifications they then use the information to construct a classification taxonomy. At one installation the engineers gave five inspectors a group of samples to classify. The inspectors each came up with slightly different classifications according to size and shape. This difference between the way the inspectors viewed the defects was not really surprising since the process is quite subjective. The surprise came when the inspectors, unknowingly, were asked to classify the same defects the next day. They all made slightly different classifications to the ones they had made the previous day.

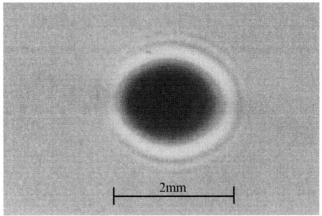

**Fig. 1a. Defect type 'bubble' in glass.**

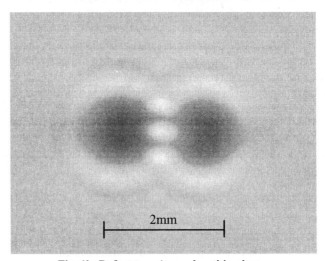

**Fig. 1b. Defect type 'ream knot' in glass.**

It is very difficult to specify a description of what is, and what is not, a defect according to parameters such as length. Similarly using samples of defects is very subjective since it relies on someone's interpretation of a group of defects. The samples provided by customers are by no means exhaustive sets of defects. Normally a limited set of samples are provided and it is expected that the people setting up the system will sensibly extrapolate from the data provided. This often causes problems. For example, the samples given to the suppliers may have all been on clear product, however the majority of the product manufactured is opaque to semi-opaque. A similar problem is the number of defects presented in the sample set. The quality control people will be able to provide a detailed and accurate list of all defect types which have occurred on a production line. Some may appear every day whereas others may seldom appear. What is important is to be able to classify correctly those that occur 99.9% of the time. (For example, the dust to defect ratio can typically be 100:1. Since you don't want to discard material which has just got dust on it, because dust is not a defect, it is important to identify dust correctly). A classification error rate of one percent on a class which is witnessed 99.9% of the time is very different to an error rate witnessed at 0.1%. An error rate as small as one percent in the largest class may render the inspection system useless. This highlights the issue of how to extrapolate information from an inadequate set of data. Most defect data is limited. The experience of the engineers is used to extend it.

Both of these methods require difficult knowledge acquisition from the expert. The result of these specifications is a system which classifies defects *abc* under *xyz* operating conditions according to some contractual agreement. Inevitably once installed in the real world either the defects change from *abc* to *def* or the operating conditions change from *xyz* to *rst*. The system is in a continual state of evolution.

Why is it difficult to capture what the expert wants? A classification made by an inspection machine allows us to assess the quality of the product being manufactured. The measure of quality is dependent upon the customer's requirements. The customer in this case maybe the end user (who would be concerned with the performance of the product) or the production staff controlling the manufacturing process (who would be concerned with the state of the production line). In many production environments there will be several different parties who all have an interest in the results of the inspection process. That is one of the reasons why it is difficult to get a standard definition of what a defect is. Many of the people involved will have different interpretations. For example, the Scientist in the Research and Development Laboratory might measure the length of a defect with a micrometer, the Engineer might use his steel rule, the Production staff might use their experience, whilst the Production manager will measure using any of these methods but will take into consideration the days production targets. Different descriptions of what constitutes a defect are available since people perceive the defects in different ways. This highlights the subjective nature of the knowledge which describes the inspection domain.

The expert from which the knowledge is acquired will not be able to give the supplier a complete body of knowledge about the environment. The supplier must therefore extract information and code it into the system in a generic form. So, given two types of defect we might assume others will be fairly similar. This mode of reasoning is similar to the way human inspectors might classify 'new' defects. This is a different approach to methods such as neural networks which have difficulty in extrapolating classifications to new defect types using knowledge of the production process. Here the extensions are being made by involving the experience of the expert.

There are two important requirements for a classification scheme within industrial inspection. The first is an appropriate mental framework which allows the capture of limited domain knowledge. The second is the ability to use the knowledge in a manner which allows reasoning about new instances in the problem domain.

## 2.2    Why is this classification different?

What is, and what is not, a defect? The immediate problem in developing a classification system is to understand or capture the information which describes the problem. In medical diagnosis, MYCIN [18] is a system which captures knowledge from experts about a particular domain. It can be described as having two underlying ideas; a rule structure with degrees of certainty, and a backward chaining, goal directed system structure. Neither of these are inherent in the expert's view of the world, rather they are conceptual structures imposed by the designer. They provide a means of expression which allow the domain expert to express some things more easily than others, and provide a framework into which that information can be fitted.

The idea of the conceptual framework above appears to be an ideal way to capture information in medical diagnosis. It is necessary to define what would be useful for automatic inspection. The environments in which these applications are being used have two key differences.

First, MYCIN works on a large, relatively stable database whereas in inspection there are many different problems each with smaller more, varying data. Figure Two illustrates the process of medical diagnosis.

The domain knowledge contains information which is accepted as given. The language used at the outset is in accordance with standard medical terminology and hence will not change through the life of the expert system. MYCIN therefore concentrates on continually finding new connections between symptoms which allow more accurate diagnosis to be made. The development work is aimed at extracting more information from a known source which always communicates in the same language.

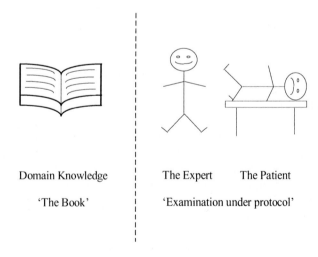

Domain Knowledge

'The Book'

The Expert        The Patient

'Examination under protocol'

**Fig. 2. The information which goes into MYCIN.**

Figure Three shows the type of information structure which would be required for an inspection expert system. Whereas medical diagnosis systems will invariably work with a single body of knowledge (historical medical data), there is no single inspection application. Rather there are a family of inspection applications each with its own special domain knowledge. In inspection the focus of attention lies in both the individual expert and the application specific domain knowledge. There is no predefined language used to talk about inspection. People use different expressions, therefore the language must be defined each time. Rather than one large database, many smaller ones are required for different environments and problems.

The second key difference is that medical diagnosis systems emulate an expert who could actually do the diagnosis. The criteria by which the expert would diagnose is the same as the rules coded into the expert system (e.g. if the stain of the organism is gram negative and the morphology is rod, etc......with a certainty level 0.8.... then an organism is Enterabacteriaceae). Hence given the information on the stain and the morphology etc., both the expert and the expert system would deduce the same result (in theory!). The information used is standard medical terminology, a language already exists for constructing a knowledge base.

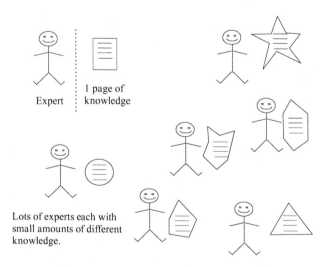

**Fig. 3. Information in an inspection expert system.**

The inspection problem is fundamentally different. There is no common language which can be used to express what constitutes a defect. The way in which a human would perceive and classify a defect is different to the method used by a machine vision system. Figure Four highlights this difference. Drawing an analogy to the MYCIN example, this would be equivalent to removing the doctors diagnosis which he obtained by prodding and poking the patient (obtaining stains, morphologies etc.) and taking obscure automated measurements using a cell counting machine which would show the number of and sizes of bacteria. Given information which is not in the terminology used by the expert (in this analogy the 'distribution of cells'), makes it difficult to make a diagnosis. The expert system no longer has an expert to model.

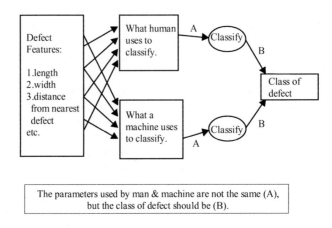

**Fig. 4. One way mapping between defect characteristics and classification.**

### 2.3    Why we need a method of representation

Parallels do exist when comparing medical diagnosis with the requirements for inspection, but the major element which does not transfer between the two is the agreed set of information which defines the structure of the system (in the case of medical diagnosis, the symptoms). In inspection this set requires defining for each application. This is an important difference and highlights the requirement for a method of representation which will enable the inspection system to work in a way which is meaningful to the user. On the one hand we have output from a machine which is detecting defects and on the other we have systems which classify defects.

Uncertainty is inherent in the inspection process. If we want to model that process then we need something which will allow us to express uncertain information. Potential tools for bridging that gap are uncertainty management techniques.

## 3    Uncertainty – Its Relation to Inspection

As previously discussed uncertainty is an inherent problem in inspection. It is necessary to integrate this uncertainty into computer systems so that they are capable of managing inspection tasks. The first process is to define the type of uncertainty present in the application domain, then apply a formalism which allows suitable representation.

## 3.1 Types of uncertainty

Krause and Clark [7] propose a classification of uncertainty which covers aspects most relevant to Artificial Intelligence applications. The typology defines a distinction where aspects of uncertainty apply to individual propositions or sets of propositions. Furthermore each of those aspects can be either lack of knowledge or from conflicting knowledge. At the next level concepts of uncertainty can be defined as: vagueness, ambiguity, anomaly, inconsistency, incompleteness, irrelevance, lack of confidence or equivocation (where propositions may be simultaneously supported and discredited). By acknowledging these aspects of uncertainty, it should be possible to identify them in real world systems. Figure five illustrates the above typology.

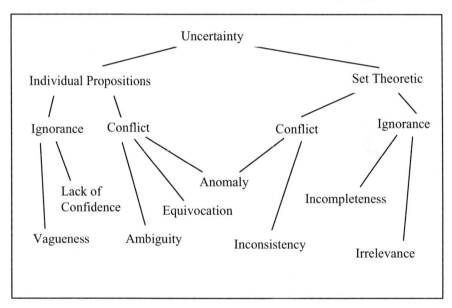

**Fig. 5. A classification of uncertainty (Krause and Clark (pg.7) [7])**

Uncertainty in inspection can predominantly be defined as: vagueness (there is no finite definition of the defect), incompleteness (the factory environment is continually changing), and ambiguity (when the measurable properties could lead to alternative classifications).

Figures One A and B show defects in glass. The images typify what might be 'seen' by a machine vision system. It is possible to construct signatures for different types of defects by analysing how they distort light. The difficulty lies in extracting the correct information to develop the signatures.

In these examples, where are the boundaries of the defect? How can the limit be detected where the light distortion stops affecting the appearance of the defect? How do the image of the light distortion and the actual defect compare? It should be noted that what the human sees and what the machine sees may not be the same. For example, the defects appear to be approximately 2mm in width. In reality the defects may appear to be larger or smaller depending on ones view of the distortion around the centre of the defect.

Traditionally people have used expressions such as:

$$if \text{ length} > 2mm \text{ } then \text{ defect type X}$$

There is a problem associated with this type of rule. Is there really a difference in appearance between a 2.00mm defect and a 2.01mm defect? In ancient Greece similar situations were known as a sorites paradox. The original sorite appeared as Zeno's paradox of the sand heap. If you take a heap of sand and remove one grain, is it still a heap? At what point does the heap stop being a heap? Which grain of sand converts the heap to a non-heap? With the rule above what length makes the change from defect X to non-defect X? Description of defects are essentially subjective and are therefore prone to vagueness.

The second type of uncertainty is incompleteness. It is very difficult to construct an accurate model of the inspection environment however this has been the primary method by which automated inspection systems have been set-up. The methods mentioned previously are only accurate when the system is initially set-up. Over time the production line will undergo natural changes. Routine maintenance work might involve changing the filters used in a process prior to the inspection stage. This might consequently cause a different type of defect to occur. Alternatively, an extra stage in production might be added to improve the process (for example, a washing unit to improve the quality of the glass). This again might create new defect types or alter the characteristics of the current types.

Another potential source of incompleteness is the inability to know your customer requirements. The primary function of inspection is to grade products. This enables the customer to buy material at an accepted quality level. The customer requirements might vary according to the current market climate and their customers. For example, if there is little product available on the market they will be more inclined to settle for lower quality product. Conversely if they have the option of buying from several suppliers they will invariably opt for high quality product.

In automotive manufacturing the process of painting cars has two key purposes. The first is to provide a protective anti-corrosion coating to the metal which is the framework of the car, and the second is for aesthetic purposes. To ensure both the criteria are met the paint finish is inspected.

There are several classes of defect associated with paint finish. Orange peel is the jargon used which describes a particular defect in the texture of paint finish. It is quite easy for the human eye to distinguish changes in the texture, the difficulty is measuring the non-uniformity. Furthermore, how do we define the characteristics when different colours and types of coating exist with different orange peel effects? The ultimate requirement in the testing for orange peel is testing for customer satisfaction. Is the paint quality of a high enough standard? Although individual textures could be classified according to examples, how can the generic case be constructed which will allow for the addition of new paint types.

Market forces will influence the type of defects to be classified. Hence there is the potential problem of incompleteness unless it is possible to predict all eventualities within the market. It is safe to assume that it is not possible to make such predictions! In reality it is not possible to define all types of defect which might occur. It is necessary to take this into consideration when organising a classification method. The inspection system should not only be robust enough to handle unknown anomalies but also have the facility to be modified.

The third type of uncertainty relating to inspection is ambiguity. This was previously defined as the case when different interpretations of a proposition were possible. In the manufacture of paper a source of defect is contamination. Here the expert is interested in what caused the defect. It could be something in the raw material or an object which has fallen onto the product. Both might look like a fibre' so how can the distinction be made?

Contamination invariably occurs when there has been some change in the process. (Another potential area of incomplete information). For example a change in raw material or some maintenance work. Taking the latter as an example, an employee Joe might have carried out some maintenance work and inadvertently caused a fault which gives rise to grease spots on the product. After the defect is remedied and he has been disciplined, he won't do it again. However in six months time, when he changes jobs, Fred comes along and the grease spots reappear. Contamination tends not to be random. It is usually caused as a result of machine problems. This highlights the difficulties which occur with defects which are process related. How is this knowledge extracted in the initial knowledge acquisition phase of the project. In the case of contamination it is not always possible to identify characteristics which would enable distinction between defect types (that is those on top of the material and those in the material).

In general, the uncertainty in many industrial applications comes from the environment in which the system exists. Since the environment is continually open to change we cannot acquire a representation which will be true for all conditions. Hence there is a requirement to reason about the information which is available and make a decision based on that information. The uncertainty therefore lies in not necessarily having a prior example of every type of defect.

In summary there are three types of uncertainty in automated inspection: vagueness, incompleteness and ambiguity. This uncertainty is a result of the subjective nature of classifying defects, which is prone to individual perception, and ignorance about possible states of the system.

---

' A fibre might be a strand of cotton from clothing or a bristle from a brush.

## 3.2    Uncertainty formalisms

Previous approaches to classification schemes which used production rules [6], suffered the restriction of inadequate data representation. The use of uncertainty techniques to overcome such representational difficulties provided a natural extension to existing models. The sections below describe how uncertainty techniques could be used to incorporate vagueness, incompleteness and ambiguity in a robust classification scheme.

### 3.2.1 A method for representing the vagueness in the data.

In the inspection of web products such as glass and plastic films many of the defects do not have crisp shapes. A typical example in glass is a bubble. The bubble itself tends to have a defined size but it is surrounded by a region of glass that distorts the light passing through. The size of that region has a significant affect on the severity of the defect but the region does not have a crisp edge. When viewed under different angles of lighting, it is possible to see changes in the pattern of distortion, this makes the distorted area larger or smaller. The border between the normal product and the defect is therefore subjective and dependent on how the measurement is taken.

The data which is available for defining defect classes is often vague. A method is required for representing expert knowledge in a descriptive manner. In this application descriptive means the ability to define expressions which capture the true meaning of a property. For example, at present boundaries are set on parameters such as length which divide objects into different classes. This might mean that defects with lengths of 2.9mm and 3.0mm are classified differently. However, if you ask any expert to distinguish between them, they won't be able to. Setting crisp boundaries on classes does not appear to be the method used by experts. What we need is a representation which allows us to capture the type of knowledge which they use.

At its simplest level, Fuzzy logic [19, 20] offers a framework for the representation of knowledge which is lexically imprecise and/or uncertain. It provides tools for representing the meaning and inferring from the kind of facts exemplified by; the area is usually high, or, a small width/length ratio usually indicates a scratch or fibre defect. A lexical representation is consistent with the language used to make final decisions about the classified product. For example, Quality Assurance are likely to assess the product as high, medium and low grades. It should be noted that the real values of these bounds are prone to change with respect to what the customer perceives to be high, medium or low grade which in turn depends on the current state of the market place.

Given that it is possible to generate fuzzy regions which correspond to possible input values for parameters such as length, width, area etc., it should also be possible to generate degrees of support for propositions defined by such parameters. For example, if a degree of support can be generated for the expression 'length is high' given an input parameter X, and a classification rule 'if length is high then defect A, B or C', it is possible to relate the degree of support for X to evidence for defects A, B and C.

Fuzzy logic provides a meaningful way of describing the expert's knowledge. What is not clear is how the formalism can be extended to incorporate some of the other sources of uncertainty. The following section looks at those sources of uncertainty and proposes a way forward.

### 3.2.2 Ambiguity and incompleteness in the data.

It was apparent from the start that it would be very difficult to define a set of parameters which would provide a complete model of the inspection task. This meant that other common approaches [1] would not be suitable. Pattern recognition techniques assume knowledge of the underlying statistical distribution or a large number of correctly classified patterns. Both these are usually unavailable and subject to change. The difficulties in applying Neural Networks highlight these problems: it is seldom possible to create a good training set, and any such set rapidly becomes out of date as requirements change. What is available is the ability to capture heuristics about the process. From these rules of thumb it is possible to generate rules which imply different defect types.

A numerical approach which incorporates methods for handling incompleteness and ambiguity is Dempster Shafer (DS), theory of evidence [16]. DS is a theory which uses a number between 0 and 1 to indicate a degree of support for a body of evidence. There are three key reasons why it seems appropriate for this application.

First is the ability to assign support to set functions rather than individual hypotheses. Being able to associate measurements in terms of sets of defects provides a good way of describing defect properties. For example, we may be able to generate a heuristic such as: 'if width/length is small then defect type {scratch, fibre}'. This rule basically states that if something has a shape which is long and thin then it could be a scratch in the material or a fibre. Being able to assign the consequent as a set of outcomes is useful since the evidence 'width/length is small' does not allow us to distinguish between the two possible defect types.

Second, the notion of making decisions based on the evidence available was intuitive to the expert. The evidence available for making decisions consists of known facts. The rejection of the law of additivity means the experts do not need to commit themselves to facts that they cannot define. This gives the experts much more freedom in constructing the knowledge they do know and brings the logic behind the classification process much closer to the method they would use themselves.

Finally, Dempster's rule of combination provides a theoretical technique for combining evidence. To combine new pieces of evidence to pre-existing hypothesis sets, we calculate the overlap, or intersection, of both the new and all the current hypothesis sets. The belief in the new subset is simply the product of the prior beliefs which constitute the newly formed subset. This subset then becomes a hypothesis set itself. Hence incomplete evidence can be updated as more information is discovered. This provides a formal method for calculating the most likely outcome given some evidence.

The difficulty in applying Dempster Shafer however is selecting a value for the degree of support associated with a piece of evidence. Shafer [16] suggests that 'an individual can make a judgement' given the circumstances surrounding a piece of evidence. In this application evidence comes from a set of measurements for each unique defect. From these measurements we need to calculate potential defect types.

The fuzzy regions described in the previous section highlighted a method for calculating degrees of support given an input from the machine. By combining the two formalism the three sources of uncertainty can be incorporated into a model for the inspection system.

### 3.3 Selecting which formalisms should be used?

The previous paragraphs describe reasons why probabilistic (Dempster-Shafer) and possibilistic (Fuzzy Set Theory) approaches could be beneficial in representing uncertain information. An important consideration in defining which formalism to use, is to identify the sources of uncertainty[2]. There may be ignorance about the data output from the system. The data could be ambiguous, it may not be possible to distinguish between two possible values. There could be other problems such as lack of confidence, error, or variability in the data. The key is to find a representation which allows the expression of uncertainty encountered in the specific application.

## 4    The Difficulty in Applying the Techniques to Inspection

It should be clear that in inspection there are applications in which there is inherent uncertainty. It is also clear that there is a body of knowledge which exists within the research community which enables such uncertain information to be expressed. What was not initially clear was how this knowledge could be applied to the inspection problem. Creating the link between the two was required.

Whilst developing an automated inspection system the first problem encountered was actually defining the problem. It is very difficult to capture generic information which describes the inspection domain. This is a classic problem encountered in many classification schemes where the products are subject to natural variation. The features which should be used to differentiate between, for example, two kinds of apple are not obvious. Actually obtaining the correct type of information in the first place is quite difficult. The uncertainty

---

[2] For example see, "Sources of uncertainty" in Reasoning Plausible [2].

techniques were useful here because they provided methods for expressing such information. They force the user to ask, "Can I express information in the form required for this formalism? If so what information can I represent?".

Equally it is not obvious how to represent the information communicated by the expert using the formalisms provided. It is not an intuitive process. Saffiotti [15] suggests there is a mismatch between the languages used in knowledge representation (production rules, taxonomies, etc.) and uncertainty management techniques (Dempster-Shafer, Bayesian, etc.). This means that if a formalism for representing uncertainty is to be used, then the user must first find a method to represent the knowledge relevant to their problem, in the framework provided by the formalism. This was a key problem in trying to implement the uncertainty techniques in this industrial application and is probably not uncommon in many industrial applications of theoretical research. The theory existed but it was not obvious how the tools could be used. The tools each have certain benefits and by fitting them to the requirements of the system, the uncertainty techniques provide a way forward in solving this problem.

Design decisions must be made which define what representation should be used. This is dependent on the application since this stage enables information relevant to the domain to be expressed in a manner which feels natural to the end user. For example, the object oriented methodology allows a form of representation within a computer language. It is possible to program in an object oriented style using a language such as FORTRAN, however it is much easier using C++ or Smalltalk. Object oriented languages make the programmer think about the structure of the information, hence the methodology fits intuitively.

At present it is difficult to express a real world problem within the constraints of the formalisms provided. When trying to implement uncertainty management techniques the task which is often the hardest is finding a representation for presenting the information to the uncertainty formalisms. The importance of highlighting the sources of uncertainty cannot be stressed enough. It was not until the three sources of uncertainty were defined that it was possible to constructively assess the best approach for defining a classification scheme. Fuzzy logic always appeared to be an intuitive method for expressing experts knowledge, however what was not clear was the method by which decisions could be made with such incomplete and ambiguous data. Dempster Shafer proved a logical step towards overcoming such sources of uncertainty. The combination of the two formalisms provided a natural extension to the rule based system which is currently in use on line. The 'new technology' therefore has the added advantage of being similar to the old and is therefore intuitive to the customer.

# 5 Conclusion

Particularly pertinent to this application, and indeed to any which involve a subjective environment, is the question of knowledge acquisition. In many cases a description of what to classify does not exist. As stated in section 2, a common assumption people make when working with inspection systems is that detailed descriptions of defects to be classified exist. That is not the case. In order to develop techniques which will allow uncertainty formalisms to be used in more widespread applications the following two points should be addressed.

To a large extent the user must work around the technology available. The opposite would be more appealing, how can the technology work around the user? Rather than programming requirements into, for example, image processing software as numerical values, it should be possible to express requirements in terms which are intuitive. The technology is available but how can it be applied? The uncertainty formalisms should enable the development of a model which fits the mental framework of those who shall use it.

Second, once a system has been developed by a knowledge engineer it is usually installed and left to operate. Since most industrial systems are prone to change it is necessary for the users of the system (rather than those who installed it) to have the facility to update the knowledge which the model describes. The process by which the model can be updated should be intuitive for the user. The representation used to express information in the model should appear natural to the users so that they can manipulate the model to suit their requirements.

At present there exists a sound theoretical basis for this work, but it is important to refine the concepts in a real world situation. For this reason the authors have set-up an experimental rig which emulates an industrial inspection environment. The purpose of the research is to classify defects in plastic films (such as OHP sheets). Developing a classification scheme has highlighted the requirements of such a model and gives an insight into how applying uncertainty techniques can improve defect classification.

The results from this study show how the theoretical ideas for representing uncertain information can be applied to real world situations. Application of the techniques also highlight the ways in which the theoretical ideas must be refined to be suitable for industrial applications.

## Acknowledgments

The author is in receipt of a Postgraduate Training Partnership Award for collaborative work at University College London and Sira Ltd. This research is funded jointly by the Department of Trade and Industry and the Engineering and Physical Sciences Research Council.

## References

1 Bayro-Corrachano E, Review of Automated Visual Inspection 1983-1993, Part II: Approaches to Intelligent Systems, *SPIE,* Vol. 2055, 1993, 159-172
2 Bonissone P, Reasoning Plausible, in 'Encyclopedia of Artificial Intelligence', S Shapiro, 1992

241

3 Chou PB, RA Rao, MC Sturzenbecker, VH Brecker, Automatic defect classification for integrated circuits, SPIE Vol. 1907 Machine Vision applications in industrial inspection, pp95-103, 1993

4 D'Haeyer J, Reliable Flaw classifiers for machine vision based quality control, SPIE Vol.2597, pp 119-130, 1995

5 Gel Count Forum - Raw Data, Image Automation Ltd., Texas, USA, June 1993

6 Holmes J, *Technical Note - Setting up the L30*, Image Automation Ltd., Sept. 1994

7 Krause P and Clark D, Representing Uncertain Knowledge an Artificial Intelligence Approach, Intellect Books, 1993

8 Lu N, Tredgold A and Fielding E, The use of machine vision and fuzzy sets to classify soft fruit, SPIE Vol. 2620, pp 663-669, 1995.

9 Luria M, Moran M, Yaffe D and Kawski J, Automatic defect classification using Fuzzy Logic, IEEE / SEMI Advanced Semiconductor Manufacturing Conference, p191-193, 1993

10 Perner P, A knowledge based image inspection system for automatic defect recognition, classification and process diagnosis, Machine Vision and Applications, 7:pp 135-147 1994

11 Petrou M, Automated intelligent inspection for quality control, Invited presentation, Sira Technology Centre Intelligent Imaging Programme, General Meeting, 7 June 1995.

12 Raafat H and Taboun S, An integrated robotic and machine vision system for surface flaw detection and classification, Computers Industrial Engineering, Vol.30, No.1 pp27-40.

13 Rao R and Jain R, A classification scheme for visual defects arising in semiconductor wafer inspection, Journal of Crystal Growth, 103 pp398-406, 1990.

14 Resin Grading and Gel Counting Technical User Forum, Image Automation Ltd., Texas, USA, June 1993

15 Saffiotti A, Issues of knowledge representation in Dempster-Shafer Theory, in Advances in the Dempster-Shafer Theory of Evidence, Ed. Yager RR, Kacprzyk J, Fedrizzi M, John Wiley, 1994.

16 Shafer G, A Mathematical Theory of Evidence, Princeton University Press, 1976

17 Sherman R, Tirosh E and Smilansky Z, An automatic defect classification system for semiconductor wafers, SPIE Vol. 1907 Machine Vision applications in industrial inspection, pp72-79, 1993

18 Shortliffe, E.H., Rule Based Expert Systems, the MYCIN Experiments of the Stanford Heuristics Programming Project, Addison Wesley 1985

19 Zadeh L, Knowledge Representation in Fuzzy Logic, pp 1-26, in An introduction to Fuzzy Logic applications in intelligent systems, ed R Yager, Kluwer 1992

20 Zimmerman HJ, Fuzzy Set Theory and its applications, Kluwer Academic Publishers, USA, 1991

# Correlation Using Uncertain and Temporal Information

John Bigham

Department of Electronic Engineering,
Queen Mary and Westfield College,
University of London,
London, E1 4NS,
United Kingdom.

J.Bigham@qmw.ac.uk

**Abstract.** This paper describes a modelling language which is suitable for the correlation of information when the underlying functional model of the system is incomplete or uncertain and the temporal dependencies are imprecise. An implementation of this approach is outlined using cost functions. If the cost functions satisfy certain criteria then an efficient and incremental approach to the control computation is possible. Possibilistic logic and probability theory (as it is used in the applications targetted) satisfy the criteria.

## 1 Introduction

This paper describes a modelling language which is suitable for the correlation of information when the underlying functional model of the system is incomplete or uncertain and the temporal dependencies are imprecise. This language has its roots in the diagnosis and maintenance of telecommunications systems and is designed to be modular and to allow the modelling of large systems. An efficient approach to implementation is outlined using cost functions which satisfy certain criteria to control computation. Possibilistic logic and probability theory (as it is used here) do.

Incompleteness in the models of artifacts usually arises from the costs of modelling and reasoning on the system at the level of detail at which it actually works. Acquiring detailed knowledge of the system behaviour and the temporal relationships can be very expensive. However the degree of completeness of a model only needs to be sufficient to discriminate between the decisions which can to be made in the application context and so incomplete models may often be sufficient. Uncertainty management is necessary to manage the risk associated with having an incomplete model.

The need to integrate uncertainty management and temporal constraint management is illustrated in the context of diagnosis in a satellite subsystem, and the limitations of a non integrated approach are used to motivate extensions to the language and reasoning system. Models are initially constructed in a logical

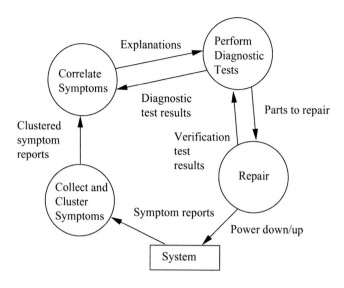

**Fig. 1.** A data flow diagram for a simple maintenance cycle

form. Logical relationships can be used to represent several different uncertainty calculi, including probability, belief functions and possibilistic logic, and to model the temporal constraints. The logical approach to modelling uncertainty builds on using "causation events" to encode uncertain happenings, typically the generation of symptoms from causes. It also allows, if required, the expression of true ignorance. The same abduction framework is used whatever calculus is used.

The result of a diagnosis is the generation of explanations that explain all the symptoms, at least to some degree of belief. An explanation is a conjunction of terms each of which represents a necessary contributory cause with a temporal imprecision constraint and a degree of belief. Multiple causes are allowed. In the current implementation, a cost function is used to focus on the least cost explanations.

## 1.1 Motivation

In many on-line diagnostic systems, fault reports are collected and clustered according to the time in which they occur. A characteristic of many applications is that there are no significantly differing propagation delays along different causal paths. Though not discussed here, even when there are no propagation delays then error reports may not be reported at the exact time and order in which they occur. The reporting time depends on the structure and programming in, for example, the maintenance control centres. Figure 1 below shows a simple maintenance cycle relevant for many such applications.

However in some cases clustering before correlation is not helpful. For example:

- There may be differing or indeterminate time delays along different causal paths
- The synchronicity of observations may allow differentiation between a single common causes for a set of observations and a set of causes.

In such cases the clustering and correlation processes have to be integrated.

*Example 1.* Consider the example shown in Figure 2 that sketches a fault impact model of some of the equipment connected to the power bus of a satellite. The uppermost shaded nodes represent the possible causes. Causal relationships between events are qualified with uncertainty degrees (here possibility $\Pi$ and necessity $N$) and temporal delays are represented as time intervals $[d_{min}, d_{max}]$, representing minimum and maximum delays between consecutive events. The uncertainty in the delay rules is interpreted as the belief in the transition. The interval effectively gives the time period during which the transition must happen if it is going to happen. For example after a temperature increase in the KU area begins (at time $\tau$ say) it can take between 5 and 60 minutes to cause watchdog software triggering. The necessity of the triggering is greater than 0.9, but if it is to trigger it must happen between $[\tau + 5, \tau + 60]$. When there is more than one arrow incident on a node the logic is "or". A Voltage Regulator connects enough Solar Arrays Sections to the power bus to meet the power consumption, and batteries are used to provide shortfall in the solar energy. The causal model expresses the knowledge about uncertain links between faults and observable events—here using possibilistic logic—and the imprecise temporal delays between the events. The model describes the dynamic behaviour of the power subsystem of the satellite. For example the failure of the protection transistor may have both an electrical and thermal impact on the satellite, with different dynamics. Electrical propagation is faster than thermal propagation. More precisely, if the Over-Voltage transistor fails then the symptom "Payload shedding" can arise via two different causal paths.                               □

In the illustration the joint possibility distributions are essentially "noisy or" logic [8], though any distribution can be modelled. Exploiting uncertainty in the causal links allows a finer description of the phenomena and the ranking of the fault hypotheses.

Payload shedding occurs either as a consequence of the unlatching of the battery management system (Batman) or the the triggering of the temperature watchdog. Once a payload has been shed it cannot be shed again. Only the first signal to shed payload can be observed. So a signal to shed as a result of thermal effects can be masked by the previous electrical signal from the Batman. The electrical path is faster but not certain, so sometimes the first signal is caused by the thermal effects.

If we do not account for the time delays, then observing payload shedding may lead us to give too much belief to Over-Voltage Transistor failure, rather than the other possible causes—an exceptional payload power request or a problem in the KU area. Using the probabilities (or necessities) ignoring the temporal

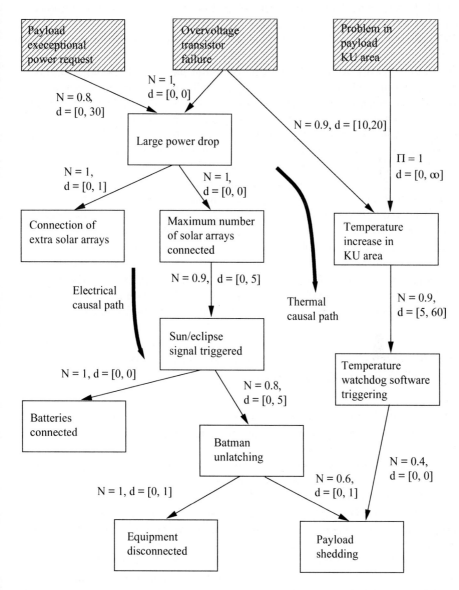

**Fig. 2.** A simplified fault impact model including uncertain and temporal information

constraints is basing the diagnosis on the assumption that every possible symptom that could be observed had enough time to be observed.

Identifying possible causes early allows us to predict possible future events and look for them, and take corrective action. The temporal information gives extra discrimination power. Suppose "Battery connected" is observed at time 195 minutes and "Payload shedding" at 200 minutes. The symptom "Payload shedding" could have been caused by an "Over-voltage transistor failure" between 15 minutes or 180 minutes ago (thermal path), or between 0 minutes to 11 minutes ago (electrical path); or of course by a "Payload exceptional power request" between 0 minutes and 41 minutes ago; or a "Problem in the payload KU area" between 5 and ∞ minutes ago. The symptom "Batteries connected" at 195 minutes is consistent with "Over-voltage failure" in [190, 195] and with "Payload shedding" being a result of the electrical path. Signs of thermal effects could now be predicted, which if observed, could discriminate further.

It can be seen that the above influence diagram identifies two ways that payload shedding can occur. Certainly to compute the belief in payload shedding this loop is important as the probability of the disjunction needs to be calculated. However when the objective is to compute possible explanations for payload shedding then, since the different possible paths to payload shedding correspond to different causal paths, it is appropriate for an explanation to be a conjunction of necessary conditions along a single causal path. The efficiency of the algorithm described to compute explanations depends on this assumption in the case of probability theory, though for possibilistic logic it does not matter.

## 2 A representation language incorporating uncertainty and temporal statements

This section describes a language suitable for representing behaviour relevant to diagnostic reasoning when that reasoning uses logical relationships, uncertain dependencies, and temporal delays.

A functional entity consists of input ports, output ports and internal attributes called states. State variables and ports have a user defined set of mutually exclusive values such as { *working, not_working* } or { *high, medium, low* }. The ports are connected to the ports of other functional entities, e.g. the power-out port of a modelled converter is connected with the power-in port of a modelled multiplexor-group. The functional entities together with these port-to-port connections are the functional model. The functional entities are called units in the modelling language. The state variable usually represents some unobservable factor which determines the behaviour. Sometimes a form of state variable is used to represent an environmental condition, such as a particular configuration or setting of the system. These are then called "environmental variables" in the implementation. Ports are labelled locally within a functional entity and so the full identification of a port is something like $F.O$, where $F$ is the name of the functional entity and $O$ is the name of a port of the functional entity $F$. There

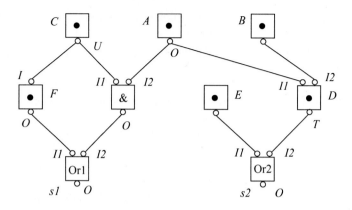

**Fig. 3.** The functional topology for a simple unit-port model

may be other ports called $O$ in different functional entities. State variables have a similar naming scheme.

When building functional models from units an output port may be linked to any number of downstream input ports, but any input port may only be connected to one upstream output port. This is to ensure that all behaviour is expressed in the units themselves and not in the connections between the ports. The connections between ports simply indicates a correspondence, and it is this separation which allows behaviour to be described locally. Units can be held in libraries which can be re-used at different places in the model, e.g. an optical link unit may be used whenever that kind of optical link is required. An output port and its associated input port(s) must all have the same domain. The representation has been used to support fault diagnosis in telecommunications systems [2].

*Example 2.* Figure 3 shows the units and ports for a simple example. For clarity this example does not include temporal dependencies. Units $A$, $B$, $C$, $D$, $E$ and $F$ have eponymous state variables each with domain {*working, not_working*} and all the ports in the model have domain {*normal, abnormal*}. The port $T$ and the outputs of the "Or" units are observable. The units $A$, $B$, $C$, and $E$ have rules which state that if the unit is not working their output port value is *abnormal*, otherwise the port value is *normal*, so:

$$A = not\_working \rightarrow O = abnormal$$
$$A = working \rightarrow O = normal$$

where $O$ is the output port of $A$. The "&" unit has input ports $I1$ and $I2$ and output port *Output* with logic:

$$I1 = abnormal \land I2 = abnormal \rightarrow Output = abnormal$$
$$I1 = normal \lor I2 = normal \rightarrow Output = normal$$

Thus both inputs have to be abnormal before the output is. (A form of built in redundancy often found in electrical systems.) The "Or" unit has input ports $I1$ and $I2$ and output port *Output* with logic:

$$I1 = abnormal \lor I2 = abnormal \rightarrow Output = abnormal$$
$$I1 = normal \land I2 = normal \rightarrow Output = normal$$

Thus if any input is anomalous then the output will be. ☐

The first rule in each set represents the nominal behaviour of a unit. When the second rule in each set is added the rules sets are covering. By covering we mean that all possible ways each output port's domain value can occur is given. $F$ and $D$ have incomplete models, specified by causation events and are described later. Rule antecedents that model the inputs to a particular port value are not required to be mutually exclusive and indeed they are not in the rules above. This differs from the model used by Poole [9] where all the antecedents are mutually exclusive. This is discussed later when "noisy or" representations are described.

Extending the notation of Konolige [6] to temporal and uncertain models, the functionality of a diagnostic tool adopting a causal model of the unit port type can be represented as a causal theory $\langle C, P, E, \Sigma \rangle$ where $C$ corresponds to propositions concerning state variable values and so represents the possible causes; $P$ corresponds to the set of possible port variable values; $E$ corresponds to possible effects (i.e. observable values, here observable port values as $E \subseteq P$.); and $\Sigma$ to the behavioural model relating the causes to the effects (i.e. how state variable values and input port values determine output port values). Causes appear in explanations of symptom sets. Explanations are described later. A typical element of $C$ is:

$$power\_supply\_1.working\_status = not\_working$$

i.e. the *working_status* state variable of functional entity *power_supply_1* (or synonymously unit *power_supply_1* ) has value *not_working*.

Following others (e.g. [1, 4]) we will use a reified propositional logic to help express our models. Let $D = C \cup P$ be the set of propositions which are temporally qualified. $D$ for example includes literals of the form $F.O = abnormal$, i.e. output port O of unit F has value *abnormal*, and $F.self = not\_working$ for the self state variable of unit $F$. Elements of $D$ can be qualified by the predicates *TRUE, FALSE, ON*, and *OFF*.

For any proposition $X \in D$ and for any time $t$, either $TRUE(X, t)$ or $FALSE(X, t)$ holds. Additionally $TRUE(X, t, t')$ means that $X$ is $TRUE$ from $t$ till $t'$, in other words:

$$TRUE(X, t, t') \equiv \forall \tau \in (t, t'] : TRUE(X, \tau)$$
$$FALSE(X, t, t') \equiv \forall \tau \in (t, t'] : FALSE(X, \tau)$$

We will sometimes need different time points to be included and excluded and so define:

$$TRUE(X, t, t') \equiv TRUE]](X, t, t') \equiv \forall \tau \in (t, t'], TRUE(X, \tau)$$
$$TRUE[](X, t, t') \equiv \forall \tau \in [t, t'], TRUE(X, \tau)$$

There are similar definitions associated with $FALSE(X, t, t')$.

In the process of generating explanations each element of $C$ may be augmented with a temporal constraint. They can be of the form:

$$TRUE[\,](unit\_name.state\_variable\_name = state\_variable\_domain\_value, t, t')$$

where the braces $[\cdot]$ indicate in the usual manner whether the end points are included or excluded. Here they are both included. An example of such a statement is:

$$TRUE]](F.self = working, -\infty, 20)$$

meaning that $F$ is working during the interval $(-\infty, 20]$. The special case of no specific temporal interval being associated with a proposition $P$ can be included as:

$$TRUE][(P, -\infty, +\infty)$$

We need to represent the event of a state variable going to a *not_working* state or to a specific fault mode state. Once a state variable has changed to *not_working*, or to a more specific fault mode, it is assumed to remain there. In what follows state variables are usually thought of as having a domain such as {*working, not_working*} or or

$$\{working, fault\_mode\_1, fault\_mode\_2, \ldots, unspecified\_not\_working\}$$

where the progression from working to another state variable value is irreversible. Events occur at an instant of time, and are expressed by the predicates $ON$ and $OFF$.

$$ON(X, t) \equiv \exists \tau, \tau' : (\tau < t < \tau') \wedge FALSE(X, \tau, t) \wedge TRUE(X, t, \tau')$$
$$OFF(X, t) \equiv \exists \tau, \tau' : (\tau < t < \tau') \wedge TRUE(X, \tau, t) \wedge FALSE(X, t, \tau')$$

An element of $D$ can now appear in expressions expressing transitions. For an element $F.self = not\_working \in C$ this could be of the form:

$$\exists t \in [t_1, t_2] : ON(F.self = not\_working, t)$$

We could have used $OFF$, but prefer to always use $ON$.

As Srinivas [10] points out, there is an implicit notion of time in a prior. We normally expect that the longer a component is in operation then the more likely it is that it will have failed. Hazard functions (see [11] for an example of their use) for individual components could be exploited in the approach described here though how this could be done is not described. The relationship between component statistics and state variables is not necessarily immediate as the model being constructed is a functional one rather than a physical one.

## 2.1 Events

A language which can be used to model systems when both uncertainty and temporal dependencies are required is described. The relationships between input port values, state variable values and the consequent output port values are represented by rules. Whether the rules express both temporal dependencies and uncertainty or solely uncertainty, the rules are assumed to be covering; possibly by construction.

The behaviour may have temporal delays and this complicates the issues as there is uncertainty associated with the times till an effect occurs as well as the uncertainty associated with whether the event occurs at all. To allow a simple understanding of the uncertainty aspects, the two aspects of uncertainty are decoupled as far as possible. The uncertainty associated with the antecedent determines if the rule is applicable but does not express any beliefs about when the effects will occur. The latter is expressed through the delays associated with the rules. In general the antecedent needs to contain predicates about temporal relationships but this will be minimised.

The approach will be described in the context of binary domains where components can be either *working* or *not_working* and ports can be either normal or abnormal. So whilst there may be a rich underlying functional model involving, say differential equations and control actions, we have mapped this model into a simpler functional model where the inputs and outputs refer to normal and abnormal. The system is assumed initially to be in a fully working state with all inputs and outputs normal. This does not mean that the system is static. Symptoms are also preclassified in terms of normal or abnormal. The richer model is some form of simulation and is used to map inputs and outputs in the simpler model to normal or abnormal by reasoning forwards from the inputs (if there are any) and hypothesized correct working behaviour in the richer model. This mapping of a richer functional model into a simpler one is not necessarily easy but common as it generally not possible to perform calculations regarding beliefs, particularly abduction, on the richer models.

We assume that a cause (or more precisely a state variable) may change only once—from *working* to *not_working* or to some specific fault mode. Different causal paths may lead to an output port which may be abnormal or normal. The effect of multiple reinforcements of *abnormal*, say, through the different paths at possibly different times can have an effect on any rules which have this port in its antecedent.

When events are considered the process can become very complex even on such simple models. To simplify matters further some assumptions about the world will be made. The model described here assumes that the only abnormal symptom at a port we will analyse is the first transition to abnormal. We will not be analysing signals of symptoms which go from normal to abnormal back to normal and so on, though the underlying model will have this as a possibility. This is quite reasonable given the abstraction level we are working at. Furthermore if the input is abnormal we have no way of saying what is normal output. We will look at the modeling of an uncertain link and a "noisy or" model depending on this assumption. Despite the simplicity of the model it is relevant to many applications.

A state variable $X$, will have domain:

$$\{\exists t : ON(X = not\_working, t), TRUE][(X = working, -\infty, +\infty)\}$$

or if $X$ is a port then the domain will be:

$$\{\exists t : ON(X = abnormal, t), TRUE][(X = normal, -\infty, +\infty)\}$$

The time of the last symptom of interest can be substituted for $+\infty$ if wanted. If the domain of $X$ is not binary and $X$ represents a state variable then one value could be:

$$TRUE][(X = working, -\infty, +\infty)$$

with other values of the form $ON(X = not\_working\_type\_i, t)$.

We will usually write $\{x, \neg x\}$ for brevity, or $\{working, not\_working\}$, or $\{normal, abnormal\}$ but they have the interpretation above. Notice that the domain does not contain any information about when $X$ becomes *not_working* or *abnormal*. Similarly the rules which give the semantics of the uncertainty rules do not involve quantification of time delays. This does not however mean that we do not use given information on time delays, just that the uncertainty semantics does not depend on knowing about the times.

Behaviour of a unit can be diverse. It depends on the nature of the inputs, the presence of synergy associated with combinations of input values and the degree of temporal overlap of input values. The latter corresponds to the duration of different combinations of input values. The synergy can manifest itself through broader applicability and hence increased likelihood of an effect or speedier reaction in certain contexts or both.

In order to keep the modeling simple, temporal relationships are not used to specify the degree of coincidence, rather lower and upper bounds are placed on the delay. The approach could be extended naturally to include statements about temporal coincidence. A consequence of the restriction is that whilst temporal synergy is not ignored (positive synergy may for example allow a reduced upper bound to delays) it is not exploited as fully as it could be. Importantly, however, it is not missed in explanations even though a more refined approach, naturally, would have more discrimination.

## 2.2 A single link

Take the case where an input port X affects an output port Z. Here we are looking at the case often modeled by a single link in an influence diagram, as illustrated in Figure 4. This could be specified by four conditional probabilities (using a notation where events are not being considered.)

$$\Pr(Z = abnormal|X = abnormal) = \alpha^*$$
$$\Pr(Z = normal|X = abnormal) = 1 - \alpha^*$$
$$\Pr(Z = abnormal|X = normal) = \beta^*$$
$$\Pr(Z = normal|X = normal) = 1 - \beta^*$$

$$X \in \{x, \neg x\} \qquad\qquad Z \in \{z, \neg z\}$$

**Fig. 4.** A link

In engineering systems the link is in fact a functional entity which is incompletely modeled and as such has behaviour. $\Pr(Z = abnormal | X = abnormal) = \alpha^*$ is affected by the "kind" of abnormality at X and the nature of propagation through the link, whilst $\Pr(Z = abnormal | X = normal) = \beta^*$ essentially only refers to a "spontaneous" fault, $\neg y$ say, occurring in the link. If explanations involving the link functional entity are sought and if there are delays associated with this "fault" it can pay to model the link with an explicit "fault" state variable. (It is not being said that this cannot be modeled using a Bayesian link by adding an explicit cause. Rather it is arguing that the explicit cause often needs to be added and discussing the distribution with which to combine the effects from upstream and the explicit cause—when there are, and when there are not, temporal dependencies.)

A simple model which expresses the only ways that $Z$ may become abnormal in terms of input port $X$ and the state variable $Y$ with domain $\{y, \neg y\}$ is:

$$((\neg x \wedge \alpha) \wedge y) \vee \neg y \leftrightarrow \neg z \tag{1}$$

where $\neg x = \exists t : ON(X = abnormal, t)$, $\neg y =: \exists t : ON(Y = not\_working, t)$, and $y = TRUE(Y = working, -\infty, +\infty)$. The model only involves one uncertain context assumption $\alpha$ (a "causation event") which can be read as "the abnormality at $X$ is of the kind to produce an abnormality at $Z$ when $Y$ is normal" and is a reflection of the granularity of the model. $Y$ is used to model effects on $Z$ which are not caused by $X$. If $Y$ were not present then $\Pr(Z = normal | X = normal) = 1$. $\neg y$ may hold for different values of the input variable $X$; $\neg y$ covers the cases $\neg x \wedge \neg y$ and $x \wedge \neg y$. In fact the delay associated with $\neg y$ need not depend on the cases and may be taken as exactly 0 as $Y$ is simply used to represent the functioning of the unit and $Y$ has no parents. The delay associated with $(\neg x \wedge \alpha) \wedge y$ is specified by the user.

More generally we may have explicit delays associated with the terms in a rule (such as $\neg x \wedge y \wedge \alpha$ and $\neg y$) which can be used to compute intervals in which the events must have occurred. For example the following rule may actually be used:

$$\exists t^* \in [t + t_1, t + t_2], (ON(X = abnormal, t) \wedge \alpha)$$
$$\wedge \ TRUE][(Y = working, -\infty, +\infty)$$
$$\vee \ \exists t^* \in [t + t_3, t + t_4], ON(Y = not\_working, t) \rightarrow ON(Z = abnormal, t^*)$$

though the uncertainty semantics comes from the simpler rule. In such a case the delay associated with $\neg y$ needs to be conservative to cover the cases.

When reasoning from observations in order to hypothesise causes we will want to determine the causes of $\neg z$ which arise at time $t$. Using the relationship:

$$((\neg x \wedge y \wedge \alpha) \vee \neg y) \leftrightarrow \neg z$$

allows us to associate an interval with $\neg x$ (and $\alpha$) of:

$$[t - \text{upper bound to delay of } (\neg x \wedge \alpha) \wedge y,$$
$$t - \text{lower bound to delay of } (\neg x \wedge \alpha) \wedge y]$$

which is interpreted as "at some time within" (in other words $\exists t$ such that at some time in the interval the literal holds). Similarly, we associate an interval $[0, t)$ with $y$ which is read as "holds during" (in other words $\forall t$ in the interval the literal holds) and we associate an interval:

$$[t - \text{upper bound to delay of } \neg y, t]$$

which is interpreted as "at some time within" with $\neg y$.

*Example 3.* Take the case where a temperature increase in the KU area can cause the temperature watchdog to trigger. If the temperature watchdog can be assumed to work perfectly then the relationship $(\neg x \wedge \alpha) \leftrightarrow z$ holds, where $\neg x$ corresponds to a temperature increase occuring at some time and $\neg z$ to the watchdog triggering at some time. $(\neg x \wedge \alpha)$ means the temperature increase occurs at some time and it is of the kind to cause the watchdog to trigger. $N(\alpha) = 0.9$. $\alpha$ really depends on $\neg x$, though this is not expressed in the formula. They are never separated so it is valid to do this.

If the watchdog trigger is not perfect and may cause triggering in the presence or absence of a temperature increase, then a model of the form:

$$((\neg x \wedge \alpha) \wedge y \vee \neg y) \leftrightarrow \neg z$$

may apply where $y$ represents the proposition that the watchdog works perfectly all the time and $\neg y$ the proposition that there is (at least) one time that the watchdog failed. Notice that $(\neg x \wedge \alpha) \wedge \neg y$ is subsumed by $\neg y$, so it is unnecessary to represent it. □

The relationship established by taking the complement of (1) is:

$$\neg(\alpha \wedge \neg x) \wedge y \leftrightarrow z \tag{2}$$
$$(\neg(\alpha \wedge \neg x) \wedge y) \vee (y \wedge x) \leftrightarrow z \tag{3}$$

(2) and (3) state the conditions under which $Z$ remains normal, not how $Z$ becomes normal. In (2) and (3), $\neg(\alpha \wedge \neg x)$ means there is not an abnormality of the right kind. Notice that we cannot take the negation into the brackets and write $(\neg\alpha \wedge \neg x)$. The negation of $\neg(\alpha \wedge \neg x)$ is $x$ (i.e. $X$ is always normal) or all cases where $X$ becomes abnormal are of the wrong kind. Below the term $\neg(\alpha \wedge \neg x)$ is written as $\neg[\alpha \wedge \neg x]$ simply to emphasise that we cannot take the

negation inside. The term $\alpha \wedge \neg x$ means that there is an abnormality of the right kind. $(\neg \alpha \wedge \neg x)$ means there is *an* abnormality of the wrong kind, but it does not mean that all abnormalities are of the wrong kind.

In (3) the term $y \wedge x$ is redundant logically. Its purpose, described below, is to allow backwards reasoning and hence the generation of explanations for symptoms. In the computational approach described later, backwards reasoning is used to create a network where each leaf, that is cause, has a time interval associated with it. Beliefs associated with multiple causes and the time intervals associated with these multiple causes are computed after the network is constructed. This involves taking the intersections of the time intervals created by the backward reasoning step being described. We replace $\neg(\alpha \wedge \neg x)$ by a representative transition for the backwards reasoning and so use the relationship:

$$((\neg \alpha \wedge \neg x) \wedge y) \vee (y \wedge x) \leftarrow z \qquad (4)$$

This allows generation of the possibilities as there is no time constraint attached to the terms in (4). The possibilities include the case where everything is working or normal. Once the possibilities are generated then the network created satisfies (2) and (3). This is explained below. In such a complementary rule the concept of a delay has no meaning. Only rules which predict abnormal port values have user specified delays. However when reasoning from an observation $z$ (i.e. $z$ is normal and has always been normal) we can still associate intervals with the literals. If the literal is positive then this corresponds to a state variable or port value always being normal and so are given temporal intervals $[0, t)$ (or $(-\infty, t)$ if we imagine the system starting not at time 0, but at some period in the past before any symptoms occur). These intervals are now read as "during" (in other words $t$ such that in the interval the literal holds). If the literal is negative then the same interval is given (namely $[0, t)$) but the interpretation is "at some time", (in other words $t$ such that at some time in the interval the literal holds). The different interpretations of the intervals are used when intersections and unions of the intervals are taken.

We wanted a simple model of a link as we want to reason backwards without generating unnecessary possibilities in order to compute possible temporal intervals to associate with fault hypotheses. The model (1) and (4) is relevant in many cases. The main restriction lies in the fact that not all multiple fault solutions are generated—even if you wanted them to be. Because $(\neg x \wedge \alpha) \wedge \neg y$ is assumed subsumed by $\neg y$ multiple faults involving functional entities above this functional entity and this functional entity will not be generated. This is arguably a good feature as we do not want to generate unnecessary possibilities. They are indeed unnecessary in most applications as the upstream causes can be found when the identified functional entity is replaced—or more precisely the physical entity or entities carrying the functionality are replaced.

*Example 4.* If the watchdog trigger is observed to become abnormal at a time t then the rule:

$$((\neg x \wedge \alpha) \wedge y) \vee \neg y \leftrightarrow \neg z$$

applies indicating that either the watchdog trigger mechanism must have itself caused the abnormality (at a time which may as well be be presumed to be time $t$), or the temperature at the input to the KU area must have increased at some time between $t - 60$ and $t - 5$ minutes ago. So the time interval associated with $\neg x$ in $(\neg x \wedge \alpha)$ is $[t - 60, t - 5)$.

If the watchdog trigger was known to have never become abnormal the rule

$$((\neg \alpha \wedge \neg x) \wedge y) \vee (y \wedge x) \leftarrow z$$

will tell us that either that the temperature was always stable and the watchdog trigger mechanism was always working correctly or the watchdog trigger mechanism was always working correctly but there was a case where the temperature increased but it was an increase of the wrong kind, i.e. it did not cause triggering. (Perhaps it was too weak.) So the time intervals associated with $x$ and $y$ in $y \wedge x$ are both $(-\infty, t)$. The interpretation is that the temperature was stable during this time period and the watchdog triggering function was working perfectly during this period. The time interval associated with $\neg x$ in $(\neg \alpha \wedge \neg x)$ is also $(-\infty, t)$, but with the interpretation that a temperature increase of the wrong kind occured in this interval. Of course in practice these events usually have small beliefs and so explanations involving them are unlikely. The computational approach aims not to generate the explanations with small beliefs until explanations with higher beliefs have been generated, and in practice tested. $\square$

Below we consider the case where different causal paths combine and "multiple fault" explanations need to be generated systematically.

## 2.3 Two input ports affecting an output port

Here there are two inputs with domains $\{normal, abnormal\}$. We will assume that uncertainty arises through granularity rather than through failure of the functional unit. The latter could be added, but a functional model with multiple inputs and with state can be built up from links as previously described and the unit to be described using a simple "noisy or" model.

Under the assumption of no state if both inputs are effectively normal then the output must be normal. The simplest model (under our assumptions) is:

$$(\neg x \wedge \alpha) \vee (\neg y \wedge \beta) \leftrightarrow \neg z$$

with complementary relationship

$$(x \wedge y) \vee (\neg[\neg x \wedge \alpha] \wedge y) \vee (x \wedge \neg[\neg y \wedge \beta]) \vee (\neg[\neg x \wedge \alpha] \wedge \neg[\neg y \wedge \beta]) \leftrightarrow z$$

or

$$(x \wedge y) \vee (\neg x \wedge (\neg \alpha \wedge y)) \vee (x \wedge (\neg y \wedge \neg \beta)) \vee ((\neg x \wedge \neg \alpha) \wedge (\neg y \wedge \neg \beta)) \leftarrow z$$

using a representative case as in (4) above for generating possibilities.

When reasoning backwards from $z$ the interval associated with $\neg x$ or $\neg y$ is $[0, t)$ and interpreted as at some time within. The intervals for $y$ and $x$ are the same but interpreted as during.

Now we have to make some assumptions about the nature of the propagation. We will assume that two events can occur at $Z$ (i.e. the effect is not masked). If the port $Z$ fans out to affect many downstream functional entities then the two causes of $\neg z$ may cause symptoms at different times. However if $Z$ is an observable then the second event is masked as far as observation is concerned but not as regards further propagation. So abduction from an observed symptom is finding the explanations of the first "symptom". Predictions of later abnormalities at the point where an abnormal symptom is observed are not necessarily inconsistent.

If there are some time delays, and even in the case where all the delays are zero, it is possible that a more liberal notion of the "right kind of $\neg x$" and the "right kind of $\neg y$" is appropriate when $\neg x$ and $\neg y$ hold simultaneously as there may be some synergy which allows a broader (reduced is conceptually possible, but ignored here) context to trigger the effect. This is called "context synergy".

*Example 5.* The inputs "Batman unlatching" and "Watchdog triggering" can cause "Payload shedding". In:

$$(\neg x \wedge \alpha) \vee (\neg y \wedge \beta) \leftrightarrow \neg z$$

$\neg x$ corresponds to the event Batman unlatching and $\neg y$ to Watchdog triggering. $\neg z$ corresponds to Payload Shedding. It is assumed that the functional unit for this dependency is implemented in physical entities which are reliable. The delay associated with $(\neg x \wedge \alpha)$, i.e. a latching of the right kind is $[0, 1]$. Different kinds of unlatching may result in different delays but they all lie in the range $[0, 1]$. The delay associated with watchdog triggering of the right kind is $[0, 0]$, i.e. it is instantaneous.

Observing shedding at time t allows us to hypothesise about the time interval Batman unlatching occurred and Watchdog triggering occurred, namely $[t-1, t]$ and $[t, t]$ respectively. Notice that we do not generate the joint case, as one is sufficient. If both have happened this will become clear after one of the faulting physical entities is replaced. If shedding is known not to have occurred then the relationship:

$$(x \wedge y) \vee ((\neg x \wedge \neg \alpha) \wedge y) \vee (x \wedge (\neg y \wedge \neg \beta)) \vee ((\neg x \wedge \neg \alpha) \wedge (\neg y \wedge \neg \beta)) \leftarrow z$$

can be used to work backwards.. This says that either the Batman has never unlatched (i.e. Batman was normal from $-\infty$ to the present time) and the Watchdog has never triggered or the Batman unlatched but it was of the wrong kind of unlatching at some time between $-\infty$ to the present time and the Watchdog has never triggered or ...

Notice that both upstream paths are kept in this case. □

A richer model which allows for a broader context to be applicable when abnormality is present at both inputs is:

$$(\neg x \wedge \alpha \wedge y) \vee ((\neg x \wedge \alpha) \wedge (\neg y \wedge \neg(\beta \vee \psi))) \vee (x \wedge \neg y \wedge \beta) \tag{5}$$
$$\vee (\neg x \wedge \neg(\alpha \vee \varphi) \wedge (\neg y \wedge \beta)) \vee (\neg x \wedge (a \vee \varphi) \wedge (\neg y \wedge (\beta \vee \psi))) \leftrightarrow \neg z$$

or equivalently:

$$(\neg x \wedge \alpha) \vee (\neg y \wedge \beta) \vee (\neg x \wedge \varphi \wedge (\neg y \wedge \psi)) \leftrightarrow \neg z \tag{6}$$

The last term gives the case where the joint occurrence of $\neg x$ and $\neg y$ are necessary for $\neg z$. This reduces the to previous model if $\varphi$ and $\psi$ do not hold. We may associate with $\varphi$ and $\psi$ a probability (say) of $\Pr(\varphi)$ and $\Pr(\psi)$. Equation (5) has complement:

$$(x \wedge y) \vee ((\neg x \wedge \neg \alpha) \wedge y) \vee ((\neg y \wedge \neg \beta) \wedge x) \tag{7}$$
$$\vee (\neg x \wedge \neg(\alpha \vee \varphi) \wedge (\neg y \wedge \neg \beta)) \vee (\neg y \wedge \neg(\beta \vee \psi) \wedge (\neg x \wedge \neg \alpha)) \leftrightarrow z$$

These relationships say *nothing* about the times and delays. They just specify all the contexts that can cause $\neg z$. Here $\varphi$ and $\psi$, where $\varphi \wedge \alpha \equiv \bot$ and $\psi \wedge \beta \equiv \bot$, are the additional contexts in which $\neg x$ can cause $\neg z$. Other models are, of course, possible.

Even if both $\neg x$ and $\neg y$ occur they do not need to overlap in the times of their effects, though there must come a time when they are both true, because of our assumption that they cannot return to either $x$ or $y$. However synergy may also make effects quicker or slower. This is temporal synergy. The time to the effect is also influenced by the degree of temporal coincidence of input values. For example in (1) if $\neg x$ occurs long before $\neg y$ and the delay associated with $\neg x$ is not long, then the delay will be that of $\neg x$ even if there would be temporal synergy when both $\neg x$ and $\neg y$ hold. The delay associated with a term such as $\neg x \wedge (\alpha \vee \varphi) \wedge \neg y \wedge (\beta \vee \psi)$ depends on how close $\neg x$ and $\neg y$ happen.

An advantage of the representation of (6) is that the time difference of $\neg x$ and $\neg y$ need not be expressed explicitly. From (5) it can be seen that minimum delay associated with each of the first two terms of (6), $(\neg x \wedge \alpha)$ and $(\neg y \wedge \beta)$, must be equal to zero. The upper bounds to these two terms will come from the bounds associated with $(\neg x \wedge \alpha) \wedge y$ and $(\neg y \wedge \beta) \wedge x$ respectively. The last term of (6) only has a meaning when $\neg x$ and $\neg y$ temporally overlap and needs to be specified by the modeller. The effect can only start when both $\neg x$ and $\neg y$ hold so it may be non zero.

If there is temporal synergy we could, as well as dividing into terms based on context (as has been done), divide into terms based on the time between $\neg x$ and $\neg y$. Then more precise intervals could possibly be attributed to the terms. However the boundaries between different cases are not easy to specify, and in the interests of parsimony we do not use temporal conditions in the terms. This means that the intervals in the relationships must specify (in the positive synergy case) the lower bounds based on maximal temporal coincidence and upper bounds on minimal temporal coincidence. So, unless temporal conditions are used as part of the terms, any temporal synergy is partially masked by the different degrees of coincidence. The approach tries to keep the models the user has to specify simple.

## 3  Finding explanations from symptoms

The reasoning process produces abductive explanations for a set of observations $O \subseteq E$. An abductive explanation for a single observation is simply a special case which is important in the implementation. An explanation is denoted by $\epsilon$ and is a conjunction of literals from $C$, each augmented by a temporal constraint and uncertainty value, such that each $\epsilon$ is consistent with $\Sigma$, ($\Sigma$ includes all the relationships between input ports, state variables and output ports and also the temporal constraints) and $\Sigma \cup \epsilon \vdash O$ to some degree of belief $> 0$. An example of an explanation is:

$TRUE(unit5.working\_status = working, -\infty, 10)$

$\wedge \exists t \in (-\infty, 20], ON(unit1.working\_status = not\_working, t)$, probability $0.05$

The $\epsilon$s generated need not be mutually exclusive (c.f. [9]). This allows explanations to retain their simplicity of interpretation. Explanations involving inconsistent assumptions are removed. Since the relationships used here are covering, the only inconsistencies are elementary mutual exclusion considerations (e.g. $\{working, not\_working\}$, $\{\alpha, \neg\alpha\}$ etc.) There are no complex no-goods—to use de Kleer's [3] terminology.

The condition "$\Sigma \cup \epsilon \vdash O$ to some degree of belief" is satisfied by the construction process described since the model is assumed covering. A *cautious explanation set* $\xi$, for $O$ is a disjunction of all the abductive explanations for $O$:

$$\xi = \bigvee_i \epsilon_i$$

where each $\epsilon_i$ is an abductive explanation. An option available in small applications is to produce a cautious explanation set, though for non trivial problems only a subset can be practically generated. In the current implementation a cost bounded ATMS (CBATMS) is used as a focusing mechanism to select low cost explanations first.

From the definition of an explanation it can be seen that the multiple fault model is being considered. In the implementation, the single fault model is included efficiently as a special case. This is managed by use of appropriate cost functions. Suppose we have observations $o_1, o_2, \ldots, o_n$, and corresponding cautious explanation sets for each individual observation $\xi_1, \xi_2, \ldots, \xi_n$. Since all observations are true and the rules are covering then:

$$\vdash o_1 \wedge o_2 \wedge \ldots \wedge o_n \equiv \xi_1 \cap \xi_2 \cap \ldots \cap \xi_n$$

Temporal intersections are used to eliminate explanations which are impossible because of the timings of the symptoms.

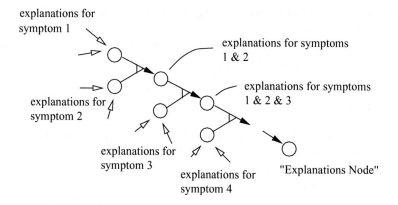

explanations for
symptom 1

explanations for symptoms
1 & 2

explanations for
symptom 2

explanations for symptoms
1 & 2 & 3

explanations for
symptom 3

explanations for
symptom 4

"Explanations Node"

**Fig. 5.** Combining networks to create explanations

## 3.1  Computing the explanations

A network is created for the individual observed symptoms by abduction on the
uncertainty relationships as outlined previously. Each hypothesis in the network
has a temporal interval associated with it by the abduction process. Since the
network is constructed for each symptom separately, much of this part of the
reasoning could be done before any symptoms are observed, and pre-constructed
networks for the symptoms of interest selected at run time. The networks for
the symptoms are then combined and explanations are generated efficiently and
incrementally using a modified ATMS algorithm.

Explanations for all the symptoms are generated by propagating in a network
created by augmenting the individual networks by justifications that combine the
networks for individual symptoms. In the figure below the general approach to
combining symptoms is shown. ATMS environments created by the propagation
process correspond to conjunctions of causes and causation events. Environments
as defined and explanations do not exactly correspond. Environments are used
to create explanations.

## 3.2  Using a cost bounded approach

Following Ngair and Provan [7], each environment, $\epsilon_i$, has a cost computed using a cost function which preserves the partial ordering on sets of assumptions
induced by set inclusion. In other words, the cost function has to satisfy:

$$\rho(\epsilon_1) \leq \rho(\epsilon_2) \text{ iff } \epsilon_1 \subseteq \epsilon_2$$

Ngair and Provan's algorithm is as follows:

1. Set the cost bound to be the lowest possible, that is the cost associated with
   the empty environment, and introduce all assumptions with cost lower or
   equal to the current bound.

2. Run the basic ATMS algorithm with the current cost bound.
3. If $l_1$ and $l_2$ are labels, then rather than $l_1 \wedge l_2$ being computed as the smallest subset in $\{\epsilon_1 \cup \epsilon_2 \mid \epsilon_1 \in l_1, \epsilon_2 \in l_2\}$, it is computed as the smallest subset in $\{\epsilon = \epsilon_1 \cup \epsilon_2 | \epsilon_1 \in l_1, \epsilon_2 \in l_2, \text{and } \rho(\epsilon) \text{ is less than or equal to the current cost bound}\}$.
4. As before, if $l_1$ and $l_2$ are labels then $l_1 \vee l_2$ is computed as the smallest subset in $\{l_1 \cup l_2\}$.

Ngair and Provan's algorithm allows the ATMS propagation and the generation of environments to be blocked and unblocked. In the context of this application the algorithm has been extended to incorporate checking for temporal consistency.

We start with the cost bound set to zero and propagate environments with a cost less than or equal to zero. When environments are constructed the temporal intersection of the time intervals relating to the same cause is taken. If a temporally consistent environment is propagated to the "explanations" node there is a solution, otherwise we increase the cost bound until a temporally consistent environment is propagated to the explanations node.

### 3.3 Difficulties with a cost bounded approach

Ngair and Provan's algorithm assumes that none of the assumptions are mutually exclusive. So, for example, if a label contains the environments $\alpha \wedge \neg \beta$ and $\alpha \wedge \beta$ this is never simplified to $\alpha$. In our case we have both *working* and *not_working* assumptions as well as the uncertainty assumptions $\alpha$, $\neg\alpha$ which appear in the rules. This is almost certainly the case in any application involving uncertainty.

However it is possible to construct useful cost functions for which resolution is not necessary (and so the cost bounded approach can be used) for the case of simple but effective criteria such as the number of not working assumptions and possibilistic logic. Later it will be also be explained that for the case of probability theory when there are different causal paths the definition of an explanation can be meaningfully simplified so that the cost bounded approach can also be taken. Arguably such a modification is more sensible when there events are time stamped.

### 3.4 Environments—explicit causation events

When a causation event is modeled explicitly then it is represented by an assumption in the ATMS. Though explicit causation events are not always needed in the modeling (particularly if possibilistic logic is used) they serve to represent the environments in a way which is not par.

An environment can be defined as a pair $[E \; \epsilon]$ where $E$ is a set of assumptions arising form causes (that is elements of $C$), and $\epsilon$ is a set of assumptions corresponding to causes which are causation events. The environment in the sense of de Kleer is the union of $E$ and $\epsilon$. For the proposition supported by environment $e$ to be believed, all the assumptions in $E$ and all the assumptions in $\epsilon$ must

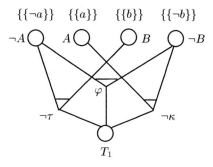

**Fig. 6.** A small ATMS network with causation events

hold. As an example, take a section of the network in Figure 6 where explicit causation events $\neg\tau$, $\varphi$, and $\neg\kappa$ are used. The label for $T_1$ is:

$$[\neg ab\ \neg\tau] + [\neg a \neg b\ \varphi] + [a \neg b\ \neg\kappa]$$

For the first environment $E$ is $\{\neg ab\}$ and $\epsilon$ is $\{\neg\tau\}$.

Suppose we define two cost functions $\rho_c$ and $\rho_{ce}$. $\rho_c$ has as its domain the explanations arising from the causes and is such that $\rho_c(E_1) \le \rho_c(E_2)$ if $E_1 \subseteq E_2$. $\rho_{ce}$ has as its domain the explanations arising from the causation events and is such that $\rho_{ce}(\epsilon_1) \le \rho_{ce}(\epsilon_2)$ if $\epsilon_1 \subseteq \epsilon_2$. These conditions are true for possibilistic logic and for probability theory if the assumptions are independent, which is a normal assumption.

Let $\rho(e) = \rho([E\ \epsilon]) = f(\rho_c(E), \rho_{ce}(\epsilon))$ for some function $f$. We will also assume that whatever $f$ is defined to be, it is such that:

$$\rho(e_1) \le \rho(e_2) \text{ if } \rho_c(E_1) \le \rho_c(E_2) \text{ and } \rho_{ce}(\epsilon_1) \le \rho_{ce}(\epsilon_2)$$

The cost bounded ATMS ensures that the cost of explanations increase monotonically as assumptions are added. The subset condition above ensures that any environment that is created as the result of combining existing environments has a cost (or lower probability/possibility/necessity, when belief is used as a cost function) that is greater than any of the environments used in the combination. This allows an incremental approach to generating explanations. For example, single fault solutions are generated before multiple fault solutions if the cost function is based on the number of causes in an explanation. When the cost bound is increased, computation proceeds from the existing explanations and partial explanations, without having to redo work already done.

## 3.5 Environments and updating rules for the CBATMS—possibilistic case

Following the approach Dubois, Lang and Prade [5] used in their Possibilistic ATMS we will extend the definition of an environment to include necessities

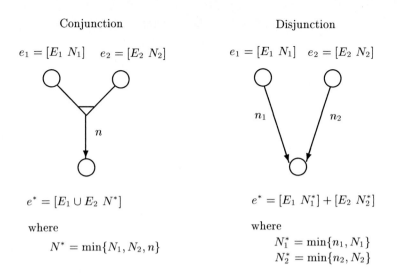

Fig. 7. Combination rules for necessities

and possibilities derived from the causation event assumptions. Now causation events can is modeled implicitly and numerical calculations are carried out in a modified ATMS propagation algorithm. However the rules behind the numerical manipulation arise from the number being a token for a logical event.

We define:

$$(N_1, \Pi_1) \geq (N_2, \Pi_2) \text{ iff } N_1 \geq N_2 \text{ or } N_1 = N_2 \text{ and } \Pi_1 \geq \Pi_2$$

An environment for a proposition is defined to be the pair $e = [E(\nu, \pi)]$ if when we believe the assumptions in $E$—the explicit assumptions—then the $(N, \Pi)$ arising from the implicit causation event assumptions is greater than or equal to $(\nu, \pi)$.

For example the environment $[\neg a \ \neg\tau\varphi]$ in Figure 7 above would now be written $[\neg a \ (\nu, \pi)]$ where $(\nu, \pi)$ is the (necessity, possibility) pair of the conjunction $\neg\tau\varphi$ of causation events $\neg\tau$ and $\varphi$. The initial value for $(\nu, \pi)$ associated with environments created for the assumptions is $(1, 1)$. For example the initial environment associated with the node $A$ above is $[\{a\} \ (1, 1)]$. In this way the $(\nu, \pi)$ of an environment keeps the propagation beliefs from the assumptions. This is independent of the beliefs in the assumptions.

If $e_1 = [E_1 \ (N_1, \Pi_1)]$ and $e_2 = [E_2 \ (N_2, \Pi_2)]$ are environments and $E_1 \subseteq E_2$ and $(N_1, \Pi_1) \geq (N_2, \Pi_2)$ then we can remove $[E_2 \ (N_2, \Pi_2)]$. This is possible as whatever $\rho$ is defined to be (within the restrictions above) as we can be sure that $\rho(e_1) \leq \rho(e_2)$. The propagation rules in Figure 7 are described in terms of necessities. The rules for possibilities are similar.

Suppose we define the following cost function:

$$\rho_1(e) = (1 - \min\{\Pi(E), \pi\}, 1 - \min\{N(E), \nu\})$$

where $e = [E \ (\nu, \pi)]$, $N(E)$ is the necessity of the conjunction of assumptions forming $E$, and $\Pi(E)$ is the possibility of the conjunction of assumptions forming $E$. The cost of a downstream node is always greater than or equal to its parents and so effective blocking can be applied using the cost. Notice that if each assumption in $E$ has $(N, \Pi) = (0, 1)$ corresponding to ignorance, then $\rho_1(e) = (1 - \pi, 1)$. If all propagations have a possibility of 1, then $\rho_1(e) = (0, 1)$ for all $e$. When using the Possibilistic CBATMS we start looking for solutions with lowest cost (typically with $(N, \Pi) = (1, 1)$ but this depends on the cost function) and gradually reduce the threshold till solutions are found.

## 3.6   Other cost functions

Several other useful cost functions are possible. For example we could choose:

$$\rho_3(e) = \omega(E)$$

where $e = [E \ \epsilon]$ and $\omega$ is the number of *not_working* assumptions in $E$. We could also select:

$$\rho^*(e) = \langle(\nu, \pi), \omega(E)\rangle$$

where $e = [E \ (\nu, \pi)]$ and again $\omega$ is the number of *not_working* assumptions. Now,

$$\langle(N_1, \Pi_1), \omega(E_1)\rangle \leq \langle(N_2, \Pi_2), \omega(E_2)\rangle$$

iff

$$(N_1, \Pi_1) \geq (N_2, \Pi_2)$$

or if

$$(N_1, \Pi_1) = (N_2, \Pi_2) \qquad \text{and} \qquad \omega(E_1) \leq \omega(E_2)$$

Notice that the sign of the inequality has been changed so that a low cost is associated with a high belief. Though there is not enough space to illustrate the point here, both of the above cost functions would not yield lower cost environments even if resolution of cause assumptions were performed. So the addition of resolution to the CBATMS propagation procedures is not necessary.

One of the benefits of a cost function such as $\rho^*$ is that it does not use any prior beliefs about causes, and it keeps ignorance regarding causes separate from the propagation beliefs. This contrasts with $\rho_1$ where ignorance in the causes swamps all the other beliefs, leading to all environments having the same cost.

## 3.7   Probability case

Probabilities are more complex to manipulate than possibilities. However if we extend the definition of an explanation to be a conjunction of causes and causation events (i.e. an environment and an explanation are synonymous) then it is not difficult to show that provided we associate each cause and each causation event with an assumption in the CBATMS then monotonicity is assured in generation of the explanations. We cannot replace causation events with numbers as was done in the possibilistic case as it is important not to multiply repeatedly when environments are combined. For example, if reasons to believe a node $X$ are captured by the environment $\alpha \wedge \beta$ and reasons to believe a node $Y$ are captured by $\beta \wedge \gamma$, then the reasons to believe $X$ and $Y$ are $\alpha \wedge \beta \wedge \gamma$, with probability:

$$\Pr(\alpha).\Pr(\beta).\Pr(\gamma)$$

not

$$\Pr(\alpha).\Pr(\beta).\Pr(\beta)\Pr(\gamma)$$

which is what would be done if numbers were used for the causation events $\alpha$, $\beta$ and $\gamma$. In the possibilistic case this is not a problem as minimums and maximums are taken. The only problem is whether a conjunction of causes and causation events is an adequate explanation. In general it is not. In practice though, it can be argued that it often is adequate when the timing of events is considered.

If we consider the symptom of payload shedding given earlier, there are two ways that this can happen; via the electrical path and via the thermal path. An explanation in terms of just causes (e.g. Overvoltage Transistor Failure) is implicitly a disjunction consisting of the different ways payload shedding could happen given the same root causes(s). Each disjunct would contain the same causes but different causation events corresponding to different paths. However the different causal paths make payload shedding occur at different times and the symptom has been triggered by events along one of the paths. The events along the other path may not even have happened yet. An explanation should be in terms of causes and causation events from a single causal path. So combination is not necessary, and indeed not desirable.

If this argument is valid for the application then environments are adequate explanations and so any cost function which provides monotonicity (without needing to consider resolution as we never need to combine paths) is adequate.

## 4   Complexity and performance

An analysis of the complexity of the algorithm has been undertaken using the number of assumptions as the cost function. The basic ATMS algorithm [3] is NP-complete. A polynomial time behaviour can be achieved using a cost function and assuming the ATMS network contains no cycles and the network is considered sparse, i.e. it has $O(q)$ connections for $q$ network nodes. (It is still polynomial for a dense network of $O(q^2)$ connections.) The order of the polynomial increases with the number of assumptions in the cost threshold. A strength of the approach is the apparent ability to scale up, and the feasibility of integration within the same computational framework both uncertainty and a form of temporal reasoning.

## 5   Conclusion

This paper has presented a knowledge representation language that can be used to represent diagnostic problems that involve uncertainty, precedence constraints and imprecise propagation delays. This is a modular system which allows models to be constructed from re-usable functional entities. Another strength of the system is that the approach to uncertain reasoning uses a cost bounded approach where appropriate cost functions can be used to limit the computation in the context of the application requirements. If the cost function and the network for each individual symptom satisfies a resolution condition then the explanations are produced with a cost which is monotonic increasing. A correlation system has been implemented in C++ and has documentation including a user's guide, a functional specification and an API specification.

## Acknowledgments

Part of this work was funded by Esprit Basic Research Action 6156 DRUMS II and Esprit Project 6083 UNITE—thanks to members of both projects. Thanks also to Shaw Green and Simon Parsons for assistance in preparing the camera-ready copy.

# References

1. M. Ghallab amd A. Mounir-Alaoui. Managing efficiently temporal relations through indexed spanning trees. In *Proceedings of the 11th International Joint Conference on Artificial Intelligence*, pages 1297–1303, 1989.
2. J. Bigham and K. Scrupps. A telecommunications maintenance application using model-based reasoning. *Electronics Letters*, 32:98–99, 1996.
3. J. de Kleer. An assumption-based TMS. *Artificial Intelligence*, 28:127–162, 1986.
4. C. Dousson, P. Gaborit, and M. Ghallab. Situation recognition: Representation and algorithms. *Automated Reasoning*, pages 166–172, 1992.
5. D. Dubois, J. Lang, and H. Prade. A possibilistic assumption-based truth maintenance system with uncertain justifications, and its application to belief revision. In J. P. Martins and M. Reinfrank, editors, *Truth Maintenance Systems*, pages 87–106. Springer Verlag, Berlin, Germany, 1990.
6. K. Konolige. Abduction versus closure in causal theories. *Artificial Intelligence*, 53:255–272, 1992.
7. T. H. Ngair and G. Provan. A lattice-theoretic analysis of assumption-based problem solving. Technical Report, Institute of System Science, National University of Singapore, 1993.
8. S. Parsons and J. Bigham. Possibility theory and the generalised Noisy OR model. In *Proceedings of the 6th International Conference on Information Processing and the Management of Uncertainty*, pages 853–858, 1996.
9. D. Poole. Probabilistic horn abduction and Bayesian networks. *Artificial Intelligence*, 64:81–129, 1993.
10. S. Srinivas. Modeling failure priors and persistence in model-based diagnosis. In *Proceedings of the 11th Conference on Uncertainty in Artificial Intelligence*, pages 507–514, 1995.
11. A. Y. Tawfik and E. Neufeld. Model-based diagnosis: A probabilistic extension. In A. Hunter and S. Parsons, editors, *Applications of Uncertainty Formalisms (this volume)*. Springer Verlag, Berlin, 1998.

# Arguing About Beliefs and Actions

John Fox[1] and Simon Parsons[2]

[1] Advanced Computation Laboratory,
Imperial Cancer Research Fund,
P.O. Box 123,
Lincoln's Inn Fields,
London WC2A 3PX,
United Kingdom.
[2] Department of Electronic Engineering,
Queen Mary and Westfield College,
University of London,
London E1 4NS,
United Kingdom.

**Abstract.** Decision making under uncertainty is central to reasoning by practical intelligent systems, and attracts great controversy. The most widely accepted approach is to represent uncertainty in terms of prior and conditional probabilities of events and the utilities of consequences of actions, and to apply standard decision theory to calculate degrees of belief and expected utilities of actions. Unfortunately, as has been observed many times, reliable probabilities are often not easily available. Furthermore the benefits of a quantitative probabilistic representation can be small by comparison with the restrictions imposed by the formalism. In this paper we summarise an approach to reasoning under uncertainty by constructing arguments for and against particular options and then describe an extension of this approach to reasoning about the expected values of actions.

## 1 Introduction

Standard decision theory [35] builds on the probabilistic view of uncertainty in reasoning about actions. The costs and benefits of possible outcomes of actions are weighted with their probabilities, yielding a preference ordering on the "expected utility" of alternative actions. However, as Tan and Pearl [40], amongst others, have pointed out, the specification of the complete sets of probabilities and utilities required by standard decision theory make the theory impractical in complex tasks which involve common sense knowledge. This realisation has prompted work on qualitative approaches to decision making which attempt to reduce the amount of numerical information required.

Work on such qualitative decision making techniques has been an established topic of research at the Imperial Cancer Research Fund since the early 80s (see [31] for a review). Our early work was partly concerned with the description of human decision processes [12] and partly with the practical development of decision systems for use in medicine [13]. Whilst the qualitative decision procedures we developed proved to have considerable descriptive value and practical promise, our desire to build decision support systems for safety-critical fields such as medicine raised the concern that our early applications were *ad hoc.* In particular we were concerned that they, in common with all other expert systems being built at the time, were not based on a rigorously defined decision theory. As a result we have put considerable effort into developing a theoretical framework for qualitative decision making. The best developed part of this is an approach to uncertainty and belief based on the idea of *argumentation.* This approach emphasizes the *construction* and *aggregation* of symbolic arguments based on the non-standard logic LA [18, 22]. This provides rules for constructing reasons to believe in and doubt hypotheses, and reasons to believe or doubt arguments.

The generality of the everyday idea of argumentation suggests that a similar approach could be taken to reasoning about actions, for instance in deciding on medical treatments or investigations. We might hope to construct arguments for and against alternative actions in the usual way, avoiding issues about the elicitation and use of numerical utilities by representing the desirability and undesirability of actions symbolically. This suggestion immediately raises two questions:

- How well does our formalisation of support and opposition transfer to reasoning about action?
- Is LA directly applicable to arguments about action or will different logics be required?

This paper attempts to provide some answers to these questions. In particular it argues that while there are similarities between arguments for and against beliefs and arguments for and against actions, there are also significant differences which amount to a requirement for additional rules for assigning values to the outcomes of actions, and for arguing the expected benefits of alternative actions. The paper then makes an initial attempt to suggest a framework for handling such rules, as well as summarising some of the applications developed using argumentation, and discussing one set of tools that are available for building such applications.

However, before starting this work, the paper first sets the discussion in context by recalling the logic of argumentation about beliefs, LA, and its relation to argumentation in general.

## 2   The logic of argument LA

Our approach to decision making was to seek a rapprochement between the purely quantitative and purely logical traditions, seeking a form of uncertainty management which people find natural, yet one which can be shown to be mathematically sound and general. This approach was based on *argumentation,* the familiar form of reasoning which is based on everyday patterns of debate. It turned out, however, that this approach was not new.

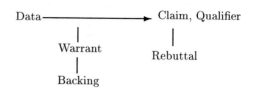

**Fig. 1.** The Toulmin argument schema

## 2.1 The nature of arguments

The philosopher Stephen Toulmin explored the question of why traditional formal models of reasoning have apparently little relevance to everyday dispute and debate, concluding that *argumentation* is a human form of reasoning distinct from both probabilistic reasoning and classical deduction. Toulmin characterised argumentation by means of the informal schema in Figure 1. This can be illustrated by the example (the italics are ours):

> in support of the *claim* that Harry is a British subject, we appeal to the *datum* that he was born in Bermuda, and ... (the claim is *warranted* by a sentence such as) ... "A man born in Bermuda may be taken to be a British subject": since, however, questions of nationality are always subject to qualifications and conditions we shall have to insert a *qualifying* "presumably" in front of the conclusion and note the possibility that our conclusion may be *rebutted* in case it turns out that both his parents were aliens or he has since become a naturalised American. Finally, in case the warrant itself is challenged, its *backing* can be put in: this will record the terms and the dates of enactment of the Acts of Parliament and other legal provisions governing the nationality of persons born in the British colonies ([42] p 104).

Two points are prominent here; the idea that in general conclusions are not certain, hence the qualifier "presumably", and that practical reasoning frequently involves contradictions among arguments (the notion of rebuttal). This is in contrast, as we have seen, to the usual approach to modeling uncertainty with a quantitative measure; Toulmin's approach anticipated the interest in symbolic representations of uncertainty in artificial intelligence and logic. Toulmin also anticipated another recent development in artificial intelligence, the desire to get to grips with the concept of contradiction. In classical logic and probability contradiction is eschewed; something cannot be both true and false nor have a probability of 0 and 1.

In attempting to address the practical problems of decision making in medical domains we faced similar problems to those identified by Toulmin. First, we have to make decisions in the face of uncertainty in situations where it is impractical to state the degree of uncertainty. Second, it is common in practical settings to have to deal with apparent contra-indications where from one point of view something is definitely the case whereas from another point of view it is definitely not the case, or at one time something is held to be true while at another it is considered false.

## 2.2 Arguments about beliefs

Toulmin's analysis was perceptive but from our point of view it is clearly inadequate since it is entirely informal. What we need is a formalisation which preserves the basic ideas while giving it sound mathematical foundations. In this section we work towards such a formalisation by providing an informal account of what our formal system, LA, provides.

We start with the notion of an argument in a standard logic such as propositional logic, first-order predicate calculus, or a modal logic such as $T$, $S4$ or $S5$ [21]. In such a logic, $L$, an argument is a sequence of inferences leading to a conclusion. If the argument is correct, then the conclusion is true. An argument:

$$G_1 \ldots G_n \vdash St$$

is correct in the logic $L$ if $St$ may be derived using the rules of inference and axioms of $L$ augmented with $G_1 \ldots G_n$. Therefore a correct argument simply yields a proposition $St$. This can be paraphrased as

$$St \text{ is true (in the context } G_1 \ldots G_n)$$

In the approach we take, this traditional form of logic based argumentation is extended in two important ways:

1. to allow arguments not only to prove propositions but also to merely indicate support for, or even doubt in, them; and
2. by explictly recording the context in which the deduction holds.

The way we do this is by borrowing from the idea of a labelled deduction system [20].

A labelled deductive system is essentially an enriched logical system, where formulae can be labelled, thereby adding structure to logical theories (usually called databases). Both formulas and labels can be manipulated independently; the exact correspondence is made explicit in the way labelled formulae are constructed by inference rules. To see how this helps, consider a situation in which we have the following pieces of information:

$$lost\_weight : a_1$$
$$lost\_weight \rightarrow cancer : r_1$$

where *cancer* is an abbreviation for "the patient has cancer", and *lost_weight* is an abbreviation for "the patient has lost weight". In a labelled deductive system we can derive the proposition *cancer* and denote this by:

$$cancer : (a_1, r_1)$$

so the label $(a1, r1)$ is a label which represents the proof of *cancer* by identifying the database items used in the proof. This takes care of recording the context of the proof; it is contained in the label.

The other thing that we need to do is to allow arguments to just indicate support for, or doubt in, propositions. Here we just use a second label which designates the confidence warranted by the arguments for their conclusions. There is nothing in the theory of labelled deductive systems which precludes the use of a number of labels, and this simple mechanism allows confidences to be expressed in a variety of representations without modifying the underlying inference system. Thus the result of a derivation is an *argument* of the form:

$$(St : G : Sg)$$

Each argument consists of a triple consisting of a Sentence $(St)$, which is the claim in Toulmin's terminology, Grounds $(G)$, which are the formulae used to justify the argument, and a Sign $(Sg)$, which is a number or a symbol which indicates the confidence warranted in the conclusion. The idea of argumentation from a database may thus be summarised by the following schema:

$$\text{Database} \vdash_{ACR} (\text{Sentence} : \text{Grounds} : \text{Sign})$$

In this schema, $\vdash_{ACR}$ is a consequence relation which defines the inference rules by which we may construct arguments for claims using the information in the database.

The use of confidences rather than logical proofs introduces a slight complication. In classical logic, if we can construct an argument (proof) for $St$ then any further arguments for $St$ are of no interest since $St$ is known to be true. If, however, we only have an indication of support for $St$ then it may be the case that additional information casts doubt on $St$. Thus we need to consider every distinct argument concerning $St$ and then carry out a process of *aggregation* to combine them. This process is also known as *flattening* since it has the effect of mapping a number of distinct arguments into a single measure. One intuitively plausible way of doing this aggregation is to assume that the more independent grounds we have for $St$, the greater our confidence in $St$ may reasonably be, and so we assess the strength of confidence in $St$ in some applications of LA by simply summing the number of arguments for $St$. Ambler [2] gives a rigorous justification for this procedure in category theoretic terms.

## 2.3   Formalising argumentation about beliefs

Having spoken informally about what LA is attempting to do, we present a formal description of LA. This is broadly the same system as that discussed in [22], but this version is less influenced by Ambler's work on the category theoretic basis of argumentation, and is more influenced by labelled deductive systems and the style of presentation used in recent work on argumentation [27, 28]. However, the differences between the two versions of the system are largely cosmetic.

We start with a set of atomic propositions $\mathcal{L}$ including $\top$ and $\bot$, the ever true and ever false propositions. We also have the set of connectives $\{\neg, \rightarrow, \wedge\}$, and the following set of rules for building the well-formed formulae (*wff*s) of the language:

- If $l \in \mathcal{L}$ then $l$ is a well-formed formula (*wff*).
- If $l$ is a *wff* then $\neg l$ is a *wff*.
- If $l$ and $m$ are *wff*s then $l \rightarrow m$ and $l \wedge m$ are *wff*s.
- Nothing else is a *wff*.

The set of all *wff*s that may be defined using $\mathcal{L}$, may then be used to build up a database $\Delta$ where every item $d \in \Delta$ is a triple $(St : G : Sg)$ in which $St$ is a *wff*, $Sg$ represents confidence in $St$, and $G$ are the grounds on which the assertion is made. With this formal system, we can take a database and use the argumentation consequence relation $\vdash_{ACR}$ defined in Figure 2 to build arguments for propositions that we are interested in. This consequence relation is defined in terms of rules for building new arguments from old. The rules are written in a style similar to standard Gentzen proof rules, with the antecedents of the rule above the line and the consequent below. Thus if the arguments above the line may be made, then the argument below the line may also be made. In detail the rules are as follows:

- The rule Ax says that if the triple $(St : G : Sg)$ is in the database, then it is possible to build the argument $(St : G : Sg)$ from the database. The rule thus allows the construction of arguments from database items.
- The rule $\wedge$-I says that if the arguments $(St : G : Sg)$ and $(St' : G' : Sg')$ may be built from a database, then an argument for $St \wedge St'$ may also be built. The rule thus says how to introduce arguments about conjunctions.
- The rule $\wedge$-E1 says that if it is possible to build an argument for $St \wedge St'$ from a database, then it is also possible to build an argument for $St$. Thus the rule allows the elimination of one conjunct from an argument.
- The rule $\wedge$-E2 is analogous to $\wedge$-E1 but allows the elimination of the other conjunct.
- The rule $\rightarrow$-I says that if on adding $(St, \emptyset, Sg)$, $\emptyset$ indicating that the triple has no grounds, to a database it is possible to conclude $St'$, then there is an argument for $St \rightarrow St'$. The rule thus allows the introduction of $\rightarrow$ into arguments.
- The rule $\rightarrow$-E says that from an argument for $St$ and an argument for $St \rightarrow St'$ it is possible to build an argument for $St'$. The rule thus allows the elimination of $\rightarrow$ from arguments and is analogous to modus ponens in standard propositional logic.

We use the term " dictionary" to describe a set of symbols which can be used to label a proposition. If we define dictionary $\mathcal{D}$ by:

$$\mathcal{D} =_{\text{def}} \{S_1, \ldots S_n\}$$

then we may write:

$$(St : G : S_i)$$

$$\text{Ax}\frac{(St : G : Sg) \in \Delta}{\Delta \vdash_{ACR} (St : G : Sg)}$$

$$\wedge\text{-I}\frac{\Delta \vdash_{ACR} (St : G : Sg) \quad \Delta \vdash_{ACR} (St' : G' : Sg')}{\Delta \vdash_{ACR} (St \wedge St' : G \cup G' : \text{comb}^{A}_{\text{conj intro}}(Sg, Sg'))}$$

$$\wedge\text{-E1}\frac{\Delta \vdash_{ACR} (St \wedge St' : G : Sg)}{\Delta \vdash_{ACR} (St : G : Sg)}$$

$$\wedge\text{-E2}\frac{\Delta \vdash_{ACR} (St \wedge St' : G : Sg)}{\Delta \vdash_{ACR} (St' : G : Sg)}$$

$$\rightarrow\text{-I}\frac{\Delta, (St : \emptyset : Sg) \vdash_{ACR} (St' : G : Sg')}{\Delta \vdash_{ACR} (St \rightarrow St' : G : \text{comb}^{A}_{\text{imp intro}}(Sg, Sg'))}$$

$$\rightarrow\text{-E}\frac{\Delta \vdash_{ACR} (St : G : Sg) \quad \Delta \vdash_{ACR} (St \rightarrow St' : G' : Sg'))}{\Delta \vdash_{ACR} (St' : G \cup G : \text{comb}^{A}_{\text{imp elim}}(Sg, Sg'))}$$

**Fig. 2.** Argumentation Consequence Relation

where $S_i$ is any symbol drawn from $\mathcal{D}$. Where there is the possibility of confusion between dictionaries we write $S_i^{\mathcal{D}}$ to denote the symbol $S_i$ from dictionary $\mathcal{D}$. Among the obvious dictionaries we may consider are sets of numbers. Dictionaries for probabilities, possibilities [8], certainty factors [39], belief functions [37] are thus straightforwardly defined. They are, respectively:

$$\mathcal{D}_{\text{probability}} =_{\text{def}} \{S : S \in [0, 1]\}$$
$$\mathcal{D}_{\text{possibility}} =_{\text{def}} \{S : S \in [0, 1]\}$$
$$\mathcal{D}_{\text{belief functions}} =_{\text{def}} \{S : S \in [0, 1]\}$$
$$\mathcal{D}_{\text{certainty factors}} =_{\text{def}} \{S : S \in [-1, 1]\}$$

Systems of argumentation which are based on LA and have semantics in terms of both quantitative probability and possibility values have been defined [22]. However, there is no requirement that we should restrict dictionaries to sets of numbers. For example we have frequently adopted one of a number of simple symbolic dictionaries. The four simplest such dictionaries are described below.

**Generic dictionary** In a standard logical proof the value "true" is assigned to a sentence if it is possible to construct a proof for it from facts which are held to be "true". However, in practical situations, prior facts, and consequently any conclusions that can be deduced from them, can be in error. To capture this idea, we therefore substitute the sign + for "true" giving the simple dictionary:

$$\mathcal{D}_{\text{generic}} =_{\text{def}} \{+\}$$

We refer to arguments with sign + as *supporting* arguments. The argument:

$$(cancer : lost\_weight : +)$$

simply says "the fact that the patient has lost weight increases my confidence in her having cancer, but I cannot say by how much". Using the generic dictionary thus means that the "force" of different arguments cannot be distinguished. Suppose we have a number of arguments whose signs are drawn from the generic dictionary. Given we cannot distinguish between the force of the arguments, it seems reasonable to assume that:

**Assumption A1** If $Args$ is any set of arguments concerning $St$, then[1]:

$$|Args \cup \{(St : G : +)\}| \geq |Args|$$

where $|Args|$ indicates the force of the set of arguments $Args$. The simple aggregation procedure mentioned above, in which we just count arguments for a proposition to assess our confidence in that proposition, conforms to this assumption.

**Bounded generic dictionary** With a large database, it will often be possible to construct a large number of arguments for a proposition. Intuitively, however, some arguments are conclusive, that is they leave no room for doubt with respect to their grounds (they may be rebutted on other grounds). To represent this we may define a more specialised dictionary, introducing an additional sign ++:

$$\mathcal{D}_{\text{bounded generic}} =_{\text{def}} \{+, ++\}$$

We refer to arguments with sign ++ as *confirming*. Informally, if we have a conclusive argument for some proposition then this argument will dominate the aggregation procedure. Thus a confirming argument is more forceful than any set of supporting arguments, and a set of confirming and supporting arguments is exactly as forceful as a single confirming argument. Thus the aggregation function is restricted by:

**Assumption A2** Let $Args$ be any set of supporting arguments concerning $St$, and $Args'$ be any set of supporting and confirming arguments concerning $St$, then:

$$|\{(St : G : ++)\}| > |Args|$$
$$|\{(St : G : ++)\}| = |Args'|$$

as well as A1. This assumption is, of course, consistent with many quantitative calculi including probability and belief functions.

---

[1] The non-strict inequality allows for limits to the force of a set of arguments, as is the case when using the bounded dictionary introduced below.

**Delta dictionary** The dictionaries discussed so far have had signs which represent belief values. At times we may also wish to reason about changes in these values. Doing this it is natural to consider both increases and decreases in value, and so the simplest delta dictionary which we make use of is:

$$\mathcal{D}_{\text{delta}} =_{\text{def}} \{+, -\}$$

in which sentences $(St : G : +)$ and $(St : G : -)$ can be interpreted as indicating, respectively, an increase or decrease in confidence in the proposition St, without indicating the degree of the increase or decrease. The use of these signs is similar to their use in qualitative probabilistic networks [44], and qualitative certainty networks [30]. We call arguments with sign $-$ *opposing* arguments.

It is possible to justify a number of aggregation procedures for arguments which use the delta dictionary. Some of these honour A1[2], and it makes sense for such procedures to also make the following assumption:

**Assumption A3** Let *Args* be any set of arguments concerning $St$, then:

$$|Args \cup \{(St : G : -)\}| \leq |Args|$$

At times when using the delta dictionary, the following rules of inference may also be used:

$$(St : G : -) \Leftrightarrow (\neg St : G : +) \tag{1}$$
$$(St : G : +) \Leftrightarrow (\neg St : G : -) \tag{2}$$

where $\neg St$ is the negation of $St$. The first of these is read as "if you have $(St : G : -)$ you may infer $\neg(St : G : +)$ and if you have $\neg(St : G : +)$ you may infer $(St : G : -)$". Using this rule means that if we have a negative argument (for instance $(cancer : young : -)$, "the young age of the patient argues against her having cancer") then this increases our overall confidence in the negated conclusion. The second rule is analogous, and together they take account of the fact that there is no rule in $\vdash_{ACR}$ for handling negation. Taken together, the rules are akin to the rule of the excluded middle, and this explains why they are not included in $\vdash_{ACR}$. We don't include them since we want to be able to build systems whose signs do not use the rule of the excluded middle.

**Bounded delta dictionary** We can also extend the delta calculus with symbols which denote increases to a maximum and decreases to a minimum value:

$$\mathcal{D}_{\text{bounded delta}} =_{\text{def}} \{++, +, -, --\}$$

We call arguments with sign $--$ *excluding* arguments. As with the bounded generic dictionary, the fact that the dictionary is bounded suggests that any flattening function should operate under the assumption:

---

[2] Note that this involves overloading the assumption by making it apply to arguments about value and arguments about changes in value. However, this seems reasonable since exactly what kind of sign is being used is always clear from the context.

**Assumption A4** Let *Args* be any set of supporting or opposing arguments concerning *St*, and *Args'* be any set of supporting, opposing and excluding arguments concerning *St*, then:

$$|\{(St : G : --)\}| < |Args|$$
$$|\{(St : G : --)\}| = |Args'|$$

Under this assumption, it is inconsistent to have both $(St : G : ++)$ and $(St : G' : --)$ for any *St*. Furthermore, when using the bounded delta dictionary, if (1) and (2) hold, then so do the following:

$$(St : G : ++) \Leftrightarrow (\neg St : G : --) \tag{3}$$
$$(St : G : --) \Leftrightarrow (\neg St : G : ++) \tag{4}$$

This completes the description of the four simplest dictionaries.

The reason that the generic dictionary is called "generic" is that it can be viewed as an abstraction of a number of quantitative uncertainty handling formalisms. Thus the "+" in the dictionary can be viewed, for instance, as either a probability, possibility or belief value, but one which is not precisely specified. A similar interpretation may be used for the delta dictionary; we can look at the "−" used there as a decrease in probability, possibility or belief without saying how much of a decrease it is. Clearly there is a limit to what can be done without identifying what kind of value is being manipulated, since the theories from which the values are taken will place some constraints on which assumptions may be valid and under what conditions they are valid.

For example, if we give a probabilistic semantics to the delta dictionary so that + represents an increase in probability [27, 28], then we get a system of argumentation which is similar in many ways to qualitative probabilistic networks [44]. With this probabilistic semantics, (1)–(4) are valid, and it is possible to determine the precise conditions under which the simple aggregation procedure of adding up arguments is reasonable [28]. Furthermore, there are delta forms for any quantitative uncertainty representation [30], and it is straightforward to show that in some of these, most notably when the signs are given a semantics in terms of possibility theory or belief functions, (1) and (4) are not valid.

As noted above, we will typically be able to build several arguments for a given proposition, and so to find out something about the overall validity of the proposition, we will flatten the different arguments to get a single sign. We can describe this in terms of a function $\mathsf{Flat}^A(\cdot)$ which maps from a set of arguments $\mathbf{A}$ for a proposition *St* from a particular database $\Delta$ to the pair of that proposition and some overall measure of validity:

$$\mathsf{Flat}^A : \mathbf{A} \mapsto \langle St, v \rangle$$

where $\mathbf{A}$ is the set of all arguments which are concerned with *St*, that is:

$$\mathbf{A} = \{(St : G_i : Sg_i) \mid \Delta \vdash_{ACR} (St : G_i : Sg_i)\}$$

| $\mathrm{comb}^A_{conj\ intro}$ | ++ | + |
|---|---|---|
| ++ | + | + |
| + | + | + |

| $\mathrm{comb}^A_{imp\ elim}$ | ++ | + |
|---|---|---|
| ++ | ++ | + |
| + | + | + |

| $\mathrm{comb}^A_{imp\ intro}$ | ++ | + |
|---|---|---|
| ++ | ++ | + |
| + | | + |

**Fig. 3.** Combinator tables for LA using the bounded generic dictionary.

and $v$ is the result of a suitable combination of the $Sg$ that takes into account the structure of the arguments. Thus $v$ is the result of applying a flattening function to the grounds and signs of all the arguments in $\mathbf{A}$:

$$v = \mathsf{flat}^A(\{\langle G_i, Sg_i \rangle \mid (St : G_i : Sg_i) \in \mathbf{A}\})$$

Often the signs $Sg_i$ and the overall validity $v$ will be drawn from the same dictionary, but it is perfectly feasible for them to be drawn from different dictionaries (so, for example, a set of arguments with numerical weights may be flattened to give a degree of support drawn from the dictionary $\{high, medium, low\}$).

Thus, if we have a set of arguments $\mathbf{A}$ for a proposition $St$, then the result of flattening is:

$$\mathsf{Flat}^A(\mathbf{A}) = \langle St, \mathsf{flat}^A\left(\{\langle G_i, Sg_i \rangle \mid (St : G_i : Sg_i) \in \mathbf{A}\}\right)\rangle$$

Together $\mathcal{L}$, the rules for building the formulae, the connectives, and $\vdash_{ACR}$ define a formal system of argumentation LA[3]. In fact, LA is really the basis of a family of systems of argumentation, because one can define a number of variants of LA by using different meanings for the connectives, different dictionaries of signs, different meanings for the dictionaries, different functions for combining signs $\mathrm{comb}^A_{conj\ elim}$, and implication $\mathrm{comb}^A_{imp\ intro}$ and $\mathrm{comb}^A_{imp\ elim}$, and different means of flattening arguments, $\mathsf{flat}^A$. Given the number of possible choices, it is possible to define a bewildering variety of different versions of LA[4]. We now describe a couple of the best understood.

The way we go about defining a new version of LA is to decide three things. First, which dictionary to use. Second, how the signs within that dictionary are to be interpreted. Third, how the connectives are to be interpreted. It should be stressed that these choices are separate; it is possible to use the same dictionary with different meanings for the signs and with different meanings for the connectives. Once the choices are made it is possible to identify how to combine the signs correctly, and to identify which additional rules of inference (such as (1)) hold. Then it is possible to determine how to flatten arguments, and under what conditions the various assumptions about flattening are reasonable.

We start by considering the use of the bounded generic dictionary in which the signs are interpreted using probability theory. In particular, we take + to

---

[3] The name stands for Logic of Argument [17].

[4] And we can complicate the picture further by defining other systems of argumentation which use different underlying logics, and so have different consequence relations $\vdash_{ACR}$. An example of such a system may be found in [26]

denote a probability of some unknown value, and ++ to denote certainty (a probability of 1). We take ∧ to be logical conjunction, and → to be material implication. With this interpretation, the combination functions required by LA are those of Figure 3. These require a little explanation. The table for $\mathsf{comb}^A_{\mathsf{conj\ intro}}$ gives the sign of the sentence $St \wedge St'$ from the signs of the sentences $St$ and $St'$. Thus, whatever the signs of $St$ and $St'$, the sign of $St \wedge St'$ is +. The table for $\mathsf{comb}^A_{\mathsf{imp\ elim}}$ gives the sign of the sentence $St'$ from the signs of the sentences $St$ and $St \to St'$. Thus if both the signs of $St$ and $St \to St'$ are ++ so is that of $St'$, and otherwise the sign of $St'$ is +. The table for $\mathsf{comb}^A_{\mathsf{imp\ intro}}$ follows directly from that for $\mathsf{comb}^A_{\mathsf{imp\ elim}}$ since it gives the sign of $St \to St'$ from that of $St$ and $St'$. In the table, $St$ is the value in the leftmost column and $St'$ is the value in the top row. This time the table includes a space, since it is impossible for $St'$ to have sign ++ when $St$ has sign +. Furthermore, it should be noted that when $St$ and $St'$ both have sign +, then the sign of $St \to St'$ could be either + or ++. Since + includes ++ (since a probability of 1 is also a probability of some value), we give the result as +. This forgiving nature of the signs allows $\mathsf{comb}^A_{\mathsf{conj\ elim}}$ to be stated as follows:

$$\mathsf{comb}^A_{\mathsf{conj\ elim}}(Sg) = Sg.$$

It is straightforward to verify that these functions are correct for this interpretation of the signs.

Since these are the only rules of inference we need to consider, we can then proceed to identifying aggregation procedures. Two obvious ones spring to mind. In the first, the function $\mathsf{flat}^A$ examines the signs $Sg_i$ and returns ++ if any of the $Sg_i$ is ++, and otherwise returns +. Thus, formally:

$$v = \begin{cases} ++ & \text{if } Sg_i = ++ \text{ for some } i \\ + & \text{otherwise} \end{cases}$$

This flattening function conforms to assumptions A1 and A2 while making no additional assumptions about the strength of arguments which are not implicit in the meaning of the signs. Note that this flattening function, in common with the others detailed in this paper, ignores the grounds. This is possible because of the use of qualitative dictionaries—at this coarse level of granularity, the interactions between arguments captured by the grounds can be ignored. However, when quantitative dictionaries are used, the grounds play an important part in flattening.

The system of argumentation described here, with the combination functions of Figure 3 and the flattening function described above, is basically that discussed in [17], though in the latter paper the meaning of the signs is less explicit than here, and the presentation is slightly different.

The second obvious aggregation procedure is slightly more complex. In this function, the $Sg_i$ come from $\mathcal{D}_{\mathsf{bounded\ generic}}$, while $v$ is just a positive number which we can consider coming from the dictionary:

$$\mathcal{D}_{\mathsf{aggregation}} =_{\mathsf{def}} \{0, 1, 2, \ldots\}$$

| $comb^A_{imp\ elim}$ | ++ | + | − | −− |
|---|---|---|---|---|
| ++ | ++ | + | − | −− |
| + | + | + | − | − |
| − | − | − | + | + |
| −− | − | − | + | + |

| $comb^A_{conj\ intro}$ | ++ | + | − | −− |
|---|---|---|---|---|
| ++ | ++ | ? | ? | −− |
| + | ? | ? | ? | −− |
| − | ? | ? | ? | −− |
| −− | −− | −− | −− | −− |

| $comb^A_{imp\ intro}$ | ++ | + | − | −− |
|---|---|---|---|---|
| ++ | ++ | + | − | −− |
| + | | + | − | |
| − | | − | + | |
| −− | | − | + | |

**Fig. 4.** Combinator tables for LA using the bounded delta dictionary.

All the procedure does is to count the number of arguments, again taking into account the fact that once one has one argument with sign ++ in favour of a sentence, all other arguments are irrelevant.

$$v = \begin{cases} \infty & \text{if } Sg_i = ++ \text{ for some } i \\ |\mathbf{A}| & \text{otherwise} \end{cases}$$

where $|X|$ gives the cardinality of the set $X$. This flattening function also conforms to assumptions A1 and A2 but in addition assumes that all arguments with sign + have equal strength[5]. Using the second aggregation function we get a version of LA which is essentially that used in the system Pro*forma* described in Section 5.

The other system we consider uses the bounded delta dictionary in which, for a formula which does not contain an implication, the sign + denotes an increase in probability, − denotes a decrease in probability, ++ denotes an increase in probability to 1 and −− denotes a decrease in probability to 0. We also have to consider what an implication means in this system, and we take a sign of ++ for $St \to St'$ to mean that if the probability of $St$ increases to 1 so does that of $St'$. We also take a sign of + for $St \to St'$ to mean that if the probability of $St$ increases so does the probability of $St'$, a sign of − for $St \to St'$ to mean that if the probability of $St$ increases the probability of $St'$ decreases, and a sign of −− for $St \to St'$ to mean that if the probability of $St$ increases to 1 the probability of $St'$ decreases to zero.

With this semantics, the combinator tables are those in Figure 4, and these can, once again, easily be proved to be correct for changes in probability [25, 28]. There are a couple of things that should be noted. First, the table for $comb^A_{conj\ intro}$ introduces the sign ? to stand for "++ or + or − or −−". This is a usual feature of qualitative systems—when you deal with abstractions, you find that eventually you need new composite abstractions because it becomes unclear

---

[5] This additional assumption is taken to be reasonable when there is no knowledge about the comparative strength of arguments.

| flat$^A$ | ++ | + | − | −− |
|---|---|---|---|---|
| ++ | ++ | ++ | ++ | |
| + | ++ | + | ? | −− |
| − | ++ | ? | − | −− |
| −− | | −− | −− | −− |

**Fig. 5.** Flattening function for LA using the bounded delta dictionary.

which abstraction is the right one. Second, the table for comb$^A_{imp\ elim}$ should be read with the sign of the antecedent being picked from the leftmost column and the sign of the implication being picked from the top column, and the table for comb$^A_{imp\ intro}$ should be read with the sign of the antecedent being picked from the leftmost column and the sign of the consequent being picked from the top row. Third, that the spaces in the latter table reflect impossible situations, and fourth that the sign given in this table is always the least specific possible, so when the implication could have sign + or ++, the table gives +.

As before, there are a number of different ways in which one can flatten arguments. One possible flattening function is one which conforms to all the assumptions introduced so far, but makes no additional assumptions. This gives the table of Figure 5, and once again this can be shown to be correct for probability theory. Here, as with the remainder of the systems discussed in this paper we define the flattening function to be binary—to generate $v$ we apply it recursively.

With these combination and flattening functions, the system we have described is essentially the system $\mathcal{NA}''$ described in [28], and similar systems which uses the delta dictionary are $\mathcal{NA}_1$ and $\mathcal{NA}_2$ in [27]. The notation used by these three systems is slightly different from that presented here because the overloading of ++, +, − and −− is overcome by the use of additional symbols to represent changes in probability.

### 2.4 Argumentation and defeasibility

The main focus of this paper is on reasoning under uncertainty in the context of making decisions. However, it is worth making a few remarks about the ways in which LA may be related to systems such as default logic and standard modal logic.

**Default logic** Suppose we can construct an argument for $St$ on the basis of a default rule. By definition a default is not guaranteed to be correct, so in this calculus the argument has the form:

$$(St : default : +)$$

If we later identify reasons to reject $St$, because we obtain an argument:

$$(\neg St : G : ++)$$

then aggregation will yield the conclusion $\neg St$ by A4 and (4). Argumentation therefore permits behaviour much like that of standard default logic, but it may also illuminate the relationship between default reasoning and quantitative uncertainty. Suppose we have a reason to doubt $St$ but not to reject it (because we can construct the argument $(\neg St : G : +)$) then, using the flattening function that counts arguments, this balances the default argument, and we are equivocal about whether $St$ or $\neg St$. If we have further arguments against $St$ then the balance of argument turns against it (3) but we can still hold both $St$ and $\neg St$ as possibilities, a behaviour similar to the normal behaviour of probabilistic, possibilistic, belief function and other quantitative calculi.

**Modal logic** The bounded delta calculus may also accommodate ideas akin to those of of modal logic. Informally, $possible(St)$ holds if we can construct an argument for $St$, and $necessary(St)$ if we can construct a bounding argument for $St$:

$$possible(St) \Leftrightarrow (St : G : +)$$
$$necessary(St) \Leftrightarrow (St : G : ++)$$

Suppose we have an argument:

$$(St : G : +)$$

which means that $possible(St)$ holds. Then, if we introduce an additional argument:

$$(\neg St : G : ++)$$

which means that $necessary(\neg St)$ holds, and if we aggregate these arguments constraints, A4 and (4) entail that $necessary(\neg St)$ dominates $possible(St)$. Turning this around if we hold $possible(St)$ then we cannot hold $necessary(\neg St)$, therefore:

$$possible(St) \Leftrightarrow \neg necessary(\neg St)$$

An analogous argument can be followed for the dual rule of modal logic:

$$necessary(St) \Leftrightarrow \neg possible(\neg St)$$

Equating modality to provability in this way echoes work on classifying arguments on the basis of the the arguments which my be built against their grounds [10, 11].

## 2.5 Soundness and completeness

So far we have neglected to say much about what it means to have an argument for a proposition beyond the fact that an argument is a *tentative proof* of the proposition and so is a proof which can fail if suitably strong arguments against the proposition can be found. However, as with any formal model of reasoning, what we would like to do is to prove that argumentation is in some sense correct, that is it generates all and only correct inferences. In other words, we would like to show that argumentation is complete and sound. To do this, however, we need to say precisely what an argument is. There are a number of ways of doing this, and three different approaches have been taken.

The first approach was based upon the commonalities between argumentation as introduced here and intuitionistic logic first pointed out by Ambler [3]. The idea was that since it is possible to give intuitionistic logic a proof-theoretic semantics in terms of category theory, this should also be possible for argumentation. Indeed this turned out to be the case. The first steps in providing this semantics are detailed in [3] which identifies the structure of the space of arguments, along with the kind of operations possible over them. The rest of the formalisation is provided in [2], which also highlights the link between argumentation and Dempster-Shafer theory [37].

The second approach was to give argumentation a model theoretic semantics. In particular, standard Kripke semantics for modal logic have been adapted by Das [7] to give a possible worlds interpretation for what it means for an argument to support a proposition to some degree.

The final semantics developed so far [27, 28] relates certain types of argumentation to probability theory by taking an argument in favour of a proposition to mean that there is evidence that the probability of the proposition increases (so the proposition becomes more likely to be true). With this interpretation, and using the bounded delta dictionary, it is possible to show that argumentation is sound and complete. Thus argumentation can capture probabilistic reasoning if required, and so it is possible to claim that, under particular conditions, argumentation is a normative theory for handling uncertainty. The probabilistic semantics has another advantage. Because it ties the notion of an argument securely to well-understood ideas about qualitative probability, it is possible to harness a number of useful results concerning qualitative probability [25, 29]. In particular, it is possible to develop a finer-grained representation of what it means to have an argument for a proposition which allows arguments of different strengths to be accommodated [27].

## 3 Towards arguments about actions

Having described the logic of argumentation LA for reasoning with uncertain information, we now consider some steps towards extending it to deal with actions in order to build a more complete decision theory. As in the previous section we begin with an informal discussion of the kinds of things we are trying to achieve.

### 3.1 An overview

At an informal level there appears to be a clear isomorphism between arguments for beliefs and arguments for actions. Suppose we wish to construct an argument in favour of treating a patient with cancer by means of chemotherapy. This might run as follows:

Cancer is an intolerable condition and should be eradicated if it occurs. It is a disease consisting of uncontrolled cell proliferation. Certain chemical agents kill cancer cells and/or reduce proliferation. Therefore we should treat cancer patients with such agents.

The steps in this argument are *warranted*[6] by some generalised (and probably complex) *theory* of the pathophysiological processes involved in cancer, and a *value system* which defines what kinds of things are tolerable, desirable and so on. The argument is not conclusive, however, since the conclusion might be rebutted by counter-arguments, as when chemotherapy is contra-indicated if a patient is frail or pregnant.

Such arguments appear compatible with LA and consequently we might consider using LA to construct such arguments. Suppose we summarise the above example in the notation of LA:

$$(St : G : +)$$

where $St$ is the sentence "the patient should be treated with chemotherapy", $G$ denotes the grounds of the argument (the sequence of steps given), and $+$ indicates that the grounds support action $St$. However this conceals some significant complexities. The notion of "support" seems somewhat different from the interpretation we have previously assigned to it. For LA we have adopted the interpretation that an argument is a conventional proof, albeit one which it is acknowledged cannot in practice be guaranteed to be correct. An argument in support of some proposition is, in other words, a proof of the proposition which we accept could be wrong. This analysis of "support" does not seem to be entirely satisfactory when reasoning about what we *ought to do* as opposed to what *is the case*. Consider the following simple argument, which is embedded in the above example:

cancer is an intolerable condition, therefore it should be eradicated

There is a possibility that this argument is mistaken, which would justify signing it with $+$ (a "supporting" argument in LA) but the sense of support seems to be different from that which is intended when we say that the intolerable character of cancer gives support to any action that will eradicate it. In other words when we say "these symptoms support a diagnosis of cancer", and "these conditions support use of chemotherapy" we are using the term "supports" in quite distinct ways. The latter case involves no uncertainty, but depends only upon some sort of statement that intolerable states of affairs ought not to be allowed to continue. If this is correct then it implies that arguing from "value axioms" is not the same thing as arguing under uncertainty and so is it inappropriate to use LA for constructing such arguments.

## 3.2  The logics of value LV and expected value LEV

How might we accommodate arguments about value within our existing framework? One possibility might be to keep the standard form and elaborate the

---

[6] The terminology harking back to Toulmin.

| The patient has colonic polyps | $(cp : G1 : ++)$ | e1 |
| polyps may lead to cancer | $(cp \to ca : G2 : +)$ | e2 |
| cancer may lead to loss of life | $(ca \to ll : G3 : +)$ | e3 |
| loss of life is intolerable | $(\neg ll : av : ++)$ | v1 |
| surgery preempts malignancy | $(su \to \neg(cp \to ca) : G4 : ++)$ | e4 |
| argument for surgery | $(su : (e1, e2, e3, e4, v1) : +)$ | ev1 |
| surgery has side-effect $se$ | $(su \to se : G5 : ++)$ | e5 |
| $\neg se$ is desirable | $(\neg se : av : +)$ | v2 |
| argument against surgery | $(\neg su : (e5, v2) : +)$ | ev2 |
| $se$ is preferable to loss of life | $(pref(se, ll) : (v1, v2) : ++)$ | p1 |
| no arguments to veto surgery | $(safe(su) : cir : ++)$ | c1 |
| surgery is preferable to $\neg$ surgery | $(pref(su, \neg su) : (ev1, ev2, p1) : ++)$ | p2 |
| commit to surgery | $(do(su) : (p2, c1) : ++)$ | a1 |

**Fig. 6.** An example argument

sentence we are arguing about to include a "value coefficient":

$$((St : +) : G : +)$$

Which might be glossed as "there is reason to believe that action $St$ will have a positively valued outcome". This may allow us to take advantage of standard LA for reasoning with sentences about the value of actions, but it does not, of course, solve our problem since it says nothing about the way in which we should assign or manipulate the value coefficients.

As a result, we currently prefer another approach, which is analogous to the decision theoretic notion of expected value. In this approach we construct compound arguments based on distinct steps of constructing and combining belief arguments and value arguments. For example, consider the following argument:

| Doing $A$ will lead to the condition $C$ | $(A \to C : G : +)$ |
| $C$ has positive value | $(C : G' : +)$ |
| Doing $A$ has positive expected value | $(A : G \cup G' : +)$ |

We can think of this as being composed of three completely separate stages as well as having three steps. The first stage is an argument in LA that $C$ will occur if action $A$ is taken, which could be glossed as "$G$ is grounds for arguing in support of $C$ resulting from action $A$". The second stage says nothing about uncertainty; it simply requires some mechanism for assigning a value to $C$, call this LV[7]. The final stage concludes that $A$ has positive expected value; to make this step we shall have to give some mechanism for deriving arguments over sentences in LA and LV, call this LEV[8].

The attraction of this scheme is that it appears to make explicit some inferences which are hidden in the other argument forms. However, it has the additional requirements that we define two new systems—LV and LEV. It seems

---

[7] The name stands for Logic of Value.
[8] The name stands for Logic of Expected Value.

to us that this is a price worth paying since making the assignment of values and the calculation of expected value explicit gives much more flexibility and so makes it possible to represent quite complex patterns of reasoning. As an example of the kind of reasoning that should be possible consider the following:

(1) The patient is believed to have colonic polyps which, while presently benign, could become cancerous.
(2) Since cancer is life-threatening we ought to take some action to pre-empt this threat.
(3) Surgical excision is an effective procedure for removing polyps and therefore this is an argument for carrying out surgery.
(4) Although surgery is unpleasant and has significant morbidity this is preferable to loss of life, so surgery ought to be carried out.

Informally we can represent this argument as in Figure 6.

There are six different forms of argument in this example which has a similar scope to the examples considered by Tan and Pearl [40]. The first are those labelled $e1$–$e5$ which are standard arguments in LA. The second are value assignments $v1$ and $v2$ which represent information about what states are desirable and undesirable. The third are expected value arguments $ev1$ and $ev2$ which combine the information in standard and value arguments. The fourth are arguments $p1$ and $p2$ which express preferences between different decision options. The fifth type of argument is the closure argument $c1$ which explicitly states that all possible arguments have been considered, and this leads to the final type of argument, the commitment argument $a1$ which explicitly records the taking of the decision. The following sections discuss some features of these arguments, in particular values and expected values.

# 4 Systems of argumentation for dealing with values and expected values

Having discussed in general terms what is required from LV and LEV, we can start moving towards an initial formal definition. We require some language for representing values. Notwithstanding the common-sense simplicity of the idea of value its formalisation is not likely to be easy. Value assignments are commonly held to be fundamentally subjective—they are based on the preferences of a decision maker rather than being grounded in some observable state of affairs.

## 4.1 Arguments about values

There are a number of possible formalisms we might consider. We might, for instance, adopt some set of modal operators, such as $desirable(St)$, where $St$ is some sentence such as "the patient is free of disease". This is the approach adopted by Bell and Huang [4]. Alternatively we might attach numerical coefficients, as in the use of quantitative utilities in traditional decision theory. We propose representing the value of a state or condition $St$ by labelling a proposition describing $St$ with a sign drawn from some dictionary $\mathcal{D}$ just as we do for beliefs. In this discussion we shall only consider qualitative value dictionaries because, as with uncertainty, we can invariably judge whether some state has positive or negative value, or is valueless, though we may not be able to determine a precise point value or precise upper and lower bounds on the value.

Another similarity with our view of uncertainty is that we can frequently assign different values to states from different points of view. For example the use of opiates is bad since they lead to addiction, but good if they are being used as an analgesic. We therefore propose to label value assignment expressions with the grounds for the assignment, for instance $St : G : V$, giving us a "value argument" analogous to the argument expressions of LA. This is not a new idea of course. For example, multi-attribute utility theory also assumes the possibility of multiple dimensions over which values can be assigned. However, the benefits of this sort of formalisation is that it may allow us to cope with situations where we cannot precisely quantify the value of a situation, and it permits explicit representation of the justifications for particular value assignments making it possible to take them into account when reasoning. The basic schema of value assignment is analogous to the standard argumentation schema:

$$\text{Database} \vdash_{VCR} (\text{Condition} : \text{Grounds} : \text{Value}) \tag{5}$$

A Basic Value Argument (BVA) is a triple defining some state, the value assigned to it, and a justification for this particular assignment. The assertions "health is good" might be represented in grounds-labelled form by:

$$(health : va : +)$$

where $va$ is a label representing the justification for the BVA.

Traditionally there has been considerable discussion of the justifications for value assignments. Any discussion has to face the difficulty that values seem to be fundamentally subjective. In discussion of beliefs there is an analogous idea of subjective probability but it is also possible to invoke the idea of long-run frequency to provide an objective basis for probability theory. There has been a similar attempt to identify an objective framework for values, in consensual values (for example social mores and legal systems), but it seems inescapable that values are grounded in opinion rather than some sort of objective estimation analogous to the chances of events. We therefore accept that a value assignment may in the end be warranted by sentences like "because I say so", "because the law says so", and "because the church says so".

In other words we have nothing new to say about the nature of the "value theories" invoked in (5). We shall simply assume that the theory provides a set of basic value assignments. Our task here is not to give or justify any particular set of value assignment sentences (any more than probability theorists are required to provide particular collections of prior or conditional probabilities) but to identify ways in which collections of such value sentences might be manipulated, aiming to take some steps towards the definition of a system LV which is

$$\text{Ax} \frac{(St : G : Sg) \in \Delta}{\Delta \vdash_{VCR} (St : G : Sg)}$$

$$\wedge\text{-I} \frac{\Delta \vdash_{VCR} (St : G : Sg) \quad \Delta \vdash_{VCR} (St' : G' : Sg')}{\Delta \vdash_{VCR} (St \wedge St' : G \cup G' : \text{comb}^{\vee}_{\text{conj intro}}(Sg, Sg'))}$$

$$\wedge\text{-E1} \frac{\Delta \vdash_{VCR} (St \wedge St' : G : Sg)}{\Delta \vdash_{VCR} (St : G : \text{comb}^{\vee}_{\text{conj elim}}(Sg))}$$

$$\wedge\text{-E2} \frac{\Delta \vdash_{VCR} (St \wedge St' : G : Sg)}{\Delta \vdash_{VCR} (St' : G : \text{comb}^{\vee}_{\text{conj elim}}(Sg))}$$

**Fig. 7.** Value Consequence Relation

analogous to LA but deals with values rather than beliefs. The assumption is that the assignment of values in sentences like "health is good" depends upon a derivation which bottoms out in some set of BVAs and that these will be propagated in the grounds of the relevant arguments.

## 4.2 Formalising argumentation about values

Having spoken informally about what LV is attempting to do, we present an initial attempt at formalizing it. This, as the observant reader will notice, is virtually identical to the definition of LA. We start with another set of atomic propositions $\mathcal{M}$ including $\top$ and $\bot$, the ever true and ever false propositions. We also have a set of connectives $\{\neg, \wedge\}$, and the following set of rules for building the well-formed formulae (*wff*s) of the language.

- If $l \in \mathcal{M}$ then $l$ is a well-formed formula (*wff*).
- If $l$ is a *wff* then $\neg l$ is a *wff*.
- If $l$ and $m$ are *wff*s then $l \wedge m$ is a *wff*.
- Nothing else is a *wff*.

Note that currently LV does not make use of the connective $\rightarrow$ since it is unclear to us what such a connective might mean. However, Shoham's recent work [38] suggests that some way of expressing conditional values may well be necessary. The set of all *wff*s that may be defined using $\mathcal{M}$, may then be used to build up a database $\Delta$ where every item $d \in \Delta$ is a triple $(St : G : Sg)$ in which $St$ is a *wff*, $Sg$ represents the value of $St$, and $G$ are the grounds on which the assertion is made. With this formal system, we can take a database and use the argumentation consequence relation $\vdash_{VCR}$ defined in Figure 7 to build arguments for propositions that we are interested in. Given the explanation of $\vdash_{ACR}$ the way this works should be clear.

Now, as before, we define dictionary $\mathcal{D}$ by:

$$\mathcal{D} =_{\text{def}} \{S_1, \ldots S_n\}$$

and so we may write:

$$(St : G : S_i)$$

where $S_i$ is any symbol drawn from $\mathcal{D}$. For values there are a couple of obvious dictionary. The first is that of numerical value, measured in whatever currency one chooses, another is that of utiles—the familiar measure of classical decision theory:

$$\mathcal{D}_{\text{money}} =_{\text{def}} \{S : S \in (-\infty, \infty)\}$$
$$\mathcal{D}_{\text{utility}} =_{\text{def}} \{S : S \in (-\infty, \infty)\}$$

However, as was the case with beliefs, our interest is primarily with qualitative dictionaries, so it is worth considering in more detail two value dictionaries which are analogous to the simple qualitative dictionaries we considered for use with LA.

**Cost benefit dictionary** The simplest useful dictionary of values allows us to talk about states that are good or desirable and states which are bad or undesirable.

$$\mathcal{D}_{\text{cost benefit}} =_{\text{def}} \{+, -\}$$

As with beliefs there are two ways we could interpret these signs. We could take $+$ to mean simply that the state has some absolute (point) positive value, but that the precise value is unknown, or we could take it to mean that we have an argument for the overall value of our goods being increased. For the moment we restrict ourselves to using absolute values, but delta values for values may be required at a later date. It would seem that good and bad states can be related through complementation rules:

$$(St : G : +) \Leftrightarrow (\neg St : G : -) \tag{6}$$
$$(St : G : -) \Leftrightarrow (\neg St : G : +) \tag{7}$$

analogous to (1) and (2) above.

**Bounded cost benefit dictionary** There also seems to be some benefit in extending the cost benefit dictionary to allow us to talk about maximal amounts of goodness (badness):

$$\mathcal{D}_{\text{bounded cost benefit}} =_{\text{def}} \{++, +, -, --\}$$

However, there seems to be a complication here. It seems straightforward to claim that there is a lower bound on badness—we might gloss this by saying certain conditions are "intolerable" such as death for instance—but an upper bound on "goodness" (for example of a bank balance) is harder to conceive of. However if we accept:

$$(St : G : ++) \Leftrightarrow (\neg St : G : --) \tag{8}$$
$$(St : G : --) \Leftrightarrow (\neg St : G : ++) \tag{9}$$

by analogy with (3) and (4), then we can obtain a reasonable interpretation for the idea of a condition which is maximally desirable as the complement of any condition that is intolerable. Furthermore sentences like "human life is priceless" arc held, by their users at least, to have some meaning. From a pragmatic point of view such statements can seem merely romantic, but if we accept the above rules it is a direct consequence of asserting that loss of life is intolerable.

Since values are derived with respect to some value theory we can contemplate different value arguments for the same sentence. In common with LA, such value arguments can be aggregated. We can describe this aggregation, as for LA, in terms of a function $\mathsf{Flat}^{\mathsf{V}}(\cdot)$ which maps from a set of value arguments $\mathbf{A}$ for a proposition $St$ from a particular database $\Delta$ to the pair of that proposition and some overall measure of validity:

$$\mathsf{Flat}^{\mathsf{V}} : \mathbf{A} \mapsto \langle St, v \rangle$$

where $\mathbf{A}$ is the set of all arguments which are concerned with $St$, that is:

$$\mathbf{A} = \{(St : G_i : Sg_i) \mid \Delta \vdash_{VCR} (St : G_i : Sg_i)\}$$

and $v$ is the result of a suitable combination of the $Sg$ that takes into account the structure of the arguments, that is $v$ is the result of applying a flattening function to the grounds and signs of all the arguments in $\mathbf{A}$:

$$v = \mathsf{flat}^{\mathsf{V}}\Big(\{\langle G_i, Sg_i \rangle \mid (St : G_i : Sg_i) \in \mathbf{A}\}\Big)$$

Often the signs $Sg_i$ and the overall validity $v$ will be drawn from the same dictionary, but it is perfectly feasible for them to be drawn from different dictionaries (so that a set of arguments with numerical values might be flattened to a value drawn from the dictionary $\{very\ expensive, expensive, cheap\}$).

There are, of course, a number of possible ways in which we might aggregate values. Numerical values might be aggregated by summation, for instance, and clearly the exact aggregation operation will depend upon the meaning of the value signs. One obvious assumption we might wish to make when using the cost benefit or bounded cost benefit dictionary is that:

**Assumption A5** If $Args$ is any set of arguments supporting and opposing arguments, then:
$$|Args| \leq |Args \cup \{(S : G : +)\}|$$

Following previous usage we might refer to the set of arguments as the *case* for $S$ being positively valued, and $|Args|$ as the *force* of these arguments. Now, a condition may be desirable on some grounds and undesirable on others, for instance if we have:

$$\Delta \vdash_{VCR} (St : G : +)$$
$$\Delta \vdash_{VCR} (St : G' : -)$$

This raises the question of how supporting and opposing arguments interact. One possibility is to make the flattening function obey the assumption:

**Assumption A6** If *Args* is any set of supporting and opposing arguments, then:

$$|Args| \geq |Args \cup \{(St : G : -)\}|$$

So that arguments with negative value bring the overall weight of a set of arguments down. In addition, we might want to assume that:

**Assumption A7** If *Args* is any set of supporting and opposing arguments, then:

$$|Args| = |Args \cup \{(St : G : -), (St : G' : +)\}|$$

so that positive and negative arguments cancel one another. This latter assumption is exactly the same as the one encoded in the flattening function for LA which counts the number of arguments. An alternative flattening, which is more in agreement with qualitative versions of classical decision theory [1, 44], is to have complementary value arguments lead to indeterminacy.

This picture is complicated slightly by the use of the bounded cost-benefit dictionary, where we have limits to values. Using this dictionary suggests the adoption of an additional assumption similar to A2 and A4:

**Assumption A8** let *Args* be any set of supporting and opposing arguments concerning *St*, and *Args'* be any set of supporting, opposing and confirming arguments concerning *St*, then:

$$|\{(St : G : ++)\}| > |Args|$$
$$|\{(St : G : ++)\}| = |Args'|$$

let *Args''* be any set of supporting and opposing arguments concerning *St*, and *Args'''* be any set of supporting, opposing and excluding arguments concerning *St*, then:

$$|\{(St : G : --)\}| < |Args''|$$
$$|\{(St : G : --)\}| = |Args'''|$$

so that an argument with maximal strength is not affected by additional information. Of course, as with A4, this means that it is inconsistent to have both $(St : G : ++)$ and $(St : G' : --)$ for any *St*.

Having discussed things in abstract terms, let's make things concrete by discussing one possible semantics for the bounded cost-benefit dictionary. In particular, we take $+$ to be some unknown positive value, and $++$ denotes some limiting unknown value (but not infinity[9]). Similarly, $-$ is some unknown negative value, and $--$ is a limiting negative value. If it helps, these can be taken to be qualitative abstractions of monetary value, with $+$ being any credit, $-$ any debit and $++$ the amount of money which if one had it, one would no longer have to worry about working for a living. We take $\wedge$ to be logical conjunction. With this interpretation, the combination function $\text{comb}^\vee_{\text{conj intro}}$ is that of Figure 8. This again uses ? as an abbreviation for "one of $++$, $+$, $-$ and $--$" (though it would probably suffice to make it just an abbreviation for "$+$ or $-$"). The

---

[9] We could use infinity, but that would make the combinator tables slightly different.

| $\mathsf{comb}^{\vee}_{\mathsf{conj\ intro}}$ | ++ | + | − | −− |
|---|---|---|---|---|
| ++ | ++ | + | + | ? |
| + | + | + | ? | − |
| − | + | ? | − | − |
| −− | ? | − | − | −− |

**Fig. 8.** The combinator table for LV using the bounded cost benefit dictionary.

| $\mathsf{flat}^{\vee}$ | ++ | + | − | −− |
|---|---|---|---|---|
| ++ | ++ | + | + | $\mathcal{C}$ |
| + | + | + | ? | − |
| − | + | ? | − | − |
| −− | $\mathcal{C}$ | − | − | −− |

**Fig. 9.** The flattening function for LV using the bounded cost benefit dictionary.

function $\mathsf{comb}^{\vee}_{\mathsf{conj\ elim}}$ for this interpretation is:

$$\mathsf{comb}^{\vee}_{\mathsf{conj\ elim}}(Sg) = \begin{cases} Sg \text{ if } Sg \in \{++, --\} \\ ? \quad \text{otherwise} \end{cases}$$

It is straightforward to verify that these functions are correct for this interpretation of the signs, and the interested reader is encouraged to do so.

We also need to define a function to flatten value arguments with this interpretation. The binary version of this flattening function is that of Figure 9. This is very similar to the table for $\mathsf{comb}^{\vee}_{\mathsf{conj\ elim}}$, but differs in that it introduces another new symbol, $\mathcal{C}$. This symbol represents a contradiction, and is at the heart of the difference between the flattening function and $\mathsf{comb}^{\vee}_{\mathsf{conj\ elim}}$. If we have two arguments $(St : G : ++)$ and $(St' : G' : --)$ then we can build an argument for $St \wedge St'$. This represents a state of affairs has one component which is completely desirable and another which is completely undesirable, and it seems reasonable to give it a value which is, roughly speaking, the sum of $++$ and $--$, and is therefore somewhere in between. We therefore use the value $?$. The intuition here is that the conjunction of a sentence with maximum positive value and one with maximum negative value has some intermediate value. Thus I may find it completely desirable to not have to work, and completely undesirable to have no income but I can put some value on the state in which I don't work and have no income.

However, if $St$ and $St'$ are the same sentence, then the two arguments contradict each other—they say that $St$ is both completely desirable and completely undesirable—no overall value for $St$ can be agreed. The intuition here is that we cannot simply cancel an argument that a condition is absolutely desirable with an argument that the same condition is absolutely undesirable. For example, in discussions of euthanasia we may have an absolute prohibition on killing; this cannot simply be cancelled out by arguing that a loved one's pain is intolerable.

There are, of course, no simple decision rules for such situations and that is why we choose to flag the situation with $C$ rather than reduce the conflict to some arbitrary value. What we need is to be able to recognise that a conflict has occurred, and then resolve it by means of some form of meta-logical reasoning, something like the opposite of circumscription, in which we introduce new assumptions or theories whose specific role is to overcome such deadlocks. In the euthanasia example, we may appeal to societal "thin end of the wedge" theories for instance in which "society's needs" were not included in the framing of the original decision.

### 4.3  Formalising argumentation about expected values

The previous section dealt with the problem of aggregation of value arguments. It remains to provide rules for deriving sentences from combinations of belief arguments and value arguments (that is arguments in LA and LV respectively). As an example of this kind of derivation, consider the following argument in LA:

$$(St : G : S)$$

meaning that we can argue for $St$ with sign $S$. Assume further that we also have the following argument in LV:

$$(St : G' : V)$$

which means that the value of $St$ is $V$. From these two arguments we wish to derive an expected value argument in LEV:

$$(St : G \cup G' : E)$$

meaning that the expected value of $St$ is $E$. Now, from a decision making point of view, arguments about expected value of states are of little interest, except in the situation where they are the *outcomes* of actions that we can choose to take or not take. As an example of the kind of thing we would like to reason about, consider combining a sentence about belief with one about action:

$$\frac{\neg cancer : v1 : V}{surgery \Rightarrow \neg cancer : e1 : S}{surgery : v1 \cup e1 : E}$$

where $\Rightarrow$ is a connective which captures the notion of applying an action so that the sentence $surgery \Rightarrow \neg cancer$ is read "the action of $surgery$ leads to the condition of $\neg cancer$" This pattern of reasoning is exactly the same as the previous one, combining a statement about beliefs (that surgery is a means of eradicating cancer, believed to degree S) with a statement about value (that a lack of cancer is a state with value V) to come up with a statement about expected value (that surgery in this case has some expected value E). However, to deal with this kind of reasoning we need to be able to talk about actions and to be able to reason backwards from the effects of actions to their causes. In particular,

$$\text{Ax}\frac{\Delta \vdash_{ACR} (St : G : Sg)\ \Delta' \vdash_{VCR} (St : G' : Sg')}{\Delta \cup \Delta' \vdash_{LEV} (St : G \cup G' : \text{comb}^{\text{L}}_{\text{ax}}(Sg, Sg'))}$$

$$\wedge\text{-I}\frac{\Delta \vdash_{LEV} (St : G : Sg)\ \Delta \vdash_{LEV} (St' : G' : Sg')}{\Delta \vdash_{LEV} (St \wedge St' : G \cup G' : \text{comb}^{\text{L}}_{\text{conj intro}}(Sg, Sg'))}$$

$$\wedge\text{-E1}\frac{\Delta \vdash_{LEV} (St \wedge St' : G : Sg)}{\Delta \vdash_{LEV} (St : G : \text{comb}^{\text{L}}_{\text{conj elim}}(Sg))}$$

$$\wedge\text{-E2}\frac{\Delta \vdash_{LEV} (St \wedge St' : G : Sg)}{\Delta \vdash_{LEV} (St' : G : \text{comb}^{\text{L}}_{\text{conj elim}}(Sg))}$$

**Fig. 10.** Expected Value Consequence Relation

from a formal point of view, we need to be able to handle the connective $\Rightarrow$. Given the well-known difficulties of building formal systems to reason about action, we will leave this for future work and only deal with combining values and beliefs about states.

With this simplification we can once again start the process of formalising the system of argumentation. We start with a third set of atomic propositions $\mathcal{N}$ including $\top$ and $\bot$, the ever true and ever false propositions. We also have the connectives $\{\neg, \wedge\}$, and the following set of rules for building the well-formed formulae (*wff*s) of the language.

- If $l \in \mathcal{M}$ then $l$ is a well-formed formula (*wff*).
- If $l$ is a *wff* then $\neg l$ is a *wff*.
- If $l$ and $m$ are *wff*s then $l \wedge m$ is a *wff*.
- Nothing else is a *wff*.

The set of all *wff*s that may be defined using $\mathcal{N}$ then defines a legal set of triples $(St : G : Sg)$ in which $St$ is a *wff* of LEV, $Sg$ represents the expected value of $St$, and $G$ are the grounds on which the assertion is made. However, LEV differs from LA and LV in that we don't build up a database of triples and build arguments from them, but build triples from existing arguments in LA and LV using the consequence relation $\vdash_{LEV}$ defined in Figure 10. Note that the consequence relation of Figure 10 differs from $\vdash_{ACR}$ and $\vdash_{VCR}$ in that the "bootstrap" rule, which allows the creation of an LEV argument from something other than an LEV argument, does not directly involve a tuple from some database. Instead it involves an argument in LA and an argument in LV. This captures the fact that any expected value argument is formed from a belief argument and a value argument.

With the consequence relation fixed, we can move on to identify suitable dictionaries. Now, our choice of dictionary is a little restricted since expected value arguments are based on both belief arguments and value arguments. Thus the meanings of the signs of expected value arguments are completely determined by the meanings of signs of their constituent belief and value arguments. Let us consider a suitable dictionary for expected value arguments built using belief

| $\mathsf{comb}^{\mathsf{L}}_{\mathsf{ax}}$ | ++ | + | − | −− |
|---|---|---|---|---|
| ++ | ++ | + | − | −− |
| + | + | + | − | − |

| $\mathsf{comb}^{\mathsf{L}}_{\mathsf{conj\ intro}}$ | ++ | + | − | −− |
|---|---|---|---|---|
| ++ | ++ | ++ | + | ? |
| + | + | + | ? | − |
| − | + | ? | − | − |
| −− | ? | − | − | −− |

**Fig. 11.** The combinator tables for LEV using the bounded expectation dictionary.

arguments whose signs are drawn from the bounded generic dictionary, and value arguments whose signs are drawn from the bounded cost benefit dictionary. This gives what we might call the bounded expectation dictionary:

$$\mathcal{D}_{\text{bounded expectation}} =_{\text{def}} \{++, +, -, --\}$$

If the belief dictionary in question is taken to be the probabilistic one discussed earlier, then the signs in the bounded expectation dictionary become qualitative abstractions of expectations (and hence the name). Suitable combinations functions are those of Figure 11. That for $\mathsf{comb}^{\mathsf{L}}_{\mathsf{ax}}$ reflects the multiplication of a belief (in the leftmost column) with a value (in the top row), while that for $\mathsf{comb}^{\mathsf{L}}_{\mathsf{conj\ intro}}$ is identical to the analogous function for LV. The function for eliminating conjunctions is:

$$\mathsf{comb}^{\mathsf{L}}_{\mathsf{conj\ elim}}(Sg) = \begin{cases} Sg \text{ if } Sg \in \{++, --\} \\ ? \quad \text{otherwise} \end{cases}$$

reflecting the indeterminacies in conjunction introduction. Once again, it is reasonably straightforward to show that these functions are correct.

In many cases a collection of qualitative expected value arguments can be aggregated under assumptions similar to those suggested for LV, and so we can again define a flattening function. As before we do this in terms of a function $\mathsf{Flat}^{\mathsf{L}}(\cdot)$ which maps from a set of expected value arguments $\mathbf{A}$ for a proposition $St$ from a particular database $\Delta$ to the pair of that proposition and some overall measure of validity:

$$\mathsf{Flat}^{\mathsf{L}} : \mathbf{A} \mapsto \langle St, v \rangle$$

where $\mathbf{A}$ is the set of all arguments which are concerned with $St$, that is:

$$\mathbf{A} = \{(St : G_i : Sg_i) \mid \Delta \vdash_{LEV} (St : G_i : Sg_i)\}$$

and $v$ is the result of a suitable combination of the $Sg$ that takes into account the structure of the set of arguments, that is $v$ is the result of applying a flattening function to the grounds and signs of all the arguments in $\mathbf{A}$:

$$v = \mathsf{flat}^{\mathsf{L}}\left(\{\langle G_i, Sg_i \rangle \mid (St : G_i : Sg_i) \in \mathbf{A}\}\right)$$

As ever, the signs $Sg_i$ and the overall validity $v$ can be drawn from the same dictionary or from different dictionaries. A flattening function suitable for the

| flat$^L$ | ++ | + | − | −− |
|----------|-----|-----|-----|-----|
| ++ | ++ | ++ | + | $\mathcal{C}$ |
| + | + | + | ? | − |
| − | + | ? | − | − |
| −− | $\mathcal{C}$ | − | − | −− |

**Fig. 12.** The flattening function for LEV using the bounded expectation dictionary.

bounded expectation dictionary is given in Figure 12. Once again, if we have expected value arguments based on conflicting values, for instance if we have $(St : G : ++)$ and $(\neg St : G' : ++)$ then such conflicts cannot be resolved within the system and as before are denoted $\mathcal{C}$.

The flattening function for LEV completes the definition of LV and LEV and we can turn to providing an example of their use.

### 4.4 Example

As an example of the kind of reasoning which LA, LV and LEV can capture, consider the following example adapted from [28]. The following database represents a career choice faced by the second author who needs to decide whether or not to concentrate his efforts on research or teaching:

$$
\begin{aligned}
&(concentrate\_on\_research : f1 : ++) &&\Delta_1 \\
&(concentrate\_on\_teaching : f2 : ++) \\
&(concentrate\_on\_research \rightarrow good\_research : r1 : +) \\
&(good\_research \rightarrow job\_in\_industry : r2 : ++) \\
&(concentrate\_on\_teaching \rightarrow good\_tutor : r3 : ++) \\
&(good\_tutor \rightarrow senior\_university\_job : r4 : ++)
\end{aligned}
$$

The facts $f1$ and $f2$ represent the possible choices, and the rules $r1$–$r4$ represent a subjective assessment of the relevant causal relations. These are expressed in LA using the bounded generic dictionary, using the probabilistic interpretation. From this information we can build the following arguments in LA by applying Ax and $\rightarrow$-E from Figure 2:

$$
\Delta_1 \vdash_{ACR} (job\_in\_industry, \{f1, r2, r2\}, +)
$$
$$
\Delta_1 \vdash_{ACR} (senior\_university\_job, \{f2, r3, r4\}, ++)
$$

which identify what the outcomes of the different career choices are, and how likely these are to come about; choosing to concentrate on teaching means a senior university job for sure, while concentrating on research means the chance of a job in industry. Now, consider we have the following value assignments in LV:

$$
\begin{aligned}
&(job\_in\_industry : f3 : +) &&\Delta_2 \\
&(senior\_university\_job : f4 : ++)
\end{aligned}
$$

which represent subjective assessments of the value of the possible outcomes expressed using the bounded cost benefit dictionary. From these we can build the arguments by applying Ax from Figure 7:

$$\Delta_2 \vdash_{VCR} (job\_in\_industry, \{f3\}, ++)$$
$$\Delta_2 \vdash_{VCR} (senior\_university\_job, \{f4\}, ++)$$

which tell us that both a senior university job and a job in industry are judged to be is totally desirable. The two related pairs of arguments can then be combined by applying Ax from Figure 10 :

$$\Delta_1 \cup \Delta_2 \vdash_{LEV} (job\_in\_industry, \{f1, f3, r1, r2\}, +)$$
$$\Delta_1 \cup \Delta_2 \vdash_{LEV} (senior\_university\_job, \{f2, f4, r3, r4\}, ++)$$

These values are expressed in the bounded expectation dictionary. From these arguments it is clear that the option to concentrate on teaching is the best since it will lead to the maximum expected value.

While this is clearly a very straightforward example to formalise, it does show why we feel the argumentation approach has some advantages. The use of the three separate systems makes it possible to separate out the belief elements from the value elements, and identify what reasoning is carried out with both. When belief and value arguments have been combined in LEV it is still clear which elements have been brought to bear. This makes it possible, for instance, to see that the reason that the option to concentrate on research loses out is because of the uncategorical relation $r1$ between concentrating on research and doing good research. This, in turn, gives the approach considerable explanatory power.

## 4.5 Soundness and completeness

As is the case for arguments about belief in the logic LA, it makes sense to ask what formal guarantees there are for arguments about values and expected values in the logics LV and LEV. The answer to this question is that there are none at the moment, and the investigation of such matters is one of the main foci of our future work on these systems. However, as remarked above, it is reasonably straightforward to obtain at least soundness proofs for both LV and LEV for the dictionaries discussed since all this involves is showing that the combination functions are correct. Furthermore, completeness proofs for systems such as LV and LEV are usually easy to obtain since they follow quite quickly from the inclusion of introduction and elimination rules for each of the connectives used.

## 4.6 Preferences and commitments

A complete decision theory is generally held to require some means of choosing between alternative actions. Despite the work outlined above the combined system LA/LV/LEV does not have such a mechanism. However, it is possible to extend the idea of arguments about values and expected values to provide one. In particular, we could use expected values to construct a preference ordering over a set of alternative actions as follows:

Condition $St$ is *preferred* to condition $St'$, $pref(St, St')$, if:

$$|\{(St : G_i : Sg_i) \mid \Delta \vdash_{LEV} (St : G_i : Sg_i)\}| \geq$$
$$|\{(St' : G_j : Sg_j) \mid \Delta \vdash_{LEV} (St' : G_j : Sg_j)\}|$$

In other words, $St$ is preferred to $St'$ if the overall force of all the expected value arguments for it is at least as great as the force of all the expected value arguments for $St'$. Transitivity of preferences is implicit in this inequality, and it is also possible to take into account the number of opposing arguments.

However we have a problem of potential instability. We could choose to act on a preference, but this preference could be transitory; wait a little longer and we might find that we can construct an argument to the effect that taking the currently preferred action could be disastrous. What is needed is some stronger condition than simply a preference for such and such an action. We would like to be able to prove that the ordering is, in fact, stable or that the benefits of achieving greater stability are outweighed by the costs. Thus we need some closure condition that says, essentially, there are no further arguments that could alter our main preference, a condition which parallels Pollock's [33] idea of a practical warrant for taking an action. Abstractly we can think of this as a "safety argument" of the form:

$$\frac{best(A) : G : ++ \quad safe(A) : cir : ++}{commit(A) : (G, cir) : ++}$$

where $best(A)$ means that aggregation of the arguments for an action $A$ has greater force than the arguments for any alternative action, and $commit(A)$ represents a non-reversible commitment for executing action $A$, for example by executing it. Informally such safety arguments might include:

- Demonstrating that there are no sources of information that could lead to arguments which would result in a different best action.
- Demonstrating that the expected costs of not committing to $A$ exceed the expected costs of seeking further information.

However, it is clear, as Pollock points out, that any system which is intended to have practical uses should take seriously the computational problems inherent in checking that no further relevant arguments can be built.

## 5 Argumentation in practice

While the work on arguments about values and expected values reported in Sections 4.2 and 4.3 is still rather preliminary, this paper being a first attempt at formalising the proposal made in [19], the work on arguments about beliefs has been applied quite widely in projects at the Imperial Cancer Research Fund. The systems to which this model has been applied include a decision support system for general medical practitioners [15], a system for interpreting medical images

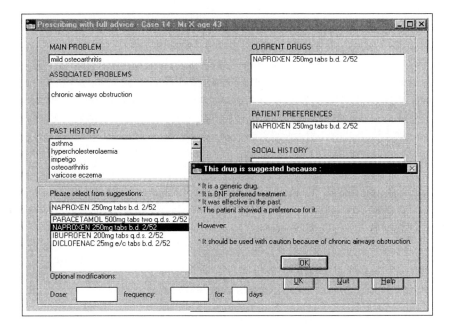

**Fig. 13.** A example consultation from CAPSULE

[41], and a system to advise on the management of acute asthma. More detail on these and other medical applications may be found in [14]. The model is also the basis for the system of argumentation used to analyse the risk of carcinogenicity of chemical compounds which is described elsewhere in this volume [23].

One recent application built using argumentation is the CAPSULE system which supports general practitioners in drug prescription. The system works in the classic expert system manner. It is equipped with information about which drugs treat which conditions and what constitutes best practice, and it is fed with information about patients. When a specific patient presents with a specific set of symptoms, CAPSULE identifies a range of drugs which are suitable, identifying for each the arguments for and against its use. The doctor can then choose the most appropriate. Figure 13 shows a typical consultation. The patient, who has a history which includes asthma, hypercholesterolaemia, impetigo, and varicose eczema has presented with mild osteoarthritis (a recurring condition). The system has identified a list of possible treatments, one of which is Naproxen. Examining the arguments for it, we find that it is a recommended treatment for four reasons. First, it is a generic drug, meaning it is not the trademarked product of a single drug company. Second, it is the treatment recommended by the BNF (the BNF being the British National Formulary, a list of drugs and the conditions they treat, which is the usual basis for prescribing decisions). Third, it has proved effective in the past (when the patient previously came to the doctor suffering from osteoarthritis). Fourth, the patient actually has a preference for it over other treatments he has tried in the past. There is also an argument against Naproxen—that it should be used with caution because of the associated problem of "chronic airways obstruction" which the patient is known to suffer from.

An evaluation of CAPSULE [43] suggests that this kind of support is extremely useful. A study was carried out in which 42 general practitioners each prescribed for 36 records based on real cases. The doctors were given 3 levels of support, a list of drugs in alphabetical order, a list of preferred drugs (decided upon by the argumentation engine), and the list of preferred drugs along with the arguments for and against. As the level of support increased, the proportion of times that the doctors agreed with a panel of experts rose from 25% to 42%, the proportion of time the doctors ignored a cheaper drug that was as effective as the one they chose fell from 50% to 35%, and the mean score (which measured how closely doctors agreed with the experts) rose from 6 (out of 8) to 6.7.

The version of CAPSULE from which Figure 13 is taken was developed using a system called Pro*forma* [16]. Pro*forma* is a generic technology for building decision support applications. It consists of the Pro*forma* language, a formal specification language in the sense used in software engineering, and a knowledge representation language. The technology also includes a number of software tools, for designing and "enacting" Pro*forma* applications. In particular, these include an editor which makes it possible to rapidly build applications from a set of standard components—plans, decisions, actions and enquiries. The use of argumentation is embedded in Pro*forma*'s decision component. All decisions are reached by building arguments for and against the decision options, and then aggregating these arguments to identify how good options are. Thus in the Pro*forma* version of CAPSULE, the system builds arguments for and against all the relevant drugs (which are precisely those for which arguments may be built) and uses an aggregation function which counts the number of supporting and opposing arguments, subtracts the second from the first, and ranks the decision options using the resulting score. This may appear to be a trivial procedure, but it does appear to be effective.

# 6 Conclusions and discussion

In order to take, or commit to, a decision we must combine or aggregate arguments in order to establish relative preferences among options. Perhaps surprisingly there is now considerable evidence that such simple decision functions are highly effective for many clinical applications (for instance [5, 24]). The most definitive study to date is that by Pradhan *et al.* who have rigorously assessed the impact of various evidence aggregation methods in medical decision making [34]. This study replicates the earlier findings cited, concluding that the correct qualitative representation of the decision has much more influence on the quality of decision making than the precision of quantitative parameters such as probabilities. We feel that this is strong evidence for the validity of argumentation as a decision making method.

This paper has built on our previous work on using argumentation to reason about beliefs towards making argumentation the basis of a complete decision theory. We identified a number of different types of argument that can participate in making decisions by reasoning about the outcome of possible actions and have suggested some ways in which these arguments may be built and combined. We believe that the framework we have outlined has the potential to integrate the best parts of traditional planning mechanisms and decision theory in the way suggested by Pollock [33] and Wellman and Doyle [45].

Furthermore, the theory seems to be capable of allowing meta-level reasoning about the structure of the decision as well as providing some means for coping with contradictory beliefs and conflicting values and for explicitly including stopping rules and commitment to particular courses of action. In addition to the obvious task of continuing the development of the foundations of this approach, there are a number of areas in which we are working. The first is to refine the set of values and expected values which may be used in order to make the system as expressive as, say, the systems proposed by Pearl [32] and Wilson [46]. The second is to investigate alternative semantics for values and expected values as, for instance, Dubois and Prade [9] have done. The third is to investigate the connections between the model we are proposing and existing means of combining plans and beliefs including the BDI framework [36] and the Domino model [6].

Much remains to be done to provide a secure foundation for this approach to reasoning and decision making but it appears to have potential merit for covering a comparable range of decisions to that addressed by classical decision theory. If this is the case, then the complete theory will provide a basis for implementing sound methods for decision making in the absence of quantitative information and the dynamic construction of the structure of the decision.

### Acknowledgments

The first part of this paper has been distilled from the work of many of our colleagues without whose efforts little of the later work would have been possible. They are Simon Ambler, Mike Clarke, Subrata Das, Morten Elvang-Gørranson, Peter Hammond, and Paul Krause. The work that led to this paper has been partially funded by a number of grants, including Esprit Basic Research Actions 3085 DRUMS and 6156 DRUMS 2, ITD/4/1/9053 RED and DTI/SERC 1822 Praxis.

# References

1. A. M. Agogino and N. F. Michelena. Qualitative decision analysis. In N. Piera Carreté and M. G. Singh, editors, *Qualitative Reasoning and Decision Technologies*, pages 285–293. CIMNE, Barcelona, Spain, 1993.
2. S. Ambler. A categorical approach to the semantics of argumentation. *Mathematical Structures in Computer Science*, 6:167–188, 1996.

3. S. Ambler and P. Krause. Enriched categories in the semantics of evidential reasoning. Technical Report 153, Advanced Computation Laboratory, Imperial Cancer Research Fund, 1992.
4. J. Bell and Z. Huang. Safety logics. In A. Hunter and S. Parsons, editors, *Applications of Uncertainty Formalisms (this volume)*. Springer Verlag, Berlin, 1998.
5. T. Chard. Qualitative probability versus quantitative probability in clinical diagnosis: a study using a computer simulation. *Medical Decision Making*, 11:38–41, 1991.
6. S. Das, J. Fox, D. Elsdon, and P. Hammond. Decision making and plan management by autonomous agents: theory, implementation and applications. In *Proceedings of the 1st International Conference on Autonomous Agents*, 1997.
7. S. K. Das. How much does an agent believe: an extension of modal epistemic logic. In A. Hunter and S. Parsons, editors, *Applications of Uncertainty Formalisms (this volume)*. Springer Verlag, Berlin, 1998.
8. D. Dubois and H. Prade. *Possibility Theory: An Approach to Computerized Processing of Uncertainty*. Plenum Press, New York, NY, 1988.
9. D. Dubois and H. Prade. Possibility theory as a basis for qualitative decision theory. In *Proceedings of the 14th International Joint Conference on Artificial Intelligence*, pages 1924–1930, San Mateo, CA, 1995. Morgan Kaufmann.
10. M. Elvang-Gøransson and A. Hunter. Argumentative logics: reasoning with classically inconsistent information. *Data and Knowledge Engineering*, 16:125–145, 1995.
11. M. Elvang-Gøransson, P. Krause, and J. Fox. Dialectic reasoning with inconsistent information. In *Proceedings of the 9th Conference on Uncertainty in Artificial Intelligence*, pages 114–121, San Mateo, CA, 1993. Morgan Kaufmann.
12. J. Fox. Making decisions under the influence of memory. *Psychological Review*, 87:190–211, 1980.
13. J. Fox, D. Barber, and K. D. Bardhan. Alternatives to Bayes? A quantitative comparison with rule-based diagnostic inference. *Methods of Information in Medicine*, 19:210–215, 1980.
14. J. Fox and S. Das. A unified framework for hypothetical and practical reasoning (2): lessons from medical applications. In *Formal and Applied Practical Reasoning*, pages 73–92, Berlin, Germany, 1996. Springer Verlag.
15. J. Fox, A. Glowinski, and M. O'Neil. The Oxford system of medicine: a prototype information system for primary care. In J. Fox, M. Fieschi, and R. Engelbrecht, editors, *AIME 87 European Conference on Artificial Intelligence in Medicine*. Springer Verlag, Berlin, 1987.
16. J. Fox, N. Johns, C Lyons, A. Rahmanzadeh, R. Thomson, and P. Wilson. Pro*forma*: a general technology for clinical decision support systems. *Computer Methods and Programs in Biomedicine*, 54:59–67, 1997.
17. J. Fox, P. Krause, and S. Ambler. Arguments, contradictions and practical reasoning. In *Proceedings of the 10th European Conference on Artificial Intelligence*, pages 623–627, Chichester, UK, 1992. John Wiley & Sons.
18. J. Fox, P. Krause, and M. Elvang-Gøransson. Argumentation as a general framework for uncertain reasoning. In *Proceedings of the 9th Conference on Uncertainty in Artificial Intelligence*, pages 428–434, San Mateo, CA., 1993. Morgan Kaufmann.
19. J. Fox and S. Parsons. On using arguments for reasoning about actions and values. In *Proceedings of the AAAI Spring Symposium on Qualitative Preferences in Deliberation and Practical Reasoning*, pages 55–63, 1997.
20. D. Gabbay. *Labelled Deductive Systems*. Oxford University Press, Oxford, UK, 1996.

21. G. E. Hughes and M. J. Cresswell. *An Introduction to Modal Logic*. Methuen, London, UK, 1968.

22. P. Krause, S. Ambler, M. Elvang-Gøransson, and J. Fox. A logic of argumentation for reasoning under uncertainty. *Computational Intelligence*, 11:113–131, 1995.

23. P. Krause, P. Judson, and M. Patel. Qualitative risk assessment fulfills a need. In A. Hunter and S. Parsons, editors, *Applications of Uncertainty Formalisms (this volume)*. Springer Verlag, Berlin, 1998.

24. M. O'Neil and A. Glowinski. Evaluating and validating very large knowledge-based systems. *Medical Informatics*, 3:237–251, 199o.

25. S. Parsons. Refining reasoning in qualitative probabilistic networks. In *Proceedings of the 11th Conference on Uncertainty in Artificial Intelligence*, pages 427–434, San Francisco, CA, 1995. Morgan Kaufman.

26. S. Parsons. Comparing normative argumentation to qualitative systems. In *Proceedings of the 6th International Conference on Information Processing and the Management of Uncertainty*, pages 137–142, 1996.

27. S. Parsons. Defining normative systems for qualitative argumentation. In *Formal and Applied Practical Reasoning*, pages 449–465, Berlin, Germany, 1996. Springer Verlag.

28. S. Parsons. Normative argumentation and qualitative probability. In *Qualitative and Quantitative Practical Reasoning*, pages 466–480, Berlin, Germany, 1997. Springer Verlag.

29. S. Parsons. On qualitative probability and order of magnitude reasoning. In *Proceedings of the 10th Florida Artificial Intelligence Research Symposium*, pages 198–203, St Petersburg, FL, 1997. Florida AI Research Society.

30. S. Parsons. *Qualitative approaches to reasoning under uncertainty*. MIT Press, Cambridge, MA, 1998.

31. S. Parsons and J. Fox. Argumentation and decision making: a position paper. In *Formal and Applied Practical Reasoning*, pages 705–709, Berlin, Germany, 1996. Springer Verlag.

32. J. Pearl. From conditional oughts to qualitative decision theory. In *Proceedings of the 9th Conference on Uncertainty in Artificial Intelligence*, pages 12–20, San Mateo, CA., 1993. Morgan Kaufmann.

33. J. L. Pollock. New foundations for practical reasoning. *Minds and Machines*, 2:113–144, 1992.

34. M. Pradhan, M. Henrion, G. Provan, B. del Favero, and K. Huang. The sensitivity of belief networks to imprecise probabilities: an experimental investigation. *Artificial Intelligence*, 85:363–397, 1996.

35. H. Raiffa. *Decision Analysis: Introductory Lectures on Choices under Uncertainty*. Addison-Wesley, Reading, MA, 1970.

36. A. Rao and M. P. Georgeff. Modelling rational agents within a BDI-architecture. In *Proceedings of the 2nd International Conference on Knowledge Representation and Reasoning*, pages 473–484, San Mateo, CA, 1991. Morgan Kaufmann.

37. G. Shafer. *A Mathematical Theory of Evidence*. Princeton University Press, Princeton, NJ, 1976.

38. Y. Shoham. Conditional utility, utility independence, and utility networks. In *Proceedings of the 13th Conference on Uncertainty in Artificial Intelligence*, pages 429–436, San Francisco, CA, 1997. Morgan Kaufmann.

39. E. H. Shortliffe. *Computer-Based Medical Consultations: MYCIN*. Elsevier, New York, NY, 1976.

40. Sek-Wah Tan and J. Pearl. Qualitative decision theory. In *Proceedings of the 12th National Conference on Artificial Intelligence*, pages 928–933, Menlo Park, CA, 1994. AAAI Press/MIT Press.

41. P. Taylor, J. Fox, and A. Todd-Pokropek. A model for integrating image processing into decision aids for diagnostic radiology. *Artificial Intelligence in Medicine*, 9:205–225, 1997.

42. S. Toulmin. *The uses of argument*. Cambridge University Press, Cambridge, UK., 1957.

43. R. T. Walton, C. Gierl, P. Yudkin, H. Mistry, M. P. Vessey, and J. Fox. Evaluation of computer support for prescribing (CAPSULE) using simulated cases. *British Medical Journal*, 315:791–794, 1997.

44. M. P. Wellman. *Formulation of tradeoffs in planning under uncertainty*. Pitman, London, UK, 1990.

45. M. P. Wellman and J. Doyle. Preferential semantics for goals. In *Proceedings of the 10th National Conference on Artificial Intelligence*, pages 698–703, Menlo Park, CA, 1991. AAAI Press/MIT Press.

46. N. Wilson. An order of magnitude calculus. In *Proceedings of the 11th Conference on Uncertainty in Artificial Intelligence*, pages 548–555, San Francisco, CA., 1995. Morgan Kaufman.

# Analysis of Multi-interpretable Ecological Monitoring Information

Frances Brazier, Joeri Engelfriet, Jan Treur

Vrije Universiteit Amsterdam
Department of Mathematics and Computer Science
Artificial Intelligence Group
De Boelelaan 1081, 1081 HV Amsterdam
Email: {frances, joeri, treur}@cs.vu.nl
URL: http://www.cs.vu.nl/~{frances,joeri,treur}

**Abstract**
In this paper logical techniques developed to formalize the analysis of multi-interpretable information, in particular belief set operators and selection operators, are applied to an ecological domain. A knowledge-based decision support system is described that determines the abiotic (chemical and physical) characteristics of a site on the basis of samples of plant species that are observed. The logical foundation of this system is described in terms of a belief set operator and a selection operator. Moreover, it is shown how the belief set operator that corresponds to the system can be represented by a normal default theory.

## 1. Introduction

In most real-life situations humans receive information that can be interpreted in many different ways. The context often determines the view with which this information is interpreted, but also other factors may be of influence. One domain in which multi-interpretable observations can be analysed using a technique based on the distinction of different views, is the domain of ecology.

Plants only grow in areas where conditions are appropriate. Knowledge of which set of factors is necessary for species to germinate and complete their life-cycle, has been acquired by experts over a large number of years. This knowledge of environmental preferences of plant species makes it possible to derive information about a terrain's abiotic (physical and chemical) characteristics on the basis of the plant species found. More specifically, experts are able to derive the abiotic conditions of the site studied in terms of acidity, nutrient value and moisture from the abiotic preferences of the species comprising the vegetation.

If knowledge on abiotic preferences of plant species is available, nature conservationists can use their knowledge of the plant species found in a specific terrain to determine the abiotic conditions. Often, however, nature conservationists responsible for terrains do not possess this detailed knowledge. An Environmental

Knowledge-based System, EKS, has been designed to support them in this decision making process. Once the abiotic conditions of a terrain have been determined, nature conservationists can then use this knowledge to manage the terrain; e.g., new measures can be derived to improve the quality of the site.

The specific domain of application in the current implementation is grasslands. The knowledge-based system, the development of which was funded by the organisations International Plant Technology Services (IPTS) and the State Forestry Department of the Dutch Ministry of Agriculture (Staatsbosbeheer), is based on knowledge acquired from experts in the fields of Plant Ecology, Eco-hydrology, and Soil Sciences. Acquiring consensus between experts on the meaning of individual plant species with respect to their specific abiotic conditions is one of the main aims of this project. The observations made in the field, a sample, can often be interpreted in different ways. To model this expert reasoning task, an approach based on belief set operators (introduced in [8]) is applied.

In this paper, the application domain is introduced in Section 2. In Section 3 the knowledge-based systems EKS is described. Section 4 introduces belief set operators and shows how the expert reasoning task can be formalized using these operators. In Section 5 the correspondence between the formalization and the system design is shown. Section 6 shows how the belief set operator describing EKS can be represented by a normal default theory. Finally, in Section 7 the reported results are discussed.

## 2. Domain of Application

Experts identify the current abiotic conditions in a terrain on the basis of plant species they encounter. The process of identification of abiotic conditions was analysed in cooperation with experts, resulting in the distinction of three tasks: (1) grouping the plant species that "belong together", (2) selecting the set of plant species experts consider most "defining", and (3) identifying the related abiotic conditions. These conditions are expressed as values for each of the abiotic factors: *acidity* (basic, neutral, slightly acid, fairly acid, acid), *nutrient value* (nutrient poor, fairly nutrient rich, nutrient rich, very nutrient rich) and *moisture* (very dry, fairly dry, fairly moist, very moist, fairly wet, very wet).

In a sample of plant species taken from an abiotic homogeneous site, a common set of abiotic conditions can be found that are shared by the plant species. A technique to determine the abiotic conditions in this case is described in Section 2.1. In practice, however, the samples often include groups of plant species that, according to the knowledge available, could not possibly grow under the same abiotic conditions. One cause could be that the knowledge about the abiotic conditions in which species can live is incomplete. Another cause could be that the sample has been taken from a heterogeneous site: a site where the abiotic conditions vary over space and time (for instance, on a site in transition between dry and wet soil). An expert needs to analyse and interpret the available information and can, for example, determine that a sub-set of the sample is most dominant. A method to determine which compatible groups of plant species can be distinguished within a sample is described in Section 2.2.

## 2.1.  Homogeneous  Sample:  Greatest  Common  Denominator

In a sample of plant species taken from a homogeneous site, at least one set of abiotic conditions can be found that is shared by all species on the site. An example of a sample of species that can all grow in a homogeneous site is used to illustrate a technique to find this set of common abiotic conditions. Examination of the plant species, depicted in Table 1, shows all possible values for each of the three abiotic factors, for each of the plant species. For example, the abiotic requirements of *Caltha palustris* L., are:
- very moist or fairly wet,
- basic, neutral or slightly acid,
- nutrient poor, fairly nutrient rich or nutrient rich terrain.

For the species *Poa trivialis* L. a terrain needs to be
- fairly moist, very moist or fairly wet,
- basic or neutral,
- nutrient rich or very nutrient rich.

If both species occur in a terrain, this implies that the terrain can only be:
- very moist or fairly wet,
- basic or neutral,
- nutrient rich.

| Species | vd | fd | fm | vm | fw | vw | bas | neu | sac | fac | ac | np | fnr | nr | vnr |
|---|---|---|---|---|---|---|---|---|---|---|---|---|---|---|---|
| | | | | Moisture | | | | Acidity | | | | | Nutrient Value | | |
| Angelica sylvestris | | | | x | x | | x | x | | | | | x | x | |
| Caltha palustris ssp palustris | | | | x | x | | x | x | x | | | x | x | x | |
| Carex acutiformis | | | | x | x | | x | x | | | | | x | x | |
| Carex acuta | | | | x | x | x | x | x | x | | | | x | x | x |
| Deschampsia caespitosa | | | x | x | x | | x | x | x | | | | x | x | x |
| Epilobium parviflorum | | | x | x | | | x | x | x | | | | x | x | |
| Equisetum palustre | | | x | x | x | x | x | x | x | | | x | x | x | |
| Galium palustre | | | | x | x | | x | x | x | | | x | x | x | x |
| Glyceria fluitans | | | | x | x | x | x | x | x | x | | | x | x | x |
| Juncus articulatus | | | | x | x | | x | x | x | | | x | x | x | x |
| Lathyrus pratensis | | | x | x | | | x | x | x | | | | x | x | |
| Myosotis palustris | | | | x | x | | x | x | x | | | x | x | x | |
| Phalaris arundinacea | | | x | x | x | x | x | x | | | | | x | x | |
| Phleum pratense ssp pratense | | | x | x | | | x | x | | | | | x | x | |
| Poa trivialis | | | x | x | x | | x | x | | | | | x | x | |
| Scirpus sylvaticus | | | | x | x | x | x | x | x | | | | x | x | |

Moisture (vd: very dry, fd: fairly dry, fm: fairly moist, vm: very moist, fw: fairly wet, vw: very wet),
Acidity (bas: basis, neu: neutral, sac: slightly acid, fac: fairly acid, ac: acid),
Nutrient value (np: nutrient poor, fnr: fairly nutrient rich, nr: nutrient rich, vnr: very nutrient rich)

**Table 1.    A  homogeneous  sample.**

Note that not only can the occurrence of a *single* species restrict the possible abiotic conditions of the terrain, but the occurrence of species *in combination* can restrict the possible abiotic conditions even further.

Analysis of the abiotic conditions for all plant species presented in Table 1 shows that only a restricted number of possibilities (but more than one) for the abiotic conditions can be found in which all of these plant species can abide. This *greatest common denominator* for the given plant species is defined by the following set of abiotic conditions:

- very moist
- basic or neutral
- nutrient rich

The combination of these plant species indicates that a terrain on which these plant species are found has to fulfill these conditions.

## 2.2. Inhomogeneous Sample: Maximal Indicative Subsets

In a sample taken from an inhomogeneous site, the sample does not have a common denominator of abiotic conditions. A real example sample is shown in Table 2, together with the possible values for the three abiotic factors for each plant species. Focusing on the acidity of a terrain shows that the plant species *Angelica sylvestris* L., for example, only grows on a basic or neutral terrain, whereas the species *Carex panicea* L., also found in the same sample, only grows on a slightly or fairly acid terrain. These two species, however, are in the same sample. One common set of possible values of the abiotic factors for all plant species can not be derived.

Further analysis of the abiotic factors of the plant species in the sample is required. Groups of plant species for which a set of shared abiotic conditions can be found are grouped together. These groups of plant species are homogeneous groups of plants as defined above in section 2.1. The largest possible homogeneous groups of plant species are called *maximal indicative subsets*.

These subsets are maximal with respect to compatibility of the plant species in the subset. In other words, all plant species in the sample that are compatible with the group of plant species in a maximal indicative subset (those plant species that can grow on a site with the same abiotic conditions), are in the subset. As shown in Table 3, in the example sample two maximal indicative sets of plant species can be distinguished. The *first maximal indicative subset* contains all plant species that can grow in

- very moist
- basic or neutral
- nutrient rich

environments. The *second maximal indicative subset* contains all plant species that can grow in

- very moist
- slightly acid
- fairly nutrient rich

environments.

| Species | Moisture | | | | | | Acidity | | | | | Nutrient Value | | | |
|---|---|---|---|---|---|---|---|---|---|---|---|---|---|---|---|
| | vd | fd | fm | vm | fw | vw | bas | neu | sac | fac | ac | np | fnr | nr | vnr |
| Angelica sylvestris | | | | x | x | | x | x | | | | | x | x | |
| Anthoxanthum odoratum | x | x | x | | | | | | x | x | | x | x | | |
| Caltha palustris ssp palustris | | | | x | x | | x | x | x | | | x | x | x | |
| Carex acutiformis | | | | x | x | | x | x | | | | | x | x | |
| Carex acuta | | | | x | x | x | x | x | x | | | | x | x | x |
| Carex nigra | | | x | x | x | | | | x | x | x | x | x | | |
| Carex panicea | | | x | x | x | | | | x | x | | x | x | | |
| Carex riparia | | | | x | x | x | x | x | | | | | | x | x |
| Cirsium oleraceum | | | | x | x | | x | x | | | | | x | x | |
| Cirsium palustre | | | x | | | | x | x | x | | | x | x | x | |
| Crepis paludosa | | x | x | x | | | x | x | x | | | | x | x | |
| Deschampsia caespitosa | | x | x | x | | | x | x | x | | | | x | x | x |
| Epilobium palustre | | x | x | x | | | | | x | | | x | x | | |
| Epilobium parviflorum | | x | x | | | | x | x | x | | | | x | x | |
| Equisetum palustre | | x | x | x | x | | x | x | x | | | x | x | x | |
| Filipendula ulmaria | | | x | | | | x | x | x | | | x | x | x | |
| Galium palustre | | | x | x | | | x | x | x | | | x | x | x | x |
| Glyceria fluitans | | | x | x | | x | x | x | x | x | | | x | x | x |
| Juncus articulatus | | | x | x | | | x | x | | | | x | x | x | x |
| Juncus conglomeratus | x | x | x | | | | | | x | x | | x | x | | |
| Lathyrus pratensis | | x | x | | | | x | x | x | | | | x | x | |
| Lotus uliginosus | | x | x | x | | | x | x | x | | | x | x | x | |
| Lychnis flos cuculi | | | x | x | | | x | x | x | | | | x | x | |
| Lysimachia vulgaris | | x | x | x | | | x | x | x | | | x | x | x | |
| Myosotis palustris | | | x | x | | | x | x | x | | | | x | x | x |
| Phalaris arundinacea | | x | x | x | x | | x | x | | | | | x | x | |
| Phleum pratense ssp pratense | | x | x | | | | x | x | | | | | x | x | |
| Poa trivialis | | x | x | x | | | x | x | | | | | x | x | |
| Scirpus sylvaticus | | | | x | x | x | x | x | x | | | | x | x | |

Moisture (vd: very dry, fd: fairly dry, fm: fairly moist, vm: very moist, fw: fairly wet, vw: very wet),
Acidity (bas: basis, neu: neutral, sac: slightly acid, fac: fairly acid, ac: acid),
Nutrient value (np: nutrient poor, fnr: fairly nutrient rich, nr: nutrient rich, vnr: very nutrient rich)

**Table 2.  An inhomogeneous sample.**

Note that the two maximal indicative subsets share a number of plants (the intersection of the two subsets). These plants have a relatively broad spectrum of environmental preferences. Note also that the conditions for the plant species that these two groups do not have in common are mutually exclusive with respect to acidity and (partially) nutrient value.

To decide which maximal indicative set is the most appropriate for a given site, additional knowledge is required. For example, in this case, the expert knows that the sample has been taken from a site that has a particular type of stratification (so-called rainwater lenses): two different layers of soil can be found on the same site. This explains the presence of the two abiotic indicative sets of plant species. Additional detailed knowledge on abiotic conditions for plant species can also be taken into account; e.g., knowledge on the optimal conditions for specific plant species.

| Species | Moisture | | | | | | Acidity | | | | | Nutrient Value | | | |
|---|---|---|---|---|---|---|---|---|---|---|---|---|---|---|---|
| | vd | fd | fm | vm | fw | vw | bas | neu | sac | fac | ac | np | fnr | nr | vnr |
| Angelica sylvestris | | | | x | x | | x | x | | | | | x | x | |
| Carex acutiformis | | | | x | x | | x | x | | | | | x | x | |
| Carex riparia | | | | x | x | x | x | x | | | | | | x | x |
| Cirsium oleraceum | | | | x | x | | x | x | | | | | x | x | |
| Phalaris arundinacea | | | x | x | x | x | x | x | | | | | | x | x |
| Phleum pratense ssp pratense | | | x | x | | | x | x | | | | | | x | x |
| Poa trivialis | | | x | x | x | | x | x | | | | | | x | x |
| Caltha palustris ssp palustris | | | | x | x | | x | x | x | | | x | x | x | |
| Carex acuta | | | | x | x | x | x | x | x | | | | x | x | x |
| Cirsium palustre | | | | x | | | x | x | x | | | x | x | x | |
| Crepis paludosa | | | x | x | x | | x | x | x | | | | x | x | |
| Deschampsia caespitosa | | | x | x | x | | x | x | x | | | | x | x | x |
| Epilobium parviflorum | | | x | x | | | x | x | x | | | | x | x | |
| Equisetum palustre | | | x | x | x | x | x | x | x | | | x | x | x | |
| Filipendula ulmaria | | | | x | | | x | x | x | | | x | x | x | |
| Galium palustre | | | | x | x | | x | x | x | | | x | x | x | x |
| Glyceria fluitans | | | | x | x | x | x | x | x | x | | x | x | x | x |
| Juncus articulatus | | | | x | x | | x | x | x | | | x | x | x | x |
| Lathyrus pratensis | | | x | x | | | x | x | x | | | | x | x | |
| Lotus uliginosus | | | x | x | x | | x | x | x | | | x | x | x | |
| Lychnis flos cuculi | | | | x | x | | x | x | x | | | | x | x | |
| Lysimachia vulgaris | | | x | x | x | | x | x | x | | | x | x | x | |
| Myosotis palustris | | | | x | x | | x | x | x | | | | x | x | x |
| Scirpus sylvaticus | | | | x | x | x | x | x | x | | | | x | x | |
| Anthoxanthum odoratum | x | x | x | | | | | x | x | | | x | x | | |
| Carex nigra | | x | x | x | | | | x | x | x | | x | x | | |
| Carex panicea | | x | x | x | | | | x | x | | | x | x | | |
| Epilobium palustre | | x | x | x | | | | x | | | | x | x | | |
| Juncus conglomeratus | x | x | x | | | | | x | x | | | x | x | | |

Moisture (vd: very dry, fd: fairly dry, fm: fairly moist, vm: very moist, fw: fairly wet, vw: very wet),
Acidity (bas: basis, neu: neutral, sac: slightly acid, fac: fairly acid, ac: acid),
Nutrient value (np: nutrient poor, fnr: fairly nutrient rich, nr: nutrient rich, vnr: very nutrient rich)

**Table 3. Maximal indicative subsets within an inhomogeneous sample.**

# 3.   The Decision Support System EKS

The above described expert knowledge on the determination of abiotic conditions on the basis of a terrain's vegetation, has been used to design a knowledge-based system to support ecologists in the upkeep of nature reserves. This knowledge-based system, the EKS system, has been modelled, specified and implemented within the compositional development method DESIRE (see e.g., [1], [4]).

## 3.1.   The Compositional Framework DESIRE

DESIRE is both a compositional development method and a modelling framework for the design and implementation of knowledge-based and multi-agent systems. A knowledge engineer is supported during all (iterative) phases of design: from initial conceptualisation to implementation, by the DESIRE development method supported by the dedicated software environment.

The development method focuses on the identification and specification of the following types of knowledge, the types of knowledge used to define a model:

(1) *process composition*
- identification of the *processes* or *tasks* involved at different levels of *process abstraction;*
- knowledge of task and role *delegation* between systems (human and/or automated): *task and role delegation;*
- knowledge of the information exchanged between processes: *information exchange;*
- knowledge of when and how processes are activated (in parallel or sequential, under which conditions): *task control;*

(2) *knowledge composition*
- identification of the types of *information* and *knowledge* used at different levels of knowledge abstraction;
- specification of the knowledge structures and the way in which they are composed;

(3) *relations between process composition and knowledge composition*
- Knowledge on which knowledge structures are used in which processes.

Initial knowledge analysis focuses on the acquisition of a shared task model: an intermediary agreed model shared by both the expert and the knowledge engineer, in which these five types of knowledge are made explicit (see [2], [3]). This knowledge is first identified at an abstract level, and refined during the further design process.

Tasks distinguished during conceptual design are modelled as components. Components can be primitive or complex: a component may encompass a number of other (either primitive or complex) components, or it may not. If not, the component is either a reasoning component with a knowledge base or a component with a so-called *alternative specification* (meaning that only its input and output are explicitly specified in the DESIRE modelling language, e.g., databases, OR-algorithms, neural networks, etc.). A knowledge-based system's behaviour as a whole is defined by the interaction between components, and between the system and its users. The DESIRE software environment consists of:

- a graphical editor to support conceptual and detailed design;
- an implementation generator that translates DESIRE specifications into executable
  code;
- an execution environment in which the translated code can be executed.

## 3.2.  Design of EKS

In Section 2, three tasks are distinguished: (1) grouping of plant species that "belong together", (2) selecting the set of plant species experts consider most "defining", and (3) identifying the related abiotic conditions.

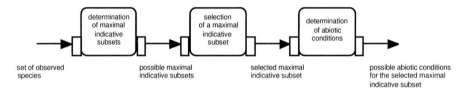

Figure 1.   The global design of EKS.

## Task Composition

These three tasks are modelled by three components as shown in Figure 1. The first task, the *determination of maximal indicative subsets*, entails analysis of the plant species in the sample and the corresponding abiotic conditions to determine maximal indicative subsets of plant species. The choice of the most defining subset is performed by the component *selection of a maximal indicative subset*. The third task, *determination of abiotic conditions*, is relatively simple, and includes the presentation of the abiotic conditions of a maximal indicative subset.

## Information Exchange

The initial information needed by the system to determine the abiotic conditions of a terrain is a list of observed plant species. This is the input for the first component. The maximal indicative sets of plant species derived in the first task are the input for the second task. The result of the selection process (the second task), one of the maximal indicative subsets, in turn, is input for the third task (determination of abiotic conditions). The final output consists of the possible abiotic conditions for the selected maximal indicative subset.

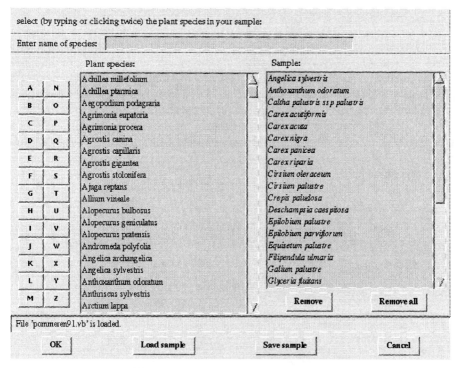

select (by typing or clicking twice) the plant species in your sample:

Enter name of species: [

| Plant species: | Sample: |

**Figure 2. Input window of EKS.**

## Task Activation
Task activation is straightforward. Completion of the first task results in activation of the second. Completion of the second task results in activation of the third. Completion of the third task results in completion of the entire task.

## Task Delegation
The first task and the third task are performed by the system. The second task is performed by the user.

## Knowledge Structures
The knowledge includes knowledge of plant species and the abiotic conditions in which they can abide, part of which is presented above in table format (see Tables 1 and 2). Each plant species has related values for each of the three abiotic factors. For reasons of efficiency, the first component is specified by an alternative specification.

The EKS-system has been developed using the DESIRE method and software environment. In addition, a graphical user interface has been designed specifically for EKS.

312

## 3.3.  User-System Interaction

Initially a user is presented with a screen with which he/she can enter the plant species found on a terrain, as shown in Figure 2. The system analyses this information, resulting in the two maximal indicative subsets of plant species. This information is presented to the user as shown in Figure 3. The overlap between the two maximal indicative subsets of plant species is presented on the screen as the list of *shared plant species*. The remaining plants are listed separately for each of the maximal indicative subsets as *abiotic indicative groups*. The user chooses which maximal subset is most appropriate. The final output of the system is a graphical presentation of the abiotic conditions for the terrain in question.

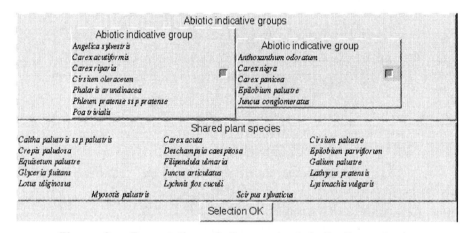

**Figure 3.    Presentation of the maximal indicative subsets.**

# 4. Formalization by a Belief Set Operator and a Selection Operator

In Section 2, three tasks are distinguished: determining groups of plants that belong together, selecting one of these groups, and then identifying its related abiotic conditions. The second task is performed by the user, and the last task is rather straightforward. As mentioned before, the first task is the most complex; it is formalized in this section. From an abstract point of view, this task can be seen as follows. The given observations together provide a partial view of the world (these observations are the plant species in the terrain). It is partial in the sense that it is not yet known which (group of) plants are most defining for the terrain. The first task consists of finding possible extensions of this partial view, by adding additional beliefs about which plants are defining (and, as said before, this can, in general, be done in multiple ways). Such forms of reasoning, in which a partial view on the world is extended to multiple (more informed) views, after which a selection from these can be made, have been formalized using belief set operators and selection operators in [8]. In this section these formalizations are related to the application at hand. To this purpose, a brief overview of the main ideas and concepts of [8] is presented.

A propositional language, $\mathbf{L}$, is assumed, together with its corresponding set of models, $\mathbf{Mod}$, and the standard (semantic) consequence relation $\vDash \subseteq \mathbf{Mod} \times \mathbf{L}$. A set of formulas which is closed under propositional consequence is called a *belief set*. A belief set can be seen as a possible set of beliefs of an agent with perfect (propositional) reasoning capabilities.

**Definition 4.1    (Belief set operator)**

a) A *belief set operator* $\mathbf{B}$ is a function $\mathbf{B} : \mathcal{P}(\mathbf{L}) \rightarrow \mathcal{P}(\mathcal{P}(\mathbf{L}))$ that assigns a set of belief sets to each set of initial facts.

b) A belief set operator $\mathbf{B}$ satisfies *inclusion* if for all $X \subseteq \mathbf{L}$ and all $T \in \mathbf{B}(X)$ it holds $X \subseteq T$. A belief set operator $\mathbf{B}$ satisfies *non-inclusiveness* if for all $X \subseteq \mathbf{L}$ and all $S, T \in \mathbf{B}(X)$, if $S \subseteq T$ then $S = T$.

The *kernel* $\mathbf{K_B} : \mathcal{P}(\mathbf{L}) \rightarrow \mathcal{P}(\mathbf{L})$ of $\mathbf{B}$ is defined by $\mathbf{K_B}(X) = \bigcap \mathbf{B}(X)$.

The first condition expresses conservativity: it means that a possible view on the world at least satisfies the given facts; the belief set operator defines a method of extending partial information (instead of, for instance, revising it). The condition of non-inclusiveness guarantees a relative maximality of the possible views. The kernel of a belief set operator yields the most certain conclusions given a set of initial facts, namely those which are in every possible view of the world. To give an example of a belief set operator, consider a set of default rules (the reader is referred to the next section for a definition of default logic). A set of initial facts, together with the default rules, gives rise to a number of extensions (which can be considered belief sets). An operator that assigns the corresponding set of extensions to each set of initial facts is a belief set operator. The kernel of this operator yields the sceptical (see e.g., [11]) conclusions.

Often, as is the case in the application, after a number of belief sets have been generated, the process will focus on (or make a commitment to) one (or possibly more) of the belief sets, because it seems the most promising, or interesting, possible view on the world. This selection process can be formalized by selection operators.

**Definition 4.2    (Selection operator and selective inference operation)**

a) A *selection   operator* $\mathbf{s}$ is a function $\mathbf{s} : \mathcal{P}(\mathcal{P}(\mathbf{L})) \rightarrow \mathcal{P}(\mathcal{P}(\mathbf{L}))$ that assigns to each set of belief sets a subset (for all $A \subseteq \mathcal{P}(\mathbf{L})$ it holds $\mathbf{s}(A) \subseteq A$) such that whenever $A \subseteq \mathcal{P}(\mathbf{L})$ is non-empty, $\mathbf{s}(A)$ is non-empty. A selection operator $\mathbf{s}$ is *single-valued* if for all non-empty $A$ the set $\mathbf{s}(A)$ contains exactly one element.

b) A *selective inference operation* for the belief set operator **B** is a function **C** : $\mathcal{P}(L) \rightarrow \mathcal{P}(L)$ that assigns a belief set to each set of facts, such that for all $X \subseteq L$ it holds **C(X)** ∈ **B(X)**

A formalization of (the first task of) the application described in this paper can be made using the notions defined above. The language **L** is the propositional language of which the atoms are the ground atoms defined by the following signature:

plant species names (**P**):  **achillea_millefolium,  achillea_ptarmica,  ....**
abiotic factors (**A**):  **moisture,  acidity,  nutrient_value**
values for each of the abiotic factors (**V**):

             **very_dry,  fairly_dry,  ......,**
             **basic,  neutral,  ......,**
             **nutrient_poor,  fairly_nutrient_rich,...  .**

Predicates:

      **occurs(P)**
      **is_negative_indication_for(P,  A,  V)**
      **has_value(A,  V)**
      **is_indicative(P)**

The constants **achillea_millefolium,  achillea_ptarmica,  ....**  represent the names of the plant species (see Figure 2). The abiotic factors are the three factors introduced in Section 2. The predicate **occurs(P)** refers to the presence of plant species **P** in the sample of the terrain (this is input to the reasoning process). The predicate **is_negative_indication_for(P, A, V)** expresses the fact that abiotic factor **A** does not have value **V**. The predicate **has_value(A,  V)** expresses the fact that factor **A** has value **V**, and **is_indicative(P)** the fact that **P** is regarded as an indicative species (giving evidence to the terrain having certain abiotic factors).

There is a set, **KB**, that consists of propositional formulae expressing knowledge (about the domain of determination of abiotic factors), which is of the following form:

• a (large) number of ground instances of:

   **is_negative_indication_for(P,  A,  V)**

These instances represent the experts' knowledge of which species may occur in terrains with certain abiotic factors.

• all ground instances of the generic rule

      **is_indicative(P)  ∧  is_negative_indication_for(P,  A,  V)**
                          →
              **¬ has_value(A,  V)**

This rule makes it possible to conclude that certain abiotic factors do not have a certain value. This derivation can be made if an indicative species has been found that does not (generally) occur in terrains for which the factor **A** has value **V**.

• statements expressing that for each abiotic attribute at least one value should apply

**has_value(moisture, very_dry)** ∨ **has_value(moisture, fairly_dry)** ∨ ...
**has_value(acidity, basic)** ∨ **has_value(acidity, neutral)** ∨ ...
**has_value(nutrient_value, nutrient_poor)** ∨
        **has_value(nutrient_value, fairly_nutrient_rich)** ∨ ...

For a given set of observed species **OBS**, i.e., input of the form
        { occurs(p) | p ∈ **OBS** }
the set
        X = KB ∪ { is_indicative(p) | p ∈ **OBS** }
may be inconsistent. That is, it may be inconsistent to assume that all observed species are indicative for the terrain. This may occur if there is an abiotic factor $A_0$ such that for all of its possible values **V**, a species **P** is observed that negatively indicates this value (which means we have both **is_indicative(P)** and **is_negative_indication_for(P, $A_0$, V)**). With the generic rule, the conclusion ¬ **has_value($A_0$, V)** is drawn for all possible values **V** of $A_0$. But this is inconsistent with the statement **has_value($A_0$, $V_0$)** ∨ **has_value($A_0$, $V_1$)** ∨ ... which is in **KB**. However, as explained earlier, the set of maximal indicative subsets containing **KB** may be considered. This is defined as follows:

**Definition 4.3    (Maximal indicative subset)**
    Let **OBS** ⊆ **P** be a given set of species
    a)  The set of species **S** ⊆ **P** is an *indicative set of species* if the theory
        KB ∪ {is_indicative(p) | p ∈ S}
    is consistent.
    b)  The set **S** ⊆ **OBS** is a *maximal indicative subset of* **OBS** if it is an indicative set of species and for each indicative set of species **T** with
    S ⊆ T ⊆ **OBS** it holds S = T.
    The *set of maximal indicative subsets* of **OBS** is denoted by **maxind(OBS)** .

Note that if **OBS** is an indicative set of species itself, there is only one maximal indicative subset of **OBS**, namely **OBS** itself.
    Based on these notions the following belief set operator can be defined.

**Definition 4.4    (Belief set operator for the application domain)**
    For a set **X** ⊆ **L**, define the *set of observations implied by* **X** by
        OBS(X) = {p | occurs(p) ∈ Cn(X)}.
    The *belief set operator* $B_{maxind}$ is defined by
        $B_{maxind}$ (X) = { Cn(X ∪ KB ∪ {is_indicative(p) | p ∈ S}) |
                                        S ∈ maxind(OBS(X)) }
    for each **X** ⊆ **L**.

Actually, here the interesting sets **X** are the sets of the form {p | **occurs(p)** ∈ **OBS**} for some set of species **OBS** ⊆ **P**.

The operator $\mathbf{B_{maxind}}$ satisfies a number of properties of well-behavedness.

**Proposition 4.5**

The belief set operator $\mathbf{B_{maxind}}$ satisfies inclusion and non-inclusiveness.

In [8], some further conditions of well-behavedness for belief set operators are introduced (generalising corresponding properties of inference operations), a number of which are listed below.

**Definition 4.6    (Properties of belief set operators)**

a) Let $\mathcal{A}, \mathcal{B}$ be sets of belief sets. The set $\mathcal{B}$ *contains more information than* $\mathcal{A}$, denoted $\mathcal{A} \leq \mathcal{B}$, if for all $T \in \mathcal{B}$ there exists $S \in \mathcal{A}$ such that $S \subseteq T$.

b) Let **B** be a belief set operator.

    1. **B** satisfies *belief monotony* if for all $X, Y \subseteq L$:
$$X \subseteq Y \Rightarrow B(X) \leq B(Y)$$

    2. **B** satisfies *weak belief monotony* if for all $X, Y \subseteq L$:
$$X \subseteq Y \subseteq K_B(X) \Rightarrow B(X) \leq B(Y)$$

    3. **B** satisfies *belief transitivity* if for all $X, Y, T \subseteq L$:
$$T \in B(X) \ \& \ X \subseteq Y \subseteq T \Rightarrow K_B(Y) \subseteq T$$

    4. **B** satisfies *belief cut* if for all $X, Y \subseteq L$:
$$X \subseteq Y \subseteq K_B(X) \Rightarrow B(Y) \leq B(X)$$

Apart from belief monotony (which should not be expected), our belief set operator is well-behaved on input sets not containing the predicates **is_negative_indication_for**, **has_value**, and **is_indicative**. The restriction on the input sets is not severe: the idea is that the input of $\mathbf{B_{maxind}}$ consists of observed plant species (i.e., sentences using the **occurs** predicate). The knowledge about abiotic factors, their values and which plant species negatively indicate a value for a factor, is contained in the definition of $\mathbf{B_{maxind}}$.

**Theorem 4.7**

The belief set operator $\mathbf{B_{maxind}}$ satisfies weak belief monotony, belief transitivity and belief cut when the input sets are restricted to those only containing the predicate **occurs**. It does not satisfy belief monotony.

**Proof**

Abbreviate $\mathbf{B_{maxind}}$ to **B**. Starting with belief monotony, consider a list of just two species, **p1** and **p2** (for simplicity), and suppose **KB** contains information which prevents **p1** and **p2** of both being indicative at the same time. This happens if there is an abiotic factor, say moisture, such that **p1** is a negative indication for a very dry terrain, and **p2** is a negative indication for all other values of moisture. Suppose

    **X** = { **occurs(p1)** },
    **Y** = { **occurs(p1), occurs(p2)** }.

Then $\mathbf{B(X)}$ contains one element (in which $\mathbf{p1}$ is indicative), and $\mathbf{B(Y)}$ contains two elements, one in which only $\mathbf{p1}$ is indicative, and one in which only $\mathbf{p2}$ is indicative. For this latter element there is no smaller set in $\mathbf{B(X)}$. Therefore, belief monotony does not hold.

Now suppose $\mathbf{X \subseteq Y \subseteq K_B(X)}$. Let $\mathbf{T \in B(X)}$, then

$$\mathbf{T = Cn(X \cup KB \cup \{is\_indicative(p) \mid p \in M\})}$$

for some $\mathbf{M \in maxind(OBS(X))}$ and $\mathbf{Y \subseteq T}$ (since $\mathbf{Y \subseteq K_B(X)}$). But as $\mathbf{X}$ and $\mathbf{Y}$ contain only the predicate $\mathbf{occurs}$ which is not present in $\mathbf{KB}$ or in $\{is\_indicative(p) \mid p \in M\}$, it must be the case that $\mathbf{Cn(Y) \subseteq Cn(X)}$, so that $\mathbf{Cn(X) = Cn(Y)}$. This implies that $\mathbf{B(X) = B(Y)}$, proving both weak belief monotony and belief cut.

If $\mathbf{T \in B(X) \& X \subseteq Y \subseteq T}$, then the same argument shows that $\mathbf{B(X) = B(Y)}$, from which immediately follows that $\mathbf{K_B(Y) = K_B(X) \subseteq T}$. This proves belief transitivity. ∎

The following proposition covers the case of an observed set of species $\mathbf{OBS}$ which has a unique interpretation:

**Proposition 4.8**

For each subset of species $\mathbf{OBS \subseteq P}$ the following are equivalent:

(i)     $\mathbf{B_{maxind}}(\{p \mid occurs(p) \in OBS\})$ contains just one element.

(ii)    the set $\mathbf{OBS}$ is an indicative set of species.

If these (equivalent) conditions are satisfied, all observed species are indicative, and the user does not need to do selection. The possible values of the abiotic factors are contained in $\mathbf{B_{maxind}}(\{p \mid occurs(p) \in OBS\})$.

If $\mathbf{B_{maxind}}(\{p \mid occurs(p) \in OBS\})$ contains more than one element, the user must select one. But even before this selection process, conclusions can be drawn: the kernel of the $\mathbf{B_{maxind}}$ operator contains the most certain conclusions, so $\mathbf{K_{B_{maxind}}}(\{p \mid occurs(p) \in OBS\})$ may be inspected. For instance, there may be two possible views in $\mathbf{B_{maxind}}(\{p \mid occurs(p) \in OBS\})$ as species have been observed which only grow in dry terrains, and other species have been observed which only grow in moist terrains. However, all of these species may indicate that the terrain is not acid, and this conclusion will be in $\mathbf{K_{B_{maxind}}}(\{p \mid occurs(p) \in OBS\})$. If acidity is all one is interested in, there is no need for selection. If one is interested also in the moistness, this selection has to take place. If one is interested in the species which are in both maximal indicative sets, one can either examine $\mathbf{K_{B_{maxind}}}(\{p \mid occurs(p) \in OBS\})$, or the intersection of the maximal indicative sets:

$$\mathbf{K_{B_{maxind}}}(X) \cap \{ is\_indicative(p) \mid p \in P \} =$$

$$\{ is\_indicative(p) \mid p \in \bigcap maxind(OBS(X)) \}.$$

So, the kernel contains the atoms $is\_indicative(p)$ precisely for $p$ in the set of shared plant species (see Figure 3, lower part), which is the intersection of the maximal indicative subsets (the two rectangles in Table 3).

# 5. Correspondence Between the Formalization and the System

The correspondence between the formalization of the expert reasoning task and the interactive knowledge-based system EKS that models the task is shown in Figure 4. The first component of the system, determination_of_maximal_indicative_subsets, is formalized by the belief set operator $B_{maxind}$ defined in Section 4 (depicted by the grey arrow at the left hand side in Figure 4). The component selection_of_a_maximal_indicative_subset (which models the selection process by the user) is formalized by a single-valued selection function $s_{user}$ (depicted by the grey arrow at the right hand side in Figure 4).

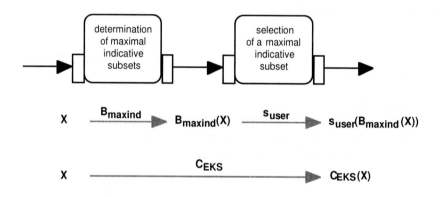

**Figure 4.** Correspondence between the formalization and the system

The composition $C_{EKS}$ of $B_{maxind}$ and $s_{user}$ defined by

$$C_{EKS}(X) = s_{user}(B_{maxind}(X)) \qquad \text{for } X \subseteq L$$

is a non-monotonic inference operation, which is selective for $B_{maxind}$ (as described in Definition 4.2b). This inference operation formalizes the reasoning of the system in interaction with the user as a whole (depicted by the grey arrow at the bottom of Figure 4). Note that from the two functions of which this overall function is composed, one is fixed and defined by the system itself (i.e., $B_{maxind}$), whereas the other can be changed dynamically, depending on the user (i.e., $s_{user}$).

# 6. Representation in Default Logic

The previous section showed how the determination of the maximal indicative sets can be formalized mathematically through the notion of a belief set operator. A specification of this belief set operator in a (well-known) logical formalism would allow for the use of proof mechanisms for this logic to be used in the application, but it would also mean that known results about this logic can be applied to this situation. In [9] and [12] default logic is used as a specification language for families of belief sets. These results can be applied to the formalization of the previous section.

To start, a brief overview of Reiter's default logic [13] is provided. Although Reiter's definitions are stated for any first-order language, here they are restricted to propositional logic, as is commonly done. So let us again assume a propositional language **L**. A *default rule* (or *default*) is an expression of the form $(\alpha : \beta_1, ..., \beta_n) / \gamma$ where $\alpha, \beta_1, ..., \beta_n$ and $\gamma$ are propositional formulae. Intuitively such a default rule means: if $\alpha$ is believed and it is not inconsistent to assume $\beta_1$ through $\beta_n$, then assume $\gamma$. A *default theory* $\Delta$ is then a pair $< \mathbf{W}, \mathbf{D} >$ with **W** a set of sentences (the *axioms* of $\Delta$) and **D** a set of default rules. The default rules are used to extend the axioms to a (larger) set of formulas, called an *extension*. The following definition of the notion of extension is slightly different but equivalent to Reiter's original definition.

## Definition 6.1 (Reiter extension)

Let $\Delta = < \mathbf{W}, \mathbf{D} >$ be a default theory. A set of sentences **E** is called a *Reiter extension* of $\Delta$ if the following condition is satisfied:

$$\mathbf{E} = \bigcup_{i=0}^{\infty} \mathbf{E}_i$$

where
$$\mathbf{E}_0 = Cn(\mathbf{W}),$$
and for all $i \geq 0$
$$\mathbf{E}_{i+1} = Cn(\mathbf{E}_i \cup \{ \omega \mid (\alpha : \beta_1,...,\beta_n) / \omega \in \mathbf{D}, \alpha \in \mathbf{E}_i \text{ and } \neg\beta_1 \notin \mathbf{E}, ..., \neg\beta_n \notin \mathbf{E} \})$$

The *set of Reiter extensions* of $\Delta$ is denoted by $Ext(\Delta)$.

Extensions of a default theory are closed under propositional provability, so $Ext(\Delta)$ is a family of belief sets. In a sense, this family is represented (or specified) by $\Delta$. For an arbitrary family of belief sets, the question can be posed whether it can be represented by a default theory.

## Definition 6.2 (Representability of a family of belief sets)

Let $\Delta = < \mathbf{W}, \mathbf{D} >$ be a default theory. A family of belief sets **F** is *representable by* $\Delta$ if $Ext(\Delta) = \mathbf{F}$. The family **F** is called *representable by a default theory* if there exists such a default theory.

In [12] the following theorem was proven (see Corollary 5.2):

## Theorem 6.3

A family **F** of theories is representable by a normal default theory if and only if $\mathbf{F} = \{\mathbf{L}\}$ or there is a consistent set of formulas **W** and a set of formulas **C** such that
$$\mathbf{F} = \{ Cn(\mathbf{W} \cup \Phi) \mid \Phi \text{ is a maximal subset of } \mathbf{C} \text{ consistent with } \mathbf{W} \}$$

In [9] the question is posed whether a belief set operator can be represented by a set of defaults. Below, the definitions in that paper are slightly generalised to deal with a restricted language as the domain of a belief set operator. Recall that **L** is the propositional language.

**Definition 6.4 (Representability of a belief set operator)**
Let $\Delta = <$ **W, D** $>$ be a default theory, and **L'** $\subseteq$ **L**. A belief set operator **B** is *representable by* $\Delta$ *for* **L'**, if for all $X \subseteq$ **L'** it holds that **B(X)** = **Ext(**$<$ **W** $\cup$ **X, D** $>$**)**. The operator **B** is called *representable for* **L'** *by a default theory* if there exists such a default theory.

Consider the family of belief sets $B_{maxind}(X)$ where **X** only consists of observations. Then Theorem 6.3 can be applied to $B_{maxind}(X)$ by setting:

> **W** = **X** $\cup$ **KB**
> **C** = { is_indicative(p) | p $\in$ OBS(X)}

Therefore the theorem implies that the belief sets of $B_{maxind}(X)$ can be described by a normal default theory. This normal default theory can actually be found by defining the set of defaults **D**:
> (occurs(p) : is_indicative(p)) / is_indicative(p)      for all species **p** in **P**.

This set of defaults is independent of **X**, so $B_{maxind}$ is representable. Let **L'** consist of all formulas of **L** which contain only the **occurs** predicate.

**Theorem 6.5**
The belief set operator $B_{maxind}$ is representable for **L'** by the default theory $<$ **KB, D** $>$.

**Proof**
Let **X** be a set of formulas containing only the **occurs** predicate. Let **X** $\cup$ **KB** be consistent (if it is not, verification is straightforward and omitted). The extensions of $<$ **KB** $\cup$ **X, D** $>$ are sets of the form **Cn(KB** $\cup$ **X** $\cup$ **S)**, where **S** is a subset of { is_indicative(p) | occurs(p) $\in$ Cn(X) }, which is maximal such that **Cn(KB** $\cup$ **X** $\cup$ **S)** is consistent. This is proved below. The sets **Cn(KB** $\cup$ **X** $\cup$ **S)** with **S** as above together comprise $B_{maxind}(X)$.
First of all, let **S** be such a maximal set, and let **E** = **Cn(KB** $\cup$ **X** $\cup$ **S)**. Then if the $E_i$ are defined as in Definition 5.1, the following holds:

$E_0$ = Cn(KB $\cup$ X),
$E_1$ = Cn($E_0 \cup$ { is_indicative(p) | occurs(p) $\in E_0$, $\neg$ is_indicative(p) $\notin$ E } )

As $E_1$ does not contain more instances of the **occurs** predicate than $E_0$ (this follows from the fact that **X** contains only the **occurs** predicate, whereas **KB** does not), $E_i = E_1$ for all $i > 1$. The claim is that
> { is_indicative(p) | occurs(p) $\in E_0$, $\neg$ is_indicative(p) $\notin$ E } = S.

Suppose **occurs(p)** $\in$ **E$_0$** and $\neg$ **is_indicative(p)** $\notin$ **E**. Then **occurs(p)** is in **Cn(X)** and **Cn(KB** $\cup$ **X** $\cup$ **S** $\cup$ { **is_indicative(p)** } ) is consistent. But as **S** was maximal with respect to these properties, **is_indicative(p)** $\in$ **S**. On the other hand, if **is_indicative(p)** $\in$ **S**, then **occurs(p)** $\in$ **E$_0$** and $\neg$ **is_indicative(p)** $\notin$ **E** (as **E** = **Cn(KB** $\cup$ **X** $\cup$ **S)** is consistent).

Now let **E** be an extension of < **KB** $\cup$ **X, D** >, then it is of the form **Cn(KB** $\cup$ **X** $\cup$ **S)**, where **S** contains (only) formulas of the form **is_indicative(p)**. Examination of **KB** (and the restriction on **X**), shows that only if **occurs(p)** $\in$ **Cn(X)** is **is_indicative(p)** $\in$ **E**. As extensions are always consistent (if each rule has a justification and the axioms are consistent), **Cn(KB** $\cup$ **X** $\cup$ **S)** must be consistent. Suppose there exists a **T** $\supset$ **S** (strict inclusion) respecting the conditions, then there must be a default rule **occurs(p) : is_indicative(p) / is_indicative(p)**, with **occurs(p)** $\in$ **Cn(X)** $\subseteq$ **E** and **Cn(KB** $\cup$ **X** $\cup$ **S** $\cup$ { **is_indicative(p)** } ) consistent, implying that $\neg$ **is_indicative(p)** $\notin$ **E**. But that means there is an applicable default rule for which the conclusion is not in **E**, contradicting the assumption that **E** is an extension. Therefore **S** must be maximal. ∎

The original formalization of the application in terms of the belief set operator **B$_{maxind}$** led to a rather direct implementation based on its definition (Definition 4.4) in the system; see Section 5. The results of the current section indicate that alternatively a theorem prover for default logic (or, rather, a program computing extensions of default theories) could be used. A highly optimised theorem prover for default logic obviates the need to optimise this part of the system ourselves. This is the subject of current work on the system.

# 7. Discussion

The outcomes of the work reported in this paper can be discussed at two levels: the level of the specific application domain and system, and at the more generic level of the logical techniques that were used.

## 7.1. Domain of Application and EKS

The multi-interpretability of samples of plant species has proven to be a central issue in this domain of application. Given the assumption that samples are always correct (the plant species named are indeed the plant species encountered), and that samples are only taken from sites which are homogeneous, the only reason for conflicting indicative information is that the specific domain knowledge on which conclusions are based is incorrect or incomplete. During the design of EKS this specific domain knowledge was continual subject of discussion between experts. The knowledge currently implemented in EKS is the result of consensus between experts, and is no longer a likely reason for conflicting indicative information.

The lack of homogeneity of a terrain is the cause of most conflicts, requiring additional expert knowledge to understand the nature of the inhomogeneity. The reason for the lack of homogeneity can, for example, be vertical stratification, as in the inhomogeneous example discussed earlier. Another possibility is the development of a terrain over time: what has and has not been done to a terrain can influence its vegetation and transitions in vegetation. Inhomogeneous terrains are more common than initially supposed: multi-interpretable samples are not the exception, but the rule. The way in which experts analyse samples from inhomogeneous terrains was at first unclear. A first model determined the, in some sense 'average', conditions for the species in the sample. This model, although originally agreed by the experts involved to be an acceptable model, did not work: experts found it difficult to interpret the outcome of the analyses. The second model displayed the ranges of conditions encountered as a kind of summary of results. However, this model was problematic for two reasons: (1) It was unclear to the user whether the ranges of conditions displayed were meant to be possible for all species or only for subsets (the difference between an *or* interpretation of a range and an *and* interpretation), (2) The different values in the ranges could not be traced back to the species on which they are based. As a result of experiencing these first two experimental models, the experts agreed that the different views of a sample were essential to the analysis of the plant species observed. EKS identifies these views and presents these views to the user. Which view is (or which views are) most appropriate requires additional heuristic (strategic) knowledge. The selection of a view is currently performed by the user of the system. Future research will focus on the acquisition of this knowledge to be able to support users in the selection process.

## 7.2. The Logical Techniques Used

The idea that information about the world can often be interpreted in different and conflicting manners was a central theme in the research reported in [14], [8]. Using techniques to formalize non-monotonic reasoning, such as default logic, often different (and often conflicting) possible outcomes of a reasoning process are obtained. In the area of research on non-monotonic reasoning, in general this is considered to be disturbing (e.g., it is called the multiple extension *problem*). To come to one set of conclusions, in the literature often the non-monotonic inference operation defined by the intersection of all possible outcomes is taken (sceptical approach), or sometimes the union of all possible outcomes (credulous approach). (The original paper on default logic, [13], however, proposed that a choice should be made for one outcome, using some mechanism outside default logic itself.)

For a particular domain such as the ecological domain addressed in this paper, both approaches are unsatisfactory: the sceptical approach often does not lead to any possible conclusions on the abiotic conditions, whereas the credulous approach often leads to inconsistent information. For reasons like these, in [14], [8] the multiple outcomes of a non-monotonic reasoning process are not considered to be a problem, but are instead exploited as a useful feature that can provide an adequate formalization of the multi-interpretability often present in real-life information. In [14] this feature is expressed by adding as an extra parameter a selection function to a default theory. In [6] and [7] a similar approach is developed, based on priority orderings between defaults. In [8] the notion of belief set operator is introduced to formalize the multiple outcomes of a non-monotonic reasoning process, and a selection operator to make a choice between the different options.

For the application domain discussed here the latter approach is more suitable, because in this approach first all alternative interpretations are generated, and the selection is made afterwards. In the approaches of [14], [6], and [7] the reasoning process itself is controlled by the selection knowledge in such a manner that only one outcome is generated, and other options remain invisible. Such strategic knowledge is not yet available. However, in the future of this project such strategic knowledge may be acquired so that not all possible options need to be generated. In that case approaches as described in [14], [6], or [7] might become useful. Another issue for future research is to characterize the domains in which the approach discussed in this paper for the ecological domain can be applied, thus generalizing the method.

## Acknowledgements

Within the EKS-project a number of persons have contributed their expertise: Frank Cornelissen, Edgar Vonk (scientific programmers); Christine Bel, Rineke Verbrugge (for parts of the analysis of the domain); Bert Hennipman and Frits van Beusekom (domain experts from IPTS); Piet Schipper, and Wim Zeeman (domain experts from Staatsbosbeheer).

## References

[1]  F.M.T. Brazier, B. Dunin-Keplicz, N.R. Jennings, and J. Treur, "Formal Specification of Multi-Agent Systems: a real-world case", in: V. Lesser (ed.), *Proc. of the First International Conference on Multi-Agent Systems, ICMAS'95*, MIT Press, Cambridge, MA, pp. 25-32. Extended version in: *International Journal of Cooperative Information Systems*, M. Huhns, M. Singh, (eds.), special issue on Formal Methods in Cooperative Information Systems: Multi-Agent Systems, vol. 6, 1997, pp. 67-94.

[2]  F.M.T. Brazier, J. Treur, and N.J.E. Wijngaards, "The Acquisition of a Shared Task Model", in: N. Shadbolt, K. O'Hara, G. Schreiber (eds.), *Advances in Knowledge Acquisition, Proc. 9th European Knowledge Acquisition Workshop, EKAW'96*, Lecture Notes in Artificial Intelligence, vol. 1076, Springer Verlag, pp. 278-289.

[3]  F.M.T. Brazier, J. Treur, and N.J.E. Wijngaards, "Modelling Interaction with Experts: the Role of a Shared Task Model", in: W. Wahlster (ed.), *Proc. European Conference on AI, ECAI'96*, John Wiley and Sons, 1996, pp. 241-245.

[4]  F.M.T. Brazier, J. Treur, N.J.E. Wijngaards, and M. Willems, "Formal Specification of Hierarchically (De)Composed Tasks", in: B.R. Gaines, M.A. Musen (eds.), *Proc. of the 9th Banff Knowledge Acquisition for Knowledge-*

*based Systems workshop, KAW'95*, Calgary: SRDG Publications, Department of Computer Science, University of Calgary, 1995, pp. 25/1-15/20.

[5] P. Besnard, *An Introduction to Default Logic*, Springer-Verlag, 1989.

[6] G. Brewka, "Adding Priorities and Specificity to Default Logic", in: C. MacNish, D. Pearce, L.M. Pereira (eds.), *Logics in Artificial Intelligence, Proceedings of the JELIA-94*, Lecture Notes in Artificial Intelligence, vol. 838, Springer-Verlag, 1994, pp. 247-260.

[7] G. Brewka, "Reasoning about Priorities in Default Logic", in: *Proceedings of the AAAI-94*, 1994.

[8] J. Engelfriet, H. Herre and J. Treur, "Nonmonotonic Reasoning with Multiple Belief Sets", in: D.M. Gabbay, H.J. Ohlbach (eds.), *Practical Reasoning, Proceedings FAPR'96*, Lecture Notes in Artificial Intelligence, vol. 1085, Springer-Verlag, 1996, pp. 331-344.

[9] J. Engelfriet, V.W. Marek, J. Treur and M. Truszczynski, "Infinitary Default Logic for Specification of Nonmonotonic Reasoning", in: J.J. Alferes, L.M. Pereira, E. Orlowska (eds.), *Logics in Artificial Intelligence, Proceedings of the Fourth European Workshop on Logics in AI, JELIA'96*, Lecture Notes in Artificial Intelligence, vol. 1126, Springer-Verlag, 1996, pp. 224-236.

[10] D. Makinson, "General Patterns in Nonmonotonic Reasoning", in: D.M. Gabbay, C.J. Hogger, J.A. Robinson (eds.), *Handbook of Logic in Artificial Intelligence and Logic Programming, Vol. 3*, Oxford Science Publications, 1994, pp. 35-110.

[11] V.W. Marek and M. Truszczynski, *Nonmonotonic logics; context-dependent reasoning*, Springer-Verlag, 1993.

[12] V.W. Marek, J. Treur and M. Truszczynski, "Representation Theory for Default Logic", to appear in *Annals of Mathematics and Artificial Intelligence*, 1997.

[13] R. Reiter, "A Logic for Default Reasoning", *Artificial Intelligence* 13, 1980, pp. 81-132.

[14] Y.-H. Tan, J. Treur, "Constructive Default Logic and the Control of Defeasible Reasoning", in: B. Neumann (ed.), *Proc. of the European Conference on Artificial Intelligence, ECAI'92*, John Wiley and Sons, 1992, pp. 299-303.

# A Local Handling of Inconsistent Knowledge and Default Bases

Salem BENFERHAT - Laurent GARCIA

IRIT, Université Paul Sabatier, 118, route de Narbonne
31062 TOULOUSE Cedex - France
email: {benferhat, garcia}@irit.fr

**Abstract:** This paper contains two parts: we first investigate the idea of reasoning, in a "local" way, with prioritized and possibly inconsistent knowledge bases. Priorities are not given globally between all the beliefs in the knowledge base, but locally within each minimal set of pieces of information responsible for inconsistencies. This local stratification offers more flexibility for representing priorities between beliefs. When this stratification is available, we show that the task of coping with inconsistency is greatly simplified, since it determines what beliefs must be removed in order to restore consistency in the knowledge base. Three local approaches are developed in this paper. The second part of the paper applies one of these three approaches to default reasoning. Our proposal for defining the specificity relation inside conflicts allows us to infer plausible conclusions which cannot be obtained if a global stratification is used. In each part, we provide a comparative study with existing inconsistency-handling approaches and with various default reasoning systems, respectively.

## 1. Introduction

An important problem in the management of knowledge-based systems is the handling of inconsistency. Inconsistency may be present for mainly three reasons:
- The knowledge base includes default rules (e.g., "birds fly", "penguins are birds", "penguins do not fly") and facts (e.g., "Tweety is a bird") and later a new information is received (e.g., Tweety is a penguin") which contradicts a plausible conclusion which could be previously derived from the knowledge base;
- In model-based diagnosis, where a knowledge base contains a description of the normal behavior of a system, together with observations made on this system. Failure detection occurs when observations conflict with the normal functioning mode of the system and the hypothesis that the components of the system are working well; this leads to diagnose what component(s) fail(s);
- Several consistent knowledge bases pertaining to the same domain, but coming from n different sources of information, are available. For instance, each source is a reliable specialist in some aspect of the concerned domain but is less reliable on other aspects. A straightforward way of building a global base $\Sigma$ is to concatenate the knowledge bases $\Sigma_i$ provided by each source. Even if $\Sigma_i$ is consistent, it is unlikely that $\Sigma_1 \cup \Sigma_2 \cup ... \cup \Sigma_n$ will be consistent also.

Gabbay and Hunter [25] claim that inconsistencies are unavoidable in the real-world and may be useful if its presence triggers suitable actions that cope with it. They give the example of overbooking in airline booking systems.

There are two attitudes with respect to inconsistent knowledge. One is to revise the knowledge base and restore its consistency. The other is to accept inconsistency and to cope with it.

The first approach, called coherence theory, can be described in two steps: ① give up some formulas of the knowledge base in order to restore its consistency, the result of this operation is one or several consistent sub-bases of the knowledge base, and ② apply classical entailment to these consistent sub-bases to deduce plausible conclusions from the knowledge base. Examples of coherence approaches which select one consistent sub-base are the possibilistic logic approach [22], Nebel's linear ordering [33], and Williams' approach [48]. Examples of approaches which use several consistent sub-bases are Rescher's notion of acceptable sub-bases [43], Brewka's preferred sub-theories [9], the complete revision function [35] and the lexicographical approach [3, 29]. Two criteria should be considered when building a coherence-based approach: the complexity of calculating the plausible conclusions and the soundness of the set of inferred conclusions. The soundness aspect depends on the considered application, and roughly speaking it means that the coherence-based approach should neither be cautious (i.e., expected conclusion should be derived), nor adventurous (i.e., unwanted conclusions should be blocked). When focusing on implementation, selecting one consistent sub-base can be very interesting (with computational complexity close to that of classical logic), while selecting several maximal consistent sub-bases is, in general, computationally very difficult (see [34, 13] for a discussion of complexity results). However, when only one consistent sub-base is systematically selected then the approach, in general, is either cautious or adventurous. The adventurous aspect is often due to the arbitrary choice of the selected consistent sub-base, while the cautiousness is due to the fact that the selected consistent sub-base is not maximal. We will illustrate this last point of view in Section 3.

The second attitude with respect to inconsistency needs a step beyond classical logic, since the presence of inconsistency enables anything to be entailed. Paraconsistent logics [15, 16] and argued systems [46, 4, 12, 23] are examples of such approaches. The idea in argued systems is to construct arguments (i.e. sets of beliefs in favour of a conclusion) and to choose the more preferred. A conclusion is derived if one of the arguments which supports this conclusion can be defended against all the arguments for its opposite conclusion.

The coherence-based approach for dealing with inconsistency may be natural when handling exceptions in default knowledge bases. For example, from a knowledge base which includes the four default rules ("birds fly", "birds have legs", "penguins are birds" and "penguins do not fly") and a fact ("Tweety is a penguin bird") which contradicts (in the sense of classical logic) the default base, it seems more intuitively reasonable to inhibit the rule "birds fly" than "penguins do not fly" to restore the consistency. Moreover, the rule "birds have legs" is not involved in an inconsistency and should be considered as useful and has to be kept. Restoring consistency also makes sense in model-based diagnosis, since it comes down to finding the reasons for a failure. In the case of multiple sources, restoring consistency looks debatable, since the goal of retaining all available information is quite legitimate in this case.

This paper is primarily devoted to the treatment of inconsistency caused by the use of default rules with exceptions rather than by the use of multiple sources of information. The next section gives the background needed for reading this paper. Section 3 investigates three coherence-based approaches for reasoning, in a "local" way, under inconsistency in knowledge bases. The idea is that when an inconsistency appears, pieces of information which are responsible for inconsistencies, called conflicts, are first identified. Then we propose to use a local stratification of conflicts so as to determine which beliefs must be removed when restoring the consistency of the knowledge base. This local stratification offers more flexibility for representing priorities between beliefs. We end this section with a comparative study with some existing inconsistency handling approaches.

The second part of the paper, Section 4, applies the inconsistency-handling techniques to reasoning with default information of the form "generally, if $\alpha$ then $\beta$" having possible exceptions. Viewing default reasoning as a particular case of inconsistency handling is not new and has been suggested by several authors (e.g., [7, 9, 8]). We start Section 4 by a discussion about the meaning of "intuitive conclusions" in default reasoning, and also by a motivation of using local approaches. Then, we apply one of the three proposed coherence-based approaches to default reasoning. We show that defining the specificity relation locally inside conflicts allows us to infer plausible conclusions which cannot be obtained if a global stratification is used. Section 5 provides a comparison with various default reasoning systems.

## 2. Definitions and notations

We consider a finite propositional language denoted by $\mathcal{L}$. We denote the classical consequence relation by $\vdash$. Greek letters $\alpha,\beta,\gamma,\ldots$ represent formulas. We denote by $\Sigma$ a set of beliefs which is not deductively closed, we call it a "belief base", following Nebel [33], while bases which are deductively closed are called "belief sets" after Gärdenfors [26]. A formula in $\Sigma$ is called a "belief" because it represents a proposition taken for granted, that does not require justification. In the presence of inconsistency, the approaches developed in this paper must be syntactic in nature, since they explicitly use formulas that appear in the belief base originally, while two inconsistent belief bases over the same language are semantically equivalent (in a trivial way).

In the present paper, the methods that cope with inconsistency are based on restoring the consistency of $\Sigma$. The preliminary step is to extract from an inconsistent belief base sets of pieces of information which are responsible for inconsistencies. The following definition is helpful to formalize this view.

**Definition 1**: A sub-base C of $\Sigma$ is said to be a *conflict* if it satisfies the two following conditions: ① $C \vdash \perp$ (C is classically inconsistent) and ② $\forall\phi\in C, C-\{\phi\}$ $\nvdash\perp$ (C is minimal w.r.t. the set inclusion relation).

In the following, we denote by $\mathbb{C}(\Sigma)$ the set of all the conflicts of $\Sigma$. In model-based diagnosis [41, p 63, Def 2.4], a conflict is called a diagnosis which is a smallest set of components such that the assumption that each of these components is faulty, together with the assumptions that all other components are behaving correctly, is consistent with the system description and the observation.

The set $\mathbb{C}(\Sigma)$ can be related to the "base of nogoods" used in the terminology of the ATMS (Assumptions-based Truth Maintenance Systems)[18]. A nogood is a minimal set of incompatible assumptions. In the ATMS, the vocabulary used to describe knowledge contains two kinds of symbols: the assumption and the non-assumption symbols[1]. Links between conflicts and nogoods can be established in the following way: let $\Sigma$ be a belief base, and let $\Sigma'$ be a new belief base obtained from $\Sigma$ by replacing each formula $\phi_i$ in $\Sigma$ by $\neg H_i \vee \phi_i$, where $H_i$ is an assumption symbol (all $H_i$ are different) and can be viewed as the source which provides the formula $\phi_i$. Then we can show that the sub-base $A = \{\phi_i \mid i=1, m\}$ is a conflict of $\Sigma$ if and only if $\mathcal{H}_A = \{H_i \mid \neg H_i \vee \phi_i \in \Sigma', \phi_i \in A\}$ is a nogood of $\Sigma'$.

Efficient algorithms for computing nogoods (hence conflicts of an inconsistent belief base) can be found in [11]. It is clear that the problem of computing conflicts is NP-complete [39], namely, there are (extreme) situations where expliciting the set of all conflicts needs an exponential time. The algorithm proposed in [11] is based on Davis and Putnam procedure [17]. Its efficiency is due to the use of particular heuristics, and has been shown experimentally by comparing it with some existing algorithms for computing nogoods in ATMS.

Restoring the consistency of $\Sigma$ comes down to *removing* some beliefs which allow to solve all the conflicts in $\mathbb{C}(\Sigma)$. A conflict is said to be *solved* if it contains one removed belief from $\Sigma$. The main problem is how to determine sets of removed beliefs. It is well known that the use of priorities between formulas is very important to appropriately revise inconsistent knowledge bases [24]. In model-based diagnosis, De Kleer [19, 20] uses prior faulty probabilities of the components to rank-order the set of all possible diagnosis. This leads to select only the most plausible ones. In the following, we will use the term "priority" or "stratification" to denote some preference relation between beliefs of the belief base. In this paper, priorities are not supposed to be given globally between all the pieces of information in the belief base, but locally inside each conflict. More precisely, we assume that each conflict C is simply divided into two layers (C, C̲), where the layer C̲ contains the least important beliefs in the conflict C. C̲ is called the least priority layer of C, and C̄ is called the most priority layer of C. The intuitive meaning of this local two-level stratification is that to solve a given conflict C, we prefer to remove from $\Sigma$ beliefs of C̲ rather than of C̄. Of course, a same belief $\phi$ can belong to two different conflicts $C_1$ and $C_2$. This same belief $\phi$ can be in the lower stratum in $C_1$ and also in the higher stratum in $C_2$. This does not lead to any contradiction but simply means that the belief $\phi$ can be removed from $\Sigma$ (due to solving $C_1$). A belief $\phi$ which is in a

---

[1] Generally, assumptions symbols correspond to the choice of the users and the non-assumption symbols often correspond to the conclusion obtained from knowledge bases and facts. For instance, in fault diagnosis, assumptions data are associated with each component which may be faulty (e.g., there is no oil, the engine belt is broken, ...) and the non-assumption symbols describe observable facts whose truth value may be kown by the user (e.g., the temperator indicator is red, ...).

higher stratum of a given conflict is not always guaranteed to be kept, except if it is always in the higher stratum of all conflicts it belongs.

This local stratification offers more flexibility for representing priorities between beliefs. It can represent a total pre-ordering, a partial ordering or a multi-ordering between beliefs as explained below.

If we consider a total pre-ordering between the beliefs of $\Sigma$, as in Pearl's system Z [38] or in possibilistic logic [22], the base $\Sigma$ is stratified in the form $\Sigma = S_1 \cup ... \cup S_n$ such that beliefs in $S_i$ have the same level of priority and have more priority than the ones in $S_j$ where $j>i$. Hence, $S_1$ contains the most important beliefs in $\Sigma$ and $S_n$ contains the least important ones. In the rest of the paper, $S_i$ are called layers or strata. From a total pre-ordering between the beliefs, the local stratification is straightforwardly defined: for each conflict C, we define $\underline{C}=(S_i \cap C)$ such that $i=\max(j \mid S_j \cap C \neq \emptyset)$. A total ordering is easy to use but in practice it is not obvious to provide a complete pre-order between all the beliefs of $\Sigma$. We come back to the discussion about a total pre-ordering in Section 3.5.

In the case of a partial ordering, the set $\underline{C}$ is defined by $\underline{C} = \{\phi \in C \mid \nexists\ \psi \in C, \phi \leq \psi\}$ (the set of minimal elements w.r.t. $\leq$). A partial ordering is more flexible than a total pre-ordering (in the sense that it is more easy to provide a partial than a total pre-order since in practice it may happen that we cannot compare two elements) but is not easy to use (see the method developed by Roos [44] or by Brewka [9] which consider all the total orderings that can be drawn from the partial ordering).

The local stratification can also represent a multi-ordering between beliefs. The multi-ordering comes from the fact that two beliefs can be compared differently according to different features. This is linked to the multi-sources fusion where sources of information are compared with respect to each feature of the knowledge described in the base. For example, if we consider the approach based on the topics [14], a conflict represents contradictory information about a given topic and the ordering between the beliefs of the conflict is determined by the priority of the sources with respect to this topic. The example given by Cholvy describes the following knowledge: Two witnesses, a woman and a man, give a description of a suspect. The woman says that the suspect is a girl wearing a Chanel suit and driving a sport Volkswagen car. For the man, the suspect is a girl wearing a dress and driving a diesel car. The idea of the approach about topics is that the sources of information are ranked according to the features that are described (topics). Here, the information given by the woman has priority over the ones given by the man when speaking about "clothing" while the priority is the contrary when speaking about "car". This example shows that the local stratification can be appropriate to represent knowledge on which several partial preference relations can be simultaneously defined.

In the next section, the local stratification defined inside conflicts is supposed to be given. In the context of default reasoning (Section 4.4.), the stratification is computed and simply corresponds to the specificity relation between default rules.

# 3. Three inferences to handle locally-stratified conflicts

The following subsections present three possibilities to restore the consistency of $\Sigma$. Two of them only retain one consistent sub-base while the last approach considers several maximally consistent sub-bases.

## 3.1. Inference relation based on undefeated beliefs

The following definition introduces the notion of (un)defeated beliefs in $\Sigma$.

**Definition 2**: A belief $\phi$ in $\Sigma$ is said to be *defeated* iff there exists a conflict C in $\mathbb{C}(\Sigma)$ such that $\phi \in \underline{C}$. It is said to be *undefeated* otherwise.

We denote by Undef($\Sigma$) the set of all undefeated beliefs in $\Sigma$. The first way to restore the consistency of $\Sigma$ is to only consider undefeated beliefs in $\Sigma$, namely the inference relation is defined in the following way:

**Definition 3**: A formula $\psi$ is said to be an *undefeated conclusion* of $\Sigma$ iff Undef($\Sigma$) $\vdash \psi$.

In terms of complexity, this method is straightforward in the sense that only the step of computing conflicts can be expensive.

When no stratification is available inside each conflict, namely, for each C in $\mathbb{C}(\Sigma)$, we have $\underline{C} = C$, the undefeated consequence relation is equivalent to the so-called free consequence relation, proposed in [2], which is based on beliefs which are not involved in any inconsistency, i.e. Free($\Sigma$)=$\{\phi \in \Sigma \mid \forall\ C \in \mathbb{C}(\Sigma), \phi \notin C\}$. Free($\Sigma$) in fact is simply the sets of all the beliefs obtained by the intersection of all maximally consistent sub-bases of $\Sigma$.

The main drawback of the undefeated inference relation is that it deletes too many beliefs. The inference is then too conservative as it is shown in the following example.

*Example 1*: Let $\Sigma = \{\alpha, \beta, \neg\alpha \vee \neg\beta, \neg\alpha \vee \delta, \neg\beta \vee \delta\}$ be the belief base. $\Sigma$ is inconsistent and the inconsistency is caused by the three first beliefs. Clearly, $\Sigma$ has one conflict A = $\{\alpha, \beta, \neg\alpha \vee \neg\beta\}$. Let us assume that $\underline{A} = \{\alpha, \beta\}$ which means that to solve the conflict A, the two beliefs $\alpha$ and $\beta$ have the same level of priority, but both have lower priority than $\neg\alpha \vee \neg\beta$. The set of undefeated formulas is Undef($\Sigma$)=$\{\neg\alpha \vee \neg\beta, \neg\alpha \vee \delta, \neg\beta \vee \delta\}$. Hence $\delta$ cannot be entailed using the undefeated consequence relation, even if it is enough to get rid either $\alpha$ or $\beta$ (and not necessary both) to restore consistency while getting $\delta$. □

It is clear that the undefeated consequence relation does not involve the idea of parsimony with respect to the removal of inconsistency, since it removes more formulas than is necessary to restore consistency.

## 3.2. Determining the first conflicts to solve

There is another limit of undefeated method: it does not take into consideration the ordering in which conflicts are solved:

*Example 2:* Let $\Sigma=\{\neg\alpha\vee\neg\beta, \psi, \neg\psi\vee\neg\beta, \alpha, \beta\}$. We have two conflicts:
$\quad$ A $= \{\psi, \neg\psi\vee\neg\beta, \beta\}$ and B $= \{\neg\alpha\vee\neg\beta, \alpha, \beta\}$.
Let us assume that $\underline{A} = \{\beta\}$ and $\underline{B} = \{\alpha, \beta\}$. There is only one way to solve the conflict A: it is to remove $\beta$. For the conflict B, we have two possibilities: either removing $\alpha$, or removing $\beta$. However the second case is debatable since $\beta$ must be removed in order to solve the conflict A. Unfortunately, the undefeated consequence relation removes all the defeated formulas and hence the belief $\alpha$ will not be kept. $\square$

In the previous example, we have seen that solving a conflict (here the conflict A) can solve other conflicts (here the conflict B). Hence, it is very important to decide which conflicts should be solved first. The following ranking indicates the influence relation between conflicts:

**Definition 4** : A conflict A has a *positive influence* on a conflict B (or solving A solves B), denoted by A $\leq_I$ B, iff $\underline{A} \cap B \neq \emptyset$ and $\underline{B}\not\subset\underline{A}$.

The previous definition is based on the most intuitive combination of the different possible elementary relations between conflicts. They can be gathered into two kinds of influence. The first one is that solving A *necessarily* solves B (that is whatever the belief of A to be deleted, B is solved); it corresponds to the case where $\underline{A} \subset B$. The second kind of influence is when solving A *possibly* solves B (the resolution of B by solving A depends on the chosen belief to delete from $\underline{A}$): this is the case when $\underline{A}\cap B\neq\emptyset$. The second case includes the first one since $\underline{A}\subset B$ implies $\underline{A}\cap B\neq\emptyset$.
$\quad$ So, Definition 4 means that a conflict A has a positive influence on a conflict B if solving A possibly solves B (see Example 3 below) but solving B does not necessary solves A.

To determine the set of the first conflicts to solve, we represent the relation $\leq_I$ by a graph G, where the nodes are the set of conflicts and an edge is drawn from A to B iff A has a positive influence on B.

**Definition 5**: A conflict A is said to be in the set of first conflicts to solve, denoted by $min(\mathbb{C}(\Sigma))$, iff there is no conflict B such that: ① there is a path from B to A, but ② there is no path from A to B.

The previous definition uses the notion of positive influence to determine what conflicts must be treated first in a given set of conflicts. The basic idea is to select the conflicts which are not influenced by other conflicts (according to Definition 4). We rather define equivalence classes: two conflicts A and B are in the same equivalence class if, in the graph, there is a path from A to B and also a path from B to A. So, we select the classes where no conflict is under the influence of a conflict of another class.

The two following approaches use $\min(\mathbb{C}(\Sigma))$ to define less conservative non-monotonic consequence relations.

## 3.3. Inference relation using first solvable conflicts

The idea in this approach is that, for each conflict C in $\min(\mathbb{C}(\Sigma))$, we remove from $\Sigma$ all the beliefs which are in $\underline{C}$, and from $\mathbb{C}(\Sigma)$ all the solved conflicts (conflicts containing at least one belief of $\underline{C}$). We iteratively repeat this step until solving all the conflicts. This approach is constructively described by the following way:

a. Let $\text{Del}\Sigma = \varnothing$, let SetC = $\mathbb{C}(\Sigma)$.
b. Repeat until SetC = $\varnothing$
    b.1. Compute $D_{min}$ = min(SetC) using Definition 5,
    b.2. For each C in $D_{min}$,
        b.2.1. $\text{Del}\Sigma = \text{Del}\Sigma \cup \underline{C}$,
        b.2.2. Remove from SetC the set of solved conflicts,
                i.e. SetC = SetC - {C' | C'$\in$SetC and C'$\cap\underline{C} \neq \varnothing$}
c. Return RFS($\Sigma$) = $\Sigma$ - $\text{Del}\Sigma$.

This algorithm determines the set of formulas to be removed from $\Sigma$; it is called $\text{Del}\Sigma$. SetC contains the conflicts that are not yet solved; initially, it contains all the conflicts of the belief base. The algorithm only computes one consistent sub-base of $\Sigma$ (containing the remaining formulas when deleting the set $\text{Del}\Sigma$). In each step, we compute the set of first solvable conflicts for the remaining conflicts, we delete all the beliefs of the less priority layer of all the first conflicts to solve and we delete all the conflicts that are then solved.

**Definition 6**: Let RFS($\Sigma$) be the sub-base of $\Sigma$ obtained by applying the previous algorithm. A formula $\psi$ is said to be a *RFS-consequence* (RFS for Removing the First Solvable conflicts) of $\Sigma$ iff $\psi$ is a classical consequence of RFS($\Sigma$).

In terms of complexity, the difficulty would come from the determination of min(SetC) (Definition 5): the problem with handling the graph is to make sure that there is no path from a variable to another variable. This means that checking if a given conclusion is a RFS-consequence of $\Sigma$ needs more time than checking if this conclusion is simply an undefeated consequence of $\Sigma$.

**Proposition 1**: If $\psi$ is an undefeated consequence of $\Sigma$ then it is a RFS-consequence of $\Sigma$.
*Proof*: The undefeated consequence relation deletes all the beliefs of the less preferred layer (those belonging to $\underline{C}$) of *all* conflicts (namely, all the undefeated beliefs) while the RFS-consequence relation deletes all the beliefs of the less preferred layer of *some* conflicts. Then, the selected sub-base for the undefeated consequence relation is included in the one selected for RFS-consequence relation. So, an undefeated consequence is also a RFS-consequence. □

The converse of the previous proposition is false. Indeed, let us consider again Example 2.

*Example 2 (continued)*: Taking again $\Sigma=\{\neg\alpha\vee\neg\beta, \psi, \neg\psi\vee\neg\beta, \alpha, \beta\}$ with two conflicts A=$\{\psi, \neg\psi\vee\neg\beta, \beta\}$ and B =$\{\neg\alpha\vee\neg\beta, \alpha, \beta\}$ and with $\underline{A}$ =$\{\beta\}$ and $\underline{B}$ =$\{\alpha, \beta\}$. Using the influence relation between conflicts, we can easily check that A $\leq_I$ B since $\underline{A} \cap B \neq \varnothing$ and $\underline{B}\not\subset A$ (moreover, B $\leq_I$ A is not true since A⊂B). Then, solving first A by removing $\beta$ from $\Sigma$ leads also to solving B. So, $\beta$ is the single belief that is deleted by RFS-consequence relation. Here, it is possible to keep the belief $\alpha$. □

However, we must notice that the RFS-consequence relation does not infer all the expected conclusions since it does not solve the problem encountered in Example 1.

Even worse, this way of solving conflicts can lead to inferring debatable conclusions as it is illustrated by the following example:

*Example 3:* Let $\Sigma=\{\neg\alpha\vee\neg\beta, \alpha, \beta, \neg\alpha\vee\delta, \neg\beta\vee\delta, \neg\delta\}$. The belief base $\Sigma$ is inconsistent. We have three conflicts: A=$\{\neg\alpha\vee\neg\beta, \alpha, \beta\}$, B=$\{\alpha, \neg\alpha\vee\delta, \neg\delta\}$ and C=$\{\beta, \neg\beta\vee\delta, \neg\delta\}$. Let us assume that $\underline{A}$=$\{\alpha, \beta\}$, $\underline{B}$=$\{\neg\delta\}$ and $\underline{C}$=$\{\neg\delta\}$.

The conflict A prefers to remove either $\alpha$ or $\beta$. The conflicts B and C prefer to remove $\neg\delta$. Moreover, note that solving A leads to solve either B or C. From these information, we intuitively prefer to get the three following possibilities to restore the consistency of $\Sigma$: remove $\{\alpha, \beta\}$, remove $\{\alpha, \neg\delta\}$ and remove $\{\beta, \neg\delta\}$.

Applying the previous algorithm, we have A $\leq_I$ B (since $\alpha\in B$ but $\neg\delta\notin A$) and A $\leq_I$ C (since $\beta\in C$ but $\neg\delta\notin A$) but, however, neither C $\leq_I$ A nor B $\leq_I$ A holds (since $\neg\delta\notin A$). Hence A is solved first, by removing both $\alpha$ and $\beta$, and hence the conflicts B and C are solved. Using the previous algorithm, we get: E=$\{\neg\alpha\vee\neg\beta, \neg\alpha\vee\delta, \neg\beta\vee\delta, \neg\delta\}$ which means that both conclusions $\neg\alpha$ and $\neg\beta$ are inferred, and also $\neg\delta$ is inferred. Clearly, this solution can be debatable.

For instance, let us assume that the previous knowledge base is about some meeting. The beliefs of the knowledge base are assumed to be provided by different sources, and the local stratification corresponds to a priori relatiability relation between the sources. We are interested to know if Annie (denoted by $\alpha$) or Brigitte (denoted by $\beta$) or Denis (denoted by $\delta$) were present in the meeting. The locally stratified conflict A expresses that Annie and Brigitte were not both in the meeting. The locally stratified conflicts B and C says that if either Annie or Brigitte was present in the meating then Denis was also. The RFS-algorithm computes the solution where neither Annie, nor Brigitte nor Denis was the meeting. Clearly, this is only one of the possible solutions. There are also other plausible solutions : the one where Annie and Denis was in the meeting or the one where Brigitte and Denis was in th meeting. □

The two last examples show that it is not suitable to delete all the beliefs of the least prioritary layer of a conflict (i.e., undefeated beliefs). With Example 1, we see that the RFS-consequence relation is still too cautious. Moreover, Example 3 shows that the RFS-consequence relation can be adventurous. The problem comes from the fact that only one consistent sub-base of $\Sigma$ is selected. In the next section, we give a way to restore consistency by deleting one and only one formula per conflict.

## 3.4. A coherence approach based on the selection of several maximal consistent sub-bases

In the two previous ways of restoring the consistency of $\Sigma$, only one consistent sub-base of $\Sigma$ is generated. This sub-base in general is not a maximally consistent sub-base of $\Sigma$. The idea in this last approach is that, rather than giving up all the beliefs with lowest priority for solving a given conflict, we remove one and only one belief per conflict. Moreover, we consider all the different possibilities and this means we compute several consistent sub-bases rather than generating one consistent sub-base. The following algorithm gives one way to construct such a consistent sub-base:

a. Let $\text{Del}\Sigma = \varnothing$, let SetC = $\mathbb{C}(\Sigma)$.
b. Repeat until SetC = $\varnothing$
    b.1. Compute min(SetC).
    b.2. Let $\phi$ a belief in $\underline{C}$ where C is in min(SetC),
        b.2.1 SetC = SetC - {C' | C'$\in$SetC and $\phi\in$C'}
        b.2.2. $\text{Del}\Sigma = \text{Del}\Sigma \cup \{\phi\}$
c. Return E = $\Sigma$ - $\text{Del}\Sigma$.

To determine all the consistent sub-bases solutions, called extensions, we have to consider all the possible cases in b.2 and all the possible cases in b.3 (i.e. we take into account all the possible combinations when we build the extensions). However, the extensions given by the previous algorithm are not always maximal.

Indeed, let us consider the following base $\Sigma = \{\neg\alpha\vee\neg\beta,\ \neg\beta\vee\neg\gamma,\ \alpha,\ \beta,\ \gamma,\ \delta,\ \neg\gamma\vee\neg\delta\}$. There are three conflicts A=$\{\neg\alpha\vee\neg\beta,\ \alpha,\ \beta\}$, B=$\{\neg\beta\vee\neg\gamma,\ \beta,\ \gamma\}$ and C=$\{\gamma,\ \delta,\ \neg\gamma\vee\neg\delta\}$. Let us assume that $\underline{A}=\{\alpha,\ \beta\}$, $\underline{B}=\{\beta,\ \gamma\}$ and $\underline{C}=\{\neg\gamma\vee\neg\delta\}$. The ordering between conflicts leads to treat A and B first (since we have three influence relations between conflicts, A$\leq_I$B, B$\leq_I$A and B$\leq_I$C, which put A and B in min(SetC) according to Definition 5). One way to solve conflicts is to delete first $\alpha$ to solve A then to delete $\beta$ to solve B and lastly to delete $\neg\gamma\vee\neg\delta$ to solve C. The obtained extension is not maximal since there is another solution which deletes $\beta$ first (hence A and B are solved) and next deletes $\neg\gamma\vee\neg\delta$ to solve C (and hence $\alpha$ is not removed).

In the following, we reduce the number of solutions by only keeping extensions that are maximal for set inclusion. Hence, it is clear that this way of restoring consistency involves an idea of parsimony with respect to the removal of inconsistencies; each extension is obtained by only removing formulas needed to restore consistency. We denote then $\mathcal{E}(\Sigma)$ the set of extensions $E_i$ which are maximal obtained using the above algorithm.

**Definition 7**: A formula $\psi$ is said to be a *universal consequence* of $\Sigma$ iff for each extension $E_i$ in $\mathcal{E}(\Sigma)$ we have $E_i \vdash \psi$.

In terms of complexity, this method is the most expensive one. This is due to the fact that several sub-bases are here computed.

*Remark*: Note that in step b.2 of the previous algorithm, one can use the work of Papini and Rauzy [36] for reducing the cardinality of $\mathcal{E}(\Sigma)$. The idea is in step b.2., we choose the ones which appear with the highest number of times in the conflicts of min(SetC). In the previous example, when dealing with min(SetC)={A, B}, the selected removed belief is $\beta$ since it is the only belief which belongs to $\underline{A}$ and $\underline{B}$. This cardinality criterion can be interesting in model-based diagnosis, in order to reduce the number of possible diagnosis. De Kleer [19] has proposed a such idea.

The following propositions link the universal consequence relation with the undefeated consequence relation and the RFS-consequence relation.

**Proposition 2**: If $\psi$ is an undefeated consequence of $\Sigma$ then it is a universal consequence of $\Sigma$. The converse is false.
*Proof*: The undefeated consequence relation deletes *all* the beliefs of the least prioritary layer of *all* conflicts (those which are undefeated) while the universal consequence relation deletes *some* beliefs of the least prioritary layer of *some* conflicts. Then, the selected sub-base for the undefeated consequence relation is included in each of the selected sub-bases for universal consequence relation. So, an undefeated consequence is also a universal consequence. For the converse, let us take the base $\Sigma = \{\neg\alpha\vee\neg\beta, \alpha, \beta, \neg\alpha\vee\delta, \neg\beta\vee\delta\}$ of Example 1. There is one conflict A={$\neg\alpha\vee\neg\beta, \alpha, \beta$} where we suppose $\underline{A}$={$\alpha, \beta$}. The undefeated consequence relation deletes {$\alpha, \beta$} and the universal consequence relation deletes either {$\alpha$} or {$\beta$}. We can then check that $\delta$ is a universal consequence while it is not an undefeated consequence. □

**Proposition 3**: The RFS-consequence relation and the universal consequence relation are not comparable.
*Counter-examples* Let us take again the base of Example 1. There is one conflict A={$\neg\alpha\vee\neg\beta, \alpha, \beta$} with $\underline{A}$={$\alpha, \beta$}. The RFS-consequence deletes {$\alpha, \beta$} and the universal consequence deletes either {$\alpha$} or {$\beta$}. We can check that $\delta$ is a universal consequence but it is not a RFS-consequence. For the converse, it is enough to consider the belief base of Example 3, where we can check that $\neg\delta$ is a RFS-consequence but it is not a universal consequence. □

### 3.5. Comparative study with other systems

It is not easy to make a comparative study with existing inconsistency-tolerant consequence relations. The reason is that, in our approach, we use a local stratification while in the existing systems the stratification (often represented by a total pre-ordering) is globally defined between all the elements of the belief base. To make a comparison possible, we restrict ourselves to the particular case where the stratification is defined globally. Let us recall that, in the case of a total pre-ordering, prioritized belief bases are of the form $\Sigma = S_1 \cup...\cup S_n$ such that beliefs in $S_i$ have the same level of priority and are more prioritary than the ones in $S_j$ where j>i. Moreover, for each conflict C, we define $\underline{C}$=($S_i \cap C$) such that i=max(j | $S_j \cap C \neq \emptyset$).

For our comparison, we consider the sets of solutions derived by every method and compare the set inclusion between them. We propose to compare our approaches to deal with inconsistency with the possibilistic logic approach [22], Nebel's linear ordering [33] and the so-called argumentative inference [4]. Other systems, like

Brewka's preferred subtheories or lexicographical inference, which have been both proposed in the context of inconsistency handling and default reasoning will be discussed in Section 5.

The possibilistic logic approach (see [22] for a detail exposition on a possibility theory and on a possibilistic logic) is a coherence-based approach which selects one consistent sub-base of $\Sigma$, denoted by $\pi(\Sigma)$, defined by $\pi(\Sigma) = S_1 \cup ... \cup S_i$ such that $\pi(\Sigma)$ is consistent but $\pi(\Sigma) \cup S_{i+1}$ is inconsistent. The rank i+1 is called the inconsistency level of $\Sigma$. If $\Sigma$ is consistent then $\pi(\Sigma)=\Sigma$. The possibilistic inference is defined as follows: $\psi$ is a possibilistic consequence of $\Sigma$ iff $\pi(\Sigma) \vdash \psi$. The idea of possibilistic logic is to keep as many formulas as possible from the more certain to the less certain until an inconsistency occurs; then, every formula that is less certain than the inconsistency level is given up even if it is not involved in an inconsistency. Clearly, the possibilistic consequence relation is drastic and the amount of removed beliefs may be important.

**Proposition 4**: If $\psi$ is a possibilistic consequence of $\Sigma$ then $\psi$ is an undefeated consequence of $\Sigma$. The converse is false.
*Proof*: It is enough to show that any belief kept by the possibilistic relation is also kept by the undefeated relation. Let us suppose that $C \in \mathbb{C}(\Sigma)$ such that $\pi(\Sigma) \cap \underline{C} \neq \varnothing$. This means that there exists $S_k \subset \pi(\Sigma)$ such that $S_k \cap \underline{C} \neq \varnothing$. Moreover, we know that $\underline{C} = (S_k \cap C)$ such that $k=\max(j \mid S_j \cap C \neq \varnothing)$. So, $\underline{C} = S_k \cap C$ and for all $S_j \cap \underline{C} \neq \varnothing$, $S_j \subset \pi(\Sigma)$ by construction of $\pi(\Sigma)$. Then, $C \subseteq \pi(\Sigma)$ hence $\pi(\Sigma)$ is inconsistent which is impossible owing to the definition of $\pi(\Sigma)$. For the converse, if we consider the base $\Sigma = S_1 \cup S_2 \cup S_3$ with $S_1 = \{\psi\}$, $S_2 = \{\neg\psi\vee\varphi, \neg\psi\vee\alpha\}$ and $S_3 = \{\neg\varphi\vee\neg\alpha, \neg\varphi\vee\beta\}$, we see that $\beta$ is an undefeated consequence but it is not a possibilistic consequence. □

**Corollary**: Propositions 1, 2 and 4 implies that, if $\psi$ is possibilistic consequence, it is a RFS-consequence and a universal consequence.

Nebel [34] has proposed a less liberal way to select one consistent sub-base. When inconsistency occurs, we give up the whole layer concerned by the inconsistency, but we continue to add layers with lower priority levels if consistency is preserved. More formally, the selected sub-base is denoted by $lo(\Sigma)$ and is computed in the following way:           $lo(\Sigma) = \varnothing$,
     for :=1 to n do    $lo(\Sigma) = lo(\Sigma) \cup S_i$ if consistent
                    $= lo(\Sigma)$ otherwise.
A formula $\psi$ is then said to be a *lo-consequence* of $\Sigma$ iff $lo(\Sigma) \vdash \psi$.

**Proposition 5**: The lo-consequence relation is not comparable with undefeated consequence relation, RFS-consequence relation and universal consequence relation.
*Counterexamples*: Using $\Sigma = S_1 \cup S_2 \cup S_3$ with $S_1 = \{\psi\}$, $S_2 = \{\neg\psi\vee\varphi, \neg\psi\vee\alpha\}$ and $S_3 = \{\neg\varphi\vee\neg\alpha, \neg\varphi\vee\beta\}$, we can check that $\beta$ is an undefeated consequence, a RFS-consequence and also a universal consequence, since there is one conflict $C = \{\psi, \neg\psi\vee\varphi, \neg\psi\vee\alpha, \neg\varphi\vee\neg\alpha\}$ where the only solution is to delete $\neg\varphi\vee\neg\alpha$. However, this conclusion is not a lo-consequence, since $lo(\Sigma) = S_1 \cup S_2$. Now let us consider the

belief base $\Sigma = S_1 \cup S_2 \cup S_3$ with $S_1 = \{\psi\}$, $S_2 = \{\neg\psi, \varphi\}$ and $S_3 = \{\neg\varphi\}$. We have $\neg\varphi$ is a lo-consequence (since $lo(\Sigma) = S_1 \cup S_3$) but it is neither an undefeated consequence, nor a RFS-consequence nor a universal consequence (since the two conflicts (i.e. $\{\psi, \neg\psi\}$ and $\{\varphi, \neg\varphi\}$) are solved by deleting $\neg\psi$ and $\neg\varphi$) .  □

Let us now compare with an argumentative consequence relation which is not a coherence-based approach since it maintains all the belief base. We choose the one given in [4]. It is based on the notion of argument defined by:

**Definition 8**: A sub-base A of $\Sigma$ is said to be an argument for $\psi$ to a prioritary rank i iff:

① $A \nvdash \bot$, ② $A \vdash \psi$, ③ $\forall \phi \in A$, $A-\{\phi\} \nvdash \psi$ and ④ $i = \mathrm{Max}\{j \mid S_j \cap A \neq \varnothing\}$.

Then $\psi$ is said to be an argued consequence of $\Sigma$ iff there exists an argument A for $\psi$ with rank i such that for any argument which supports $\neg\psi$ with rank j, we have j>i.

**Proposition 6**: Argumentation is not comparable with our three inference relations.
*Counterexamples*: Taking the base $\Sigma = S_1 \cup S_2 \cup S_3$ with $S_1 = \{\neg\alpha\vee\neg\beta\}$, $S_2 = \{\alpha, \beta, \neg\delta\vee\beta\}$ and $S_3 = \{\delta\}$, we can check that $\neg\delta$ is an argued consequence (since the only argument that supports $\neg\delta$ (i.e. $\{\neg\alpha\vee\neg\beta, \alpha, \neg\delta\vee\beta\}$) is of rank 2 and is preferred to the only one supporting $\delta$ (i.e. $\{\delta\}$) which is of rank 3). But this conclusion is neither an undefeated consequence, neither a RFS-consequence nor a universal consequence. There are indeed two conflicts $A=\{\neg\alpha\vee\neg\beta, \alpha, \beta\}$ and $B=\{\neg\alpha\vee\neg\beta, \alpha, \neg\delta\vee\beta, \delta\}$ (where the stratification implies that $\underline{A} = \{\alpha, \beta\}$ and $\underline{B} = \{\delta\}$ and the only influence is A has a positive influence on B). The undefeated consequence relation deletes all the beliefs of $\underline{A}$ and $\underline{B}$ (i.e. $\alpha$, $\beta$ and $\delta$). Then $\neg\delta$ is not an undefeated consequence. The RFS-consequence relation deletes all the beliefs of $\underline{A}$ (i.e. $\alpha$ and $\beta$). Then $\neg\delta$ is not a RFS-consequence. The universal consequence relation deletes one belief of $\underline{A}$ then one belief of $\underline{B}$ if necessary (i.e. either $\alpha$, or $\beta$ and $\delta$). Then $\neg\delta$ is not a universal consequence.
Now, taking the base $\Sigma = S_1 \cup S_2 \cup S_3$ with $S_1 = \{\phi\}$, $S_2 = \{\neg\phi\}$ and $S_3 = \{\neg\phi\vee\psi, \phi\vee\neg\psi\}$, we can check that $\psi$ is an undefeated consequence, a RFS-consequence and a universal consequence (since solving the only conflict, i.e. $\{\phi, \neg\phi\}$, leads to delete the belief $\neg\phi$) but $\psi$ is not an argued consequence (since the argument supporting $\neg\psi$ has the same rank, i.e. 3, as the argument supporting $\psi$).  □

The following hierarchy summarizes the cautiousness relation between the different consequence relations studied here when the stratification is given globally between all the conflicts. The edges denote the inclusion-set relation between the set of results deduced by each consequence relation. The top of the diagram thus corresponds to the most conservative inferences.

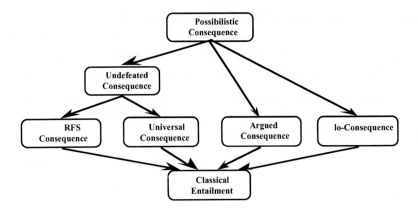

Figure 1

The proofs between the consequence relations other than Undefeated Consequence, RFS-Consequence and Universal Consequence can be found in [4]. When $\Sigma$ is consistent, we can easily check that all the consequence relations collapse to classical logic.

## 4. Application to default reasoning

We propose to apply the idea of local reasoning with inconsistency, presented in the previous section, to dealing with rules having possibly some exceptions. Viewing default reasoning as a special case of inconsistency handling is not new and has been suggested by several authors (e.g. [7, 9]). Of course we need to clarify how to define a conflict in the context of default reasoning, how to stratify it and which nonmonotonic consequence relation should be used for inferring plausible conclusions.

Default rules considered here are all of the form "generally, if $\alpha$ then $\beta$", denoted by $\alpha \rightarrow \beta$, where $\alpha$ and $\beta$ are propositional formulas. The implication "$\rightarrow$" is a *non-classical* arrow, and it should not be confused with the material implication ($\neg \alpha \vee \beta$). Default rules considered in this paper can be viewed as a special case of Reiter's normal default rules [40]. A *default base* is a set $\Delta = \{\alpha_i \rightarrow \beta_i, i=1,..., n\}$ of default rules. For any set of default rules A, we denote by $\Sigma_A$ the set of classical propositional formulas such that $\Sigma_A = \{\neg \alpha_i \vee \beta_i \mid \alpha_i \rightarrow \beta_i \in A, i=1,..., n\}$ contains the material counterparts of the default rules in A. $\Sigma$ only contains classical propositional formulas. To make sure that all the conflicts corresponding to the fact $\mathcal{F}$ are taken into account, the fact is represented by the set of its prime implicates denoted by $\mathcal{F} = \{p_1, p_2, ..., p_n\}$. The whole belief base $\Sigma$ will be then denoted by $\Sigma = \Sigma_A \cup \mathcal{F}$.

The two next sections give a brief discussion about "intuitive" conclusions in default reasoning and gives some motivation of using a local approach in the context of default reasoning.

## 4.1 Discussion about "intuitive" deduction

It is well known that there is no agreement about the notion of "intuitive" conclusion between existing default reasoning systems, even if the default base contains only few rules. This divergence between the existing systems can be mainly explained by the following points:

- The cautiousness and the adventurous aspect of default reasoning systems are often due to the incomplete way of describing the knowledge, and to the assumptions made by the systems to complete this knowledge.

- Intuitive conclusions depend on the meaning assigned to propositional symbols. Two different meaning assignments to propositional symbols in the same set of rules can lead to different sets of intuitive conclusions. Indeed, when we give a precise meaning to the symbols in a default base, we are leaning to infer conclusions which are based on general information about the real world that are not explicitly mentioned in the default base. We will illustrate this situation later in Example 4 and in the example of Figure 2.

- The interpretation of default rules is not the same in the existing systems. For instance, in Adam's $\varepsilon$-semantics [1] and Pearl's System Z [38], a default rule $\alpha \rightarrow \beta$ is interpreted by the following constraint $P(\beta|\alpha) > 1-\varepsilon$. There are two implicit assumptions in this interpretation: the rate of exceptions is very small and the domain associated to $\alpha$ (namely, the set of worlds where $\alpha$ holds) must be very large. Clearly, these two assumptions are not the basis of Reiter's default logic. This means that for instance the rules "generally, student of a class X are male" cannot be encoded using this probabilistic interpretation. Indeed, if we encode this rule by $P(\text{male\_stud\_class\_X} \mid \text{stud\_class\_X}) > 1-\varepsilon$, where P is a probability measure, then this implies that the number of the students in the class X is very large, which is of course not true. Another natural probabilistic interpretation, that we call majority interpretation, is to replace $P(\beta|\alpha) > 1-\varepsilon$ by $P(\beta|\alpha) > 1/2$. However, if we define a non-monotonic inference relation based on all the probability distributions satisfying the constraints $P(\beta_i|\alpha_i) > 1/2$ for all $\alpha_i \rightarrow \beta_i$ of $\Delta$, then this inference will not satisfy the rationality postulate proposed in [28], namely postulates of System P; see [37] for counter-examples. Recently, it has been shown by Benferhat et al. [6], that it is possible to recover rules of System P using this interpretation (i.e., majority interpretation) by considering a class of probability distribution proposed by Snow [45] under the name "Atomic Bound Systems". The natural question is then if it is always possible to build a probability distribution which is an "Atomic Bound Systems" for any set of default rules?

This section does not aim to provide a deep discussion about the notion of "intuitive" conclusion, but just tries to explain with simple default bases (where the used symbols have no a priori meaning) which assumptions are assumed when a given conclusion is considered as plausible.

Before starting the analyzing of some default bases, we consider the following principle as fundamental:

**Auto-deductivity principle:** For any default $\alpha \rightarrow \beta$, if we observe $\alpha$ and only $\alpha$ then $\beta$ must be considered as intuitive.

We see later that this principle is not satisfied by all default reasoning systems such as Reiter's default logic.

Now, let us start with the following example.

*Example 4*: Let us consider a simple default base containing only one default rule $\Delta = \{x \rightarrow y\}$. Given an observed fact $\neg y$, we are interested to know if x (resp. $\neg x$) follows or not.

• Clearly, accepting x is non-intuitive and disagrees with the idea of default reasoning where it is preferred to believe in normal situations rather than in the exceptional ones.

• Now if we assume that $\neg x$ is plausible then this means that the contraposition rule (from $\alpha \rightarrow \beta$ deduce $\neg\beta \rightarrow \neg\alpha$) is accepted. This conclusion can be justified since $\neg y$ does not contradict our belief base. Moreover accepting $\neg x$ means that the rule $x \rightarrow y$ has a very small number of exceptions. Some systems like System Z [38], Geffner's conditional entailment [27] infer such a conclusion. A possible meaning assignment to the symbols that agrees with this inference is to interpret x by "student" and y by "has got a student card". If we consider a person which does not have got a student card, we lean to infer that this person is not a student.

• If *neither x nor $\neg x$* is inferred, then this means that we do not decide between the two previous cases. This is a cautious attitude. This make sense in probabilistic (infinitesimal or majority) interpretation of default theories. If we use a majority interpretation of default rules, then it is both possible to construct a probability distribution where $P(y|x)>0.5$ and $P(x|\neg y)>0.5$ and another where $P(y|x)>0.5$ and $P(\neg x|\neg y)>0.5$. Some systems, like Reiter's default logic [40] or System P [28], have this attitude. A possible meaning assignment that justifies this cautious attitude is to consider the rule "a human walks". If the fact is "an object which does not walk", it is natural to adopt a cautious attitude where we do not choose between "being a human" or "not being a human". In fact, it depends on the universe of discourse. If it is only (or mainly) composed of humans, then intuitively, from "non-walk" we prefer to deduce "being human". However, if the universe of discourse is the real world where we are, when giving "a non-walking object", we prefer to infer plausibly that it is not a human. Clearly, information about the universe of discourse of the different symbols should be a parameter of any default reasoning system.

The following consistency principle is accepted in our approach:

**Consistency principle:** When an observed fact does not contradict the default base, then plausible conclusions are exactly the same as the ones of classical logic; hence, all the properties of the classical logic are considered as valid.

The following examples consider the case when adding a fact contradicts the default base.

*Example 4 (continued):* We add a second default rule $(y \rightarrow z)$ to the base of Example 4 and obtain $\Delta = \{x \rightarrow y, y \rightarrow z\}$.

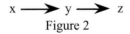

Figure 2

Given a fact $x \wedge \neg z$, we are interested to know if y can be inferred or not? Let us consider two cases:

• From $x \wedge \neg z$, we prefer inferring $\neg y$. This intuitively means that the rule $x \rightarrow y$ meets more exceptions than the rule $y \rightarrow z$ (namely, we prefer to give priority to $y \rightarrow z$ rather

than to x→y). Intuitive situation of this case can be obtained by interpreting $x$ by "students", $y$ by "young" and $z$ by "have a special rate for travelling". The fact that "Tom is a student and has no special rates for travelling" leads intuitively to prefer concluding that "Tom is not young". The reason is that the rule "young people have special rates for travelling" accepts a very small number of exceptions, while it is not very surprising to find some students which are not young. Another situation is to interpret $x$ by "humans", $y$ by "walk" and $z$ by "have feet". Given a human who does not have feet, we plausibly infer that he doesn't walk. This is due to the fact that the rule "persons who are walking have feet" allows few exceptions, indeed even none.
• If from $x \wedge \neg z$, we prefer to infer y then applying the contraposition rule to y→z in this case can be debatable. Let us interpret x by "Danish people", y by "tall people" and z by "play basket-ball". In the presence of Bjarne Riis (who is Danish and does not play basket-ball), one would like to infer that he is a tall person. The reason is that it is less surprizing to find a tall person which does not play basket-ball rather than to find a small Danish person. Note that in this example the domain associated to "being Danish", "being tall" and "playing base-ball" has not the same size, but this is not explicitly mentioned in the default base. A probabilistic interpretation where y is inferred from $x \wedge \neg z$ can be the following. Let us denote by $|\alpha|$ the number of complete situations (e.g. classical interpretations) where $\alpha$ holds. Let us assume that the two default rules are interpreted in terms of proportion such that $|x \wedge y|/|x|=|y \wedge z|/|y|=a$ with $a>0.5$. This assumption is strong since in practice not all rules have the same rate of exceptions. When there is no information about the proportion of $\alpha$ being $\beta$, we assume that $|\alpha\beta|=|\alpha\neg\beta|$. We want to compare $|xy\neg z|$ and $|x\neg y\neg z|$ so as to determine the amount of x and $\neg z$ being y and the amount of x and $\neg z$ being $\neg y$. Then, using the previous assumptions, we find that $|xy\neg z|=a.(1-a)>|x\neg y\neg z|=(1-a)/2$, since $a>0.5$, and hence, the conclusion y is preferred. An example of default reasoning system where y is inferred from $x \wedge \neg z$ is Reiter's default logic.

Of course there is also a cautious attitude where neither y nor ¬y is inferred. Most of the existing systems (e.g. System P [28], System Z [38], Boutilier's approach [8], ε-belief functions [5]) adopt this attitude.

The previous example shows that the meaning assignment to propositional symbols can alter our decisions. It also illustrates the need of providing explicit information to get a desired conclusion. This can be done by adding some ordering or independence relation between default rules.

Another reason why y should be preferred to ¬y in Figure 2 is to use the specificity principle. Indeed the rule x→y is preferred to the rule y→z, since the class x is more specific then the class y, using Touretzky's definition. The following well-known triangle example illustrates the specificity principle:

*Example 4 (continued):* Now, let us expand the example of Figure 2 by adding the rule x→¬z. So, we have Δ = {x→y, y→z, x→¬z}.

Figure 3

This is the famous penguin example when x is interpreted by "penguin", y by "birds" and z by "fly". Given an observed fact x then it is well agreed that y and ¬z are plausible conclusions of Δ. The main argument used to justify these conclusions is that the class x is more specific than the class y.

The default base of Figure 3 with the fact x is similar in some way to the default base of Figure 2 with the fact x∧¬z. The difference is about ¬z: in Figure 2, ¬z is in the fact $\mathscr{F}$ while, in Figure 3, ¬z is deduced from the fact x and the rule x→¬z.

However we have no problems to intuitively conclude y in Figure 3 while this conclusion in general does not follow in Figure 2! Let's notice that Reiter's default logic doesn't allow to infer ¬z and, hence, Reiter's default logic does not satisfy the auto-deductivity principle.

Let us now study the importance of specificity beside the length of the path of deduction. For this, let us consider the example given in the following Figure 4: Δ={a1→a2, a2→a3, a3→a4, a1→¬a4}.

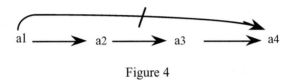

Figure 4

We want to know what must be deduced from a1. Let us give two interpretations to propositional symbols.

A possible meaning assignment to $a_i$ is: a1 is "penguin", a2 is "bird", a3 is "has feathers" and a4 is "fly". Here, we want to deduce that a penguin has feathers. This solution follows the idea of Touretzky [47] or Moinard [32], where they justify this conclusion by applying the specificity principle. Another meaning is to consider that a3 is interpreted by "moving in the sky" (the other variables have the same meaning). Here, we want to deduce that a penguin does not move in the sky (since, intuitively, it is very surprising to find a non-flying object moving in the sky).

This example can be seen as an extension of the example of Figure 2 but here the facts a2 and a4 are not given but deduced. So, it should be natural to keep on deducing the same results (that is a3).

The reason why some systems like Pearl's System Z [38] or Geffner's system [27] do not deduce a3 from this base is that their definition of specificity is based on the notion of contradiction between rules i.e. a rule is specific if, when it is verified, there is an inconsistency due to the presence of other rules. Namely, these definitions do not take into account the fact that the specificity can also exist between classes when no exception explicitly holds. If we take the default base Δ={A→B, B→C}, the two rules are not conflicting but A→B is more specific than B→C using Touretzky's definition of specificity.

*Example 4 (continued):* Irrelevance
Now let us again consider the example of Figure 3. We assume that the language contains four propositional symbols x, y, z and v (where v does not appear in the default base). We are interested to know if from a fact *x and v* we get ¬z or not? Some systems, like System P [28], do not allow z or ¬z to be deduced. This cautious attitude is justified by the fact that we have no information to decide if "x and v" is an

exceptional x with respect to the property "¬z" or not. This problem is known as the irrelevance problem. In the following, we consider the next principle as valid:

**Irrelevance Principle:** Let δ be a propositional formula composed of propositional symbols which do not appear in the default base; if some conclusion ψ is a plausible consequence of a given fact φ w.r.t. Δ, then ψ is also a plausible consequence of a more specific fact φ∧δ w.r.t. Δ.

## 4.2. Why a local approach?

We have seen in the previous section that the inference of debatable conclusions can be due to some assumptions used by default reasoning systems in the absence of complete information. However some systems, like System Z [38] (or equivalently the rational closure [30], or the possibilistic approach based on the specificity principle [2]), infer debatable conclusions that are due to the global handling of inconsistency appearing when we learn some new fact. To illustrate this situation, let us consider the following example:

*Example 5 (ambiguity):* Let Δ = {q→p, r→¬p}. This is the famous Nixon diamond example: "Republicans normally are not pacifists" and "Quakers normally are pacifists". Clearly, from q we prefer to infer p, and from r we prefer to infer ¬p and this is justified by the auto-deductivity principle. But however, if we are interested to know if Nixon, who is a Republican and a Quaker, is a pacifist or not, then we prefer to say nothing. This is intuitively satisfying. Now let us add to this example three further rules (not related to pacifism), which give more information about Quakers: "Quakers are Americans", "Americans like base-ball" and "Quakers do not like base-ball". So, let Δ = {q→p, r→¬p} ∪ {q→a, q→¬b, a→b}. This is illustrated by the following Figure 5:

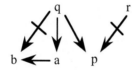

Figure 5

Given a fact q∧r, we have two conflicts, one A = {r∧q, q→p, r→¬p} is related to the pacifism and the other B={q, q→a, q→¬b, a→b} is related to playing base-ball. These two conflicts are independent and, hence, from q∧r we prefer to infer a,¬b but neither p nor ¬p is intuitively considered as a plausible conclusion. Some systems like System Z, prefer to infer p rather than ¬p. The reason is that the two conflicts are not handled independently but globally, and hence, in System Z, for the conflict B the class q is a specific class and is given a higher priority over all the general classes especially over the class r, therefore the debatable conclusion p is inferred!  □

There is another reason where handling default information locally is recommended. It concerns the case of default bases containing cycles.

*Example 6*: Let's take the example of the base $\Delta=\{Y{\rightarrow}S, S{\rightarrow}F, F{\rightarrow}Y\}$ which corresponds to the following default rules: "young people are students", "students like to have fun" and "people who like to have fun are young". It is illustrated by the following Figure 6.

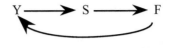

Figure 6

A global treatment of rules does not allow us to make a difference between the rules and put the three rules in the same level. This is intuitively satisfying when considering specificity globally (with respect to Touretzky's idea). Considering the fact $Y{\wedge}{\neg}F$, a global treatment does not allow S to be inferred. With a local treatment, from the fact $Y{\wedge}{\neg}F$, only the two rules $Y{\rightarrow}S$ and $S{\rightarrow}F$ are involved in the inconsistency and we do not take into account the rule $F{\rightarrow}Y$ (namely, $F{\rightarrow}Y$ is not activated). Priority is given to the rule $Y{\rightarrow}S$ upon $S{\rightarrow}F$ using Touretzky's specificity principle. Then, S can be inferred. □

## 4.3. Determination of conflicts

In default reasoning, a distinction is made between the default base $\Delta$ and the fact $\mathcal{F}$. We assume that $\mathcal{F}$ and $\Sigma_\Delta{}^2$ are separately consistent, but however $\Sigma = \mathcal{F} \cup \Sigma_\Delta$ is generally inconsistent. We need to clarify how to define conflicts of this base (more precisely, what beliefs are involved in the conflicts).

First, we represent a fact by the set of its prime implicates $\mathcal{F}=\{p_1, p_2, ..., p_n\}$. We use this representation to make sure that we consider all the minimal sets of information that lead to a conflict by taking into account the part of the fact involved in the inconsistency. Let us consider Example 4: to compute the conflicts given the fact "Quaker Republican" $(q{\wedge}r)$, we must consider the conflicts due to the fact "Quaker" $(q)$, the ones due to the fact "Republican" $(r)$ and the ones due to the fact "Quaker Republican" $(q{\wedge}r)$. This leads to consider the conflict about "liking base-ball" (corresponding to "Quaker") and the conflict about "pacifism" (corresponding to "Quaker Republican"). Here, the fact is $\mathcal{F}=\{q, r\}$. The computation of conflicts consider all the possible combinations of prime implicates of the fact (in our example, the possible combinations are $\mathcal{F}_1=\{q\}$, $\mathcal{F}_2=\{r\}$ and $\mathcal{F}_3=\{q, r\}$).

A conflict is a minimal inconsistent sub-base (Definition 1) of $\mathcal{F} \cup \Sigma_\Delta$. $\mathcal{F}$ and $\Sigma_\Delta$ are supposed to be separately consistent. This implies that each conflict C contains a non-empty subpart of $\mathcal{F}$, denoted by $C_\mathcal{F}$, and also a non-empty subpart of $\Sigma_\Delta$, denoted by $C_\Delta$. Since the fact is considered as a sure piece of information, we only stratify $C_\Delta$ involved in each conflict, namely, we always have $\underline{C}{\subset}C_\Delta$ and $\underline{C}{\cap}C_\mathcal{F}=\varnothing$.

---

[2] We recall $\Sigma_\Delta$ is the classical counterpart of the default base $\Delta$, obtained by replacing the non-classical arrow "$\rightarrow$" by a material implication in each default of $\Delta$.

Taking again Example 4, there are two conflicts A and B such that $A_{\mathcal{F}}=\{q\}$ and $A_\Delta=\{\neg q\vee a,\ \neg q\vee\neg b,\ \neg a\vee b\}$ and $B_{\mathcal{F}}=\{q,\ r\}$ and $B_\Delta=\{\neg q\vee p,\ \neg r\vee\neg p\}$. A natural stratification on these conflicts is $\underline{A}=\{\neg a\vee b\}$ and $\underline{B}=\{\neg q\vee p,\ \neg r\vee\neg p\}$.

The following section gives how to stratify default rules inside conflicts.

## 4.4. Specificity-based default ranking

In this section, we propose a new definition of specificity which will be used to stratify conflicts. This definition extends the so-called tolerance relation, used in System Z [38], in order to take into account the specificity relation between non-conflicting defaults. Let A be a sub-base of $\Delta$, and $A_T$ be the set of default rules tolerated[3] by A. Then we propose to select a unique non-empty sub-base of $A_T$, denoted by $\underline{A}$, composed of rules, called taxotolerated rules, with the general antecedent classes. More formally:

**Definition 9**: A default rule $\varphi\rightarrow\psi$ in A is said to be *taxotolerated* if:
① $\varphi\rightarrow\psi \in A_T$ (i.e., $\varphi\rightarrow\psi$ is tolerated by A), and
② there is no default rule $\varphi'\rightarrow\psi' \in A_T$ with $\varphi\neq\varphi'$ such that $\{\varphi,\ \psi\} \cup \Sigma_A \vdash \varphi'$, where $\Sigma_A$ is the material counterpart of A obtained by turning rules in A into strict rules that is $\Sigma_A=\{\neg\alpha_i\vee\beta_i \mid \alpha_i\rightarrow\beta_i\in A\}$.

If there is no taxotolerated default rules in A then we simply let $\underline{A}=A_T$. For instance, if $A=\{a\rightarrow b,\ b\rightarrow a\}$ then if we apply the previous definition, none of these two rules will be taxotolerated, even if both of them are tolerated.

It is easy to check that taxotolerated default rules are the most general ones in A. Indeed a rule is taxotolerated if activating this rule (by considering true its antecedent) does not activate any other rule. This definition of taxotolerance extends the definition of specificity relation given by Touretzky [47], when antecedents and consequents of rules are not necessarily propositional symbols but general formulas. It also, by definition, refines the tolerance relation of System Z. For example, if we take the following base $\Delta=\{x\rightarrow y,\ y\rightarrow z\}$, then both rules are tolerated in System Z but, with our definition, $x\rightarrow y$ is not taxotolerated and is then specific.

## 4.5. Inferring plausible conclusions

We will neither use the undefeated consequence relation nor the RFS-consequence relation to deal with default information. The reason is that the first one is conservative (see Example 1) while the latter can lead to non-intuitive and adventurous conclusions as it is shown by the following example: let $\Delta=\{p\rightarrow b,\ p\rightarrow\neg f,\ b\rightarrow f,\ mw\rightarrow f\}$ be the base and let $\mathcal{F}=\{p,\ mw\}$ be the fact, where p, b, f and

---

[3] A default rule d of A is tolerated by A iff there exists an interpretation $\omega$ which satisfies d and which falsifies none of the default rules of A (where $\omega$ satisfies $d=\alpha\rightarrow\beta$ if $\omega \models \alpha\wedge\beta$ and $\omega$ falsifies $\alpha\rightarrow\beta$ if $\omega \models \alpha\wedge\neg\beta$).

mw respectively mean "penguins", "birds", "fly" and "have metal wings". If we consider a penguin which has metal wings, we are in situation of ambiguity and we have no reason to choose between f and ¬f. We have two stratified conflicts: A={$\underline{A}$={p→¬f, mw→f}, $\overline{A}$ =∅} and B={$\underline{B}$={b→f}, $\overline{B}$ ={p→b, p→¬f}}. Clearly, A has a positive influence on B, then A is solved first. Unfortunately, the RFS-consequence removes all the formulas of $\underline{A}$={p→¬f, mw→f} from $\Sigma_\Delta$, the remaining base is {p→b, b→f}, and, considering the fact $\mathscr{F}$, this leads to infer *f*.

Now, we want to apply the algorithm of Section 3.4. We have explained what represents $\Sigma$, we have defined the set $\mathbb{C}(\Sigma)$. It remains to determine $\underline{C}$ for each conflict C (this also allows to determine the set min(SetC)). This is done simply applying our definition of taxotolerance (Definition 9).

**Definition 10**: Let C = C$_\mathscr{F}$ $\cup$C$_\Delta$. Let A={$d_{\phi_i}$ | $\phi_i \in$ C$_\Delta$} be the sub-base of $\Delta$ associated to C$_\Delta$ (i.e.; $d_\phi$ is the default rule in the default base $\Delta$ whose material counterpart is $\phi$). A belief $\phi$ of C$_\Delta$ is in $\underline{C}_\Delta$ iff the default $d_\phi$ associated to $\phi$ is taxotolerated by the sub-base A.

In the case where there is no belief in $\underline{C}$, which corresponds to the situation where there is no default rule which is taxotolerated, we let $\underline{C}$=C$_\Delta$. An example of this case is the base $\Delta$={⊤→x, x∨y→¬x}. In this case, we put all the beliefs in $\underline{C}$.

*Notation*: In the rest of this paper, we will use **UC** to denote our proposed default reasoning system based on the use of the universal consequence relation applied in default reasoning with a stratification of conflicts given by Definition 10.

*Example 5 (continued)*: Let $\Delta$ = {q→p, r→¬p, q→a, q→¬b, a→b} and $\mathscr{F}$={q, r}. Clearly, $\Sigma$={q, r, ¬q∨p, ¬r∨¬p, ¬q∨a, ¬q∨¬b, ¬a∨b} is inconsistent and has two conflicts A={q, r, ¬q∨p, ¬r∨¬p} and B={q, ¬q∨a, ¬q∨¬b, ¬a∨b}. Considering {q→p, r→¬p}, the two rules are taxotolerated and we have $\underline{A}$ = {¬q∨p, ¬r∨¬p} while considering {q→a, q→¬b, a→b}, only the rule a→b is taxotolerated and we have $\underline{B}$={¬a∨b}. We obtain $\mathbb{C}(\Sigma)$ = {A = ($\underline{A}$={¬q∨p, ¬r∨¬p}, $\overline{A}$ = {q, r}), B = ($\underline{B}$={¬a∨b}, $\overline{B}$ = {q, ¬q∨a, ¬q∨¬b})}. Applying the algorithm of Section 3.4., we get two maximal extensions: E$_1$={q, r, ¬q∨p, ¬q∨a, ¬q∨¬b} and E$_2$={q, r, ¬r∨¬p, ¬q∨a, ¬q∨¬b}. From these extensions, a and b are deduced but neither p nor ¬p is inferred. This complies with the intuition. □

*Example 6 (continued)*: Let $\Delta$ = {Y→S, S→F, F→Y} with the fact $\mathscr{F}$ = {Y, ¬F}. We have one conflict for $\Sigma$ = {Y, ¬F, ¬Y∨S, ¬S∨F, ¬F∨Y} which is A = {Y, ¬F, ¬Y∨S, ¬S∨F}. The definition of taxotolerance computes $\underline{A}$={¬S∨F}. Then, applying the algorithm of Section 3.4. deduce S. □

Next section compares our method (i.e., **UC**) with other existing default reasoning systems.

## 5. Examples, discussions and comparative study

We will use the notation **DL** for designating Reiter's normal default logic [40], **DS** for Delgrande and Schaub's approach [21], **BPT** for Boutilier's [8] proposal to use Brewka's preferred subtheories [9], **LEX** for the lexicographical ordering suggested by Lehmann [29] and equivalently proposed in [3].

*Default logic, Delgrande and Schaub's extension*

We only consider normal default logic since in our approach it is not possible to represent general default rules of the form $\alpha : \beta / \gamma$, with $\beta \neq \gamma$. The notion of extensions used in our approach to define the universal consequence relation is not the same as the one used in **DL**. In our definition, an extension is a maximal consistent sub-base of $\mathcal{F} \cup \Sigma_\Delta$ while, in Reiter's definition, it is not the case (see Example 7, below).

The two following examples show that **DL**, in some situations, is conservative because some intuitive conclusions, obtained by the universal consequence relation, cannot be deduced using **DL**.

*Example 7:* Let $\Delta = \{x \rightarrow y\}$ and $\mathcal{F} = \{\neg y\}$. We are interested to know if $\neg x$ can follow from $\Delta$ and $\mathcal{F}$. In our **UC** system $\neg x$ is inferred. In **DL** (and also in System P [28]), *neither x nor ¬x are inferred.* □

*Example 8:* **DL** does not use specificity criteria to prefer one extension over the other. Let $\Delta = \{p \rightarrow b, b \rightarrow f, p \rightarrow \neg f\}$. **UC** has no problem to infer b and ¬f from $\Delta$ and $\mathcal{F} = \{p\}$. In **DL**, neither f nor ¬f is inferred. Basically, in **DL**, there are as many extensions as ways to solve conflicts among defaults and no priority (specificity) is used to block unwanted conclusions. □

Of course, there are variants of **DL** where ¬f follows from p and the default base $\Delta$. These variants address correctly specificity handling by an appropriate use of semi-normal default logic. Delgrande and Schaub [21], following ideas of Reiter and Criscuolo [42], have suggested transforming, using Pearl's System Z, rules whose antecedent is in the general classes into semi-normal defaults. Specific rules remain unchangeable. Then, they use semi-normal default logic to do inferences. **DS** rectifies many of the shortcomings of **DL** but, however, in some situations, like the one of Example 7, it is still cautious (e.g., from $\Delta = \{x \rightarrow y\}$ and $\mathcal{F} = \{\neg y\}$ we do not get ¬x even if $\{\neg y, \neg x \vee y\}$ is consistent).

The following example explains that **UC** and **DL** (or **DS**) have different behaviours in front of an inconsistent set of default rules. Inconsistency here is understood in the sense of Pearl [38] (or Adams [1])[4].

---

4  A set of defaults $\{\alpha_i \rightarrow \beta_i \mid i=1,n\}$ is said to be inconsistent if it doesn't exist a probability distribution such that $\forall i \in 1,n$ $P(\beta_i \mid \alpha_i) \geq 1-\varepsilon$ where $\varepsilon$ is an infinitesimal positive number. A typical example of an inconsistent default base is $\{\alpha \rightarrow \beta, \alpha \rightarrow \neg \beta\}$.

348

*Example 9* [31]: Let $\Delta=\{T \rightarrow x, x \vee y \rightarrow \neg x\}$ and $\mathcal{F}=\varnothing$. This default base is classically inconsistent. With **UC**, we only restore consistency by considering the two extensions $E_1=(\{x\})$ and $E_2=(\{\neg x \wedge \neg y\})$. Neither x nor $\neg x$ is then obtained. In **DL** (and also in **DS**), only one extension is generated and then x is obtained.  □

*System Z*

System Z [38] proceeds in the following way: first, it partitions the set of default rules $\Delta$ in $(\Delta_1,...,\Delta_n)$ (this partition is based on a definition of specificity called *tolerance* where $\Delta_1$ contains the most specific rules and $\Delta_n$ the most general rules), and next, for a given fact $\mathcal{F}$, System Z selects one sub-base $E=\Sigma_{\Delta_1}\cup...\cup\Sigma_{\Delta_i}$ of $\Sigma$ such that: $\mathcal{F}\cup\Sigma_{\Delta_1}\cup...\cup\Sigma_{\Delta_i}$ is consistent but $\mathcal{F}\cup\Sigma_{\Delta_1}\cup...\cup\Sigma_{\Delta_{i+1}}$ is inconsistent (we recall that $\Sigma_{\Delta_i}$ is the classical form of the base $\Delta_i$). An inference in System Z is simply defined by: $\psi$ follows from $\Delta$ w.r.t. $\mathcal{F}$ if $\psi$ is a classical consequence of $\mathcal{F}\cup E$ (so, the definition of entailment is the same as the possibilistic logic machinery). System Z is equivalent to possibilistic logic approach proposed in [2] and Lehmann's rational closure [30].

System Z has two limits: in some situations it is adventurous and in other situations it is cautious. Indeed, in Example 5, System Z infers the non-intuitive conclusion p from (q∧r) while in our approach neither p nor ¬p is inferred (which is satisfying). Moreover, System Z can be cautious and more precisely suffers from the so-called "blocking property inheritance" problem[5], illustrated by the following default base (extended from the base of Example 8): $\Delta=\{p\rightarrow b, b\rightarrow le, p\rightarrow\neg f, b\rightarrow f\}$ where b→le means that generally birds have legs. System Z does not allow to infer that "penguins have legs" even if the rule b→le is not in any conflict. In **UC** we get this intuitive conclusion since **UC** only removes the formulas involved in an inconsistency and nothing more.

*Brewka's preferred sub-theories*

Boutilier [8] uses Brewka's preferred sub-theories [9] in System Z to define a new nonmonotonic inference relation. The idea is to start with the default base $(\Delta_1,...,\Delta_n)$ stratified by System Z and to construct a preferred sub-theory E from $\Delta$ by adding to the set of observed facts $\mathcal{F}$ as many formulas of the set $\Delta_1$ as possible (with respect to the consistency criterion) then as many formulas as possible of the set $\Delta_2$, and so on. Lastly, Boutilier defines the set of plausible conclusions as a set of assertions which holds in all preferred sub-theories of $\Delta$. This approach partially remedies to the blocking inheritance problem, but however it increases the set of plausible conclusions provided by System Z. Hence, using preferred sub-theories will not block the inference of adventurous conclusions produced by System Z (e.g. Example 5).

---

[5] When a subclass is an exception to a class for a precise property, it can inherit none of the properties of the class (even if it is not an exception for these properties).

The following example gives a situation where a conclusion is derived using **UC** while it cannot be obtained by applying Brewka's preferred sub-theories.

*Example 10:* Let $\Delta = \{x{\rightarrow}y, y{\rightarrow}z\}$ and $\mathcal{F}=\{x{\wedge}\neg z\}$. We are interested to know if y can be inferred or not. **UC** infers y, while **BPT** neither infer y nor $\neg$y.   □

*Other systems*

The system **LEX** is based on selecting some preferred sub-theories which contains a highest number of formulas with lower rank (see [29, 3] for more details). This approach is satisfactory in model-based diagnosis (see [19]) but in default reasoning this approach can be adventurous. Indeed, not only it generates undesirable conclusions, like in Example 5, but can be very syntax dependent. For example, duplicating the same formula can change the set of plausible conclusions. For instance, if we take a variant of Nixon diamond example, namely $\Delta=\{q{\rightarrow}p, r{\rightarrow}\neg p, e{\rightarrow}p\}$ (where e means ecologist), applying **LEX** to the given fact $e{\wedge}q{\wedge}r$ leads to infer p, while **UC** preserves ambiguity by inferring neither p nor $\neg$p.

Moreover, in Example 10, none of the following systems, **LEX**, $\varepsilon$-belief functions [5] and Geffner's system [27], allow us to infer the conclusion y from the fact "$x{\wedge}\neg z$".

Lastly, the following example shows a case where Geffner's conditional entailment [27] infers a conclusion which cannot be obtained by our **UC** system.

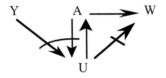

Figure 7

If we take the example of the default base $\Delta=\{A{\wedge}Y{\rightarrow}U, U{\rightarrow}A, U{\rightarrow}\neg W, A{\rightarrow}W\}$ of Figure 7, Geffner's conditional entailment deduces $\neg$W from $A{\wedge}Y$ while it is not possible to obtain it by our method (the minimality of the conflict leads to not consider the rule $U{\rightarrow}A$ and, then, to not make a difference in term of specificity between $U{\rightarrow}\neg W$ and $A{\rightarrow}W$). It is not easy to say if inferring "$\neg$W" is intuitive or not. This depends again on the meaning given to the symbols. Geffner provides an interpretation of propositional symbols where inferring $\neg$W is preferred: A stands for "adults", U "university students", W "work" and Y "young". However, we can also give another meaning where the intuition is the opposite. For example, if U means "university persons" and if Y means "teacher", we want to infer that W follows from $A{\wedge}Y$ ("adults teachers work").

## 6.   Conclusion

The proposed notion of local and coherence-based approach to inconsistency handling and default reasoning is appealing for several reasons. First, it reduces to the classical logic in the case of consistency. Next, our approach to dealing with conflicts is local and hence independent conflicts are solved separately. This is not easy to do with approaches based on a global handling of inconsistency, like System Z, where some formulas are removed while they are outside the conflicts. Thirdly, the local stratification offers more flexibility for representing priorities between beliefs. Fourthly, it is modular in the sense that the step of computing the specificity ordering of the defaults is independent of the step of solving conflicts. Hence, if one prefers another definition of specificity, then it is not very hard to adapt our method.

The choose between the three proposed local approaches depends on the considered application. If we are in real-time applications, then it is recommended to use the non-defeated inference, which never provides adventurous conclusions. The price to pay is that some plausible conclusions of the knowledge base will not be deduced. If we want to have a more adventurous approach with a reasonable time of computation then RFS-consequence relation can be appropriate. The price to pay is that some conclusions can be erroneous. If time has not a lot of importance or if the size of the knowledge base is reasonable then **UC** appears to be particularly attractive. It is not too cautious and avoids inferring unwanted conclusions.

A future work will be to apply the local techniques presented in this paper to model-based diagnosis, where contrary to the existing approaches (like GDE system [20]), the metaknowledge concerning the failure of the components is not given in terms of probability (which is generally not available) but simply is given locally by specifying inside the conflict which are the most suspicious ones.

## Acknowledgements

We would like to thank Didier DUBOIS, Simon PARSONS, Henri PRADE and the anonymous referees for their useful comments.

## References

1. E.W. Adams (1975). *The logic of conditionals*. D. Reidel.

2. S. Benferhat, D. Dubois and H. Prade (1992). Representing default rules in possibilistic logic. *Proc. of the 3rd Inter. Conf. on Principles of Knowledge Representation and Reasoning (KR'92)*. 673-684.

3. S. Benferhat, C. Cayrol, D. Dubois, J. Lang and H. Prade (1993). Inconsistency management and prioritized syntax-based entailment. *Proc. of the 13th Inter. Joint Conf. on Artificial Intelligence (IJCAI'93)*. 640-645.

4. S. Benferhat, D. Dubois and H. Prade (1995). How to infer from inconsistent beliefs without revising? *Proc. of the 14th Inter. Joint Conf. on Artificial Intelligence (IJCAI'95)*. 1449-1455. Extended version of this paper: Some syntactic approaches to the handling of inconsistent knowledge bases: a comparative study. *Technical report IRIT/94-55-R*.

5. S. Benferhat, A. Saffiotti and P. Smets (1995). Belief functions and default reasoning. *Proc. of Uncertainty in Artificial Intelligence (UAI'95)*. 19-26.

6. S. Benferhat, D. Dubois et H. Prade (1997) Possibilistic and standard probabilistic semantics of conditional knowledge. Proc. of the 14th National Conf. on Artificial Intelligence (AAAI'97), pp. 70-75.

7. W. Bibel (1985). Methods of automated reasoning. *Fundamentals in Artificial Intelligence*, LNCS 232.

8. C. Boutilier (1992). What is a Default priority? *Proc. of the 9th Canadian Conf. on Artificial Intelligence (AI'92)*. 140-147.

9. G. Brewka (1989). Preferred subtheories: an extended logical framework for default reasoning. *Proc. of the 11th Inter. Joint Conf. on Artificial Intelligence (IJCAI'89)*. 1043-1048.

10. G. Brewka (1994). Reasoning about priorities in default logic. *Proc. of the 1994 National Conf. on Artificial Intelligence (AAAI'94)*. 940-945.

11. T. Castell, C. Cayrol, M. Cayrol and D. Le Berre (1996). Using the Davis and Putnam procedure for an efficient computation of preferred models. *Proc. of the 12th European Conference on Artificial Intelligence (ECAI'96)*. 350-354.

12. C. Cayrol (1995). On the relation between argumentation and non-monotonic coherence-based entailment. *Proc. of the 14th Inter. Joint Conf. on Artificial Intelligence (IJCAI'95)*. 1443-1448.

13. C. Cayrol and M.C. Lagasquie-Schiex (1994). On the complexity of non-monotonic entailment in syntax-based approaches. *Proc. of Workshop ECAI'94 on Algorithms, Complexity and Commonsense Reasoning*.

14. L. Cholvy (1995). Automated reasoning with merged contradictory information whose reliability depends on topics. *Proc. of the 1995 European Conference on Symbolic and Quantitative Approaches to Reasoning under Uncertainty (ECSQARU'95)*.

15. N. C. A. Da Costa (1963). Calcul propositionnel pour les systèmes formels inconsistants. *Compte Rendu Acad. des Sciences (Paris)*, 257. 3790-3792.

16. N.C.A. Da Costa and D. Marconi (1987). An overview of paraconsistent logic in the 80s. *Monografias da Sociedade Paranense de Matematica*.

17. M. Davis and H. Putnam. A computing procedure for quantification theory. *Journal of the Assoc. for Computing Machinery*, 7. 201-215.

18. J. De Kleer (1986). An assumption-based TMS. *Artificial Intelligence*, 28. 127-162.

19. J. De Kleer (1990). Using crude probability estimates to guide diagnosis. *Artificial Intelligence*, 45. 381-391.

20. J. De Kleer and B. C. Williams (1987). Diagnosing multiple faults. *Artificial Intelligence*, 32. 97-130.

21. J. P. Delgrande and T. H. Schaub (1994). A general approach to specificity in default reasoning. *Proc. of the 4th Inter. Conf. on Principles of Knowledge Representation and Reasoning (KR'94)*. 146-157.

22. D. Dubois, J. Lang and H. Prade (1994). Possibilistic logic. *Handbook of Logic in A. I. and Logic Programming*, vol. 3. 439-513.

23. M. Elvang-Goransson, P. Krause and J. Fox (1993). Dialectic reasoning with inconsistent information. *Proc. of Uncertainty in Artificial Intelligence (UAI'93)*. 114-121.

24. R. Fagin, J. D. Ullman and M. Y. Vardi (1983). On the semantics of updates in database. *Proc. of the 2nd ACM SIGACT-SIGMOD Symp. on the Principles of Databases Systems*. 352-365.

25. D.M. Gabbay and A. Hunter (1991). Making inconsistency respectable (Part 1). *Fundamentals of Artificial Intelligence Research*, LNAI 535. 19-32.

26. P. Gärdenfors (1988). *Knowledge in flux - Modeling the dynamic of epistemic states*. MIT Press.

27. H. Geffner (1992). *Default reasoning: Causal and conditional theories*. MIT Press.

28. S. Kraus, D. Lehmann and M. Magidor (1990). Nonmonotonic reasoning, preferential models and cumulative logics. *Artificial Intelligence*, 44. 167-207.

29. D. Lehmann (1993). Another perspective on default reasoning. *Technical report*. Hebrew University, Jerusalem.

30. D. Lehmann and M. Magidor (1992). What does a conditional knowledge base entail? *Artificial Intelligence*, 55. 1-60.

31. D. Makinson (1989). General theory of cumulative inference. *Non-monotonic reasoning*, LNCS 346. 1-18.

32. Y. Moinard (1987). Donner la préférence au défaut le plus spécifique. *Proc. of the 6th Conf. on Reconnaissance des Formes et Intelligence Artificielle (RFIA'87)*. 1123-1132.

33. B. Nebel (1991). Belief revision and default reasoning: syntax-based approaches. *Proc. of the 2nd Inter. Conf. on Principles of Knowledge Representation and Reasoning (KR'91)*. 417-428.

34. B. Nebel (1994). Base revision operator and schemes: semantics representation and complexity. *Proc. of the 11th European Conference on Artificial Intelligence (ECAI'94)*. 341-345.

35. O. Papini (1992). A complete revision function in propositional calculus. *Proc. of the 10th European Conference on Artificial Intelligence (ECAI'92)*. 339-343.

36. O. Papini and A. Rauzy (1995). Révision : mettons un bémol. *Revue d'Intelligence Artificielle*, vol. 9, n°4. 455-473.

37. J. Pearl (1988) Probabilistic Reasoning in Intelligent Systems: Networks of Plausible Inference. Morgan Kaufmann, San Mateo, CA.

38. J. Pearl (1990). System Z: A natural ordering of defaults with tractable applications to default reasoning. *Proc. of the 3rd Conf. on Theoretical Aspects of Reasoning about Knowledge (TARK'90)*. 121-135.

39. G. M. Provan (1988). The computational complexity of assumption-based truth maintenance systems. *Technical report*. University of British Columbia, Vancouver.

40. R. Reiter (1980). A logic for default reasoning. *Artificial Intelligence*, 13. 81-132.

41. R. Reiter (1987). A theory of diagnosis from first principles. *Artificial Intelligence*, 32. 57-95.

42. R. Reiter and G. Criscuolo (1981). On interacting defaults. *Proc. of the 7th Inter. Joint Conf. on Artificial Intelligence (IJCAI'81)*. 270-276.

43. N. Rescher (1976). *Plausible Reasoning: An introduction to the theory and practice of plausibilistic inference*. Van Gorcum.

44. N. Roos (1992). A logic for reasoning with inconsistent knowledge. *Artificial Intelligence*, 57. 69-103.

45. P. Snow (1996) Standard probability distributions described by rational default entailment. Technical Report.

46. S. Toulmin (1956). *The uses of argument*. Cambridge University Press.

47. D. S. Touretzky (1984). Implicit ordering of defaults in inheritance systems. *Proc. of the 1984 National Conf. on Artificial Intelligence (AAAI'84)*. 322-325.

48. M. A. Williams (1996). Towards a Practical Approach to Belief Revision: Reason-Based Change. *Proc. of the 5th Inter. Conf. on Principles of Knowledge Representation and Reasoning (KR'96)*. 412-421.

# The XRay System: An Implementation Platform for Local Query-Answering in Default Logics[*]

Pascal Nicolas[1] and Torsten Schaub[1,2]

[1] LERIA, Faculté de Sciences, Université d'Angers, 2 Boulevard Lavoisier,
F-49045 Angers Cedex 01, pascal.nicolas@univ-angers.fr
[2] Institut für Informatik, Universität Potsdam, Postfach 60 15 53, D-14415 Potsdam,
torsten@cs.uni-potsdam.de

**Abstract.** We present an implementation platform for query-answering in default logics, supporting local proof procedures. We describe the salient features of the corresponding system, called XRay, and provide some major theoretical underpinnings. The deductive power of XRay stems from its usage of Prolog Technology Theorem Proving Techniques (PTTP). This is supported by further enhancements, such as default lemma handling, regularity-based truncations of the underlying search space, and further configurable features. The computational value of these enhancements is backed up by a series of experiments that provide us with valuable insights into their influence on XRay's performance. The generality of the approach, allowing for a (simultaneous) treatment of different default logics, stems from a novel model-based approach to consistency checking.

## 1 Introduction

In many AI applications, default reasoning plays an important role since many subtasks involve reasoning from incomplete information. Starting with [24], the last 17 years have provided us with a profound understanding of the underlying problems and have resulted in a number of well-understood formal approaches to default reasoning. During the development of our proof system for query-answering in default logics, called XRay, we draw heavily on this knowledge. XRay's deductive power, however, is mainly due to our efforts at implementing default reasoning by means of advanced classical theorem proving techniques: Unlike other approaches that address the implementation of default reasoning by encapsulating the underlying theorem prover as a separate module, we pursue a rather different approach by integrating default reasoning into an existing automated theorem prover. In particular, we were able to adapt a very interesting implementation technique for our purposes, namely the *Prolog Technology Theorem Proving* approach (PTTP) [31], which allows us to take advantage of todays highly efficient Prolog systems.

To be more precise, we are interested in query-answering in default logics and hence we elaborate on proof procedures that allow for determining whether

---

[*] This is a revised and largely extended version of [28].

a formula has a default proof from an underlying default theory. This question was first addressed in [24]. Other authors like [30, 22, 11] are primarily interested in computing entire conclusion sets from which queries are then (roughly) answerable by memberships tests. As opposed to such bottom-up computations, our approach strictly proceeds in a top-down manner, starting from the given query. This is why we center it around *local proof procedures* that allow for validating each inference when it is performed. As already put forward in [24], this is feasible in the presence of the property of semi-monotonicity, among other options such as stratification techniques [1, 7]. This property allows us to consider a relevant subset of default rules while answering a query. Note that in the absence of such a property a proof procedure must necessarily consider all default rules in the given theory.

The basic compilation techniques needed for default reasoning were introduced in [26] while focusing on the somehow greatest common fragment of default logics given by normal default theories (see below). The corresponding implementation was sketched in [27]. Our present contribution thus concentrates

- on generalizing the aforementioned approach towards full-fledged default logics,
- on providing experimental analysis of the enhancements conceived for improving XRay's performance, and
- on describing XRay's basic usage and some selected implementation details.

We start in Section 2 by giving a brief introduction to the basic concepts of default logic and we describe XRay's fundamental compilation techniques. Section 3 and 4 focus on XRay's salient features and their computational value, respectively. For simplicity, the exposition in the first half of the paper is mainly given by appeal to so-called normal default theories. Section 5 addresses the treatment of full-fledged default logics by means of an extended model-based approach to consistency checking. Section 6 provides a closer look at XRay's functionality by detailing diverse file interfaces.

## 2 Background and basic compilation techniques

This section gives a very brief overview of the basic formal and technical underpinnings needed for understanding the principles of our system. The interested reader is referred to the given literature for a detailed introduction to the concepts sketched in this section.

Let us first give some concepts of default logic required for a basic understanding of XRay's capabilities: Default logic augments classical logic by *default rules* (*defaults* for short) for sanctioning inferences that rely upon given as well as absent information. Knowledge is represented in default logics by *default theories* $(D, W)$ consisting of a (for simplicity) consistent set of formulas $W$ and a set of defaults $D$; both of which are taken to be propositional in the sequel. A default $\frac{\alpha : \beta}{\gamma}$ has two types of antecedents: A *prerequisite* $\alpha$ which is established if $\alpha$ is derivable and a *justification* $\beta$ which is established if $\beta$ is "consistent"

356

(see below). If both conditions hold, the *consequent* $\gamma$ is concluded by default.[3] A set of such conclusions is called an *extension* of an initial set of facts. Given a default theory $(D, W)$, any such extension $E$ is a deductively closed set of formulas containing $W$ such that, for any $\frac{\alpha : \beta}{\gamma} \in D$, if $\alpha \in E$ and $\neg\beta \notin E$ then $\gamma \in E$.

While we treat general default theories in Section 5, we confine ourselves for simplicity in what follows to so-called *normal* default theories, containing normal defaults $\frac{\alpha : \gamma}{\gamma}$ only. A *default proof* $D_\varphi$ for a formula $\varphi$ from a normal default theory $(D, W)$ is a finite sequence of defaults $\langle \frac{\alpha_i : \gamma_i}{\gamma_i} \rangle_{i \in I}$ such that

$$W \cup \{\gamma_i \mid i \in I\} \vdash \varphi$$

and for all $i \in I$:

$$W \cup \{\gamma_0, \ldots, \gamma_{i-1}\} \vdash \alpha_i \tag{1}$$
$$W \cup \{\gamma_0, \ldots, \gamma_{i-1}\} \nvdash \neg\gamma_i \tag{2}$$

Condition (1) spells out that $D_\varphi$ has to be *grounded* in $W$. Condition (2) expresses an incremental notion of *consistency*. One can show that $\varphi \in E$ for some extension $E$ of $(D, W)$ iff $\varphi$ has a default proof $D_\varphi$ from $(D, W)$. As an example, consider the statements "students are adults", "adults usually have a driving license", and "having a driving license usually implies being able to drive a car". The corresponding default theory along with fact $S$ for students is

$$\left( \left\{ \frac{A : L}{L}, \frac{L : C}{C} \right\}, \{S, S \to A\} \right) . \tag{3}$$

For instance, we can show $C$ (or that, given $S$, "students are able to drive a car") by means of default proof

$$\left\langle \frac{A : L}{L}, \frac{L : C}{C} \right\rangle . \tag{4}$$

The formal basis of **XRay**'s query answering procedure rests on a *connection calculus*[4] for characterizing default proofs [25]; it is based on the idea that a default $\frac{\alpha : \beta}{\gamma}$ can be decomposed into a *classical implication* $\alpha \to \gamma$ along with two proof-theoretic conditions on the usage of the resulting clauses: *admissibility* (accounting for groundedness) and *compatibility* (enforcing consistency). In the sequel, let $C_W$ be the clausal representation of $W$ and let $C_D$ be the set of clauses $\{\neg\alpha, \gamma\}$ obtained from the implications $\alpha \to \gamma$ corresponding to defaults $\frac{\alpha : \beta}{\gamma}$ in $D$. (Wlog. we assume that a default consists of atomic components only; such an atomic format is always obtainable by appropriately introducing new atomic propositions (see [25] for details).) In our example, we get the following sets of clauses:

$$C_W = \{\{S\}, \{\neg S, A\}\} \quad \text{and} \quad C_D = \{\{\neg A, L\}, \{\neg L, C\}\} . \tag{5}$$

---

[3] We use $\alpha, \beta, \gamma$ throughout the paper for referring to the respective components.

[4] Connection calculi are structure-oriented formal proof systems. See [5, 6] for details.

The key observation that led to **XRay** was that this approach allows to apply Prolog technology. This is due to the fact that the aforementioned connection calculus can be mapped onto *model elimination*[5] (ME) [19] which is itself implementable by means of Prolog Technology Theorem Provers (PTTPs) [31]. The idea (illustrated in Figure 1) is then to translate a default theory along with query into a Prolog program and a Prolog query such that the original query belongs to an extension of the default theory iff the Prolog query is derivable from the Prolog program. (In PTTP, the original queries are actually a part of

Default logic
  program

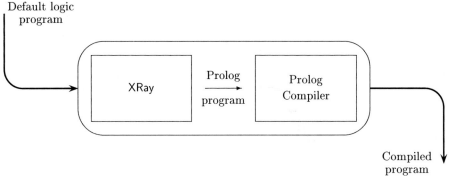

Compiled
program

**Fig. 1.** The outer architecture of **XRay**.

the knowledge base; they are subsequently posed by special query predicates, as detailed at the end of this section.)

As regards classical theorem proving, our implementation follows the approach taken by Mark Stickel's PTTP [32]. PTTP can be seen as an extension of Prolog that provides a proof system for full first order predicate calculus. To this end, Prolog's input resolution has to be basically enriched by possibilities to reason by contraposition and to reason by cases via reduction steps. (Recall that ME essentially consists of input resolution augmented by the possibility to apply reduction steps (for details see [19]).) This can be achieved by a mechanism translating clauses into a Prolog program encoding both features. For integrating the concepts of admissibility and compatibility this translation has to be extended appropriately.

To explain this, let us first give an idea of the Prolog rules produced by **XRay**, given Default theory (3) from Section 1.[6] For reference, the rules are preceded by numbers:

---

[5] Model elimination furnishes another formal proof system that can be seen as belonging to the family of connection calculi, while being rather algorithmic. See [19, 6] for details.

[6] Following PTTP's syntax, a and not_a stand for $A$ and $\neg A$ etc. Thus, eg. not_a stands for $\neg adult$.

```
(1) s(Anc,(Mod,Mod)).
(2) a(Anc,(ModI,ModO)) :-          (4) not_a(Anc,(Mod,Mod)) :-
        NewAnc = [a|Anc],                  member(a,Anc).
        s(NewAnc,(ModI,ModO)).
(3) not_s(Anc,(ModI,ModO)) :-      (5) s(Anc,(Mod,Mod)) :-
        NewAnc = [not_s|Anc],              member(not_s,Anc).
        not_a(NewAnc,(ModI,ModO)).
(6) l(Anc,(Mod,NewMod)) :-         (7) c(Anc,(Mod,NewMod)) :-
        a([],(Mod,Mod1)),                  l([],(Mod,Mod1)),
        model(l,Mod1,NewMod).              model(c,Mod1,NewMod).
```

Neglecting for the time being the second argument of each (Prolog-)literal, it is easy to see that rules (1)–(5) were generated from $C_W$, as given in (5), according to Stickel's approach: Rules (1)–(3) encode all contrapositives for clauses in $C_W$ to enable reasoning by contraposition. That is, rules (1)–(3) are refinements of s, a :- s, and not_s :- not_a, whereas rules (4) and (5) implement reduction steps, allowing for inferences with ancester subgoals.[7] To this end, the first argument, namely Anc, of each literal is used to memorize ancestor goals. (For further details on the translation of classical formulas in the PTTP approach the reader is referred to [32].)

Let us now turn to the translation of the set of defaults in (3) along the lines detailed in [26]: Rules (6) and (7) result from translating the elements of $C_D$, as given in (5). As mentioned above, this translation has to take care of the concepts of admissibility and compatibility. As shown in [25], admissibility can be implemented as follows: First, one has to guarantee that whenever a clause $\{\neg\alpha,\gamma\} \in C_D$ is used as input clause, only $\gamma$ is resolved upon. Therefore XRay generates only one so-called $\delta$-rule, namely a Prolog rule of form $\gamma : -\alpha$, corresponding to contrapositive $\gamma \leftarrow \alpha$. Second, the derivation used to prove $\alpha$ must not contain reduction steps with ancestor goals of $\alpha$. This is guaranteed by setting the list memorizing ancestor goals to the empty list (cf. Prolog rule (6) and (7)).

For implementing compatibility, we use a model-based approach guaranteeing at each point of a derivation that there is a model satisfying $W$ as well as all justifications of defaults used in this derivation. To this end, each literal is augmented by a second argument for propagating models. Furthermore, we use the predicate model/3 that, given a model Mod and the justification $\gamma$ of a (normal)[8] default $\delta$, checks whether there is a new model NewMod such that NewMod satisfies $\gamma$, too.[9] If this is not the case model/3 fails since the use of the rule generated from $\delta$ violates compatibility. (This approach is elaborated upon in Section 5 for treating general defaults.)

The above material only provides XRay's basic recipe for transforming a default theory $(D, W)$. The rules generated by XRay are in fact much more

---

[7] Recall that a reduction step allows to solve a goal if it is complementary to one of its ancestor goals.

[8] Eg. in constrained default logic, this requires testing $\beta \wedge \gamma$ for underlying $\frac{\alpha\,:\,\beta}{\gamma}$.

[9] See Section 5 for a formal specification of model/3.

complex. For instance, **XRay** adds further arguments and predicates in order to implement regularity checks and lemma handling (see Section 6). For query answering, **XRay** must also be able to transform queries: Following PTTP, **XRay** generates for a query $\varphi$ a rule of the form `query :- ` $\varphi(\dots)$, where '...' stands for the additional arguments discussed above. This allows the user to pose the initial query $\varphi$ via the Prolog query `?-query`. Without going into details, rule `query :- ` $\varphi(\dots)$ is further enriched by predicates, for instance for finding an initial model of $W$ and proof printing.

## 3   XRay's salient features: An overview

Let us now describe some salient features of our implementation. First of all, let us have a closer look at the **XRay** module given in Figure 1; its inner structure is given in Figure 2. **XRay** is built upon Mark Stickel's PTTP. The basic adaptions

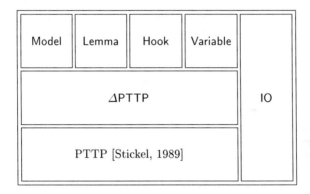

**Fig. 2.** XRay's inner architecture.

for handling defaults are done in module $\Delta$PTTP.

One of the major enhancement situated in the latter module is given by the enforcement of *regularity*, which is an indispensable technique for ME-based proof systems (eg. see [15]). It forbids that a subgoal is identical to one of its ancestor goals. For our implementation, this tool had to be adapted to what we call *blockwise regularity*. Blockwise regularity requires (i) that no subgoal is equal to one of its ancestors except if a $\delta$-rule was used in between, and (ii) that after applying a $\delta$-rule $\gamma$ :- $\alpha$, it must not be used for proving $\alpha$. This form of regularity prunes away large parts of the search space; it furthermore guarantees completeness because every infinite branch of a derivation necessarily violates blockwise regularity. The blockwise regularity check is an permanent feature of **XRay**.

In contrast to such an immanent feature, **XRay** allows us to decide at compile-time whether we check first a default's justification for consistency or whether we prove first its prerequisite. This amounts to switching the tasks specified by Condition (1) and (2) in Section 2. Alternatively, we could thus obtain for $\delta$-rules (6) and (7):

```
(6') l(Anc,(Mod,NewMod)) :-        (7') c(Anc,(Mod,NewMod)) :-
        model(l,Mod,Mod1),                 model(c,Mod,Mod1),
        a([],(Mod1,NewMod)).               l([],(Mod1,NewMod)).
```

As we will see below, this task switching may have an important influence on the performance depending on the considered example. This compile-time switch is also located in Module $\Delta$PTTP.

Another valuable enhancement is provided by *lemma handling* as an important means for eliminating redundancy in ME-based theorem proving (eg. see [15]). This task is however more difficult in our context, since proofs may depend on defaults. Therefore, XRay distinguishes between *static* and *dynamic lemmas* (cf. [17]). A static lemma may be kept along with its underlying consistency assumptions throughout a whole derivation (and even beyond); this requires verifying compatibility each time such a lemma is used. Instead, the validity of dynamic lemmas expires as soon as one of the defaults used in their proof is withdrawn. Thus, they are usable without any consistency checks. The latter form of lemmas may result in a significant speed-up, while they practically never harm the proof search due to their restricted viability (cf. Section 4). Lemma handling is an optional feature of XRay, providing many parameters. Among them, we are able (i) to choose between dynamic, static, or both types of lemmas, (ii) to parameterize the type of lemmas, such as default consequents or selected predicates, and (iii) to choose the syntactic format of lemmas, like unit or disjunctive lemmas.[10] All these features are provided by module Lemma.

Before entering the experimental results, we mention that (i) XRay deals with formulas in negation normal form; a more comfortable front-end comprising a default logic programming language is available and sketched in Section 6 (Module IO), (ii) XRay provides separate query compilation (Module IO), (iii) it supports variable handling over a finite universe (Module Variable), and (iv) it allows for conditional insertion of Prolog code (Module Hook). A trivial application of the latter is a debugger that is implemented by adding spy-points at specifiable locations of the compiled default logic program.

## 4 The computational value of lemma handling and task switching: A case study on Hamiltonian cycle problems

This section provides some selected experiments illustrating some of the major features of XRay along with their influence on XRay's performance. All subsequent test examples are expressed via non-normal default theories in constrained

---

[10] Although one may generate both types, only unit lemmas are currently supported for subsequent usage.

default logic [13]; this is arguably the variant of default logic closest to normal default theories. [11]

To begin with, we have selected a "meaningful" example, `people`, that is a taxonomic knowledge base comprising 62 formulas, including disjunctive integrity constraints, implications, and defaults. Yet, in order to provide a systematic series of tests, we have moreover decided to treat an artificial yet generic set of examples. This allows us to study the general influence of XRay's parameters on its performance. However, instead of totally arbitrary default theories that arguably lack significance, we have decided to treat the problem of finding a Hamiltonian cycle in a graph. This problem is interesting because its size is easily parameterizable, it is graph- and complexity-theoretically well-studied, and it has already been subject to encodings in default logic [10].

Formally, given a graph $G = (V, E)$ where $V$ is a vertex set and $E$ a set of oriented edges between vertices in $V$, an *Hamiltonian cycle* in $G$ is a cycle meeting each vertex of $V$ exactly once. Here, we consider only complete and irreflexive graph $G = (V, E)$ with $n$ vertices $v_1, \ldots, v_n$. Following the approach of [10], we define the translation of an Hamiltonian cycle problem in $G$ into a constrained default theory $(D, W)$ such that:

$$\begin{aligned}
W &= \{vstd(v_1)\} \\
D &= \{go(v_i, v_j) \mid i = 1, \ldots, n \text{ and } v_j \in \Gamma^+(v_i)\} \\
&\quad \cup \{goback(v_i, v_1) \mid i = 2, \ldots, n\}
\end{aligned}$$

where $\Gamma^+(v) = \{(v, w) \in E \mid w \in V\}$ and

$$go(v_i, v_j) = \frac{vstd(v_i) : \neg move(v_i, v_1) \wedge \ldots \wedge \neg move(v_i, v_{j-1}) \wedge \neg move(v_i, v_{j+1}) \wedge \ldots \wedge \neg move(v_i, v_n)}{move(v_i, v_j) \wedge vstd(v_j)}$$

and

$$goback(v_i, v_1) = \frac{vstd(v_i) : \neg move(v_1, v_i) \wedge \ldots \wedge \neg move(v_{i-1}, v_1) \wedge \neg move(v_{i+1}, v_1) \wedge \neg move(v_n, v_1)}{move(v_i, v_1) \wedge vstdtwice(v_1)}$$

Intuitively, an Hamiltonian cycle is a path through a graph that "visits" all vertices and that comes back to the starting vertex. So, the underlying meaning of the used predicates are the following:

- $vstd(v_i)$ is true if vertex $v_i$ is visited. In $W$ we only have $vstd(v_1)$ to represent the fact that the starting vertex is $v_1$ (this choice is arbitrary and does not affect the existence or non-existence of a solution).
- for every edge $(v_i, v_j)$ in the graph, $go(v_i, v_j)$ can be read as: if the vertex $v_i$ is visited, and if it is possible to check that no move from $v_i$ to another vertex $v_j \neq v_i$ has been made, then the vertex $v_j$ is visited and we record the move from $v_i$ to $v_j$ (these defaults are useful to visit only one time every vertex).

---

[11] The technical underpinnings for handling this variant are given in Section 5; this section is dedicated to the evaluation of the concepts given in the last section.

– $goback(v_i, v_1)$ are special "go-defaults" to close the Hamiltonian cycle by going back to the first vertex. This is why we use $vstdtwice(v_1)$ to express that $v_1$ has to be visited two times since the searching cycle starts from $v_1$.

The problem of finding a Hamiltonian cycle in $G$ is then equivalent to the existence of a default proof of query

$$vstdtwice(v_1) \wedge (\textstyle\bigwedge_{i=1}^{n} vstd(v_i))$$

from $(D, W)$.

In the sequel, we denote by ham_n the default theory corresponding to a graph with $n$ vertices. Let us note that ham_n contains only one fact in $W$ and $n^2 - 1$ defaults. This results for ham_15, for instance, in an intermediate Prolog code (provided by XRay) containing 904 rules and 404430 bytes.

We give in Table 1 some experimental results where each item contains a time measure in seconds, comprising system and user time, along with the length of the resulting proof in parentheses. The test series vary in two respects, leading

| ordering | adm–com | | com–adm | |
|---|---|---|---|---|
| lemma | no lemmas | lemmas | no lemmas | lemmas |
| people | 0.08 (64) | 0.08 (50) | 0.09 (64) | 0.08 (50) |
| ham_4_min | 0.01 (36) | 0.0 (21) | 0.01 (36) | 0.0 (21) |
| ham_4_max | 424.03 (36) | 16.99 (21) | 1.34 (36) | 0.5 (21) |
| ham_5_min | > 1000 | > 1000 | 0.12 (52) | 0.06 (26) |
| ham_5_max | > 1000 | > 1000 | 7.51 (52) | 1.66 (26) |
| ham_6_min | > 1000 | > 1000 | 0.37 (71) | 0.15 (31) |
| ham_6_max | > 1000 | > 1000 | 330.53 (71) | 69.72 (31) |
| ham_7_min | > 1000 | > 1000 | 1.03 (93) | 0.25 (36) |
| ham_7_max | > 1000 | > 1000 | > 1000 | > 1000 |
| ham_8_min | > 2000 | > 2000 | 11.83 (118) | 1.76 (41) |
| ham_8_max | > 2000 | > 2000 | > 2000 | > 2000 |
| ham_10_min | > 2000 | > 2000 | 27.91 (177) | 5.38 (51) |
| ham_10_max | > 2000 | > 2000 | > 2000 | > 2000 |
| ham_20_min | > 5000 | > 5000 | > 5000 | 309.4 (101) |
| ham_20_max | > 5000 | > 5000 | > 5000 | > 5000 |

**Table 1.** Experimental results (on Linux Bi-PentiumPro, 200MHz, 256 MB).

to four different columns: The first two columns contain results obtained when checking first admissibility and subsequently compatibility, indicated by (**adm–com**); the order of tasks is switched in the columns headed by (**com–adm**). Furthermore, the columns differ as concerns the usage of dynamic lemmas, indicated by **lemmas**. As regards the test series, we have actually constructed for each problem ham_n ten different randomly selected permutations of the set of defaults. From these test series, we give for each column the minimal (`ham_n_min`) and maximal (`ham_n_max`) times obtained over these ten permutations.[12]

This witnesses the important influence of "programming" the knowledge base, since the same problem, for instance `ham_8`, can be solved in a time varying from 2 seconds (in `ham_8_min`) to more than 2000 seconds (in `ham_8_max`) in the last configuration. We have pushed this a bit further by doing 200 permutations over the default set in `ham_8`. The minimum test vector[13] obtained was 0.05 (118), 0.02 (41), 0.04 (118), 0.02 (41). This phenomenon is due to the fixed search strategy imposed by the underlying SLD-resolution of the Prolog system. In order to diminish this influence, we stick with PTTP's iterative deepening proof search (although blockwise regularity guarantees a finite search space).

Let us now take a closer look at Table 1. First of all, we observe that the use of dynamic lemmas always reduces the proof length and even more importantly the time spent for finding this proof. The latter is testified by the fact that no matter whether we check admissibility or compatibility first, we always improve (sometimes even by an order of magnitude) on the elapsed time. The impact of lemma handling on the proof (and in particular its length) is illustrated by Figure 3 and Figure 4, where the proof in `ham_4` is given first without and then with the use of lemmas.[14] In these figures, `ext`, `red`, `unit`, `default`, and `dyn-lemma` indicate the application of an extension, reduction, unit, default, or dynamic lemma inference, respectively. In fact, we observe that the subproofs of `gamma(4, (move(1, 3), vstd(3)))` and `gamma(7, (move(3, 2), vstd(2)))` in Figure 3 are entirely replaced in Figure 4 by using the corresponding default lemmas, since both of them have already been solved when proving `ext(vstd(4))`. Since XRay uses PTTP's iterative deepening approach to proof search, we are actually assured to obtain always shortest proofs.

As impressively witnessed by Table 1, the usage of dynamic lemmas has a significant influence on resolving Hamiltonian cycle problems. On the other hand, dynamic lemmas practically never harm the proof search due to the restricted viability of dynamic lemmas, as testified, for instance, by a failing query[15] to `ham_4` yielding test vector 3964.03 (—), 191.64 (—), 17.69 (—), 4.64 (—). Technically, this is due to the fact that (propositional unit) lemmas are treatable as unit clauses; hence a lemma's failure does not lead to any backtracking.

Another significant speed-up on Hamiltonian cycle problems is obtained by verifying compatibility before admissibility. In our particular case, this is due to the rather large conjuncts as justifications. So, when it comes to guaranteeing compatibility, the subsequent proof search becomes constrained by the justifications of the default rule at hand; in this way, we may discard a large number of putatively applicable yet incompatible defaults in the course of the rest of the proof search. The inverse phenomenon (albeit with a largely different significance) is sometimes observed on our taxonomic knowledge base, where

---

[12] These tests sets are automatically generated by a separate module of XRay [3].

[13] Such a vector corresponds to a line in Table 1.

[14] These proof trees are optionally generated by an extra module [33].

[15] A failing query was obtained by adding `fail` to the end of the successful query.

```
ext(query)
 |--ext(vstd(4))
 |  |--default(gamma(3, (move(2, 4), vstd(4))))
 |     |--ext(alpha(3, vstd(2)))
 |        |--ext(vstd(2))
 |           |--default(gamma(7, (move(3, 2), vstd(2))))
 |              |--ext(alpha(7, vstd(3)))
 |                 |--ext(vstd(3))
 |                    |--default(gamma(4, (move(1, 3), vstd(3))))
 |                       |--ext(alpha(4, vstd(1)))
 |                          |--unit(vstd(1))
 |--ext(vstd(3))
 |  |--default(gamma(4, (move(1, 3), vstd(3))))
 |     |--ext(alpha(4, vstd(1)))
 |        |--unit(vstd(1))
 |--ext(vstd(2))
 |  |--default(gamma(7, (move(3, 2), vstd(2))))
 |     |--ext(alpha(7, vstd(3)))
 |        |--ext(vstd(3))
 |           |--default(gamma(4, (move(1, 3), vstd(3))))
 |              |--ext(alpha(4, vstd(1)))
 |                 |--unit(vstd(1))
 |--unit(vstd(1))
 |--ext(vstdtwice(1))
    |--default(gamma(15, (move(4, 1), vstdtwice(1))))
       |--ext(alpha(15, vstd(4)))
          |--ext(vstd(4))
             |--default(gamma(3, (move(2, 4), vstd(4))))
                |--ext(alpha(3, vstd(2)))
                   |--ext(vstd(2))
                      |--default(gamma(7, (move(3, 2), vstd(2))))
                         |--ext(alpha(7, vstd(3)))
                            |--ext(vstd(3))
                               |--default(gamma(4, (move(1, 3), vstd(3))))
                                  |--ext(alpha(4, vstd(1)))
                                     |--unit(vstd(1))
```

**Fig. 3.** Proof tree for query $vstd(4) \land vstd(3) \land vstd(2) \land vstd(1) \land vstdtwice(1)$ from ham_4 without lemma handling and setting **com–adm**.

the choices of the inference engine are only rarely corrected by the subsequent compatibility check.

In view of using XRay for realistic applications, we can finally draw the following conclusions from our experimental results:

- default reordering, at least locally, may enhance the performance,
- using dynamic lemmas always improves the efficiency of XRay,
- checking compatibility before admissibility can be a good way to speed up the search in presence of defaults with rather complex justifications.

## 5  Addressing different default theories (simultaneously)

Up to now, we have described the XRay system along with its major features mainly from the perspective of normal default theories. This section goes now

```
ext(query)
  |--ext(vstd(4))
  |  |--default(gamma(3, (move(2, 4), vstd(4))))
  |     |--ext(alpha(3, vstd(2)))
  |        |--ext(vstd(2))
  |           |--default(gamma(7, (move(3, 2), vstd(2))))
  |              |--ext(alpha(7, vstd(3)))
  |                 |--ext(vstd(3))
  |                    |--default(gamma(4, (move(1, 3), vstd(3))))
  |                       |--ext(alpha(4, vstd(1)))
  |                          |--unit(vstd(1))
  |--ext(vstd(3))
  |  |--dyn_lemma(gamma(4, (move(1, 3), vstd(3))))
  |--ext(vstd(2))
  |  |--dyn_lemma(gamma(7, (move(3, 2), vstd(2))))
  |--unit(vstd(1))
  |--ext(vstdtwice(1))
     |--default(gamma(15, (move(4, 1), vstdtwice(1))))
        |--ext(alpha(15, vstd(4)))
           |--ext(vstd(4))
              |--dyn_lemma(gamma(3, (move(2, 4), vstd(4))))
```

**Fig. 4.** Proof tree for query $vstd(4) \wedge vstd(3) \wedge vstd(2) \wedge vstd(1) \wedge vstdtwice(1)$ from ham_4 with lemma handling and setting **com–adm**.

largely beyond this fragment and supplies us with the theoretical underpinnings and the specification of our treatment of non-normal default theories. Importantly, this generalization affects Module **Model** (cf. Figure 2) only. This is because full-fledged default logics, like classical [24], justified [20], constrained [13], or rational default logic [21], differ only in the way they address consistency. For implementing such a variety of systems, we can thus restrict our attention to the treatment of consistency, while relying for the implementation of further default logic specific techniques like deduction and groundedness on those developed for normal default theories. Since our approach is however founded on a local proof machinery, it cannot treat default theories needing an inspection of all default rules for proving a query. The resulting restriction is made precise below.

For implementing a variety of systems, we have actually two alternatives: Either we address each variant in turn, or we provide a technique general enough to cover all of them. The latter option is clearly the more generic one. Apart from the fact that it allows for realizing the first option anyway, it has moreover the advantage that we may *mix* multiple conceptions of default logics in the same setting. This is why we have chosen to pursue the more general approach. This undertaking benefits from the fact that its theoretical underpinnings have already been established in [4], where a context-based framework for default logics was proposed. In this approach each variant of default logic corresponds to a fragment of a more general and uniform default reasoning system, called *contextual default logic*.

## 5.1 Introducing contextual default logic.

In this approach, one considers roughly three sets of formulas: A set of facts $W$, an extension $E$, and a certain *context* $C$ such that $W \subseteq E \subseteq C$. The set of formulas $C$ is somehow established from the facts, the default conclusions, as well as from all underlying consistency assumptions, given by the justifications of all applied defaults. For those familiar with the aforementioned default logics, this approach trivially captures the application conditions found in existing default logics: For $\frac{\alpha : \beta}{\gamma}$, eg. $\alpha \in E$ and $\neg\beta \notin E$ in the case of classical default logic, and $\alpha \in E$ and $\neg(\beta \wedge \gamma) \notin C$ in constrained default logic. This motivates an extended notion of a default [4]: A *contextual default* $\delta$ is an expression of the form

$$\frac{\alpha_W \mid \alpha_E \mid \alpha_C \; : \; \beta_C \mid \beta_E \mid \beta_W}{\gamma}$$

Taking $x \in \{W, E, C\}$, formula $\alpha_x$ is called $x$-prerequisite, also $Prereq_x(\delta)$, $\beta_x$ is called $x$-justification, also $Justif_x(\delta)$, and $\gamma$ is the consequent, also $Conseq(\delta)$.[16] For convenience, we omit tautological components; a non-existing component must thus be identified with a tautology. Very roughly, such a rule applies wrt the aforementioned sets $W$, $E$, and $C$, if $\alpha_W \in W$, $\alpha_E \in E$, $\alpha_C \in C$, and $\neg\beta_C \notin C$, $\neg\beta_E \notin E$, $\neg\beta_W \notin W$. The reader is referred to [4] for further formal details, such as the definition of a contextual extension.

In fact, [4] show that classical, justified, and constrained default logic are embedded in contextual default logic. [18] extends these embeddings to rational default logic. For brevity, we exemplarily give the resulting mappings and refer the reader to [4, 18] for the corresponding equivalence results: For a default theory $(D, W)$, define

$$\Phi_{\mathsf{DL}}(D, W) = \left( \left\{ \frac{\mid \alpha \mid : \mid \beta \mid}{\gamma} \; \middle| \; \frac{\alpha : \beta}{\gamma} \in D \right\}, W \right) \qquad \text{(Classical default logic)}$$

$$\Phi_{\mathsf{JDL}}(D, W) = \left( \left\{ \frac{\mid \alpha \mid : \gamma \mid \beta \wedge \gamma \mid}{\gamma} \; \middle| \; \frac{\alpha : \beta}{\gamma} \in D \right\}, W \right) \qquad \text{(Justified default logic)}$$

$$\Phi_{\mathsf{CDL}}(D, W) = \left( \left\{ \frac{\mid \alpha \mid : \beta \wedge \gamma \mid\mid}{\gamma} \; \middle| \; \frac{\alpha : \beta}{\gamma} \in D \right\}, W \right) \qquad \text{(Constrained default logic)}$$

$$\Phi_{\mathsf{RDL}}(D, W) = \left( \left\{ \frac{\mid \alpha \mid : \beta \mid\mid}{\gamma} \; \middle| \; \frac{\alpha : \beta}{\gamma} \in D \right\}, W \right) \qquad \text{(Rational default logic)}$$

Then, the translated contextual default theory yields the same extensions as obtained in the original default logic.

These embeddings extend to variants of default logic relying on labeled formulas (or *assertions* [8]): [13] shows that constrained and cumulative default logic [8] are equivalent modulo representation. The same is shown by [14] for classical and Q-default logic [14], and by [18] for rational and CA-default logic [14], respectively.

As a brief example [23], suppose we have defaults saying that a robot's arm is usable, unless it is broken and we are told that one of the robot's arms, the left one or the right one, is broken. For repairing, the mechanic relies on the following defaults: if it is possible that the arm's failure is caused by hardware

---

[16] These projections extend to sets of contextual defaults in the obvious way.

failure then take the tool-box; if it is possible that it is due to a software problem then take the laptop. In our setting, hard- and software errors cannot appear simultaneously. Encoding the latter defaults by appeal to $\Phi_{JDL}$ and the former with $\Phi_{CDL}$ yields:

$$\left( \left\{ \frac{||: \neg Bl \wedge Ul \, ||}{Ul}, \quad \frac{||: \neg Br \wedge Ur \, ||}{Ur}, \quad \frac{||: To \,|\, Ha \wedge To \,|}{To}, \quad \frac{||: La \,|\, So \wedge La \,|}{La} \right\}, \{Bl \vee Br, \neg Ha \vee \neg So\} \right)$$

This encoding attributes stronger consistency constraints to the justifications of the first two defaults than to those of the last two default rules. As a consequence, we obtain two extensions, one containing Ul, To, and La and another with Ur, To, and La due to different types of justifications. That is, we obtain that, no matter which arm is usable, we take both toolbox and laptop.

## 5.2 Default proofs in contextual default logic

As discussed in the introductory section, we address query-answering by means of a top-down proof procedure; such a procedure is arguably most powerful if it is executable in a *local* fashion that allows for verifying the validity of each inference step when it is performed. In default logics, such localness is most effectively guaranteed by the property of *semi-monotonicity*, which is notably enjoyed by normal default theories, on which we focused in the previous sections. In accord with this, we restrict our attention to contextual default theories supporting a local formation of default proofs: We call a contextual default theory $(D, W)$ *semi-monotonic* if we have for any two subsets $D'$ and $D''$ of $D$ with $D'' \subseteq D' \subseteq D$ that if $(E'', C'')$ is a contextual extension of $(D'', W)$, then there is a contextual extension $(E', C')$ of $(D', W)$ such that $E'' \subseteq E'$ and $C'' \subseteq C'$. Actually, justified and constrained default logic enjoy semi-monotonicity in full generality. Clearly, this carries over to the corresponding fragments of contextual default logic, so that our approach applies immediately to these default logics. Notably, this extends to the union of the respective default theories; thus allowing for treating some default rules according to justified default logic and others according to constrained default logic. For classical and rational default logic, on the other hand, we must restrict ourselves to semi-monotonic fragments. (Such fragments should be determinable by appropriate stratification techniques; a concrete adaptation of such techniques remains however future work.)

For furnishing an appropriate proof theory, we account next for the notion of a default proof suitable for (semi-monotonic) contextual default logic. In view of the above embeddings, we may restrict ourselves to contextual default rules of the following form: [17]

$$D^\star = \left\{ \frac{|\alpha| \; : \; \beta_C \,|\, \beta_E \,|}{\gamma} \right\}$$

---

[17] This is because neither of $\Phi_{DL}$, $\Phi_{RDL}$, $\Phi_{CDL}$, or $\Phi_{RDL}$, respectively, do make use of $W$- and $C$-prerequisites nor $W$-justifications.

Then, according to [29], a default proof for a formula $\varphi$ from a semi-monotonic contextual default theory $(D, W)$ with $D \subseteq D^\star$ is a finite sequence of contextual default rules $\langle \delta_i \rangle_{i \in I}$ such that

$$W \cup \{ Conseq(\delta_i) \mid i \in I \} \vdash \varphi$$

and for all $i \in I$:

$$W \cup Conseq(\{\delta_0, \ldots, \delta_{i-1}\}) \vdash Prereq_E(\delta_i) \tag{6}$$

$$\left\{ \begin{array}{c} W \cup Conseq(\{\delta_0, \ldots, \delta_i\}) \cup Justif_C(\{\delta_0, \ldots, \delta_i\}) \nvdash \neg Justif_E(\delta_k) \\ \text{for } k \in \{0, \ldots, i\} \end{array} \right\} \tag{7}$$

By semi-monotonicity and compactness, $\varphi$ is then in some extension of $(D, W)$ iff there is a default proof for $\varphi$ from $(D, W)$. Clearly, the derivation of $\varphi$ from $W$ and $\langle \delta_i \rangle_{i \in I}$ as well as Condition (6), that is groundedness of $\langle \delta_i \rangle_{i \in I}$, are treated as with standard normal default theories. This witnesses the fact that we can concentrate on the implementation of Condition (7).

It is instructive to verify that the above specification reduces to that given in Section 2 when treating normal default theories. Another simplification is observed when regarding Condition (7) in case of constrained default logic due to the absence of $E$-justifications: [18]

$$W \cup Conseq(\{\delta_0, \ldots, \delta_{i-1}\}) \cup Justif_C(\{\delta_0, \ldots, \delta_{i-1}\}) \nvdash \neg Conseq(\delta_i) \vee \neg Justif_C(\delta_i)$$

## 5.3 Specification of the compatibility check

Let us now turn to the actual topic of this section: The implementation of various default logics by an enhanced approach to consistency. As indicated above, we pursue a model-based approach to reduce computational efforts of successive consistency checks. In fact, a model provides us with a compact representation of the consistency of a (partial) default proof at hand. For normal default theories $(D, W)$, we start with an initial model $m$ of $W$. Whenever a (normal) $\delta$-rule $\gamma$ :- $\alpha$ is used, we check whether $m$ satisfies $\gamma$. If this easy test succeeds, we continue with $m$. If not, a new model (of $W, \gamma$ and all justifications involved so far) is generated or, if this fails too, backtracking is engaged. To find models, we use a variant of the Davis-Putnam procedure [12]. Further improvements to minimize the search space for finding models are detailed in [9, 29]. Among them, we rely on so-called *model-matrices* representing all possible models.[19] Importantly, such a matrix can be significantly reduced during a derivation (i) by using information gathered during the proof search by means of lemma techniques and (ii) by continued applications of reductions, such as unit-resolutions and subsumptions. This leads to a drastic reduction of the search space for finding new models, as argued in more detail in [9].

---

[18] To be precise, all $E$-justifications are tautological rather than non-existent.

[19] A matrix represents a formula in conjunctive normal form. An open path through such a matrix gives a partial model of the underlying formula.

For normal default theories, it is actually sufficient to furnish a single model of the premises in $W$ satisfying all default conclusions in a proof at hand (cf. Condition (2)). In the presence of putatively contradictory $E$-justifications, however, we need more complex model structures for guaranteeing compatibility. In fact, we need now several models of $W$, all of which must entail the consequents and the $C$-justifications of the defaults involved in the current derivation, while there must be at least one model of each $E$-justification among them. Observe that the models covering $E$-justifications are not necessarily distinct; distinctness is only necessary in the presence of contradictory $E$-justifications.

Let us make this precise in the sequel. For a formula $\phi$ and a set of models $M$, we write $M \models \phi$ if $m \models \phi$ for all $m \in M$; and $M \not\models \phi$ if $m \models \neg\phi$ for some $m \in M$. For a set of formulas $S$, we define its set of models as $Mod(S)$. For sets of formulas $S$ and $T$, we define [20]

$$Mod_S(T) = \begin{cases} \bigcup_{\phi \in T} Mod(S \cup \{\phi\}) & \text{if } T \neq \emptyset \\ Mod(S) & \text{otherwise} \end{cases}$$

For a set of formulas $W$ and a sequence of contextual defaults $\langle \delta_i \rangle_{i \in I}$ of form $\frac{\lfloor \alpha \rfloor : \beta_C \lfloor \beta_E \rfloor}{\gamma}$ (sufficient in view of the above translations), we are then interested in selecting individual members from the model set $Mod_S(T)$ obtained by taking

$$S = W \cup Conseq(\{\delta_i \mid i \in I\}) \cup Justif_C(\{\delta_i \mid i \in I\})$$
$$\text{and} \quad T = Justif_E(\{\delta_i \mid i \in I\}) .$$

For readability, we abbreviate this set of models by $M_W(I)$; in analogy, we denote its subset $\{m \in M_W(I) \mid m \models Justif_E(\delta_i)\}$ by $M_W^i(I)$ for $i \in I$. In fact, for non-empty $I$, $M_W(I)$ equals $\bigcup_{i \in I} M_W^i(I)$, each of which covers a different $E$-justification in $Justif_E(\{\delta_i \mid i \in I\})$.

For illustration, consider the model set induced by the first aforementioned extension:

$$Mod_{W \cup \{UI, To, La\} \cup \{\neg Bl \wedge Ul\}} (\{Ha \wedge To, So \wedge La\})$$

where $W = \{Bl \vee Br, \neg Ha \vee \neg So\}$. This set of models is actually composed of two distinct sets, those satisfying $Ha \wedge \neg So$ and those satisfying $So \wedge \neg Ha$. Such model sets furnish the *domain* from which we select individual models witnessing the compatible application of defaults.

Now, in order to characterize compatible default proofs $\langle \delta_i \rangle_{i \in I}$ from a set of premises $W$, we consider non-empty subsets $M$ of $M_W(I)$ such that $M \cap M_W^i(I) \neq \emptyset$ for all $i \in I$; and we use $\sqsubseteq_I$ to indicate by writing $M \sqsubseteq_I M_W(I)$ that this structural set inclusion property holds. Observe that for non-empty $I$ the existence of such a set $M$ implies that all underlying sets $M_W^i(I)$ are non-empty. This guarantees that $M$ contains at least one model for each $E$-justification $Justif_E(\delta_i)$. In case $I$ is empty, we also deal with a non-empty subset $M$ of $M_W(\emptyset) = Mod(W)$; we write $M \sqsubseteq_\emptyset M_W(\emptyset)$. The non-emptiness of $M$ is guaranteed, since $W$ is assumed to be consistent.

---

[20] This is the semantic counterpart to the notion of pointwise closure used in [4].

The following Function $\nabla$ gives a formal specification of the predicate `model/3` used by XRay for consistency checking in the general case [29]:[21] For contextual default $\delta_i = \frac{|\alpha| : \beta_C |\beta_E|}{\gamma}$ and some index set $I = K \cup \{i\}$, $\nabla$ maps triples of form $\langle M, W, \langle \delta_k \rangle_{k \in K} \rangle$ with $M \sqsubseteq_K M_W(K)$ onto triples of the same format if $\beta_C$ and $\beta_E$ are "consistent"; it yields $\bot$ otherwise:

$$\nabla(\delta_i, \langle M, W, \langle \delta_k \rangle_{k \in K} \rangle) =$$

$$= \begin{cases} \langle M, W, \langle \delta_i \rangle_{i \in I} \rangle & \text{if } M \models \gamma \wedge \beta_C \text{ and } m \models \beta_E \text{ for some } m \in M \\ \langle M', W, \langle \delta_i \rangle_{i \in I} \rangle & \text{if } M \not\models \gamma \wedge \beta_C \text{ or } m \not\models \beta_E \text{ for all } m \in M \\ & \quad \text{and for } M' \sqsubseteq_K M_W(K), \\ & \quad M' \models \gamma \wedge \beta_C \text{ and } m' \models \beta_E \text{ for some } m' \in M' \\ \bot & \text{if there is no } M'' \sqsubseteq_K M_W(K), \\ & \quad M'' \models \gamma \wedge \beta_C \text{ and } m'' \models \beta_E \text{ for some } m'' \in M'' \end{cases}$$

Observe that $M' \sqsubseteq_K M_W(K)$ implies $M' \neq \emptyset$ even though $K = \emptyset$ due to the consistency of $W$. In fact, we may restrict our attention to singleton sets $M'$ in the absence of $E$-justifications. $M'$ must contain multiple models when dealing with inconsistent $E$-justifications. In the worst case, that is when dealing with $n$ pairwisely inconsistent $E$-justifications, $M'$ includes at most $n$ distinct models.

## 5.4   Experiments

For experimental analysis, we have developed a tool to build generic contextual default theories in order to be able to parameterize the number of model switches during query answering. In fact, we must generate a new model whenever we apply a default whose justification is denied by the current set of models. Since we deal with different sorts of justifications, it is moreover interesting to study the influence of different compatibility tests. We present here two test series, one with 50 and another with 100 defaults, each of which contains additionally 50 and 100 binary clauses, respectively, provoking a fixed number of model switches. This gives a putative search space for models of $2^{50}$ and $2^{100}$. All defaults are necessary for proving the query. The number of effectuated model generations is indicated in the first column of the tables combined in Table 2. We distinguish three major test cases comprising defaults having (i) only $C$-justifications, (ii) only $E$-justifications, (iii) both $C$- and $E$-justifications. In case (iii), we distinguish model generations provoked by $C$- or $E$-justifications. These cases are listed in order in the columns headed by $\beta_C$, $\beta_E$, and $\beta_C + \beta_E$. The column headed by $\beta_C + \beta_E$ distinguishes between switches causes by $C$- (left column) or $E$-justifications (right column). Each item contains a time measure in seconds, comprising system and user time

Note that the two limiting cases are given in the first and last line, representing no model switches and consecutive model switches. We observe that model

---

[21] That is $\nabla(\delta, X) = Y$ iff `model`$(\delta, X, Y)$, where $X$ and $Y$ are complex structures including one or multiple models.

| #/50 | $\beta_C$ | $\beta_E$ | $\beta_C + \beta_E$ | |
|---|---|---|---|---|
| 1 | 3.6 | 2.6 | 5.7 | 4.4 |
| 10 | 3.6 | 8.1 | 7.6 | 9.3 |
| 25 | 8.0 | 18.8 | 9.8 | 19.1 |
| 50 | 11.9 | 31.3 | 18.0 | 35.2 |

| #/100 | $\beta_C$ | $\beta_E$ | $\beta_C + \beta_E$ | |
|---|---|---|---|---|
| 1 | 11.1 | 9.4 | 38.5 | 28.5 |
| 25 | 16.3 | 66.3 | 42.2 | 87.6 |
| 50 | 46.6 | 132.1 | 92.5 | 166.2 |
| 100 | 102.7 | 260.7 | 135.6 | 330.4 |

**Table 2.** Experimental results on different types of consistency conditions

switches caused by $E$-justifications are more expensive than those caused by $C$-justifications. This reflects the fact that the latter impose a stronger consistency constraint than the former, as witnessed by the second case in the specification of $\nabla$. In addition, the exclusive use of $C$-justifications makes us treat in turn a single yet different model at all instances, while in our setting each proof including $n$ model switches provoked by $E$-justifications involves $n$ distinct models. Hence, except for the case of a single model switch, $C$-justifications behave better than $E$-justifications. The aforementioned exception is due to the fact that $C$-justifications are added to the primary matrix (comprising the initial set of facts and the consequents and $C$-justifications of all applied default rules) which is subject to consecutive reductions. These efforts however are rapidly amortized with an increasing number of model switches. Finally, we mention that we observed on non-artificial examples like taxonomic knowledge bases and even Hamiltonian circuit problems very few model switches which indicates the feasibility of our approach in practice.

## 6   A closer look at XRay's functionality

This section aims at giving a flavor of how XRay is used in more concrete terms. For this, we sketch the different file interfaces starting from the initial knowledge base file, over XRay's direct input file, up to the resulting Prolog code handed over by XRay to a standard Prolog compiler. This is done by regarding the files corresponding to the two examples treated in Section 2 and 5, respectively.

Figure 5 gives the formalization of the students example (cf. Section 2) in the knowledge representation language furnished by XRay's (current)[22] front end [2]. The first part contains the involved classical formulas, while the second part, delineated by begin(nd) and end(nd), comprises normal default rules in a simplified format omitting the respective justifications. Also, an initial query is supplied. To a turn, this knowledge base is parsed and translated into XRay's (real) input format. As already mentioned in Section 2, this format is strongly based on PTTP's syntax; thus allowing for formulas in negation normal form. The result is given in Figure 6. The first two lines comprise the negation normal

---

[22] This interface is still under development. This is why we refrain from giving a more complete description.

```
default_theory(students)
                              % classical formulas
    begin(classic)
       student.
       student -> adult.
    end(classic)
                              % normal default rules
    begin(nd)
       license :- adult.
       car :- license.
    end(nd)
                              % initial query
    query :- car.
end(students)
```

**Fig. 5.** `students.dth` : Knowledge base in the students example (processed by XRay's front-end).

```
student.
not_student ; adult.

license   :-   adult    :   ( license | true ).
car       :-   license :   ( car     | true ).

query :- car.
```

**Fig. 6.** `students.kb` : XRay's (real) input file in the students example.

forms of the classical formulas in Figure 5, while the last two rules are in fact contextual default rules representing the normal default rules in Figure 5. Any component of such a rule can be itself an arbitrary complex formula in negation normal form. In this simple case, the query rule remained unaffected. This file is then compiled by XRay into a standard Prolog program, as given in Figure 7 after applying a pretty-printer [16]. In connection with the Eclipse Prolog system, this compilation is launched by

```
[eclipse 2]: xray(students).
```

In fact, the compiled initial query is written into a separate file, since it is subject to further recompilation whenever subsequent queries to the same knowledge base are given. A query is then posed by typing Prolog query `?- query.` (see Figure 8).

The result of the compilation of knowledge base `students.kb` is given in Figure 7; it is obtained along the line described in Section 2. However, this concrete Prolog code reveals a couple of details suppressed in Section 2. First, the imple-

373

```
student(A,_,_,_,_,B,B,_,_):-
    identical_member(student, A),!,fail.
student(_,A,_,B,B,C,C,D,E):-
    identical_member(not_student, A),!,
    D = [reduction(not_student)|E].
student(_,_,_,A,A,B,B,C,D):-
    C = [unit(1 : student)|D].

not_student(_,A,_,_,_,_,B,B,_,_):-
    identical_member(not_student, A),!,fail.
not_student(A,_,_,B,B,C,C,D,E):-
    identical_member(student, A),!,
    D = [reduction(student)|E].
not_student(A,B,C,D,E,F,G,H,I):-
    (F >= 1, J is F - 1),
    K = [not_student|B],
    H = [extension(2 : not_student)|L],
    not_adult(A, K, C, D, E, J, G, L, I).

not_adult(_,A,_,_,_,_,B,B,_,_):-
    identical_member(not_adult, A),!,fail.
not_adult(A,_,_,B,B,C,C,D,E):-
    identical_member(adult, A),!,
    D = [reduction(adult)|E].

adult(A,_,_,_,_,_,B,B,_,_):-
    identical_member(adult, A),!,fail.
adult(_,A,_,B,B,C,C,D,E):-
    identical_member(not_adult, A),!,
    D = [reduction(not_adult)|E].
adult(A,B,C,D,E,F,G,H,I):-
    (F >= 1, J is F - 1),
    K = [adult|A],
    H = [extension(2 : adult)|L],
    student(K, B, C, D, E, J, G, L, I).

gamma(A,B,_,_,C,_,_,D,D,_,_):-
    identical_member(gamma(A, B), C),!,fail.
gamma(A,license,_,_,B,C,D,E,F,G,H):-
    (E >= 1, I is E - 1),
    J = [gamma(A, license)|B],
    G = [default(3 : (license :- adult : justification([[license]], [])))| K],
    alpha(3, adult, [], [], J, C, L, I, F, K, H),
    model(justification([[license]], []), L, D).
gamma(A,car,_,_,B,C,D,E,F,G,H):-
    (E >= 1, I is E - 1),
    J = [gamma(A, car)|B],
    G = [default(4 : (car :- license : justification([[car]], [])))| K],
    alpha(4, license, [], [], J, C, L, I, F, K, H),
    model(justification([[car]], []), L, D).

alpha(3,adult,_,_,_,A,B,C,D,E,F,G):-
    (D >= 1, H is D - 1),
    F = [extension(3 : alpha(3, adult))|I],
    adult([], [], A, B, C, H, E, I, G).
alpha(4,license,_,_,_,A,B,C,D,E,F,G):-
    (D >= 1, H is D - 1),
    F = [extension(4 : alpha(4, license))|I],
    license([], [], A, B, C, H, E, I, G).
```

```
license(A,_,_,_,_,_,B,B,_,_):-
    identical_member(license, A),!,fail.
license(_,A,_,B,B,C,C,D,E):-
    identical_member(not_license, A),!,
    D = [reduction(not_license)|E].
license(A,B,C,D,E,F,G,H,I):-
    (F >= 1, J is F - 1),
    K = [license|A],
    H = [extension(3 : license)|L],
    gamma(3, license, K, B, C, D, E, J, G, L, I).

car(A,_,_,_,_,_,B,B,_,_):-
    identical_member(car, A),!,fail.
car(_,A,_,B,B,C,C,D,E):-
    identical_member(not_car, A),!,
    D = [reduction(not_car)|E].
car(A,B,C,D,E,F,G,H,I):-
    (F >= 1, J is F - 1),
    K = [car|A],
    H = [extension(4 : car)|L],
    gamma(4, car, K, B, C, D, E, J, G, L, I).
```

**Fig. 7.** `students.ckb` : XRay's output in the students example (after pretty-printing).

mentation of blockwise regularity is witnessed by the first rule of each Prolog procedure. Second, XRay uses PTTP's iterative deepening search, as indicated by the arithmetic Prolog subgoals, like (E >= 1, I is E - 1), used for counting inferences. (Note that this is theoretically obsolete for the propositional case when verifying regularity; it is nonetheless useful for finding short proofs.) Finally, default rules are subject to a transformation, turning a $\delta$-rule ($\gamma$ :- $\alpha$ : $\beta$) (informally) into three rules ($\gamma$ :- gamma), (gamma :- alpha : $\beta$), and (alpha :- $\alpha$) in order to handle non-atomic components $\alpha, \beta, \gamma$ (cf. Section 2) by introducing new atomic components gamma, alpha for default rules.

The standard (linear) proof format obtained when proving query car is given in Figure 8.

```
[eclipse 3]: query.
proved by:
  extension(5 : query)
  extension(4 : car)
  default(4 : (car :- license : justification([[car]], [])))
  extension(4 : alpha(4, license))
  extension(3 : license)
  default(3 : (license :- adult : justification([[license]], [])))
  extension(3 : alpha(3, adult))
  extension(2 : adult)
  unit(1 : student)
yes.
```

**Fig. 8.** Proof (in linear format) of query car.

For a complement, let us take a look at the realization of the robot example, discussed in Section 5. The resulting knowledge base is given in Figure 9. This example comprises two different interpretations of default rules. Default rules that are to be treated as in justified default logic are regrouped between begin(jd) and end(jd), while those to be treated as in constrained default logic are enclosed in begin(cd) and end(cd).

The result of the syntactical analysis of file robot.dth is given in Figure 10. The resulting file, robot.kb, has the same format as the one given in Figure 6; it is a list of formulas in negation normal form, contextual default rules, and a Prolog rule comprising the initial query. These logical expressions correspond to the contextual default theory given in Section 5 for the robot example.

## 7 Conclusion

The XRay system can be looked at from different perspectives: First, it is a general implementation platform for query-answering in default logics, supporting local proof procedures. Second, it is an enhancement of an existing theorem

```
default_theory(robot)
                              % classical formulas
    begin(classic)
       brokenleft or brokenright.
       not hardware or not software.
    end(classic)
                              % default rules in Justified Default Logic
    begin(jd)
       toolbox :- true : hardware.
       laptop  :- true : soft.
    end(jd)
                              % default rules in Constrained Default Logic
    begin(cd)
       usableright :- true : not brokenright.
       usableleft :- true : not brokenleft.
    end(cd)
                              % initial query
    query :- toolbox and laptop and usableleft.
end(robot)
```

**Fig. 9.** robot.dth : Knowledge base in the robot example.

```
brokenleft    ; brokenright.
not_hardware ; not_software.

toolbox :- true : ( toolbox | hardware , toolbox ).
laptop  :- true : ( laptop | soft     , laptop ).

usableright :- true : ( not_brokenright , usableright | true ).
usableleft  :- true : ( not_brokenleft  , usableleft | true ).

query :- toolbox, laptop, usableleft.
```

**Fig. 10.** robot.kb : XRay's (real) input file in the robot example.

prover, PTTP, by means for handling different types of default information. And finally, it can be seen as a logic programming system going beyond Horn-logic by integrating disjunction and classical as well as (different) default negation(s).

In this paper, we described three salient features of XRay: (i) its usage of advanced yet transposed automated theorem proving technology for enhancing the overall performance, (ii) its capacity of handling (simultaneously) multiple variants of default logic by means of an extended model-based approach to consistency checking, and (iii) its basic functionality by means of its principle file interfaces.

Moreover, our experimental analysis provided us with insights into the computational value of different enhancements of the standard approach, such as default lemma handling and task switching. We showed that dynamic lemmas are an extremely valuable tool for improving the performance of the system. Notably, our experiments have furthermore shown that the usage of such dynamic lemmas practically never harms the reasoning process due to their restricted viability; and this even in failing query answering.

Another valuable enhancement is furnished by the capability of switching the verification of groundedness and consistency (or admissibility and compatibility, respectively) at compile-time. The application of either option depends on whether the search for default proofs is better guidable by looking first for grounded or consistent proofs, respectively. However, in view of the impressive improvements observed on Hamiltonian circuit problems, it seems to be preferable to take consistency as a first class constraint on the proof search.

# References

1. K. Apt, H. Blair, and A. Walker. Towards a theory of declarative knowledge. In J. Minker, editor, *Foundations of Deductive Databases and Logic Programming*, chapter 2, pages 89–148. Morgan Kaufmann Publishers, 1987.

2. Alain Baudry, Emmanuel Bezagu, Raphael Pieroni, and Denis Pithon. Analyseur syntaxique xray. Student project report (licence informatique), Department of Computer Science, University of Angers, 1997.

3. Richard Beilleau and Styve Jaumotte. Environnement de tests. Student project report (licence informatique), Department of Computer Science, University of Angers, 1997.

4. P. Besnard and T. Schaub. An approach to context-based default reasoning. *Fundamenta Informaticae*, 23(2-4):175–223, 1995.

5. W. Bibel. *Automated Theorem Proving*. Vieweg Verlag, Braunschweig, second edition, 1987.

6. W. Bibel. *Deduction: Automated Logic*. Academic Press, London, 1993.

7. N. Bidoit and C. Froidevaux. General logical databases and programs: Default logic semantics and stratification. *Information and Computation*, 91(1):15–54, 1991.

8. G. Brewka. Cumulative default logic: In defense of nonmonotonic inference rules. *Artificial Intelligence*, 50(2):183–205, 1991.

9. S. Brüning and T. Schaub. A model-based approach to consistency-checking. In Z. Ras and M. Michalewicz, editors, *Proceedings of the Ninth International Symposium on Methodologies for Intelligent Systems*, volume 1079 of *Lecture Notes in Artificial Intelligence*, pages 315–324. Springer Verlag, 1996.

10. P. Cholewiński, V. Marek, A. Mikitiuk, and M. Truszczyński. Experimenting with nonmonotonic reasoning. In *Proceedings of the International Conference on Logic Programming*. MIT Press, 1995.

11. P. Cholewiński, V. Marek, and M. Truszczyński. Default reasoning system DeReS. In *Proceedings of the Fifth International Conference on the Principles of Knowledge Representation and Reasoning*. Morgan Kaufmann Publishers, 1996.

12. M. Davis and H. Putnam. A computing procedure for quantification theory. *Journal of the ACM*, 7:201–215, 1960.

13. J. Delgrande, T. Schaub, and W. Jackson. Alternative approaches to default logic. *Artificial Intelligence*, 70(1-2):167–237, 1994.
14. L. Giordano and A. Martinelli. On cumulative default logics. *Artificial Intelligence*, 66(1):161–179, 1994.
15. C. Goller, R. Letz, K. Mayr, and J. Schumann. SETHEO V3.2: Recent Developments. In A. Bundy, editor, *Proceedings of the Conference on Automated Deduction*, volume 814 of *Lecture Notes in Artificial Intelligence*, pages 778–782. Springer Verlag, 1994. System abstract.
16. Michael Jolivet and Nicolas Jeanneau. Pretty printer. Student project report (licence informatique), Department of Computer Science, University of Angers, 1997.
17. T. Linke and T. Schaub. Lemma handling in default logic theorem provers. In C. Froidevaux and J. Kohlas, editors, *Proceedings of European Conference on Symbolic and Quantitative Approaches to Reasoning and Uncertainty*, volume 946 of *Lecture Notes in Artificial Intelligence*, pages 285–292. Springer Verlag, 1995.
18. T. Linke and T. Schaub. Towards a classification of default logics. *Journal of Applied Non-Classical Logics*, 7(4), 1997. To appear.
19. D. Loveland. *Automated Theorem Proving: A Logical Basis*. North-Holland, New York, 1978.
20. W. Łukaszewicz. Considerations on default logic — an alternative approach. *Computational Intelligence*, 4:1–16, 1988.
21. A. Mikitiuk and M. Truszczyński. Rational default logic and disjunctive logic programming. In A. Nerode and L. Pereira, editors, *Proceedings of the Second International Workshop on logic Programming and Non-monotonic Reasoning.*, pages 283–299. MIT Press, 1993.
22. I. Niemelä. Towards efficient default reasoning. In C. Mellish, editor, *Proceedings of the International Joint Conference on Artificial Intelligence*, pages 312–318. Morgan Kaufmann Publishers, 1995.
23. D. Poole. What the lottery paradox tells us about default reasoning. In R. Brachman, H. Levesque, and R. Reiter, editors, *Proceedings of the First International Conference on the Principles of Knowledge Representation and Reasoning*, pages 333–340, Los Altos, CA, May 1989. Morgan Kaufmann Publishers.
24. R. Reiter. A logic for default reasoning. *Artificial Intelligence*, 13(1-2):81–132, 1980.
25. T. Schaub. A new methodology for query-answering in default logics via structure-oriented theorem proving. *Journal of Automated Reasoning*, 15(1):95–165, 1995.
26. T. Schaub and S. Brüning. Prolog technology for default reasoning. In W. Wahlster, editor, *Proceedings of the European Conference on Artificial Intelligence*, pages 105–109. John Wiley & sons, 1996.
27. T. Schaub, S. Brüning, and P. Nicolas. XRay: A prolog technology theorem prover for default reasoning: A system description. In M. McRobbie and J. Slaney, editors, *Proceedings of the Conference on Automated Deduction*, volume 1104 of *Lecture Notes in Artificial Intelligence*, pages 293–297. Springer Verlag, 1996.
28. T. Schaub and P. Nicolas. An implementation platform for query-answering in default logics: The XRay system, its implementation and evaluation. In J. Dix, U. Furbach, and A. Nerode, editors, *Proceedings of the Fourth International Conference on Logic Programming and Non-Monotonic Reasoning*, volume 1265 of *Lecture Notes in Artificial Intelligence*, pages 442–453. Springer Verlag, 1997.
29. T. Schaub and P. Nicolas. An implementation platform for query-answering in default logics: Theoretical underpinnings. In Z. Ras, editor, *Proceedings of the*

*Tenth International Symposium on Methodologies for Intelligent Systems*, Lecture Notes in Artificial Intelligence. Springer Verlag, 1997. To appear.

30. C. Schwind. A tableaux-based theorem prover for a decidable subset of default logic. In M. Stickel, editor, *Proceedings of the Conference on Automated Deduction*. Springer Verlag, 1990.

31. M. Stickel. A Prolog technology theorem prover. In M. Stickel, editor, *Proceedings of the Conference on Automated Deduction*, volume 449 of *Lecture Notes in Artificial Intelligence*, pages 673–674. Springer Verlag, 1990.

32. M. Stickel. A Prolog technology theorem prover: A new exposition and implementation in prolog. In A. Miola, editor, *Proceedings of the International Symposium on Design and Implemetation of Symbolic Computation Systems*, volume 429 of *Lecture Notes in Computer Science*, pages 154–163. Springer Verlag, 1990.

33. Jérome Vieron and Nicolas Torzec. Arbre de preuve. Student project report (licence informatique), Department of Computer Science, University of Angers, 1997.

# Model-Based Diagnosis:
# A Probabilistic Extension

Ahmed Y. Tawfik[1] and Eric Neufeld[2]

[1] Wilfrid Laurier University
[2] University of Saskatchewan

**Abstract.** The present study treats model-based diagnosis as an uncertain reasoning problem. To handle the uncertainty in model-based diagnosis effectively, a probabilistic approach serves as a point of departure. The use of probabilities in diagnosis has proved beneficial to the performance of diagnostic engines.

We extend the use of probabilities to reflect the aging processes affecting component lifetimes. Unexpected failures signal unusual operating conditions possibly due to the failure of other subsystems. The diagnostic system architecture proposed here is capable of detecting failures that are difficult to detect using a conventional diagnostic engine.

Moreover, ascribing a statistical interpretation to nonmonotonic reasoning, allows us to use a hybrid (probabilistic-logical) inference engine at the heart of this system.

## 1  Diagnosis and Uncertain Reasoning

Diagnosing a system is the process of identifying a set of components whose failure explains the faulty system performance. Generally, model-based diagnosis consists of a cyclic process of making assumptions (regarding the faultiness or faultlessness of components), predicting the system behavior under these assumptions, observing actual system behavior, and adjusting the assumptions. This cycle is repeated until a set of faulty components is identified, and the failure of this set of components explains the observed abnormal behavior. As described, model-based diagnosis is deducing some hidden properties based on some observed ones and a causal understanding of the function of the system and its components.

Hidden properties cannot be determined with certainty. Hence the assumptions made regarding which components might be faulty are at best uncertain. Another source of uncertainty is introduced in the diagnostic cycle by the prediction phase. The behavior of a faulty component is hard to predict. It can be identical to the correct behavior for some inputs, but very different from it given another input. However, the faulty behavior is constrained by physical constraints. Attempts to perform diagnosis based on the correct behavior alone, have typically generated a large number of possible diagnoses, including some physically impossible ones. The incorporation of failure modes into the system description has been driven by the need to weed out physically impossible diagnoses [9]. Another constraint that is usually imposed on nonmonotonic diagnostic engines is the minimality constraint. A set of components forming a diagnosis $\Delta$ is minimal if it does not contain any component $X$ such that the set $\Delta - X$ can explain the observed behavior. Other potential sources of uncertainty in a diagnostic process are the unreliability of observations, the stochastic nature of the system under diagnosis, and intermittent failures.

Here, we approach the diagnostic problem as a problem of reasoning under uncertainty. The problem readily yields itself to probabilistic approaches [17], [12], and [24]. Moreover, a statistical interpretation for nonmonotonic reasoning allows us to consider nonmonotonic systems, such as GDE [10], as performing some form of uncertain reasoning. Casting diagnosis as a problem of reasoning under uncertainty justifies both the minimality and failure mode requirements. Adding components to a minimal diagnosis reduces the probability of the set (the probability of a diagnosis is the product of the independent probabilities of failure of its components) which justifies the minimality requirement. Moreover, the probability of a physically impossible failure mode is zero, which guarantees the elimination of any explanation involving such failure modes.

Further advantages can be achieved from a probabilistic formulation of diagnosis. These advantages include choosing the most informative tests using entropy measures [10], reducing the time required for diagnosis and the costs of diagnosis [17], and optimizing the diagnostic decision making to maximize some utility [8]. The following paragraphs shed some light on these advantages, and the rest of this work introduces a new one: the detection of premature failures resulting from the failure of other subsystems.

A diagnostic engine has to determine which measurement to take next. One approach to guiding the diagnostic process is to select the measurement that would provide most information [10]. Using a probabilistic representation, it is easy to select such measurement based on entropy. The minimum entropy corresponds to maximum information.

Performing the most informative test first is attractive because it allows the diagnostic engine to limit the search and therefore provide a superior average performance. However, in practical situations, performing the most informative test may be too costly, or difficult. Choosing to optimize cost instead of information results in a different strategy for selecting the measurement/test to perform next. The decision tree appropriate for analyzing the next measurement decision has a branch corresponding to each test. Each test has a cost and a duration associated with it. Each component has a probability of failure. Tests determine the status of tested components. The minimum average testing cost (or duration) can be achieved by testing the components with the highest probability of failure to testing cost (testing duration) ratio [17]. More elaborate decision-theoretic approaches create diagnosis and repair plans optimized to minimize down time, costs due to failure, and repair costs [8]. These techniques rely heavily on the availability of probabilistic information.

## 2 What is the probability of failure?

Knowing the probability of failure of each component is crucial for efficient, cost effective, and correct diagnosis. The question that this section deals with the nature of the probability of failure. As a first step towards the answer, consider the following example:

An electric vehicle EV has a battery system and an electric motor. A set of controls adjusts the speed. The vehicle is equipped with a charger to recharge the batteries. Battery failures are more frequent than connector failures. Properly designed motors and controls rarely fail.

The average lifetime of lead-acid EV batteries is two years or 24,000 miles given the current technology [14]. Electric motors are usually designed to provide 20,000 hours of operations at full load [6].

Over-charging, extreme weather conditions, and high discharge rates can result in premature failure of batteries. Corrosion and salt build up is a common connector failure in some environments. Excessive heating, a large number of restartings, or over-loading are factors that can reduce the life of a motor. Controls are sensitive to heating and mechanical shocks.

The above passage gives a realistic description of failure diagnosis of EVs. The type of information provided in each paragraph is different. The first paragraph provides static, time independent information. The relatively high frequency of battery failures make the battery the prime suspect any time an EV does not start. Knowing the newness of components makes the static knowledge less useful. For example, it is unreasonable to suspect a new battery. It is also unreasonable to ignore the possibility of a connector failure when the conditions are right for corrosion.

The second paragraph introduces the failure dependence on time. The temporal nature of lifetimes cannot be overlooked. An adequate representation must express the changes of the probability of failure with time. Unless otherwise specified, the environmental and operating conditions are assumed to be 'normal'. We define 'normal' conditions as the conditions taken into consideration in the design. Normal conditions for a mining vehicle are different from those for a city driving one.

The third paragraphs describes some factors affecting failure. These factors can have dramatic effects on the probability of failure. In general, different factors may interact. We need to represent for each component $c_i$ the probability of failure $P_{c_i|K}(t)$ where $K$ represents known environmental factors such as temperature and humidity, functional factors such as hours of continuous operation, and load; and inherent conditions such as material and manufacturing process.

The probability of failure is a continuously changing quantity that depends on time and operating conditions. Previous attempts to capture the notions underlying the probability of failure such as component aging can be divided into three categories: qualitative stages approaches, reliability measures, and survival models. The qualitative stages approach tries to divide the component life into stages such as new, young and old [26]. A new component can have a relatively high probability of failure due to manufacturing defects, a young component has a lower failure probability. This probability gets high again for old ones due to aging. This coarse grain temporal quantization introduces discontinuities in the failure distribution. Failure mechanisms tend to build-up gradually with time and therefore can be better represented using a continuous distribution. Setting the age thresholds between stages can be problematic. Moreover, this qualitative representation does not lend itself easily to adjustments to account for operating factors affecting lifetimes.

The Mean Time Between Failures (MTBF) is a reliability measure. It is used for model-based diagnosis [28]. Expressing the lifetime as a single number $MTBF$, does not provide information about the failure distribution. Moreover, the industrial norms for reporting $MTBF$ assume that:

- components are not operated beyond the recommended end-of-life,
- devices are operated under normal conditions, and
- systems have not been subjected to damage or abuse [18].

Unfortunately, these assumptions do not apply in a diagnostic context. With the exception of critical components, most components are usually used until they fail. The actual operating conditions are not ideal and damages are not uncommon. Another class of problem stems from the nature of 'means'. In many practical situations failure rates tend to have large variances. Common failure rate (hazard) functions such as the bathtub, the exponential or the log-normal (non-monotonic) in Figure 1 illustrate the large variance property. In such situations the mean time is not informative.

We represent the probability of failure using survival analysis. Survival analysis represents the probability that an event takes place. Here, the event we are interested in is the failure of a component. This event occurs at a time represented by the random variable $T$. It is therefore appropriate to express the probability of failure as a function of time. The advantages of using survival analysis are numerous. In addition to solving the problems discussed above, survival functions can be deduced from historical data using widely available software tools [16]. They can also be estimated based on an understanding of the physical effects of aging[3].

In this quick overview of survival analysis, we assume continuous time, but the basic ideas are also valid for discrete time. Allison [1] provides a good introduction to the subject.

The temporal distribution of failure can be expressed as a survival function $S(t)$, a probability density function $f(t)$, a probability distribution $F(t)$, or a hazard function $h(t)$. The probability density function $f(t)$ is defined as

$$f(t) = \lim_{\Delta t \to 0} \frac{Pr(t \leq T < t + \Delta t)}{\Delta t} \tag{1}$$

---

[3] The approach presented here is still of some use if we have a ranking of the failure likelihood and how this ranking changes with time.

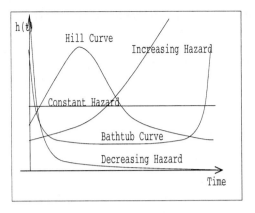

**Fig. 1.** Some Typical Hazard Functions

where $T$ is the failure time.

The probability distribution function $F(t)$ is the probability that the failure occurs before $t$ and is defined in terms of $f(t)$ as

$$F(t) = Pr(T \leq t) = \int_0^t f(x)dx. \tag{2}$$

The survival function $S(t)$ is the probability that the failure occurs after time $t$ and is defined as

$$S(t) = Pr(T \geq t) = \int_t^\infty f(x)dx. \tag{3}$$

The hazard function $h(t)$ is the rate at which the failure occurs and it is defined as

$$h(t) = \lim_{\Delta t \to 0} \frac{Pr(t \leq T < t + \Delta t | T \geq t)}{\Delta t}. \tag{4}$$

We can also deduce that $h(t) = \frac{f(t)}{S(t)}$. By substitution and integration we find that

$$S(t) = e^{-\int_0^t h(x)dx}. \tag{5}$$

From the above equations, we can draw several useful conclusions. First, simple relations exist between the four functions and they can be deduced from one another. Actually knowing one of the functions fully specifies the others. Second, the survival function can take any shape based on the corresponding hazard function. For example, a constant hazard would result in an exponentially decreasing survival probability. Third, the analysis assumes that failure occurs once. This may be true in some cases, but does not take repair actions into consideration. Here, we shift the survival function in time to start at the repair time for replaced components. Repair is not necessarily a replacement procedure; special repair models apply in such situations [2]. Fourth, the equations described do not consider the effect of variables other than time. The solution to this problem requires the use of models that replace $h(t)$ by a conditional version $h(t|X_1 \ldots X_n)$ where $X_i$ is in general a time varying factor affecting the survival. These factors are sometimes called explanatory variables.

The vulnerability of a component $c$ over a period $\langle t, t + \delta t \rangle$ is given by

$$\frac{S_t(c) - S_{t+\delta t}(c)}{S_t(c)}.$$

For short $\delta t$ this probability approximately equals $h(t)\delta t$.

## 2.1 Survival Models

Survival analysis is a useful tool for temporal probabilistic reasoning in general . Some earlier works which considered the use of survival techniques for temporal representation, reported some difficulties [11]. To overcome these difficulties, we use regressive survival models. Regressive survival models express the probability of an event conditioned on observations and other events, to account for events' interaction. The proper choice of survival model guarantees that each factor is accounted for appropriately.

Attaching causal semantics to the statistical models makes it easier to integrate these models in a knowledge based system. Causal models assume that events trigger effects either immediately or after a time lag. The effects produced by an event may be affected by other events. The causal ordering specifies a temporal relation between events and effects such that the effect of an event cannot precede the event itself.

Two causal relationships, namely *RESULT* and *ENABLE* are sufficient to describe the causal interactions underlying the models [21]. *RESULT* establishes a cause-effect relationship between an event and a state. A state *ENABLEs* an event if it is a necessary condition for the event to take place. For example, *RESULT* can be used to indicate that 'rust may cause a metal joint to fail', while *ENABLE* is used to express that humidity is necessary for rust to form. The less formal notation, '$X$ is a *RESULT* of $C_1 \vee \cdots \vee C_n$', is used instead of '$RESULT(X, C_1 \vee \cdots \vee C_n)$' for improved readability whenever possible, and similarly for *ENABLE*. A state is said to *DISABLEs* an event if it prevents the event taking place. The remainder of this subsection introduces some common survival models relevant to diagnosis.

**Competing Risks Model** As the name suggests, the competing risks model represents two or more potential risks racing to achieve a failure, but the success of one of the risks inhibits the others. $C_1 \vee \cdots \vee C_n$ *result* in state $S$ and state $S$ *DISABLEs* $C_1, \cdots, C_n$ from succeeding. For example, $S$ may be death and $C_1, \cdots, C_n$ are potential causes for death. However $S$ is not necessarily a final state. It may be one that just briefly blocks the other competing causes. For example, consider the case of two infections with the same virus. The state *anti-bodies present in blood* blocks *second infection*. Competition is a relation between events and in the statistical analysis of this model the nature of $S$ does not affect the analysis. According to the underlying causal model, this statistical model applies to many situations. See [19] for possible application areas.

Berzuini [5] represents competing events using networks of dates. Two competing events $C_1$ and $C_2$ produce effects at $T_1$ and $T_2$. $T_1$ and $T_2$ are temporal random variables of known distributions.

The result $X$ occurs at $\min(T_1, T_2)$. The failure density for $X$ which is the *RESULT* of the competition of two causes with failure densities $f_1$ and $f_2$, is given by:

$$f(t) = f_1(t)S_2(t) + f_2(t)S_1(t) \tag{6}$$

where the survival functions $S_1$ and $S_2$ are defined as above. Survival analysis provides a compact and efficient way to represent and evaluate the overall effect of competing events.

**Proportional Hazard Model** The proportional hazards model is one of the more widely used survival models. It is a parametric model that allows the effect of environmental and other factors to be taken into consideration. First proposed by Cox [7], it assumes that the natural logarithm of the ratio of the conditional hazard function (in the presence of explanatory variables) to the hazard $h_0(t)$ (in their absence) is a linear weighted sum of the risks or

$$h(t|X_1 \ldots X_m) = h_0(t)e^{\sum_i^m \beta_i X_i(t)}. \tag{7}$$

To overcome the limitations implied by the linearity assumption of this model, nonlinear mapping functions may be used such that the hazard function remains a linear combination of the mapped factors. For example, an engine is more likely to fail when operated at an unusually high temperature. The hazard function therefore becomes

$$h(t|high\_temperature) = h_0(t)e^{\beta z}$$

where $z$ represents the temperature and $\beta$ is a parameter that reflects the effect of temperature on the engine's failure probability. $h_0(t)$ is calculated in the absence of high temperature. This new function models the effect of *temperature* on *engine-lifetime*. The causal interpretation of this model can be viewed, as in the previous cases, through the introduction of a state. The *high_temperature* *RESULT*s in the engine state *less heat dissipation* and the event *engine-fails* is then more likely to happen quickly.

**Accelerated Time** A serious limitation of the proportional hazard model described above is that it assumes time invariant effect of the factors, which is not true in many cases. The effect produced by a certain factor depends on time. In such cases, it is possible to replace the parameters $\beta$ with functions $\beta(t)$. Techniques supporting such models have only recently been proposed by West [29] for continuous time and Singer and Willett [27] for discrete time. An alternative model for dealing with effects of explanatory variables on lifetime is to consider a different time scale $t'$ and find a relation $m(t, X_1, \ldots, X_n)$ between a normal

time unit, say a second, and its corresponding scaled time unit under the effect
of the factors. This is done by assuming that the failure time depends on the explanatory variables. A commonly used function is $log(T) = \sum_i \beta_i X_i$. Kalbfleisch
and Prentice [19] give a detailed description of this model. This model is also
similar to the location-scale model [20]. Substituting $t'$ for $t$ in the original survival function produces the new function in the presence of the factors. The effect
of a higher speed on the probability that a car runs out of gas can be accounted
for using this model. In this case, event *double the speed RESULTs* in the car
*consuming more gas* and the event *out-of-gas* occurring sooner.

**Additive Storage Model** Systems may fail due to the accumulation of stress.
To model this type of failure, consider a fixed capacity reservoir with an incoming
flow (in-flow) and an out-going flow (out-flow). The capacity of the reservoir
is the maximum stress the system can tolerate without failure. The incoming
flow is the additive stress applied to the system and the out-flow reflects the
ability of the system to recover from stressful situations. Systems with adequate
recovery can tolerate large stresses occurring over a long duration. They may
fail however when the the same stress is concentrated during a shorter duration.
The special case of unlimited recovery corresponds to systems that would only
fail if the instantaneous stress applied to them exceeds the maximum stress they
can tolerate. Systems with no recovery let the stress add up until failure. The
use of different release rules (for the out-flow) can be motivated by the fact
that most systems exhibit different patterns. Metals have unlimited recovery to
tensile stresses within the elastic region and have no recovery once the stress
exceeds a critical value causing plastic deformation.

Some systems can learn how to deal with stress. These systems include adaptive systems and many biological systems. This behavior can be modeled in the
storage context by a reduction in the amount of stress resulting from an occurrence of this risk once the system has survived a similar risk. This process may
be permanent (as in the case of measles) or temporary (as for the case of flu).

For storage models, the causal model assumes collaboration, and the events
have an additive *RESULT* but limited persistence (due to recovery). This model
can be seen as a temporal variant of the Noisy OR-Gate model [22]. Storage
models have been used to model dams, warehouses and similar systems. Glynn
[13] gives a detailed analysis of a discrete-time storage process. The classification
of systems response to stress is inspired by the treatment in [4].

## 3 Uncertain Reasoning with Changing Defaults

The failure probabilities as estimated using survival analysis serve as diagnostic
temporal constraints. They are used in mapping knowledge about components'
age and operating conditions to a set of assumptions regarding their vulnerability to failure. Components are divided into two sets $COMP_V$ and $COMP_P$

based on this probability. A simple clustering algorithm[4] starts by placing the component with the highest failure probability in $COMP_V$ and the one with the lowest probability in $COMP_P$. Other components belong to one set or the other depending on their probabilities. A component is placed in $COMP_V$ if its probability is numerically closer to the highest probability value than the lowest one.

Knowing the probabilities of failure for all components, it is time to get to the diagnosis task. A probabilistic representation such as a probabilistic ATMS [10], or a Bayesian network [22] can be used at this point. Instead, given a statistical interpretation to defaults, any nonmontonic diagnostic engine can be used. To illustrate this, Theorist is used here.

Theorist is a general nonmonotonic reasoning tool [23]. Let $F$ be a set of facts and $D$ a set of defaults. A scenario is a consistent set $S = F \cup A$ where $A \subseteq D$ constitutes the assumptions chosen from the possible defaults. Theorist finds all explanations of a formula $g$, namely scenarios that logically imply $g$. In diagnosis, the possible assumptions for component $c_i$ are $OK(c_i)$ or $FAULTY(c_i)$ (never both)[5]. A diagnosis is a set of $FAULTY$ assumptions consistent with the facts known about the behavior of correct and faulty components, and explaining the observed behavior $O$.

In a dynamic world, facts and defaults change with time. Changes are, in general, uncertain but constrained. It is practically impossible to predict the exact moment when a particular change occurs but the possible changes are physically constrained. For example, a functional light bulb can burn-out but a burnt-out bulb cannot recover. In other terms, functionality of an $OK$ bulb persists for a duration while the failure of a $FAULTY$ bulb persists forever. To represent temporal evolutions and persistence, we need in addition to the facts $F$ and the defaults $D$ a set of constraints $C$. The constraints provide a mapping from the knowledge available at time $t$ to a set of facts and defaults possible at this time.

$$C : K_t \rightarrow F_t, D_t$$

In diagnosis, possible defaults are $OK$ and $FAULTY$. Different components are more likely to fail at different times according to age, operating or environmental conditions. The diagnostic constraints have to map knowledge about components' age and operating conditions to a set of assumptions regarding their vulnerability to failure. In fact, this process consists of dividing the components set $COMP$ into two subsets: the set of vulnerable components $COMP_V$ and the set of perfect components $COMP_P$. In some situations a third set $COMP_F$ includes the components known to have failed and not been replaced.

Many default inferences are based on statistical notions [3]. The default em 'birds fly' may indicate that a large percentage of birds fly. Using a similar interpretation, it is possible to assume that a component is vulnerable if a significant

---

[4] We are currently considering more elaborate algorithms to maximize the probability of having the failed component in the set $COMP_V$.

[5] $FAULTY$ is similar to *abnormal* in Reiter's formulation of the problem [25].

percentage of components may fail at this age when operated under given conditions.

# 4 Model Generation

A diagnostic engine uses a system description $SD$ and a set of observations $O$ to find the defective components whose failures explain the observed behavior. The $SD$ includes failure modes as well as a description of the correct behavior of components [9]. Many diagnostic systems make some implicit assumptions regarding the vulnerability of components: for example, connecting wires are generally assumed perfect. Instead of making such assumptions, we start with a general system description where all components are vulnerable. Depending on the failure probabilities, new partial models are dynamically generated. Each partial model allows only components that are presently vulnerable to fail while other components are considered perfect.

The general model consists of statements describing the normal behavior as well as the failure modes of different components. The description language consists of two predicates $STATUS$ and $OK$. $STATUS$ describes the condition of various components. For example, $STATUS(switch, on)$ indicates that the switch is in the on position. $STATUS$ is also used to describe the behavior of a component. For example, the following rule describes an inverter:

$$STATUS(in, X) \Rightarrow STATUS(out, \neg X).$$

The rule above describes a perfect inverter, the description of a vulnerable inverter includes in addition to the normal behavior, the failure modes. $FAULTY$ is added for convenience and it means not $OK$.

$$STATUS(in, X) \wedge OK(inverter) \Rightarrow STATUS(out, \neg X).$$

$$STATUS(in, X) \wedge FAULTY(inverter) \Rightarrow STATUS(out, X).$$

In addition to the rules describing the behavior, default rules allowing all vulnerable components to be considered $OK$ or $FAULTY$, but never both, take the form

$$\forall \ x \in COMP_V, \ ASSUME \ OK(x).$$
$$\forall \ x \in COMP_V, \ ASSUME \ FAULTY(x).$$
$$\forall \ x \ ASSUME \ FAULTY(x) \Rightarrow \neg OK(x).$$

Comparing the descriptions of the vulnerable inverter and the perfect one, the perfect inverter behaves like an $OK$ inverter, except we do not have to assume that it is $OK$.

The model generator first divides the components into two sets: the vulnerable set $COMP_V$ and the perfect set $COMP_P$. This partitioning is done according to the probability of failure using the clustering algorithm described earlier. Starting from a detailed model where all components are vulnerable, we generate a concise model by removing all statements describing the failure modes of components in $C_p$. Those statements are easy to identify because they contain $\cdots \wedge FAULTY(c_i) \cdots$ where $c_i \in COMP_P$. The conjunction term $OK(c_i)$ is removed because $c_i$ is now assumed perfect. The resulting model is concise and it is very likely that it would contain the failed components.

It is still possible to have the failed component in the set $COMP_P$. This can result from the nature of probabilities or a wrong probability estimate. By the nature of probability we mean that a low probability still indicates a possibility. A wrong failure probability estimate can result from ignoring a risk factor. In both cases, we expand the set $COMP_V$ by including components from $COMP_P$ until we find the failed component(s).

## 5  Unexpected Failures

Diagnosis is sometimes defined as the process of finding the failed component. Here, we argue that in some cases finding the failed component is not necessarily all what we expect from a clever diagnostic engine. For example, if an EV does not start because its 1.5 years old battery has failed, it is reasonable to replace the battery without further investigations. However, if the new battery fails one month later, then this failure will probably surprise us and prompt us to think that the charger is defective.

To automate this type of reasoning, we need to:

- represent lifetimes,
- detect surprising failures, and
- reason about them.

We explained earlier how to represent lifetimes. Detecting surprises involves quantifying and measuring surprise. Reasoning about possible causes for a surprise constitutes an important dimension of diagnostic reasoning. Surprises allow us to discover the causes of unanticipated failures.

### 5.1  Surprises

A surprise is the occurrence of an event that is very unlikely to happen. The surprise index is a measure of the degree of surprise associated with the occurrence of an event. Among surprise measures, Weaver's index and Good's index are more appropriate here for reasons of simplicity and numeric significance. Weaver's surprise index [15] expresses surprise as:

$$Surprise = \frac{\sum_i (p_i)^2}{p_r}.$$

The summation is over all mutually exclusive possible outcomes and $p_r$ is the probability of the event that actually occurs. The surprise index values ranges from zero to infinity. A value between zero and one corresponds to the case of a likely outcome occurring. Values greater than one indicate a surprise. The larger the index the more astonishing the surprise is.

Less likely outcomes are more surprising than the more probable ones. However, the surprise index is a better indicator of the degree of surprise than the probability of the event by itself. The following example illustrates how the surprise index works. While it is not surprising at all that *someone* wins the lottery it is a big surprise if *I* win. Let there be $n$ tickets sold to an equal number of persons and let us assume that the draw is among the sold tickets. The probability of winning for each individual is then $1/n$. Let X be a person unknown to us. The surprise index for the proposition $X$ *won the lottery* is then

$$Surprise = \frac{n(1/n)^2}{1/n} = 1.$$

The proposition *I won the lottery* has only two possible outcomes actually winning or not with probabilities $1/n$ and $(1 - 1/n)$. For these two outcomes, the surprise associated with winning is

$$Surprise = \frac{(1/n)^2 + (1 - 1/n)^2}{1/n} = n - 2 + 2/n.$$

For a large $n$ the surprise is very large, while there is no surprise at all if $n = 1$ (why be surprised to win if there is only one ticket sold?). The surprise index measures how unlikely an outcome is compared with other possible outcomes. Surprises are therefore representation dependent.

A single fault assumption is equivalent to assuming that component failures are mutually exclusive. In this case, the surprise associated with the failure of one component $c_r$ is given by

$$Surprise = \frac{\sum_{\forall c_i}(P_t(c_i))^2}{P_t(c_r)\sum_{\forall c_i}P_t(c_i)}.$$

The summation in the denominator of the above equation is a normalization factor introduced because the sum of probabilities does not necessarily add up to one. The surprise associated with multiple faults is more easily expressed in terms of the logarithmic surprise index. The surprise associated with the failure of two components $r1$ and $r2$ is given by

$$Surprise = \sum_{c_i} P_t(c_i)(\log(P_t(c_i)) - \log(P_t(c_{r1}))) +$$
$$\sum_{c_i} P_t(c_i)(\log(P_t(c_i)) - \log(P_t(c_{r2}))).$$

For the logarithmic surprise index, a value of zero or less indicates no surprise. A positive value indicates surprise.

Unsurprising failures need not be processed any further. For a moderately high surprise index, replacement of the failed component and monitoring its performance are sensible decisions. Consider the surprise associated with the failure of a certain component $c_i$ after $x$ hours of operation to be $S_{c_i}(x)$ If $S_{c_i}(x)$ is moderate, it may be advantageous and more cost effective to note the failure and monitor $c_i$ closely. To implement this strategy, we use a leaky surprise bucket (an additive storage model) to store moderate surprises. If they occur frequently, their accumulation would be equivalent to a high surprise, and it would trigger a full investigation. Infrequent moderately surprising failures are ignored as they leak from the bucket over time (according to a release rule).

Two threshold surprise values $S_{c_i L}$ and $S_{c_i M}$ are chosen for each component $c_i$. Surprises higher than the low surprise threshold $S_{c_i L}$ but less than the moderate surprise threshold $S_{c_i M}$ are stored in the surprise accumulator. Surprises higher than $S_{c_i M}$ prompt a more careful and detailed investigation into the causes of failures. Setting surprise thresholds depends on the properties of the lifetime distribution of the component and economic factors such as the replacement cost as opposed to the cost of additional measurements.

Assuming a single threshold for each component separating surprising failures from non surprising ones, the total cost is the sum of two terms. The first represents the cost of a false surprise. Such false surprises are more frequent for lower threshold values. The cost of a false surprise is the cost encountered in performing further tests to verify that the unexpected failure is not caused by an external factor $f$. The second term represents the cost of additional failures resulting from a hazard that has not been investigated. This cost is higher for higher threshold values.

The proper setting of the threshold depends therefore to a large extent on the costs and on the probability that a component fails due to an external factor. The setting of thresholds in the case of the two thresholds explained earlier can be analyzed in a similar fashion.

## 5.2 Reasoning about surprising failures

Once the decision to further investigate a surprising failure is taken, the diagnostic engine proceeds to find possible explanations for the surprising failure. The first step is to check survival models for risk factors affecting the failed component. Let $R$ be the set of risk factors. Any factor $r \in R$ can have caused the failure. It is also possible that a number of risk factors have collaborated in causing the failure. For reasons of parsimony, efficiency and practicality we prefer the explanation involving the smallest number of risk factors. We therefore start by looking at singletons then couples and so on. For simplicity, we assume that the risks can only be present or absent as opposed to identifying their actual levels. For each set of risks being considered, the probabilities of failure are generated in the presence of the risks. The presence of the risks are also added to the models. If the presence of a risk factor can be verified against sensor observations, such observations are also included. The process ends when an explanation is found or the possibilities are exhausted. In the former case, the risk is eliminated, if at all possible, or the survival model is set to take the presence of this factor into account when calculating the probabilities. The absence of explanations indicates that the unexpected failure is purely caused by random chance.

# 6 Example

*A simple flashlight circuit consists of a light bulb (light), a switch (sw) and a battery (bat) connected in series with wires (w1,w2 and w3). The probability distributions for the lifetime of the bulb and the battery are normal with means of 1000 and 20 hours respectively. The variances are 200 and 5 for the bulb and the battery. The wiring and the switch rarely fail but their probability of failure is high initially due to burn-in faults. Then it drops as these defects usually affect the torch during the first few hours of operation. The failure probability finally rises again with aging. The wires have a constant hazard of 0.000001.*

The general model for this circuit considers all components as vulnerable. A Theorist rule base corresponding to the general model consists of the following rules:

```
fact ok(bat) and ok(w1) => status(w1,on).
fact ok(bat) and ok(w3) => status(w3,on).

fact status(w1,on) => ok(bat) and ok(w1).
fact status(w3,on) => ok(bat) and ok(w3).

fact status(w1,X) and status(sw,on) and ok(sw) and
          ok(w2) => status(w2,X).
fact not ok(sw) and ok(w2) => status(w2,off).
fact ok(sw) and not ok(w2) => status(w2,off).

fact status(w2,on) and status(w3,on) and ok(light) =>
          status(light,on).
fact status(w2,off) and ok(light) => status(light,off).
fact status(w3,off) and ok(light) => status(light,off).
fact not ok(light) => status(light,off).

fact not status(X,on) =>  status(X,off).

default ok(X).
default faulty(X).
fact faulty(X) => not ok(X).
```

For the light bulbs the failure density function is

$$f_{light}(t) = \frac{1}{\sqrt{400\pi}}e^{-0.5((t-1000)/200)^2},$$

and that of the switch is given by

$$f_{bat}(t) = \frac{1}{\sqrt{10\pi}}e^{-0.5((t-20)/5)^2}.$$

The hazard function for the switch is

$$h_{sw}(t) = \frac{0.005}{0.0033t + 0.5} + 0.0015 \exp(0.0033t - 5)$$

which corresponds to a bathtub hazard function.

To illustrate how this approach works, we consider three situations: expected failure, unexpected failure and preventive maintenance.

*Scenario 1. A torch fails; the switch and the bulb have operated for 500 hours; the age of the battery is 16 hours.* Using the hazard distribution given, the probability of failure of the switch during its $500^{th}$ hour is 0.0023. The probability of failure of the bulb during the same period is 0.000092. The probability of failure of the battery during its $16^{th}$ hour is 0.013.

The model generator assumes that the battery is the only vulnerable component and generates the following model

```
fact ok(bat) => status(w1,on).
fact ok(bat) => status(w3,on).

fact status(w1,on) => ok(bat).
fact status(w3,on) => ok(bat).

fact status(w1,X) and status(sw,on) => status(w2,X).

fact status(w2,on) and status(w3,on) => status(light,on).
fact status(w2,off)  => status(light,off).
fact status(w3,off)  => status(light,off).

fact not status(X,on) =>  status(X,off).

default ok(X).
default faulty(X).
fact faulty(X) => not ok(X).
```

Theorist finds *faulty(bat)* as the only explanation for *status(switch,on) and status(light,off)*. Replacing the battery verifies the explanation. The surprise index in this case is equal to

$$\frac{(0.013)^2 + (0.000092)^2 + (0.0023)^2 + 3(0.000001)^2}{0.013} = 0.0134.$$

A normalization step is required here because the sum of probabilities is less than one. The normalized index is

$$\frac{0.013}{0.013 + 0.0023 + 0.000092 + 0.000003} = 0.87.$$

This low surprise index indicates that the failure of the battery at this time is not surprising at all.

*Scenario 2. The torch fails again four hours after the battery is replaced.*

The probabilities of failure of the bulb and the switch have not changed much, but that of the battery is now practically nil ($7 \times 10^{-5}$). The model generator generates a model where the switch is the only suspect, but the result of testing the switch indicates that it is not faulty. The model is expanded to include the bulb. It turns out that the bulb has failed. The normalized surprise index in this case is 24.07 . This value is high enough to prompt further investigations. Vibrations and high voltage are two risk factors for light bulbs. Measuring the voltage of the new battery indicates that it is defective because it is somehow generating 9 Volts instead of 1.5 Volts. An accelerated time failure model justifies the failure of the bulb at this time due to high voltage.

*Scenario 3. The torch with a new light bulb and battery is now to be used by a space exploration mission, for a duration of five hours. Because the weight is at premium, unnecessary spare parts cannot be supplied. Any component that may fail during the next five hours is to be replaced by another with lower failure probability.*

The component with the highest probability of failure during the five hours mission is the switch. Unfortunately, replacing it will raise the probability of failure about 10 times. It is therefore safer to leave it. Vibrations are a risk factor for the light bulb as mentioned earlier. For this reason, it may be necessary to take a spare bulb and try to avoid exposing the torch to vibrations. The new battery stands a chance of $3 \times 10^{-4}$ of failing during this period.

## 7   Discussion and Conclusion

This work shows the role that uncertain reasoning plays in diagnostic problem solving. Statistical models are introduced as tools for representing and reasoning about the failure probability of a device under given operating conditions. While the diagnostic process itself is carried out within a nonmonotonic framework, the approach presented here strives to keep the qualitative models accurate because they are more faithful to the probabilistic model. These models also help in explaining unexpected failures. The dynamic system descriptions are more relevant, concise, and accurate than their static counterparts. The notion of surprise is used to point out to the system unusual failures. Finding out the reasons for a surprising failure is part of the diagnosis that has generally been overlooked.

## Acknowledgments

The authors acknowledge the support of Wilfrid Laurier University, the University of Saskatchewan, and the Natural Sciences and Engineering Research Council of Canada NSERC.

## References

1. P. Allison. *Event History Analysis*. Sage, Beverly Hills, 1984.

2. H. Ascher and H. Feingold. *Repairable Systems Reliability.* Marcel Dekker, Lecture Notes in Statistics, New York, 1984.

3. F. Bacchus. On probability distributions over possible worlds. In T. Levitt, L. Kanal, and J. Lemmer, editors, *Uncertainty in Artificial Intelligence*, volume 4 of *Machine Intelligence and Pattern Recognition 9*, page 217. North-Holland, 1990.

4. F. Bastani, I. Chen, and T. Tsao. Reliability of systems with fuzzy failure criterion. In *IEEE Annual Reliability and Maintainability Symposium*, pages 442–448, Anaheim, California, 1994.

5. C. Berzuini. Representing time in causal probabilistic networks. In *Uncertainty in Artificial Intelligence 5*, pages 15–28. Elsevier Science Publishers B.V., 1990.

6. E. Brancato. Estimation of lifetime expectancies of motors. *IEEE Electrical Insulation Magazine*, 8(3):5–13, May/June 1992.

7. D. Cox. Regression models and lifetables. *Journal of the Royal Statistical Society*, B34:187–220, 1972.

8. B. d'Ambrosio. Real-time value-driven diagnosis. *Telematics and Informatics*, 12(3):171, 1995.

9. J. de Kleer and B. Williams. Diagnosis with behavioral modes. In *Proceedings of the International Joint Conference on Artificial Intelliegence (IJCAI-89)*, pages 1324–1330, 1989.

10. J. de Kleer and B. Williams. Diagnosing multiple faults. In *Readings in Model-Based Diagnosis*, pages 100–117. Morgan Kaufmann Publishers, San Mateo,CA, 1992.

11. T. Dean and M. Wellman. *Planning and Control.* Morgan Kaufmann, San Mateo, California, 1991.

12. H. Geffner and J. Pearl. An improved constraint-propagation algorithm for diagnosis. In *Proceedings of the $10^{th}$ International Joint Conference on Artificial Intelligence (IJCAI-87), Milan, Italy*, 1987.

13. J. Glynn. A discrete-time storage process with a general release rule. *Journal of Applied Probability*, 26:566–583, 1989.

14. GNB Battery Co, 829 Parkview Bvd.,Lombard, IL 60148. *High performance lead-acid EV Battery.*

15. I.J. Good. *Good Thinking: The Foundations of Probability and Its Applications.* University of Minnesota Press, Minneapolis, 1983.

16. F. Harrell and R. Goldstein. A survey of microcomputer survival analysis software: The need for an integrated framework. *The American Statistician*, 51(4):360, 1997.

17. D. Heckerman, J. Breese, and K. Rommelse. Decision-theoretic troubleshooting. *Communications of the ACM*, 38(3):49–57, 1995.

18. IBM Almaden Storage Group. *MTBF – a measure of OEM disk drive reliability,* January 1996. Available from http://www.almaden.ibm.com:80/storage/oem/tech/mtbf.htm.

19. J. Kalbfleisch and R. Prentice. *The Statistical Analysis of Failure Time Data.* John Wiley and Sons, New York, 1980.

20. J. Lawless. *Statistical Models and Methods for Lifetime Data.* John Wiley, New York, 1982.

21. M. Pazzani. *Creating a Memory of Causal Relationships : An Integration of Empirical and Explanation-Based Learning Methods.* LEA Publishers, Hillsdale, NJ, 1990.

22. J. Pearl. *Probabilistic Reasoning in Intelligent Systems: Networks of Plausible Inference.* Morgan Kaufmann, San Mateo, CA, 1988.

23. D. Poole. A logical framework for default reasoning. *Artificial Intelligence*, 36(1):27–47, 1988.

24. D. Poole. Representing diagnsotic knowledge for probabilistic Horn abduction. In *Proceedings of the 12$^{th}$ International Joint Conference on Artificial Intelligence (IJCAI-91), Sydney, Australia*, 1991.

25. R. Reiter. A theory of diagnosis from first principles. *Artificial Intelligence*, 32:57–95, 1987.

26. P. Rhodes and G. Karakoulas. A probabilistic model-based method for diagnosis. *Artificial Intelligence in Engineering*, 6(2):86–99, 1991.

27. J. Singer and J. Willett. It's about time: Using discrete-time survival analysis is to study duration and the timing of events. *Journal of educational statistics*, 18(2):155, 1993.

28. S. Srinivas. Modeling failure priors and persistence in model-based diagnosis. In *Proceedings of the Eleventh Conference on Uncertainty in Artificial Intelligence*, pages 507–514. Morgan Kaufmann, 1995.

29. M. West. Modeling time-varying hazards and covariate effects. In J. Klein and P. Goel, editors, *Survival Analysis: State of the Art*. Nato ASI Series, Kluwer Academic Publisher, Dordrecht, Netherlands, 1991.

# Background to and Perspectives on Possibilistic Graphical Models [*]

Jörg Gebhardt[1] and Rudolf Kruse[2]

[1] Dept. of Mathematics and Computer Science, University of Braunschweig
38106 Braunschweig, Germany
[2] Dept. of Computer Science, Otto-von-Guericke University
39106 Magdeburg, Germany

**Abstract.** Graphical modelling is an important tool for the efficient representation and analysis of uncertain information in knowledge-based systems. While Bayesian networks and Markov networks from probabilistic graphical modelling have been well-known for about ten years, the field of *possibilistic graphical modelling* appears to be a new promising area of research. Possibilistic networks provide an alternative approach compared to probabilistic networks, whenever it is necessary to model uncertainty *and* imprecision as two different kinds of imperfect information. Imprecision in the sense of multivalued data has often to be considered in situations where information is obtained from human observations or non-precise measurement units. In this contribution we present a comparison of the background and perspectives of probabilistic and possibilistic graphical models, and give an overview on the current state of the art of possibilistic networks with respect to propagation and learning algorithms, applicable to data mining and data fusion problems.

## 1 Introduction

One major aspect concerning the acquisition, representation, and analysis of information in knowledge-based systems is the development of an appropriate formal and semantic framework for the effective treatment of uncertain and imprecise data [26]. A task that frequently appears in applications is to describe a state $\omega_0$ of the world as specificly as possible using a tuple of instantiations of a finite number of variables (attributes), based on available *generic knowledge* and application-dependent *evidential knowledge*. As an example we mention medical diagnosis, where $\omega_0$ could be the current state of health of a person, characterized by relationships between different attributes like diseases, symptoms, and relevant attributes for observation and measurement. For a most specific description of $\omega_0$ we use generic knowledge (medical rules, experience of medical doctors, databases of medical sample cases) and additional evidential knowledge about the person under consideration (the instantiations of those variables or attributes that can be found by asking and examining this person).

---

[*] This work is an update of contributions made to ECAI'96 and ECSQARU/FAPR'97

*Imprecision* in the sense of multivalued data comes into our considerations, when generic knowledge about dependencies among variables is relational rather than functional, and when the actual information on the current state does not result in a single tuple of variable instantiations, but rather in a set of alternatives. This means that we only know that the current state is definitely one element of this set of alternatives, but we have no preferences that help us in selecting the "true" element. In the case of medical diagnosis the set of alternatives could be the set of diseases that the medical doctor regards as possible explanations for the observed symptoms, without making any preferences among these diseases. If imprecision is modelled by sets of alternatives, then it is reasonable to see preferences in the way that they reflect the uncertainty about identifying the current state $\omega_0$ within its *frame of discernment* $\Omega$, which is the product of the domains of all variables under consideration and thus the set of all possible candidates for $\omega_0$.

*Uncertainty* arises in this context from the fact that in most cases there are no crisp functional or relational dependencies among the involved variables, but only imperfect relationships that can be quantified by degrees of confidence. If, for example, the symptom *temperature* is observed, then various disorders might explain this symptom, and the medical doctor will assign his preferences to them. The modelling of this kind of uncertainty is done in an adequate calculus, for instance with help of a probabilistic approach, with concepts taken from non-standard uncertainty calculi like possibility theory, but also in a purely qualitative way by fixing a reasonable preference relation. The origin of uncertainty and the problem of allocating appropraite degrees of confidence is due to phenomena like randomness, but also to the fusion of conflicting, partially inconsistent pieces of information, provided by heterogeneous sources having different levels of reliability. A discussion of relevant concepts of parallel combination and uncertainty modelling is beyond the scope of this paper. For more details on this topic, we refer to [20].

For simplicity, we restrict ourselves to *finite* domains of variables. Generic knowledge about $\omega_0$ is assumed to refer to the uncertainty about the truth value of the proposition $\omega = \omega_0$, which is specified for all alternatives $\omega$ of $\Omega$. Such knowledge can often be formalized by a *distribution function* on $\Omega$, for example a probability distribution, a mass distribution, or a possibility distribution, depending upon the uncertainty calculus that best reflects the structure of the given knowledge.

The consideration of evidential knowledge about $\omega_0$ corresponds to *conditioning* the available generic knowledge, and therefore to conditioning a given prior distribution defined on $\Omega$. Conditioning is often based on the instantiation of particular variables. In our example of medical diagnosis we could think of instantiating the variable *temperature* by measurement with a medical thermometer. The conditioning operation leads to an inference process that has the task to calculate the posterior marginal distributions for the non-instantiated variables.

In addition to inference and decision making aspects it is of particular interest to answer the question of how generic knowledge is obtained. In automated induction of knowledge this problem is quite easy to handle, if there is a database of sample cases that serves as an input for learning algorithms which determine a distribution function on $\Omega$ that best fits the database.

Since multidimensional frames of discernment $\Omega$ in applications of practical interest tend to be intractable as a whole because of their high cardinality, the aim of efficient methods for knowledge representation and the respective inference and learning algorithms is to take advantage from *independencies* that may exist between the variables under consideration.

Independencies support decomposition techniques that reduce operating on distributions to low-dimensional subspaces of $\Omega$. The field of *graphical modelling* provides useful theoretical and practical concepts for an efficient reasoning under uncertainty [44, 4, 28, 40]. Applications of graphical models can be found in a variety of areas such as diagnostics, expert systems, planning systems, data analysis, and control. For an overview, see [6].

In the following, we will investigate graphical modelling from the viewpoint of the uncertainty calculus of *possibility theory*. In Section 2 we discuss some principal aspects of graphical modelling. Section 3 gives an introductory example of how to interpret databases of (imprecise, multivalued) sample cases in terms of *possibility distributions*. Theoretical underpinnings of *possibilistic graphical models* with their basic concepts of *possibilistic conditional independence, conditional independence graphs, factorization*, and *decomposition* are summarized in Section 4. Referred to these foundations, Section 5 deals with efficient algorithms for *evidence propagation* in possibilistic graphical models. In Section 6, we focus on a specific data mining problem, which is how to *induce possibilistic graphical models* from databases of sample cases. Finally, Section 7 is for clarifying the benefits and limits of possibilistic graphical models when compared to their probabilistic counterparts.

## 2   Graphical Models

A graphical model for the representation of uncertain knowledge consists of a qualitative and a quantitative component. The *qualitative (structural)* component is a graph, for example a directed acyclic graph (DAG), an undirected graph (UG) or a chain graph (CG). In a unique way it represents the conditional independencies between the variables represented by the nodes of the graph. For this reason, it is called the *conditional independence graph* of the respective graphical model. The *quantitative* component of a graphical model is a family of distribution functions on subspaces of $\Omega$, whose structure is determined by the conditional independence graph. The distribution functions specify the uncertainty about the values of the projections of $\omega_0$ on the corresponding subspaces. In the case of a DAG, conditional distribution functions are used in order to quantify the uncertainty relative to each component value of tuple $\omega_0$, dependent of all possible instantiations of the direct predecessors of the node identified with this component. On the other hand, an UG with induced hypergraph structure is the appropriate choice, if non-conditional distributions are preferred. For each hyperedge, such a distribution is defined on the common product domain of the variables whose identifying nodes are contained in the respective hyperedge.

Figure 1 shows an example of a conditional independence graph for an application, where expert knowledge represented by a graphical model successfully has been used to improve the results of modern cattle breeding programs [30]. The main purpose is genotype determination and parentage verification for pedigree registration. The application refers to the F-blood group system which controls 4 blood group factors for blood typing. The graphical model consists of 21 attributes (variables) that are relevant for determining the genotypes and verifying the parentage of Danish Jersey cattle.

The conditional independence graph reflects the dependencies and independencies that exist between the observable variables (lysis factors, phenogroups of stated dam and stated sire), and those variables that are relevant for the intended inference process (especially genotype, dam correct, and sire correct). The involved variables have at least two, and at most eight possible values for instantiation. The genotypes, for example, are coded by $F1/F1$, $F1/V1$, $F1/V2$, $V1/V1$, $V1/V2$, and $V2/V2$, respectively.

The conditional independence graph in Figure 1 can be interpreted as follows: Selecting any two nodes of the graph, their underlying variables are independent given any instantiation of all other variables whose number with respect to a topological order that agrees with the graph is not greater than the maximum of the order numbers of the two selected nodes. The topological order is chosen in that there is no arc from a node to another node with a smaller order number. *Conditional independence* refers to the uncertainty calculus that the graphical model is based on. In the case of a probabilistic graphical model this means conditional independence of the random variables that are represented by the nodes in the graph. The common distribution function of these random variables is supposed to satisfy all independence relations expressed by the conditional independence graph. For this reason, the distribution has a factorization, where the probability of each elementary event obtained by a full instantiation of all variables equals a product of conditional probabilities in lower-dimensional subspaces. These factors are the probabilities of the single random variables given the instantiations of their parent variables in the directed acyclic graph (DAG) [28, 44].

In the example shown in Figure 1, the decomposition provided by the mentioned factorization leads to the simplification that the user of the graphical model only needs to specify 306 conditional probabilities in subspaces of at most three dimensions, whereas the 21-dimensional frame of discernment $\Omega$ has 92 876 046 336 elements.

In the concrete application, the 306 needed conditional probabilities were specified on the base of statistical data and the experience of experts. The resulting probabilistic graphical model therefore consists of the DAG in Figure 1 as the qualitative part, and a family of 21 conditional probability distributions.

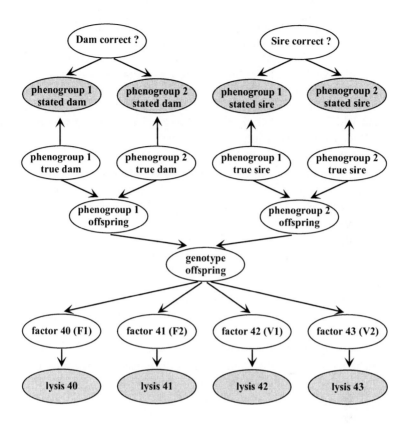

Fig. 1.: Graphical model for genotype determination and parentage verification of Danish Jersey cattle in the F-blood group system

The aim of this type of graphical model is automated evidence propagation with a final step of decision making. Given, for instance, the lysis factors of a particular calf, and instantiating the corresponding variables (lysis 40, lysis 41, lysis 42, and lysis 43), the task is to calculate the posterior distributions of the other variables, especially the genotype and the variables on the parentage.

From an operational point of view, there are efficient algorithms for evidence propagation which are implemented in some commercial software tools. We will refer to this topic in more detail in Section 5. The two following sections will investigate graphical modelling in the sense of the above given example, but using a *possibilistic* instead of a probabilistic approach.

## 3   Possibility Theory and Possibilistic Networks

A *possibilistic network* is a graphical model whose quantitative component is defined by a family of possibility distributions. A *possibility distribution* $\pi$ is represented as a mapping from a referential set $\Omega$ to the unit interval. If $\pi$ is used as an imperfect specification of a current state $\omega_0$ of a part of the world, then $\pi(\omega)$ quantifies the degree of possibility that the proposition $\omega = \omega_0$ is true. From an intuitive point of view, $\pi(\omega) = 0$ means that $\omega = \omega_0$ is impossible, and $\pi(\omega) = 1$ says that this proposition is regarded as being possible without restriction. Any intermediary possibility degree $\pi(\omega) \in (0, 1)$ indicates that $\omega = \omega_0$ is true with restrictions, which means that there is evidence that supports this proposition as well as evidence that contradicts it.

Similar to the fact that one can find a variety of approaches to the semantics of subjective probabilities, there are different ways of introducing the semantics of the concept of a possibility distribution. In this context, we mention possibility distributions as the epistemic interpretation of fuzzy sets [46], the axiomatic approach to possibility theory with the aid of possibility measures [11, 12], and possibility theory based on likelihoods [10]. Integrated in Dempster–Shafer theory, possibility distributions are regarded as contour functions of consonant belief functions [35], and in the framework of set–valued statistics, they are read as falling shadows [42].

One can also find some interpretations of possibility theory that owe nothing to probability theory. In this connection we mention possibility as *similarity*, where the interpretation is clearly related to metric spaces [32, 31, 33], and possibility as *preference*, mathematically justified by comparable possibility relations [13].

Introducing possibility distributions as information-compressed representations of databases of sample cases, it is convenient to interpret them as (non-normalized) one–point coverages of random sets [21], which leads to a very promising semantics of possibility distributions [15, 16, 20]. With this approach it is quite simple to prove Zadeh's *extension principle* [45] as the adequate way of extending set-valued operations to their corresponding generalized operations on possibility distributions. It turns out that the extension principle is the only way of operating on possibility distributions that is consistent with this semantic background. For more technical details, see [14].

In this contribution we show an example that demonstrates how a database of sample cases is transformed into a possibility distribution. We therefore reconsider our blood group determination example of Danish Jersey cattle in Figure 1.

Table 1 represents a part of a database that is reduced to five attributes:

| lysis 40 | lysis 41 | lysis 42 | lysis 43 | genotype offspring |
|----------|----------|----------|----------|--------------------|
| $\{0, 1, 2\}$ | 6 | 0 | 6 | $V2/V2$ |
| 0 | 5 | 4 | 5 | $\{V1/V2, V2/V2\}$ |
| 2 | 6 | 0 | 6 | $*$ |
| 5 | 5 | 0 | 0 | $F1/F1$ |

Table 1.: Database with four sample cases

The three first rows specify imprecise sample cases, the fourth row shows a precise one. In row 1, we have three tuples $(0, 6, 0, 6, V2/V2)$, $(1, 6, 0, 6, V2/V2)$, and $(2, 6, 0, 6, V2/V2)$. They specify those states that have been regarded as possible alternatives when observing the calf that delivered the first sample case. These three tuples are the possible candidates for the state of this calf, concerning the relationship between lysis factors and genotype. In a similar way, the second row shows two possible states with respect to the second sample calf. An unknown value in the third row is indicated by *.

Assuming that the four sample cases in Table 1 are in the same way representative for the specification of relationships between the five selected attributes, it is reasonable to fix their probability of occurrence to $1/4$.

From a probabilistic point of view, we may apply the *insufficient reason principle* to the database, stating that alternatives in multivalued sample cases are equally likely, if preferences among these alternatives are unknown. Uniform distributions on multivalued sample cases lead to a refined database of $3 + 2 + 6 + 1 = 12$ data tuples, where, for instance, $(2, 6, 0, 6, V2/V2)$ has an occurrence probability of $1/3 * 1/4 + 0 + 1/6 * 1/4 + 0 = 3/24$.

In a possibilistic interpretation of the database, we obtain for the same tuple a degree of possibility of $1/4 + 0 + 1/4 + 0 = 1/2$, since this tuple is considered as being possible in the first and in the third sample, but it is excluded in the two other samples. Calculating the possibility degrees for all tuples of the common domain of the five selected attributes, we get an information-compressed interpretation of the database in form of a possibility distribution.

# 4 Theoretical Foundations of Possibilistic Networks

Graphical models take benefits of conditional independence relations between the considered variables. The basic aim is to reduce operations on distribution functions from the multidimensional frame of discernment $\Omega$ to lower-dimensional subspaces, so that the development of efficient inference algorithms is supported. The starting point of theoretical investigations for graphical models is to find an appropriate concept of *conditional independence* of variables relative to the uncertainty calculus under consideration. Such a concept allows to introduce *conditional independence graphs* and to search for appropriate *factorization* and *decomposition* techniques. We will consider these topics in more detail in the following subsections, referred to the uncertainty calculus of possibility theory.

## 4.1 Possibilistic Conditional Independence

While the notion of probabilistic conditional independence has been well-known for a long time, there is still some need for discussion of analogous concepts in the possibilistic setting. The main reason for it comes from the fact that possibility theory is suitable for the modelling of two different kinds of imperfect knowledge (uncertainty and imprecision), so that there are at least two alternative ways of approaching independence. Additionally, the various proposals for the semantics of possibility distributions allow the foundation of different concepts of independence. For an overview, we refer to [5]. Nevertheless, all these proposals agree to the following general definition:

Given three disjoint sets $X$, $Y$, and $Z$ of variables (attributes), where $X$ and $Y$ are both not empty, $X$ is called *independent* of $Y$ given $Z$ relative to a possibility distribution $\pi$ on $\Omega$, if any additional information on the variables in $Y$, formalized by any instantiations of these variables, does not change the possibility degrees of the common tuples of values of the variables in $X$, whatever particular instantiation of the variables in $Z$ is chosen.

In other words: If the $Z$-values of $\omega_0$ are known, then additional restrictive information on the $Y$-values of $\omega_0$ is useless for getting more information on possible further restrictions of the $X$-values of $\omega_0$.

From an operational point of view, the independence condition may also be read as follows: Suppose that a possibility distribution $\pi$ is used to imperfectly specify the state $\omega_0$. Given any crisp knowledge about the $Z$-values of $\omega_0$, this distribution is conditioned with respect to the corresponding instantiations of the variables in $Z$. The projection of the resulting possibility distribution $\pi$ on the $X$-values equals the possibility distribution that we obtain if we condition $\pi$ with respect to the same instantiation of the variables in $Z$ and any instantiation of the variables in $Y$, and then project the conditioned possibility distribution on the $X$-values.

How *conditioning* and *projection* have to be defined, depends on the chosen semantics of possibility distributions: If we view possibility theory as a special case of *Dempster-Shafer theory*, by interpreting a possibility distribution as a representation of a consonant belief function or a nested random set, then we obtain the concept of conditional indpendence of sets of variables in possibilistic graphical models from the so-called *Dempster conditioning* [35]. On the other hand, if we regard possibility distributions as (non-normalized) one-point coverages of random sets, as we did it in Section 3 for the possibilistic interpretation of databases of sample cases, then we have to choose the conditioning and the projection operation in conformity with the extension principle. The resulting type of conditional independence corresponds to *conditional possibilistic non-interactivity* [22]. For more details on this axiomatic approach to possibilistic independence, we refer to [5].

It should be pointed out that the above mentioned two types of conditional independence satisfy the *semi-graphoid-axioms* which have been established as the basic requirements to any reasonable concept of conditional independence in graphical models [28]. Possibilistic conditional independence in the Dempster-Shafer approach even satisfies the *graphoid-axioms* [29], in analogy with the case of probabilistic conditional independence.

## 4.2 Possibilistic Conditional Independence Graphs

Confining to conditional possibilistic non-interactivity as our appropriate concept of conditional independence, it is straight-forward to define what we call a conditional possibilistic independence graph:

An undirected graph with $V$ as its set of nodes is called *conditional independence graph* of a possibility distribution $\pi$, if for any non-empty disjoint sets $X$, $Y$, and $Z$ of nodes from $V$, the separation of each node in $X$ from each node in $Y$ by the set $Z$ of nodes implies the possibilistic independence of $X$ from $Y$ given the condition $Z$.

This definition makes the assumption that the so-called *global Markov property* holds for $\pi$ [44]. In contrast to probability distributions, where the equivalence of global, local, and pairwise Markov property can be verified, the possibilistic setting establishes the global Markov property as the strongest of the three properties, so that it should be selected as the basis for the definition of possibilistic conditional independence graphs [14].

## 4.3 Treatment of Directed Graphs

Similar to other fields of graphical modelling, a directed acyclic possibilistic conditional independence graph (see Figure 1) can be transformed to its associated undirected *moral graph* [27], which is obtained by eliminating the direction of all arcs in the DAG, and by "marrying" all parent nodes with the aid of additional combining edges. Figure 2 is a modified representation of the DAG in Figure 1, where the new edges in the moral graph are indicated by the dotted lines.

The moral graph satisfies a subset of the independence relations of the underlying DAG, so that using the moral graph in the worst case is connected with a loss of independence information. *Triangulation* of the moral graph, which perhaps causes further loss of independence information, yields an UG whose hypergraph representation is a *hypertree*. The hyperdeges of this hypertree correspond to the nodes of the *tree of cliques* that is associated with the triangulated moral graph. The tree of cliques that may be constructed from the DAG in our blood group determination example is shown in Figure 3. For more information on such graph-theoretical problems, we mention [6].

## 4.4 Factorization and Decomposition

Section 2 has already indicated that in applications of reasonable complexity multidimensional joint domains $\Omega$ are intractable as a whole. Efficient knowledge representation and reasoning techniques should therefore take advantage from decomposition operations that reduce considerations to lower–dimensional subspaces of $\Omega$. In database theory such decompositions are often guided by functional dependencies. Decomposition based on independence relations between variables has extensively been studied in the field of probabilistic graphical models [27]. A very important result is the reformulation of the *Hammersley–Clifford–Theorem* [23] that verifies a one–to–one correspondence between the

406

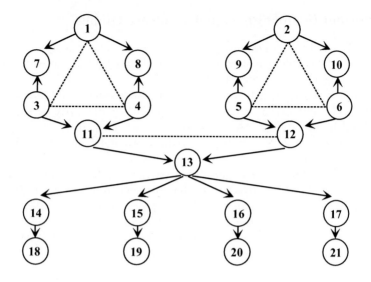

Fig. 2.: Modified representation of the DAG in Figure 1

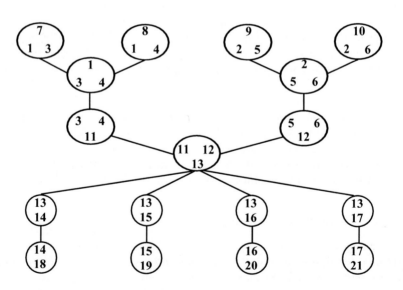

Fig. 3.: Tree of cliques of the triangulated DAG in Figure 1

(pairwise equivalent) Markov properties of a strictly positive probability distribution $p$ on $\Omega$ and the representability of $p$ as a product of functions that depend only on the variables in the maximal cliques of the conditional independence graph of $p$. The proof of a possibilistic counterpart of this theorem is given in [14]:

A possibility distribution $\pi$ on $\Omega$ has a decomposition into complete irreducable components, if the decomposition is referred to a triangulated conditional independence graph $G$ of $\pi$. The *factorization* of $\pi$ relative to this decomposition is characterized in the way that $\pi$ has a representation as the minimum of its projections on the maximal cliques of $G$. This result coincides with the decomposition of probability distributions, when the minimum operator is substituted by the product, and when degrees of possibility are changed to probabilities.

## 5 Evidence Propagation in Possibilistic Networks

Depending upon the structural properties of the conditional independence graph and thus the decomposability of the particular distribution function of a graphical model, it is possible to develop efficient algorithms for evidence propagation.

In the example from Figure 1 the major task is to get information about the genotype and the correctness of assumed parentage of a given calf under consideration. Available evidential knowledge refers to the eight grey nodes in Figure 1. It is based on measuring the lysis factors and determining the phenogroups of the stated parents. Generic knowledge is coded by the family of distribution functions that specifies the quantitative part of the graphical model. Conditioning the underlying decomposed distribution function with respect to the instantiations of the above mentioned eight variables yields an imperfect specification of the state $\omega_0$ of the considered calf, which consists of the 21 attributes involved in Figure 1.

Propagation algorithms that carry out the conditioning process and the calculation of the posterior marginal distributions are based on locally communicating node- and edge-processors that realize the global information exchange in the whole network. The typical propagation algorithms differ from each other with respect to the special network structures they support, but in most cases they are applicable independently from the given uncertainty calculus; there is only the need to adapt elementary operations like conditioning and projection relative to the particular framework [27, 28, 37].

A quite general approach to uncertain reasoning under imprecision in so-called *valuation-based networks* which can be applied, for example, to upper and lower probabilities [43], Dempster–Shafer theory of evidence [8, 9, 35, 36, 41], and possibility theory [46, 11, 12] has been proposed in [38, 40, 39] and implemented in the software tool PULCINELLA [34].

An example of a well-known interactive software tool for probabilistic reasoning in trees of cliques is HUGIN [1]. A similar approach is implemented in POSSINFER [17] for the possibilistic setting. The efficiency of propagation is obvious, since distributing all the necessary information on instantiated variables needs only two traversals through the tree of cliques. In our blood group determination example all operations are referred to subspaces with a maximum of three dimensions.

## 6  Learning Possibilistic Networks from Data

If expert knowledge is not sufficient to fully specify the structural as well as the quantitative part of a possibilistic graphical model, then the question arises whether this specification can also be induced with the aid of a database of (imprecise, multivalued) sample cases. More particularly, the learning task consists of finding the best approximating decomposition of the possibility distribution that is generated from the database, relative to a chosen class of possibilistic graphical models. Structure learning can be referred to DAG structures [19] as well as hypertree structures [18]. For quantifying the approximation quality, one needs a *measure of nonspecificity* for the information represented by a possibility distribution. While probabilistic measures of uncertainty usually are based on Shannon entropy, the origin of possibilistic measures of nonspecificity is *Hartley information*. Theoretical considerations on this topic can be found in [18].

The addressed learning problem is NP-hard in the case of non-trivial classes of graphical models, even if we restrict to n-ary relations that can be regarded as special cases of n–dimensional possibility distributions. For this reason, in analogy to learning probabilistic graphical models, heuristics are not avoidable. On the other hand, the approximation quality of the calculated graphical model can efficiently be found, so that a quantification of the loss of specificity that has to be tolerated when dealing with a family of lower-dimensional possibility distributions instead of the original possibility distribution is available.

Using an adequate representation of the possibility distribution $\pi$ induced by the database, a greedy learning algorithm based on the theoretical results in [18] approximates an optimal hypertree decomposition of $\pi$ in $O(n^k m r^k)$ time, where $n$ is the number of variables, $m$ the number of sample cases in the database, $r$ the maximum cardinality of the individual domains of the considered variables, and $k$ the maximum number of nodes that one wants to deal with in each hyperedge. This algorithm has successfully been applied to the blood group determination example. Network induction was based on an artificial database for the 21 attributes, generated from a real database for 9 attributes, and additional expert knowledge. The database consists of 747 sample cases with a large number of incomplete or imprecise cases inside. For more details, we refer to [14]. General experiences with possibilistic graphical models and possibilistic learning are summarized in the next section.

## 7  Discussion: Probabilistic vs. Possibilistic Models

Probability theory and possibility theory both provide concepts for the treatment of uncertain data. The existing controversy between the application domains of possibility and (subjective) probability, especially the Bayesian approach (cf. [7, 3]), comes from the fact that both calculi aim to model comparable aspects of uncertainty handling. Nevertheless, the following summary of characteristic properties identifies advantages of each of the two frameworks:

## Probability Theory

- serves for the *exact* modelling of uncertain, but *precise* data. Imprecise data that provide sets of alternatives without any underlying preference structure among these alternatives are not representable by single probability distributions. Appropriate additional assumptions, for example applying the insufficient reason principle, have to be made in order to transform imprecise data into sets of precise data.

- supports the modelling of imprecision by using families of probability distributions. Related approaches refer, for instance, to probability intervals, upper and lower probabilities, and random sets, respectively. Unfortunately, these approaches often give rise to crucial complexity problems, so that they are of limited power for efficient reasoning in knowledge–based systems.

- has its main application domains, where statistical data are available, or expert knowledge can be quantified in terms of subjective probabilities. The normative character of probabilistic modelling for handling precision under uncertainty supports the surely most justified and transparent form of decision making.

## Possibility Theory

- serves for the *approximative (information-compressed)* modelling of uncertain and/or *imprecise (multivalued)* data. Imprecision is due to the occurrence of sets of possible alternatives, without making any unjustified assumptions about unknown preferences among these alternatives. Information compression, for example by using the (non–normalized) one–point coverage instead of the random set itself, is necessary to support efficiency of operations when handling uncertainty and imprecision together. This is made explicit by interpreting a possibility distribution with the semantics we mentioned in Section 3.

- supports the modelling of precision under uncertainty in that a possibility distribution may be regarded as the one-point coverage of a random set that represents a probability distribution. On the other hand, due to the mentioned loss of information in calculating the one-point coverage, for precision under uncertainty the more effective and reasonable way of modelling is to use a probabilistic instead of a possibilistic approach.

– has its main application domain in those fields of uncertainty modelling, where a relevant part of the available information is imprecise, and should be considered as being imprecise, without any simplifying assumptions. The proposed semantic background of possibility theory (see [15, 14, 20]) provides a basis for well–founded techniques of possibilistic inference and possibilistic decision support, although possibility theory primarily is viewed as a framework for knowledge representation.

Probabilistic as well as possibilistic graphical models are equipped with efficient evidence propagation and learning algorithms of comparable complexity. Nevertheless, considering the special aspects of graphical modelling and the individual properties of the two addressed calculi, the following differences can be found:

*Probabilistic graphical models*

– support exact evidence propagation under uncertainty, since dealing with precise data does not make it necessary to tolerate any loss of information in order to be efficient. The exactness of the reasoning process has the advantage that probabilistic graphical models are very helpful for decision making, even when operating on exceptional events with a very low probability of occurrence. Avoiding the treatment of imprecision allows to focus on a sensitive consideration of uncertainty aspects. Nevertheless, sometimes this tends to be an overmodelling. A typical example is medical diagnosis, where evidence propagation in probabilistic graphical models often results in the necessity of choosing sets of alternative instantiations of decision variables in order to reach a probability that an expert accepts as his comfort level for decision making. This means that uncertain reasoning with precise data does not always prevent us from obtaining imprecise decisions.

– can be induced by databases of sample cases, where the respective learning algorithms make use of approximation techniques or greedy search methods to circumvent the inherent complexity of the learning problem. In most approaches it is required that the cases in the database are precise and complete (without missing values). A problem that is still pending concerns the availability of treatable performance measures, for example the evaluation of the representational quality of the induced graphical model relative to the database, and the minimum number of sample cases needed in order to reach this quality.

*Possibilistic graphical models*

– support approximate evidence propagation under uncertainty and imprecision. The necessity of information compression may lead to an undermodelling of the available knowledge, so that the quality of decision support is reduced by nonspecific results of the reasoning process. Referred to the possibilistic interpretation of a database of sample cases, a typical situation for the potential inability of decision making occurs when reasoning with events that are only rarely supported by the database. This behavior is welcome in systems, where exceptions indicate noisy information rather than interesting dependencies. A benefit of considering, but not overestimating exceptions consists in supporting the stability of approximate reasoning techniques.

– can be induced by databases of sample cases that may consist of imprecise as well as missing values. Due to the NP–hardness of the learning problem, possibilistic structure identification algorithms need to use approximation or greedy search methods in order to be efficient. Performance evaluation refers to measuring the nonspecificity of the possibility distribution associated with the delivered graphical model, compared to the nonspecificity of the possibility distribution associated with the referential database. Note that due to the information compression step, those uncertain dependencies that are only weakly supported by the database, may no longer be extractable from the interpreting possibility distribution. In this case, the learning algorithm will provide a good decomposition, but it has no chance to identify structural properties that have been lost during the information compression step.

## 8  Summary

The above discussion has indicated that probabilistic and possibilistic graphical models both are useful in quite different domains of knowledge representation, which makes them cooperative rather than competitive. For this reason, any attempt to defend one framework against the other is rather destructive than constructive, at least in case that one is more interested in supporting the various facets of dealing with imperfect information in knowledge–based systems than trying to push particular scientific communities. It is therefore one topic of future work to study in which way probabilistic and possibilistic data, obtained from expert knowledge and/or databases of sample cases, can be combined and then represented as the quantitative part of a unified type of graphical model.

## 9  Acknowledgements

The concepts and methods of possibilistic graphical modelling presented in this paper were applied within the CEC-ESPRIT III BRA 6156 DRUMS II (Defeasible Reasoning and Uncertainty Management Systems) and in a cooperation with Deutsche Aerospace for the conception of a data fusion tool [2]. Furthermore, the learning algorithms have been considered in the conception of a data mining tool that is developed in the research center of the Daimler-Benz AG in Ulm, Germany.
Finally, the authors want to express their sincere appreciation to the reviewers for their fruitful comments.

412

# References

1. S.K. Andersen, K.G. Olesen, F.V. Jensen, and F. Jensen. HUGIN — A shell for building Bayesian belief universes for expert systems. In *Proc. 11th International Joint Conference on Artificial Intelligence*, pages 1080–1085, 1989.
2. J. Beckmann, J. Gebhardt, and R. Kruse. Possibilistic inference and data fusion. *Proc. 2nd European Congress on Fuzzy and Intelligent Technologies*, pages 46–47, 1994.
3. J. Bezdek, editor. Fuzziness vs. probability. Again (!?). *IEEE Transactions on Fuzzy Systems* 2, 1994.
4. W. Buntine. Operations for learning graphical models. *J. of Artificial Intelligence Research*, 2:159–224, 1994.
5. L.M. de Campos, J. Gebhardt, and R. Kruse. Axiomatic treatment of possibilistic independence. In C. Froidevaux and J. Kohlas, editors, *Symbolic and Quantitative Approaches to Reasoning and Uncertainty, Lecture Notes in Artificial Intelligence 946*, pages 77–88. Springer, Berlin, 1995.
6. E. Castillo, J.M. Gutierrez, and A.S. Hadi. *Expert Systems and Probabilistic Network Models*. Series: Monographs in Computer Science. Springer, New York, 1997.
7. P. Cheeseman. Probability versus fuzzy reasoning. In: L.N. Kanal and J.F. Lemmer, editors, *Uncertainty in Artificial Intelligence*, 85–102. North–Holland, Amsterdam, 1986.
8. A.P. Dempster. Upper and lower probabilities induced by a multivalued mapping, *Ann. Math. Stat.*, 38:325–339, 1967.
9. A.P. Dempster. Upper and lower probabilities generated by a random closed interval, *Ann. Math. Stat.*, 39:957–966, 1968.
10. D. Dubois, S. Moral, and H. Prade. A semantics for possibility theory based on likelihoods. Annual report, CEC–ESPRIT III BRA 6156 DRUMS II, 1993.
11. D. Dubois and H. Prade. *Possibility Theory*. Plenum Press, New York, 1988.
12. D. Dubois and H. Prade. Fuzzy sets in approximate reasoning, Part 1: Inference with possibility distributions. *Fuzzy Sets and Systems*, 40:143–202, 1991.
13. D. Dubois, H. Prade, and R.R. Yager, editors, *Readings in Fuzzy Sets for Intelligent Systems*. Morgan Kaufman, San Mateo, CA, 1993.
14. J. Gebhardt. Learning from Data: Possibilistic Graphical Models. *Habilitation Thesis, University of Braunschweig*, Germany, 1997.
15. J. Gebhardt and R. Kruse. A new approach to semantic aspects of possibilistic reasoning. In M. Clarke, S. Moral, and R. Kruse, editors, *Symbolic and Quantitative Approaches to Reasoning and Uncertainty*, pages 151–159. Springer, Berlin, 1993.
16. J. Gebhardt and R. Kruse. On an information compression view of possibility theory. In *Proc. 3rd IEEE Int. Conf. on Fuzzy Systems (FUZZIEEE'94)*, pages 1285–1288, Orlando, 1994.
17. J. Gebhardt and R. Kruse. POSSINFER — A software tool for possibilistic inference. In D. Dubois, H. Prade, and R. Yager, editors, *Fuzzy Set Methods in Information Engineering: A Guided Tour of Applications*, pages 407–418. Wiley, New York, 1996.
18. J. Gebhardt and R. Kruse. Tightest hypertree decompositions of multivariate possibility distributions. In *Proc. Int. Conf. on Information Processing and Management of Uncertainty in Knowledge-Based Systems (IPMU'96)*, pages 923–927, Granada, 1996.

19. J. Gebhardt and R. Kruse. Automated construction of possibilistic networks from data. *J. of Applied Mathematics and Computer Science*, 6(3):101–136, 1996.

20. J. Gebhardt and R. Kruse. Parallel combination of information sources. In D. Gabbay and P. Smets, editors, *Handbook of Defeasible Reasoning and Uncertainty Management Systems*, Vol. 1: Updating Uncertain Information. Kluwer, Dordrecht, 1997 (to appear).

21. K. Hestir, H.T. Nguyen, and G.S. Rogers. A random set formalism for evidential reasoning. In I.R. Goodman, M.M. Gupta, H.T. Nguyen, and G.S. Rogers, editors, *Conditional Logic in Expert Systems*, pages 209–344. North–Holland, 1991.

22. E. Hisdal. Conditional possibilities, independence, and noninteraction. *Fuzzy Sets and Systems*, 1:283–297, 1978.

23. V. Isham. An introduction to spatial point processes and Markov random fields. *Int. Stat. Rev.*, 49:21–43, 1981.

24. F. Klawonn, J. Gebhardt, and R. Kruse. Fuzzy control on the basis of equality relations with an example from idle speed control. *IEEE Transactions on Fuzzy Systems*, 3:336–350, 1995.

25. R. Kruse, J. Gebhardt, and F. Klawonn. *Foundations of Fuzzy Systems*. Wiley, Chichester, 1994.

26. R. Kruse, E. Schwecke, and J. Heinsohn. *Uncertainty and Vagueness in Knowledge Based Systems: Numerical Methods*. Artificial Intelligence. Springer, Berlin, 1991.

27. S.L. Lauritzen and D.J. Spiegelhalter. Local computations with probabilities on graphical structures and their application to expert systems. *Journal of the Royal Stat. Soc., Series B*, 2(50):157–224, 1988.

28. J. Pearl. *Probabilistic Reasoning in Intelligent Systems: Networks of Plausible Inference (2nd edition)*. Morgan Kaufmann, New York, 1992.

29. J. Pearl and A. Paz. Graphoids – A graph based logic for reasoning about relevance relations. In B.D. Boulay et al., editors, *Advances in Artificial Intelligence 2*, pages 357–363. North–Holland, Amsterdam, 1991.

30. L.K. Rasmussen. Blood group determination of Danish Jersey cattle in the F-blood group system. *Dina Research Report 8*, Dina Foulum, 8830 Tjele, Denmark, November 1992.

31. E.H. Ruspini. The semantics of vague knowledge. *Rev. Internat. Systemique*, 3:387–420, 1989.

32. E.H. Ruspini. Similarity based models for possibilistic logics. *Proc. 3rd Int. Conf. on Information Processing and Mangement of Uncertainty in Knowledge Based Systems*, 56–58, 1990.

33. E.H. Ruspini. On the semantics of fuzzy logic. *Int. J. of Apprximate Reasoning*, 5, 1991.

34. A. Saffiotti and E. Umkehrer. PULCINELLA: A general tool for propagating uncertainty in valuation networks, In: B. D'Ambrosio, P. Smets, and P.P. Bonisonne, editors. *Proc. 7th Conf. on Uncertainty in Artificial Intelligence*, 323–331, Morgan Kaufmann, San Mateo, 1991.

35. G. Shafer. *A Mathematical Theory of Evidence*. Princeton University Press, Princeton, 1976.

36. G. Shafer and J. Pearl. *Readings in Uncertain Reasoning*, Morgan Kaufman, San Mateo, CA, 1990.

37. G. Shafer and P.P. Shenoy. Local computation in hypertrees. Working paper 201, School of Business, University of Kansas, Lawrence, 1988.

38. P.P. Shenoy. A Valuation-based Language for Expert Systems, *Int. J. of Approximate Reasoning*, 3:383–411, 1989.

39. P.P. Shenoy. Valuation Networks and Conditional Independence, *Proc. 9th Conf. on Uncertainty in AI*, 191–199, Morgan Kaufman, San Mateo, 1993.

40. P.P. Shenoy and G.R. Shafer. Axioms for Probability and Belief-function Propagation. In: R.D. Shachter, T.S. Levitt, L.N. Kanal, and J.F. Lemmer, editors. *Uncertainty in AI*, 4:169–198, North Holland, Amsterdam 1990.

41. P. Smets and R. Kennes. The transferable belief model. *Artificial Intelligence*, 66:191–234, 1994.

42. P.Z. Wang. From the fuzzy statistics to the falling random subsets, In P.P. Wang, editor. *Advances in Fuzzy Sets, Possibility and Applications*, 81–96, Plenum Press, New York, 1983.

43. P. Walley. *Statistical Reasoning with Imprecise Probabilities*, Chapman and Hall, 1991.

44. J. Whittaker. *Graphical Models in Applied Multivariate Statistics*. Wiley, 1990.

45. L.A. Zadeh. The concept of a linguistic variable and its application to approximate reasoning. *Information Sciences*, 9:43–80, 1975.

46. L.A. Zadeh. Fuzzy sets as a basis for a theory of possibility. *Fuzzy Sets and Systems*, 1:3–28, 1978.

# How Much Does an Agent Believe:
# An Extension of Modal Epistemic Logic*

Subrata K. Das

Charles River Analytics
55 Wheeler Street
Cambridge, MA 02138
sdas@cra.com

**Abstract:** Modal logics are often criticised for their coarse grain representation of knowledge of possibilities about assertions. That is to say, if two assertions are possible in the current world, their further properties are indistinguishable in the modal formalism even if an agent knows that one of them is true in twice as many possible worlds as compared to the other one. Epistemic logic, that is the logic of knowledge and belief, cannot avoid this shortcomings because it inherits the syntax and semantics of modal logics. In this paper, we develop an extended formalism of modal epistemic logic which will allow an agent to represent its *degrees of support* about an assertion. The degrees are drawn from qualitative or quantitative dictionaries which are accumulated from agent's a priori knowledge about the application domain. A possible-world semantics of the logic is developed by using the accessibility *hyperelation* and the soundness and completeness results are stated. The abstract syntax and semantics are illustrated and motivated by an example from the medical domain.

## 1 Introduction

In recent years there has been growing interest within AI community to build intelligent agents [24, 27]. Several proposals, notably the work of Rao and Georgeff [25], have emphasized on building intelligent agents capable of hypothetical reasoning, that is, reasoning with beliefs and goals. The major shortcomings in these approaches as well as in the work of traditional modal epistemic logic [17, 4, 11, 16, 22, 21] is the coarse grain representation of beliefs about assertions. In other words, if two assertions are believed in the current situation, their further properties are indistinguishable even if an agent knows that one of them is true in twice as many possible worlds as compared to the other one. The paper addresses this problem by developing a logic $\mathcal{L}_{rs}$ which extends epistemic logic and allows an agent to represent its *degrees of support* about an assertion. The context in which this work was carried out and its practical applications can be found in [7, 8, 12].

We extend the syntax of traditional modal epistemic logic by including an indexed modal operator $\langle sup_d \rangle$ for support. In this way, we can model an argument which merely

---

* The author completed this work while working at the Imperial College, University of London. The author would like to thank his colleagues in the RED project, John Fox and Paul Krause of Imperial Cancer Research Fund, for many helpful comments. The project was supported under the DTI/SERC project ITD 4/1/9053: Safety-Critical Systems Initiative.

supports a proposition, but does not necessarily warrant an agent committing to believe in that proposition. For example, an argument for $peptic\_ulcer$ using the formula

$$\langle bel \rangle upper\_abdomen\_pain \rightarrow \langle sup_d \rangle peptic\_ulcer$$

states that if a patient is believed to have pain in upper abdomen then there is an amount of support $d$ for the patient having peptic ulcer. The extended modal logic is given a uniform possible world semantics by introducing the novel concept of an accessibility *hyperelation* which will be described fully in this paper.

As will become clear, the modality $\langle sup_d \rangle$ (in particular the level of support $d$) is monotonic. This is sufficient reason [10] for us to need to distinguish the level of support $d$ from a measure of uncertainty in the general case. Consequently, this work should not be considered in the same terms as, for example, the work on probabilistic logic discussed in [23, 1, 26, 14]. Nevertheless, what we *are* able to do is to offer a framework in which levels of support may be taken from one of a variety of different qualitative, semi-qualitative and quantitative "dictionaries" which may be supplied with aggregation operations for combining levels of support (see Appendix A for details). These *aggregation* operations can give us back some of the properties we would expect of an uncertainty measure when the agent uses them to generate or confirm its beliefs in a proposition, based on sets of supports for and against (for the negation of) that proposition.

Essentially, the aggregation process allows an agent to accumulate evidence for and against a proposition and then combine them to provide an overall judgement. Whether an agent accepts such a judgement from a mechanical process will depend on the nature of that agent. We shall describe a *rational* agent as one who accepts an assertion as a belief if the process generates enough combined evidence for the assertion. A *strict* agent, in contrast, will not believe an assertion unless such an aggregation process generates the highest support possible.

The rest of the paper is organised as follows. The syntax of the system $\mathcal{L}_{rs}$ which allows beliefs and supports to be represented is detailed in section 2. We then establish an adequate set of properties for the support operator and its relationship to the concept of knowledge and belief through a set of axioms in section 3. An extended possible world semantics of $\mathcal{L}_{rs}$ through *hyperelation* is then presented in section 4. Having presented the semantics time is taken to illustrate the abstract model definition with an example in section 5. The soundness and completeness result of $\mathcal{L}_{rs}$ is then established in section 6. The proofs of the propositions and theorems stated here can be found in the longer version which is available on request.

## 2  Syntax of $\mathcal{L}_{rs}$

Suppose $\mathcal{P}$ is the set of all propositions which includes the special symbol $\top$ (true) and $D$ is an arbitrary *dictionary* of symbols which will be used to label the propositions. In general, a dictionary will be a semi-lattice with the partial order relation $\leq$. For simplicity, we shall consider a dictionary as a chain with one distinguished element $\triangle$ known as the *top element* to represent the highest support for arguments. For example, elements ++ and 1 are the top elements of the two dictionaries $dict(Qual)$ and $dict(Prob)$ respectively. A number of different dictionaries for reasoning under uncertainty have been discussed in [13, 19], together with their mathematical foundations and their relation to classical probability and other uncertainty formalisms.

The modal operator of $\mathcal{L}_{rs}$ corresponding to belief is $\langle bel \rangle$. In addition, for each dictionary symbol $d \in D$, we have a modal operator $\langle sup_d \rangle$ for support. The *formulae* (or *assertions*) of $\mathcal{L}_{rs}$ are as follows:
- propositions are formulae.
- $\langle bel \rangle F$ is a formula, where $F$ is a formula.
- $\langle sup_d \rangle F$ is a formula, where $F$ is a formula and $d \in D$.
- $\neg F$ and $F \wedge G$ are formulae, where $F, G$ are formulae.
We take $\perp$ (false) to be an abbreviation of $\neg \top$. Other logical connectives are defined using '$\neg$' and '$\wedge$' in the usual manner.

## 3 Axioms of $\mathcal{L}_{rs}$

We consider every instance of a propositional tautology to be an axiom of $\mathcal{L}_{rs}$. This set includes instances of propositional tautologies that may involve any number of the modal operators, for example, $\langle bel \rangle p \rightarrow \langle bel \rangle p$. We also have the *modus ponens* inference rule, that is, $F$ and $F \rightarrow G$ entails $G$. We adopt a set of standard axioms of belief which can be found in [4, 11, 16, 22]:

**Axiom 1** $\neg \langle bel \rangle \perp$

**Axiom 2** $\langle bel \rangle F \wedge \langle bel \rangle (F \rightarrow G) \rightarrow \langle bel \rangle G$

**Axiom 3** $\langle bel \rangle F \rightarrow \langle bel \rangle \langle bel \rangle F$

**Axiom 4** $\neg \langle bel \rangle F \rightarrow \langle bel \rangle \neg \langle bel \rangle F$

Axiom (1) expresses that an inconsistency is not believable by an agent. The derivation of the symbol $\perp$ from the database implies inconsistency. Axiom (2) states that an agent believes all the logical consequences of its beliefs, that is, an agent's beliefs are closed under logical deduction. Axiom (3) represents positive introspection, that is, an agent believes that s/he believes in something. On the other hand, axiom (4) represents negative introspection, that is, an agent believes that s/he does not believe in something. We also have the rule of necessitation for beliefs:

**Inference Rule 1** *if* $\vdash F$ *then* $\vdash \langle bel \rangle F$

**Proposition 1.** *The following are theorems of $\mathcal{L}_{rs}$:*
$\langle bel \rangle (F \wedge G) \leftrightarrow \langle bel \rangle F \wedge \langle bel \rangle G$
$\langle bel \rangle F \vee \langle bel \rangle G \rightarrow \langle bel \rangle (F \vee G)$
$\langle bel \rangle F \rightarrow \neg \langle bel \rangle \neg F$

There is no support for an inconsistency and the following axiom reflects this property:

**Axiom 5** $\neg \langle sup_d \rangle \perp$, *for every* $d \in D$

Support is closed under tautological equivalence by preserving degrees:

**Inference Rule 2** *if* $\vdash F \leftrightarrow G$ *then* $\vdash \langle sup_d \rangle F \leftrightarrow \langle sup_d \rangle G$, *for every* $d \in D$

Support operators can be combined to obtain a single support operator by using the following axiom:

**Axiom 6** $\langle sup_{d1} \rangle F \wedge \langle sup_{d2} \rangle (F \to G) \to \langle sup_{d1 \otimes d2} \rangle (F \wedge G)$

where $\otimes : D \times D \to D$ is the function for computing supports for assertions derived through material implications. The axiom states that if $d_1$ and $d_2$ are supports for $F$ and $F \to G$ respectively then $\otimes(d_1, d_2)$ (or equivalently $d_1 \otimes d_2$ in infix notation) is a derived support for $F \wedge G$. The function $\otimes$ can be considered as ordinary multiplication when $D$ is $dict(Prob)$. In a more general semi-lattice structure dictionary, $d_1 \otimes d_2$ can simply be taken as the greatest lower bound of $d_1$ and $d_2$. Note that, within such a structure, $d \otimes \triangle = d$, for every $d \in D$.

A *rational agent* believes in something which has support with the top element of the dictionary. Thus, the following axiom should be considered for a rational agent:

**Axiom 7** $\langle sup_\triangle \rangle F \to \langle bel \rangle F$

This axiom, of course, assumes that an assertion and its negation are not simultaneously derivable with the top element as support, that is, an integrity constraint [5] as follows:

**Proposition 2.** $\vdash \langle sup_\triangle \rangle F \wedge \langle sup_\triangle \rangle \neg F \to \perp$.

It is difficult to maintain consistency of a database in the presence of this formula, particularly when the database is constructed from different sources; mutual inconsistency and mistakes sometimes need to be tolerated. In these circumstances, it might be left to the agent to arbitrate over what to believe or not believe.

An agent might believe in something even if the database derives no support for it. We call an agent who does not believe in something unless there is support with the top element a *strict agent*. Thus, the following axiom is considered for a system implementing a strict agent:

**Axiom 8** $\langle bel \rangle F \to \langle sup_\triangle \rangle F$

In a strict system, a tautology has always the highest support and the support operator is closed under believed implications:

**Proposition 3.** *if* $\vdash F$ *then* $\vdash \langle sup_\triangle \rangle F$, *and*
$\vdash \langle sup_d \rangle F \wedge \langle bel \rangle (F \to G) \to \langle sup_d \rangle (F \wedge G)$.

## 4   Semantics of $\mathcal{L}_{rs}$

A *model* of $\mathcal{L}_{rs}$ is a tuple

$$\langle W, V, R_b, R_s \rangle$$

in which $W$ is a set of possible worlds, $V$ is a *valuation* which associates a world to a set of propositions which are true in that world. Symbolically,

$$V : W \to \Pi(P)$$

where $P$ is the set of propositions and $\Pi(P)$ is the power set of $P$. The relation $R_b \subseteq W \times W$ relates each world $w$ to a set of worlds considered possible by the agent from $w$. Finally, $R_s$ is a *hyperelation* which is defined as

$$R_s \subseteq W \times D \times \Pi(W)$$

Semantically, if $\langle w, d, W' \rangle \in R_s$ and $w$ is the current world then there is an amount of support $d$ for moving to one of the worlds in $W'$ from the world $w$. The set $W'$ is a non-empty subset of the set $R_b(w)$ of possible world from $w$, where $R_b(w) = \{w' \in W : wR_bw'\}$.

An assertion is a *belief* of an agent at a world $w$ if and only if it is true in every possible world accessible from the world $w$ by $R_b$. Note that the members of $R_s$ have been considered of the form $\langle w, d, W' \rangle$ rather than $\langle w, d, w' \rangle$. The main reason is that the derivability of an assertion of the form $\langle sup_d \rangle F$ from the current state of a knowledge base supports the set of possible worlds where $F$ is true as opposed to a single world. Thus, an assertion is *supported* at a world $w$ if and only if there is some amount of support for *the* subset of the set of possible worlds from $w$ where it is true.

Formally, given a model $\mathcal{M} = \langle W, V, R_b, R_s \rangle$, truth values of formulae with respect to a world $w$ are determined by the rules given below:

$\models_{\mathcal{M}}^{w} \top$

$\models_{\mathcal{M}}^{w} p$ iff $p \in V(w)$.

$\models_{\mathcal{M}}^{w} \langle sup_d \rangle F$ iff there exists $\langle w, d, W' \rangle$ in the relation $R_s$ such that $\models_{\mathcal{M}}^{w'} F$, for every $w' \in W'$, and $\not\models_{\mathcal{M}}^{w'} F$, for every $w' \in R_b(w) - W'$.

$\models_{\mathcal{M}}^{w} \langle bel \rangle F$ iff for every $w'$ in $W$ such that $wR_bw'$, $\models_{\mathcal{M}}^{w'} F$.

$\models_{\mathcal{M}}^{w} \neg F$ iff $\not\models_{\mathcal{M}}^{w} F$.

$\models_{\mathcal{M}}^{w} F \wedge G$ iff $\models_{\mathcal{M}}^{w} F$ and $\models_{\mathcal{M}}^{w} G$.

A formula $F$ is said to be *true* in model $\mathcal{M}$, written as $\models_{\mathcal{M}} F$, if and only if $\models_{\mathcal{M}}^{w} F$, for every world $w$ in $W$. A formula $F$ is said to be *valid* with respect to a class of models $\Gamma$, written as $\models_{\Gamma} F$, if $F$ is true in every model in $\Gamma$. If a formula $F$ is valid with respect to every class of model then we simply write $\models F$.

If we are allowing axioms (1)-(4) in a system the standard set of properties which will be possessed by the accessibility relation $R_b$ are the the following:

**Model Property 1** $R_b$ *is serial, transitive, euclidean.*

The fact that an agent does not believe in something inconsistent guarantees the existence of a possible world which is the seriality property. The explanation of $R_b$ being transitive and euclidean can be found in [3, 20].

The hyperelation $R_s$ satisfies the following properties:

**Model Property 2** *for every $w$ in $W$ and $d$, $d_1$, $d_2$ in $D$, the relation $R_s$ satisfies the following conditions:*

1. *if $\langle w, d, W' \rangle \in R_s$ then $W' \neq \emptyset$.*
2. *if $\langle w, d_1, W_1 \rangle$, $\langle w, d_2, W_2 \rangle \in R_s$ then $\langle w, d_1 \otimes d_2, W_1 \cap W_2 \rangle \in R_s$, provided $W_1 \cap W_2 \neq \emptyset$.*

3. *if* $\langle w, \triangle, W' \rangle \in R_s$ *then* $W' = R_b(w)$.
4. $\langle w, \triangle, R_b(w) \rangle \in R_s$.

These restrictions on $R_s$ can be summarised as follows. If there is an amount of support $d$ for moving to one of the worlds in $W'$ then the worlds of $W'$ are realised by the agent. Thus $W'$ cannot be empty which is property (a). The property (b) simply composes evidences for worlds using the function $\otimes$ defined earlier. The property (c) says that if one is sure about supporting a set of possible worlds $W'$ from $w$ with the highest support $\triangle$ then $W'$ ought to be the set of all possible worlds from $w$, that is, $R_b(w)$. Given the current world $w$, an agent has to move to one of the possible worlds accessible from $w$ by $R_b$. In other words, the changed world always belongs to $R_b(w)$ and thus there is always the highest support for moving to one of the worlds in $R_b(w)$ from any given world $w$ which confirms the property (d).

## 5 A worked example

This section provides an example which illustrates the semantics presented in the previous section. First of all, we consider the dictionary $D$ as $dict(Prob)$ and $D'$ (as mentioned in Appendix A) is $D$ itself. Suppose the current world $w_0$ is described by a database consisting of the following formulae

$\langle bel \rangle (elderly \wedge weight\_loss) \rightarrow \langle sup_{d1} \rangle cancer$
$\langle bel \rangle smoker \rightarrow \langle sup_{d2} \rangle cancer$
$\langle bel \rangle positive\_biopsy \rightarrow \langle sup_{d3} \rangle cancer$
$\langle bel \rangle upper\_abdomen\_pain \rightarrow \langle sup_{d4} \rangle peptic\_ulcer$
$\langle bel \rangle young \rightarrow \langle sup_{d3} \rangle (\neg cancer \wedge \neg peptic\_ulcer)$
$\langle bel \rangle pain\_after\_meals \rightarrow \langle sup_{d5} \rangle (cancer \wedge peptic\_ulcer)$

The *knowledge* ($\equiv F \wedge \langle bel \rangle F$) at $w_0$ is the above set of formulae together with the following set of facts:

$\{young, smoker, upper\_abdomen\_pain, weight\_loss\}$

The valuation $V$ on $w_0$, that is, $V(w_0)$ is defined as the above set of facts. Since the decision is to establish one of 2 candidates *cancer* and *peptic_ulcer*, there will be $2^2$, that is, four possible worlds $w_1$, $w_2$, $w_3$ and $w_4$ whose valuations are as follows (see figure 1):

$V(w_1) = V(w_0) \cup \{cancer\}$
$V(w_2) = V(w_0) \cup \{peptic\_ulcer\}$
$V(w_3) = V(w_0) \cup \{cancer, peptic\_ulcer\}$
$V(w_4) = V(w_0)$

Parts of the relations $R_b$ and $R_s$ in the model definition from $w_0$ are respectively defined as the following two sets:

$\{\langle w_0, w_1 \rangle, \langle w_0, w_2 \rangle, \langle w_0, w_3 \rangle, \langle w_0, w_4 \rangle\}$
$\{\langle w_0, d2, \{w_1, w_3\} \rangle, \langle w_0, d4, \{w_2, w_3\} \rangle, \langle w_0, d2, \{w_4\} \rangle\}$

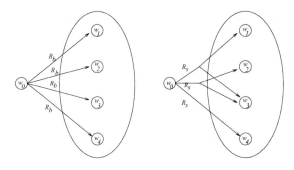

**Fig. 1.** A view to the possible worlds.

The supports for the mutually exclusive possibilities are computed by the aggregation process (using the domain knowledge that $cancer$ and $peptic\_ulcer$ are almost mutually exclusive candidates) as follows:

- total support for $C_1(cancer \land \neg peptic\_ulcer) = \mathcal{A}(\{\langle C_1, G_1, d2\rangle\}) = d2$
- total support for $C_2(\neg cancer \land peptic\_ulcer) = \mathcal{A}(\{\langle C_2, G_2, d4\rangle\}) = d4$
- total support for $C_3(cancer \land peptic\_ulcer) = 0$
- total support for $C_4(\neg cancer \land \neg peptic\_ulcer) = \mathcal{A}(\{\langle C_4, G_4, d4\rangle\}) = d2$

where each $di$ is drawn from $dict(Prob)$ and the grounds $G_1, G_2$ and $G_4$ are respectively the following three:

$smoker \rightarrow cancer$
$upper\_abdomen\_pain \rightarrow peptic\_ulcer$
$young \rightarrow \neg cancer \land \neg peptic\_ulcer$

Aggregation of arguments (see the appendix) introduces a hierarchy of preferences [6] among the set of all possible worlds accessible from $w$ by the relation $R_b$. Assuming that $d4$ is less than $d2$, the preference relation $\prec$ among the set of possible worlds is derived as $w_3 \prec w_2$, $w_2 \prec w_1$ and $w_2 \prec w_4$. The maximally preferred possible worlds are $w_1$ and $w_4$. This yields a dilemma. In case the agent cannot gather any more evidence, s/he may commit to $w_4$ by preferring $w_4$ to $w_1$. This involves adding $\neg cancer$ and $\neg peptic\_ulcer$ to the current state of the database as either beliefs or knowledge depending on the strength of support and agent's confidence. We add only beliefs to keep the belief revision option open in case of a wrong diagnosis.

Alternatively, if we now add an additional evidence $\langle bel\rangle positive\_biopsy$ into the database that would increase the total support for $C_1$ to $\mathcal{A}(\{\langle C_1, G_1, d2\rangle, \langle C_1, G'_1, d3\rangle\})$ which is $d2 + d3 - d2 \times d3$, where the additional ground $G'_1$ for $C_1$ is $positive\_biopsy \rightarrow cancer$. Note that the two arguments for $cancer$ are constructed using independent pieces of evidence $smoker$ and $positive\_biopsy$. The revised valuation on each $w_i$ will be as before except $positive\_biopsy$ changes its truth value. The relations $R_s$ will be redefined as

$$\{\langle w_0, d2, \{w_1, w_3\}\rangle, \langle w_0, d4, \{w_2, w_3\}\rangle, \langle w_0, d2, \{w_4\}\rangle, \langle w_0, d3, \{w_1, w_3\}\rangle\}$$

Since $w_1$ is the only world preferred to the rest of the possible worlds, the agent considers $w_1$ as the goal world and commits to it. Changing to the committed world from the current world involves adding $cancer$ and $\neg peptic\_ulcer$ to the database as the agent's beliefs. Adding $\langle bel \rangle cancer$ to the database will trigger the decision for cancer treatment among $surgery$ and $chemotherapy$ and the agent continues reasoning as before with the relevant knowledge.

## 6   Soundness and completeness

The technique adopted in this section for establishing soundness and completeness of $\mathcal{L}_{rs}$ is similar to the one for the class of normal logics in [3]. Suppose, $\Gamma_{rs}$ is the set of all models satisfying the properties (1) and (2). First of all, the following two propositions prove that the validity in a class of models is preserved by the use of the rule of inference and the axioms of $\mathcal{L}_{rs}$.

**Proposition 4.** *For every formulae $F$ and $G$:*
*if $\models F$ then $\models \langle bel \rangle F$*
*if $\models F \leftrightarrow G$ then $\models \langle sup_d \rangle F \leftrightarrow \langle sup_d \rangle G$*

**Proposition 5.** *Axioms (1)-(7) are valid with respect to the class of models $\Gamma_{rs}$.*

The above set of propositions establishes the basis of the soundness result. In order to prove the completeness result, the class of canonical models is relevant.

**Definition 6.** A model $\mathcal{M} = \langle W, V, R_b, R_s \rangle$ of $\mathcal{L}_{rs}$ is called a *canonical model*, written as $\mathcal{M}_c$, if and only if
(1) $W = \{w : w$ is a maximal consistent set in logic $\mathcal{L}_{rs}\}$.
(2) For every $w$, $\langle bel \rangle F \in w$ if and only if for every $w'$ in $W$ such that $w R_b w'$, $F \in w'$.
(3) For every $w$, $d$ and $W'$, $\langle sup_d \rangle F \in w$ if and only if there exists $\langle w, d, W' \rangle \in R_s$ such that $F \in w'$, for every $w'$ in $W'$.
(4) For each proposition $p$, $\models^w_{\mathcal{M}_c} p$ if and only if $p \in w$.

**Proposition 7.** *Let $\mathcal{M}_c = \langle W, V, R_b, R_s \rangle$ be a canonical model of $\mathcal{L}_{rs}$. Then, for every $w$ in $W$, $\models^w_{\mathcal{M}_c} F$ if and only if $F \in w$.*

Therefore, the worlds in a canonical model for $\mathcal{L}_{rs}$ will always verify just those sentences they contain. In other words, the sentences which are true in such a model are precisely the theorems of $\mathcal{L}_{rs}$.

**Theorem 8.** *Let $\mathcal{M}_c = \langle W, V, R_b, R_s \rangle$ be a canonical model of $\mathcal{L}_{rs}$. Then $\vdash F$ if and only if $\models_{\mathcal{M}_c} F$, for every formula $F$.*

The existence of a canonical model for $\mathcal{L}_{rs}$ is shown by the existence of a proper canonical model defined as follows.

**Definition 9.** A model $\mathcal{M} = \langle W, V, R_b, R_s \rangle$ of $\mathcal{L}_{rs}$ is called a *proper canonical model*, written as $\mathcal{M}_{pc}$, iff

(1) $W = \{w: w$ is a maximal consistent set in logic $\mathcal{L}_{rs}\}$.

(2) For every $w$ and $w'$, $wR_bw'$ if and only if $\{F : \langle bel \rangle F \in w\} \subseteq w'$.

(3) For every $w$, $d$ and $W'$, $\langle w, d, W' \rangle \in R_s$ if and only if $\{\langle sup_d \rangle F : F \in \cap W'\} \subseteq w$.

(4) For each proposition $p$, $\models_{\mathcal{M}_{pc}}^w p$ if and only if $p \in w$.

By definition, a proper canonical model exists and the following proposition establishes that a proper canonical model is a canonical model.

**Proposition 10.** *Suppose* $\mathcal{M}_{pc}$ *is a proper canonical model of* $\mathcal{L}_{rs}$ *as defined above. Then* $\mathcal{M}_{pc}$ *is also a canonical model.*

**Theorem 11.** *If* $\mathcal{M}_{pc}$ *is a proper canonical model of* $\mathcal{L}_{rs}$ *then the model satisfies properties (1) and (2).*

The following soundness and completeness theorem establishes the fact that $\mathcal{L}_{rs}$ is determined by $\Gamma_{rs}$.

**Theorem 12.** *For every formula* $F$, $\vdash_{\mathcal{L}_{rs}} F$ *iff* $\models_{\Gamma_{rs}} F$.

A *normal* system, denoted as $\mathcal{L}_{norm}$, is obtained from the system $\mathcal{L}_{rs}$ by excluding axioms (7) and (8). Similarly, a *rational* (resp. *strict*) system, denoted as $\mathcal{L}_r$ (resp. $\mathcal{L}_s$), is obtained from the system $\mathcal{L}_{rs}$ by excluding axiom (8) (resp. axiom (7)). Suppose, $\Gamma_{norm}$ is the set of all models satisfying the properties (1) and (2a-b). Similarly, $\Gamma_r$ (resp. $\Gamma_s$) is the set of all models satisfying the properties (1) and (2a-b-c) (resp. (1) and (2a-b-d)).

**Corollary 13.** *For every* $F$, $\vdash_{\mathcal{L}_{norm}} F$ *iff* $\models_{\Gamma_{norm}} F$.

**Corollary 14.** *For every formula* $F$, $\vdash_{\mathcal{L}_r} F$ *iff* $\models_{\Gamma_r} F$.

**Corollary 15.** *For every formula* $F$, $\vdash_{\mathcal{L}_s} F$ *iff* $\models_{\Gamma_s} F$.

# 7 Conclusion

We have developed an extended formalism of modal epistemic logic which allows an agent to represent degrees of support for an assertion. This framework forms a part of the domino decision making model which has already been successfully applied in the domains of cancer and asthma protocol management [7, 8, 12]. $\mathcal{L}_{rs}$ is an extension of the epistemic part of $LR^2L$ developed in [9]. Like the proposals in [2, 15], the framework integrates closely the degrees of support with the underlying logic. Our approach breaks up the traditional coarse grain representation of knowledge of possibilities about assertions followed in standard BDI-architectures [25, 27]. Therefore, the formalism provides a promising framework for the design of intelligent agents. We have also presented versions of the formalism to model what we have called rational and strict agents. A possible-world semantics of the logic has been developed by using the accessibility hyperelation and the soundness and completeness results have been established.

# References

1. F. Bacchus. *Representing and reasoning with probabilistic knowledge.* MIT Press, 1990.
2. P. Chatalic and C. Froidevaux. Lattice-based graded logic: a multimodal approach. In *Proceedings of the Conference Conference on Uncertainty in Artificial Intelligence*, pages 33–40, 1992.
3. B. Chellas. *Modal Logic.* Cambridge University Press, 1980.
4. P. R. Cohen and H. Levesque. Intention is choice with commitment. *Artificial Intelligence*, 42, 1990.
5. S. K. Das. *Deductive Databases and Logic Programming.* Addison-Wesley, 1992.
6. S. K. Das. A logical reasoning with preference. *Decision Support Systems*, 15:19–25, 1995.
7. S. K. Das, J. Fox, D. Elsdon, and P. Hammond. Decision making and plan management by autonomous agents: theory, implementation and applications. In *Proceedings of the International Conference on Autonomous Agents*, California, February 1997.
8. S. K. Das, J. Fox, P. Hammond, and D. Elsdon. A flexible architecture for autonomous agents. *to appear in the Journal of Experimental and Theoretical Artificial Intelligence*, 1997.
9. S. K. Das, J. Fox, and P. Krause. A unified framework for hypothetical and practical reasoning (1): theoretical foundations. In D. M. Gabbay and H. J. Ohlbach, editors, *Proceedings of the International Conference on Formal and Applied Practical Reasoning*, pages 58–72. Springer-Verlag, June 1996.
10. D. Dubois and H. Prade. Non-standard theories of uncertainty in knowledge representation and reasoning. *The Knowledge Engineering Review*, 9:399–416, 1994.
11. R. Fagin and J. Y. Halpern. Belief, awareness and limited reasoning. *Artificial Intelligence*, 34:39–76, 1988.
12. J. Fox and S. K. Das. A unified framework for hypothetical and practical reasoning (2): lessons from medical applications. In *Proceedings of the International Conference on Formal and Applied Practical Reasoning*, pages 73–92. Springer-Verlag, June 1996.
13. J. Fox, P. J. Krause, and S. Ambler. Arguments, contradictions and practical reasoning. In *Proceedings of the European Conference on Artificial Intelligence*, August 1992.
14. P. Hajek, L. Godo, and F. Esteva. Fuzzy logic and probability. In *Proceedings of the 11th European Conference on Uncertainty in Artificial Intelligence*, pages 237–244, 1995.
15. J. Halpern and M. Rabin. A logic to reason about likelihood. *Artificial Intelligence*, 32:379–405, 1987.
16. J. Y. Halpern and Y. O. Moses. A guide to the modal logics of knowledge and belief. In *Proceedings of the 9th International Joint Conference on Artificial Intelligence*, pages 480–490, 1985.
17. J. Hintikka. *Knowledge and Belief.* Cornell University Press, 1962.
18. P. Krause and D. Clark. *Representing Uncertain Knowledge: An artificial intelligence approach.* Intellect, Oxford, 1993.
19. P. J. Krause, S. J. Ambler, M. Elvang-Goransson, and J. Fox. A logic of argumentation for uncertain reasoning. *Computational Intelligence*, 11:113–131, 1995.
20. E. J. Lemmon. *An Introduction to Modal Logic.* Basil Blackwell, 1977.
21. J. J. Meyer and W. van der Hoek. *Epistemic Logic for AI and Computer Science.* Cambridge Tracks in Theoretical Computer Science. Cambridge University Press, 1995.
22. J.-J. Ch. Meyer, W. van der Hoek, and G. A. W. Vreeswijk. Epistemic logic for computer science: a tutorial (part one). *EATCS*, 44:242–270, 1991.
23. N. J. Nilsson. Probabilistic logic. *Artificial Intelligence*, 28:71–87, 1986.
24. H. S. Nwana. Software agents: an overview. *The Knowledge Engineering Review*, 11:205–244, 1996.

25. A. S. Rao and M. P. Georgeff. Modelling rational agents within a BDI-architecture. In *Proceedings of the Conference on Knowledge Representation and Reasoning*, pages 473–484, 1991.
26. N. Wilson and S. Moral. A logical view of probability. In *Proceedings of the 11th European Conference on Artificial Intelligence*, pages 386–390, 1994.
27. M. Wooldridge and N. R. Jennings. Intelligent agents: theory and practice. *The Knowledge Engineering Review*, 10:1–38, 1995.

# A Argumentation and aggregation

In classical logic an argument is a sequence of inferences leading to a conclusion. The usual interest of the logician is in procedures by which arguments may be used to establish the validity (truth or falsity) of a formula. In LA, a logic of argument [13, 19], arguments do not necessarily prove formulae but may merely indicate support for (or doubt about) them. Also in classical logic, so long as we can construct *one* argument (proof) for $F$, any further arguments for $F$ are of no interest. In our system all distinct arguments of candidates are of interest (intuitively, the more arguments we have for $F$ the greater is our knowledge about the validity of $F$). We therefore distinguish distinct arguments by identifying the unique grounds of each (essentially a normalised proof term in LA [19]) and a sign drawn from some dictionary which indicates the support provided to $F$ by the argument. A simple form of argument for $F$ we have constructed in [7, 8] is by $\langle bel \rangle G \rightarrow \langle sup_d \rangle F$, where $d$ is a support for the candidate $F$ on the *ground* $G \rightarrow F$. For example, in the context of argument for *cancer* by

$$\langle bel \rangle (elderly \wedge weight\_loss) \rightarrow \langle sup_{d1} \rangle cancer$$

$F$ is *cancer*, the ground is *elderly* $\wedge$ *weight_loss* $\rightarrow$ *cancer* and the support is $d1$. This argument states that if a medical decision making agent believes that the patient is elderly and suffered weight loss then a support $d1$ is conferred on the patient having cancer.

Suppose an agent has a set of arguments for and against a set of mutually exclusive alternative beliefs under consideration whose signs are drawn from a single dictionary. The agent can *aggregate* these arguments to yield a sign representing the agent's overall confidence in each of the candidates. Every dictionary has a characteristic aggregation function for aggregating arguments. Consider the argument presented above and

$$\langle bel \rangle smoker \rightarrow \langle sup_{d2} \rangle cancer$$

Considering the dictionary of probability as

$$dict(Prob) =_{def} [0, 1]$$

The two arguments can be aggregated by using a special case of Dempster's epistemic probability [18] giving the value $d1 + d2 - d1 \times d2$. This formula can be generalised incrementally if there are more than two arguments for the candidate *cancer*. There is no requirement that we should restrict dictionaries to $dict(Prob)$. Among the obvious dictionaries we may consider is

$dict(Qual) =_{def} \{+, ++\}$

where $\langle sup_+ \rangle F$ means an argument for $F$ and $\langle sup_{++} \rangle F$ means an argument that $F$ is definitely true.

In general, suppose an agent has a set of arguments for and against a set of mutually exclusive alternative beliefs, $C$, (candidates, that is, alternative beliefs or plans under consideration) whose signs are drawn from a single dictionary $D$. The agent can *aggregate* these arguments to yield a sign drawn from $D'$ which represents the agent's overall confidence in each $C$. The general form of an aggregation function as

$$\mathcal{A} : \Pi(C \times G \times D) \rightarrow C \times D'$$

where $\Pi$ stands for "power set" and $G$ is the set of all grounds. If $D$ is $dict(Qual)$ then $D'$ is the set of non-negative integers whereas $D'$ is $D$ itself when we consider $dict(Prob)$ as $D$. In the former case, $\mathcal{A}$ assigns an aggregation number to each alternative beliefs, giving a total preference ordering over the options. This suggests a simple rule for taking a decision; choose the alternative which maximises this value.

If we allow both $F$ and $\neg F$ to occur in the support then by applying our usual aggregation algorithm we compute total evidence for $F$ (say, $d1$) and $\neg F$ (say, $d2$) separately. If we have used the dictionary $dict(Prob)$ then we have the following cases:
- total evidence for $F$ is $d1 - d2$ if $d1 > d2$;
- the total evidence for $\neg F$ is $d2 - d1$ if $d2 > d1$;
- dilemma if $d1 = d2$
- inconsistent if $d1 = d2 = \infty$.

If we have used the dictionary $dict(Prob)$ then we have the following cases:
- total evidence for $F$ is $d1(1 - d2) \div (1 - d1 \times d2)$;
- total evidence for $\neg F$ is $d2(1 - d1) \div (1 - d1 \times d2)$;
- dilemma if $d1 = d2$;
- inconsistent if $d1 \times d2 = 1$.

# Safety Logics

John Bell and Zhisheng Huang

Applied Logic Group
Computer Science Department
Queen Mary and Westfield College
University of London, London E1 4NS, UK
{jb, huang}@dcs.qmw.ac.uk

**Abstract.** In this paper we begin the analysis and formalisation of common sense reasoning about safety. To begin with we analyse *absolute* safety, and use and extend the framework of Dynamic Logic in order to develop a formal possible-worlds semantics and logic for it. We then extend the analysis to *normal* safety. We introduce *Defeasible Dynamic Logic* in order to give possible-worlds semantics and logic for normal safety, and define a preferential entailment relation defined in order to represent common sense reasoning about the normal termination of actions. We conclude with a discussion of the relationship between safety, obligation, rationality and risk, and outline some extensions to the present work.

## 1 Introduction

Attempting to develop a formal theory of reasoning about safety is a complex task; as reasoning of this kind may involve common sense reasoning about action and change, time, beliefs, goals, obligations, rationality, etc. In this paper we begin this task by abstracting away from many of these features in order to develop a formal theory which captures what we consider to be the essential features of what we call *absolute safety*. In order to do so, we use and extend the framework of Dynamic Logic [8] to provide a possible-worlds semantics and a logic for absolute safety. We then extend this theory to include reasoning about *normal safety*. We introduce *Defeasible Dynamic Logic* and use this to give a possible-worlds semantics and logic of normal safety. We then show how common sense reasoning about the normal termination of actions can be represented by means of a preferential entailment relation. In conclusion, we discuss the relationships between safety, obligation, rationality and risk, and outline some extensions to the present work.

## 2 Absolute Safety

We start with disasters and the idea of a *disastrous state*. A disastrous state is one in which some fact, which the agent considers to be disastrous, is true. It is assumed that such states are abhorrent to the agent and that the agent tries to avoid them if at all possible. For instance, a typical medical safety-critical system would consider states in which the patient dies as a result of treatment to be disastrous, and would try to avoid them at all costs. We further assume that the application domain is such that there is no question as to which states the agent considers to be disastrous. Of course, what counts as a disastrous state may be context-dependent. For example, the agent might consider a state in which it has missed a plane to be disastrous if it has a non-transferrable ticket, but it need not do so if there is another flight and the ticket is transferrable. A *disastrous action* can now be defined to be an action which *always* leads to a disastrous state. We then define a *dangerous action* to be an action which *may* lead to a disastrous state, and a *dangerous state* to be state in which every action which the agent can perform – every action which is open to the agent – is dangerous. Note that disastrous actions (states) are thus dangerous actions (states). Finally, we define a *safe action* (a *safe state*) to be an action (a state) which is not dangerous.

As an example of these definitions consider an agent who is learning to swim, and suppose that the agent is alone in the pool. The agent's goal is to enjoy its swim, and, naturally, the agent considers that its death by drowning would be a disaster; that is, the agent takes states in which it has drowned to be disastrous states. The agent enjoys swimming, regardless of whether it is swimming in shallow or deep water. Swimming is shallow water is safe; the agent is never in danger of drowning because it can always stand up. However, if the agent is in deep water this action is no longer open to it and all its attempts to stay afloat amount to helpless floundering. Consequently it is in danger of drowning no matter what action it takes, and will do so unless someone comes to its aid. Swimming in deep water is therefore dangerous (or unsafe) for the agent. Note that being in deep water is only unsafe because *all* of the actions open to the agent are dangerous. If, for example, the agent could capture a buoy whenever it wanted – that is, if a safe action were available to the agent – then swimming in the deep end would be safe.

This notion of safety is an *absolute* one : an action is safe only if there is absolutely no possibility of it leading to a dangerous state. In everyday life almost all actions are dangerous, as there is always some (though perhaps remote) possibility that the action will lead to a disastrous state. So practice we are usually interested in actions which are *normally* safe. However, it is useful to start with the formalisation of absolute safety for two reasons. Firstly, it is fundamental to the development of safety-critical systems. Systems of this kind involve domains where safety is paramount, and therefore the ability to reason about it rigorously is highly desirable. Fortunately such systems typically also involve controlled environments; domains in which it is often possible and useful to assume, in order to simplify the reasoning task at hand, that many of the less likely dangers of daily life will not arise. In the sequel we give an example of reasoning of this kind in a (fictional) nuclear power station, where the task is to show that a plan for disabling the reactor is absolutely safe; assuming that natural disasters, acts of sabotage, etc. do not impede the execution of the plan. The second reason for starting with absolute safety is methodological. The formalisation of absolute safety provides the conceptual and theoretical basis on which the subsequent analysis of normal safety, builds.

## 2.1 The language $\mathcal{SL}$

We have chosen to formalise absolute safety in Dynamic Logic [8], as this offers a powerful tool for formalizing actions using classical logic and Kripke semantics. In particular, states are represented as possible worlds, and actions are represented as accessibility relations between worlds. The crucial distinction between the necessary and the possible consequences of actions in our informal analysis is thus readily and naturally formalised.

We begin by defining the language $\mathcal{SL}$. Let $P$ be a set of primitive propositions, and $PA$ be a set of primitive actions. We will use the Roman letters $a, b, \ldots$ (with or without subscripts or superscripts) to denote actions, and lower case Greek letters $\phi, \psi, \ldots$ (with or without subscripts or superscripts) to denote formulas.

**Definition 1 (Actions).** The set of (composite) actions $Acts$ is, as usual, defined to be the smallest set which is closed under the following syntactic rules:

- If $a \in PA$ then $a \in Acts$
- If $a, b \in Acts$ then $(a \cup b), (a; b) \in Acts$

Here $\cup$ is the non-deterministic choice operator (so $a \cup b$ means "do either $a$ or $b$ non-deterministically"), and ';' is the sequence operator (so $a; b$ means "do $a$ and then do $b$").

**Definition 2 (The language $\mathcal{SL}$).** The language $\mathcal{SL}$ is the minimal set of formulas which satisfies the following conditions:

- If $p \in P$ then $p \in \mathcal{SL}$.
- If $\phi, \psi \in \mathcal{SL}$ then $\neg\phi \in \mathcal{SL}$ and $\phi \wedge \psi \in \mathcal{SL}$.
- If $a \in Acts$ and $\phi \in \mathcal{SL}$ then $\langle a \rangle \phi \in \mathcal{SL}$.
- If $\phi \in \mathcal{SL}$ then $\mathbf{Dis}\phi \in \mathcal{SL}$ and $\mathbf{Dan}\phi \in \mathcal{SL}$.
- If $a \in Acts$ then $\mathbf{Dis}(a) \in \mathcal{SL}$ and $\mathbf{Dan}(a) \in \mathcal{SL}$.

Informally, $\langle a \rangle \phi$ states that doing $a$ makes $\phi$ possible, that is $\phi$ *may* be true after action $a$ is taken. Then $[a]\phi$ is defined as $\neg\langle a \rangle\neg\phi$. Thus $[a]\phi$ states that doing $a$ makes $\phi$ inevitable; that is, $\phi$ *will* be true after action $a$ is taken. A sentence of the form $\mathbf{Dis}\phi$ ($\mathbf{Dan}\phi$) means that $\phi$ is disastrous (dangerous). Similarly $\mathbf{Dis}(a)$ ($\mathbf{Dan}(a)$) means that action $a$ is disastrous (dangerous). The safety operators are then introduced by definition:

$$\mathbf{Safe}(a) \stackrel{\text{def}}{\Longleftrightarrow} \neg\mathbf{Dan}(a)$$
$$\mathbf{Safe}\phi \stackrel{\text{def}}{\Longleftrightarrow} \neg\mathbf{Dan}\phi$$

Recall that our analysis of safety started with disastrous states. We therefore
extend the standard Kripke models of propositional Dynamic Logic by adding a
disastrous-worlds function. In our analysis we also want to view actions as being
temporally forwards-directed, with each action leading from an earlier world to a
set of later worlds. On this view, an action followed by its inverse (e.g. the *pickup*
and *putdown* operators in STRIPS) can be conceived as leading to a new world
which differs from the original one only in that the time stamp has changed;
that is, time has moved on. It also seems natural to require that the underlying
model of time is a tree, in which each branch represents a possible outcome of a
sequence of actions.

**Definition 3 ($\mathcal{SL}$-models).** A *model for $\mathcal{SL}$* is a tuple $M = \langle W, \{R^a\}_{a \in PA}, D, V \rangle$
where

- $W$ is a (non-empty) set of possible worlds,
- $R^a \subseteq W \times W$ is a binary accessibility relation for each primitive action
  $a \in PA$,
- $D : W \to \mathcal{P}(W)$ assigns to each world $w$ the set $D(w)$ of worlds which are
  disastrous with respect to $w$, and
- $V : P \to \mathcal{P}(W)$ is the usual valuation function.

As usual, we extend the accessibility relation for primitive actions, $R^a$, to one for
composite actions, $R^a_+$. For simplicity, $R^a_+$ will usually be written as $R^a$ where
there is no danger of ambiguity.

- $R^a_+ = R^a$ (where $a$ is primitive)
- $R^{a \cup b}_+ = R^a_+ \cup R^b_+$
- $R^{a;b}_+ = R^a_+ \circ R^b_+$ (composition of relations)

Finally, we require that the global accessibility relation $R = \{\langle w, w' \rangle : wR^a_+ w'$ for
some $a\}$ is a *chronology* – that is, that $R$ is a backwards-linear (or anti-convergent)
partial order.

Intuitively $wR^a_+ w'$ means that world $w'$ is one possible outcome of doing
action $a$ in world $w$. In order to capture the idea of the consequences of an
action *leading to* a disastrous state, we define the *trace* of each action $a$ from
each world $w$. The trace of $a$ from $w$, is a tree rooted at $w$, each branch of which
represents a course of events which might result from doing $a$ at $w$. Thus $a$ may
lead to a disastrous world (state) if there is such a world on some branch of the
trace of $a$ from $w$. Formally, let $R^a w = \{w' \in W : \langle w, w' \rangle \in R^a_+\}$ be the set
of all possible outcomes of doing the (possibly compound) action $a$ at $w$. Then
$Trace(a, w)$ is defined as follows.

- $Trace(a, w) = \langle w, w \rangle \cup \{\langle w, w' \rangle : w' \in R^a w\}$ where $a$ is primitive
- $Trace((a \cup b), w) = Trace(a, w) \cup Trace(b, w)$
- $Trace((a;b), w) =$
  $Trace(a, w) \cup \bigcup_{w' \in R^a w} Trace(b, w') \cup (Trace(a, w) \circ \bigcup_{w' \in R^a w} Trace(b, w'))$

For brevity's sake we will write $w_1 R^a w w_2$ if $\langle w_1, w_2 \rangle \in Trace(a, w)$; thus, $w_1 R^a w w_2$ states that $w_1$ occurs no later than $w_2$ on a branch in the trace of $a$ from $w$.

**Definition 4 (Semantics for $\mathcal{SL}$).** Let $M = \langle W, \{R^a\}_{a \in PA}, D, V \rangle$ be an $\mathcal{SL}$-model. Then a sentence $\phi$ is true at a world $w$ in $M$ (written $M, w \models \phi$, or, equivalently, $w \in [\![\phi]\!]_g^M$) as follows.

$$M, w \models p \quad \text{iff } w \in V(p) \text{ where } p \text{ is primitive}$$
$$M, w \models \neg \psi \quad \text{iff } M, w \not\models \psi$$
$$M, w \models \psi \wedge \chi \quad \text{iff } M, w \models \psi \text{ and } M, w \models \chi$$
$$M, w \models \langle a \rangle \psi \quad \text{iff } \exists w'(w' \in R^a w \text{ and } w' \in [\![\psi]\!]_g^M)$$
$$M, w \models \mathbf{Dis}\psi \quad \text{iff } [\![\psi]\!]_g^M \subseteq D(w)$$
$$M, w \models \mathbf{Dis}(a) \quad \text{iff } \forall w_1(w R^a w w_1 \Rightarrow$$
$$\exists w_2((w_1 R^a w w_2 \text{ or } w_2 R^a w w_1) \text{ and } w_2 \in D(w)))$$
$$M, w \models \mathbf{Dan}(a) \quad \text{iff } \exists w'(w R^a w w' \text{ and } w' \in D(w))$$
$$M, w \models \mathbf{Dan}\psi \quad \text{iff } \forall w_1(w_1 \in [\![\psi]\!]_g^M \Rightarrow$$
$$\forall a(R^a w_1 \neq \emptyset \Rightarrow \exists w_2(w_1 R^a w_1 w_2 \text{ and } w_2 \in D(w))))$$

As usual, a sentence $\phi$ is said to be true in a model $M$ (written $M \models \phi$) if $M, w \models \phi$ for all worlds $w$ in $M$, and $\phi$ is said to be valid (written $\models \phi$) if $\phi$ is true in all models.

The truth condition for dangerous states is a bit tricky. It can be paraphrased as follows: at world $w$, a state $\phi$ is a dangerous state iff every performable action in the state is dangerous with respect to $w$.

## 2.2 The Safety Logic SL

The logic of safety, **SL**, consists of the following axioms, definitions and inference rules.

### Axioms

(PC) All propositional tautologies (expressed in $\mathcal{SL}$)
(A1) $\neg \langle a \rangle \bot$
(A2) $\langle a \rangle (\phi \vee \psi) \rightarrow \langle a \rangle \phi \vee \langle a \rangle \psi$
(A3) $\langle a; b \rangle \phi \leftrightarrow \langle a \rangle \langle b \rangle \phi$
(A4) $\langle a \cup b \rangle \phi \leftrightarrow \langle a \rangle \phi \vee \langle b \rangle \phi$

(D1) $\mathbf{Dis}\bot$
(D2) $\mathbf{Dis}(\phi \vee \psi) \rightarrow \mathbf{Dis}\phi \vee \mathbf{Dis}\psi$
(D3) $\mathbf{Dis}\phi \wedge \mathbf{Dis}\psi \rightarrow \mathbf{Dis}(\phi \vee \psi)$
(D4) $\mathbf{Dis}(a \cup b) \leftrightarrow \mathbf{Dis}(a) \wedge \mathbf{Dis}(b)$

(DA1) $\mathbf{Dan}\phi \wedge \mathbf{Dan}\psi \rightarrow \mathbf{Dan}(\phi \wedge \psi)$
(DA2) $\langle a \rangle \phi \wedge \mathbf{Dis}\phi \rightarrow \mathbf{Dan}(a)$

(DA3) $\mathbf{Dan}(a \cup b) \leftrightarrow \mathbf{Dan}(a) \vee \mathbf{Dan}(b)$
(DA4) $\mathbf{Dan}(a) \vee (\langle a; b \rangle \phi \wedge \mathbf{Dan}\phi) \rightarrow \mathbf{Dan}(a; b)$
(DA5) $\mathbf{Dan}\phi \wedge \phi \wedge \neg [a] \bot \rightarrow \mathbf{Dan}(a)$

(DD1) $\mathbf{Dis}\phi \rightarrow \mathbf{Dan}\phi$
(DD2) $\mathbf{Dis}(a) \rightarrow \mathbf{Dan}(a)$

## Definitions

(A5) $\langle a \rangle^* \phi \leftrightarrow \langle a \rangle \phi \vee \phi$ (where $a$ is primitive)
(A6) $\langle a \cup b \rangle^* \phi \leftrightarrow \langle a \cup b \rangle \phi \vee (\langle a \rangle^* \phi \vee \langle b \rangle^* \phi) \vee \phi$
(A7) $\langle a; b \rangle^* \phi \leftrightarrow \langle a; b \rangle \phi \vee \langle a \rangle^* \phi \vee \langle a \rangle \langle b \rangle^* \phi \vee \phi$
(A8) $[a]\phi \leftrightarrow \neg \langle a \rangle \neg \phi$

(SAdf) $\mathbf{Safe}(a) \leftrightarrow \neg \mathbf{Dan}(a)$
(SSdf) $\mathbf{Safe}\phi \leftrightarrow \neg \mathbf{Dan}\phi$

## Inference Rules

(MP) From $\phi$ and $\phi \rightarrow \psi$ infer $\psi$
(NECA) From $\phi$ infer $[a]\phi$
(MONA) From $\langle a \rangle \phi$ and $\phi \rightarrow \psi$ infer $\langle a \rangle \psi$
(SPD) From $\psi \rightarrow \phi$ infer $\mathbf{Dis}\phi \rightarrow \mathbf{Dis}\psi$
(SPDS) From $\psi \rightarrow \phi$ infer $\mathbf{Dan}\phi \rightarrow \mathbf{Dan}\psi$

## Theorems and Derived Rules

(SPS) From $\phi \rightarrow \psi$ infer $\mathbf{Safe}\phi \rightarrow \mathbf{Safe}\psi$
(SS1) $\neg\mathbf{Safe}\bot$
(SS2) $\mathbf{Safe}(\phi \wedge \psi) \leftrightarrow \mathbf{Safe}\phi \wedge \mathbf{Safe}\psi$
(SS3) $\mathbf{Safe}(\phi \wedge \psi) \rightarrow \mathbf{Safe}(\phi) \vee \mathbf{Safe}(\psi)$
(SA1) $\mathbf{Safe}(a \cup b) \leftrightarrow \mathbf{Safe}(a) \wedge \mathbf{Safe}(b)$
(SA2) $\mathbf{Safe}(a; b) \rightarrow \mathbf{Safe}(a)$
(SA3) $\mathbf{Safe}(a) \wedge \langle a \rangle^* \phi \rightarrow \neg \mathbf{Dis}\phi$
(TA1) $\phi \rightarrow \langle a \rangle^* \phi$

The axioms (A1)-(A4) and the inference rules (NECA) and (MONA) are those of Dynamic Logic. Axiom (D1) states that logical inconsistency is a disaster. (D2) states that disasters are decomposable under disjunction. (D3) states that if two states are disastrous (simultaneously), then one of them must be disastrous. (D4) states that action $a \cup b$ is disastrous exactly when actions $a$ and $b$ are disastrous. (DA1) states that dangerous states are closed under conjunction. (DA2) states that if one possible outcome of the action is disastrous, then the action is dangerous. (DA3) reiterates that dangerous actions are closed under disjunction. (DA4) states that if a sub-action is dangerous, then the whole sequence of the action is dangerous as well. (DA5) says that all actions which can be taken in a dangerous state are dangerous. (DD1) and (DD2) state that all disastrous states and actions are dangerous. The axioms (A5)-(A7) extend the operator $\langle \cdot \rangle$ to the more general operator $\langle \cdot \rangle^*$. Informally, $\langle a \rangle^* \phi$ states that $\phi$ is possible after some sub-action of action $a$. The inference rule (SPD) states that any state which implies a disastrous state is also disastrous, and (SPDS) states that the same applies to dangerous states. Some of the properties of safe actions and states are listed as theorems. (SA2) and (SA3) are of particular interest. (SA2) states that if an action sequence $a; b$ is safe, then action $a$ is safe. It does *not* generally follow that it is safe to do $b$; as doing $a$ may lead to dangers which are not otherwise apparent. Similarly, (SA3) states that a safe action can never lead to a disastrous state; although it may lead to a dangerous one.

**Theorem 5 Soundness of SL.** *The logic* **SL** *is sound for the class of* $\mathcal{SL}$-*models.*

*Proof.* The proofs for most axioms and inference rules are straightforward from the definitions. For example, proof for (DD1) is as follows. Suppose that $M, w \models$ **Dis**$\phi$, then, by the truth condition, we have $[\![\phi]\!]_g^M \subseteq D(w)$. For any $w_1 \in [\![\phi]\!]_g^M$ and any action $a$, we have $w_1 Raw_1 w_1$ by the definition of a trace. So $w_1 Raw_1 w_1$ and $w_1 \in D(w)$. So, for any $w_1 \in [\![\phi]\!]_g^M$ and any action $a$, there exists a world $w_1$ such that $w_1 Raw_1 w_1$ and $w_1 \in D(w)$. So, by the truth condition for dangerous states, we have $M, w \models$ **Dan**$\phi$.

It is not possible to prove the completeness of **SL** by means of the standard method of canonical models because $\mathcal{SL}$ lacks the required expressive power. For example, from the truth condition for dangerous actions, we know that if an action $a$ is dangerous, then there exists a state $\psi$ such that $\psi$ is accessible via the action $a$ (written $\langle a \rangle^* \psi$), and $\psi$ is disastrous, namely, the following "axiom" holds:

(DA$^+$) **Dan**$(a) \rightarrow \langle a \rangle^* \psi \wedge$**Dis**$\psi$ for some formula $\psi$.

However, the higher-order existential quantification in this axiom cannot be expressed in $\mathcal{SL}$, or in a sensible rule schema. Similarly, the truth condition for dangerous states involves universal quantification over actions. However, $\mathcal{SL}$ does not permit this.

Despite its incompleteness, **SL** can be used to formalise interesting and useful reasoning about absolute safety.

*Example 1.* Consider the imaginary nuclear power-station pictured in Figure 1. The area $A1$ represents those parts of the power-station which should be kept radiation-free. This area surrounds the area $A3$ which contains the nuclear reactor, and which is thus an area of high radioactivity. The area $A2$ acts as a "radiation lock" between $A1$ and $A3$; it provides access between the two areas, and is designed to prevent radioactivity spreading from area $A3$ to area $A1$. Area $A2$ contains safety suits $S1$ and $S2$ which are designed to protect against

434

radioactivity. If an agent is wearing one of these suits, the agent can go into area $A3$ safely. But if the agent goes into area $A3$ without a suit, the agent will be exposed to a lethal dose of radiation. Agents who are wearing safety suits are not allowed to enter area $A1$, as the residual radiation on the suits would contaminate area $A1$. An accident has occurred, the reactor is out of control and is heading towards melt-down. The only remaining way of disabling it is by means of switch $S$ in area $A3$. Our agent, $Stan$, who is currently located in area $A1$, has to form and execute a plan for doing this safely.

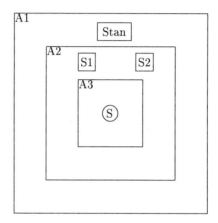

**Fig. 1.** Power-station Example

The initial state can be described as follows:

$(Init)$ $Agent(Stan) \land Suit(S1) \land Suit(S2) \land Switch(S) \land Object(S1) \land Object(S2) \land Object(S) \land Area(A1) \land Area(A2) \land Area(A3) \land In(Stan, A1) \land In(S1, A2) \land In(S2, A2) \land In(S, A3) \land \neg Radiated(Stan) \land \neg Radioactive(A1)$

The safety constraints can be represented as follows:

$(C1)$ $In(Stan, A3) \land \neg(Wearing(Stan, S1) \lor Wearing(Stan, S2)) \to Radiated(Stan)$

$(C2)$ $In(S1, A1) \lor In(S2, A1) \to Radioactive(A1)$

Thus $Stan$ gets a lethal dose of radiation if he enters $A3$ without a suit, and area $A1$ becomes radioactive if a suit is brought into it.

We will thus say that $Stan$'s actions are safe if they do not violate $(C1)$ and $(C2)$:

$(SA)$ **Safe**$(a) \leftrightarrow \neg\langle a\rangle^* Radiated(Stan) \wedge \neg\langle a\rangle^* Radioactive(A1),$

and define a safe shutdown state as follows:

$(SS)$ **Safe**$Shutdown \leftrightarrow$
$Shutdown \wedge In(Stan, A1) \wedge \neg Radiated(Stan) \wedge \neg Radioactive(A1)$

In order to reason about action and change, we will, for present purposes, adopt the extended STRIPS-approach used in SIPE [6, 15]. The available actions (operators) are as follows. An agent can move between areas, or move to an object in an area, or move away from an object in an area.

- $Move(a, a1, a2)$.
  - Preconds: $Agent(a) \wedge Area(a1) \wedge Area(a2) \wedge In(a, a1) \wedge \neg \exists x NextTo(a, x)$.
  - Additions: $In(a, a2)$.
  - Deletions: $In(a, a1)$.
- $Move(a, a1, x)$.
  - Preconds: $Agent(a) \wedge Area(a1) \wedge Object(x) \wedge In(a, a1) \wedge In(x, a1)$.
  - Additions: $NextTo(a, x)$.
- $Move(a, x, a1)$.
  - Preconds: $Agent(a) \wedge Object(x) \wedge Area(a1) \wedge In(a, a1) \wedge In(x, a1)$.
  - Deletions: $NextTo(a, x)$.

An agent can also put on or take off a protective suit.

- $Enrobe(a, s)$.
  - Preconds: $Agent(a) \wedge Suit(s) \wedge NextTo(a, s)$.
  - Additions: $Wearing(a, s)$.
  - Deletions: $NextTo(a, s)$.
- $Disrobe(a, s)$.
  - Preconds: $Agent(a) \wedge Suit(s) \wedge Wearing(a, s)$.
  - Additions: $NextTo(a, s)$.
  - Deletions: $Wearing(a, s)$.

Finally, an agent can disable the reactor.

- $Disable(a, s)$.
  - Preconds: $Agent(a) \wedge Switch(s) \wedge NextTo(a, s)$.
  - Additions: $Shutdown$.

In STRIPS, an action $a$ occurs in a state $\Sigma$. If the preconditions of $a$ are true when $a$ occurs, then $a$ succeeds. The resulting state $\Sigma'$ is obtained by adding the additions of $a$ to $\Sigma$ and removing the deletions of $a$ from $\Sigma$. In SIPE, $\Sigma$ may, in effect, also contain domain rules; such as the safety constraints $(C1)$ and $(C2)$. Indeed, in the present example we also need the following domain rules to describe a ramification of the move-area action:

(C3)   $In(a, a1) \wedge Wearing(a, s) \to In(s, a1)$
(C4)   $Object(o) \wedge In(o, a1) \wedge a1 \neq a2 \to \neg In(o, a2)$

Thus, if an agent is wearing a safety suit when it moves from one area to another, then the suit should go with the agent.[1] The presence of domain rules complicates the update process; as it is necessary, after the earlier revisions, to add the consequents of any domain rules that are applicable, and then delete any literals which were in $\Sigma$ and whose complements have been added by the domain rules. We will refer to this process as a "SIPE update".

Let us assume that *Stan* produces the following non-linear plan:

($\pi$)   $Move(Stan, A1, A2); (\pi_1 \cup \pi_2); Move(Stan, A2, A1)$

where

$\pi_1 = Move(Stan, A2, S1); Enrobe(Stan, S1); Move(Stan, A2, A3);$
$Move(Stan, A3, S); Disable(Stan, S); Move(Stan, S, A3);$
$Move(Stan, A3, A2); Disrobe(Stan, S1); Move(Stan, S1, A2)$

$\pi_2 = Move(Stan, A2, S2); Enrobe(Stan, S2); Move(Stan, A2, A3);$
$Move(Stan, A3, S); Disable(Stan, S); Move(Stan, S, A3);$
$Move(Stan, A3, A2); Disrobe(Stan, S2); Move(Stan, S2, A2)$

Our task is to formalise this plan and to show that it is safe; that is, that it satisfies (SA) and (SS). We can represent an action $a$ in $\mathcal{SL}$ as the sentence $\Sigma \to [a]\Sigma'$; where $\Sigma$ is a conjunction of sentences of $\mathcal{SL}$ which describes the state in which $a$ occurs and which implies the preconditions of $a$, and $\Sigma'$ is the appropriate SIPE-update of $\Sigma$. We will not attempt to formalise the inference process which produces the SIPE-update. We will thus assume, (SIPE), that for each state $\Sigma$ which is produced by the plan and which implies the preconditions of an action $a$ in the plan, we have the sentence $\Sigma \to [a]\Sigma'$; in this example it is clear what $\Sigma'$ is in each case. Given $\Sigma$, $a$ can thus be applied, (SIPE) and (MP), to give $[a]\Sigma'$. For conciseness, we will abbreviate $\Sigma \to [a]\Sigma'$ to $\Sigma[a]\Sigma'$. Our task is thus to prove that

(SAS)   **Safe**$(\pi) \wedge \Sigma[\pi]\Sigma' \wedge (\Sigma' \to$**Safe**$Shutdown)$

where $\Sigma$ is the initial state description (*Init*) conjoined with the domain rules $(C1) - (C4)$.

Here is an outline of the proof. The plan $\pi$ in effect consists of a plan involving suit $S1$ and a plan involving suit $S2$:

---

[1] For convenience we have occasionally used first-order formulae in the prepresentation of the problem. These are easily translated into suitable, if long-winded, sentences of $\mathcal{SL}$.

$\pi_{S1} = Move(Stan, A1, A2); \pi_1; Move(Stan, A2, A1)$
$\pi_{S2} = Move(Stan, A1, A2); \pi_2; Move(Stan, A2, A1)$

It is sufficient to prove that $\pi_{S1}$ and $\pi_{S2}$ both satisfy $(SAS)$; as it then follows from the theorem (SA1) and the theorem:

$(SA4)\quad [a]\phi \wedge [b]\phi \rightarrow [a \cup b]\phi$

that $\pi$ satisfies $(SAS)$. As the two plans are similar, we will outline the proof of the case for $\pi_{S1}$ only.

We have the following action-application rule:

(App) From $\Sigma$ and $\Sigma[a]\Sigma'$ infer $[a]\Sigma'$

And, by means of (MONA), (A3)-(A8), and propositional reasoning, we can derive the following action-sequence rule:

(Seq) From $\Sigma[a]\Sigma'$ and $\Sigma'[b]\Sigma''$ infer $\Sigma[a;b]\Sigma''$.

In order to show that **Safe**$(\pi_{S1})$, we can use (MONA), (App), (Seq), $(SIPE)$ and $\Sigma$ to successively show that:

$[Move(Stan, A1, A2)]\neg Radiated(Stan) \wedge \neg Radioactive(A1)$
$[Move(Stan, A1, A2); Move(Stan, A2, S1)]\neg Radiated(Stan)\wedge\neg Radioactive(A1)$
$\ldots$
$[\pi_1]\neg Radiated(Stan) \wedge \neg Radioactive(A1)$.

Then, by (MONA), (A5)-(A8), and propositional reasoning, we can obtain the desired conclusion:

$\neg\langle\pi_{S1}\rangle_N^* Radiated(Stan) \wedge \neg\langle\pi_{S1}\rangle_N^* Radiated(A1)$.

To complete the proof for $\pi_{S1}$, we can repeatedly use (Seq), and $(SIPE)$ to show that in $\Sigma[\pi_{S1}]\Sigma'$, $\Sigma'$ is $\Sigma \wedge Shutdown$. And so, by propositional reasoning and $(SS)$, we have $\Sigma' \rightarrow$**Safe**$Shutdown$ as required. □

Despite its usefulness, the incompleteness of **SL** is a problem. For example, given the semantics, an action may be safe, but an automated theorem prover using **SL** may fail to prove that it is. This might mean that an action is bot taken when it should have been.

It is interesting to compare our analysis of absolute safety with work on reasoning about safety in Theoretical Computer Science. In particular, Manna and Pneuli [12] use temporal logic in order to study safety properties of programs.

Safety properties are properties which hold at every state in the execution of a program. For example, partial correctness is a safety property as it requires that every terminating $\phi$-computation terminates in a $\psi$-state; it is thus (canonically) expressed as a safety formula; as a formula of the form $\Box p$ where $p$ is a past formula. By contrast, total correctness is a guarantee property as it requires that every $\phi$-computation terminates in a $\psi$-state; it is thus (canonically) expressed as a guarantee formula, a formula of the form $\Diamond p$. While they are interested in properties of programs, we are concerned with common sense reasoning about safety and thus with giving semantics and a logic for the common sense notions of safe, dangerous and disastrous actions and states. For example, our definition of a safe action as one which never leads to a disastrous state captures a central feature of practical reasoning about the safety of actions, namely the avoidance of disasters.

## 3 Normal Safety

We have defined an *absolute* notion of safety, in which an action is safe only if there is absolutely no possibility of it leading to a dangerous state. In everyday life almost all actions are dangerous, as there is always *some* (perhaps remote) possibility that any such action will lead to a disastrous state. So in practice we are interested in actions which are *normally* safe; that is, in actions which do not normally lead to disastrous states. For example, it is not absolutely safe to fly by major airlines (because, there is always the possibility, however remote, of a crash) but it is normally safe to do so (as flights do not normally crash). In this section we extend the theory of safety to reasoning of this kind by adding a dimension of normality to the concepts introduced in the previous section. For example, a *normally* dangerous action is one which, in the normal course of events, may lead to a disastrous state, and a *normally* dangerous state is one in which every action which is open to the agent is, in the normal course of events, dangerous.

### 3.1 The Language $\mathcal{SL_N}$

In order to formalise the normal aspect, we introduce *Defeasible Dynamic Logic* by adding an abnormality operator, $Ab$, and a defeasible necessity operator, $[\cdot]_N$ to $\mathcal{SL}$.

**Definition 6 (The language $\mathcal{SL_N}$).** $\mathcal{SL_N}$ is defined by replacing $\mathcal{SL}$ with $\mathcal{SL_N}$ everywhere in Definition 2, and by adding the clauses:

- If $a \in Acts$ then $Ab(a) \in \mathcal{SL_N}$.
- If $a \in Acts$ and $\phi \in \mathcal{SL_N}$ then $[a]_N\phi \in \mathcal{SL_N}$.
- If $\phi \in \mathcal{SL_N}$ then $\mathbf{Dis}_N\phi \in \mathcal{SL_N}$ and $\mathbf{Dan}_N\phi \in \mathcal{SL_N}$.
- If $a \in Acts$ then $\mathbf{Dis}_N(a) \in \mathcal{SL_N}$ and $\mathbf{Dan}_N(a) \in \mathcal{SL_N}$.

Intuitively, $Ab(a)$ means that action $a$ has ended abnormally, $[a]_N\phi$ states that $\phi$ holds in all normal outcomes of $a$, $\mathbf{Dis}_N\phi$ ($\mathbf{Dan}_N\phi$) states that $\phi$ is normally disastrous (normally dangerous), and $\mathbf{Dis}_N(a)$ ($\mathbf{Dan}_N(a)$) states that action $a$ is normally disastrous (normally dangerous). The additional operators are then defined as follows:

$$\langle a\rangle_N\phi \overset{\text{def}}{\Longleftrightarrow} \neg[a]_N\neg\phi$$
$$\mathbf{Safe}_N(a) \overset{\text{def}}{\Longleftrightarrow} \neg\mathbf{Dan}_N(a)$$
$$\mathbf{Safe}_N\phi \overset{\text{def}}{\Longleftrightarrow} \neg\mathbf{Dan}_N\phi$$

Thus $\langle a\rangle_N\phi$ states that $\phi$ holds in some normal outcome of $a$, and $\mathbf{Safe}_N(a)$ ($\mathbf{Safe}_N\phi$) states that action $a$ (state $\phi$) is normally safe.

$\mathcal{SL}$-models are extended to $\mathcal{SL}_\mathcal{N}$-models by adding the function $AB$ which returns the set of actions which have ended abnormally at each world.

**Definition 7 ($\mathcal{SL}_\mathcal{N}$-models).** An $\mathcal{SL}_\mathcal{N}$-model is a tuple $M = \langle W, \{R^a\}_{a\in PA}, AB, D, V\rangle$, where:

- $W$, $\{R^a\}_{a\in PA}$, $D$ and $V$ are as in Definition 3, and
- $AB : W \to \mathcal{P}(Acts)$ assigns to each world $w$ the set of actions which have ended abnormally at $w$. $AB$ is required to satisfy the following conditions on compound actions:
  - $a;b \in AB(w)$ iff $\exists w', w''(w'' R^a w'$ and $w' R^b w$ and $b \in AB(w))$, and
  - $a\cup b \in AB(w)$ iff $\exists w'(w' R^a w$ and $a \in AB(w)$, or $w' R^b w$ and $b \in AB(w))$.

The conditions on $AB$ ensure that if an action $a;b$ has ended abnormally at a world $w$ then $b$ has ended abnormally at $w$, and that if an action $a \cup b$ has ended abnormally at $w$ then one of the actions $a$ or $b$ has ended abnormally at $w$.

The truth conditions for the normal safety operators are defined in terms of the notion of the *normal trace*, $Trace_N(a, w)$, of an action $a$ from a world $w$. Informally, $Trace_N(a, w)$ is the sub-tree of $Trace(a, w)$ consisting of all branches of $Trace(a, w)$ in which events unfold normally, that is, of all branches which contain no worlds in which any sub-action of $a$ ends abnormally. Formally, $Trace_N(a, w)$ is defined analogously to $Trace(a, w)$, except that $R^a_N w = \{w' \in W : \langle w, w'\rangle \in R^a_+$ and $a \notin AB(w')\}$ replaces $R^a w$ everywhere in the definition. In like manner we also abbreviate $\langle w_1, w_2\rangle \in Trace_N(a, w)$ to $w_1 R_N w w_2$.

**Definition 8 (Semantics for $\mathcal{SL}_\mathcal{N}$).** Let $M = \langle W, \{R^a\}_{a\in PA}, AB, D, V\rangle$ be an $\mathcal{SL}_\mathcal{N}$-model. Then a sentence $\phi$ is true at a world $w$ in $M$ (written $M, w \models \phi$, or, equivalently, $w \in [\![\phi]\!]^M_g$) as in Definition 4 with the following additions.

$M, w \models Ab(a)$     iff $a \in AB(w)$

$M, w \models [a]_N\psi$     iff $\forall w'(w' \in R_N^a w \Rightarrow w' \in [\![\psi]\!]_g^M)$

$M, w \models \mathbf{Dis}_N\psi$     iff $M, w \models \mathbf{Dis}\psi$

$M, w \models \mathbf{Dis}_N(a)$     iff $\forall w_1(wR_N^a ww_1 \Rightarrow$
$$\exists w_2((w_1 R_N^a ww_2 \text{ or } w_2 R_N^a ww_1) \text{ and } w_2 \in D(w)))$$

$M, w \models \mathbf{Dan}_N(a)$ iff $\exists w'(wR_N^a ww' \text{ and } w' \in D(w))$

$M, w \models \mathbf{Dan}_N\psi$    iff $\forall w_1(w_1 \in [\![\psi]\!]_g^M \Rightarrow$
$$\forall a(R^a w_1 \neq \emptyset \Rightarrow \exists w_2(w_1 R_N^a w_1 w_2 \text{ and } w_2 \in D(w))))$$

## 3.2 The Safety Logic $\mathbf{SL_N}$

The logic of (absolute and) normal safety, $\mathbf{SL_N}$, is obtained by adding the following axioms and inference rules to the absolute safety logic $\mathbf{SL}$.

### Axioms

(AN1) $[a]_N\top$

(AN2) $[a]_N(\phi \wedge \psi) \leftrightarrow [a]_N\phi \wedge [a]_N\psi$

(AN3) $[a;b]_N\phi \leftrightarrow [a]_N[b]_N\phi$

(AN4) $[a \cup b]_N\phi \leftrightarrow [a]_N\phi \wedge [b]_N\phi$

(AN5) $[a]_N\phi \leftrightarrow [a](\neg Ab(a) \rightarrow \phi)$


(AB1) $Ab(a;b) \rightarrow Ab(b)$

(AB2) $Ab(a \cup b) \leftrightarrow Ab(a) \vee Ab(b)$


(DN1) $\mathbf{Dis}_N\phi \leftrightarrow \mathbf{Dis}\phi$

(DN2) $\mathbf{Dis}_N(a \cup b) \leftrightarrow \mathbf{Dis}_N(a) \wedge \mathbf{Dis}_N(b)$


(DAN1) $\mathbf{Dan}_N\phi \wedge \mathbf{Dan}_N\psi \rightarrow \mathbf{Dan}_N(\phi \wedge \psi)$

(DAN2) $\langle a \rangle_N\phi \wedge \mathbf{Dis}_N\phi \rightarrow \mathbf{Dan}_N(a)$

(DAN3) $\mathbf{Dan}_N(a \cup b) \leftrightarrow \mathbf{Dan}_N(a) \vee \mathbf{Dan}_N(b)$

(DAN4) $\mathbf{Dan}_N(a) \vee (\langle a;b \rangle_N\phi \wedge \mathbf{Dan}_N\phi) \rightarrow \mathbf{Dan}_N(a;b)$


(DDN1) $\mathbf{Dis}_N\phi \rightarrow \mathbf{Dan}_N\phi$

(DDN2) $\mathbf{Dis}_N(a) \rightarrow \mathbf{Dan}_N(a)$


(DDAN1) $\mathbf{Dis}(a) \rightarrow \mathbf{Dis}_N(a)$

(DDAN2) $\mathbf{Dan}_N(a) \rightarrow \mathbf{Dan}(a)$

(DDAN3) $\mathbf{Dan}_N\phi \rightarrow \mathbf{Dan}\phi$

### Definitions

(PosN) $\langle a \rangle_N\phi \leftrightarrow \neg[a]_N\neg\phi$

(SAdf) $\mathbf{Safe}_N(a) \leftrightarrow \neg\mathbf{Dan}_N(a)$

(SSdf) $\mathbf{Safe}_N\phi \leftrightarrow \neg\mathbf{Dan}_N\phi$

(AN6) $\langle a\rangle_N^*\phi \leftrightarrow \langle a\rangle_N\phi \vee \phi$ (where $a$ is primitive)
(AN7) $\langle a \cup b\rangle_N^*\phi \leftrightarrow \langle a \cup b\rangle_N\phi \vee (\langle a\rangle_N^*\phi \vee \langle b\rangle_N^*\phi) \vee \phi$
(AN8) $\langle a;b\rangle_N^*\phi \leftrightarrow \langle a;b\rangle_N\phi \vee \langle a\rangle_N^*\phi \vee \langle a\rangle_N\langle b\rangle^*\phi \vee \phi$
(AN9) $[a]_N\phi \leftrightarrow \neg\langle a\rangle_N\neg\phi$


## Inference Rules

(MONAN) From $[a]_N\phi$ and $\phi \rightarrow \psi$ infer $[a]_N\psi$
(SPDSN) From $\psi \rightarrow \phi$ infer $\mathbf{Dan}_N\phi \rightarrow \mathbf{Dan}_N\psi$

## Theorems and Derived Rules

(PAN) $\langle a\rangle_N\phi \leftrightarrow \langle a\rangle(\phi \wedge \neg Ab(a))$
(SPSN) From $\phi \rightarrow \psi$ infer $\mathbf{Safe}_N\phi \rightarrow \mathbf{Safe}_N\psi$
(SSN1) $\neg\mathbf{Safe}_N\bot$
(SSN2) $\mathbf{Safe}_N(\phi \wedge \psi) \leftrightarrow \mathbf{Safe}_N\phi \wedge \mathbf{Safe}_N\psi$
(SSN3) $\mathbf{Safe}_N(\phi \wedge \psi) \rightarrow \mathbf{Safe}_N\phi \vee \mathbf{Safe}_N\psi$
(SAN1) $\mathbf{Safe}_N(a \cup b) \leftrightarrow \mathbf{Safe}_N(a) \wedge \mathbf{Safe}_N(b)$
(SAN2) $\mathbf{Safe}_N(a;b) \rightarrow \mathbf{Safe}_N(a)$

The axioms (AN1)-(AN9), (AB1), (AB2), (PosN) and the inference rule (MONAN) give our Defeasible Dynamic Logic. The remaining axioms and inference rule state properties of the defeasible safety operators and the relationship between them and the absolute safety operators. Some of the properties of normally safe actions and states are listed as theorems.

**Theorem 9 Soundness of $\mathbf{SL_N}$.** *The logic $\mathbf{SL_N}$ is sound for the class of $\mathcal{SL_N}$-models.*

### 3.3 Chronologically Minimising Abnormalities

While it is now possible to distinguish between absolute safety and normative safety and to reason about normative safety, we still do not have a complete account of common sense reasoning about it. For example, in reasoning that it is normally safe to fly, we make the default assumption that, given that the usual preconditions hold (the plane is airworthy, has been fuelled, etc.), the flight will be a normal one. In order to represent this aspect of common sense reasoning about actions, we will, following [13], define a preferential entailment relation. Intuitively, we prefer models in which events unfold normally. Technically, we restrict consideration to models in which abnormalities occur as late as possible; that is, to models which are chronologically most normal.[2]

---

[2] An interesting alternative approach to the representation of common sense reasoning about actions in the framework of Dynamic Logic is given in [5]. An argument for

**Definition 10.** Let $M = \langle W, \{R^a\}_{a \in PA}, AB, D, V \rangle$ and $M' = \langle W', \{R^{a'}\}_{a \in PA}, AB', D', V' \rangle$ be $\mathcal{SL_N}$-models with respective chronologies $R$ and $R'$. $M$ and $M'$ are said to be *comparable* if $W = W'$, $R = R'$ and $D = D'$. $M$ is said to be *chronologically more normal than* $M'$ (written $M \prec M'$) if $M$ and $M'$ are comparable and there is a world $w \in W$ such that:

- for any world $w' \in W$ such that $w \neq w'$ and not $wRw'$,
  - $AB(w') = AB'(w')$ and
  - $\{p \in \Phi_0 : w' \in V(p)\} = \{p \in \Phi_0 : w' \in V'(p)\}$,
- for any action $a$, $M', w \models Ab(a)$ if $M, w \models Ab(a)$, and
- for some action $a$, $M', w \models Ab(a)$ and $M, w \not\models Ab(a)$.

Thus $M \prec M'$ if $M$ and $M'$ are comparable, $M$ and $M'$ agree on all worlds which precede or are unrelated to some world $w$ in their common chronology, every action that ends abnormally at $w$ in $M$ also ends abnormally at $w$ in $M'$, and there is at least one action which ends normally at $w$ in $M$ and which ends abnormally at $w$ in $M'$.

**Definition 11.** An $\mathcal{SL_N}$-model $M$ is a *chronologically most normal model* (a *c.m.n.-model*) of a sentence $\phi$ if $M \models \phi$ and there is no model $M'$ such that $M' \models \phi$ and $M' \prec M$. Similarly, $M$ is a c.m.n.-model of a set of sentences $\Theta$ if $M \models \Theta$ and there is no model $M'$ such that $M' \models \Theta$ and $M' \prec M$.

**Definition 12 (Normal entailment).** A set of sentences $\Theta$ *normally entails* a sentence $\phi$ (written $\Theta \approx \phi$) if $M \models \phi$ for any c.m.n.-model $M$ of $\Theta$.

*Example 2.* Let $\Theta$ be the theory:

$$\langle fly \rangle Arrive \wedge \langle fly \rangle Crash$$
$$[fly](Crash \rightarrow \neg Arrive)$$
$$[fly](\neg Ab(fly) \rightarrow Arrive)$$
$$\mathbf{Dis}(crash)$$

Thus, flying may result in arrival but it might also end with a crash, if a flight crashes it does not arrive, flights normally arrive, and crashes are disastrous. Then: $\Theta \approx \neg\mathbf{Safe}(fly) \wedge \mathbf{Safe}_N(fly)$. Given $\Theta$, we can conclude by default that it is not absolutely safe to fly, but that it is normally safe to do so. □

Notice that we have moved from proof theory to pragmatics (i.e. reasoning on the basis of the set of intended models of the theory in question). This might seem to make the prospects of automation even more remote. However, it is worth investigating the possibility of using the model-building approach suggested in [1]. If successful, this approach would overcome the problem of the incompleteness of **SL** and **SL$_N$**.

---

the use of chronological minimisation in *predictive* common sense reasoning about actions is given in [3].

# 4 Safety, Obligation, Rationality and Risk

In conclusion we discuss some of the relationships between safety, obligation, rationality and risk, and indicate how the present work might be extended to include these.

It is interesting to consider the relationship between obligation and safety. A central idea here is that of a *safety procedure* or *protocol*. Protocols are designed to maintain safety and have to be revised if they are found to lead to dangerous states. Protocols impose deontic restrictions on agents, as the agents involved are (normally) obliged to follow them. For example, in hospitals medical staff are (normally) obliged to follow protocols when treating patients; see, e.g, [7]. In order to formalise these constraints we could add the deontic operators **Obl** and **Per** to $\mathcal{SL_N}$. Intuitively, **Obl**$(a)$ states that action $a$ is obligatory, and **Per**$(a)$ states that action $a$ is permitted. Of course we have to provide appropriate formal semantics for these operators. One trick might be to introduce an action operator, $Do$, and then use the standard possible-world semantics for deontic operators; for example, **Obl**$(a) \stackrel{\text{def}}{\Longleftrightarrow}$ **Obl**$Do(a)$. We can then, for example, state that only procedures which are normally safe can be followed:

$$\mathbf{Per}(a) \rightarrow \mathbf{Safe}_N(a).$$

The problem with this approach is that it may not always be *rational* to do only safe actions. For example if a patient has reached a critical stage, it may be that an *unsafe* treatment is the only option. So, in exceptional circumstances agents must be able to override protocols. Moreover, in domains where safety is not considered critical, it is often rational to do things which are not even normally safe. For example, an investor may risk money on an unsafe investment as this promises to bring in a greater return than any safe alternative, or an adult may risk their life trying to save that of a child. Indeed, in much of everyday life it is rational to take risks; that is to do dangerous things. In the case of protocols, we thus want the imperative to state that only rational actions are permitted:

$$\mathbf{Per}(a) \rightarrow \mathbf{Rat}(a).$$

The problem now is to give a semantic account of the rationality operator. One starting point is the AI-planning theory of practical rationality outlined in [2] which begins with the following definition:

A resource-bounded agent behaves rationally if it reasons and acts so as to achieve as many of its goals, in their comparative order of importance to the agent, as is possible given the resources available to it and the constraints in force.

In this paper we will simplify the theory dramatically. The relevant components are an agenda of goals, a planner which produces plans for these goals, and a scheduler which chooses the best plan to execute.

The agenda can be formalised using the preference semantics developed in [9, 11]. In order to incorporate them, two components need to be added to our models:

- $cw : W \times P(W) \to P(W)$ is a function, which selects the set $cw(w, [\![\phi]\!]_g^M)$ of closest worlds to $w$ in which $\phi$ is true, and
- $\succ \subseteq P(W) \times P(W)$ is a preference relation on sets of worlds.

We can then introduce the preference operator $\mathbf{P}$ and give its truth conditions as follows:

$$M, w \models \phi \mathbf{P} \psi \text{ iff } cw(w, [\![\phi \wedge \neg\psi]\!]_g^M) \succ cw(w, [\![\psi \wedge \neg\phi]\!]_g^M).$$

So $\phi\mathbf{P}\psi$ is true at $w$ if every closest $\phi\wedge\neg\psi$-world to $w$ is preferred to every closest $\psi\wedge\neg\phi$-world to $w$. The truth condition thus formalises von Wright's *conjunction expansion principle* for preferences. We can now formalise the agenda by writing $\phi\mathbf{P}\phi'$ to indicate that goal $\phi$ is preferred to goal $\phi'$.

In order to represent the planner we will, for present purposes, simplify and assume that there is only one possible plan (action) which will achieve each goal. We can therefore define the plan $a$ which will achieve goal $\phi$ as:

$$Plan(a, \phi) \overset{\text{def}}{\iff} [a]\phi \wedge \forall b(b \neq a \to \neg[b]\phi).$$

We can then define a preference ordering on plans according to the desirability of the goals they are designed to achieve:

$$a \succ_d b \overset{\text{def}}{\iff} Plan(a, \phi) \wedge Plan(b, \psi) \wedge \phi\mathbf{P}\psi$$

A plan (action) can then be defined to be executable if it is possible given the resources available: $Exec(a) \overset{\text{def}}{\iff} \neg[a]\bot$. The scheduler should then execute the most preferred executable plan:

$$\mathbf{Rat}(a) \overset{\text{def}}{\iff} Exec(a) \wedge \neg\exists b(Exec(b) \wedge b \succ_d a).$$

It may be important to reason about degrees of risk; for example, an investor should take reasonable risks. In order to represent this kind of reasoning, the operator $Sat$ can be added to the language, where, intuitively, $Sat(a)$ means that the risk associated with action $a$ is acceptable. Models can be extended to include a function which associates an appropriate level of risk with each action at each world:

$$SR : W \times Acts \to \omega$$

Then, letting $Risk(a, w)$ be the number of branches in the (normal) trace of $a$ from $w$ which contain at least one disastrous world, we can supply truth conditions for the new operator as follows.

$$M, w \models Sat(a) \text{ iff } Risk(a, w) \leq SR(a, w)$$

The most preferred, executable action could then be defined to be rational if the degree of risk involved is acceptable:

$$\mathbf{Rat}(a) \overset{\text{def}}{\iff} Exec(a) \wedge \neg\exists b(Exec(b) \wedge b \succ_d a) \wedge Sat(a).$$

# Acknowledgements

This research formed part of the RED project (Decision Support Systems: Safety and Liability) and was supported by the United Kingdom Engineering and Physical Sciences Research Council under grant number GR/H 12348. Earlier versions of parts of this paper appeared in [4] and [10]. We would like to thank everyone who has commented on it.

# References

1. Bell, J., Pragmatic Reasoning; A Model-Based Theory. In M. Masuch and L. Polos (eds.) *Applied Logic: How, what and why?*, Kluwer Academic Publishers, Amsterdam, 1995, pp. 1-28.
2. Bell, J., A Planning Theory of Practical Rationality. Proceedings of the AAAI-95 Fall Symposium on Rational Agency, M.I.T., 1995. Fehling, M. (ed.), pp. 1-4.
3. Bell, J., Prediction Theories, manuscript.
4. Bell, J., and Huang, Z., Safety Logics II : Normative Safety, *Proceedings of the 12th European Conference on Artificial Intelligence, ECAI96*, W. Wahlster (ed.), John Wiley and Sons, London, 1996, pp. 293-297.
5. Dunin-Keplicz, B., and Radzikowska, A., Epistemic Approach to Actions with Typical Effects. Proceedings of *ECSQARU'95*. Froidevaux, C., and Kholas, J., (Eds). Lecture Notes in Artificial Intelligence No. 946. Springer, Berlin, 1995, pp. 180-188.
6. Fikes, R., and Nilsson, N., STRIPS: A New Approach to the Application of Theorem Proving to Problem Solving, *Artificial Intelligence* 2, 1971, pp. 189-209.
7. Hammond, P., and Sergot, M., Computer Support for Protocol-Based Treatment of Cancer. Proceedings of the 2nd International Conference on the Practical Applications of Prolog, London, 1994.
8. Harel, D., Dynamic Logic, in: D. Gabbay and F. Guenthner, (eds.), *Handbook of Philosophical Logic*, Vol.II, (D. Reidel publishing company, 1984), 497-604.
9. Huang, Z., *Logics for Agents with Bounded Rationality*, ILLC Dissertation series 1994-10, University of Amsterdam, 1994.
10. Huang, Z., and Bell, J., Safety Logics I : Absolute Safety. Proceedings of Common Sense '96. Buvac, S., and Costello, T., (eds.), pp. 59-66.
11. Huang, Z., Masuch, M., and Pólos, L., ALX: an action logic for agents with bounded rationality, *Artificial Intelligence* **82** (1996), pp. 101-153.
12. Manna, Z., and Pneuli, A., *Temporal Verification of Reactive Systems, Vol. II: Safety*, Springer Verlag, Berlin, 1995.
13. Shoham, Y. *Reasoning About Change*, M.I.T. Press, Cambridge, Massachusetts, 1988.
14. von Wright, G., *The Logic of Preference*, (Edinburgh, 1963).
15. Wilkins, D., *Practical Planning*. Morgan Kaufmann, San Mateo, California, 1988.

# Modeling Uncertainty with Propositional Assumption-Based Systems*

Rolf Haenni

Institute of Informatics
University of Fribourg
CH–1700 Fribourg, Switzerland

Phone: +41 (0)26 300 83 31
Fax: +41 (0)26 300 97 26
E-Mail: rolf.haenni@unifr.ch
WWW: www-iiuf.unifr.ch/tcs

**Abstract.** This paper proposes assumption-based systems as an efficient and convenient way to encode uncertain information. Assumption-based systems are obtained from propositional logic by including a special type of propositional symbol called assumption. Assumptions are needed to express the uncertainty of the given information. Assumption-based systems can be used to judge hypotheses qualitatively or quantitatively. This paper shows how assumption-based systems are obtained from causal networks, it describes how symbolic arguments for hypotheses can be computed efficiently, and it presents ABEL, a modeling language for assumption-based systems and an interactive tool for probabilistic assumption-based reasoning.

## 1 Introduction

Propositional logic is an efficient and convenient way to encode knowledge or information. In particular, uncertainty can be incorporated into propositional knowledge by including assumptions. Judging a hypothesis in the light of the given assumption-based knowledge means finding arguments (i.e. a sufficient number of assumptions) which allow a prove of the hypothesis. Assumption-based reasoning is therefore the process of computing arguments for which a given hypothesis can be deduced from the available knowledge.

The computation of arguments for certain hypotheses is essentially a task that involves deduction and theorem proving. A variety of established methods and procedures exist for deduction in propositional logic. In particular, the concept of **assumption-based truth maintenance systems** (ATMS) provides the basic elements for assumption-based reasoning (de Kleer, 1986; Reiter & de Kleer, 1987). A traditional ATMS is restricted to Horn clauses (clauses with at most one non-negated atom) and it accepts only single literals as queries. The

---

Research supported by grant No.2100–042927.95 of the Swiss National Foundation for Research.

fundamental ATMS problem is to identify the contexts of assumptions in which queries hold. R. Reiter proposed the concept of a **clause management systems** (CMS) – a generalization of de Kleer's original ATMS – which is no longer restricted to Horn clauses (Reiter & de Kleer, 1987). Other interesting works about truth maintenance systems, clause management systems, and probabilistic assumption-based reasoning are (Laskey & Lehner, 1989), (Provan, 1990), (Inoue, 1991), (Siegel, 1987), and (Kohlas & Monney, 1993).

This paper uses the notion of **assumption-based systems** (ABS) (Kohlas & Monney, 1993; Haenni, 1996), which turns out to be a special case of the general evidence theory (Kohlas, 1995; Haenni, 1996). Section 2 starts with an intuitive prescription of transforming uncertain causal relations into assumption-based propositional logic. Causal networks are often used to represent patterns of influence among variables. Representing knowledge by causal relations covers therefore a number of different applications in the domain of uncertain reasoning. Then, Section 3 introduces assumption-based systems formally. It describes how arguments for hypotheses can be computed efficiently. Finally, Section 4 presents ABEL, an interactive modeling tool for probabilistic assumption-based reasoning.

## 2 Modeling Uncertain Causal Relations

Causal or inference networks are used in a number of areas to represent patterns of influence among variables. They consist of connected causal relations. A causal relation can be regarded as a rule of the form "if *cause*, then *effect*". Examples of causal relations are: "if there is some rain tonight, then the grass will be wet tomorrow", "if the next bingo-number is 7, then my wife wins 100 dollars", or "if my father returns late at night, then my mother gets angry". Thus, causality can be seen as any natural ordering in which knowledge of an event influences the opinion concerning another event. This influence can be logical, physical, temporal, or simply conceptual (Lauritzen & Spiegelhalter, 1988).

### 2.1 From Causal Networks to Propositional Logic

Causes and effects can be modeled as variables with finite domains. These variables are the nodes of the network. Causal relations between two variables are the edges. Figure 2.1 depicts a causal network consisting of only two nodes $C$ and $E$. Usually, nodes are represented as circles and causal relations between them as arrows (Kohlas & Monney, 1995).

**Fig.** 2.1. Causal relation between two variables $c$ and $e$.

The concept of directed acyclic graphs is an appropriate mathematical structure to describe causal networks. A pair $\mathcal{G} = (\mathcal{N}, \mathcal{E})$ is called **directed graph** if $\mathcal{N}$ is a set of nodes and $E \in \mathcal{E}$ are **directed edges**, i.e. pairs $(n_i, n_j)$ of nodes, $n_i, n_j \in \mathcal{N}$. Directed edges $(n_i, n_j)$ are depicted as arrows from $n_i$ to $n_j$.

In a directed graph $\mathcal{G} = (\mathcal{N}, \mathcal{E})$ a **directed chain** from $n_1$ to $n_{q+1}$ is a sequence of edges $E_1, \ldots, E_q$ such that $E_k = (n_k, n_{k+1})$ for $k = 1, \ldots, q$. $n_1$ is called the **initial endpoint** and $n_{q+1}$ the **terminal endpoint** of the directed chain. A **directed cycle** is a directed chain in which no edge appears twice in the sequence of edges and in which the two endpoints are the same. If a directed graph $\mathcal{G}$ has no cycles, then it is called **directed acyclic graph**. Figure 2.2 shows two directed graphs. The one on the left is acyclic, the one on the right is not.

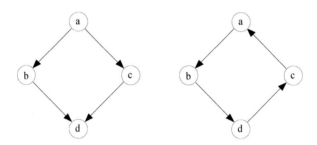

**Fig.** 2.2. Two directed graphs.

Generally, a variable of a causal network can have any domain. In the following, only problems with binary variables are considered, i.e. variables with possible values 1 (true) and 0 (false). If the cause $c$ of a causal relation is true, then the effect $e$ of the relation is also true. This can be expressed as a logical implication $c \to e$. Binary variables of a causal network are therefore represented by propositional symbols.

Consider the directed acyclic graph on the left side of Figure 2.2. If it is interpreted as a causal network, then $a$, for example, is cause for $b$ and $c$, whereas $b$ and $c$ are causes of $d$. Such multiple causes or multiple effects can be interpreted as conjunctions or as disjunctions. Thus, four different cases are possible:

(1) If cause $c$ is true, then all effects $e_1$ to $e_n$ are also true:

$$c \to e_1, \; c \to e_2, \; \cdots \; , c \to e_n. \tag{2.1}$$

(2) If cause $c$ is true, then at least one effect $e_1$ to $e_n$ is also true:

$$c \to e_1 \vee e_2 \vee \cdots \vee e_n. \tag{2.2}$$

(3) If at least one of the causes $c_1$ to $c_n$ is true, then effect $e$ is also true; besides $c_1$ to $c_n$ there are no other causes of $e$:

$$c_1 \rightarrow e, \ c_2 \rightarrow e, \ \cdots, c_n \rightarrow e,$$
$$e \rightarrow c_1 \vee c_2 \vee \cdots \vee c_n. \tag{2.3}$$

(4) If all causes $c_1$ to $c_n$ are true, then effect $e$ is also true; this is the only way to cause $e$:

$$c_1 \wedge c_2 \wedge \cdots \wedge c_n \rightarrow e,$$
$$e \rightarrow c_1, \ e \rightarrow c_2, \ \cdots, e \rightarrow c_n. \tag{2.4}$$

According to Figure 2.3, different graphical representations are used to distinguish these cases.

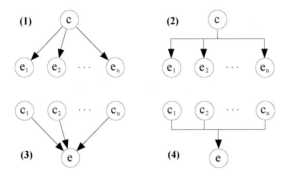

**Fig.** 2.3. Multiple causes and multiple effects.

In (3) and in (4) it is assumed that besides $c_1$ to $c_n$ there are no other causes for $e$. This is called **accountability condition** (Pearl, 1988). It states that the model explicitly contains all causes that may produce $e$. Logically, this can be expressed through implications from $e$ to $c_i$. Such implications pointing to the opposite direction are important especially for diagnostics analyses.

Some or all of the causal relations of a causal network may be uncertain. In such cases, effects are only caused under some circumstances. This type of uncertainty can be expressed by **assumptions**. A rule like "if cause $c$ is true, then effect $e$ is true under some circumstances $a$" can be transformed into $c \wedge a \rightarrow e$. $a$ represents the assumption that the necessary circumstances are present. If all causal relations of Figure 2.3 are assumed to be uncertain, then the following logical implications are produced:

(1') If cause $c$ is true, then – under some circumstances $a_i$ – effect $e_i$ is also true:

$$c \wedge a_1 \rightarrow e_1, \ c \wedge a_2 \rightarrow e_2, \ \cdots, c \wedge a_n \rightarrow e_n. \tag{2.5}$$

(2') If cause $c$ is true, then – under some circumstances $a$ – at least one effect $e_1$ to $e_n$ is also true:

$$c \wedge a \rightarrow e_1 \vee e_2 \vee \cdots \vee e_n. \qquad (2.6)$$

(3') If cause $c_i$ is true, then – under some circumstances $a_i$ – effect $e$ is also true; besides $c_1$ to $c_n$ there are no other causes of $e$:

$$c_1 \wedge a_1 \rightarrow e, \ c_2 \wedge a_2 \rightarrow e, \ \cdots, c_n \wedge a_n \rightarrow e,$$
$$e \rightarrow (c_1 \wedge a_1) \vee (c_2 \wedge a_2) \vee \cdots \vee (c_n \wedge a_n). \qquad (2.7)$$

(4') If all causes $c_1$ to $c_n$ are true, then – under some circumstances $a$ – effect $e$ is also true; this is the only way to cause $e$:

$$c_1 \wedge c_2 \wedge \cdots \wedge c_n \wedge a \rightarrow e,$$
$$e \rightarrow c_1, \ e \rightarrow c_2, \ \cdots, e \rightarrow c_n, e \rightarrow a. \qquad (2.8)$$

If in case (3') other (unknown) causes of $e$ are possible, then an additional assumption $a_{n+1}$ has to be introduced. $a_{n+1}$ describes the uncertainty whether unknown causes of $e$ are present.

(3'') If cause $c_i$ is true, then – under some circumstances $a_i$ – effect $e$ is also true; besides $c_1$ to $c_n$ other causes of $e$ are possible:

$$c_1 \wedge a_1 \rightarrow e, \ c_2 \wedge a_2 \rightarrow e, \ \cdots, c_n \wedge a_n \rightarrow e, a_{n+1} \rightarrow e$$
$$e \rightarrow (c_1 \wedge a_1) \vee (c_2 \wedge a_2) \vee \cdots \vee (c_n \wedge a_n) \vee a_{n+1}. \qquad (2.9)$$

According to this intuitive prescription, all relations of a causal network can be transformed into a set of material implications. This system of logical formulas can be used to judge hypotheses about variables of the causal network. Arguments for such hypotheses are expressions consisting of assumptions about the uncertain circumstances of the causal relations. They can be used to make **predictions** of effects or to give **explanations** (diagnoses) of observed effects.

## 2.2 Example 1: Chest Clinic

A doctor has to decide whether a patient, who complains about shortness-of-breath, suffers from bronchitis, lung cancer, or tuberculosis. This fictitious example was first mentioned in (Lauritzen & Spiegelhalter, 1988) in order to illustrate the use of Bayesian networks. Here, the same example is applied to the field of assumption-based reasoning.

The doctor's medical knowledge helps him to find the causes of the patient's symptoms. His knowledge is composed of what he learned at medical school and of what he knows from his practical experience. It can be summarized as follows (Lauritzen & Spiegelhalter, 1988):

"Shortness-of-breath (dyspnoea) may be due to tuberculosis, lung cancer, or bronchitis, or none of them, or more than one of them. A recent visit to an under-developed country increases the chances of tuberculosis, while smoking is known to be a risk factor for both lung cancer and tuberculosis. The results of a single chest X-ray do not discriminate between lung cancer and tuberculosis; nor does the presence or absence of dyspnoea."

In Figure 2.4 this small piece of fictitious medical knowledge is shown as causal network. Direction of causality is from top to bottom. Note that some effects have more than one cause and that some causes produce more than one effect. Thus, multiple causes are interpreted as disjunction, whereas multiple effects are interpreted as conjunction.

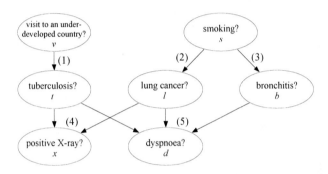

**Fig.** 2.4. Causal network for the fictitious example.

All causal relations of Figure 2.4 are uncertain. Furthermore, it is assumed that for all effects there are other (unknown) causes. Thus, the strategy described in $(3'')$ has to be used in order to obtain the following set of logical implications:

$$(1) \quad v \wedge a_1 \to t, \quad a_2 \to t, \quad t \to (v \wedge a_1) \vee a_2; \tag{2.10}$$

$$(2) \quad s \wedge a_3 \to \ell, \quad a_4 \to \ell, \quad \ell \to (s \wedge a_3) \vee a_4; \tag{2.11}$$

$$(3) \quad s \wedge a_5 \to b, \quad a_6 \to b, \quad b \to (s \wedge a_5) \vee a_6; \tag{2.12}$$

$$(4) \quad t \wedge a_7 \to x, \quad \ell \wedge a_8 \to x, \quad a_9 \to x,$$
$$\quad x \to (t \wedge a_7) \vee (\ell \wedge a_8) \vee a_9; \tag{2.13}$$

$$(5) \quad t \wedge a_{10} \to d, \quad \ell \wedge a_{11} \to d, \quad b \wedge a_{12} \to d, \quad a_{13} \to d,$$
$$\quad d \to (t \wedge a_{10}) \vee (\ell \wedge a_{11}) \vee (b \wedge a_{12}) \vee a_{13}. \tag{2.14}$$

## 2.3 Example 2: Burglary

The example considered here is a small story around the alarm system of Mr. Holmes' house (Pearl, 1988):

"A burglary in Mr. Holmes' house generates an alarm if the alarm system is functioning. But the alarm may also be caused by an earthquake or by other (unspecified) reasons. The neighbors of Mr. Holmes, Dr. Watson and Mrs. Gibbons, phone Mr. Holmes in the case of an alarm. Possibly, Dr. Watson may also phone Mr. Holmes as a joke. Mrs. Gibbons is hard of hearing, and she may possibly not be able to hear the alarm. Furthermore, if Mr. Holmes' daughter is at home, then she surely will phone too in the case of an alarm. Finally, if there is an earthquake and if the earthquake is registered, then there is a confirmation of it on the radio."

In Figure 2.5 the above story is shown as a causal network.

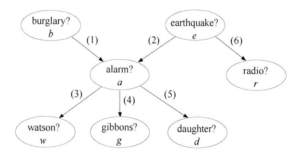

**Fig.** 2.5. Causal network for the burglary example.

Using the strategy described in $(3'')$ leads to the following set of logical implications:

$$
\text{(1)} \quad b \wedge a_1 \to a, \quad e \wedge a_2 \to a, \quad a_3 \to a,
$$
$$
a \to (b \wedge a_1) \vee (e \wedge a_2) \vee a_3; \tag{2.15}
$$
$$
\text{(2)} \quad a \wedge a_4 \to w, \quad a_5 \to w, \quad w \to (a \wedge a_4) \vee a_5; \tag{2.16}
$$
$$
\text{(3)} \quad a \wedge a_6 \to g, \quad a_7 \to g, \quad g \to (a \wedge a_6) \vee a_7; \tag{2.17}
$$
$$
\text{(4)} \quad a \wedge a_8 \to d, \quad a_9 \to d, \quad d \to (a \wedge a_8) \vee a_9; \tag{2.18}
$$
$$
\text{(5)} \quad e \wedge a_{10} \to r, \quad a_{11} \to r, \quad r \to (e \wedge a_{10}) \vee a_{11}. \tag{2.19}
$$

# 3  Assumption-Based Systems

This section introduces the notion of assumption-based systems formally. Basically, an assumption-based system is a set of propositional formulae, where a subset of the propositions is declared as assumptions. Therefore, this technique profits from the expressiveness of propositional logic and the advantages of existing deduction techniques based on resolution. Assumption-based systems can be used to treat queries about the given knowledge, i.e. to find arguments in favor or against certain hypotheses. The examples of the previous section show how assumption-based systems are obtained from causal networks.

## 3.1 Representing Uncertainty by Propositional Logic

Propositional logic with uncertain assumptions provides a concise language for describing uncertain information. Let $P = \{p_1, \ldots, p_q\}$ and $A = \{a_1, \ldots, a_r\}$ be two disjoint sets of propositional symbols. The elements of $P$ are called **propositions** and the elements of $A$ **assumptions**. $N = P \cup A$ is the entire set of symbols considered. Let $Q \subseteq N$ be a subset of $N$. The corresponding set of negated symbols is denoted by $\sim Q$. $Q^\pm = Q \cup \sim Q$ represents the set of all literals of $Q$. The corresponding set of all well-formed logical formulae in $Q$ is denoted by $\mathcal{L}_Q$.

The set $\Sigma = \{\xi_1, \ldots, \xi_s\}$ is a set of clauses on the literals $N^\pm$. Note that a more general framework in which $\Sigma$ consists of arbitrary logical formulas can always be transformed into an equivalent framework consisting only of clauses. $\Sigma$ is called a **knowledge base** and it represents the available information. The conjunction $\xi = \xi_1 \wedge \cdots \wedge \xi_s$ is a logical representation of $\Sigma$. If $\Sigma$ is empty, then $\xi = \top$. A clause $\xi_i \in \Sigma$ is a statement of the available information. It restricts the possible truth values of the propositional symbols appearing in $\Sigma$. A triple $\mathcal{A} = (P, A, \Sigma)$, where $P$ and $A$ are disjoint sets of propositional symbols and $\Sigma$ is a set of clauses on the literals in $N^\pm$, is called **assumption-based system** (ABS).

The assumptions involved in the clauses of $\Sigma$ are necessary to express the uncertainty of the corresponding statements. The examples of Section 2 show how assumptions differ from "normal" propositions, and how they are used to represent uncertainty.

## 3.2 Hypotheses and Arguments in Assumption-Based Systems

Given an assumption-based system $\mathcal{A} = (P, A, \Sigma)$, one may be interested in certain hypotheses $h$ about the knowledge contained in $\mathcal{A}$. Such hypotheses can be expressed as logical formulae in $\mathcal{L}_N$. What can be learned from $\Sigma$ about the possible truth of $h$? If some assumptions are considered to be either true or false, then $h$ can possibly be deduced from $\Sigma$. Such a combination of true and false assumptions can be regarded as an **argument** in favor of $h$. Arguments are therefore conjunctions of literals of assumptions, or, more generally, logical formulae in $\mathcal{L}_A$. This is the link to the general evidence theory (Haenni, 1996): the possible hypotheses are logical formulae in $\mathcal{L}_N$, and the possible arguments are logical formulae in $\mathcal{L}_A$.

In view of these remarks consider a logical formula $a \in \mathcal{L}_A$, such that $a \wedge \xi \models h$, where $\xi$ is the conjunction of the clauses contained in $\Sigma$, and $h \in \mathcal{L}_N$ represents a hypothesis. The formula $a$ allows us to deduce $h$ from $\Sigma$. It is called **supporting arguments** for $h$ relative to $\Sigma$. If $a$ is the coarsest (least precise) supporting argument of $h$, i.e. if there is no other supporting argument $a'$ of $h$ with $a \models a'$ and $a \neq a'$, then $a$ is called **quasi-support** of $h$ relative to $\Sigma$, denoted by $qs(h, \Sigma)$. It can be shown (Kohlas & Monney, 1995) that quasi-support satisfies the following conditions ("$\equiv$" means "logically equivalent"):

(Q1) $qs(\top, \Sigma) \equiv \top$,

(Q2) $qs(h_1 \wedge h_2, \Sigma) \equiv qs(h_1, \Sigma) \wedge qs(h_2, \Sigma)$,
(Q3) if $h_1 \models h_2$, then $qs(h_1, \Sigma) \models qs(h_2, \Sigma)$,
(Q4) $qs(h_1, \Sigma) \vee qs(h_2, \Sigma) \models qs(h_1 \vee h_2, \Sigma)$.

In many cases $qs(\bot, \Sigma)$ will be different from $\bot$. If $a$ is a supporting argument for $\bot$, i.e. if $a \wedge \xi \models \bot$, then $a$ is in contradiction to the knowledge base $\Sigma$ and should be eliminated from quasi-support. The **support** of $h$ relative to $\Sigma$ is defined by

$$sp(h, \Sigma) \equiv qs(h, \Sigma) \wedge \sim qs(\bot, \Sigma), \qquad (3.1)$$

and an argument $a$ with $a \models sp(h, \Sigma)$ and $a \not\models qs(\bot, \Sigma)$ is called **proper argument** of $h$. Support satisfies the following properties (S1) to (S4):

(S1) $sp(\top, \Sigma) \equiv \sim qs(\bot, \Sigma)$,
(S1') $sp(\bot, \Sigma) \equiv \bot$,
(S2) $sp(h_1 \wedge h_2, \Sigma) \equiv sp(h_1, \Sigma) \wedge sp(h_2, \Sigma)$,
(S3) if $h_1 \models h_2$, then $sp(h_1, \Sigma) \models sp(h_2, \Sigma)$,
(S4) $sp(h_1, \Sigma) \vee sp(h_2, \Sigma) \models sp(h_1 \vee h_2, \Sigma)$.

It may also be interesting to consider arguments against a hypothesis $h \in \mathcal{L}_N$, in other words, arguments in favor of $\sim h$. A formula $a \in \mathcal{L}_A$ is called a **refuting argument** of $h$ if $a \wedge \xi \models \sim h$. If $a$ is a refuting argument of $h$, and there is no other refuting argument $a'$ of $h$ with $a' \models a$ and $a' \neq a$, then $a$ is called the **doubt** in $h$ relative to $\Sigma$, denoted by $db(h, \Sigma)$. Doubt is obtained from quasi-support and vice versa:

$$db(h, \Sigma) \equiv qs(\sim h, \Sigma), \qquad (3.2)$$
$$qs(h, \Sigma) \equiv db(\sim h, \Sigma). \qquad (3.3)$$

From (Q1) to (Q4) it follows that the following conditions (D1) are valid for doubt:

(D1) $db(\bot, \Sigma) \equiv \top$,
(D2) $db(h_1 \vee h_2, \Sigma) \equiv db(h_1, \Sigma) \wedge db(h_2, \Sigma)$,
(D3) if $h_1 \models h_2$, then $db(h_2, \Sigma) \models db(h_1, \Sigma)$,
(D4) $db(h_1, \Sigma) \vee db(h_2, \Sigma) \models db(h_1 \wedge h_2, \Sigma)$.

A formula $a \in \mathcal{L}_A$ is called a **possible argument** of $h$ if it is not a refuting argument of $h$, i.e. if $a \wedge \xi \not\models \sim h$. If $a$ is a possible argument of $h$, and if there is no other possible argument $a'$ of $h$ with $a \models a'$ and $a' \neq a$, then $a$ is called the **plausibility** of $h$ relative to $\Sigma$, denoted by $pl(h, \Sigma)$. It corresponds to the negated quasi-support of the negated hypothesis,

$$pl(h, \Sigma) \equiv \sim qs(\sim h, \Sigma), \qquad (3.4)$$
$$qs(h, \Sigma) \equiv \sim pl(\sim h, \Sigma), \qquad (3.5)$$

and it satisfies the conditions (P1) to (P4):

(P1) $pl(\bot, \Sigma) \equiv \bot$,

(P2) $pl(h_1 \vee h_2, \Sigma) \equiv pl(h_1, \Sigma) \vee pl(h_2, \Sigma)$,
(P3) if $h_1 \models h_2$, then $pl(h_1, \Sigma) \models pl(h_2, \Sigma)$,
(P4) $pl(h_1 \wedge h_2, \Sigma) \models pl(h_1, \Sigma) \wedge pl(h_2, \Sigma)$.

If a formula $a \in \mathcal{L}_A$ is either a supporting argument, a proper argument, a refuting argument, or a possible argument of a hypotheses $h$, then it is called a **symbolic argument** of $h$. $\mathcal{L}_A$ is therefore the set of all possible symbolic arguments.

If the symbolic arguments are computed for a given hypothesis, then it is also possible to transform this qualitative measure into a corresponding quantitative measure by assigning prior probabilities to the assumptions (Kohlas & Monney, 1994). Then, instead of support, doubt, and plausibility we speak of **degree of support**, **degree of doubt**, and **degree of plausibility**. Note that degree of support correspond to the notion of **belief** in Dempster-Shafer's theory of evidence (Dempster, 1967; Shafer, 1976). The technique used for this computation is not discussed in this paper, see (Kohlas & Monney, 1994; Kohlas, 1994; Bertschy & Monney, 1996). Examples of so-called **numerical arguments** are given in Subsections 4.1 & 4.2.

To illustrate the idea of symbolic arguments, consider three implications $a_1 \rightarrow p$, $a_2 \rightarrow q$, and $p \rightarrow \sim q$. Let $a_1, a_2$ be assumptions and $p, q$ propositions, i.e. $A = \{a_1, a_2\}$ and $P = \{p, q\}$. The knowledge base is therefore given by $\Sigma = \{\sim a_1 \vee p, \sim a_2 \vee q, \sim p \vee \sim q\}$. Let $q$ be the hypothesis to be judged. For this situation we get the following symbolic arguments:

$$qs(q, \Sigma) = a_2, \tag{3.6}$$
$$qs(\bot, \Sigma) = a_1 \wedge a_2, \tag{3.7}$$
$$sp(q, \Sigma) \equiv qs(q, \Sigma) \wedge \sim qs(\bot, \Sigma) = a_2 \wedge \sim a_1, \tag{3.8}$$
$$db(q, \Sigma) \equiv qs(\sim q, \Sigma) = a_1, \tag{3.9}$$
$$pl(q, \Sigma) \equiv \sim db(q, \Sigma) = \sim a_1. \tag{3.10}$$

## 3.3 Representing and Computing Symbolic Arguments

The previous subsections introduced an evidence theory based on propositional logic. It assigns arguments (represented by formulae in $\mathcal{L}_A$) to hypotheses (represented by formulae in $\mathcal{L}_N$) in the sense of the general evidence theory (Kohlas, 1995). Now, there are at least two important questions to be answered:

(1) How can symbolic arguments be represented or stored efficiently?
(2) How are arguments computed from the knowledge base and the given hypothesis?

These questions are discussed in the following two subsections.

**Representing Symbolic Arguments.** How can symbolic arguments be represented efficiently? Note that in all cases (quasi-support, support, etc.) symbolic

456

arguments are ordinary logical formulae $a \in \mathcal{L}_A$. Thus, the question to be discussed here can be answered more generally by considering how logical formulae (i.e. their corresponding equivalence classes) can be represented efficiently.

Let $f$ be a logical formula in $\mathcal{L}$. To represent $f$ efficiently, a semantically equivalent formula $f' \equiv f$ is needed such that the number of propositions or logical operators contained in $f'$ is as small as possible. To simplify the problem, $f'$ can be restricted to consist only of conjunctions $\wedge$, disjunctions $\vee$, and negations $\sim$. Furthermore, in order to obtain conformity, $f'$ is assumed to be either in disjunctive normal form (DNF) or in conjunctive normal form (CNF). Thus, the problem is to transform an arbitrary logical formula $f$ into an equivalent DNF or CNF $f'$ such that the number of propositional symbols or the number of terms in $f'$ is small or minimal. The disjunction $\psi(f)$ of all non-trivial prime implicants of $f$ or the conjunction $\varphi(f)$ of all non-trivial prime implicates of $f$ are usually good solutions (Haenni, 1996). The minimal or the shortest DNF or CNF is obtained from $\psi(f)$ or $\varphi(f)$ by eliminating different combinations of redundant terms. This is often difficult and expensive, and in most cases it is not worthwhile. Thus, either $\psi(f)$ or $\varphi(f)$ is selected to represent a formula $f$. An algorithm for computing prime implicants and prime implicates is described in (Haenni, 1996).

In the case of $f$ being a symbolic argument, i.e. $f \in \mathcal{L}_A$, the disjunction $\psi(f)$ of all non-trivial prime implicants is the more interesting representation than the conjunction $\varphi(f)$. If for example $f$ is the quasi-support of $h$, then the conjunctions contained in $\psi(f)$, i.e. the prime implicants $\Psi(f)$, are always supporting arguments of $h$. Thus, it is often more convenient to treat a symbolic argument $f$ as a set, namely the set $\Psi(f)$ of non-trivial prime implicants of $f$. From this point of view, a symbolic argument is a set of conjunctions of literals of different assumptions.

Let $C_A$ denote the set of conjunctions of zero, one, or more literals of different assumptions in $A^{\pm}$. The elements of $C_A$ represent equivalence classes of arbitrary conjunctions of literal of assumptions. The "empty" conjunction, i.e. a conjunction with zero literals, represents the tautology $\top$. $C_A$ is a partially ordered set with the logical entailment $\models$ as its ordering relation. If $A$ contains $r$ elements, then $C_A$ contains $3^r$ different conjunctions. Figure 3.1 shows the partially ordered set $C_A$ for $A = \{a_1, a_2\}$.

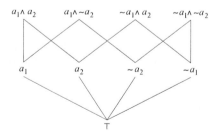

**Fig.** 3.1. Example of a partially ordered set.

The implicants of an arbitrary formula $f \in \mathcal{L}_A$ form a subset $F \subseteq C_A$. If $f$, for example, is the quasi-support of a hypothesis $h \in \mathcal{L}_N$, then $F$ forms the set of all supporting arguments of $h$. $\mu F$ denotes the subset of conjunctions in $F$, which subsume no other conjunction of the set, i.e. which are minimal within the set, and obviously $\mu F = \Psi(f)$. In the following $\mu F$ is used to represent symbolic arguments.

Figure 3.2 shows the subset $F \subseteq C_A$ for the symbolic argument $f = a_1 \vee a_2$. $F$ is entirely determined by the minimal conjunctions $a_1$ and $a_2$, i.e. $\mu F = \Psi(f) = \{a_1, a_2\}$.

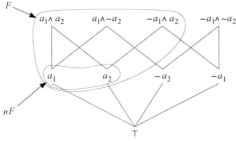

**Fig.** 3.2. Subsets $\mu F \subseteq F \subseteq C_A$ of a partially ordered set.

Each possible symbolic argument $f \in \mathcal{L}_A$ has a corresponding set $\mu F \subseteq C_A$ of minimal conjunctions, and, inversely, each set $\mu F$ of minimal conjunctions represents a symbolic argument. Furthermore, a conjunction of literals of assumptions can also be regarded as a set: the set of its literals. Therefore, the entire theory of assumption-based systems can also be developed in terms of sets of literals and set-operations, rather than in terms of logical formulae and logical operations.

The minimal elements $\mu F$ of a subset $F \subseteq C_A$ can also be interpreted in the following sense. Let $a \in C_A$ be an arbitrary conjunction of literals of different assumptions. $L(a)$ denotes the corresponding set of literals. An assumption $a_i \in A$ is called **positive** relative to $a$, if $a_i \in L(a)$; it is called **negative** relative to $a$, if $\sim a_i \in L(a)$; and it is called **irrelevant** relative to $a$, if $a_i \notin L(a)$ and $\sim a_i \notin L(a)$. Each assumption $a_i \in A$, $i = 1, \ldots, r$, is thus either positive, negative, or irrelevant relative to $a$. $A^+(a)$, $A^-(a)$, and $A^\pm(a)$ denote the sets of positive, negative, and irrelevant assumptions relative to $a$ respectively. Let $F \subseteq C_A$, for example, represent the quasi-support of a hypotheses $h \in \mathcal{L}_N$. Every conjunction $a \in \mu F$ allows us to prove $h$. If a specific $a \in \mu F$ is used to prove $h$, then the statements corresponding to the assumptions in $A^+(a)$ have to be true, the statements of $A^-(a)$ have to be false, and the statements of $A^\pm(a)$ can be either true or false, i.e. they are irrelevant. This interpretation is possible for all kinds of symbolic arguments. From this point of view, representing symbolic arguments as sets of prime implicants has also an important semantical meaning.

**Computing Symbolic Arguments.** This subsection describes how symbolic arguments are determined from a given assumption-based system $\mathcal{A} = (P, A, \Sigma)$.

It proposes a method that generates the quasi-support of a hypothesis $h \in \sim C_N$, in which $\sim C_N$ denotes the set of possible clauses over $N^{\pm}$, $N = P \cup A$. This method is based on a theorem stated in (Reiter & de Kleer, 1987). The theorem assumes that the set $\Phi(\xi)$ of prime implicates of $\xi$ is known. $\xi$ is the logical form of $\Sigma$ and instead of $\Phi(\xi)$ one can also write $\Phi(\Sigma)$.

Reiter's and de Kleer's theorem uses a set-oriented view for the clauses contained in $\Phi(\Sigma)$ and for the conjunctions involved in the symbolic arguments. Thus, consider the following notation: if $f$ and $g$ are two clauses, then $f - g$ denotes the subclause of $f$, which is obtained when all literals present both in $f$ and $g$ are eliminated from $f$.

**Theorem 1.** *(Reiter & de Kleer, 1987) Let $\Phi(\Sigma)$ be the set of prime implicates of a given knowledge base $\Sigma$. If $h$ is a clause in $\sim C_N$, then the prime implicants of the quasi-support $\Psi(qs(h, \Sigma))$ are given by*

$$\Psi(qs(h, \Sigma)) = \mu\{\sim(f - h) \in C_A : f \in \Phi(\Sigma)\}. \qquad (3.11)$$

According to this theorem, one way to determine quasi-supports for clauses is to compute the prime implicates of $\Sigma$ and then to filter the prime implicants of the quasi-support out of them.

If the hypothesis $h$ is not restricted to be a clause, then property (Q2) helps to determine the quasi-support. First, $h$ has to be transformed into a conjunctive normal form $h = h_1 \wedge \cdots \wedge h_k$, in which $h_i$, $i = 1, \ldots, k$, are all clauses. Then $qs(h_i, \Sigma)$, $i = 1, \ldots, k$, for all these clauses can be obtained through (3.11), and from (Q2) follows that the quasi-support of $h$ is simply the conjunction

$$qs(h, \Sigma) \equiv qs(h_1, \Sigma) \wedge \cdots \wedge qs(h_k, \Sigma). \qquad (3.12)$$

Although this method generates the quasi-support of a hypothesis $h$, it can also be used to generate support, doubt, and plausibility. They are obtained indirectly from quasi-support and equations 3.1 to 3.4.

The method described in this subsection to generate symbolic arguments like quasi-support is only appropriate for a knowledge base $\Sigma$ with a relatively small number of prime implicates. Generally, the time needed to compute prime implicates grows exponentially with the size of $\Sigma$. Thus, the computation of the prime implicates for a large knowledge base will be too expensive or even impossible. Nevertheless, it is often possible to decompose a large set $\Sigma$ into small sets $\Sigma_1, \ldots, \Sigma_r$ with $\Sigma = \Sigma_1 \cup \cdots \cup \Sigma_r$. Such a decomposition puts the problem of computing symbolic arguments into the framework of valuation networks (Shenoy & Shafer, 1990). Instead of working on a large knowledge base, valuation networks allow local computations on smaller sets. This idea is further developed in the following subsection.

## 3.4 Assumption-Based Systems in Valuation Networks

An assumption-based system $\mathcal{A} = (P, A, \Sigma)$ represents some information or knowledge relative to the statements expressed by the propositional symbols contained in $P$. Sometimes it will be useful or necessary to marginalize (focus) the assumption-based system $\mathcal{A}$ to a smaller set $P' \subseteq P$ of propositional symbols. If two or more assumption-based systems are given, then it will be important to combine them into a new combined assumption-based system as well. This subsection discusses two operations for assumption-based systems called **marginalization**, and **combination**. This puts assumption-based systems into the framework of **valuation networks** (Shenoy & Shafer, 1990) where operations of marginalization and combination are important. If a decomposition $\Sigma_1, \ldots, \Sigma_r$ is given, then every sub-knowledge $\Sigma_i$ (i.e. its corresponding assumption-based system $\mathcal{A}_i$) forms a **valuation** in the sense of Shenoy's idea of valuation networks. It is easy to show that assumption-based systems satisfy the necessary axioms that allow local computation in valuation networks (Haenni, 1996). Therefore, the idea how to compute symbolic arguments efficiently is the following:

(1) Find a decomposition $\Sigma_1, \ldots, \Sigma_r$ and construct a corresponding valuation network.
(2) Propagate the valuations locally through the network (inward and outward phase).
(3) Compute symbolic arguments from the resulting marginals using the methods of Subsection 3.3.

**Marginalization.** Let $\mathcal{A} = (P, A, \Sigma)$ be an assumption-based system. The marginalization of the information contained in $\mathcal{A}$ to a subset $P' \subseteq P$ can be defined in terms of the given knowledge base $\Sigma$. This leads to a new assumption-based system $\mathcal{A}' = (P', A, \Sigma')$. $\Sigma'$ is derived from $\Sigma$ by eliminating sequentially all propositional symbols not belonging to $P'$ (Kohlas & Moral, 1995).

Let $P^* = P - P' = \{p_1, \ldots, p_k\}$ be the set of proposition to be eliminated from $\Sigma$. Generally, the elimination of a proposition $p \in P^*$ from $\Sigma$ involves the computations of all possible resolvents for $p$. If $\xi_i$ is a clause containing the positive literal $p$ and $\xi_j$ a clause containing the negative clause $\sim p$, then the **resolvent** $\rho(\xi_i, \xi_j)$ can be formed by eliminating $p$, $\sim p$ and all multiple occurrences of literals from $\xi \vee \xi_j$. $\rho(\xi_i, \xi_j)$ is set to $\top$ if $\xi_i$ and $\xi_j$ contain other pairs of negated literals besides $p$ and $\sim p$.

To describe the elimination of a proposition $p \in P^*$ from $\Sigma$, three sets $\Sigma_p$, $\Sigma_{\sim p}$, and $\Sigma_{-p}$, all subsets of $\Sigma$, are defined as follows:

$$\Sigma_p = \{\xi_i \in \Sigma : p \in \xi_i\}, \tag{3.13}$$
$$\Sigma_{\sim p} = \{\xi_i \in \Sigma : \sim p \in \xi_i\}, \tag{3.14}$$
$$\Sigma_{-p} = \{\xi_i \in \Sigma : p, \sim p \notin \xi_i\} = \Sigma - (\Sigma_p \cup \Sigma_{\sim p}). \tag{3.15}$$

Now, the new set $\Sigma_{-\{p\}}$ obtained after eliminating $p$ is:

$$\Sigma'_{-\{p\}} = \mu(\Sigma_{-p} \cup \{\rho(\xi_i, \xi_j) : \xi_i \in \Sigma_p, \xi_j \in \Sigma_{\sim p}\}). \tag{3.16}$$

The marginalization $\Sigma' = \Sigma_{-P^*}$ is obtained from $\Sigma$ by eliminating the propositions $p_i \in P^*$, $i = 1, \ldots, k$, in any order. The new assumption-based system

$\mathcal{A}' = (P', A, \Sigma')$ is called **marginal** of $\mathcal{A}$ to $P'$, denoted by $\mathcal{A}^{\downarrow P'}$. It satisfies the property of transitivity (Shenoy & Shafer, 1990), i.e. for $P'' \subseteq P' \subseteq P$

$$(\mathcal{A}^{\downarrow P'})^{\downarrow P''} \equiv \mathcal{A}^{\downarrow P''}. \tag{3.17}$$

**Combination.** Up to now, an assumption-based system $\mathcal{A} = (P, A, \Sigma)$ was fixed. Now, suppose that there are two (or more) assumption-based systems $\mathcal{A}_1 = (P_1, A_1, \Sigma_1)$ and $\mathcal{A}_2 = (P_2, A_2, \Sigma_2)$, $P_1 \cap A_2 = \emptyset$, $P_2 \cap A_1 = \emptyset$, which may be combined into a new system $\mathcal{A} = \mathcal{A}_1 \otimes \mathcal{A}_2 = (P, A, \Sigma)$. The symbol $\otimes$ denotes the combination. The new system is clearly determined by $P = P_1 \cup P_2$, $A = A_1 \cup A_2$ and $\Sigma = \mu(\Sigma_1 \cup \Sigma_2)$. Thus, to combine two assumption-based systems essentially means to form the union between $\Sigma_1$ and $\Sigma_2$ and to eliminate all subsuming clauses.

The combination of assumption-based systems is idempotent (i.e. $\mathcal{A} \otimes \mathcal{A} = \mathcal{A}$), commutative (i.e. $\mathcal{A}_1 \otimes \mathcal{A}_2 = \mathcal{A}_2 \otimes \mathcal{A}_1$), and associative (i.e. $(\mathcal{A}_1 \otimes \mathcal{A}_2) \otimes \mathcal{A}_3 = \mathcal{A}_1 \otimes (\mathcal{A}_2 \otimes \mathcal{A}_3)$). Another important property is the distributivity of marginalization over combination (Shenoy & Shafer, 1990):

$$(\mathcal{A}_1 \otimes \mathcal{A}_2)^{\downarrow P_1} \equiv \mathcal{A}_1 \otimes (\mathcal{A}_2)^{\downarrow P_1 \cap P_2}. \tag{3.18}$$

## 3.5 Assumptions as Hypotheses

Generally, the hypotheses to judge are formulae in $\mathcal{L}_N$, $N = P \cup A$, i.e. they can contain both propositions and assumptions. Now, the special case will be studied in which the hypothesis $h$ consists only of assumptions. This simplifies some computations. Let $h_1$ and $h_2$ be two formulae in $\mathcal{L}_A$, i.e. expressions composed of assumptions. In this case the following properties for quasi-support, support, doubt, and plausibility are satisfied (Kohlas *et al.*, 1996):

(Q4') $qs(h_1 \vee h_2, \Sigma) \equiv qs(h_1, \Sigma) \vee qs(h_2, \Sigma)$,
(S4') $sp(h_1 \vee h_2, \Sigma) \equiv sp(h_1, \Sigma) \vee sp(h_2, \Sigma)$,
(P4') $pl(h_1 \wedge h_2, \Sigma) \equiv pl(h_1, \Sigma) \wedge pl(h_2, \Sigma)$,
(D4') $db(h_1 \wedge h_2, \Sigma) \equiv db(h_1, \Sigma) \vee db(h_2, \Sigma)$.

These properties replace (Q4), (S4), (D4), and (P4) from Subsection 3.2. Note that any logical formula $f$ is equivalent to $f \vee \bot$ and to $f \wedge \top$. This leads to the following important theorem:

**Theorem 2.** *(Kohlas* et al., *1996) If $\mathcal{A} = (P, A, \Sigma)$ is an assumption-based system and $h_A$ a formula in $\mathcal{L}_A$, then the symbolic arguments are given by:*

$$qs(h_A, \Sigma) \equiv h_A \vee qs(\bot, \Sigma), \tag{3.19}$$
$$sp(h_A, \Sigma) \equiv h_A \wedge {\sim}qs(\bot, \Sigma), \tag{3.20}$$
$$db(h_A, \Sigma) \equiv h_A \wedge qs(\bot, \Sigma), \tag{3.21}$$
$$pl(h_A, \Sigma) \equiv h_A \wedge {\sim}qs(\bot, \Sigma). \tag{3.22}$$

Thus, the problem of finding the symbolic arguments for a hypothesis $h_A \in \mathcal{L}_A$ mainly consists in finding the quasi-support of the contradiction. In many applications (especially in diagnostics problems) the interesting question can be expressed by a formula in $\mathcal{L}_A$. In such cases it is enough to have efficient methods to determine $qs(\bot, \Sigma)$.

From Theorem 2 follows that for hypotheses $h_A \in \mathcal{L}_A$, support and plausibility are always the same:

$$sp(h_A, \Sigma) \equiv pl(h_A, \Sigma). \tag{3.23}$$

The results of Theorem 2 can also be applied in a more general case, where a hypothesis $h \in \mathcal{L}_N$ has to be judged. Often, $h$ can be decomposed into two hypotheses $h_N \in \mathcal{L}_N$ and $h_A \in \mathcal{L}_A$, such that $h = h_N \wedge h_A$. Thus, quasi-support and support are obtained through:

$$qs(h, \Sigma) \equiv (h_A \wedge qs(h_N, \Sigma)) \vee qs(\bot, \Sigma), \tag{3.24}$$
$$sp(h, \Sigma) \equiv h_A \wedge qs(h_N, \Sigma) \wedge \sim qs(\bot, \Sigma). \tag{3.25}$$

Similarly, if the hypothesis $h \in \mathcal{L}_N$ can be decomposed into $h_N \in \mathcal{L}_N$ and $h_A \in \mathcal{L}_A$, such that $h = h_N \vee h_A$, then doubt and plausibility are obtained through:

$$db(h, \Sigma) \equiv (\sim h_A \wedge qs(\sim h_N, \Sigma)) \vee qs(\bot, \Sigma), \tag{3.26}$$
$$pl(h, \Sigma) \equiv h_A \wedge \sim qs(\sim h_N, \Sigma) \wedge \sim qs(\bot, \Sigma). \tag{3.27}$$

In all of these cases it is sufficient to use the methods presented in Subsection 3.3 in order to determine the quasi-support of $h_N$ (or $\sim h_N$) and the quasi-support of the contradiction. If $h_N$ is much simpler than the original $h$, then it is often less efficient to apply the methods directly on $h$. For example, if $h = a_1 \wedge p \vee a_2 \wedge p$ is the hypothesis to be judged, $a_1, a_2 \in A$, $p \in P$, then $h = (a_1 \vee a_2) \wedge p = h_A \wedge h_N$ with $h_A = a_1 \vee a_2$ and $h_N = p$. In this example it would be easier to determine $qs(p, \Sigma)$ and $qs(\bot, \Sigma)$ instead of $qs(a_1 \wedge p \vee a_2 \wedge p, \Sigma)$.

## 4 ABEL – A New Language for Assumption-Based Reasoning

This section describes ABEL (Anrig et al., 1997a; Anrig et al., 1997b) which is both, a new modeling language for assumption-based systems and an interactive tool for assumption-based reasoning[1]. Given an assumption-based system and some additional facts or observations, the aim of ABEL is to compute symbolic and numerical arguments for the user's hypotheses (see Figure 4.1). ABEL was designed and implemented at the University of Fribourg for the Macintosh platform. It results from a research project leaded by the author of this paper. The program is written in CLOS (Common Lisp Object System), and it is therefore easily portable to different platforms. Examples of ABEL models can be found in the following two subsections and in (Anrig et al., 1997a).

---

[1] The software can be obtained through the author's home page.

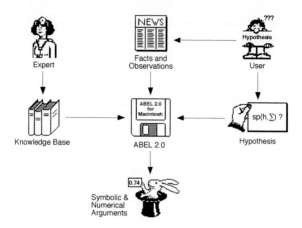

**Fig.** 4.1. Using ABEL to compute symbolic and numerical arguments.

The user interface of ABEL is a multiple-window-environment based on the Macintosh Common Lisp (MCL) programming interface. There are two different window types (Anrig *et al.*, 1997a):

(1) **Modeling windows** are editors to model and develop assumption-based systems. Usual Macintosh editor features, such as text scrolling and mouse-based editing, are included. In addition, parenthesis matching and smart indentation are possible. The compilation of the ABEL model contained in a modeling window can be started by an appropriate command on the ABEL menu bar.

(2) A special window called **transcript** is used for most interaction between the user and the system. As soon as the user types an ABEL command or a query in the transcript window, ABEL reads and interprets the expression, prints the result, and detects and reports possible errors.

Figure 4.2 shows a screenshot of the ABEL environment showing a modeling and a transcript window for the example discussed in Subsection 4.2.

ABEL is based on three other computer languages: (1) from **Common Lisp** (Steele, 1990) it adopts **prefix notation** and therewith a number of opening and closing parentheses; (2) from **Pulcinella** (Saffiotti & Umkehrer, 1991) it uses the idea of the commands `tell`, `ask`, and `empty`; and (3) from an existing ABEL prototype (Lehmann, 1994; Haenni, 1996) it inherits the concept of **modules** and the syntax of the queries.

Working with ABEL usually involves three sequential steps:

(1) The given information is expressed using the command `tell`. The resulting model is called **basic knowledge base**. It describes the part of the available information that is relatively constant and static in course of time such as rules, relations, or dependencies between different statements. It consists of

**Fig.** 4.2. A screenshot of the ABEL environment.

one or several lines called **instructions**. The contents of an instruction can be a **definition** of types, variables, assumptions, or modules, a **statement**, i.e. a rule or another part of the basic knowledge base, or an application of a **module**. The sequence of instructions is interpreted as a conjunction. The syntax of a `tell`-command is the following:

```
(tell <instr-1>
      ...
      <instr-n>)
```

Every instruction can be seen as a piece of information. Therefore, the command `tell` is used to add new pieces of information to the existing basic knowledge base. Note that the instructions of a `tell`-command can be distributed among several `tell`-commands.

(2) In order to complete the model, **observations** or **facts** are added to the basic knowledge base. Observations describe the actual situation or the concrete circumstances of the problem. Note that observations may change in course of time. It is therefore important to separate observations from the basic knowledge base. ABEL provides a command `observe` to specify observations. It expects a sequence of ABEL statements. The sequence is interpreted as a conjunction.

```
(observe <stm-1>
         ...
         <stm-n>)
```

Statements given by `observe`- and `tell`-commands are treated similarly. The difference is that `observe`-statements can be deleted or changed independently when new observations were made. To change an observation, the same statement with the new values has to be re-written. The `empty`-command can be used to delete observations.

(3) Queries about the actual knowledge base are expressed using the command `ask`. Generally, there are two different types of queries: (a) it can be interesting to get the available information about certain variables; and (b) it can be interesting to get symbolic or numerical arguments in favor or against certain hypotheses. In both cases, several queries can be treated at once:

```
(ask <query-1>
     . . .
     <query-n>)
```

In the first case, a query is simply an ABEL expression. This type of query is useful, for example, in constraint satisfaction problems (consider (Anrig *et al.*, 1997a) for examples). The second way to state queries is important in problems of assumption-based reasoning, when different types of arguments may be of interest. The respective keywords in ABEL are `sp`, `qs`, `pl`, `db`. A hypothesis is an ABEL statement. Arguments are conjunctions of normal or negated assumptions. It is also possible to ask for numerical arguments like **degree of support**, **degree of quasi-support**, **degree of plausibility**, or **degree of doubt** (Haenni, 1996); the respective keywords in ABEL are `dsp`, `dqs`, `dpl`, `ddb`. A numerical argument is obtained by computing the probability for the corresponding symbolic argument. This computation is based on prior probabilities specified in the definition of the assumptions.

In this paper the language is not discussed further. For a precise language description refer to (Anrig *et al.*, 1997a).

In the case of a query, i.e. if the user formulates a hypothesis, then ABEL starts the inference mechanism and computes corresponding symbolic or numerical arguments. The inference mechanism is based on modules for the following seven tasks:

(1) Compile the ABEL model into a corresponding set of clauses. Transform the clauses into an appropriate internal representation. Report possible errors.
(2) Apply a method called Tree-Alg to transform the hypergraph given by the variables contained in the clauses into a covering hypertree (Kohlas & Monney, 1995).
(3) Construct from the hypertree a corresponding valuation network (Shenoy & Shafer, 1990) and choose an arbitrary root. Distribute the clauses among the nodes of the network, i.e. decompose the knowledge base.

(4) Propagate the clauses through the network towards the root using Shenoy's message-passing scheme (Shenoy & Shafer, 1990; Kohlas & Moral, 1995) (only inward phase). This delivers the marginal for the root of the network.

(5) Select from the network an appropriate node that can be used to answer the query. Perform the outward propagation from the root to this node.

(6) Use the resulting clauses obtained from the node selected in step (5) to compute the symbolic arguments for the hypothesis. Display the results in a convenient form.

(7) Possibly, transform the symbolic arguments into corresponding numerical arguments.

The techniques implemented in ABEL for performing step (1) to step (7) are not discussed further. In the two remaining subsections, in order to illustrate the use of ABEL, we present the corresponding ABEL models for the examples introduced in Section 2.

## 4.1 Example 1: Chest Clinic

Consider the chest clinic example from Section 2.2. The knowledge base is a set of material implications resulting from the corresponding causal network. In ABEL, material implications can be expressed as follows (Anrig *et al.*, 1997a):

```
(-> <condition> <conclusion>)
```

The two expressions `<condition>` and `<conclusion>` are either atomic symbols (propositions or assumptions) or composed logical formulas. Furthermore, if we suppose the probabilities

$$p(a_1) = 0.1, \ p(a_2) = 0.01, \ p(a_3) = 0.2, \ p(a_4) = 0.1, \ p(a_5) = 0.3,$$
$$p(a_6) = 0.1, \ p(a_7) = 0.9, \ p(a_8) = 0.8, \ p(a_9) = 0.1, \ p(a_{10}) = 0.9,$$
$$p(a_{11}) = 0.8, \ p(a_{12}) = 0.7, \ p(a_{13}) = 0.1,$$

for the assumptions involved in the model, then the knowledge base can be encoded as follows:

```
(tell
  (var visit tuberculosis x-ray lung-cancer smoker
       bronchitis dyspnoea binary)
  (ass a1 a6 a9 a13 binary 0.1)
  (ass a2 a4 binary 0.01)
  (ass a3 binary 0.2)
  (ass a5 binary 0.3)
  (ass a7 a10 binary 0.9)
  (ass a8 a11 binary 0.8)
  (ass a12 binary 0.7)

  (-> (and visit a1) tuberculosis)
  (-> a2 tuberculosis)
```

```
(-> tuberculosis (or (and visit a1) a2))

(-> (and smoker a3) lung-cancer)
(-> a4 lung-cancer)
(-> lung-cancer (or (and smoker a3) a4))

(-> (and smoker a5) bronchitis)
(-> a6 bronchitis)
(-> bronchitis (or (and smoker a5) a6))

(-> (and lung-cancer a7) x-ray)
(-> (and tuberculosis a8) x-ray)
(-> a9 x-ray)
(-> x-ray (or (and lung-cancer a7) (and tuberculosis a8) a9))

(-> (and tuberculosis a10) dyspnoea)
(-> (and lung-cancer a11) dyspnoea)
(-> (and bronchitis a12) dyspnoea)
(-> a13 dyspnoea)
(-> dyspnoea (or (and tuberculosis a10) (and lung-cancer a11)
                 (and bronchitis a12) a13)))
```

If the doctor observes that the patient who suffers from dyspnoea is a smoker
and that he has visited an under-developed country recently, then $d$, $s$, and $v$
can be added as observations to the basic knowledge base:

```
(observe dyspnoea smoker visit)
```

Now, symbolic or numerical arguments for hypotheses like "Does the patient
suffer from tuberculosis?", "Does the patient suffer from bronchitis?", etc., may
be of interest. For the hypotheses $t$ (tuberculosis) and $b$ (bronchitis) the system
reports the following results (Anrig *et al.*, 1997a):

```
? (ask (sp tuberculosis))          ? (ask (sp bronchitis))
QUERY: (SP TUBERCULOSIS)           QUERY: (SP BRONCHITIS)
   56.5% : A1 A10                      49.2% : A12 A5
   13.2% : A1 A12 A5                   16.4% : A12 A6
   10.0% : A1 A11 A3                   11.2% : A11 A3 A5
    6.3% : A1 A13                       7.0% : A13 A5
    5.7% : A10 A2                       6.3% : A1 A10 A5
    4.4% : A1 A12 A6                    3.7% : A11 A3 A6
    1.3% : A12 A2 A5                    2.3% : A13 A6
    1.0% : A11 A2 A3                    2.1% : A1 A10 A6
    0.6% : A13 A2                       0.6% : A10 A2 A5
    0.5% : A1 A11 A4                    0.6% : A11 A4 A5
    0.4% : A12 A2 A6                    0.2% : A10 A2 A6
    0.1% : A11 A2 A4                    0.2% : A11 A4 A6

? (ask (dsp tuberculosis))         ? (ask (dsp bronchitis))
QUERY: (DSP TUBERCULOSIS)          QUERY: (DSP BRONCHITIS)
   0.206                              0.591
```

From symbolic support the doctor gets configurations of assumptions that allow him to explain or deduce the hypothesis. In contrast, numerical degrees of support help to judge and compare the results quantitatively. Here, bronchitis is almost three times as credible as tuberculosis.

## 4.2  Example 2: Burglary

Consider the burglary example from Section 2.3. Again, if we suppose probabilities for the assumptions $a_1, \ldots, a_{11}$, for example

$$p(a_1) = 0.9,\ p(a_2) = 0.9,\ p(a_3) = 0.1,\ p(a_4) = 0.7,\ p(a_5) = 0.3,\ p(a_6) = 0.1,$$
$$p(a_7) = 0.1,\ p(a_8) = 0.7,\ p(a_9) = 0.3,\ p(a_{10}) = 0.9,\ p(a_{11}) = 0.1,$$

then the problem can be modeled as follows:

```
(tell
    (var burglary alarm earthquake watson gibbons daughter radio binary)
    (ass a1 a2 a10 binary 0.9)
    (ass a4 a8 binary 0.7)
    (ass a3 a6 a7 a11 binary 0.1)
    (ass a5 a9 binary 0.3)

    (-> (and burglary a1) alarm)
    (-> (and earthquake a2) alarm)
    (-> a3 alarm)
    (-> alarm (or (and burglary a1) (and earthquake a2) a3))

    (-> (and alarm a4) watson)
    (-> a5 watson)
    (-> watson (or (and alarm a4) a5))

    (-> (and alarm a6) gibbons)
    (-> a7 gibbons)
    (-> gibbons (or (and alarm a6) a7))

    (-> (and alarm a8) daughter)
    (-> a9 daughter)
    (-> daughter (or (and alarm a8) a9))

    (-> (and earthquake a10) radio)
    (-> a11 radio)
    (-> radio (or (and earthquake a10) a11)))
```

Suppose now that Mr. Holmes receives a phone call from his neighbor Dr. Watson who tells him that there is an alarm sound from the direction of Mr. Holmes's house. Furthermore, suppose that there is no announcement of an earthquake on the radio.

```
(observe watson (not radio))
```

Now, symbolic and numerical arguments for some hypotheses may be of interest.
Here, Mr. Holmes will be mostly interested in whether there is a burglary or not.
Some of the possible queries produce the following results:

```
? (ask (sp burglary))
QUERY: (SP BURGLARY)
    90.0% : A1 A10 A4 (NOT A11) (NOT A3) (NOT A5)
    10.0% : A1 A4 (NOT A11) (NOT A2) (NOT A3) (NOT A5)
? (ask (sp earthquake))
QUERY: (SP EARTHQUAKE)
   100.0% : A2 A4 (NOT A1) (NOT A10) (NOT A11) (NOT A3) (NOT A5)
? (ask (dsp burglary))
QUERY: (DSP BURGLARY)
    0.482
? (ask (dpl burglary))
QUERY: (DPL BURGLARY)
    1.000
? (ask (dsp earthquake))
QUERY: (DSP EARTHQUAKE)
    0.005
? (ask (dpl earthquake))
QUERY: (DPL EARTHQUAKE)
    0.105
```

There is a relatively strong degree of support of 0.482 for a burglary, but only a
very weak support for an earthquake. Mr. Holmes should therefore immediately
call the police and return to his house.

## 5  Summary

This paper introduces the framework of propositional assumption-based reasoning. It shows how a set of uncertain causal relations can be transformed into a corresponding assumption-based system. This technique is illustrated by two examples which are often used in AI literature. Then, the paper describes a valuation-based method for computing symbolic arguments for a given hypothesis. This method is implemented in ABEL, an interactive tool for probabilistic assumption-based reasoning. The paper describes ABEL and demonstrates how it can be used for solving the examples mentioned before.

The actual work consists in improving the modeling language and the ABEL solver. The language has already been extended and today it supports also discrete and numerical variables (Anrig et al., 1997a). For example, ABEL allows now mixed expressions of the form $w \in \{q, r, s\} \wedge \sim a \rightarrow (x^2 + 3y \leq z)$. Clearly, this improves the expressiveness of the formalism and enlarges the field of possible applications significantly. But the idea behind is still the same: finding symbolic or numerical arguments for hypotheses given some knowledge.

Future work will mainly focus on approximation strategies for big models with modular structures.

# References

Anrig, B., Haenni, R., & Lehmann, N. 1997a. *ABEL – A New Language for Assumption-Based Evidential Reasoning under Uncertainty.* Tech. Rep. 97–01. University of Fribourg, Institute of Informatics.

Anrig, B., Haenni, R., Kohlas, J., & Lehmann, N. 1997b. Assumption-based Modeling using ABEL. *In:* Gabbay, D., Kruse, R., Nonnengart, A., & Ohlbach, H.J. (eds), *First International Joint Conference on Qualitative and Quantitative Practical Reasoning; ECSQARU–FAPR'97*Springer, for Lecture Notes in Artif. Intell.

Bertschy, R., & Monney, P.A. 1996. A Generalization of the Algorithm of Heidtmann to Non-Monotone Formulas. *Journal of Computational and Applied Mathematics,* **76**, 55–76.

de Kleer, J. 1986. An Assumption-based TMS. *Artificial Intelligence,* **28**, 127–162.

Dempster, A. 1967. Upper and Lower Probabilities Induced by a Multivalued Mapping. *Ann. Math. Stat.,* **38**, 325–339.

Haenni, R. 1996. *Propositional Argumentation Systems and Symbolic Evidence Theory.* Ph.D. thesis, Institute of Informatics, University of Fribourg.

Inoue, K. 1991. An Abductive Procedure for the CMS/ATMS. *Pages 34–53 of:* Martins, J.P., & Reinfrank, M. (eds), *Truth Maintenance Systems, Lecture Notes in A.I.* Springer.

Kohlas, J. 1994. *Mathematical Foundations of Evidence Theory.* Tech. Rep. 94–09. Institute of Informatics, University of Fribourg.

Kohlas, J. 1995. Mathematical Foundations of Evidence Theory. *Pages 31–64 of:* Coletti, G., Dubois, D., & Scozzafava, R. (eds), *Mathematical Models for Handling Partial Knowledge in Artificial Intelligence.* Plenum Press.

Kohlas, J., & Monney, P.A. 1993. Probabilistic Assumption-Based Reasoning. *In:* Heckerman, & Mamdani (eds), *Proc. 9th Conf. on Uncertainty in Artificial Intelligence.* Kaufmann, Morgan Publ.

Kohlas, J., & Monney, P.A. 1994. *Probabilistic Assumption-Based Reasoning.* Tech. Rep. 94–22. Institute of Informatics, University of Fribourg.

Kohlas, J., & Monney, P.A. 1995. *A Mathematical Theory of Hints. An Approach to the Dempster-Shafer Theory of Evidence.* Lecture Notes in Economics and Mathematical Systems, vol. 425. Springer.

Kohlas, J., & Moral, S. 1995. *Propositional Information System.* Working Paper. Institute of Informatics, University of Fribourg.

Kohlas, J., Monney, P.A., Anrig, B., & Haenni, R. 1996. *Model-Based Diagnostics and Probabilistic Assumption-Based Reasoning.* Tech. Rep. 96–09. University of Fribourg, Institute of Informatics.

Laskey, K.B., & Lehner, P.E. 1989. Assumptions, Beliefs and Probabilities. *Artificial Intelligence,* **41**, 65–77.

Lauritzen, S.L., & Spiegelhalter, D.J. 1988. Local Computations with Probabilities on Graphical Structures and their Application to Expert Systems. *Journal of Royal Statistical Society,* **50**(2), 157–224.

Lehmann, N. 1994. *Entwurf und Implementation einer annahmenbasierten Sprache.* Diplomarbeit. Institute of Informatics, University of Fribourg.

Pearl, J. 1988. *Probabilistic Reasoning in Intelligent Systems.* Morgan Kaufmann Publ. Inc.

Provan, G.M. 1990. A Logic-Based Analysis of Dempster-Shafer Theory. *International Journal of Approximate Reasoning,* **4**, 451–495.

Reiter, R., & de Kleer, J. 1987. Foundations of Assumption-Based Truth Maintenance Systems. *Proceedings of the American Association in AI*, 183–188.

Saffiotti, A., & Umkehrer, E. 1991. *PULCINELLA: A General Tool for Propagating Uncertainty in Valuation Networks*. Tech. Rep. IRIDIA, Université de Bruxelles.

Shafer, G. 1976. *The Mathematical Theory of Evidence*. Princeton University Press.

Shenoy, P.P., & Shafer, G. 1990. Axioms for Probability and Belief Functions Propagation. *In:* Shachter, R.D., & al. (eds), *Uncertainty in Artificial Intelligence 4*. North Holland.

Siegel, P. 1987. *Représentation et Utilisation de la Connaissance en Calcul Propositionel*. Ph.D. thesis, Université d'Aix-Marseille II. Luminy, France.

Steele, G. L. 1990. *Common Lisp – the Language*. Digital Press.

# Author Index

# Subject Index

# Lecture Notes in Artificial Intelligence (LNAI)

# Lecture Notes in Computer Science